Praise for *Hitchhiker's Guide to SQL Server 2000 Reporting Services*

"The ultimate resource for both DBAs and developers on SQL Server Reporting Services; this book and DVD will guide you from installation, security, report design, and deployment to developing extensions."

—Gert E.R. Drapers
Software Architect
SQL Server Development
Microsoft Corporation

"Bill Vaughn and Peter Blackburn have created a masterful work of Reporting Services documentation, which includes tips, tricks, and product insights that you just won't find anywhere else."

—Bryan Keller
Programmer-Writer
SQL Server Reporting Services
Microsoft Corporation

"An insightful, informative, and sometimes irreverent look into the world of Reporting Services, *Hitchhiker's Guide to SQL Server 2000 Reporting Services* provides plenty of walk-throughs, examples, tips, and tricks to help you get the most out of the product. Peter and Bill take you step by step through the various features of Reporting Services, pointing out pitfalls and best practices along the way. An excellent addition to any Reporting Services library."

—Michelle Larez
Technical Writer
SQL Server Reporting Services
Microsoft Corporation

"Although it is called *Hitchhiker's Guide to SQL Server 2000 Reporting Services*, I like to think of it in more of a movie context as *Bill and Peter's Excellent Adventure*. Get ready for a totally excellent quest to get the most out of your SQL Server Reporting Services deployment."

—Brian Welcker
Group Program Manager
SQL Server Reporting Services
Microsoft Corporation

Hitchhiker's Guide to SQL Server 2000 Reporting Services

Microsoft Windows Server System Series

Books in the **Microsoft Windows Server System Series** are written and reviewed by the world's leading technical authorities on Microsoft Windows technologies, including principal members of Microsoft's Windows and Server Development Teams. The goal of the series is to provide reliable information that enables administrators, developers, and IT professionals to architect, build, deploy, and manage solutions using the Microsoft Windows Server System. The contents and code of each book are tested against, and comply with, commercially available code. This series should be an invaluable resource for any IT professional or student working in today's Windows environment.

TITLES IN THE SERIES

Paul Bertucci, *Microsoft SQL Server High Availability,* 0-672-32625-6 (Sams)

Peter Blackburn and William R. Vaughn, *Hitchhiker's Guide to SQL Server 2000 Reporting Services,* 0-321-26828-8 (Addison-Wesley)

William Boswell, *Learning Exchange Server 2003,* 0-321-22874-X (Addison-Wesley)

Bill English, Olga Londer, Shawn Shell, Todd Bleeker, and Stephen Cawood, *Microsoft Content Management Server 2002: A Complete Guide,* 0-321-19444-6 (Addison-Wesley)

Don Jones, *Managing Windows® with VBScript and WMI,* 0-321-21334-3 (Addison-Wesley)

Sakari Kouti and Mika Seitsonen, *Inside Active Directory, Second Edition: A System Administrator's Guide,* 0-321-22848-0 (Addison-Wesley)

Shyam Pather, *Microsoft SQL Server 2000 Notification Services,* 0-672-32664-7 (Sams)

For more information please go to www.awprofessional.com/msserverseries

Hitchhiker's Guide to SQL Server 2000 Reporting Services

Peter Blackburn

William R. Vaughn

✦✦ Addison-Wesley

Boston • San Francisco • New York • Toronto • Montreal
London • Munich • Paris • Madrid
Capetown • Sydney • Tokyo • Singapore • Mexico City

The publisher offers discounts on this book when ordered in quantity for bulk purchases and special sales. For more information, please contact:

  U.S. Corporate and Government Sales
  (800) 382-3419
  corpsales@pearsontechgroup.com

For sales outside of the U.S., please contact:

  International Sales
  international@pearsoned.com

Visit Addison-Wesley on the Web: www.awprofessional.com

Library of Congress Cataloging-in-Publication Data

Blackburn, Peter, 1967–
  Hitchhiker's guide to SQL Server 2000 Reporting Services / Peter
Blackburn, William R. Vaughn.
      p. cm.
   Includes bibliographical references and index.
   ISBN 0-321-26828-8 (pbk. : alk. paper)
  1. Client/server computing. 2. SQL server. I. Vaughn, William R. II.
Title.

  QA76.9.C55B53 2004
  004'.36—dc22

                                2004017832

Text printed on recycled and acid-free paper.

ISBN 0321268288

3 4 5 6 7 8 CRS 07 06 05

3rd Printing   February 2005

Contents

Chapter 7   Report Layout and Design 317

Chapter 8   The Chart and Matrix Controls 387

Chapter 13   Writing a Custom Data Processing Extension . . . 605

Foreword

Business Intelligence is one of those genuinely interesting and useful technologies that is unfortunately dramatically underused in companies and organizations. For far too long, Business Intelligence has been both too expensive and esoteric to achieve widespread adoption. I started in this industry at Dynamics Associates in 1979. We didn't even use the term Business Intelligence back then. Just the same, what we call BI today began as an industry of specialists building specialty software for other specialists. The companies were small, often academic, and mostly clustered around Cambridge (MIT), Palo Alto (Stanford University), and Ann Arbor (University of Michigan).

Over seven years ago, we in the SQL Server group at Microsoft asked ourselves: "What would a mass market Business Intelligence (BI) industry look like?" We knew some obvious things already. For example, the software had to be easy to use and deploy. It had to be cost-effective to acquire and maintain. It had to integrate with common back-end data sources and with popular desktop tools.

At that time, BI was a best-of-breed market. We believed back then that success in "BI for the Masses" would require 24x7 BI servers, not the norm then. We also believed that embedded BI would be a key element in driving data and BI capabilities into new job functions and that application developers and IT departments would want professional-grade BI development tools. But mostly we believed that for companies to make the substantial BI bet that we envisioned, they would demand an integrated, end-to-end BI platform, including servers and clients.

Now it's July 2004, seven years later. Did we deliver that platform? I claim that Microsoft SQL Server and Microsoft Office comprise that platform for most companies. Clearly we are building the platform in increments. We started with Analysis Services, Data Transformation Services, and Excel. Next we added Data Mining. The Office team added more BI features in Excel and SharePoint Portal Server. And most recently we added Reporting Services.

Like our other BI components, Reporting Services has been a labor of love. Nothing lights up the faces of our developers, testers, and program managers like seeing a customer successfully use our product. Our teams are extremely small. Passion and energy are our investment capital. Happy customers are our ultimate source of funding.

BI for the Masses is a huge vision. It is a journey, as trite as that expression has become. We cannot accomplish this mission with outstanding software alone. To succeed, we need a community. We are blessed with excellent partners. Companies like ProClarity, Panorama, Cizer, MIS AG, OutlookSoft, and Geac have been with us every step of the way, adding value on top of our platform. We are blessed with a great user population, including customers and consultants who contribute generously to our public newsgroups and to our user group, PASS (Professional Association for SQL Server). And we are blessed with talented educators who write the articles, website content, and books that help make our platform real for so many users.

Bill Vaughn and Peter Blackburn are two of the finest authors in our community. Bill and I go back about eight years to a time when I managed ADO (that's a separate, long story) and he was my customer on the Visual Basic team. I know Peter from his partnership with Bill and from his prolific contributions to our newsgroups.

> Bill Vaughn and Peter Blackburn are two of the finest authors in our community.

These guys are pros. This is no quick dash-off book. Bill and Peter worked Reporting Services to death to learn everything they could to help you successfully deploy and use the product. I learned new things when I read it. I think it's fair to say that some of the developers on our team feel like Bill and Peter go under the covers too much. My advice to you, the reader, is to learn from their exploration; but remember, we *will* change some of the internals sooner or later. We pledge always to protect your investment in our programming interfaces. Use all the externally visible functions and web services to your heart's content. But, as Bill and Peter warn repeatedly, be careful when poking around inside the ReportServer database.

You can be assured that Bill and Peter took a very independent view of our product. I winced several times while reading the draft manuscript. As much as it hurts when someone calls our baby ugly, we learn from criticism and use it to build better and better products.

These two comments aside, I heartily recommend this book. The authors provide sage and practical advice on getting the most from Reporting Services. For example, using "Run as…" to test your reports the way your users will see them. Or how to optimally split work between the Report Server and the database server.

The first chapter alone is worth the price of admission. Chapter 4 is a most thorough walk-through of the Report Manager and all of the functionality it exposes.

Read Chapter 5 twice. It covers in great depth the concept of "minimum permissions required," which is one of the keys to keeping your corporate computing environment secure. Reporting Services is a very powerful environment. It makes a wealth of corporate information available to huge numbers of users in an easy, efficient, and cost-effective way. However, human nature is such that we tend to get excited and forget the implications of all that power and the potential access the ease of use could allow. Any deployment of Reporting Services demands careful thought and deliberate action to ensure no accidental loss of data or inadvertent granting of permissions. Reporting Services is not by its nature insecure; it is locked down by default, and you will want to open things up a bit as a convenience to your users. But pay attention. Read Chapter 5. Twice.

Make use of the appendixes and the DVD. They contain valuable tutorials and walk-throughs, including media clips of some of the more involved configuration settings. For example, we recommend using SSL. If you've never set that up, you will appreciate Appendix A and the Guide me! narrated screen capture demonstrations.

I hope you enjoy this book and profit from reading it. It is fast-paced for a technical book, and witty. The authors, as much as they goad us, also poke plenty of fun at themselves. I'm not sure I would ever admit to sending myself nearly a terabyte of e-mail. Read the footnotes too. They contain interesting nuggets and occasional cultural and technical (Edlin) references—plus Yiddish! By the way, "futz" is from the Yiddish "arumfartsn zikh." I'll leave the reader to Google that…

> I heartily recommend this book. The authors provide sage and practical advice on getting the most from Reporting Services.

> Read Chapter 5 twice.

> This book is an important addition to the Reporting Services community.

As I said earlier, we at Microsoft depend on our communities for the ultimate success of our products. Reporting Services is significant to our Business Intelligence strategy. This book is an important addition to the Reporting Services community.

Bill Baker
General Manager, SQL Server Business Intelligence
Microsoft Corporation
Redmond, Washington
July 2004

Preface

How This Book Came to Life

In the late summer of 2003, although in the sands of time it seems a lifetime away on another planet in a parallel universe, the warmth of the late afternoon sun was beaming down on Bill and me, while we sat in the gardens of a hotel near the campus of the Microsoft UK headquarters. We'd just given a number of successful presentations at a VBUG developer's conference, and we were both "high" on the post-conference euphoria. One of the sessions I had presented was on Reporting Services for Yukon—that's SQL Server 2005, but at that stage it was still in alpha builds. The Reporting Services session had been well received, and, as always when Reporting Services is first shown to developers, there was a noisy and palpable interest from the developer community, so many desperately clamoring to be released from the chains of other obtuse reporting software they were compelled to use. Fortunately, Microsoft had announced it was decoupling Reporting Services from the SQL Server 2005 project to be able to release it early. It was designed to work with SQL Server 2000, so there was quite some excitement in the air.

Ahem! By the way, Bill, I wasn't serious. It was an idle pipe dream, just like, "When I grow up I'm going to be an astronaut."

–Peter

Is that why we put an astronaut spacewalking on the cover of the book? Or is it because in the end we took the rocket science out of Reporting Services?

–Bill

As we sat there and ordered more drinks, I idly suggested that we could very *easily* write a book on Reporting Services—after all, there was nothing *too* complicated to Reporting Services. It's so intuitive that it couldn't take us long to turn out a 200-page book.

Bill seized the idle, naïve chatter at face value, and a few months later, after lengthy negotiations with Addison-Wesley, we started writing this book. We figured it would be done a few weeks after the product release, and we could spend a leisurely spring lecturing and collecting royalties.

What I didn't know was that Peter was thinking about 200 pages of microfiche.

–Bill

Anyway, soon after we got started, my life stopped—perhaps just my old life—and a time warp began; I'm an awful *lot* older now, and strangely my grandparents seem much younger than me. You see, that initially conceived "easy" 200 pages mushroomed as we covered more ground in the technical detail we'd be proud to put our names to. I tried telling Bill that I always assumed that Sondra Scott, our acquisitions editor at Addison-Wesley, really had 4-point type in mind when calculating 200 pages.

Who Is This Book For?

This book is for you if you do anything with Reporting Services.

When we are asked this question we usually answer "yes." This book is for you if you do anything with Reporting Services and value the enterprise security of your systems. So, that includes anyone from a user or manager with little technical knowledge to a report developer or systems integrator, right up to and including the Reporting Services rocket scientists working with Microsoft. We kid you not; we were privileged to have worked very closely indeed with the Microsoft Reporting Services development team as we wrote this book, and get e-mails from members of the team asking us how we had implemented certain functionality, and we also fed back a lot of information to Microsoft as we wrote the book. In fact, one of the reasons we held back from publishing too soon after the launch of Reporting Services was because as a result of feedback we had given, certain security-related functionality was scheduled to be placed in Service Pack 1. At that point, we realized too many issues needed resolution to rush the book to press. We could not in good conscience publish a book that did not give the reader the complete story. Since it includes detailed information on what Service Pack 1 fixes (and what it doesn't), it will prove to be the most current book on the market. Even if you've bought another Reporting Services book, we're certain that this book will be well worth the price.

Report Server Administrators and DBAs

Yes, this book is most especially for you and the developers you support. Reporting Services is a great product, and it gives users a lot of long–sought after powerful functionality. *But*, and this is a big but, if you as a DBA implement Reporting Services in an insecure way, you might as well post the SA password and your private data on a public newsgroup or display it in Times Square for the world to see. We appreciate that Reporting Services calls for skills that fall outside the hitherto usual skill set of a DBA. Because of this we've gone to great lengths to ensure that we explain the skills you'll need in an easy-to-read but concise way. You see, Reporting Services is a product that also requires IIS skill. Many DBAs are gurus with the Query Analyzer and SQL Profiler. They're used to interrogating poorly coded T-SQL in stored procedures, rhythmically tut-tutting as they see yet more unbelievably clumsy T-SQL programming. However, when it comes to IIS, .NET programming, and SOAP, some DBAs break out in a cold sweat and freeze when developers start talking "OOP." Well, hey, relax! We'll walk you through all of these dark alleys with a 20,000 candle-power light and an armed escort.

Chapter 1 gives you insight into all the components of Reporting Services. Chapter 2 talks you through installing Reporting Services, showing you how to ensure that you choose the right accounts. This way you don't leave a back door open to your databases for all the (evil/curious/adventurous) ASP.NET developers in your organization. It also talks you through how to ensure that the Reporting Services website has an SSL certificate. This is very important. We firmly encourage you to set up Reporting Services with an SSL certificate. If you don't, we are aware of sniffing vulnerabilities that can be targeted to extract credentials as they are passed around the network. During Reporting Services installation, an SSL certificate is required by default and for excellent, important reasons. Microsoft goes to great lengths to encourage you to use SSL—they really want your data to be secure (and so do we). You have to take personal responsibility if you uncheck the SSL checkbox and install without SSL.

Chapter 4 is a good source of information, as most DBAs will be responsible for administering the Report Server. All the features are explained in an incremental way. No, you won't need to write any reports, but a lot goes into the configuration of a Report Server to ensure that correct security is established, and that data source Connection strings are configured correctly.

> Chapter 5 is also an absolute must read for DBAs.

While you might not be that bothered about writing reports, Chapter 5 is also an absolute must read for DBAs. Here we strongly encourage you to switch off Integrated Security on the Report Server so that you can sleep at night. Chapter 5 will give you all the ammunition you need to make sure when you sit in those management meetings and a user is trying to get your boss to force you to switch Integrated Security back on, you'll be able explain the risks. You should also make sure they give you these orders in writing, countersigned by the manager's mother: *"Yes, I know my son is a manager with no technical background or understanding whatsoever, but he really does want you to enable Integrated Security. I'll take full responsibility for him. —Mom"*

Now, many DBAs have only just taken the lid off Visual Basic for Applications (VBA), and to a large extent we have DTS to thank for that. However, there is no VBA for Reporting Services. If you want to do any scripting work, you need to do that with Visual Basic .NET and the report scripting tool called rs.exe. The report scripting tool uses the Report Server's SOAP interface, so you'll also find the magic of Chapter 9¾ quite helpful.

Report Users/Managers

If you see yourself as just a user of reports and already have Reporting Services installed, of most interest to you in this book will be Chapter 1, in which we deal with an overview of the technology, and Chapter 4, in which we go through in detail how to use the Report Manager. Chapter 4 is good to be able to work through in a tutorial style because you'll see most of the functionality of the Report Manager, assuming that your report Administrator has enabled it. And if certain features are not enabled you'll know what privileges you want to petition him or her for.

Report Authors

> Bill Baker (General Manager of SQL Server Business Intelligence) suggests in the Foreword that it's a great idea to read Chapter 5 more than once.

If you want to create reports, in addition to Chapters 1 and 4, where report users should concentrate initially, you'll want to take the tutorial through Chapter 3 where we show you how to use the built-in report wizard. Working through this chapter will give you a grounding before you look at Chapter 5. Chapter 5 is pretty important because it explains the security considerations you need to bear in mind, but to begin to appreciate it you do need a good foundation. Bill Baker (General Manager of SQL Server Business Intelligence) suggests in the Foreword that it's a great idea to read Chapter 5 more than once. Certainly after you have worked through Chapters 6 and 7 you'll have a greater appreciation for why Chapter 5 is so important, especially if you want to keep your enterprise secure. As you become more proficient you'll want to experiment with charts and Matrix tables—those are covered in Chapter 8.

Report Developers

Once you're off the launch pad and feel confident in creating reports, you'll want to start pushing the envelope of what you can do with Reporting Services to make your productivity much better. In Chapter 9, we show you how and where you create report and project templates so that you can bring a consistent look and feel to your reports. We also show you how you can have styles applied to reports at runtime by creating your own .NET assemblies—and indeed we show you all you need to know about code access security as it is implemented in Reporting Services. Code access security is a complex topic, but we have gone to extreme lengths to lower the access bar to your understanding it—and if you work through it you'll feel you're head and shoulders above your colleagues. If you're already a code access security guru, Chapter 9 is still worth working through. You see, in Reporting Services there are a number of peculiarities about how code access security is implemented. As an added benefit of working through code access security, you'll probably find that you can then leverage what you have learnt to other .NET programming that you do. You'll be well on your way to becoming a .NET guru yourself.

Web Developers

If you're planning on utilizing Reporting Services with your own web applications, Chapter 10 will be of interest to you as it deals with how to use the Report Server via its URL interface—which is probably the best way to go. However, you may indeed be tempted to use the Reporting Services SOAP interface, so be sure to study Chapter 9¾. Yes that's 9¾, but it's not where you might suspect it is, so you'll have to look in the right place for it. A clue: 9¾ is not between Chapters 9 and 10.

Systems Integrators

Now, here's the scoop. Say you already have your own application and you want to add reporting functionality to it. You look at Microsoft Report Manager, and it doesn't do just what you'd like it to do. You know it would if only you could customize it, change the colors, and most importantly, specify the way parameters are collected from your users. You see, natively the Report Manager doesn't support multiple column selects. Well, the choice is yours. You might try to build your own Report Manager, which is a tedious amount of work, depending on how much functionality you are going to put into it. Or you can phone Microsoft and ask for the source code to the Report Manager. You'll probably hear the same thing we did, but Addison-Wesley won't print it—it wasn't very nice (something about open source being the bane of the industry). Or you can spend literally a few minutes tweaking the Report Manager by updating its cascading style sheets and implementing HTML behavior files to work with your custom parameter user interfaces. Well, Chapter 11 takes you behind the scenes and shows you how to do it. Yes, it's possible (and fairly likely) that Microsoft will come back and tweak things later; but hey, 30 minutes customizing the Report Manager is a short-time investment as opposed to 30 person-months building your own Report Manager to get the same functionality, isn't it? Besides, we plan on making some tools available to help make the customizations even easier, so do check on our website (www.SQLReportingServices.NET). We also hope to take a proof of concept that we have working in our labs to a production product that enables people to do server-side printing from the Report Manager. Stay tuned.

Peter's concept of time is a bit skewed. I know what "basketball" minutes are, but "Peter" minutes are a lot longer. When Peter says "a few minutes," he really means a long afternoon that stretches into dinnertime.

–Bill

Hardcore Guru Developers

If you have a unique source of data that you want to leverage, you'll need to figure out how to write your own Data Processing extension. We walk through the Microsoft example and explain how to make it work. Without our help you'll find it a bit tough—Microsoft left off a bit of information here and there. Next, we carefully guide you through the process of writing a Data Processing extension to generate reports from the Windows event logs in your Domain. You don't have to be a hardcore developer to work through Chapter 13, but if you follow the example, you'll be a very accomplished report programmer by the end of it.

The DVD

Narrated Guide me! sessions permit the reader to see Reporting Services in action.

When documenting a product as visually rich as Reporting Services, one of the problems is how to describe the *visual* aspects of the product. To address this challenge we recorded dozens of Camtasia screen capture sessions and provided them on the DVD that ships with the book. These narrated Guide me! sessions permit the reader to see Reporting Services in action while we walk through setup, report creation, using the Report Manager, creating subscriptions and Snapshots, and many other aspects of Reporting Services. In the accompanying DVD, we have gone much further to redefine the concept of what a technical book should provide. Our video demonstrations not only explain but also *show* how to navigate safely through some of the more difficult and confusing parts of the technology. The demonstrations walk the reader step by step through complex wizards by showing every step in motion—with instructor voices in the background—which creates a virtual classroom experience. These demonstrations are provided in a form that any Windows system can play. The DVD also includes lots of code samples, selected white papers, and supplementary text. This is truly a work that takes the reader far beyond the official Microsoft documentation.

Also included on the DVD are products and samples from several third-party companies that work closely with Reporting Services.

Thanks to the generosity of the Microsoft SQL Server team, we also include a demonstration version of Reporting Services that you're free to install and use on your own system.

www.SQLReportingServices.NET

When you purchase this book, you are provided with an individual code that enables you to register for access to Premium Content areas of our website and have access to our support newsgroups, discussion groups, and special offers. If you visit this site you'll see hundreds of threads that discuss common (and some not so common) questions and answers (if there is one). We regularly post responses here, as do many other experienced Reporting Services DBAs and developers. This is also where we'll be posting updates to any report examples, new templates, and add-ins that we might build or discover. You can also ask questions about the examples in the book (there are several dozen).

So what are you standing here reading the Preface for? Take several copies of the book over to the counter and buy them for your colleagues.

Peter Blackburn
Huntingdon, UK
July 2004

> I wanted to create a book from which developers with almost any level of experience could get inside information.

A Note from William Vaughn, Coauthor

My original Hitchhiker's Guide series was started with the intent of providing a different approach to technical documentation and learning. When *Hitchhiker's Guide to Visual Basic and SQL Server* was published, I had been developing and presenting SQL Server, Visual Basic, and other technical courseware at Microsoft University for more than five years. Because I found this environment somewhat stifling, I wanted to create a book from which developers with almost any level of experience could get *inside* information—facts not shared by the Microsoft documentation or courseware. The idea was to provide fundamental information for developers just getting started, as well as advanced information for those more up to speed with the technology. The books not only told readers *how* to do something but *why*. I always included my own opinions and best practices based on decades of experience, real-world customer interaction, and direct contact with the development teams at Microsoft. The books also provided a solutions-oriented approach that showed the reader how a problem was actually solved—not endless lists of objects, properties, methods, and events. I also wanted the books to be easier to read than the Microsoft documentation, which had to be technically generic, politically correct, and (so it seemed) dull. Sure, some of the quips I used in the Hitchhiker's Guides were not understood by some Clevelandites or C++ developers, but they're both tough groups to get through to.

Sometimes the Hitchhiker's Guides brought "issues" (okay, bugs) to light that weren't always complimentary to Microsoft, and from time to time, I would hear low rumbling noises from the vicinity of the development and marketing teams on the Redmond campus (within artillery range of my house). However, once they understood that I was writing to "typical" developers in an attempt to help them better understand and use the tools, Microsoft began to understand how valuable the books could be and provided more and more assistance—and inside information. Eventually, Microsoft Press began publishing the Hitchhiker's Guide series—jabs, issues, one-liners, and all. *Hitchhiker's Guide to Visual Basic and SQL Server* was in its sixth edition when I retired from Microsoft in 2000 to focus on mentoring, writing, and lecturing.

At this point, I wanted to continue the popular Hitchhiker's Guide series, but I was waiting for the right subject, publisher, and technical resources. By happenstance, I met Peter Blackburn when he was assigned as technical editor for my ADO.NET book. Peter, who lives in the United Kingdom, proved to be an invaluable resource because of his vast technical depth and thorough understanding of SQL Server, Windows, security, and the web. We soon became good friends, despite the language barrier (he's a C# fan). What you might not appreciate is that Peter has the same dry "English" sense of humour that I do.

When Peter approached me about doing a book on Reporting Services, I was initially hesitant, as my interests had shifted away from reporting. However, Peter's enthusiasm and in-depth knowledge of the Reporting Services technology convinced me. I agreed to help if he could provide the technical details.

Frankly, Peter is the primary author of this book. My contribution has been to rework the material to match the tone and readability of the Hitchhiker's Guide series. I also have edited the content to provide a "less-experienced" point of view so it can be more easily understood by those not as versed in the inner workings of Windows, security, the web, SOAP, CAS, LSMFT (and several other acronyms), Visual Studio .NET, and Reporting Services.

Who Should Buy This Book?

We think *Hitchhiker's Guide to SQL Server 2000 Reporting Services* is designed to address the needs of database administrators (DBAs), application developers, and their managers who are:

- Getting up to speed on Reporting Services and need a quick tutorial on how to get started and how to setup simple single-server installations or a web farm
- Planning to administer a Reporting Services installation where an in-depth understanding of the Report Manager, Report Designer, subscription model, security issues, report caching, and custom extensions is needed
- Learning to write and deploy reports using the Visual Studio .NET Report Designer
- Trying to solve Reporting Services installation, design, configuration, security, or subscription problems
- Importing reports from Microsoft Access or other platforms to Reporting Services
- Writing programs using the Reporting Services SOAP interface
- Designing their own custom Data Processing extensions and understanding how the extensions work
- In need of up-to-the minute fixes and workarounds for newly discovered issues as well as advice and Reporting Services developer community support

As you can see, Peter and I have ventured far off the beaten track. That's because we want this book to be the definitive source on Reporting Services. We understand that not all of our readers are familiar with SQL Server or Visual Studio, so we also provide easy-to-follow steps to get readers up to speed quickly—regardless of their experience level.

William R. Vaughn
Redmond, Washington
July 2004

Acknowledgments

Bill Vaughn

The person I must acknowledge most of all on this project is my friend and coauthor, Bill Vaughn. The writing of this book has in real terms taken many man-years of work time, if one were to take 40 hours as a man-week. Literally, I've rarely stopped working on this project other than to sleep, and I've been the cause of many of Bill's sleepless nights. Bill, without your constant encouragement, patience, understanding, and ability to take my technical output to the next level of prose and presentation, then I think I'd have left this as an unfinished work many months ago and gone out consulting. Heaven knows it's more profitable.

Peter Blackburn

(By Bill Vaughn) I haven't known Peter that long—only four or five years. But in that relatively short period of time I have grown to respect him on many levels. He's become a close friend—far beyond being my coauthor. Peter's greatest qualities are his insight, honesty, and integrity. He stridently challenges us to protect ourselves against those who would steal, pilfer, and vandalize our data. He's told me about many situations where chinks in the security were to be found and how easy it would be to get in—but his scruples prevented him from capitalizing on leveraging those security flaws. I'm just glad he's on "our" side. We're about to launch out on a new book—this time I'll be the principal author—but I don't know that I could do it without Peter to make sure I get the technical details right and to keep me on track with some of the uglier aspects of Visual Studio—like C# and (ugh) XML.

Microsoft Reporting Services Development Team

We were very privileged throughout the writing of this book to have direct access to many members of the development team. The relationship has been a symbiotic one. It can be frustrating to write about a product, how to use it, and how to work around its foibles, and have to turn around and present work for technical review by the very folks who then go and change the product (to correct the foibles, issues, and bugs). However, it does result in a better product, and it certainly enabled us to produce a book of much higher quality than would otherwise have been possible. So we'd like to acknowledge the members of Jason Carlson's team whom Jason permitted to give generously of their time. This book has been greatly enriched through the input the team provided.

Brian Welcker, *Microsoft Reporting Services Group Program Manager*

Brian gave very generously of his time, led the technical review of our manuscript, and provided us with access to members of his own team. Brian, while you could have made it easier and simply given us the source code, we are grateful and acknowledge your input, speedy responses to our queries, and detailed comments on the chapters. It must not go unnoticed or unacknowledged that many of your e-mails to us were timed in the early hours of your morning and from an IP address that clearly indicated you were working from home. Or was it a satellite link to your yacht? Thank you for taking our suggestions and feedback into account and ensuring that answers to our issues were always found, especially when some of those answers escaped your encyclopedic knowledge of the product. We understand why you consulted Chris Hays on Transparency not being a color because we needed him to explain it to us about 50 times before we eventually got the message. Anyway, thanks also for resolving many of our issues in Service Pack 1, and for scheduling some of the others to Service Pack 2 and the Yukon release. We know that you diligently worked through our prose and examples. Our book could simply not have happened in the quality it has without the constant support and assistance you provided.

Tudor Trufinescu, *Microsoft Reporting Services Development Lead*

Tudor technically reviewed many of the more complex topics, and we know we provided him with ample cause (many times over) to give birth to several litters of kittens. Tudor, we really didn't have the source code—we worked it out for ourselves. However, we did learn a lot of IL. Well, Tudor, we tried to be honest. As a result, we have to warn our readers that the undocumented features we discuss are not supported and may (will) change, as Bill Baker mentioned in the Foreword, so hopefully you can cancel the contract on us? We really do appreciate your rapier-like focus and explanations about the perplexing way some of the esoteric features work or don't work. Readers, especially those of you who are DBAs, Tudor would like you to learn to use the SOAP interface rather than go dipping into the Report Server database with T-SQL. Tudor mentioned to us that if the only tool you know how to use is a hammer then everything looks like a nail. We understand and encourage using Microsoft supported interfaces. But sometimes you know a DBA's gotta do what a DBA's gotta do to a database. And yes, when they do it they know they are on their own. Meddle with the Report Server database with extreme caution, and ensure you have a backup first. Thanks, Tudor.

Robert Bruckner, *Microsoft Reporting Services Developer*

Robert (when he wasn't hobnobbing with premier ranking European politicians) took time out to help us with the chapter on charting. Robert, your input was especially useful in that it identified for us the additional features of the Dundas Chart control that were to be enabled in SP1, before any documentation was available. Robert also provided us with a number of tips and directions to inside passageways to some of the more obscure features of the Chart control. Vielen Dank!

Chris Hays, *Microsoft Reporting Services Program Manager*

We had much fun with Chris during the development stages, when we'd banter and exchange hacks we'd found to get around certain limitations. Chris wanted to know at one stage if there was a competition for his crown as the King of the Sleazy Hacks. Chris, take a look at our Chapter 11 on customizing the Report Manager. Are there any better hacks, or do we now own the crown? Thanks for your help, Chris. By the way, folks, those of you who get confused about setting colors in the Report Designer, Chris is the guy who has done the most for the human race in helping the understanding that in the Report Designer "Transparent is NOT a color"—it's the absence of a color, and "Nothing at all" gets put into the RDL when you choose Transparent; it's not a string literal. Thanks for that "see-through" explanation, Chris.

Heidi Steen, *Microsoft Reporting Services Documentation Manager*

Bryan Keller, *Microsoft Reporting Services Programmer Writer*

Michelle Larez, *Microsoft Reporting Services Technical Writer*

Heidi reviewed several of our chapters herself and kindly enabled Michelle Larez and Bryan Keller, members of her team, to review other chapters. Thank you, Heidi! These are the folks who wrote the Reporting Services Books Online Documentation. Their review of our manuscript was invaluable, and as with the development team the relationship has proven to be very symbiotic. As we went along, we gave feedback on what we noticed was awry in the BOL documentation, and they let us know when we had the wrong end of the stick in our chapters. Perhaps to the outside world some of our interactions would appear to be how a study group might study together for an examination, as some issues came up that permitted us to all to take a metaphorical stick to the development team at certain points, from different angles.

Michelle very (very) diligently worked through chapters relating to the use of the Report Designer. Michelle also gave us invaluable and detailed stylistic feedback, which enabled us to alter the structure so that it fit together much better. Thank you, Michelle!

Now, Bryan. Bryan reviewed many of our programming chapters, and we know that proved time consuming. We did hit a few brick walls in some areas, and Bryan very kindly copied code samples that he was working on for the next product, which went some of the way toward enabling us to gain a clearer understanding. For certain, without Bryan's generous help and availability we might never have got to the bottom of some of the topics we covered. So, thank you, Bryan.

Alexandre Mineev, *Microsoft Reporting Services Developer*

We need to thank Alex for the clarity he brought us when reviewing the code access security chapter. There were a few improvements that he suggested and we adopted. Code access security is a fairly complex issue to get one's head around, and we have gone to great lengths to make it easy for readers. Alex, the comment you fed back to our publishers as you reviewed the content: "Overall, great chapter. Easy to read, contains a lot of useful info and no water!" made our heads swell. Thanks for the kind words and the feedback.

Donovan Smith, *Microsoft Reporting Services Test Lead*

Daniel Reib, *Microsoft Reporting Services Developer*

Mike Schetterer, *Microsoft Reporting Services Test Lead*

Bruce Johnson, *Microsoft Reporting Services Tester*

Albert Yen, *Microsoft Reporting Services Development Lead*

During the writing of this book, these guys helped us identify issues that we had flagged as bugs. And we appreciate the time and explanations you all took when responding to our e-mails. Thanks, guys!

Bill Baker, *Microsoft General Manager SQL Server Business Intelligence*

By championing our book, Bill broke down a number of barriers to the development, testing, and documentation teams. All along the way, if we had problems, he was able to get us back on track with the right people and resources. He also wrote a very complimentary Foreword for the book sometime between a family bar mitzvah and a trip to the emergency room. We sure hope it wasn't the bugs we uncovered that made you ill.

Douglas Milnes

Douglas Milnes gave freely of his spare time to work through some of our chapters, approaching them as a complete novice to Reporting Services, which he still is. (No, that bit is not true, but it sounded funny and Douglas laughed along with us when we'd said that. He's actually now very accomplished with Reporting Services.) This enabled us to take feedback from someone not contaminated with a longstanding relationship with the product prior to reading our content and enabled us to pay attention to structure and to content that was missing. Douglas also filmed (and refilmed and refilmed) many of the screen demonstrations following the instructions in the book, enabling us to do the editing and voice more quickly. And we must not forget the time that Douglas devoted to getting the book's website, www.SQLReportingServices.NET, up and running.

John Salichos

John is a Reporting Services developer who lives in Greece. John also gave his time to discuss and dissect with us various bugs that we'd unearthed during the early development stage, and we used him as a sounding board before we'd call in a bug to see if he could reproduce it too.

Sondra Scott

Sondra Scott, who was an acquisitions editor at Addison-Wesley at the time, signed us up. Sondra talked us into this project (and two others). This was a process that took her over five years to accomplish, but it paved the way for what we hope to be a long-term relationship with Addison-Wesley. Sondra spent countless hours discussing the industry with us—learning what we wanted in an author/publisher relationship. Without her, we probably would not have signed. Thanks.

The Addison-Wesley Team

Of course, the book would not have been done at all without you guys and gals. Thanks for putting up with us and our tirades and quirky style. Let's hope this is only the first in a long series of successful books.

Ildikó Blackburn

Well, what can I say? Writing a book won't make me a millionaire, even if we do have a Harry Potter chapter in the book. But were it not for me being a "kept" man I would not have been able to devote 100 percent of my waking hours to this project, and the project could not have happened. Ildikó, being a SQL Server consultant servicing many of the UK clients of Geac, is actually well placed to understand the technical details of this book, and on many occasions she provided input while doing the vacuuming around me. I'll let you the reader find the references in the prose. Toward the end of the project, I was indeed getting very depressed with the overwhelming work still to do, and the poor quality of my recording microphone picking up RF from my monitors. Ildikó went out and replaced my CRT monitors with two 21-inch LCD pivot monitors, and a professional studio recording microphone, boom, preamp, and mixing desk. When we went into the microphone store, we explained to the salesman that I was trying to record voice onto a computer for various videos. I told him that I was frustrated that the present microphone I had was pathetic and was constantly picking up the noise of my fans. The salesman expressed that he understood how noisy and frustrating fans can be. I mean, we even talked with him about water cooling and refrigeration—and at some considerable length too. Unfazed by this, he sold us a top-of-the-range microphone. However, it was as Ildikó was paying that it came to light that the salesman discreetly asked her who I was and which rock band I was from. He told her he recognized me and knew I was famous, but he just didn't want to embarrass himself or insult me by asking me himself. Turns out, you see, the salesman thought the noisy "fans" in question were my adoring groupies. So if in the background of the DVD recordings you hear throngs of screaming young people eager for my next words, you know that it's only my other fans! Anyway, that was a bit of a digression, but thank you, Ildikó, for your constant support and encouragement, and seeing me through the really dark times when the going on this book was tough.

Marilyn Vaughn

Marilyn is Bill's wife, and she has been very understanding of the pressures that this book has placed on Bill. When I have been in Redmond, Marilyn has kindly accommodated me, providing more pleasant surroundings than I could have had being stuck in some hotel. Thank you for the home away from home, Marilyn.

(By Bill Vaughn) Marilyn has (again) helped keep the kids, dogs, cats, and kittens out of my office while the job of writing a 200-page book that was supposed to take four months stretched to 700+ pages and almost a year. While she didn't go out and buy me a new set of monitors (sigh), she did get me out of the house and back on my feet when I got cabin fever. She's also my bookkeeper and does the whole job without a computer (miraculous). Thanks.

Peter Blackburn
Huntingdon, UK
July 2004

About the Authors

PETER BLACKBURN has worked in the computer industry since 1981. He studied computer science at Cambridge University, England, where he received an M.A. Through his consulting company, Boost Data Limited, Peter has designed, built, and implemented small and large-scale database systems, including reporting systems based on SQL Server. He has contributed countless hours to the development and honing of Microsoft Reporting Services and remains directly involved with the development team, and he is a Microsoft MVP. He supports developers through newsgroups and beta programs, and trains teams of developers working with SQL Server and Reporting Services. Having worked closely with .NET since before its launch, Peter and Boost Data have ensured the technical accuracy of many leading .NET books. Peter lives in the United Kingdom and travels all over the world to consult, speak, and provide support for his fellow developers, fellow MVPs, his writing team, and Microsoft itself.

    WILLIAM R. VAUGHN has worked in the computer industry since 1972. He holds a bachelor's degree in computer science from Mary Hardin-Baylor and a master's degree in interdisciplinary studies from the University of Texas. He's also been awarded an honorary Ph.D. from the University of Advancing Computer Technology in Tempe, Arizona. He began working for the Windows developer liaison team at Microsoft in 1986. For 14 years he worked in various divisions at Microsoft, including Microsoft University and the Visual Basic documentation, Visual Studio marketing, and Internal Technical Education teams, before retiring in 2000 to form his own company, Beta V Corporation. Bill has written six editions of the popular *Hitchhiker's Guide* (Microsoft Press) and several books for APress, including the bestseller *ADO Examples* *and Best Practices*. He writes lead articles for *SQL Server Magazine*, *Hardcore Visual Studio*, *MSDN Magazine*, *Visual Studio Magazine*, and others. He also writes a biweekly editorial for *Processor.com Magazine*. Bill is a top-rated speaker at conferences worldwide, including keynotes and sessions at VSLive, TechEd, DevWeek, Dev Connections, SQL Connections, VBUG, PASS, and many others. He is a Microsoft MVP.

CHAPTER 1

An Overview

This chapter puts Microsoft SQL Server 2000 Reporting Services in context. You'll learn about its architecture and its place in the world and get a brief overview of its features and functionality. This *is* an important chapter because it helps you understand why Reporting Services is more than just an alternative (or supplement) to Crystal Reports and how it can make your life easier.

We know you're chomping at the bit to get started—and perhaps you've already installed the software, snooped around, and tried out a report or two. Hopefully you've extracted a copy of the symmetric encryption key and have the backup off-site, along with the backup file password. Yes? Good. Now we're ready to dispel any prejudices or misconceptions your explorations have generated.

Security is (or should be) very important to you; at least we know your boss is concerned with security. All along the way, we'll show you how to secure your data and reports in ways that the documentation doesn't mention or only touches upon. We'll discuss encryption and topics that seem pretty far removed from "reporting," but without these protections, you might as well post reports exposing your company secrets on the 20-foot newsreader board in Times Square.

Guide me!

NOTE We've spent quite a bit of time creating audio-annotated screen capture demonstrations of aspects of Reporting Services. You'll find these demos on the accompanying DVD. We call these Guide me! videos. If you need help on a section, look for the Guide me! icon in the margin.

What Is Microsoft SQL Server 2000 Reporting Services?

At long last, developers have a brand-new server-based reporting solution from Microsoft built from the ground up, almost completely but not entirely in .NET managed code. Without being *too* enthusiastic, we can say that Reporting Services enables extremely straightforward, centrally managed, rapidly developed, easily extended, scalable, secure, fixed as well as interactive, proactive as well as passive database reporting to a variety of (extensible) output formats, from *any* database or data source (and not just SQL Server) whose learning curve is hardly a curve; it's almost flat. <Whew!> Best of all, it's free! Well, let's qualify that statement a little: it's included with the SQL Server Standard or better license at no additional cost.

Not having taken the Microsoft red pill,[1] we can freely draw comparisons to other reporting products on the market. One of the first that undoubtedly flashes into everyone's minds is Crystal Reports. In contrast to Crystal Reports, Reporting Services is a product that Microsoft definitely got right from the outset. We see a new age dawning of assault on Crystal practitioners. Stand by to be assimilated—resistance is futile.

Okay, if you are at the pinnacle of pushing Crystal to its functional feature limits, you may well find that Crystal offers additional functionality over Microsoft Reporting Services, even if it's expensive and awkward to learn and use. However, we think that the vast majority of developers and power users in the market want reporting that's easy to use, learn, and develop with. Microsoft Reporting Services certainly delivers that.

What Is the Source of the Report Data?

Before we go any further, we want to reinforce the message that although the product name includes the moniker "SQL Server 2000" as in "Microsoft SQL Server 2000 Reporting Services," in fact SQL

---

[1] Or been on their payroll.

released now, as in right now, with the current version of SQL Server 2000. Microsoft appeared to take that feedback to heart, and in June 2003 it was publicly announced at the TechEd Conference in Dallas: Rosetta for SQL Server 2000 would indeed be released at the end of 2003. We're both glad that Rosetta was untied from Yukon because we don't expect this innovative version of SQL Server to appear for another year (or so).

–Peter

Server 2000 is required only as the catalog repository for the deployed (managed) reports and their metadata, and not necessarily as the *only* data source that those reports can be based on.

In fact, right out of the box Reporting Services includes built-in support to generate reports from a number of data sources through what the Reporting Services folks call ***Data Processing extensions***. Think of them as another form of .NET Data Providers; they're based on the same technology. Data is extracted from SQL Server and Oracle as well as any other database management system (DBMS) that can be accessed via either OLE DB providers or ODBC drivers using Data Processing extensions. This means that most commercial data stores are accessible because there are managed .NET Data Providers as well as OLE DB or ODBC drivers for virtually every serious data source. These providers are available from Microsoft or from the DBMS manufacturers and third-party data provider vendors such as DataDirect (and others).

Reporting Services is designed with an open architecture. No, Microsoft does not publish the source code,[2] but under the covers, Reporting Services' Data Processing extensions utilize a subset of easily understood .NET Data Provider interfaces. If you can get or write a .NET Data Provider for a custom data source (something that's moderately easy), Reporting Services can connect to and generate reports on that custom data source.[3] We'll discuss this in more detail in Chapter 13 where we'll show you our implementation to report on the Windows system event logs.

Reporting Services: The Main Components

In a nutshell, to author a report, the developer creates a ***report definition*** using the Report Designer add-in to Visual Studio .NET 2003 or a third-party authoring tool.[4] While under development, each

---

[2]   Like *that* will happen…

[3]   Writing a .NET Data Provider in managed code is much easier than writing an ODBC driver, unlike writing an OLE DB data provider, which requires a Ph.D. in nuclear physics and abstract reasoning.

[4]   See the DVD for a list of these tools as well as working examples of their RDL generators.

Delving into the intermediate language (IL) of these components (which is, of course, expected of a potty-trained geek like me) leads one to conclude that C# was the developer's language of choice.
–Peter

Yes, but those folks were C++ geeks and not smart enough to learn Visual Basic .NET.
–Bill

OK, Bill, I'll let you win. The Visual Basic .NET geeks can be smarter, if that's what you want, but the C# geeks will remain richer. "Developers who program primarily in C# earn 26 percent more than those who develop primarily in Visual Basic .NET." (www.fawcette.com/ vsm/2003_06/ magazine/features/ salarysurvey/)
–Peter

Yes, but C# programs take 28 percent longer to write, so they spend more time at the office while the Visual Basic programmers are out having a life.
–Bill

Nice try, but if you read the article, this was based on hourly rates.
Peter

report definition is maintained in its own XML file, which is given the file extension of "RDL". We'll tell you more about RDL later on; however, succinctly, RDL files contain the layout, graphics, connection, and query information as well as Report Parameter definitions and almost all other report logic. Using the Report Designer, developers can author, tune, and refine reports without having to access the Report Server. At design time, reports can be "previewed" using the Report Designer, which provides a close approximation of what the finished report will look like when rendered by the Report Processor.

Once a report definition is complete, the report is published, or "deployed," to a Report Server where it becomes a compiled ***managed report***. At this point, the DBA or report administrator can decide how and to whom a report is to be made available.

The Report Server exposes a SOAP[5] interface, through which these managed reports can be programmatically manipulated. Straight out of the box, there is a fully functional Report Manager. This is an ASP-based application that sits on top of the Report Server's SOAP interface and provides a user-friendly GUI environment with which to manage reports. Additionally, there is a Report Scripting Utility (rs.exe) that enables you to execute scripts that make calls to the SOAP interface.

We'll show you how to launch managed reports from code or simply tune up or customize the existing Report Manager. When it's time to view a managed report, the compiled report definition is fed to the Report Processor, which fetches the data, merges it with the report layout, renders the report into a selected format, and streams back the result. Reports can be processed on demand or according to customizable schedules. It's all really very simple. But don't close the book yet. There are a few more details that you'll want to know.

Reporting Services is composed of a number of well-integrated components, most of which are written in .NET managed code. Some of these components we'll be exploring, and we shall see that they consist of open and extensible subcomponents. The overall look and feel of the Reporting Services Report Designer is reminiscent of web (ASP) application development in Visual Studio .NET or the

---

[5]   We discuss how to manipulate reports through SOAP in Chapter 9¾.

Report Designer in Microsoft Access—but it's far more flexible. To build a report you first define the location of the source of its data, lay out some controls on the report surface, and bind those controls to the data. For much of this, it's all drag and drop. When the report is generated, the Report Server extrudes the report in much the same way that the ASP.NET engine returns HTML from a web page. But Reporting Services does not stop there. It can also render reports in a variety of other ways, as we'll soon explain.

Here are the main components of Reporting Services:

- A Visual Studio .NET 2003 add-in **Report Designer** for authoring reports. As we'll show you in Chapters 3, 6, and 7, this is alarmingly reminiscent of the Report Designer in Microsoft Access.[6] It extends Visual Studio .NET 2003 to permit developers to define Reporting Services DataSets, specify a query and layout, and preview and deploy the report definitions, which are saved to report definition (RDL) files in the project and then when deployed, are saved to the Report Server database as intermediate language (IL).
- An ASP.NET XML Web Service–based **Report Server** works in conjunction with a .NET Windows System ReportServer Service to process and provide managed reports in a variety of rendered output streams and stores its configuration, processing information, and other metadata in SQL Server.
- An ASP.NET web application–based **Report Manager** for centralized report management is an important tool for DBAs, developers, and users. It's designed for report management and is an ideal and secure platform for users to select and launch reports. The Report Manager permits developers or database administrators (DBAs) to define or modify Data Sources, locate and organize reports, and create **Subscriptions**, which permit reports to be e-mailed on a scheduled basis. We detail the Report Manager in Chapter 4.

Figure 1.1 gives you the basic idea how the basic Reporting Services components fit together.

---

[6] It's almost as if both SQL Server Reporting Services and Access were written by the same company.

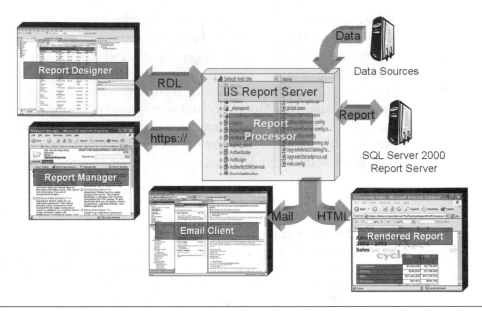

Figure 1.1 SQL Server Reporting Services Overview

Writing Reports: The Report Designer

WYSIWYG—what you see is what you get. Goodness, haven't we come a long way since the Apple Macintosh?
 –Peter

Peter does not remember (he was in primary school) when WYSIWYG appeared on CPT word processors, which predate the Apple Macintosh.
 –Bill

Reporting Services comes with a WYSIWYG Report Designer add-in to Visual Studio .NET 2003 (as shown in Figure 1.2) to aid in the construction of report definitions. The Report Designer provides a new set of Business Intelligence Project types containing two out-of-the-box templates: a Report Project wizard and a blank report project—we'll show you how to create your own Report Templates in Chapter 9. No, Visual Studio .NET doesn't have to be the Rolls Royce (or Cadillac) version to host the Reporting Services add-in. The inexpensive Visual Basic .NET 2003 Standard (or Academic) version is sufficient.

The Report Designer is as intuitive and easy to use as the Microsoft Access Report Designer, but it's far more powerful. The typical report-authoring approach is to create a Reporting Services DataSet (which, by the way, is not to be confused with an ADO.NET DataSet). This DataSet is connected to the source of the data through a Reporting Services Data Source, which is effectively a Connection string. Once the underlying data is provided for the report, the next step is to visually lay out the report controls, binding them to the underlying data, customize their properties, and preview the report. All of this can be done without having to involve the Reporting Services server.

Once you're ready, you can ask the Report Designer add-in to "deploy" either the report definition or the whole report project, which might contain several report definitions, to the designated IIS[7] server (where your Reporting Services virtual directories are hosted). This creates one or more managed reports on your server—one for each report in your project—and creates any Data Sources that are needed. At this point, users can execute any reports your report DBA has enabled to be visible. This chapter gives you an overview of this process, and Chapters 6 through 9 deal with the process in greater depth.

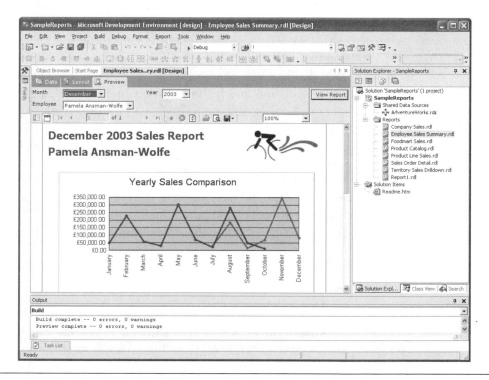

Figure 1.2 The Visual Studio .NET Report Designer Previewing a Report—Rendered in the UK

---

[7] Folks, we assume you know what most of the acronyms like IIS, ODBC, and ASP mean. If you don't, you're going to have considerable trouble with what we're talking about. We'll define the new ones, but the rest can be Googled pretty easily.

Define the Data Source

Usually, when creating a new report definition, you first wire up the report to its data source or sources. Data sources are typically SQL Server, Oracle, or other DBMS-style servers, but they can be anything exposed with a .NET Data Provider, or by ODBC or OLE DB. This means you can get report data from flat text files, spreadsheet files, Microsoft Access MDB files, or virtually any source of data. Sure, a report can extract information from several independent data sources, but if you need to JOIN data together from different data sources you'll need to do that through SQL Server's linked database facility.

Once you choose your data source, you need to create a report Data Source that connects to it and manages the credentials needed to access its data. Building a report's Data Source is very similar to creating an ADO.NET Connection string, and the Report Designer makes intuitive use of the very same Visual Studio .NET 2003 Data Link applet[8] dialog when creating report Data Sources. This applet assists in the validation and testing of the Connection string, driver choice, user credentials, and other driver-specific or provider-specific options. Sure, a report can have several Data Sources. A report's Data Source can also be created as a stand-alone object that can be shared among several reports (a "shared" Data Source), or alternatively it can be directly embedded and thus specific to a report. In Chapter 5, and again in Chapter 6, we'll discuss the security implications of embedded passwords in Data Sources and managed reports. Frankly, you won't see a single chapter that doesn't mention security in one context or another.

Create a DataSet

Typically, with a Data Source in place, you can create a query to populate a Reporting Services DataSet with data on which to base a report. So, as in ADO.NET, you need to create a SELECT query to return data from one or more tables (or views) or (better still) name a stored procedure and its parameters. One point to keep in mind: until the SQL Server 2005 version, the Reporting Services "DataSet"

---

[8] The Data Link applet is the dialog that appears when you create a new connection in the Server Explorer or double-click on a UDL file.

does not expose the same functionality as the ADO.NET DataSet. You can't "just" take an existing ADO.NET DataSet and pass it to a Reporting Services Report—at least not yet (unless you build a custom Data Processing extension, as we discuss in Chapter 13).

The Report Designer offers two ways to help build the SQL for your query: the default "generic" query designer, and the more familiar GUI-based Visual Design Tools' Query Builder. Figure 1.3 shows the generic query designer. It permits you to enter any ad hoc SQL query desired, including stored procedures—just change the command type on the toolbar over to stored procedure. To execute the SQL entered, click on the red ! icon. The generic designer might not be as easy to use as its GUI-based cousin, but it does not balk at complex queries as long as the syntax is understood by the target DBMS that the Data Source connects to.

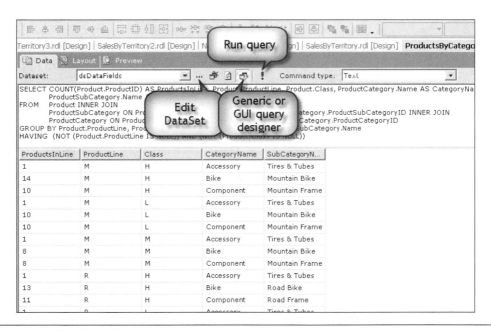

Figure 1.3 The Generic Query Designer

You toggle the designer of choice by clicking the 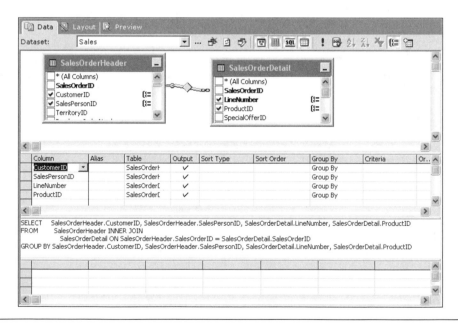 icon on the toolbar, as shown in Figure 1.3. The problem with this icon is that its tool tip always says "generic query designer" instead of toggling as it should. We expect this problem to disappear quietly in a Service Pack, although it didn't appear to be fixed in Service Pack 1.

The GUI-based query designer—which you may already be familiar with if you've used Access, Visual Basic 6.0, or Visual Studio .NET—makes it a breeze to create simple table-based DataSets (see Figure 1.4). Once you venture beyond the bounds of the GUI-based designer's ability to parse your query, you'll have to go back to the generic designer or resort to using stored procedures or views.

You get an *A* if you noticed we said DataSets, plural. Yes, a report definition can use any number of separate DataSet objects— each obtaining data from the DBMS to which they are connected through their respective Data Sources. And yes, their underlying queries can have input and output parameters, which can be bound to lookups, can be fixed values, can be strongly typed, can have defaults, can have configurable prompt strings, can be included in expressions, and much, much more.

Figure 1.4 The GUI-Based Data Tools Query Designer

The cognoscenti[9] who read our last book, *ADO.NET Examples and Best Practices for C# Programmers*, might have thought that the DataSet we're talking about here is the *classic*[10] ADO.NET DataSet. However, the Reporting Services DataSet doesn't implement all the features you may have seen before in an ADO.NET DataSet; it implements only the streamlined subset of the features that the development team needed immediately. For the next version release of Reporting Services, we are confident that the DataSet element will be more fully implemented.

One of the features that isn't there at the moment is DataSet support for multiple resultsets. However, you can take several approaches if you want to work with multiple resultsets; for example, you might write a custom Data Processing extension or deal with this entirely on the server in a stored procedure by performing an ugly call out to a middleware component.

Visually Lay Out the Report Controls

The Visual Studio .NET Report Designer add-in provides nine report "controls" (called **Report Items**) on the Toolbox palette (see Figure 1.5). The spec and BOL usually refer to these as controls, so we will too. Just understand that these "items" are not the same as the controls you use with other Visual Studio projects, and so you can't, at present, add custom controls to the toolbox and use them within a report definition. We understand that extensibility is a feature that's not too far off.

These report controls can be dragged and dropped from the Toolbox palette onto the report definition layout surface. (Behind the scenes, the report's RDL definition is synchronized as the report design is visually manipulated and configured.)

---

[9] cognoscenti (noun): A person with superior, usually specialized knowledge or highly refined taste; a connoisseur.

[10] Ha! DataSets have formally been around only since October 2001, and already we're calling them classic.

Figure 1.5 The Report Designer Toolbox Report Controls

The Layout tab is where you can most easily set the properties of your report's controls, just as you might do when designing a web or Windows form. Reporting Services permits you to place these controls virtually anywhere on the report. Be careful, though. Sizing the report can be tricky, as we'll discuss in Chapter 7.

Thankfully, there are enough report controls to build most types of report. For example, you'll find a Chart control that can build charts for every appetite, including line, column, area, and carborich (bar, pie, and doughnut), along with the scatter, bubble, and stock types, including colorful 3D and explosive effects. Yes, these are the same chart types you've feasted on for years. We dedicate all of Chapter 8 to the Chart control.

You'll also find ways to lay out your report data using tabular layouts. For example, Reporting Services includes a Table control (shown in Figure 1.6) that lets you merge cells, create and sort multiple grouping rows, and enable report interaction with compelling drilldown into other areas of the same report and drill through onto other reports. For example, if you wanted the rendered report to be filtered on a particular postal code, you'll find it's easy to create a dropdown list or simple dialog to enter this parameter at runtime, just before the report is rendered. That's because, just like programs, these reports can be interactive. Yes, we also said "merge cells," and, what's more, it's possible to embed charts within tables, or tables within tables.

Data | Layout | Preview

| Header |
| Detail |
| Footer |

Figure 1.6 The Table Control in the Visual Studio .NET IDE

Another slick feature of the Visual Studio .NET 2003 Reporting Services Report Designer is that it supports dragging a Field into a cell in the Detail, Header, or Footer section of a Table control. When you do, the Designer does a lot of the binding legwork for you. For example, if you drag a Field into a cell in the Footer section, the Report Designer places the Field name in the Header cell and binds a sensible aggregate into the Footer cell; if it's not the aggregate you had in mind, you can always override it.

Oh, Fields! We forgot to mention that once a report has one or more DataSets, the Designer places their columns (AKA *Fields*) into a palette indexed by a DataSet combo box (as shown in Figure 1.7). This makes it easy to drag and drop selected Fields directly onto the report definition, at which time the Report Designer automatically wires up the bindings for you—just as with the Table control. Nope, there's nothing preventing you from the drudgery of manually binding controls to DataSet Fields if that's what helps you sleep better (or if you're being paid by the hour).

Figure 1.7 The Fields Palette Window

There's also another tabular data layout report control: the Matrix control (see Figure 1.8). And no, it's not supplied or licensed from the Wachowski Brothers, although it does provide a somewhat transcendental interactive user experience to intuitively drill into columns and rows. And no, it does not show data in long, scrolling columns of unrecognizable green characters, unless Mr. Smith gets involved.[11] Chapter 8 discusses the Matrix control.

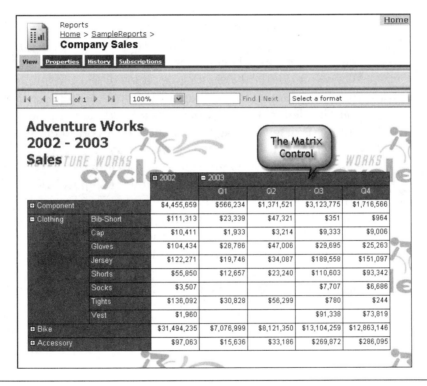

Figure 1.8 The Matrix Control Rendered in a Report

---

[11] Now, if you haven't heard of *The Matrix*, and the characters Neo, Trinity, and Mr. Smith mean nothing to you, then you have certainly led a geek-sheltered life and have missed out on a great trilogy of films. Take a look at http://whatisthematrix.warnerbros.com/.

We almost forgot to mention the most fundamental report controls from the Report Items toolbar because we simply took them for granted. As you know, no report would be complete without Line and Rectangle controls as well as data-bindable Textbox and Image controls.

In traditional report writers (such as Microsoft Access or Crystal Reports), you work with horizontal bands in the report that span the page and repeat for each row of data being shown. In contrast, Reporting Services uses a more Visual Basic forms-like approach. Here report controls can be hosted, or "parented," in data regions, which grow at runtime while other controls are automatically repositioned to make room. The advantage of this approach is that you can define multiple floating data regions, and not just above and below each other, as you do in banded reports. These data regions can appear virtually anywhere in the body of a report in any configuration (as shown in Figure 1.9). Think of the report definition as simply a container, or "form," for the parts of a report (the display controls) that sit between the report header and footer.

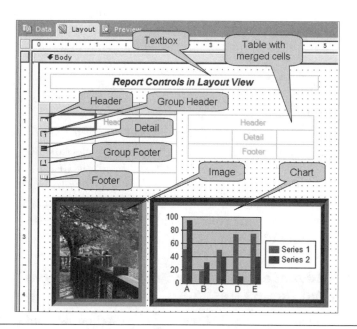

Figure 1.9 The Layout View with Two Side-by-Side Table Controls, an Image Control, and a Chart Control

As is to be expected, in Reporting Services, Report Designer can specify *PageHeader* and *PageFooter* sections in the report definition. These go at the top and bottom of report pages, and, naturally, a main *Body section* is positioned between the page header and page footer. Chapter 7 has a diagram (Figure 7.3) that shows how these areas are laid out. It's worth emphasizing that the body is not bindable to a DataSet, so the body can't repeat once for each record as the body does in Microsoft Access reports. Although this takes some folks by surprise, it's one of the most empowering features of Reporting Services.

We've mentioned the Table and Matrix tabular controls, and these certainly repeat for each record within themselves. However, not all reports call for tabular representations; many have a free-form repeating requirement, which Reporting Services provides via the List control. List controls can host other controls, and the List repeats once for each record in the DataSet to which it is bound.

In Reporting Services jargon, List, Table, and Matrix Report Items (controls) are *data regions*. What makes the tool so powerful is that these data regions can be laid out side by side (as shown in Figure 1.9), or even defined hierarchically within one another. The latter feature supports data that you want to be independently sorted, grouped, and filtered at the data region level.

You can lay out reports that need snaking columns (like a newspaper) by setting the *Columns* property on the report definition to the number of columns you want. Reports can also contain *Subreport* controls, which are basically reports within reports—and the nesting can get several layers deep before choking. There's also a wizard that takes the tough work out of translating and importing reports from Microsoft Access. A minor disappointment for us is that there isn't any out-of-the-box wizardry to translate, import, and then flush Crystal Reports out of our systems. We'll be happy to discuss converting your Crystal Reports (and Access Reports). See the website 12 for details.

Advanced Features: Programmability in the Report Designer

What a report looks like on the screen (how it's *rendered*) is controlled by a plethora of report definition and report control properties and

---

[12] See www.SQLReportingServices.NET.

the chosen Rendering extension. Although you can set many of these properties to permanent fixed values at design time, you can also set many of them to Visual Basic .NET expressions, which are evaluated when a managed report is prepared for rendering. It's also possible to make custom Visual Basic .NET code methods for use in any expression; to do this, you create Visual Basic .NET shared functions and paste them into the report's *Code* property. We show how to do that in Chapters 7 and 9.

This programmability makes it possible to do convoluted things, such as conditionally changing the text color in a Textbox control, but only when rendered by a specific user, only when the values are within certain ranges, or only when rendered on a Thursday afternoon between 3 and 4 PM by a certain user. This would be handy if you are a report programmer going into a review meeting with your boss at 3:30 and want to make an impact. Of course, the business logic possibilities are endless, and you'll probably have more serious requirements to implement!

No, you don't need to be jump qualified to be considered a "paraprogrammer."
–Bill

But it sure helps to be jump qualified if you are going to write poor queries for reports that take every cycle of CPU— so that when the DBA and supporting security officers show you the exit on the 42nd floor (the window) you can survive to bring another corporation's servers to its knees. So it's a good idea to either learn how to program properly or how to jump.
–Peter

Why use Visual Basic .NET and not C# (or both)? Well, behind the scenes a single .NET assembly is created for each managed report (using `System.CodeDom`). This assembly contains all the expressions and properties as property methods. It was a lot easier for Microsoft's developers to require that one and only one language assembly be compiled and used. Visual Basic .NET was chosen as being a slightly more user-friendly expression language, especially with paraprogrammers. By default, these expressions embedded in the report definition are given only Execute permission; this helps to prevent someone from creating a ***Trojan report*** by using an expression squirreled away that deletes files in the background, installs a virus, or bumps up your salary by 45 percent. By default, the Report Server does not permit access to the file system from custom code in expressions. Yes, a System Administrator might relax this, but this breach of the security dike would then apply to all expressions in all managed reports. We strongly advise against it, because there are other, more controlled ways to solve this problem.

What if you want to create some custom code that can be used by *all* reports? Well, the facility exists to create your own custom code class library assemblies in any Common Language Runtime (CLR) language, strongname them, reference them in the report definition's *References Collection* property, instantiate any specific classes, and subsequently use the class methods, or shared functions, in report expressions. The System Administrator must install each of these assemblies and grant them specific permissions. These can be as restrictive as None, denying any ability to run; can be Execute only, which relaxes a little more to permit the code to run in a restricted sandbox; can be completely unrestricted Full Trust; or any combination of specific permissions. All this is achieved through code access security (CAS). If a System Administrator granted sufficient privileges to an assembly, a *Mission Impossible*–style report could be created that, when rendered, would promptly *fdisk* the system in 30 seconds. But such a scenario is enabled only if the System Administrator has permitted it by breaching the security seals and leaving the door open. In Chapter 9 we'll show in detail how to work with expressions and custom assemblies and how to assign strong-names, and set code access security permissions.

We suggest using the principle of least privilege—that is, grant only the permissions needed to do the immediate tasks and no others. Full Trust permission should not be given arbitrarily, and this requires administrators to use fine-grained permissions. For example, if an assembly needs permission to open a certain file, it should be granted permissions only to that file and not to the whole hard drive, nor should it be fully trusted.

Document Maps

For large reports that extend over many pages, it's possible to create a navigable hierarchical tree view called a **Document Map**. Populating the nodes of this tree is as easy as putting a value into the *Label* property on any of the controls to be included in the Document Map (see Figure 1.10). This can be a fixed literal value, or, as just discussed, it can result from a calculated expression. If any labels have been set in any of the controls, the Document Map is deployed in a pane when the generated report is rendered in a browser. The *Label* property can also be bound to a DataSet Field. We'll show you this in action in Chapter 7.

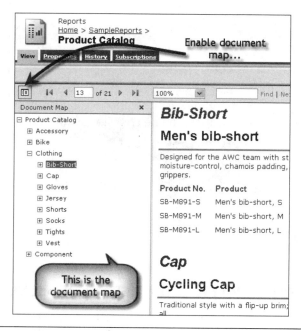

Figure 1.10 A Document Map and Report as Rendered in a Browser

Previewing in the Designer

After you have visually laid out the report controls on the report definition, the Report Designer lets you render and debug the report locally using data collected from the Data Source(s). When using the Preview tab in the designer as shown in Figure 1.11, the Report Designer does not access the Reporting Services server—it uses its own renderer. After you deploy your reports, recheck how the Reporting Services Rendering extension displays the report—we've noticed some subtle (and some not so subtle) differences.

TIP When you design reports, be sure to limit the number of rows to be used when previewing the report in the Report Designer. If you don't, there's a good chance you'll lock up Visual Studio .NET while it tries to render a 50,000-page report. In Chapter 3 we discuss how to limit the number of rows returned in a query, but while you're practicing, be sure to use a parameter-focused query or a `TOP` expression. If you really do want all 50,000 pages, don't forget to remove any row restriction before you deploy the report.

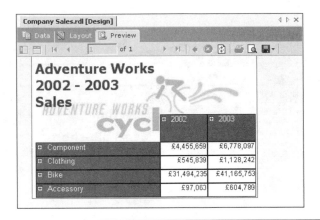

Figure 1.11 Previewing a Report in the Visual Studio .NET IDE

Previewing with the RSReportHost Utility

You can preview your report in the Report Designer Preview pane (as shown in Figure 1.11) by clicking the Preview tab in the Designer. This is great most of the time, but if you're developing with custom assemblies that you are also editing and redeploying, you *won't* want to use this technique. That's because the Visual Studio .NET process loads the custom assembly and doesn't unload it until you close down the Visual Studio .NET development environment. As a result, you won't be able to update the custom assembly you're working on until you've restarted Visual Studio. To address this issue, Microsoft provides the RSReportHost utility, which you call by setting the Solution Configuration to DebugLocal and selecting Debug on the project, or on a specific report. (Note that if you try this out with the Microsoft-supplied samples, there is not a "DebugLocal" Solution Configuration option, so you may have to create one—the crucial part is ensuring that the *TargetServerURL* property on the project remains blank. This ensures that when you try to debug, the RSReportHost starts instead. Figure 1.12 shows the Project properties page for the "Charting" project setup to use RSReportHost to preview the report design.

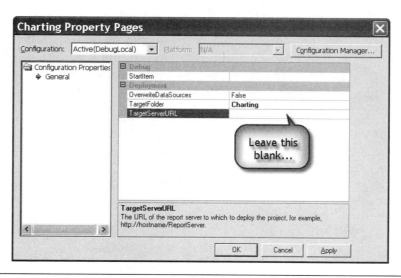

Figure 1.12 Setting the Report Project Properties for the "Charting" Report

When the RSReportHost utility starts, it loads itself and your custom assembly into a new process space, and it renders the report (as shown in Figure 1.13). When you close RSReportHost, that process space is unloaded, along with your custom assembly, so you'll then be able to work on any desired changes to your custom assembly.

Note that in rendered generated reports, currency formatting can adapt automatically to the current locale of the user browsing the report. That's the way that the Microsoft-supplied samples have been setup in the sample report definitions, but it is *not* the way we advise working. Guess where Figure 1.11 and Figure 1.13 were rendered? Unfortunately, these values are stored in the database using the currency datatype, not even as dollar amounts and not British pounds sterling. If you manage different types of currencies, we recommend that you explicitly embed any currency symbol directly into the Textbox control's *Format* property, possibly even based on the result of evaluating a report expression. If you are going to format a Textbox as "currency," placing a "c" in the Textbox's *Format* property (as Microsoft did in its samples) has the following effect: If the *Language* property is not set on that textbox, or it's set to "default," the report renderer defers to the *Language* property setting on the report definition. If the *Language* property is not set or left as "default," the language of the user's web browser is used as the language from which the currency symbol and formatting would be used. Clear? Leaving the rendering choice of currency symbol to the browser could be problematic, to say the least—especially if the rendered report is an invoice!

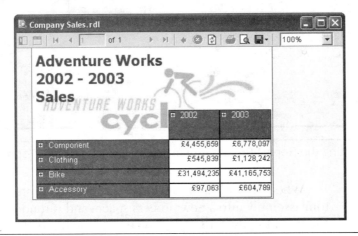

Figure 1.13 Previewing in the RSReportHost Utility

RDL: Report Definition Language

As we mentioned earlier, while you're designing a report, the Report Designer maintains the definition of the report in an "open" human-readable Report Definition Language (RDL) file (see Figure 1.14). RDL files are laid out in an XML format using an open published XSD schema. (Developers can indeed extend RDL by adding their own elements and attributes.) When a report definition is being edited visually in the Report Designer, the underlying RDL file is automatically kept synchronized. Sure, it's also possible to edit the RDL file directly, and those changes are immediately reflected in the Designer. Diehard gurus won't use the Report Designer; they'll use Visual Notepad, or even Edlin![13]

---

[13] Edlin, for the young whippersnappers, was an old command-line text editor. In fact, it still works in the command prompt shell.

The more serious corollary of an open RDL standard is that other report design tools can be built that extrude RDL or translate other proprietary reporting file formats to RDL. You'll then be able to verify the resulting RDL against the published XSD schema. You may even have ideas about enabling your own custom application to create or modify RDL files.

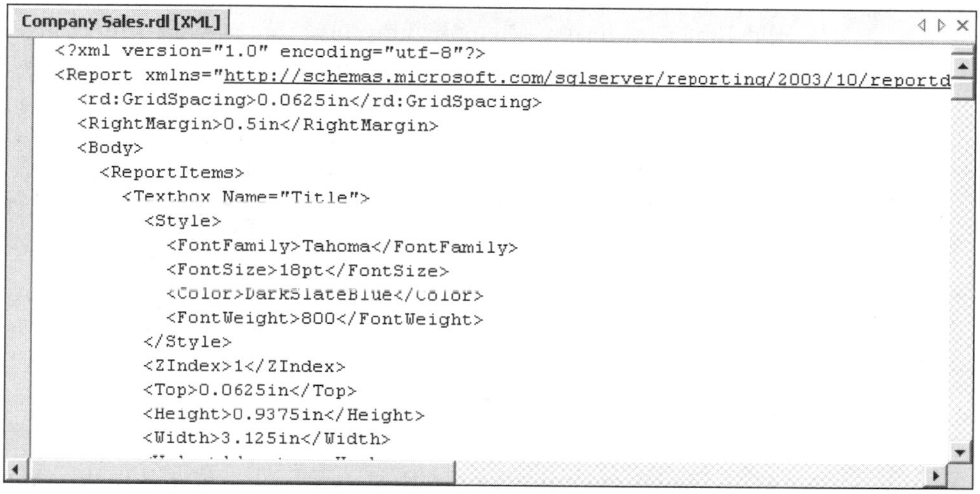

Company Sales.rdl [XML] ◁ ▷ ✕

```xml
<?xml version="1.0" encoding="utf-8"?>
<Report xmlns="http://schemas.microsoft.com/sqlserver/reporting/2003/10/reportd
  <rd:GridSpacing>0.0625in</rd:GridSpacing>
  <RightMargin>0.5in</RightMargin>
  <Body>
    <ReportItems>
      <Textbox Name="Title">
        <Style>
          <FontFamily>Tahoma</FontFamily>
          <FontSize>18pt</FontSize>
          <Color>DarkSlateBlue</Color>
          <FontWeight>800</FontWeight>
        </Style>
        <ZIndex>1</ZIndex>
        <Top>0.0625in</Top>
        <Height>0.9375in</Height>
        <Width>3.125in</Width>
```

Figure 1.14 A Sample of RDL Code in a Report Definition

RDS: Report Data Source Files

Report Data Source (RDS) files provide a mechanism to share Data Sources on a Report Server scale. Like report Data Sources, **shared Data Sources** hold a Connection string and user credentials. These **user credentials** provide access to the underlying data—they're simply the User ID and Password or options that prompt the user for user name and password. These credentials determine whether the DBMS permits your report's DataSets to access the database and further grant or deny access to the underlying database tables, views, functions, or stored procedures. Shared Data Sources can be created in the Report Designer (in Visual Studio .NET), in the Report Manager, or programmatically through the SOAP interface (as we describe in Chapter 9¾). However, the Report Designer only permits a restricted subset of Report Data Source features to be configured. There is much greater capability (albeit a more awkward interface) when configuring deployed report-specific or shared Data Sources with the Report Manager.

There are a number of mechanisms you can use to specify, manipulate, and persist connection credentials. In Chapter 3 we show you how to create a shared Data Source using the Report Designer wizard, and in Chapter 4 we illustrate how to manipulate Data Sources in the Report Manager. Chapter 5 discusses serious security issues in a deployed production environment, and Chapters 6 and 7 discuss the use of Data Sources in the development environment. After reading these chapters, you'll see that each credential persistence approach has far-reaching consequences. To ensure that you don't leave the door open to Trojan reports or other security risks, you should get a good handle on this information before launching your first production environment.

The Report Server

After you've used the Report Designer to design and build a report definition or report project (which might contain any number of report definitions, shared Data Sources, and resources such as graphic files), you deploy it by sending its RDL (or RDS if a shared Data Source, or the resource file if a graphic) to the ASP.NET-based ***Report Server***. Before attempting to deploy a report, it's crucial to configure two properties on each report project in Visual Studio .NET 2003: the target URL of the Report Server, and the notional folder to which you wish to deploy. You'll also want to reference an appropriate StartItem report, as shown in Figure 1.15.

To deploy a project or a single report within a project, right-click the project or report name and choose Deploy. Once a report definition is complete and deployed to the Report Server, it becomes a ***managed report***.

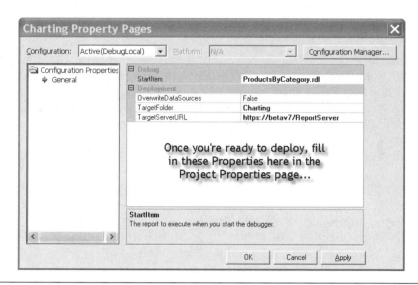

Figure 1.15 The Project Properties Page—Ready for Deployment

I say "XML-like" because although some of these files look like XML, if you try to put in XML comments—for example, `<!--A Comment-->`—this can choke SQL Server, and the exception messages can be pretty cryptic. We'll discuss these configuration files later in this chapter.
–Peter

The Report Server exposes Reporting Services' SOAP endpoint, and Visual Studio .NET deploys the report and shared Data Sources and resource files by simply making calls to SOAP methods. All these report definitions, shared Data Sources, and resource files are organized in the Report Server in a logical folder hierarchy, over which is an extensive role-based security system integrated with Computer/Domain Users and Groups.

If you're developing your own tools or being paid by the hour and you want to build your own .NET application to deploy reports, you can call the SOAP interface from your own programs. We'll show you how in Chapter 9¾.

The Report Server uses a SQL Server 2000 database to retain almost all of its metadata. In fact, the only modifiable metadata retained outside SQL Server are any custom assemblies and supporting files you may have written that the report references, along with a handful of XML-like configuration files for the web and Windows services and security policies.

SQL Server and SOAP

Although Reporting Services uses SQL Server as its own data store and you can get at the Reporting Services' own tables and stored procedures, we should warn you that the *only* officially supported interface is SOAP. The reason is that as the product progresses, Microsoft might (is likely to) change/tune/alter/repair/enhance/refine the underlying schema of the Reporting Services database and the definitions of the stored procedures. Microsoft has confirmed that the SOAP interfaces will be backwardly supported but says that the use of SQL Server by Reporting Services for its data store is a (publicly undocumented) implementation detail subject to change. So if you feel inclined to fiddle directly within the Reporting Services ReportServer database with T-SQL, be warned that a next version or Service Pack could (and probably will) break your code. This is a little frustrating because calling out to a SOAP interface from T-SQL in SQL Server 2000 is not as trivial as it will be in the next version of SQL Server (SQL Server 2005).

Rendering Extensions

In addition to SOAP-type HTTP and HTTPS calls, the Report Server's ASP.NET web server component dutifully responds to specially formatted URL Request Strings by streaming requested reports over HTTP or HTTPS in an amazing number of rendering formats. The rendering formats that a Report Server can generate are governed by the Rendering extension assemblies installed and registered on the system. Out of the box there are six Rendering extensions: HTML (3.2, 4.0, MHTML), XML, CSV, IMAGE (BMP, EMF, GIF, JPEG, PNG, TIFF), EXCEL, and PDF.[14]

Stop and think for a moment about where we are. At this point, we have the ability to design and render a report in a variety of formats, which can target a number of potential platforms and devices. We should also emphasize that there is no additional separate license fee to pay to Adobe for the PDF report generation, and there is a way to extract an HTML table fragment stream, which you can

---

[14] Sometimes we assume too much—as in we assume you know what these acronyms mean. If you don't, try this website: www.geocities.com/ikind_babel/babel/babel.html. It defines all of them.

incorporate directly into one of your own web pages without having to use an IFrame control.[15]

But as if that were not enough, in true TV shopping style—"Wait! There's more!"—you also get the ability to create and register any of your own custom Rendering extensions. So, for example, if you have a commercial requirement that your reports be rendered on Wireless Application Protocol (WAP)-enabled phones, you can write a .NET Rendering extension assembly for Reporting Services to do so. But be warned—developing Rendering extensions is hard, at least in our opinion. Configuring the Report Server to use a new Rendering extension is as simple as placing your custom rendering assembly in the right folder and delicately editing a few XML configuration files. We suggest you investigate the existing Rendering extensions, such as using Extensible Stylesheet Language Transformations (XSLT) with an XML-rendered report. This might satisfy your requirements without the need to write a new extension.

Does anyone still have a WAP phone? Do yourself a favor and get a Smartphone or PocketPC phone. I was one of the first to use WAP technology and blew a load of dough writing WML servers and translators. Thanks, Nokia, for nothing!
–Peter

Delivery Extensions

So far we've talked about being able to extract a rendered report stream in response to a specially formatted URL, but the Report Server need not always be shy and passive. Reporting Services does have the ability to break out of its box and start spamming preconfigured and presumably consenting recipients over SMTP[16] at preset scheduled times or only when the data changes.

And if benevolent spam is not enough, the Report Server can even proactively save rendered reports onto a UNC[17] file share on a certain schedule or when data changes. Yes, it even takes care of any credentials it might need to use to access that share, and it can set access credentials on the saved file to restrict access to a certain computer or domain user or group. It can also be configured to overwrite any previous file or to incrementally number files so as not to overwrite any previous file.

---

[15] An IFrame is a pesky little web control that enables you to host one web page inside another. Not all web browsers support IFrames.

[16] SMTP stands for Simple Mail Transfer Protocol (e-mail).

[17] UNC stands for Universal Naming Convention. These are shares that start with `\\<Server>\<share>`.

Both delivery features are provided through what are called **Delivery extensions**, and yes, you can write your own .NET Delivery extension assembly to proactively deliver reports elsewhere. For example, you can send to an FTP[18] service, post it using NNTP[19] to a newsgroup, or dispatch an SMS message to a WAP-enabled phone, with the embedded link pointing to where you use your WAP Rendering extension. The extensible delivery possibilities are endless, and they are, for the most part, much easier to develop than Rendering extension assemblies.

What About Printing Delivery Extensions?

We have, however, discovered a small fly in the ointment. In the initial release version there isn't an out-of-the-box Delivery extension to send reports directly to a printer. Thankfully, the Microsoft development team has not left us completely high and dry; they provide project code samples in C# and Visual Basic .NET that show how to make a Delivery extension that targets a printer.

If you stop to think for a moment about how many printers there are in the world and how many different printer drivers there are to take advantage of the plethora of hardware-specific configurable options—such as duplex printing, paper size selection, input and output trays, color printing, margin settings, collation, stapling, binding, faxing, scaling, even the number of copies that should be printed—it would have been a mammoth undertaking for the development team to have created a generic printer Delivery extension that would cater to every possible option, and time constraints pushed this part of the development out to the next version. Our guess is that printer manufacturers and third-party ISVs[20] will write their own printer Delivery extensions that take advantage of their hardware's features to make them fully available to Reporting Services. The Delivery extension sample provided by the Reporting Services developers works by rendering the report as an image and sending that to the printer. This is certainly not the most efficient way to solve the problem—being more

---

[18] File Transfer Protocol
[19] Network News Transport Protocol
[20] Independent software vendors

"crude but effective," as Seven of Nine might say.[21] All of this said, we are working on a server-side printing extension that can be called directly from the Report Manager when viewing a report, so be sure to check our website www.SQLReportingServices.NET for news.

The SQL Server Agent and ReportingServicesService.exe Windows Service

The Report Server is not alone when it comes to its ability to push report content through Delivery extensions. It's aided and abetted by two friends: the SQL Server Agent and another Windows system service that you'll see in your task manager as the tautological ReportingServicesService.exe, which is a .NET Windows system service. These provide an infrastructure that enables possible load balancing in a web farm environment when you're pushing scheduled content out via Delivery extensions. (For more on web farms, see Chapter 2.)

While the SQL Server Agent creates entries in the ReportServer database's Event table at scheduled times, it's the ReportingServicesService.exe Windows system service that polls the database every 10 seconds to see if there are any entries in this table and takes appropriate action. Chapter 2 tells you how you can configure the polling interval.

The Report Processor

The **Report Processor** is the thoroughbred workhorse[22] of the Reporting Services team (see Figure 1.16). It's only used to process managed (deployed) reports. It's responsible for querying data, assembling the report into the Intermediate Format (IF) Binary Large Object (BLOB), and extruding the report to the client. This is where the various extensions come into play. For example, a Data Processing extension is used during report processing to query the report's Data Sources. Data and layout are combined by the Report

---

[21] Don't know what the ASP.NET guru Doug Seven would say, though.

[22] It's not a donkey or obstinate ass that's difficult to get to do what you want.

Processor and saved to the database in the IF. Only at this stage does the Rendering extension come into play. The benefit of this approach is that all the querying and processing work is done once, after which different renderers can be called—all of which can work from the same IF BLOB. This Intermediate Format can be persisted behind the scenes in the ReportServer database to enable reports to be rendered from cached versions, historic versions, or Snapshots. The fundamental difference between immediate in-demand, cached Snapshots and history is simply where and how long a generated report is stored and managed. (You'll learn more about report history and Snapshots shortly.) The key to the Intermediate Format is that all the heavy lifting is done once, and that it's device (renderer) independent.

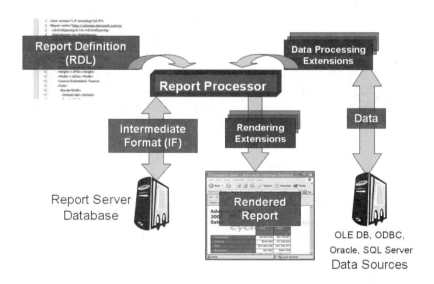

Figure 1.16 The Report Processor

Caching Intermediate Format

To obtain some performance gains and scalability, the Report Server can cache the generated report IF in a SQL table within the Report Server database—assuming that the credentials used in the report's Data Sources are not derived from Windows Authentication security

(SSPI) or by prompting the user. If caching is enabled on a managed report, the report can be delivered much more quickly after it has been requested the first time because the Report Server doesn't have to query all the Data Sources again; it need only render the IF into the requested stream type. Reports can be cached for a configurable number of integer minutes to a maximum of 2,147,483,647— approximately 4,083 years, by which stage we doubt you'll still be bothered (assuming your system stays up that long). For a higher degree of control, the cache can be expired on a report-specific schedule or on a schedule shared with other objects.

For parameterized cache-enabled reports, the Report Server creates IF images and caches the report each time it's requested by means of parameter values that have not already been used, compiled, and cached. In other words, the cache is uniquely indexed on a report and on the parameter values with which it was executed. Reports remain in the cache until they expire or are explicitly flushed from the cache.

Caching Snapshots

The first time a report is executed, it can take a very long time, especially if a lot of number crunching is required in the report's queries or if you asked for all 50,000 customers. Microsoft has provided an alternative to deal with this contingency: the ability to populate the cache with an Intermediate Format Snapshot from a report executed at a scheduled time. Again, the schedule can be specific to a report or can be shared with other objects and must use hard-coded credentials. This approach is designed to support preparation of reports in off-peak hours.

Caching History

The Report Server can maintain a historic archive of Intermediate Format report Snapshots that can be repeatedly rendered at any time in the future—assuming that the system is still up when it's time to render the report. This *history* can be unlimited—or, more accurately, limited—by what SQL Server can provide in storage space. The Report Server can generate Snapshot reports on shared schedules or on a report-specific schedule.

The Report Execution Timeout Governor

Preparing the Intermediate Format for reports can take considerable time, especially if there is a lot of data to collect or if complex processing is required. Fortunately, the Report Server provides the option to time out the execution of a report and cancels it with a *polite*[23] message to the user. This Report Execution Timeout setting is set in seconds, and there is a default for the whole Report Server; this default can be overridden on a report-by-report basis.

The default timeout is close to 60 seconds. The Report Server evaluates running jobs at 60-second intervals. Every 60 seconds, the server compares actual process time against the report execution timeout value. If the processing time for a report exceeds the report execution timeout value, report processing stops. If you specify a timeout value that is less than 60 seconds, the report may execute in full if processing starts and ends during the quiet part of the cycle when the Report Server is not evaluating running jobs. For example, if you set a timeout value of 10 seconds for a report that takes 20 seconds to run, the report will process in full if report execution starts early in the 60-second cycle. You can set the *RunningRequestsDbCycle* setting in the RSReportServer.config file to change how often running jobs are evaluated.

The Report Manager

So far we've given an overview of designing reports and deployment to a Report Server. We've said little about how these deployed reports can be managed while in the Report Server, nor how a user might choose a report to run. Well, to do this Microsoft provides a Report Manager ASP.NET web application. The Report Manager provides an attractive interface that acts as a wrapper to the URL calls and SOAP methods of the Report Server.

---

[23] Perhaps a politically correct translation of what the DBA would really like to say to users who execute queries that bring their 8-way processor/3-terabyte RAM system to its knees.

The Report Manager can be accessed on its default URL of http/https://<server>/Reports. What users see rendered in their web browsers depends on the security permissions they have been assigned; reassuringly, users can perform administrative functions *only* if they have Administrative privileges. In Chapter 4 we'll discuss Report Manager security and explain how to setup Administrative and User account roles. The Report Manager really comes into its own as a user application that enables users to choose from and execute the managed reports that they have permissions to access.

Managing Security Permissions

The Reporting Services security permissions system is extensive and is based on assigning **roles** to Windows domain, local machine user, or group accounts. Here's how it works. At the lowest level of granularity, the various **tasks** that can be performed are identified, and these tasks can be aggregated into various defined roles by an Administrator or someone with appropriate privileges.

Out of the box there are four defined roles—Browser, Content Manager, My Reports, and Publisher—providing permissions very much along the lines of what their names imply. Because these roles are constructed from a selectable list of task operations that can be performed, it is possible to define new roles consisting of different subsets of tasks. Keep in mind that by default ordinary users have no rights; only those who have Administrator rights can access these roles unless you modify the permissions for your selected accounts.

Managing Folders

As mentioned earlier, the Report Server maintains managed reports and shared Data Sources in notional folders, and the Report Manager lets users navigate these folders. Depending on security permissions, the person browsing can create new folders and can delete, move, hide, rename, and edit the descriptions of folders or reports. Of course, if the person browsing doesn't have permission to see a report or folder, then it isn't visible when the *user* views the Report Manager. In addition, it is possible to set permissions for users and configure the Report Server to maintain folders on a per-user basis on a model similar to the My Documents folder on the Windows file system. This model enables users to have their own My Reports folders for their own reports (independent of other users) that they alone can see.

Managing Shared Data Sources

Subject to permissions, any shared Data Sources can be managed by a user through the Report Manager. Users can change credentials and Connection strings in the Data Sources on a live Report Server without invoking a development tool.

Managing Linked Reports

One of the cool Report Server features that the Report Manager exposes is the ability to create, name, delete, and manage *linked reports*. This is a report description that doesn't have any RDL of its own. The concept here is very similar to the way a shortcut operates in the Windows file system. The Report Manager enables linked reports to have different default values, different visibility for parameters, and different security than those of the underlying report to which they are linked, and it provides a placeholder for a user to execute. Alas, for a linked report, it is not possible to establish Data Sources or credentials that differ from the ones used by the real underlying report. Now that *would* be interesting.

Managing Shared Schedules

We have referred to schedules several times in different contexts. The Report Manager provides a mechanism for creating system-wide schedules that can be shared wherever a schedule can be used and can be managed from a central point.

Managing the Cache, Snapshots, History, and Report Execution Timeout

When we discussed the Report Server, we mentioned caching Snapshots and creating historic Snapshots. Yes, you can use the Report Server SOAP interface to configure these, but you'll probably be relieved to know that the Report Manager provides a UI wrapper around the SOAP interface to let you easily configure these and many other features without needing to resort to programming.

At the site level, someone with Administrator privileges can create defaults using the Report Manager to set the maximum execution time in seconds that a server should spend rendering each report before it decides to abandon it and return a message to the user. This site default can also be overridden on each report.

Subscriptions

Users with the requisite permissions can *subscribe* to managed reports using the Report Manager. This means that selected users can configure a managed report to be delivered to them via one of the installed Delivery extensions (such as Report Server File Share) or by e-mail on a personal or a shared schedule. With additional permissions a user can configure a *data-driven subscription*, where configuration information and distribution lists can be derived from a query on a table.

Help

All the pages that constitute the Report Manager have context URL links to HTML help pages. If the Report Manager is going to be deployed in the default location where users select and execute reports, it is reassuring to know that an out-of-the-box help system is provided. If you are going to build your own report management system, you'll need to budget time to explain how it works and possibly provide your own online help system.

Extending the Report Manager

The Report Manager is intended to be a closed, black-box solution. Because of this Microsoft has not released the source code. In our opinion, the Report Manager is a delightful application, but there are some rough edges that you may find that you want to smooth out. In this respect, not all the settings that one might like to adjust from the Report Manager are provided. Although some of these may be added at a later stage, at the moment a System Administrator may have to delicately futz around with the XML-like configuration files or find a custom application that does it. Another irritation that comes to mind is that there is very little control over the layout of the ASP.NET controls that are used to collect the parameters in a report.

Microsoft's official position is that you should make your own Report Manager if you don't like the way the Report Manager works. To some extent, Microsoft helps by providing some sample starter applications. The problem is that it's a heck of a lot of work to build all the functionality that the Report Manager application provides when you want to add only a few bells and whistles.

Well, because we are not on the red pill we spoke of earlier, we can be mischievous and tell you how to pry open the Report Manager black box and provide the degree of customization you might want. This certainly takes much less effort than creating a whole Report Manager application. Of course this approach is hostage to Microsoft changing things, as it is at liberty to do in the future. However, the approach we'll show you in Chapter 11 enables you to make easy modifications now, and if Microsoft comes back and breaks your toys later (as we told you it might), at least you'll be able to incorporate them into your own Report Manager should you be forced to build one.

Versions of Reporting Services

There are four versions of Reporting Services to choose from: the Standard Edition, the Enterprise Edition, the Developer Edition, and the Evaluation Edition. Except for the Standard Edition, all provide the same feature set and differ only in EULA[24] license terms and time-bomb duration before the code stops working:

- The Evaluation Edition stops working after 120 days and is licensed only for evaluating the product.
- The Developer Edition differs from the Enterprise Edition only in that it's licensed for development but not for production use.

---

[24] End-User License Agreement

- The Standard Edition and the Enterprise Edition are the only editions licensed for production use and for using the features described in this chapter.
- The Standard Edition is limited in that it does not support web farms, custom security extensions, report history, and data-driven subscriptions, and it's limited to not more than four processors and 2 GB of RAM.

Summary

This chapter gives you a brief tour of Reporting Services and enough detail to get you started toward a better understanding of the technology. Reporting Services runs on an IIS system and requires a SQL Server 2000 system to manage its databases. Visual Studio .NET plays a role as the host for the Report Designer add-in, and it can be used to build Data Sources, queries, and report definitions and to deploy them. The underlying Report Server and its Data Processing and Rendering extensions help capture report data from a variety of data sources and publish managed reports in a variety of formats. Next, we'll show you how to install Reporting Services.

NOTE Microsoft recommends that you avoid use of the underscore character in computer names as the Report Server does not persist the session state information on these systems—unless they have been patched with Internet Explorer Patch MS01-055. See "Preparing to Install" in the Reporting Services documentation for more information.[25]

---

[25] http://msdn.microsoft.com/library/default.asp?url=/library/ en-us/RSinstall/htm/gs_installingrs_v1_8k82.asp

CHAPTER 2

Installing and Configuring Reporting Services

As we discussed in Chapter 1, Reporting Services is dependent on ASP.NET version 1.1 hosted on IIS, and on SQL Server 2000 SP3a Standard Edition and later. Reporting Services won't work, and is not supported, on SQLExpress or MSDE Editions of SQL Server, and there's a different version specifically for Yukon (SQL Server 2005). Sure, you can use SQLExpress, MSDE or a non-SQL Server database as a data source—just not as the Reporting Services Catalog.

In this chapter, we discuss various installation setups you can use to install and configure Reporting Services. For the most part, this process is managed by the Setup.exe installation wizard, so expect to be prompted for a number of configuration options that determine how, where, and whether each segment of the Reporting Services package will be installed. We know that there are a variety of ways to install Reporting Services, so we've tried not only to address the common case, but also provide hints and techniques to be used for some of the more sophisticated installation scenarios. To make this process as painless as possible, we've broken this chapter down into several sections:

- **Installation Pathways and Preparation:** This section discusses things you need to consider for each of the configuration scenarios—typical or not. Here we show additional details and considerations regarding SSL configuration and other security issues, separate IIS and SQL Server systems and instances, and using the command-line installation option.
- **Step by Step: Installing Reporting Services on a Server with IIS:** This section assumes a typical development machine running IIS, SQL Server, and a Visual Studio .NET tool. It walks

through the Setup wizard step by step and discusses how to respond to each dialog.

- **After Installation—Tuning and Reconfiguring:** This section discusses the various configuration files and the command-line tools used to manipulate the files and perform other security and maintenance tasks. If you choose to use Secure Sockets Layer (SSL) (as we recommend) and you also decide to force SSL for all communications with the Report Manager and Report Server, you should revisit the Tuning and Reconfiguring section after the installation wizard completes, which allows you to tune the config files and change the SecureConnectionLevel.

- **Testing the Installation:** This section shows step by step how to verify that your Reporting Services installation is ready to produce reports. Testing helps you install the sample reports using Visual Studio .NET and verify that you can successfully deploy and retrieve reports with a browser.

- **Installing Reporting Services on a Web Farm:** This section walks through the process of setting up Reporting Services on a web farm. This configuration uses several linked IIS servers to share the same Report Server database.

- **Removing Reporting Services:** In case you need to uninstall Reporting Services, this section discusses the mechanisms and side effects of the tear-down process.

Installation Pathways and Preparation

Before we get started, we need to mention the most important prerequisite: the website that hosts the Reporting Services ought to support SSL and therefore needs an SSL web server certificate. In Appendixes A and B, we've included a detailed walkthrough and an article written for MSDN that should prove useful to you if you need further guidance in installing an SSL web server certificate and (if necessary) setting up your own certificate services. Be sure to check out the DVD content as well because we've provided plenty of short media clips on different aspects and issues associated with installation and configuration.

There are two major parts of installation: Server components and client components. The client components are needed by developers to design reports, provide some report programming and database samples, as well as provide a suite of command-line tools to administer the Report Server. These client components are not needed for your users to *run* reports—all they need is a web browser (HTML 3.2 and later).

Operating System Choices

Reporting Services can be installed on the recent breeds of Microsoft operating systems as shown below. We categorize these in two groups: "server" and "workstation" operating systems. Server operating systems include Windows Server 2003, Windows Small Business Server 2003, and Windows 2000 Server. Workstation operating systems include Windows XP Professional and Windows 2000 Workstation.

For test and development situations, we feel that workstation operating systems are suitable platforms, and Windows XP Professional can be an ideal platform for a single machine where you can safely install all of the Reporting Services components and expect reasonable performance and up-to-date functionality. However, take note that Windows XP has a default maximum limit of 10 concurrent connections to its IIS server. This is usually adequate when you're testing as a single user but can prove to be very limiting and frustrating in some development situations. For example, as we'll see in Chapter 4, you may hit this barrier of 10 connections when you want to test accessing the Report Server and Report Manager concurrently under the context of different users. Consider that each web browser session consumes at least two IIS connections and often as many as four. All too frequently, we've seen that connections can hang and block the IIS server, which reports this stoppage by returning a 403.9 error code message (Too many users connected). Sometimes, even after the performance monitor (Perfmon) shows that all connections to IIS have been released, new connections still generate strange errors.

To address this issue, the first and most important thing we recommend for production environments is to use an operating system from the group of server OSs listed above. These server-class operating systems are designed for "serving" and don't have a limit on the possible number of connections to IIS. We recommend that you use either Windows Server 2003 or Windows 2000 Server for your production server. However, Windows Server 2003 is more secure.

If you must use Windows XP and want to address 403.9 errors that have blocked the IIS server, you can take either of two approaches, depending whether or not you want a treatment or cure. The "treatment" approach is to restart IIS, either at the command prompt with the IISRESET command, through the Services MMC snap-in or through the IIS MMC snap-in. Restarting IIS usually alleviates the problem—albeit temporarily. The "cure" is to delve into the Windows XP IIS metabase and increase the maximum connection limit to no greater than 40 connections. No, you can't go beyond 40 connections because IIS is hard-coded to explicitly slam you directly back down to 10 if you try to go above 40. In our development situations, we found it frustrating to work with the 10-connection governor for any extended period of time, but once raised to 40 in normal development scenarios we found it adequate to resolve IIS 403.9 (Too many users connected) errors. See Appendix D for the steps to take to update the IIS metabase. Microsoft also suggests that you make the IIS connection timeout shorter, and we show you how to do that in Appendix D.

NOTE *Installing Reporting Services on Domain Controllers* When installing Reporting Services on a Windows 2003 server that is also a domain controller, no manual configuration is necessary for Reporting Services to install and run properly. However, on a domain controller on Windows 2000 Server, while Reporting Services installs properly it is not automatically activated. In this case, you'll need to perform the following steps, either before or after running Setup, in order to properly configure Reporting Services to run on a domain controller:

1. Grant Impersonate Privilege to the IWAM_<machine> account. For more information, see the Knowledge Base Article "IWAM Account Is Not Granted the Impersonate Privilege for ASP.NET 1.1 on a Windows 2000 Domain Controller with SP4" (KB 824308).
2. Remove the IWAM_<machine> account from the Guest group. Guest users cannot store or maintain encrypted content. For more information, see the Knowledge Base Article "Roaming Profiles Cannot Create Key Containers" (KB 265357). Then reboot the computer.

All on One Machine (Typical Development Scenario)

Guide me!

One approach to installation is to simply execute[1] the Reporting Services Setup.exe without using command-line arguments and install everything on a single machine, accepting all the wizard's defaults. (In this case, you need to do this with Local Administrator privileges.) The Setup.exe installation wizard inspects the local machine and performs an initial check, looking for any "missing" components, some of which the wizard might be prepared to update for you—for example, the .NET Framework, although it will only report other missing dependencies in a dialog when it cannot find a qualifying version of SQL Server 2000. These components are "missing" based on the bold assumption that your intention is to install the Reporting Services, Report Designer add-in utilities, documentation, and sample reports all on the same machine. This is the simplest installation approach, assuming you are targeting a development machine that already has the following Setup:

- A Visual Studio .NET 2003 Development Tool installed (e.g., Visual Basic .NET 2003)
- SQL Server 2000 Developer Edition[2] or better with Service Pack 3a
- Internet Information Server (IIS) with ASP.NET 1.1[3]
- An enabled Default website *with an SSL web server certificate installed*

NOTE It's best to make sure the IIS service is running on your system before installing Reporting Services. (IIS is called the "World Wide Web Publishing" service in the Services management console (MMC)). If you already installed Reporting Services (before IIS), you'll need to use a command prompt. Navigate to *C:\Windows\Microsoft.NET\ Framework\v1.1.4322* and execute `aspnet_regiis -i.` to register ASP.NET in the IIS metabase.

---

[1] Why do programs start working when you "execute" them, but people stop working?
[2] The SQLExpress, MSDE or Personal Editions of SQL Server can't host Reporting Services.
[3] The RTM readme says Reporting Services Setup requires that version 1.1.4322 of ASP.NET be registered with IIS.

Setting up a machine with these prerequisites[4] should be straightforward enough. The only thing that might trip you up is the installation of an SSL web server certificate that we casually slipped in there—especially if you've not had much exposure to IIS and Certificate Services. Please, don't install Reporting Services without an SSL certificate. Yes, the wizard will let you uncheck Require an SSL Certificate, but be prepared to tell your manager why you needlessly (and carelessly) exposed your data and potentially your systems to the world. Keep in mind that there are situations in which user credentials (logon name and password) need to be passed to and from the Report Server and Report Manager—even if you're simply updating data sources with the Report Manager. If you don't have SSL installed, those credentials can be harvested by evil people. Think about how careful you should be when entering credit card details into a web form. The same degree of care should be applied to any user credentials that you enter into web forms such as the Report Manager. Microsoft gives you all the tools and the Setup wizard defaults to remain secure, so there can be no excuse if you choose to be reckless. Sure, Reporting Services works without SSL, and perhaps in a development environment you might be tempted to go without this degree of protection—but we still don't recommend this approach. If you've not used SSL in production before, it would be a good idea to experiment with it in a development environment first

It's possible to separate the installation into several phases and place the Report Designer on machines where Visual Studio .NET 2003 is installed (and licensed), and install the Reporting Services (Report Manager and Report Server) on any machines running IIS. In a web farm environment, you can have several machines hosting the Reporting Services Server components, all accessing the same Report Server database catalog. The present license arrangements (as we understand them) require you to have a SQL Server license (either per seat or per CPU[5]) for each server that hosts the Reporting Services Server components (Report Manager and Report Server),

---

[4] The installation wizards (should) take care of other prerequisites such as installing the 1.1 version of the .NET Framework—however, the readme.htm puts a shadow on this assertion.

[5] Machine or CPU licensing is selected during SQL Server Setup.

[6] EULA (noun): End-User License Agreement.

I know Bill Vaughn has worn out three pairs of spectacles going over the minutiae of the United States EULA[6] paragraph 12, rereading and rereading it. Beats counting sheep, doesn't it, Bill?

–Peter

Well, did you notice in paragraph 54 that the EULA grants rights to your first-born child in servitude to Microsoft?

–Bill

whether or not you have SQL Server installed on that machine. In the case of per seat licensing, that means each user that accesses the Reporting Services or the Design Tools will need a CAL (Client Access License). No, we're not licensing experts (or lawyers), and of course licensing is a complex subject, so read your licensing conditions very carefully.

If installation doesn't go smoothly, you may need to use some of the command-line administration tools and delicately futz[7] with some configuration files. We explain those tools in brief later in this chapter, but we can't cater to every single caveat here, especially because new caveats can be created by Service Packs. For the latest information, take a look at our website (www.SQLReportingServices.NET) and join our community, as we'll be doing our best to help folks out there stay current on evolving Reporting Services technology.

Installing Only the Report Designer Add-In

Guide me!

The Report Designer add-in for Visual Studio .NET is used to interactively design reports (as we discussed in Chapter 1). If you want to install just the Report Designer add-in to a target machine, run the Reporting Services Setup.exe file, but ensure beforehand that you already have a Visual Studio. NET 2003 Development Tool like Visual Basic .NET installed. Don't worry when the wizard reports that ASP.NET, IIS, or the Default website are not installed if you deliberately don't have them on the target machine—they aren't needed to install and use the Report Designer add-in. On the wizard's Feature Selection dialog, just choose that you only want the Report Designer. It's probably a good idea to install the Books Online (BOL) help file as well because it can be hosted in the Visual Studio .NET designer. In Chapter 4, we'll show you how to customize your Visual Studio .NET Help search interface to find topics in the Reporting Services help files.

You may be asked for a 25-character CD key if the wizard can't detect a qualifying version of SQL Server on the target machine—so make sure you have the CD key from your SQL Server handy.

---

[7] futz (verb): Manipulate, fix, experiment with, tune, play with.

(If you've mislaid the hard copy of the CD key—you should be able to locate it in the registry of the SQL Server machine under *HKLM\SOFTWARE\Microsoft\Microsoft SQL Server\80\ Registration:CD_Key*). We'll first use the Design Tools in Chapter 3 when we show how to use Design wizards, and we really go to town with the Report Designer in Chapter 6. After installation, if you have issues deploying reports, and you're getting messages like: "The underlying connection was closed: Could not establish trust relationship with remote server." chances are you need to deploy using HTTPS and include the same URL embedded in the SSL web server certificate.

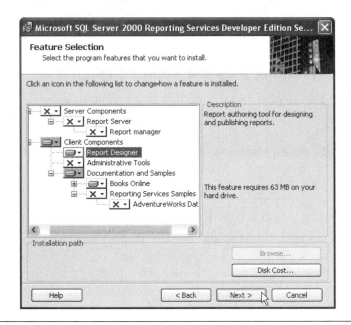

Figure 2.1   Select the Portions of Reporting Services That You Wish to Install

Installing Only the Sample AdventureWorks2000 Database

You can install the Sample AdventureWorks2000 database on a target SQL Server by running Setup on the server and selecting just the AdventureWorks2000 database from the Feature Selection dialog (see Figure 2.1). After the AdventureWorks2000 database is installed, only administrators will be able to get at the data to produce reports from it, so don't forget to add domain groups to the database and at least assign them to the SQL Server db_datareader role.

Installing Reporting Services on a Server with IIS

In a production environment you probably won't want to install the Sample Databases or the Design Tools onto a production SQL Server or IIS server. However, before you run Setup (the installation wizard), step through this checklist:

1. Decide which IIS server is to host the Reporting Services. Initially, the IIS server must have the Default website enabled.
2. Check that the IIS server has an SSL web server certificate. If `http://<Server>/Postinfo.html` returns a web page, but `https://<Server>/Postinfo.html` does not, you need to install an SSL certificate. For detailed information on installing SSL, see Appendixes A and B and watch the video clips.
3. Decide where the Reporting Services' own catalog database is going to be installed. This needs to be SQL Server 2000 with at least SP3a—not Yukon, MSDE, or Personal Editions. This SQL Server need not be on the same server as the IIS components, but if it is, you economize on the SQL Server licences that you'll need.
4. Do you have sufficient privileges on your database? Make sure you have an account that is a member of the sysadmins role on the SQL Server to use during installation.
5. If you need to run Setup with command-line options, consider our security caveats, and especially consider encrypting any Setup ini file.
6. Launch the installation wizard from a non-network path.

Which Account Is Running the Install Wizard?

During installation of Reporting Services, the bootstrapper installation wizard logs on to the SQL Server used to host the Report Server catalog databases with the wizard's account credentials, using

"Trusted" connection SSPI security. This means the target SQL Server must expose a login account that corresponds to the rights granted to the user running the wizard. As we said earlier, it's easiest if the wizard is run with Administrator credentials as SQL Server automatically creates a login account for all system administrators. If the domain administrator won't let you have access to the Administrator account and you choose to use an ordinary Domain User account, it must belong to the System Administrators (sysadmin) SQL Server Security "Server Role" (at least during the install). The wizard will check up on you to ensure that it is and won't continue if it isn't.[8] (If you're a trainee SQL Server guru, you might think that the Database Creators (dbcreator) SQL Server Security "Server Role" would be sufficient. However, the bootstrapper installation wizard also needs to make a couple of calls to the sp_addrole stored procedure, in addition to creating the Reporting Services databases. Accounts that are only members of the Database Creators (dbcreator) role can't do that.)

Of course, using a trusted connection is by far the most sensible route from a security standpoint, but there may be situations where you have the SQL Server in one Active Directory Domain, the Reporting Services in another Active Directory Domain, and no formal Active Directory Trust between the two Domains. Perhaps you have no Active Directories at all. In this case, it means that you won't be able to add the Domain User Account under which you are running the installation wizard to the SQL Server System Administrators SQL Server Security "Server Role." Thus, the wizard won't be able to create the database catalogs. We told you it would be easier just to steal the Administrator's password. Don't worry, you are not pooched—there is a solution. You can instruct the wizard to use a SQL account that belongs to the sysadmin role instead. To do this, launch the Setup installation wizard and provide a few command-line options: RSSETUPACCOUNT and RSSETUPPASSWORD. We discuss these options in the next section.

---

[8] We've found that when the wizard catches you, things work best if you cancel the install, make the changes to the account on the SQL Server, and then start the install again.

Security Bulletin 1

If you put sensitive information into an ini file—things like the credentials of a SQL Server sysadmin account, as when setting the `RSSETUPACCOUNT` and `RSSETUPPASSWORD` options, practice safe computing. Setting ACLs on files should be your first line of defense, but you should also be concerned about what happens to those files when they are deleted.

Before you edit and save any values in your copy of the template file, encrypt your copy of the file (right-click it, select Properties, on the General tab click the "Advanced" button, and then select Encrypt contents to secure data). In addition, consider the permissions on this option file. Why? Well, if you don't follow our advice you might as well just write the SA password on a Post-it note and stick it on the monitor for all to see. Consider that when you delete an unencrypted ini file, any credentials or other information it contained could be easily "harvested" from the disk. A wealth of utilities floating around the Internet (for free) are for doing just that, as anyone watching one of the crime shows on TV would know.

Security Bulletin 2

We also hope that if you are going to be using a SQL Server account for the Setup (i.e., setting the `RSSETUPACCOUNT` and `RSSETUPPASSWORD` options) that you have assigned an SSL certificate to the SQL Server and have configured the SQL Server to force encryption. If you haven't, you should be aware that SQL Authentication, which is what will by default be used over an unencrypted connection, is fairly insecure. One final thought for the paranoid:

After the installation, you can always change the Password for the SQL Server account that you used during installation—just don't rely on this approach. It only takes someone listening to grab the credentials while on the wire and immediately create their own backdoor sysadmin account. Yes, folks, we've seen this kind of thing happen in some environments when the door was only open for a few seconds. (Sleep well tonight.)

Installing Reporting Services on Web Farms

It's possible to scale out and configure a number of IIS servers to all use the same Report Server database. Such a configuration is called a ***web farm***. Web farm configurations are only available to the Developer/Enterprise/Evaluation versions of SQL Server, but there are licensing restrictions on use of the Developer or Evaluation versions in production. If during the installation you instruct the wizard to use a pre-existing Report Server database, the wizard asks if you want to setup a web farm and leads you through the installation steps. There may be occasions when you want to take a stand-alone Reporting Services installation and create or join it to an existing web farm. With some configuration file editing and some command-line utilities (`rsconfig.exe`, `rsactivate.exe`, and possibly `rskeymgmt.exe`), you'll be able to get it to work. We briefly discuss some these utilities to provide an overview of what they do in "Installing Reporting Services on a Web Farm," later in this chapter.

Licensing Your Reporting Services Installation

As with the installation of the Report Designer, if the wizard cannot find a qualifying[9] installed SQL Server 2000, it asks you for the 25-character product key of a qualifying version. To comply with the license agreement, you need a SQL Server 2000 server license for every machine on which the Reporting Services *Server* components are installed. If you decide to split the installation so that the Reporting Services SQL Server Catalog is on one machine and the IIS Report Manager and Report Server are on another machine, you'll need two SQL Server 2000 server licenses—but only one if you run them on the same box. As we said earlier, we're not licensing experts, and licensing arrangements change and are different from locale to locale, so please check your license arrangements carefully. For development purposes only, our solution is that we subscribe to MSDN Universal, which includes SQL Server Developer Edition,[10] which has sufficient rights and licenses for our development machines—but the MSDN Universal is not licensed for any production purposes.

---

[9] Qualifying versions do not include SQL Server Express, MSDE or Personal Editions. Yes, these versions can be reported from and used as data sources, but they are not licensed to host the Reporting Services Catalogs, and the installation wizard is hard-coded not to install onto them.

[10] SQL Server Developer Edition can be purchased for $49.

Command-Line Options for the Installation Wizard

It's possible to run the installation wizard from a Command prompt window and provide some or all of the options to the wizard—it's even possible to do a completely silent install. The command-line options are typically supplied as parameters to Setup.exe or through an ini file. You'll find a template ini file in your Reporting Services distribution media. The template is well documented and explains all of the options. It's convenient (and a good idea) to copy this template and edit the values you need. Next, launch the Setup.exe wizard from a command prompt with `setup.exe /settings myoptions.ini`— assuming myoptions.ini is your file based on the template.ini.

Preparing Your System to Run the Setup Wizard

If you've already received an SSL web server certificate from a public Certificate Authority or from an Enterprise Certificate Services Certificate Authority within your Active Directory Domain and created and installed an SSL web server certificate for the web server hosting Reporting Services, you'll have little to do but answer a few simple questions in the following Reporting Services Setup dialogs. If not, then you might need to take a couple of side trips to make sure this SSL infrastructure is installed. We've provided a detailed explanation of the steps you'll need to take to enable SSL security for your website in Appendix A, "Using SSL to Protect Your Data," and Appendix B, "Using Secure Sockets Layer for Reporting Services." Better yet, watch the Guide me! narrated screen capture demonstration that shows how to do this.

Step by Step: Installing Reporting Services on a Server with IIS

With SSL in place, you're ready to proceed with the Reporting Services Setup. As we discussed earlier, the default prerequisites for the Report Services installation specify the target machine has IIS, ASP.NET 1.1, and a Default website (with an SSL web server certificate). So, we are working with either Windows 2000 Server, Windows Server 2003 configured as an Application Server, or

Windows XP with IIS enabled. You'll also need connection credentials to an instance of SQL Server 2000, which has at least Service Pack 3a applied. Make sure you setup a properly permissioned login ID. To do all of this, you're going to need to use the sysadmin role[11] as described below, but only for the installation. This means that if you don't have sufficient permission, you need to get your SQL Server SA to do this for you.

If you are installing Reporting Services on a machine that:

- Belongs to an Active Directory Domain
- The SQL Server hosting the Reporting Services catalog database is in the same Domain
- You haven't messed around with your SQL Server security settings
- You are installing under an account that has Admin privileges

If all of the above are true, the major roadblocks to a successful installation have been addressed. However, if you stepped off that line, encountered some setup issues, or want to perform unattended installs, you might have to return to the earlier section that discusses the issues you're likely to encounter.

Stepping Through the Setup Wizard

The Component Update dialog appears when you first start the Reporting Services Setup wizard. It automatically checks to make sure that the "Microsoft SQL Server Reporting Services Setup Support Files" and other dependencies are installed. This dialog also runs when you restart Setup to uninstall or reconfigure Reporting Services. According to readme_en.htm, you'll have to have ASP.NET 1.1.4322 registered with IIS. You'll also need to ensure that MDAC 2.6 or later has been installed, which should not be a problem as this version of MDAC (or later) is included with all of the recent versions of Windows and is installed with Visual Studio .NET.

This dialog is followed by a Registration Information dialog asking you to personalize your installation. There's no clear use for this information, but we expect it's salted away in the registry somewhere.

---

[11] Use the SA login or a login that's a member of the sysadmin fixed role.

Next, you'll see a Feature Selection dialog, which permits you to select how much of Reporting Services should be installed and where to install it. This dialog determines whether the Server components, the client components, or both should be installed. If some prerequisites are not met, the features that depend on them are missing from the component tree. For example, no IIS means no Server features, and no Visual Studio means no Report Designer. If you're installing Reporting Services on a development system, we strongly suggest including the Reporting Services Samples and AdventureWorks database, as we will be using these to illustrate how Reporting Services works. You don't have to install Reporting Services onto the machine hosting the SQL Server Report Server database catalog (but the machine will need a SQL Server license).

Remember, all you need for Reporting Services is a machine running IIS server, ASP.NET 1.1, and a Default website with an SSL web server certificate. This system can be Windows 2000 Server or a Windows Server 2003 configured as an Application Server. It can even be a Windows XP system if you install IIS. The Reporting Services Setup program will check to make sure most of these requirements are in place when first started—all except the SSL certificate. Because you might not have an SSL web server certificate, we'd better tell you what you need to know about Secure Sockets Layer (SSL).

Reporting Services Windows and Web Service Account Installation Options

The next dialog (shown in Figure 2.2) specifies the accounts under which the ReportServer Services will run. This dialog can sometimes seem a little tautologically[12] confusing, and it's easy to lose track of which service uses which account, so let's take a deep breath and make a start.

---

[12] tau·tol·o·gy (noun): A redundant repetition of a meaning in a sentence or idea using different words.

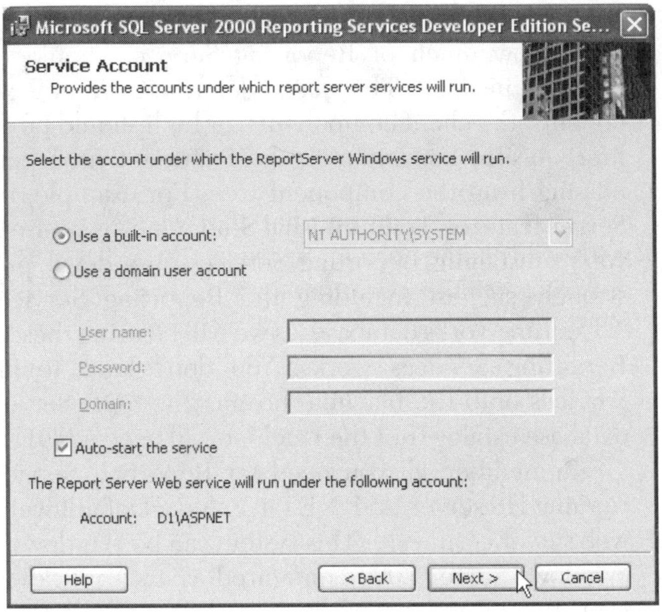

Figure 2.2 Selecting the Account for the ReportServer Windows Service

- **The ReportServer Windows service,** a Windows service, can execute under a number of accounts, depending on which operating system it's running on. On Windows 2000 and Windows XP, you can configure this to be either a Domain Account or the Local System Account (NT AUTHORITY\ SYSTEM). On Windows Server 2003, there is an additional choice of running this with the Network Service Account (NT AUTHORITY\NETWORK SERVICE). We recommend that you use the Local System Account on Windows 2000 and Windows XP and that you choose Network Service Account on Windows Server 2003. This choice will make more sense in a minute.
- **The Report Server web service** is presently an ASP.NET program, so by default it's run under the account configured for the ASP.NET Worker Process (aspnet_wp.exe). On Windows XP and Windows 2000, this (by default) is a local user account

on the machine called ASPNET. On Windows Server 2003, the ASP.NET Worker Process is run under the Network Service Account (NT AUTHORITY\NETWORK SERVICE). If you have changed this account in machine.config, chances are Setup will not be able to run correctly.

There is also an account that we need to concern ourselves with—this is the account whose credentials the Report Server web service and the ReportServer Windows service both use to access the Report Server database. If you followed our recommendation and are running the Windows Report Service under a Local System or Network Service, you have several choices for the credentials for the Report Server web service:

1. The same account that the Windows Report Service is running under
2. A Domain User Account
3. A SQL Login account

If you are running Windows 2000 but didn't accept the recommendation, and you decided you knew better and used a Domain Account for the ReportServer Windows service, your only option is to access the report database using SQL Login credentials or use the same Domain Account that you specified for the Windows service. In addition, your reports will not be able to use prompted or stored Windows credentials to access remote data sources; they would have to use SQL credentials. If you use a SQL account, Setup creates it if it does not exist and assigns the correct SQL permissions to it. It also assigns the required SQL permissions to any account you use. However, using a SQL Login can be considered a security vulnerability unless you also have enabled Encryption on your SQL Server. Why? We knew you were going to ask that (again). This security vulnerability is mostly due to the fact that SQL Login credentials are not as secure as trusted connections or Domain credentials, which have more security features built in—things like making sure passwords are unique and are replaced regularly, and SQL Authentication is much easier to crack than Windows Domain Credentials from a hacking point of view. Another factor here is the cavalier attitude some folks have when passing around and using the SQL Server SA account password. Ah! You mean, why can't you use a Domain Account? Well, the answer is that it is a limitation of Windows 2000, and also the infrastructure of Reporting Services—so, it is because it is…unfortunately.

If you are on Windows Server 2003, then party on, but use the Network Service Account (NT AUTHORITY\NETWORK SERVICE) rather than the Local System Account (NT AUTHORITY\SYSTEM) for the Reporting Services Windows service, as it has fewer privileges but is sufficient for Reporting Services and is therefore somewhat more secure.

Auto-Starting the Reporting Services Service

At the bottom of the Service Account dialog, you'll find a checkbox that specifies whether or not to auto-start the service. If you uncheck this box, the Reporting Services service will have to be started on first use. For development systems, this might be a good idea to reduce the amount of overhead the service consumes.

Choosing the Reporting Services Virtual Directories

The next dialog you'll encounter in the Reporting Services Setup wizard asks you to specify the virtual directories on which Reporting Services and Report Manager are accessible (as shown in Figure 2.3). Throughout the book and DVD examples, we'll use the defaults of "ReportServer" for the Reporting Server virtual directory and "Reports" for the Report Manager virtual directory.

You may have already gathered that the Report Manager and the Report Server are installed in virtual directories on the Default website of an IIS server. By default, Reporting Services Setup assumes that the website that you want to install on has a web server certificate issued to it and supports SSL. This is great if your website supports SSL, but it may possibly send you off in a diversionary spin if it doesn't, and on a substantial time-consuming learning curve if IIS configuration minutiae are outside of your hitherto core experience. This is especially true if you don't have an experienced IIS administrator on hand to bully or cajole into setting up the SSL for you.

Unless you uncheck the Use SSL checkbox in the installation wizard (which is shown checked in Figure 2.3), you won't be able to install with the wizard—that is, unless you have SSL already installed. Take heart, because Appendix A will give you a *boost* with instructions and a Guide me! video, and if that still isn't enough to get you going we offer correspondence and onsite consultancy services for a modest fee.

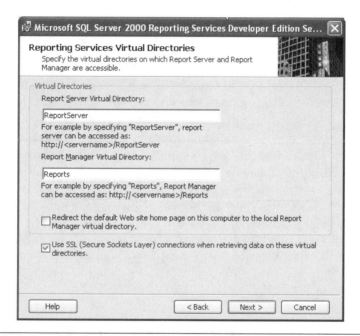

Figure 2.3 If You Don't Have SSL Installed, You Won't Get Past This Installation Dialog Without Removing the Check from "Use SSL"

Why Is Secure Sockets Layer (SSL) Important?

SSL provides the ability for an IIS server to encrypt network traffic, and makes it possible for a browser to interact with a website (securely) using *HTTPS*. Web sites *should* be using HTTPS and SSL when you provide your credit card details. The theory is that if the network traffic is encrypted it makes it more difficult for anyone who intercepts that traffic to decrypt it—assuming that they don't possess the keys. The cost of having SSL (apart from the certificate mentioned in Appendixes A and B) is a slight dent in performance.

In the Reporting Services context, one important role for SSL is effective encryption of any user credentials that might need to be passed to Reporting Services to enable it to gain access to a managed report's underlying data. While there may be other approaches and better practices, which we'll talk about elsewhere, it is possible to pass these credentials in the URL or in an HTTP POST. If you don't have SSL and therefore are not using HTTPS, those credentials will traverse the network in plaintext and be a trivial exercise for evil folks to harvest.

As we said in Chapter 1, you'll discover that in order to access many of the more important SOAP interface web methods, you'll have to have SSL enabled on the IIS server. If you choose to write your own custom applications using the SOAP methods, you'll find you have secure and complete access to the whole SOAP interface, but only if you have SSL enabled on the Reporting Services website.

Appendix A walks you through the process of setting up SSL on your website and provides a great deal of detailed information on the minutiae you might need to consider if you haven't done this before. Appendix B is an MSDE article we wrote on installing SSL and a certificate service that might also prove beneficial. We're going to assume from this point forward that you've created and installed an SSL certificate for your website.

Selecting the Report Server Database and Credentials

The next dialog exposed by the Reporting Services Setup wizard (as shown in Figure 2.4) asks you to specify the SQL Server to host the Reporting Services database. Remember to address the correct instance using the <instance>\<server name> notation. Next, supply (or accept) the name of the Reporting Services database—the default is "ReportServer." If the wizard finds this database on the Report Server, it stops and demands that you change the name or remove the existing database. Otherwise, it creates a new ReportServer (2.31 MB) and a ReportServerTempDB (1.24 MB) database. As we'll discuss later, if you uninstall Reporting Services, the database is not removed (among other things) so you'll have to clean up your system after the uninstall wizard runs.

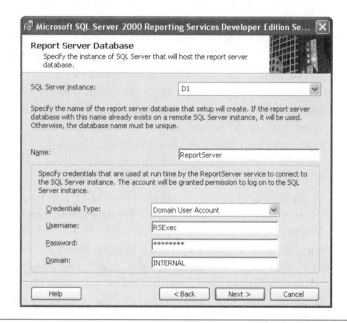

Figure 2.4 Select the Report Server Database and the Domain Account That Accesses It

Which Accounts—Best Practice Summary

Windows 2000 and Windows XP

- Run the Windows service under NT AUTHORITY\SYSTEM.
- Use a Domain Account for the services to access the SQL Reporting Services database.

Windows Server 2003

- Run the Windows service under NT AUTHORITY\NETWORK SERVICE.
- Use a Domain Account for the services to access the SQL Reporting Services database.

SMTP Mail Configuration

The next dialog you'll encounter (shown in Figure 2.5) asks you to specify how Reporting Services should contact you via e-mail. It's important to establish these linkages so that Reporting Services can pass reports via mail and notify you if there are problems with the server. This section discusses how to specify the SMTP and "From" address as well as how to edit elements in the RSReportServer.config file to ensure mail is delivered as expected.

As discussed in Chapter 1, Reporting Services supports a number of delivery extensions, including SMTP,[13] that can be used to send reports via e-mail. During the Setup process, you'll be asked to configure two parts of the SMTP configuration: the SMTP server and the e-mail address that the Report Server will use as a "From" address. Note that the SMTP server address is either an IP Address or a resolvable network name to an SMTP service.

If you want to enhance your *From* address, you can provide a free-text name and specify the e-mail address in < > brackets, as shown in the Setup dialog in Figure 2.5. We've provided "smtp.boost.net" as our SMTP server address. We also used "Boost Report Server <Reports@boost.net>" as the From address. However, we suggest that you *don't* use these addresses for your server as the boost mail server won't guarantee that you'll get your e-mail—use your own SMTP server address.

When e-mail arrives in the destination mailbox, it shows (in this case) as being from "Boost Report Server" and masks the e-mail address (as shown in Figure 2.6). If you have a web farm installation, you could use different names with the same e-mail address in the From address—but if that's the case, be sure to see "Installing Reporting Services on a Web Server" later in this chapter.

No, you don't really need to create an Exchange mailbox for the From address—that is, unless you want to monitor the "non-delivery" reports sent back to this e-mail address, or read the replies your users might send the Report Server.

---

[13] SMTP: Simple Mail Transfer Protocol, a protocol for servers to send electronic mail among themselves.

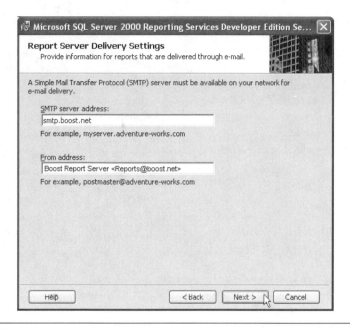

Figure 2.5 SMTP Setup Dialog

✉	!	🗋	▽	🔋	From	Subject	Sent ▽	Size
	✉				Boost Report Server	Product Catalog was executed at 24/12/2003 01:20:06	Wed 24/12/2003 01:20	2 KB
	✉				Boost Report Server	Report2 was executed at 24/12/2003 01:20:06	Wed 24/12/2003 01:20	4 KB
	✉				Boost Report Server	Product Catalog was executed at 24/12/2003 01:19:13	Wed 24/12/2003 01:19	2 KB

Figure 2.6 Reports in an E-Mail Inbox with Enhanced "From" Names

Once the SMTP installation phase is over, the only way to change the SMTP server and the e-mail address is to edit elements in the RSReportServer.config[14] file under the Report Server Email extension node. Shown in Listing 2.1, on the next page, is the raw default configuration resulting from the SMTP installation wizard. If you want to enhance the e-mail name after having already run the wizard, notice that "<" is represented as < and ">" as >, just like in HTML!

---

[14] You'll find the RSReportServer.config file in *\Program Files\Microsoft SQL Server\ MSSQL\Reporting Services\ReportServer.*

Listing 2.1 The RSReportServer.config File

```xml
<Extension Name="Report Server Email" Type="Microsoft.ReportingServices.
EmailDeliveryProvider.EmailProvider,ReportingServicesEmailDeliveryProvider">
  <MaxRetries>3</MaxRetries>
  <SecondsBeforeRetry>900</SecondsBeforeRetry>
  <Configuration>
    <RSEmailDPConfiguration>
      <SMTPServer>smtp.boost.net</SMTPServer>
      <SMTPServerPort></SMTPServerPort>
      <SMTPAccountName></SMTPAccountName>
      <SMTPConnectionTimeout></SMTPConnectionTimeout>
      <SMTPServerPickupDirectory></SMTPServerPickupDirectory>
      <SMTPUseSSL></SMTPUseSSL>
      <SendUsing></SendUsing>
      <SMTPAuthenticate></SMTPAuthenticate>
      <From>Boost Report Server&lt;Reports@boost.net&gt;</From>
      <EmbeddedRenderFormats>
        <RenderingExtension>MHTML</RenderingExtension>
      </EmbeddedRenderFormats>
      <PrivilegedUserRenderFormats></PrivilegedUserRenderFormats>
      <ExcludedRenderFormats>
        <RenderingExtension>HTMLOWC</RenderingExtension>
        <RenderingExtension>NULL</RenderingExtension>
      </ExcludedRenderFormats>
      <SendEmailToUserAlias>True</SendEmailToUserAlias>
      <DefaultHostName></DefaultHostName>
      <PermittedHosts></PermittedHosts>
    </RSEmailDPConfiguration>
  </Configuration>
</Extension>
```

We don't actually like the default installation for e-mail because after <MaxRetries> at set intervals the mail can fail. We prefer using an alternative that makes use of the SMTP Windows service and its pick-up directory, as this can be more robust and takes the pressure off Reporting Services to make delivery. We tell you how you can configure that in Appendix C, "Configuring SMTP."

Report Server Samples Setup

If you checked the samples option in the Feature Selection dialog, the Setup wizard asks you where the 72.63 MB AdventureWorks2000 database should be installed. Normally, this is installed on the Report Server host SQL Server, but it can be sited anywhere there's room and connectivity. As with the earlier steps, the user running Setup must have permission to create databases on the specified SQL Server instance. If this database exists on the target instance, you'll have to delete it before proceeding or point to another target server.

Licensing Mode

The next dialog should be familiar to anyone who has installed SQL Server before—it asks you to specify how you intend to license Reporting Services.

Ready to Install

Up to this point, the wizard has done nothing as far as actually installing anything on the target servers. When you click Install on the Ready to Install dialog, the wizard completes the Setup process. Once the installation wizard completes, you might want to take a few more steps to further improve the security of your Reporting Services installation. If you installed and accepted SSL (by default), any credentials passed back and forth between the server and the browser are protected by SSL and are secure. However, if the reports themselves are of a sensitive nature, you might want to force all communications to be over SSL, including managed report delivery. To achieve this degree of security, there are a number of additional steps you need to take:

- The RSWebApplication.config file <ReportServerURL> element contains the correct URL for your Report Server.
- The RSReportServer.config file has the SecureConnectionLevel set to 3.
- The RSReportServer.config file has the correct URL for your Report Server.

The location of these files and details on how to change them is located in the section "After Installation—Tuning and Reconfiguring," later in this chapter.

As we've said, Reporting Services installation can be a fairly complex operation (especially if you want to protect your data), so there are a few things that could go wrong. We have seen many of these issues as we've worked extensively with the Setup wizard and configuration files, so we should be able to help you build a safe server. To help validate your server installation, we provide an outline of steps to verify that you're ready to start creating, deploying, and publishing reports. See "Testing the Installation" near the end of this chapter.

Installing Reporting Services in a Non-Default Website

The ordinary installation wizard installs Reporting Services as two virtual directories to the Default website. If you're installing to a development system on Windows XP, you don't have anything other than the Default website anyway. However, if you're installing to a server operating system such as Windows 2000 Server or Windows Server 2003, you can manually create a completely separate website on the server just for Reporting Services. This certainly makes it easier to manage, as it is separated from the Default website, and it enables you to do things like stop and start such a website independently of any others your server may be hosting. It also permits you to install an SSL certificate specifically for the Reporting Services website.

If you are using Windows 2000 Server, you'll have to perform a normal install to the Default website, and subsequently create a completely new and empty website (not virtual directory), sign it with an SSL certificate (not mandatory but it is if you want to be one of our friends), and then create two virtual directories: one called "Reports" and the other "ReportServer." At this point, you can compare all the properties of the Reports and ReportServer virtual directories and copy them over—one property at a time—to the new directories. You haven't quite finished by this stage as you must also install the ASP.NET 1.1 client-side scripts to your website by executing `aspnet_regiis.exe` from the correct .NET framework and with the correct parameter. At the command prompt, navigate to *%windir%\Microsoft.NET\Framework\v1.1.4322* and execute `aspnet_regiis -c`. Once all of this is done, you can now remove the Reports and ReportServer virtual directories on the Default website. And finally, you'll need to change the URLs in the RSWebApplication.config (<ReportServerUrl>) and RSReportServer.config (<UrlRoot>) files to reflect the URL where you are putting the virtual directories. This is why we told you about those elements earlier!

Windows Server 2003 has a nice "back door" route that can simplify some of the steps. Perform an ordinary installation of Reporting Services to the Default website. Next, take backups of the Reports and ReportServer virtual directories by right-clicking on each of them, and then under All Tasks select Save configuration to a file. You can then go to your new website, and under New select New virtual directory from file, and use each of the backups to create new virtual directories. You can then remove the virtual directories from the Default website. Yes, you still need to execute `aspnet_regiis -c` as described above, and you still need to edit the RSWebApplication.config and RSReportServer.config files.

Installation Log Files

During installation, the install wizard records all of its actions and checks to log files it maintains in a file called RSStp_.cab in *\Microsoft SQL Server\80\RS Setup Bootstrap\Log*. In case there were any confusing setup issues or failure points that baffled you, these log files will be a lot more helpful and humanly readable to the average administrator than BSOD[15] dumps are.

---

[15] BSOD: Blue Screen of Death. This used to result from catastrophic failures of drivers and so on in the operating system, and huge dumps of the memory core would be moved to a file. Fortunately, we've not been plagued by any BSODs for a while.

Runtime Trace Log Files

There are three runtime trace log files that are created by default, and they all live in *Microsoft SQL Server**<SQL Server Instance>*\\ *Reporting Services**LogFiles*. They all take the name form of `<logfilename><awkward US timestamp>`.log. Okay, why is this so awkward? Well, it seems to be `<month number>_<day of Month number>_<Year>_<Hours>_<Minutes>_<Seconds>`.

Here's an example: ReportServer__01_02_2004_18_50_47.log. It would have been ever so convenient if instead an ISO date format had been used, such as yyyymmddhhnnssReportServer.log. Such a format would not have confused Europeans and Antipodeans and also would have more easily permitted sorting in the explorer and scripting programs…. Ah well, that aside you need to know what these log files trace, how you can configure how much detail they record, and what automated maintenance is performed on them.

The logs are:

- Report Server web service—ReportServer<datetime>.log
  See the <RSTrace> element in the web.config file in \\Microsoft SQL Server\\MSSQL\\Reporting Services\\ReportServer
- Report Manager—ReportServerWebApp<datetime>.log
  See the <RSTrace> element in the web.config file in \\Microsoft SQL Server\\<instance>\\Reporting Services\\ReportManager
- Report Server Windows Service—<datetime>.log
  See <RSTrace> in ReportingServicesService.exe.config in \\Microsoft SQL Server\\<instance>\\Reporting Services\\Bin

Within the various web.config files, you'll notice that you can configure the log filename, file size, and retention times. You'll also find a peer element to <RSTrace> called <system.diagnostics> and within that an element <switches> with an attribute of DefaultTraceSwitch set to a default of 3. While the file itself documents in a comment possible values of <!-- 1 = error, 2 = warning, 3 = info, 4 = verbose -->, you can switch off logging entirely by setting this to 0.

If you are troubleshooting, it can be quite handy to attach a debugger to the aspnet_wp.exe process as new entries are echoed to the debug output window as well as written to the file. If you've not done this before, we have a video demo for you to watch.

After Installation—Tuning and Reconfiguring

After you've completed the Setup wizard, you might find it necessary to go back and change some of the settings. One approach you might consider is to uninstall and reinstall Reporting Services to make some of these changes. However, we don't encourage that as there are a number of splinters left behind that make this problematic. See the section later in this chapter on uninstalling before taking that route. You can change the configuration files as described here—if you're careful.

In any case, if you're using SSL security as we suggested, we recommend that you change both the RSReportServer.config and RSWebApplication.config files to include the correct URL and SecureConnectionLevel settings. These changes are described in detail below.

The Reporting Services Configuration Files

RSReportServer.config

We've already talked quite a bit about the configuration items in the RSReportServer.config file—its default location is *\Program Files\Microsoft SQL Server\MSSQL\Reporting Services\ ReportServer*. We should mention a few more elements before discussing the other configuration files.

You can control which instance of SQL Server the Report Server web and Windows services uses through the `<InstanceId> MSSQL.1</InstanceId>` element—MSSQL.1 is, of course, the default instance. When the Report Services file is created, a GUID `<InstallationID>` is created to uniquely identify an instance of the installation. This same GUID is used to index the encryption keys table we spoke of earlier. You may need to adjust other entries in the RSReportServer.config file—for example, when you want to create custom extension assemblies. However, we'll cover those elsewhere in the book.

SSL Configuration After Install

Ah! So you didn't listen to us about how to install SSL, or you installed oblivious to the importance of SSL and now want to be able to reconfigure to use SSL without having to take the pain of uninstall followed by reinstall. Well, you are in luck because this is controlled in the RSReportServer.config file by the entry: `<Add Key="SecureConnectionLevel" Value="3"/>` where the Value can be set as follows:

- 3 is the most secure—use SSL for absolutely everything
- 2, secure—use SSL for rendering but don't insist on it for all SOAP calls
- 1, basic security—accept HTTP but reject any calls that might be involved in the passing of credentials
- 0, the least secure—don't use SSL at all

The Report Server redirects the browser to HTTPS as needed, depending on the value of SecureConnectionLevel.

RSWebApplication.config

The Report Manager's main configuration file is RSWebApplication.config. By default, you'll find this file in the *\Program Files\Microsoft SQL Server\MSSQL_\Reporting Services\ ReportManager* folder. The most important thing this file contains is the URL configuration used by the Report Manager to contact the Report Server. If you change the address name of the Report Server, you'll have to come here to hook up the Report Manager. The entry you'll be looking for is

```
<ReportServerUrl>http://rs1.boost.net/ReportServer</ReportServerUrl>
```

(Replace rs1.boost.net with your own server name!)

Reporting Services BOL[16] version 1 tells you not to modify this setting.

---

[16] BOL: The Books Online master help file included with Reporting Services.

Another entry in this file determines the maximum number of requests that can come from each user at a given point in time. With the `<MaxActiveReqForOneUser>` element the default is 20 concurrent requests per user. There is a similar entry in the RSReportServer.config file too.

When the Report Manager encounters an error, it can display an error message with a link off to the Microsoft website for further updated information. You can control whether your users are presented with the link to this Microsoft site by adjusting the `<DisplayErrorLink>` element. The default is "true."

RSReportDesigner.config

The Report Designer also has a configuration file: RSReportDesigner.config. This is located in the *Program Files \\Microsoft SQL Server\\80\\Tools\\Report Designer* folder. For the most part, this file lists the custom data, designer, and render extensions. The entries that it contains are generally related to any custom extensions that you would like to run.

The Policy Configuration Files

In the Report Manager, Report Server, and Report Designer main configuration files, we studiously avoided mentioning the "policy level" keys so that we could deal with them here. There are three XML-like policy files: rspreviewpolicy.config for the Designer, rsmgrpolicy.config for the Report Manager, and rssrvpolicy.config for the Report Server. These configuration files determine how Reporting Services manages Code Access Security (CAS). For the most part, this is how Reporting Services implements security and trust in the CLR code assemblies that it's prepared to load and execute. We'll provide more detail on CAS when we deal with writing a custom extension and how you can declare what permission features your assembly needs—such as registry access, file system access, or network access. CAS also determines how someone installing your assembly can determine how much trust they want to give your assembly, and prevent it from doing unapproved things. This is all governed by the contents of the aforementioned policy files.

Policy Files Are *Not* XML Files

Policy files might look like hierarchical XML files, but they don't contain XML headers and, indeed, they certainly don't support XML comments <!- - - ->

If when you end up editing them (as we will) you enter comments or (heaven forbid) change the case on something like "Url="$CodeGen$/*"" to "Url="$CODEGEN$/*"" you can expect trouble. The problem is that when things come tumbling down, you can get messages telling you that there are fatal errors in Machine.config, which you probably haven't touched. So if you get there, you won't have to suffer the pain we did, and boy did it hurt—two days of ripping ASP.NET to bits with Machine.config, and all because of a measly XML comment we'd put in a policy file to remind us what the previous value was.

The Reporting Services Command-Line Utilities

In some cases, you might need to tune or reconfigure the Reporting Services installation using one of the command-line tools. Each of these are provided to address one or more issues that can crop up in "off-the-beaten-path" (non-typical) installations.

Activation...rsactivate.exe

No, this is not some new-fangled license-related activation spy-ware scheme; it is a clever way to protect credentials. You don't normally need to be concerned about activation unless you are manually configuring a web farm, but you might need it to complete a problematic installation if you're using a non-default IIS configuration or if other required components are configured in a way that Setup does not expect. (This is a known issue with the first release and is high on the agenda to be addressed in future releases.) In most single-system installations, the installer takes care of activation for you, but we're still going to tell you what it is all about here so that you'll be aware of what goes on.

Reporting Services encrypts (both Windows and SQL) credentials that it uses in Reports and Data Sources. The technique is a reversible encryption using a symmetric key. Yes, it needs to be reversible—because how else is it going to be able to use those credentials if it can't work out what they are? During the installation, the Reporting Services Windows service co-operates with the

Reporting Services web service and generates the symmetric keys, which can be inspected in the Report Server Database Keys table. You should be able to see at least two entries there; one for the web service and one for the Windows service. If you create a web farm, you'll see further entries in the Keys table for each Windows service and web service in the farm. Until the web service and Windows service have been activated, neither can make use of content that has encrypted credentials. Reporting Services activates (which means that it shares between all the web and Windows services involved in the web farm the symmetric key) on first use of the web service. That said, sometimes things don't quite work out for some reason, and you may have to do surgery with the Reporting Services command-line tool `rsactivate`.

Key Management...rskeymgmt.exe

Microsoft provides an administrator's command-line utility, `rskeymgmt.exe`, to manage the symmetric key. For example, it's possible to use the `rskeymgmt` tool to back up the symmetric key to an encrypted file. To achieve this, `rskeymgmt` enlists the help of the Windows Reporting Service—so you have to make sure that the service and the SQL Server are both running. You can store the 52-byte backup key file on floppy or other removable media. Don't forget to ensure you also securely retain the password you use to encrypt the file—otherwise it's all a bit pointless.

You can also use `rskeymgmt.exe` to rip out *all* encrypted content from the Report Server by calling `rskeymgmt.exe -d`. Just before you do, be aware that this not only removes each encrypted copy of the symmetric key from the Keys table, but it also removes all encrypted credentials that shared Data Sources and reports use, and you are going to have to put them all back in. Note that subscriptions retain a pointer to encrypted credentials specified for the managed report's Data Source. After you run `-d` (and respecify your stored credentials), you have to manually open each subscription and resave it.

To "restore" a symmetric key using rskeymgmt.exe, you call it with the "apply" parameter, `-a`, and supply the backup file and password you used. If you removed encrypted content using rskeymgmt.exe –d, reapplying the symmetric key from a backup will restore only the key—it can't restore the deleted credentials; they're gone forever. However, if it is your desire to only temporarily remove access to encrypted credentials, you could directly delete all rows in the SQL Server Keys table where the Client column is greater than or equal to 0. This will effectively remove the key, and as such the encrypted credentials will not be able to be unencrypted until you reapply the backup copy of the key.

Tips for `rskeymgmt.exe` and `rsactivate.exe`

We experimented quite extensively with the Reporting Service command-line utilities. One thing we found helpful (when things were a little more challenging than usual) was to restart IIS (which can be done with the command-line `IISRESET`) and also to restart the Report Server Windows service.

What Is `rsconfig.exe`?

Well, we know that the Report Server web and Windows services must access the Report Server database, and to do that these services must use some form of Windows or SQL Login credentials. Those credentials are stored in an encrypted format in an XML-like configuration file called RSReportServer.config, which you'll find in the *\Program Files\Microsoft SQL Server\MSSQL\Reporting Services\ReportServer* folder.

The `rsconfig.exe` command-line tool provides a one-way mechanism to encrypt and store any updated credentials in the configuration file. It's also used to specify credentials used for unattended processing for reports that do not use credentials. As you know, you can choose "No credentials" for a report definition or managed report's Data Source. This creates a security hole because the Report Server had to log on to the remote database server using its own credentials. This has been fixed by the introduction of a requirement for credential information—users must now run `rsconfig` with the –e option to specify a –u user name and –p password that the Report Server uses to log on to a remote data server.

Report Server Windows Service Polling

Scheduled Jobs, be they subscriptions or snapshots, are managed by the SQL Server Agent. However, it's the Report Server Windows service that processes these reports. On the off chance that there is some processing to do, the Report Server Windows service polls the database every 10 seconds (by default). Okay, so you might think that the Microsoft development team has taken a shortcut here, as polling instinctively feels like the wrong approach. You could be forgiven for thinking that all the Microsoft developers needed to do was to put the Windows service to sleep and wake it up with a signal. For example, by creating a signaling procedure with the COM invoking the sp_OACreate stored procedure, or with an extended procedure. That might seem simple enough, but what if the Report Server's web components are on a server that does not host the Reporting Services database? In this case, you not only have to cross process boundaries, you've got to get onto another machine. Ah, DCOM? .NET Remoting? A bespoke IP message? (What about firewalls?) Notification Services? Or MSMQ? This is more apparent if you consider the web farm scenario, in which none of the machines know about other machines in the farm. Any machine in the farm can pull an event from the database queue. Who decides which machine gets the event? What if a machine goes down? Does the controller ping them to see if they want the event? So this seemingly simple situation becomes more complicated to program and more complicated to install and troubleshoot, and the polling solution that we have for now is probably the best compromise. We agree that a pull model works best in this scenario.

However, if you don't like the idea of polling every 10 seconds, then there is something you can do about it. In the RSReportServer.config file, you can change the polling element by editing `<Polling-Interval>10</PollingInterval>`.

Testing the Installation

If you installed with SSL enabled, you'll probably find that there is a change you'll need to make to the sample reports Microsoft provides. In most cases, you'll need to correct the project's TargetServerURL to reflect the https:// address of your Report Server.

Let's quickly show you how to use Visual Studio .NET to load, build, and deploy the sample reports. These reports will help verify several aspects of the install and give you a degree of confidence that your installation has succeeded. Let's step through the process:

1. Start Visual Studio .NET on your development system.
2. Open the SampleReports.sln solution file (File|Open| Project…). The installation wizard gave you the option of installing the sample reports—we assume you chose to install the report samples. If you changed the path where these were installed, you're on your own, but if you used the default location, you'll find these samples at *C:\Program Files\Microsoft SQL Server\MSSQL\Reporting Services\Samples\Reports*.
3. Open the Solution Explorer for the SampleReports project, as shown in Figure 2.7.

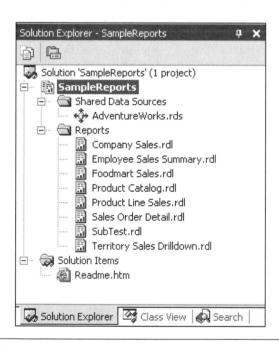

Figure 2.7 The Solution Explorer Window for SampleReports

4. Change the SampleReports TargetServerURL to the URL of your IIS ReportServer virtual directory. To access this property, right-click the SampleReports project in the Solution Explorer and choose Properties. If you're using SSL security, the URL needs to specify https:// instead of http://. Because the IIS ReportServer might not be on the developer's local system—and it's likely not to be—you also need to set the correct server name instead of "localhost."

   Figure 2.8 shows how we changed the TargetServerURL to https://betav1/reportserver so that it targets the Betav1 IIS ReportServer virtual directory. This name must match the Common Name you specified in the IIS SSL certificate. Click OK to close the Property page and apply the changes.

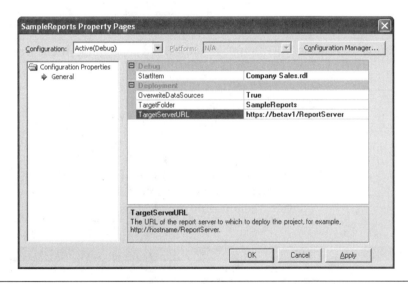

Figure 2.8 Change the TargetServerURL to Point to the Correct IIS ReportServer Virtual Directory

5. Deploy the SampleReports project, paying close attention to the Output window. To start deployment, right-click on the SampleReports project and choose Deploy. After the SampleReports project is built, each report definition should deploy one at a time, as shown in Figure 2.9.

Figure 2.9 The Visual Studio .NET Output Window Shows the Deployment Was Successful

6. Use a browser to address the TargetServerURL you entered above. Remember, this is the IIS ReportServer virtual directory. For our test, we'll use https://betav1/reportserver. If this works, you should get a page that looks something like Figure 2.10. If you get a Page Not Found error or a permissions error, you have missed a step somewhere or you don't have sufficient rights to see this server.

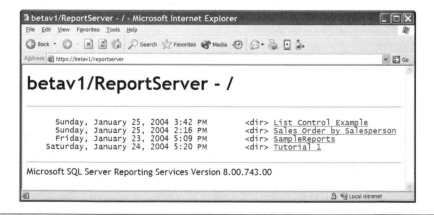

Figure 2.10 Using a Browser to Address the ReportServer Virtual Directory

7. To view one or more of the sample reports, click on the SampleReports link. This should show a list of the sample reports you just deployed, as shown in Figure 2.11.

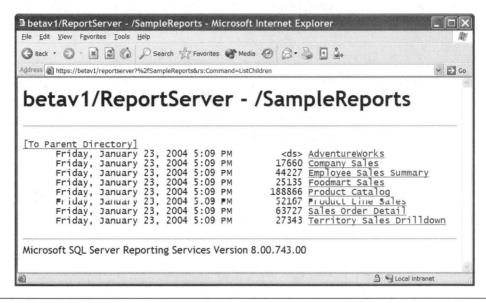

Figure 2.11 The betav1/ReportSever SampleReports Directory

8. Click on one of the reports in the list to get Reporting Services to render the report. After a window appears that tells you the report is being generated, the selected report should be rendered in the browser. We selected Company Sales, and Figure 2.12 shows how this is rendered in the browser.
9. As a final step, you might like to check that the SQL Server Agent is running, in addition to the Report Services Windows service—as they both are used with Report Subscription. We'll tell you more about that in Chapter 4, however, so don't get overly worried about it here.

Once you've completed these steps, you should be ready to continue with the rest of the book with a degree of confidence that you can create, deploy, and view reports in a browser. We'll get into more detail on developing, managing, publishing, and fine-tuning reports in subsequent chapters.

Figure 2.12 The Company Sales Report as Rendered in a Browser

Installing Reporting Services on a Web Farm

This section is for people running the SQL Server Enterprise, Developer, or Evaluation versions who want to share the Report Server database with a number of IIS servers and so create a web farm. Before you follow any of these steps, you first need to perform one normal installation of Reporting Services because the steps show you how to add additional IIS servers to an already working installation.

Web Farm Installations

You can take two approaches when installing Reporting Services technology on a web farm.

> 1. During the installation wizard, specify that the SQL Server instance to contain the Report Server database is already located on another machine.

2. Take a preconfigured Reporting Services installation and change the DSN Connection to the Report Server databases and the account credentials that should be used to connect to that database—in the RSReportServer.config file.

We'll walk you through both of these configuration options.

Specify a Different SQL Server Instance

This first approach is fairly straightforward, but it has a restriction: both systems have to be in the same domain or in trusted domains. To start with, prior to running Reporting Services Setup, use Enterprise Manager on the target SQL Server to create a new Domain user named "WebFarmUser" (as shown in Figure 2.13). Next, give this user permission to log in to the Reporting Services database and assign that user to the RSExec role in those catalogs. During Reporting Services installation, specify that the SQL Server instance that you want to be used is located on the SQL Server machine with the WebFarmUser user account.

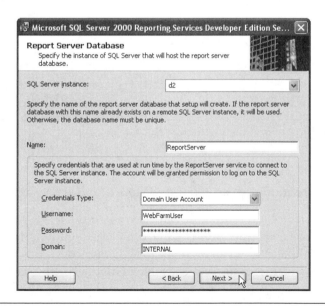

Figure 2.13 "D2" Is a Secondary Development Server Where Reporting Services Was Already Installed. This Screen Was Captured While Executing Setup on Server "D1"

Once you specify a different server to host the SQL Server instance, the installer recognizes this is not a local Report Server database, and assumes that this is a web farm installation. At this point, you'll be presented with an additional dialog (as shown in Figure 2.14) to capture details of an already working installation in the web farm and login details to that installation. These details are used by the wizard to ensure that the symmetric key is correctly configured for the new member of the farm.

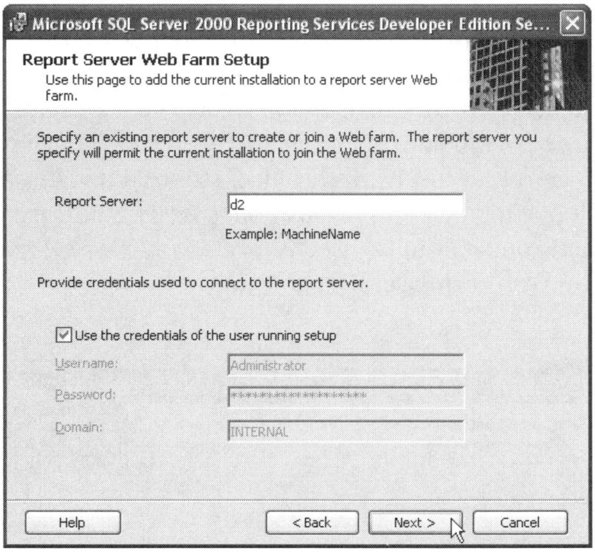

Figure 2.14   Specifying a Pre-Existing Report Server

Reconfigure an Existing Reporting Services Configuration

The other route you can take to setup a Reporting Services web farm configuration is to take an existing Reporting Services installation and change the DSN Connection to the Report Server databases and the account credentials that should be used to connect to those databases. These changes are made to the RSReportServer.config file. The problem is that the details you need to change are encrypted in the file, so you have to use the rsconfig.exe command-line tool and specify the information. For example, the following command-line statement shows how to make the needed changes:

```
rsconfig.exe -c -s <Server Hosting RS DB> -d <RS Database Name>┘
-a Windows -u "<Domain Name>\<User>" -p "<password>"
```

- Having done this, next you need to use Enterprise Manager against the SQL Server hosting the ReportServer database. Here you enable the account you've just specified to log in to the Server with access to the ReportServer and ReportServerTempDB databases. You also need to make this account a member of the RSExec role in both the ReportServer and ReportServerTempDB databases.
- Restart the Report Server Windows service, and restart IIS (you can restart IIS at the command line with IISRESET)
- If you are changing the database that a Report Server used to use, you might like to disable the old database at this point.
- Try to call up the Report Server or the Report Manager in the browser. At this point, it should fail—telling you that the Report Server installation is "not initialized." Don't let that worry you unduly. This is a good sign, as it confirms that you are no longer pointing at any previous installation. However, if you get a message about bad passwords, you need to revisit the rsconfig command line utility and review the account name and password you used. You also need to double-check that you made that account a member of the RSExec role in the two databases as described.
- As a further check, look in your RSReportServer.config file and find the GUID in the <InstallationID> node. Note the GUID and examine the Keys table in the ReportServer

database. You should be able to find two entries with this GUID. You'll find only one if you haven't tried to access the Report Server or Report Manager via the browser yet.

- Assuming that you have found the two entries in that Keys table (in addition to the other entries that will be in there from the other members of the farm), you should now be able to "initialize" or "activate" this installation. The easiest way to do this is to log on to any other machine that is already working in the web farm and execute `rsactivate`. No, you can't do this on the machine you are trying to get to join the farm.

```
rsactivate -m <machine to be added> -u <Administrator User>
-p <Password>
```

- Retry accessing the Report Server in the browser on the newly added machine.

At this point, you should be able to have a working Reporting Services configuration on your web farm.

Removing Reporting Services

To uninstall or reconfigure Reporting Services, you can simply start the Setup wizard again using Windows Control Panel Add/Remove Programs. This launches a new dialog (as shown in Figure 2.15) that permits you to change the installed components or remove Reporting Services. Be aware that if you try to uninstall, the wizard doesn't do a complete tear down. It seems that after running the uninstall program you're going to have to get down on your hands and knees and pick a few splinters out of the system by hand.

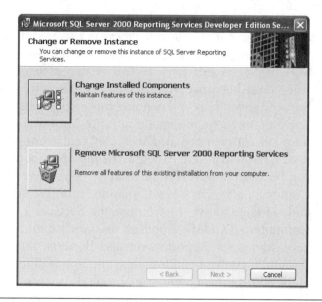

Figure 2.15 Relaunching the Setup Wizard from Add/Remove Programs

Removing the Splinters Left Behind After Uninstall

Let's start with the databases created to support Reporting Services and host your reports. One of the problems is that the Reporting Services database can contain user data that you really want to keep. Just because the application is being uninstalled doesn't necessarily mean that you want to remove your user data too. In a web farm configuration, the uninstall routines can't tell if this is the last machine being uninstalled. Just imagine the chaos if, when uninstalling Microsoft Word, it also removed all your Word documents. In the same way, the uninstall program leaves the ReportServer and the ReportServerTempDB (or whatever you renamed them during installation) databases behind, so you (might) need to delete them by hand.

Deleting all of the things Reporting Services has installed and configured on your SQL Server can be problematic and tedious. This is especially true if you had any Scheduled Report jobs or

Subscription jobs. That's because these jobs have entries for the SQL Server Agent squirreled away in the MSDB database. Here's a warning: don't go digging into MSDB to remove any Report Services SQL Server Agent jobs. It's much easier to make these changes using the Enterprise Manager by navigating to Management | SQL Server Agent | Jobs and deleting those dead jobs manually. You will, however, need to go digging into the Master and the MSDB databases to remove the RSExec roles that were created during the install, but you'll have to delete the members of the role first.

But wait, there is a bit more to tear down. If you launch the Component Services MMC snap-in from the Administrative Tools, and navigate down to Component Services | Computers | <My Computer> | COM+ Applications, you'll find at least a pair of IIS applications for ReportServer and Reports. We say at least a pair because if you've been installing and uninstalling you'll see a pair of applications for each time you installed! You can safely remove these from the system, although in order to do so you'll need to select each application's Properties dialog and uncheck Disable deletion on the Protection tab. This will permit you to delete them.

Reporting Services Documentation Refresh

Shortly after releasing Reporting Services, Microsoft released a refresh to the documentation. To achieve consistency in the formal documentation among the nine language translations in which SQL Server is released, the documentation team had to freeze the documentation while the product was still under active development. So if you want to have documentation that more accurately reflects the released product, take a hike over to www.microsoft.com and search for RSDocRefresh.msi. The article is titled "Reporting Services Books Online January 2004 Update" and (currently) links from http://go.microsoft.com/fwlink/?LinkId=29077. You can simply download the RSDocRefresh.msi and double-click on it to install. After installation, expect Visual Studio .NET 2003 to take some time when you next open it to update its help file indexes.

Reporting Services Service Pack 1

To keep the download as small as possible, Reporting Services Service Pack 1 (SP1) doesn't install the Documentation Refresh. So be aware that you'll need to install the Documentation Refresh separately.

SP1 is supplied as a single executable, and it upgrades all versions of Reporting Services (Enterprise, Developer, Standard, and Evaluation). It also updates all the installation configurations. To install it, simply execute it on the development machines and servers. While it's independent of Service Pack 4 for SQL Server 2000, Microsoft recommends that SQL Server Service Pack 4 be applied first—once it's released. We guess this means that you may need to re-apply the Reporting Services Service Pack after you've installed SQL Server Service Pack 4. <Sigh> However, *do not* postpone installing Reporting Services Service Pack 1—it contains certain security enhancements that we strongly advise be applied.

Summary

In this chapter, we discussed some of the more common setup scenarios—from installing everything on one development system to installing the various Reporting Services components on different machines. We also walked you through a number of configuration and testing steps that should help you get started with Reporting Services more quickly and with fewer hassles.

While we can't give advice for every conceivable configuration, we invite you to participate in our community at www.SQLReportingServices.NET. Here you can let us know any issues you encounter, and we'll try to help you solve them. You might also share with us any solutions you find for particular problems. As Reporting Services evolves, we envisage that the most up-to-date best practice suggestions will be posted on our website.

TIP *A Final Suggestion* Whatever Reporting Services installation configuration you have built, we strongly recommend that you use the rskeymgmt.exe utility, back up the symmetric key to offline storage, and secure it along with the password you used to encrypt the file.

CHAPTER 3

Creating Your First Report with the Report Designer Wizards

This chapter walks you step by step through the process of creating your first report with the ***Reporting Services Report Designer***. We want to acquaint you with this process before you try it yourself and get frustrated with the minutiae. You'll discover in this chapter that there are myriad configurable options that determine how your report queries data, how it looks, and how it is deployed. You'll see how to preview a report and how to tune the configured options after the report is created with the wizards. Recall that in Chapter 1 we outlined how to use the Report Designer to create a report description, save it to an RDL report definition file in your Visual Studio .NET project, and deploy the report to the Report Server where it becomes a "managed" report.

The Visual Studio .NET Reporting Services Designer add-in includes a Report Project wizard and a Report wizard. What's the difference? Well, the Report Project wizard creates a new project and subsequently calls the Report wizard—whereas the Report wizard can be called independently when a new report is added to a pre-existing Report Project. We leave the discussion of Report wizard customizations to Chapter 9, so if you're already confident with using these wizards and know their foibles, feel free to skim this chapter.

A couple of key points we'll highlight in this chapter: When working with the wizards, it's important to set the application name correctly on the data source object. In addition, we'll show where the Report wizard overrides any sort ordering you might have specified in your SQL query, and we detail how to unpick it. We also will be using the same query that we use for a Table report in a Matrix report, so if you're new to "cross-tab" reports you'll find this chapter a light introduction. Some of the menus (especially for the property pages of the Table control and Matrix control) are buried very deeply, so working through this chapter might help if you have jumped in a little too quickly and can't seem to make the drilldowns work the way you intended.

Guide me!

NOTE Media clips on the DVD, the Guide me! narrated screen capture demonstrations, show how these wizards were driven. This is another good place to start, particularly if you're new to Visual Studio .NET.

Creating a Table Report with the Report Project Wizard

Let's get started with our first report. Here you'll see that Reporting Services relies heavily on wizards to build Report Data Source (RDS) files. In some cases wizards call other wizards, so it's easy to get lost and confused. Stay close behind us—we'll lead you through this maze.

First, we're going to show how to use the Report Project wizard, which launches the Report wizard to query the AdventureWorks2000[1] sample database. You'll be making a tabular drilldown report of AdventureWorks suppliers, to show the amounts purchased from each supplier each month of each year, and to show the number of individual purchase orders.

---

[1] The AdventureWorks2000 sample database you'll find with the Reporting Services installation media—it's like the NorthWind sample database on steroids; much larger; and more thought given to data normalization, but it's still pretty challenged (in our opinion).

Start up a new Visual Studio .NET project, and follow these steps:

1. **Launch the Report Project Wizard Template in Visual Studio .NET from the File | New | Project Menu (as Shown in Figure 3.1):** This is a template available under Business Intelligence Projects. (If you don't have Business Intelligence Projects listed, you probably have not installed the Reporting Services Designer add-in, so you might need to take a trip back into Chapter 2 and see how to install it).

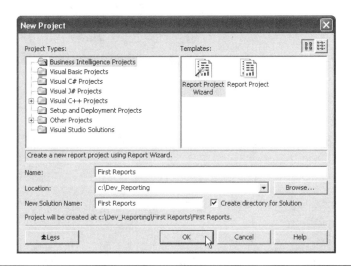

Figure 3.1 Starting the Report Project Wizard in the Reporting Services Add-In

2. **Complete the Project Boilerplate:** This names the project and indicates where to create the folder for the project files. Click OK to proceed to the next step.

3. **Define the Data Source:** Most reports are based on information retrieved from one or more data management systems, and access to these resources might be (should be) gated by access (user) credentials. Because of this, the wizard's first step is to collect the connection and user details. The Data Source enables Reporting Services to find the data

and collect login credentials, which enables access to the DBMS managing the data. The combination of connection details and credentials is called a ***Data Source***. A Data Source can be embedded in a report definition's RDL file, in which case only the specific managed report can use it. Or it can be created as a stand-alone object that can be shared by a number of report definitions or deployed managed reports (see the overview discussion on RDS files in Chapter 1). In our example, we've already installed the AdventureWorks2000 sample database on our Development SQL Server "D1," so we'll connect to that with the Microsoft SQL Server Data Processing extension using a trusted connection. We'll call our DataSource "dsAdventureWorks" and mark it to be shared (as shown in Figure 3.2). Enter these values for the New Data Source and the Type option from the drop-down list. Leave the "Make this a shared data source" box checked, and click Next to proceed to the next step.

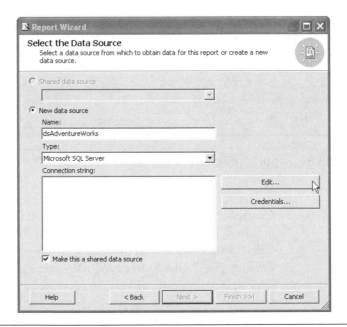

Figure 3.2 Selecting and Configuring a Report Data Source

The Edit button on this wizard page is the route through to a dialog (as shown in Figure 3.3) that you may have seen before. This is the Data Link Properties dialog, which makes it easy to define and test the Connection string and Credentials using a graphical UI.

NOTE *Using Integrated Security Can Be a Security Risk* We've selected Use Windows NT Integrated security (SSPI security) in the dialog in Figure 3.3. As we'll make crystal clear (pardon the pun) in Chapter 5, there are a number of security issues that you should take into account before using SSPI security in a deployed report. We've found that it's possible to create a "Trojan" report, but we'll leave the details to Chapter 5.

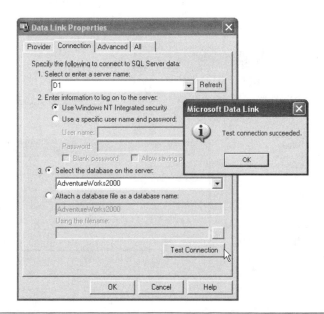

Figure 3.3 The Data Link Properties Dialog Captures Data Source Properties

4. Set the Application Name Property on All Data Sources: Just before we leave the *Data Link* properties, we're going to hop on over to the All tab and set an *Application Name* property to the name of our Data Source, rdsAdventureWorks2000 (as shown in Figure 3.4). This means that if we should ever want or need to trace connection activity on the target SQL Server with the SQL Profiler, we'll be able to identify and even filter the connection by the Application Name. If we don't set an Application Name, it defaults to .NET SQL Data Provider, and filtering by Application Name would then include all the other "polluting" connections from developers who didn't bother to set their Application Name.

TIP *Setting the Application Name in the Connection String* If you forget to set the *Application Name* property in the Data Link Properties dialog, you can always enter it manually into the Connection string—just remember to delimit it with a semicolon (;).

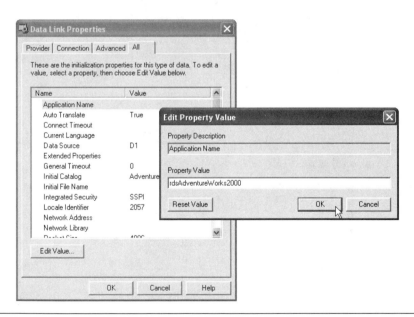

Figure 3.4 Setting the Application Name in the "All" Data Link Properties Dialog

Click OK in the Data Link Properties dialog. At this point, a Connection string is displayed in the Report wizard dialog (as shown in Figure 3.5).

Figure 3.5 The Completed Connection String as Created by the Data Link Properties Dialog

NOTE Under the covers there's a bit of magic taking place. We mentioned in Chapter 1 that Reporting Services connects to data sources using .NET Data Provider technology. There is no standard User Interface wizard for connecting to managed providers, so the smart folks in the Reporting Services development team leverage the OLE DB data link dialog. When they get the OLE DB connection string back from the dialog, they attempt to morph that into a .NET provider connection string. If they can replace the OLE DB provider type with SQL, Oracle, or ODBC, then they will. If it can't be replaced, they leave the OLE DB provider type intact.

5. Design the Query: At this step of the Report wizard, you need to provide the query that returns data from the Data Source for the report definition. In Chapter 6, we'll discuss several best practices for designing report queries and explain why we're not in favor of using dynamic SQL to execute directly against server tables as the Report wizard encourages. You SQL Server gurus just need to keep cool for a while—all will be revealed in time.

If you can write a near-perfect T-SQL SELECT statement, just enter the SQL directly into the Query string textbox on this page of the wizard (as shown in Figure 3.6). The wizard doesn't execute your proposed query, but it does submit it to the server to verify the syntax before permitting you to move on to the next step.

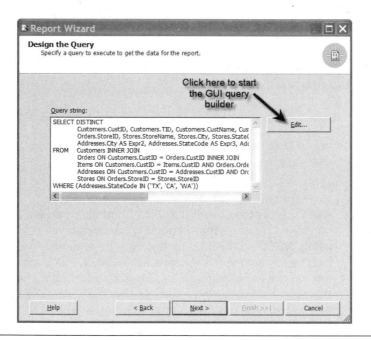

Figure 3.6 Entering the SQL SELECT Statement Directly into the Wizard

6. **Using the Graphical User Interface (GUI) Query Designer:** On the other hand, if you think that you might benefit from visually selecting tables and columns (report fields), and setting query criteria, sorting orders, and group-by clauses by constructing the query in a GUI[2] environment, you might be tempted to hit the Edit button on the Design the Query dialog, as shown in Figure 3.6. This launches the Visual Design Tools' Query Builder in another window that you'll probably want/need to maximize (as shown in Figure 3.7).

However, the first thing that might worry you once you get into the Query Builder is that there is no menu and no toolbar, and you'll be staring at a dialog window with four near-empty panes. To get you started, we'll give you a hint: Click Add Table… by using the right mouse button context menu in the top pane. This enables you to select data source tables to be included in your query, as shown in Figure 3.7.

NOTE When you're building a report, information shown in the report can be drawn from a wealth of data sources. This data can be exposed in the form of database tables (as the Query Builder exposes), or more likely in the form of stored procedures or views. Most experienced database developers and DBAs expose data through stored procedures or views to protect the data and to improve performance and scalability. If you open the Query Builder, right-click to add tables, and don't see any database tables exposed, don't be alarmed. It means your DBA is on the ball and has hidden all of the base tables to protect the company's data. In this case (as we'll discuss later in Chapter 6), you'll have to generate your reports from whatever data sources your DBA provides. If you are trying to see data in the AdventureWorks2000 database, you may need to ensure that your user account has permission to access the database and its objects—you or a DBA will need to do that on the SQL Server with the Enterprise Manager.

---

[2] GUI: Graphical User Interface

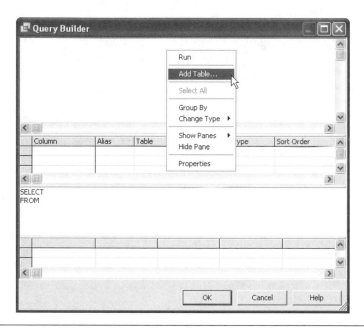

Figure 3.7 Choosing Data Source Tables to Be Included in the Report Query

7. **Testing Your Query and Limiting the Rowset Size:** If you want to execute the T-SQL query in the Query builder—just while you're designing—you'll find it very helpful (if not essential) to limit the number of rows returned. This is accomplished by choosing Properties from the Query Builder's context menu and setting the TOP option as shown in Figure 3.8, or by directly editing the T-SQL and adding a TOP statement after the SELECT (as shown in Figure 3.8). A TOP expression simply tells the data source server that you only want to return the top N rows generated by the query. Remember to remove the TOP expression from your query once you're happy with the results—unless your report is supposed to include only the top N rows.

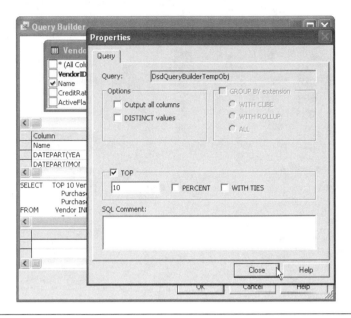

Figure 3.8 Setting the TOP Expression to Limit the Number of Rows Returned During Testing

NOTE Our aim in this book is not to teach you SQL, as there are plenty of other books around for that. Our favorites are by Joe Celko, a wise old sage who's been around databases since before Codd.

If you're following this example and don't understand the SQL, simply copy the SQL verbatim from Figure 3.9 into the Query Builder. If you want to test the query and see what rows are returned, right-click on the dialog and click Run. This executes the SQL SELECT and populates the bottom results window. If you're satisfied with the results, hit OK to accept the generated query and you'll be returned to the wizard with the query pane filled in (as shown in Figure 3.10).

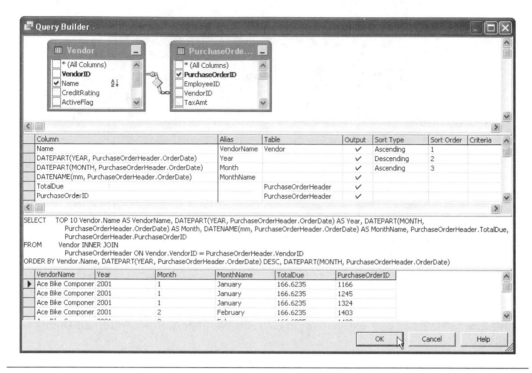

Figure 3.9 The Query Builder After Having Clicked Run

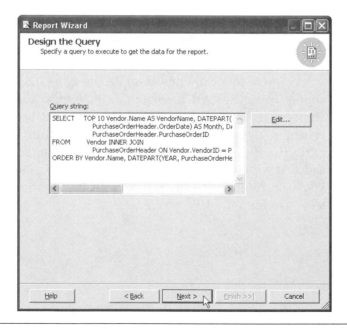

Figure 3.10 The Report Wizard Query String Dialog (with TOP Clause)

8. **Remove the TOP Expression:** Don't forget that when you're done designing and testing you'll probably want to remove the TOP row limitation by removing it from the Query string textbox. This leaves the unfettered query, as shown in Figure 3.11.

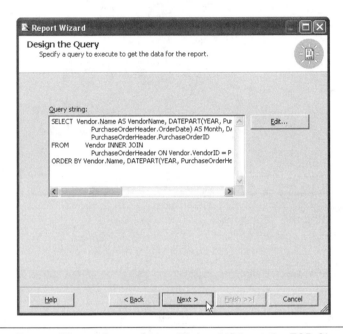

Figure 3.11 The Report Wizard Query String Dialog (Without the TOP Clause)

9. **Select the Report Type:** In the next step, the wizard asks us to choose a report type. (We described each of these types in Chapter 1.) Because we've set out to write a tabular report, we chose Tabular, as shown in Figure 3.12.

10. **Select Group-By Fields:** In the next dialog, the Report wizard permits us to select which fields Reporting Services uses to group the data. Because we want to make this a drill-down report, we need to group by these selected fields (as shown in Figure 3.13). Note that Month is just a number to sort by. We don't really need it, so we could have left it out of the output in Figure 3.9.

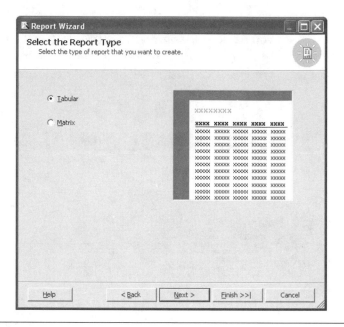

Figure 3.12 Choosing the Report Type

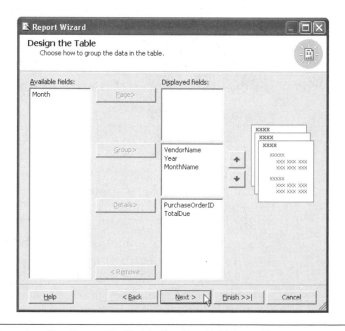

Figure 3.13 Choosing the Group-By Fields for Our Drilldown Report

11. **Choose a Report Table Layout:** Our next Report wizard step determines which Table Layout type we want. Because we want to use a drilldown table, we're forced to select Stepped over Block, otherwise the Enable drilldown option is disabled. In this case, we chose to include subtotals because the wizard doesn't always do sensible things with our data—it subtotals the PurchaseOrderID field. Apparently, the wizard is unable to distinguish the fact that although PurchaseOrderID is a numeric field, we really only want subtotals on the Total Due. Fortunately, we'll be able to substitute other aggregates once the wizard is complete. For example, we'll be able to specify Count() rather than Sum() on the PurchaseOrderID fields in each grouping. Figure 3.14 shows the wizard options we selected for the report's Table Layout type.

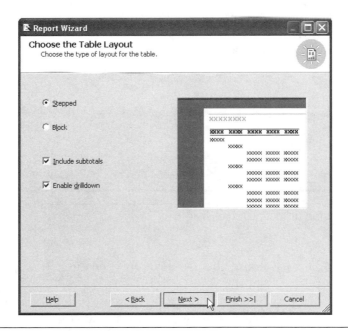

Figure 3.14 Setting the Table Layout Options

12. **Choose the Table Style:** As we near the end of the wizard, the Choose Table Style dialog (shown in Figure 3.15) permits us to choose a Table Style to use when constructing our

report definition. For this example, we chose Casual. A visual layout of the report is shown (albeit intentionally blurry). You'll notice that on our options we have an additional Table Style that you probably don't have—Boost Bold. We'll tell you more about how you can define your own table styles and modify the built-in Report wizard Style Templates in Chapter 9.

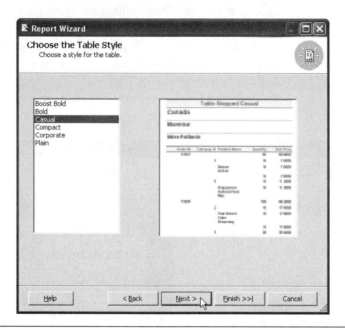

Figure 3.15 Choosing a Casual Table Style

13. Choose the Deployment Location: If you're running the Report Project wizard—as opposed to using the Report wizard to add a new report definition to an existing project—the wizard asks how the Report Server is to deploy the report (as shown in Figure 3.16). You provide a folder name to use on the Report Server—this is where the

report is deployed. If you followed our advice in the installation chapter, you should have an SSL web server certificate installed, so you should update the default URL generated (`http://localhost/ReportServer`) to the correct HTTPS path, in addition to providing a Deployment folder.

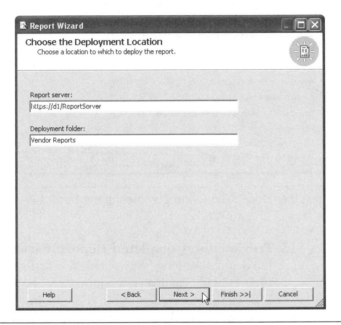

Figure 3.16 Choosing a Deployment Location

14. **Choose the Report Name:** The final step of the Report wizard (shown in Figure 3.17) shows a summary of what the wizard is going to do. Set the report name (which is the name of the report definition's RDL file and the name that in the next chapter we'll see is used by the Report Manager to refer to the managed report post deployment) and indicate that you want to preview the fruits of your labor by checking the Preview report checkbox.

Figure 3.17 Providing the Report Name and Completing the Report Wizard

15. Preview the Completed Report: Fanfare music and roll the drums—at long last we have our first report (as shown in Figure 3.18). The Preview window of the Visual Studio .NET IDE Report Designer add-in shows our new report.

16. Examine the Generated Report: Ah, wait. Vinyl record zip and clatter sound. Okay, what went wrong? As shown in Figure 3.18, we drilled down a reasonable way into Advanced Bicycles and into February 2001, but a few things look rather odd. First, if you recall our original SELECT query, we set up alternative ordering—the Years should be in *descending* order, but clearly they are not. Remember, we predicted that subtotals on PurchaseOrderIDs would look strange, and they certainly do. However, the formatting on the Total Due column also is askew—showing four–decimal-place currency. Ah, no, that's not right. But look! The Report wizard has "intelligently" parsed the camelcase[3] SQL query field names

---

[3] Camelcase is the colloquial name given to strings that have embedded uppercase letters; for example, ThisIsCamelCase.

by inserting a space character between upper- and lowercase letters and used these for the report's Table control's column names. For example, MonthName was changed to Month Name. We're going to tell you how to polish up this report definition without getting into too much detail. We'll have to leave more complete explanations until the next chapter, when we discuss making reports by hand and manipulating a Table control.

So, to start "fixing" things, select the Layout tab in the Designer. This should reveal something similar to Figure 3.19.

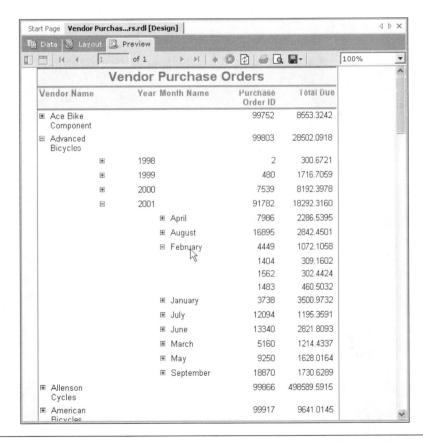

Figure 3.18 Visual Studio .NET Report Designer Add-In's Preview Report Window

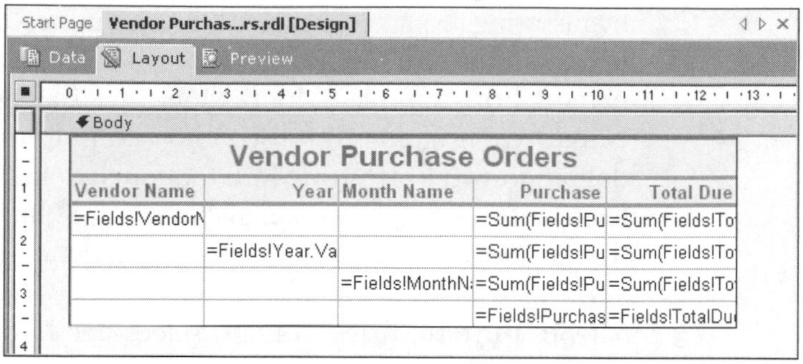

Figure 3.19 Viewing the Report Layout in the Visual Studio .NET Report Designer

17. **Correct the Aggregates:** We can see that we have a grid—or rather a Table control—and we can see that the Purchase Order Id Column is using aggregates of Sum() (under Total Due). This isn't what we wanted, and aggregating or summing Purchase Order IDs doesn't make any sense, so let's change these over to Count() by clicking in those cells on the grid and editing them directly.

Figure 3.20 shows more of the Table control. Down the left side are icons that indicate if the row is a header (as the icon immediately next to Vendor Name indicates) or if it is a grouping row (as the icons incorporating "1, 2, 3" indicate). The detail row is indicated by an icon on the left-hand side with three horizontal black lines.

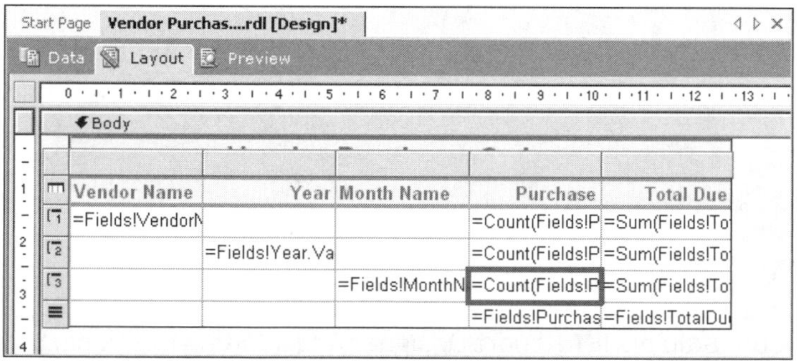

Figure 3.20 Examining the Left-Hand Column Row-Type Icons

18. **Correct Column Formatting:** Figure 3.21 shows how we can improve the formatting of the Total Due column by clicking the mouse in the table header and subsequently setting the *Format* property. Just as in Microsoft Excel, you can set this for each cell separately. As we will see in Chapter 8, *Format* properties respect .NET formatting, so one could simply set a "c" for currency type. This means when rendering a report, the column is formatted as currency and uses a currency symbol. However, in this example we're going to use a template of "#,###.00" to avoid a debate on which currency format to use. We continue this discussion in the Chapter 8.

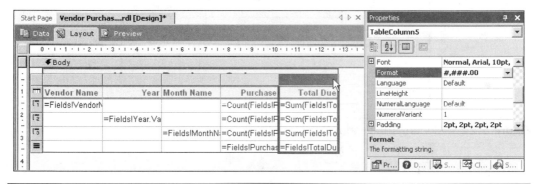

Figure 3.21 Changing the Format of a Set of Columns

19. **Tune Sorting and Grouping:** The only tasks that remain are to polish up the report definition and discuss sorting within the groupings. It turns out that the Table control has its own groupings, and those groups can be sorted. By default, the groups are sorted in ascending order. To be fair to the Reporting Services programmers, they have no way of knowing whether you've already sorted the data being presented, as we did in our query. Because of this, they provided built-in sorting capabilities within each group on the table. Our issue with this, and it's one that you should take to heart, is that if you're issuing a query against a relational data source that is fully optimized for searching and sorting data, you should do your sort ordering on the database server as

part of the query. Runtime sorting within the table on Reporting Services (as the wizard has done) is problematic and has in fact overridden our SQL sort order.

To remove report-driven sorting, choose the Layout table by clicking in the top-left header box, as shown in Figure 3.22, or select it directly out of the Property drop-down list. Next, on the Properties pane, choose the additional property pages available to you by selecting the icon, as shown in Figure 3.23.

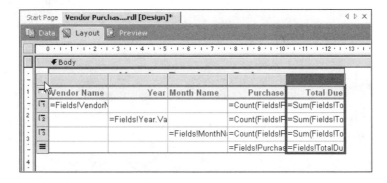

Figure 3.22 Selecting the Vendor Purchase Table Layout

Figure 3.23 Table1 Property Pages Icon

Clicking the Property Pages icon launches the Table Properties dialog. Alternatively, you can right-click on the top-left corner handle of the table and then select Properties. Next, we navigate to the Groups page by selecting the Groups tab, as shown in Figure 3.24.

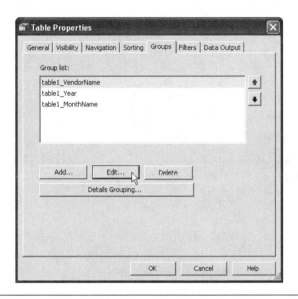

Figure 3.24 The Groups Tab in the Table Properties Dialog

We edit each group in turn by selecting it and clicking the Edit button, which reveals the Grouping and Sorting Properties dialog, and on those pages we need to navigate to the Sorting tab (as shown in Figure 3.25). Consider that sorting at this level is not the same as sorting on the table level. If you're feeling like a deep-sea diver, you have our sympathies—especially if you've been holding your breath—but we're nearly done.

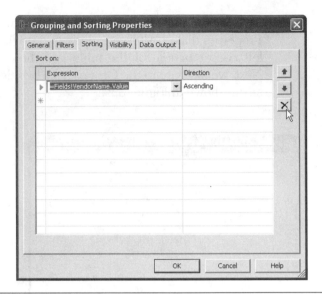

Figure 3.25 The Sorting Tab in the Grouping and Sorting Properties Dialog

In the Sorting tab of the Grouping and Sorting Properties dialog, choose the sorting expression and delete it. Don't forget to delete the sorting expressions for each table grouping before returning to the surface.

20. **Preview the Corrected Report:** If you've followed us so far and are back on dry land, you should now be able to choose the Preview tab in Visual Studio .NET and see something that looks a little more polished, as shown in Figure 3.26.

21. **Deployment:** If the Report wizard is executed from within the Report Project wizard, the project already knows where to deploy (remember Figure 3.16). If you need to update the deployment information, you'll find it on the First Reports project properties. As we've made a few changes, we need to deploy the finished report definition to the Report Server, so right-click on the Report (Project or Solution) in Visual Studio .NET Solution Explorer (as shown in Figure 3.27)—depending on how much of the

solution you want to (re)deploy—and choose the appropriate deploy option from the right mouse button context menu. This creates a managed report in the Reports database. You can test your report in the Report Manager by addressing https://<Your Server>/Reports in your browser—assuming that you listened to us in the last two chapters and installed an SSL web server certificate. If you didn't, you can use http://, but be sure your résumé is current.

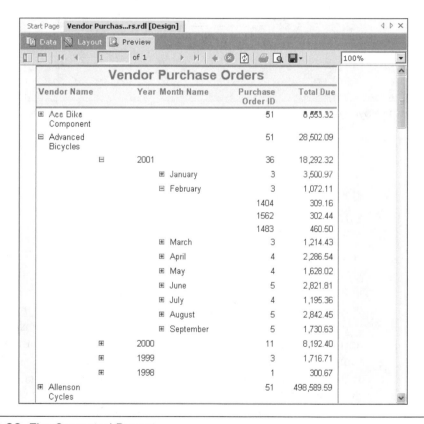

Figure 3.26 The Corrected Report

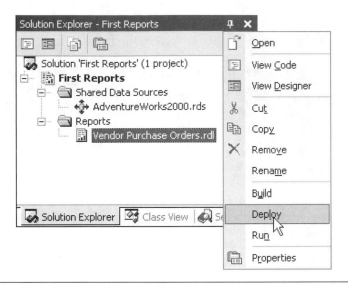

Figure 3.27 Deploying a Report

Creating a Matrix Report with the Report Project Wizard

If you study the output of the Table-based report in Figure 3.26, you'll see that it's not very easy to compare a supplier's purchase values in a particular month and in a selected year. If you displayed years in different columns, and the months in rows (more or less pivoting the table on its side), the report would be easier to read and understand. Well, it's fairly easy to make those changes. Those familiar with PivotTables and T-SQL's WITH CUBE and WITH ROLLUP features probably have a head start on achieving this kind of representation.

Reporting Services provides the ability to take a modest result-set (such as the one generated when we used the wizard earlier) and through a Matrix report permit the report programmer (you) to select which resultset fields are wanted for rows and which are wanted for columns, while still permitting the report viewer to drill into either. To illustrate this, we're going to take a short trip into the Report wizard again to build a matrix version of our report. Before we get going you can save yourself some effort if you copy the T-SQL for the query we used when creating the tabular Vendor Purchase Orders report into an empty Notepad window. You can get to the SQL by opening the report in the Designer and selecting the Data tab. This will save you some time later on when we need to define the report's query.

Guide me!

Here are the steps to build our Matrix report:

1. **Launch the Report Wizard:** Open up the First Reports project in the ReportWizard Solution that we created earlier, select the Reports node, right-click it, and select Add New Report, as shown in Figure 3.28. This launches the Report wizard.

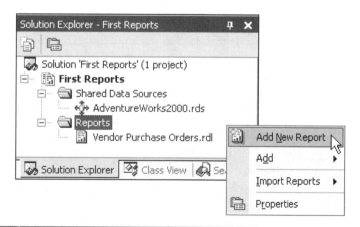

Figure 3.28 Add a New Report to the Project

2. **Select the Data Source:** As we already have a shared Data Source, let's use it (AdventureWorks2000), as shown in Figure 3.29.

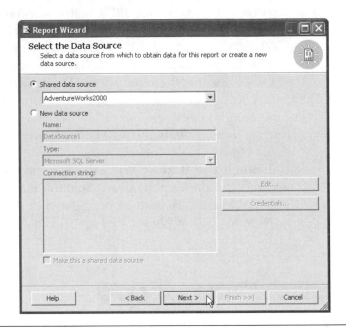

Figure 3.29 Choosing the Shared Data Source

3. **Design the Query:** If you listened to our advice and you have the query on your clipboard and/or in a Notepad window, you can just paste it directly into the Query string textbox, as shown in Figure 3.30. If you didn't listen <sigh>, then follow the steps to Design the Query in the previous example.

4. **Select the Report Type:** At this step of the wizard, this time we chose the Matrix control, as shown in Figure 3.31.

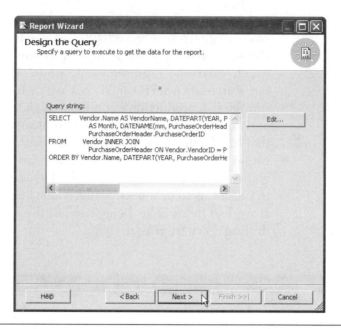

Figure 3.30 The Report Query as Pasted in from the Previous Example

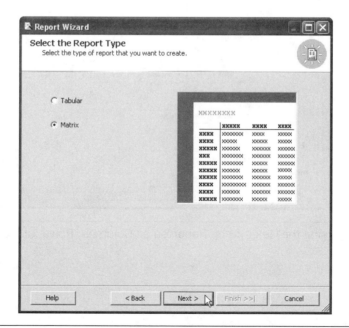

Figure 3.31 Choosing the Matrix Report Type

5. Design the Matrix Control: At the next stage of the wizard (shown in Figure 3.32), we get the opportunity to choose which fields we want represented as Columns and which we'd like represented as Rows. We could include the PurchaseOrderID field, but we're trying to keep this simple. In a production example, we would not use dynamic SQL queries such as these, but we'll tell you more about that in Chapter 6. Not only that, but in a production application, we'd only be returning the fields we were actually going to use in the report. We've selected Enable drilldown to permit us to drill into VendorName and see the months. If we had more fields being used in the Columns, we'd be drilling down from Year.

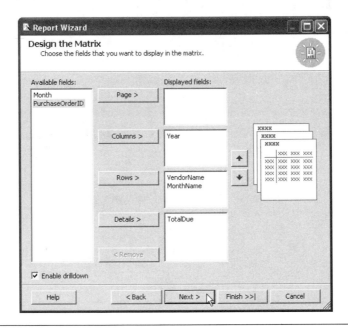

Figure 3.32 Choosing the Fields to be Reported as Columns, Rows, and Details

6. **Choose the Matrix Control Style:** As with the first example, we're going to choose the Casual style, as shown in Figure 3.33, and lobby to encourage you to use the techniques and code provided in Chapter 9 that show how to create your own style templates for the wizard.

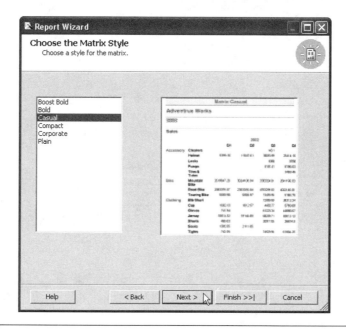

Figure 3.33 Setting the Style for the Matrix Report

7. **Completion:** Figure 3.34 shows the final summary of what we've asked the wizard to do for us. In this final wizard dialog, we choose a name for the report, select to preview it, and hit the Finish button to allow the Report wizard to perform its magic.

Figure 3.34 Setting the Matrix Report Name and Asking the Wizard to Preview the Report

8. **The Preview:** Figure 3.35 shows what the wizard has done. As we can see, the wizard has not respected the sort order (ORDER BY clause) we defined on the query and has implemented its own defaults on top of ours. We can see that while the amounts are formatted we're not thrilled with how it was done. In this case, the amounts are set to four decimal places (a bit strange for currency), and not enough room has been left for a nice aesthetic look when you drill into the vendor. The wizard *has* indeed brought us quite a long way, and we can set about polishing up the report in the Layout view.

9. **Spit and Polish:** To correct the skimpy column width, use the Layout view to drag the first column wider, as shown in Figure 3.36.

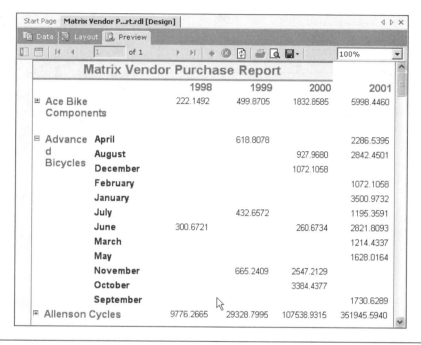

Figure 3.35 The First Preview of Our Matrix Report

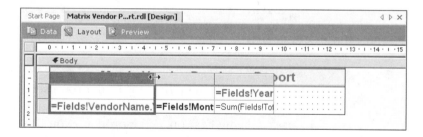

Figure 3.36 Resizing the VendorName Report Column

Now let's select the Matrix control's cell (as shown in Figure 3.37) where the totals are displayed. Change the *Format* property to use a mask of "#,###.00" so that the currency values are shown in the report with two decimal digits.

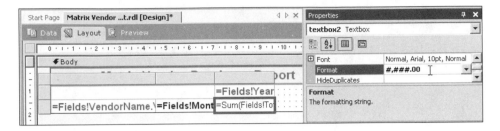

Figure 3.37 Changing the Currency Column to Format the Value Correctly

Next, select the Year column (as shown in Figure 3.38) and configure the *TextAlign* property to Right—to improve the look of this financial data. (You can also enlist the help of a Report Formatting Toolbar.)

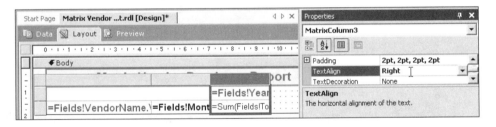

Figure 3.38 Setting the Year Column's *TextAlign* Property

Next, let's clean up the Sort Order representation on the groupings—just as with a Table Report you'll need your deep-sea diving gear on as the property you need to change is deeply buried. Start by selecting the Matrix control's report description layout in the Layout tab by clicking in the top-left header box (as shown in Figure 3.39), or simply choose the Matrix control from the properties list.

Next, launch the Matrix control's Property Pages from the icon on the Properties pane (as shown in Figure 3.40), or right-click the top-left corner handle of the Matrix control and select Properties.

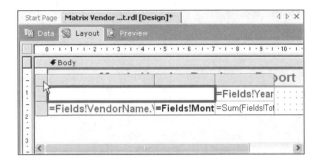

Figure 3.39 Select the Matrix Report in the Layout Tab of the Report Designer

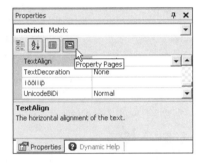

Figure 3.40 Opening the Matrix Properties Page

Once the Matrix control Properties page is displayed, we need to visit each group in turn, as shown in Figures 3.41 through 3.43. This time, once we have Rows and Columns groupings selected, we need to click Edit and remove the sorting expression, as shown in Figure 3.44. If we had not sensibly ordered our initial query, then this would be the place to deal with the sort orders. But as we've said before, it's best to do sorting directly on the server when querying for the data rather than having the Reporting Services code sort the data while processing the report definition or managed report.

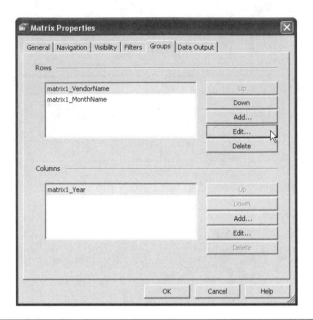

Figure 3.41 Drilling Down into the Groups to Get at the Sort Expression

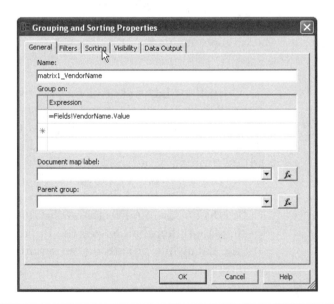

Figure 3.42 Drilling Down from the General Tab to Get at the Sort Expression

Figure 3.43 The Sort Expression to Be Removed

Figure 3.44 Clear the Sort Expression

Before we leave these ocean floor–level properties, let's define another column grouping of All Years. This column is the one we want to display above the breakdown for each year. Let's program the report so that we can drill down into All Years before the breakdowns become visible. To accomplish this, select Add… in the Matrix control's Properties dialog on the Columns (Figure 3.45) and then complete the *Name* and the *Expression* properties in the Grouping and Sorting Properties dialog that pops up. The expression we're choosing here is just a static string of All Years (as shown in Figure 3.46). After we've created the column, we need to move it to the top (as shown in Figures 3.47 and 3.48).

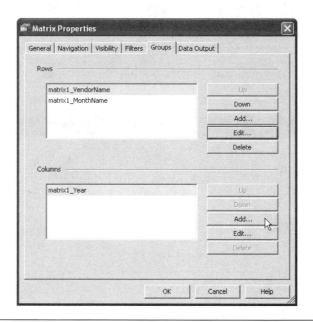

Figure 3.45 Add a New Column Grouping at This Level

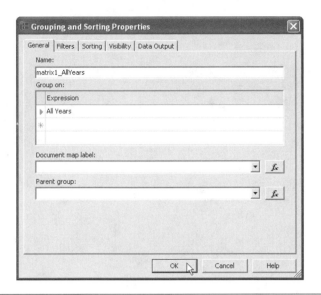

Figure 3.46 Define the New Column Grouping as "All Years"

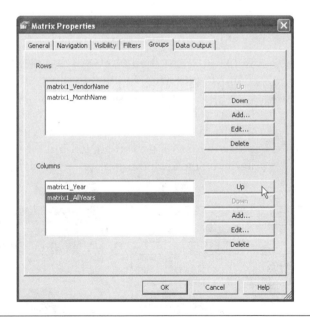

Figure 3.47 The New Column Grouping Now Appears as a Group Column

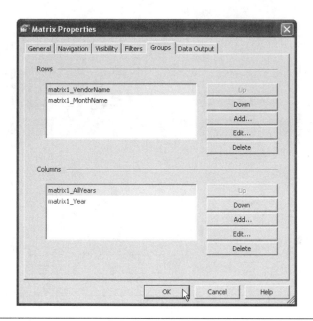

Figure 3.48 Moving the All Years Group to the Top of the List

Now, this part might be confusing because before you can wire up All Years to be the toggle item to drill into the Year breakdown, you need to close all these property page dialogs. Next, you need to name the cell to which All Years is bound (Figure 3.49). The problem is that the Property Page wizard dialog is not intelligent enough to know the name of the cell it is going to create to bind the All Years grouping to until you close all these pages. <Big sigh!>

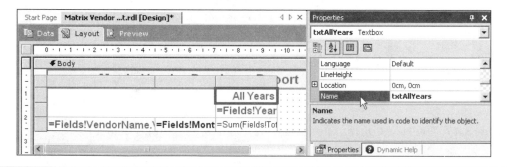

Figure 3.49 Naming the Cell to Bind to the All Years Group

Once you've named the All Years cell, you have to navigate right back to the Matrix control's Properties Groups page and choose Edit (again!) on the Year Column group (as shown in Figure 3.50).

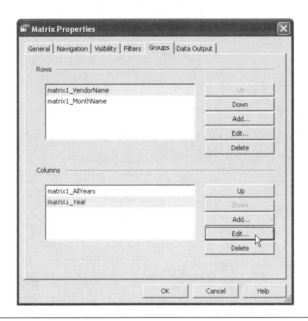

Figure 3.50 Re-editing the Matrix Properties

On the properties page that comes up, navigate to the Visibility tab, marking the initial visibility as Hidden and that its visibility can be toggled by txtAllYears (as shown in Figure 3.51).

At last! You can close all these properties pages (again), come back up to the surface of Visual Studio. NET, and select the Preview tab. The initial view should look similar to Figure 3.52.

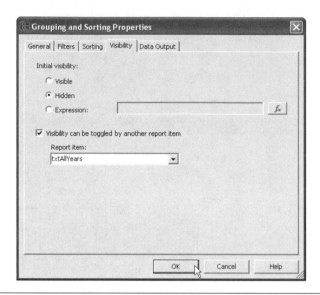

Figure 3.51 Setting the Visibility Attribute for the All Years Item

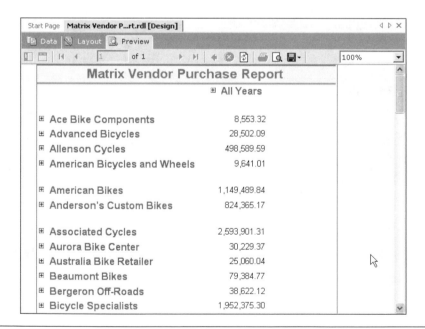

Figure 3.52 The Initial Matrix Report View After Adding the All Years Item

If we drill into some columns and rows, we can see the effect, as shown in Figure 3.53.

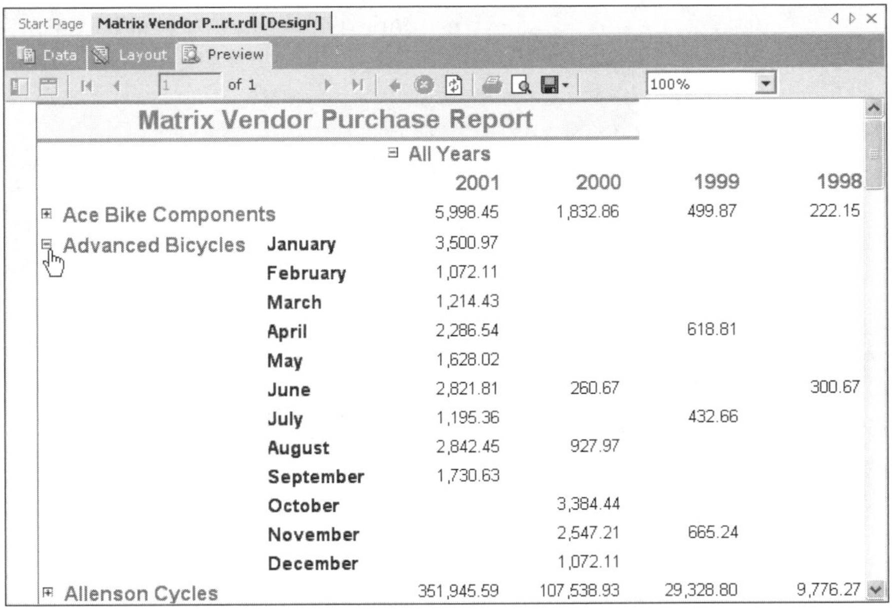

Figure 3.53 The Matrix Report When You Drill into a Selected Column

10. **Deploy the Matrix Control Report:** You can now deploy the Matrix control Report from the Visual Studio .NET Solution Explorer—just select the report and choose Deploy from the right mouse button context menu.

Summary

In this chapter, we gently introduced you to the Report Project wizard and the Report wizard. We've seen that these wizards can go a substantial way toward helping you create tabular interactive reports using a Table or a Matrix control. We've also shown you the Visual Design Tools' Query Builder and mentioned some of its foibles and some ways in which you can cope with them. For demonstration purposes, we used the same query for both reports, but we cautioned you that in production systems it's not a good practice to return fields that are not used. If we were more diligent, we'd now go back and instruct the underlying queries not to output those fields that we didn't use. However, as we'll discuss in more detail in Chapter 6, using dynamic queries directly against database tables in production systems is not one of our best practices.

One best practice (that we did show you here) is to try to have any sorting performed on the database server—rather than by Reporting Services. Database servers are really designed specifically to sort and organize data. No, it's not that Reporting Services is at all "bad" at sorting; in fact, it compares favorably with SQL Server when sorting fields that are not indexed. But by the time data is in Reporting Services, there are no indexes for the sort to leverage. To accomplish this, we also had to show you how to clear the sorting expression that the Report wizards force upon you. The same principle also applies to grouping, and the query that underlies the Matrix report could possibly have been more optimally prepared and grouped on the server rather than by Reporting Services.

CHAPTER 4

Using the Report Manager

The Reporting Services Report Manager is an attractive web-based user interface (UI) wrapper around the Reporting Server's SOAP and URL interfaces. The Report Manager performs both as a Report Server administrator's and end user's tool, and it uses a role-based permission system. This means that administrators can establish roles that limit what managed reports end users can see or change using the Report Manager's administrative functions. Unless an administrator enables a specific "task" for a User or a Domain Group, users gaining access to the Report Manager won't be able to access specifically selected managed reports or perform administrative tasks. We'll work through the details of how to setup these roles and permission hierarchies in this chapter. Remember that a *managed* report (a term Microsoft coined) is simply a report that's been deployed to the Report Server and made visible to those users with sufficient rights. The term "managed" has nothing to do (really) with "managed code." This chapter talks about working with (managing) these managed reports. Think you can manage it?

This chapter is a "must-read" for your company's DBAs or security administrators, even if they never expect to create a single report.

NOTE *How to Read This Chapter* This chapter leads you through a series of steps that creates a user account we call TestUser. As the chapter progresses, we gradually grant rights to this user, so in the end the account has almost as many rights as an administrator. If you skip parts of the chapter, you might miss steps that grant specific rights to the TestUser account and not understand why some of the Report Manager features do not seem to be visible or enabled. We encourage you to work through these steps to get a firm understanding of the permission hierarchy. Again, because of serious security concerns, we cannot recommend that you simply grant your user blanket rights and expect your reports or database to remain secure.

Hopefully, you've successfully installed the Reporting Services and the Report Manager, as explained in Chapter 2. If you haven't, this chapter won't make much sense, and the examples won't work all that well—okay, they won't work at all. You'll also benefit more from this chapter if you've installed the sample AdventureWorks2000 database, as discussed in Chapter 2. If you're a developer, you'll benefit by installing the Visual Studio .NET Report Designer and the AdventureWorks sample reports. It wouldn't hurt to have also followed our discussion of using the report wizards in Chapter 3. However, in any case you'll need a baseline (functional) Report Server that contains some deployed test reports with which you can safely experiment.

NOTE *Install the Sample Reports Using RS* A script execution tool (`rs`) can be used to simplify the process of installing the sample reports. The script PublishSampleReports.rss is located in the *\Program Files\Microsoft SQL Server\MSSQL\Reporting Services\ Samples\Scripts* folder. These scripts are Visual Basic .NET programs that can be run with `rs` from the command prompt as:
`rs -i PublishSampleReports.rss -s https://<Server>/ reportserver -v parentFolder="Sample Reports".`
You C# folks will just have to figure it out.

The route that we've mapped out for this chapter's journey is to show how to use the Report Manager as a typical user in a single web browser window, while at the same time performing Administrative Tasks as an administrator in another web browser window. This is sort of a Reporting Services version of patting your head and rubbing your stomach at the same time. But this approach will save you time and shoe leather transferring between machines or continually logging on and off. Next, we'll explain Reporting Services security *Item-level* and *System-level* roles and how to assign them to managed reports and Users/Groups. Along the way, we'll discuss the changing functional scenery as we continually increase the level of rights provided to a user—until we've elevated that user as far as possible.

NOTE When we refer to a **Data Source** in this and other chapters, we're talking about the report component used to connect to a database—a **data source**. We'll try not to confuse you any more than absolutely necessary.

By the end of the chapter, you should have a good grasp of the Report Manager's functionality. As we go, we'll be snitching to you about tips and techniques that we hope will save you time and protect your data. Listen carefully, especially when we tell you about interesting stuff that happens when you delete shared Data Sources, or when you administer security through Domain Groups.

Guide me!

NOTE This chapter walks you through a long series of steps that are (for the most part) captured in their entirety with Guide me! narrated screen capture demonstrations. You might find it helpful to reference the DVD and drill down to the individual Guide me! sessions that show how each step is done as you read through the chapter.

Understanding the Role-Based Security Model

One of the fundamental lessons we've learned while working with Reporting Services is that it can break through the security boundaries you and your DBA have built around your database. Along the way, we've discovered that when improperly managed, Reporting Services can permit SQL injection attacks and easy access to confidential or otherwise sensitive data. We've also learned that Reporting Services provides plenty of security mechanisms for you—but it's up to you to leave them enabled or turn them on in the first place. We'll show you how to best leverage these security features by spending quite a bit of time setting up user permissions with the Report Manager. Many of these features are implemented through Computer or Domain User Accounts and Groups. This section discusses how to setup these accounts and grant just enough permission to them to permit selected users to see the data they're entitled to see—and no more.

NOTE *Report Manager Performance* We've noticed that it can take quite some time to get the Report Manager started when first invoked or after it's been idle for an extended period. This is because the ASP.NET assemblies used to implement Reporting Services (for example, the web services) must be recompiled if they are not in memory. Once loaded, response times drop to near-zero. Sometimes you'll have to press F5 (refresh) if the browser seems to be hung waiting for Report Manager to start, and other times you may find that closing the web browser completely and opening it again is all that's needed.

Launching the Report Manager as a User and as an Administrator

By now, you've probably already used the Report Manager while testing report deployment in Chapters 2 and 3, so you may be familiar with its URL of https://<server>/Reports.[1] When presented in a web browser, the Report Manager maps to its default or "Home" starting point of https://<server>/Reports/Pages/Folder.aspx. When you access the Report Manager, what you see in your browser depends (for the most part) on which user account accesses the Report Manager—that is, which Reporting Services role-based permissions have been assigned to the user account through the Report Manager's role-based security system, or to any of the Active Directory Domain (or Local Computer) Security Groups that include the User account as a member. Before we start experimenting with these accounts, we need to take a short diversion.

Launching the Web Browser Under Different Credentials

Guide me!

When administering a Report Server, we find it helpful to be able to test and see the effect of our changes on the target User or Group. It helps to see what a typical user sees in *his or her* browser without having to log off the system as a developer or administrator user and

---

[1] Or http://<server>/Reports if you haven't followed all our suggestions from Chapter 2.

log back on as a humble domain or computer user, just to see if something has worked. For those glued to their office swivel chair, this approach eliminates the need to actually get up and walk to the other side of the room[2] to use another machine!

To address this problem, we like to create a number of shortcuts on our desktop or menus that make use of `RunAs.exe`. This permits us to launch programs such as Internet Explorer[3] in the context of another user. Using this technique, we can have several active web browser sessions open on the same machine concurrently addressing the Report Manager—each effectively running as a different user, with each user's own Favorites and home page settings intact.

TIP Don't skip over this step. It's important to gaining an understanding of how the permission hierarchy works and affects the functionality of the Report Manager.

To implement these shortcuts, setup a test user account within the Windows Domain or on the local computer, which is permissioned similarly to your ordinary target users. Next, create a Windows shortcut, and when asked for the program's "location," provide the following incantation but don't forget to insert appropriate values for the <DOMAIN> and <TestUser>. If you're on Windows 2000, you can't use this shortcut because /savecred doesn't work. For Windows XP and later, create the following shortcut:

```
%windir%\system32\runas.exe /profile /user:<DOMAIN>\<TestUser>↵
/savecred "C:\Program Files\Internet Explorer\iexplore.exe"
```

Once the shortcut has been created, it won't have a nice icon by default, so you might want to change it by right-clicking the shortcut and after selecting Properties, select the Change Icon button (you'll

---

[2] And our wives wonder why we're nearly crippled after pounding the keyboard all day.

[3] If you don't want to test with Internet Explorer, you can try this for your particular browser—just put the path to your poison in the command-line shortcut we'll discuss in a moment. However, we have not had particularly good results using Netscape. It does not support HTML 4.0, so a number of the pages do not render correctly.

find an appropriate one in the iexplorer.exe file). If you are using Windows XP or Windows 2003, you'll be able to include the savecred parameter (if you're not, just omit it). The savecred (save credentials) parameter determines how Windows caches the user credentials. That is, the very first time that you execute the shortcut, you'll probably see a command prompt that asks for the indicated User's password. If you use the savecred option, Windows stores this encrypted password in your own user profile, so any subsequent executions of that shortcut should run smoothly without prompting for the password each time—until the password is changed.

The profile parameter ensures that the user profile whose credentials you are impersonating is loaded, so any changes that you might make in that particular Internet Explorer window (for example, setting the home page) are persisted only to that user's profile, not your own. For a real professional look on Windows XP and Windows 2003, you can stop the command-line window from flashing on your screen (even momentarily) by setting the shortcut properties to start minimized. Notice that the Internet Explorer browser launched with this technique (as shown in Figure 4.2) does not have "rounded" edges like a normal Windows XP window. This makes it easier to know that this is your special TestUser window. We set the home page for this window to address Report Manager to make it even easier to use.

TIP *Increase IIS MaxConnections* If you're using Windows XP as a development host for Reporting Services and have not increased the number of IIS connections that Windows XP can support from 10 to 40, be sure to read Appendix D. If you don't increase the connections, you'll probably use up the 10 available connections very quickly. Once all the available connections are in use and waiting to time out, any new connection attempt from the web browser gets a 403.9 error from IIS, and it complains about too many users being connected. What it really means is that the limit of 10 connections has been exceeded. Don't say we didn't warn you. We've found that once the connections are increased to 40, the problem goes away, as this is sufficient for most of our genuine development purposes.

So let's go take a look at the Report Manager using the web browser with our two different User accounts: your own development account (which, hopefully, has Administrative privileges[4]) on the Report Server and your new TestUser account, which has no Reporting Services privileges—at least not initially. Assuming that you've deployed the Microsoft Sample Reports within the last 24 hours, your development/administrator account should see the SampleReports folder with a green !NEW moniker when you access the Report Server using the Report Manager, as shown in Figure 4.1.

Guide me!

The process we're about to describe is shown in several Guide me! demonstrations.

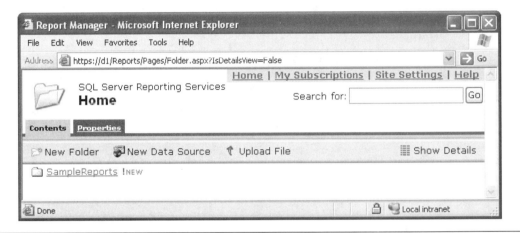

Figure 4.1 The Report Manager as Viewed by an Administrator/Content Manager

Assuming that the test user is not a member of the BUILTIN\ Administrators Group or any other group and has yet to have permissions assigned in the Report Manager, when you access the Report Server as the test user you'll see, as shown in Figure 4.2, almost nothing at all! Using the test user's web browser, click on the

---

4 You don't need Domain or Local Computer Administrator privileges to administer a Report Manager, other than for one small feature in relation to managing aggregated My Reports folders from all users—but we'll explain that at the end. As we'll see in this chapter, Content Manager role and Reporting Services System Administrator role membership can be provided to any User without that user needing to be a Domain or Local Computer Administrator.

Home hyperlink in the Report Manager—it won't do anything because you're already in the Home folder. The *My Subscriptions* hyperlink won't be very exciting either—it won't show you any subscriptions. So that only leaves *Help*—and you'll find that clicking it will take you to a context-sensitive *Help* hyperlink in another browser window. Try it and see!

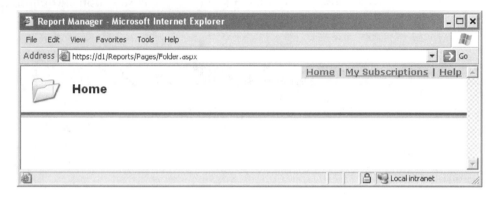

Figure 4.2 The Report Manager as Viewed by a Test User with No Permissions[5]

The reason for the difference is that after a default installation, the BUILTIN\Administrators Group is assigned a Reporting Services System Administrator role and also assigned the Content Manager role on the root Home folder in the Reporting Services notional folder

---

[5] If your TestUser is seeing folders at this point, someone has possibly provided Reporting Services role permissions either directly to the TestUser on the root folder or to a Domain or Computer Group to which the TestUser belongs. Of course, this could be Reporting Services role permissions assigned to the Domain Users group. It's probably best not to remove that role assignment if it is placed there for a reason by an Administrator. The solution might be to either create a Local Computer TestUser account (if you are on a development platform on Windows XP), or talk to your Domain Administrators and ask them for a test account that is not a member of any of the domain groups that may have been assigned Reporting Services roles, but which has logon permissions. Ultimately, you can still work through this chapter with a TestUser account that can see more than nothing at the start—you just need to keep going (adding more rights) until you add a role permission that exceeds those given to the group. It is pretty pointless working through this chapter solely with an Administrative account that can by default do everything.

structure. These default permissions permeate the items and subfolders throughout the folder hierarchy. This means a Member of the BUILTIN\Administrators Group has permission to do anything. For obvious reasons, it's not possible to lock out members of the BUILTIN\Administrators Group. Although you might change or even delete the roles assigned to the BUILTIN\Administrators Group, members of BUILTIN\Administrators are always capable of giving themselves rights, modifying or re-creating roles for themselves even when the system might appear as if they initially have no rights. (Don't jump the gun and make the test user a member of the BUILTIN\Administrators Group to test that out just yet—there are things you need to be aware of when assigning Reporting Service Roles to Groups.)

Assigning a Role to a User Account

Well, let's get you started by enabling your TestUser account to at least see that there are reports in the Report Server. We'll start by assigning roles directly against the TestUser account rather than adding to any Groups of which TestUser is a member. Yes, in a production environment you'd probably want to follow our best-practice advice and assign Reporting Service Roles at the Group level. This saves you the trouble of keeping the User accounts synchronized with your organization's staff churn. However, for optimization reasons, IIS caches certain security information, and it can take up to 15 minutes for IIS to respect a Group membership change. We'll explain this fully a bit later, so for now just follow along as we lead you through assigning Reporting Services Roles on a User account.

1. As illustrated in Figure 4.1, open the Report Manager in a web browser under an Administrator's credentials. This is done by addressing https://<server>/Reports using your Administrator browser shortcut. If you already had the Report Manager open and you've been burrowing off into the folders, make sure that you've come back to Home by clicking on the *Home* hyperlink.
2. Select the Properties tab. You should see that the BUILTIN\ Administrators Group has been assigned the Role of Content Manager on the Home folder (as shown in Figure 4.3). By

default, this Role Assignment is effectively propagated to all of its child objects and folders under the Home folder hierarchy. The Content Manager role (as we'll see) is the most privileged[6] that can be assigned to a managed report.

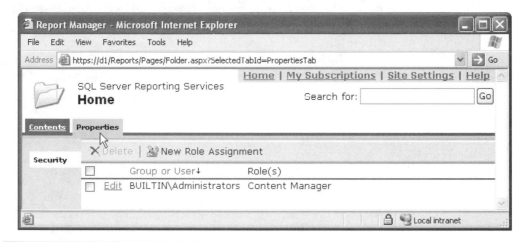

Figure 4.3 An Administrator/Content Manager's View of the Security Properties on the Home Folder and All Child Objects

3. Click New Role Assignment, which appears on the toolbar, and enter your TestUser account, including appropriate Computer or Domain Name. Select the Browser role and click the OK button.

TIP *If You're Already Lost...* If instead of New Role Assignment you see Edit Item Security on the toolbar, you're probably trying to define properties on the SampleReports folder rather than on the Home folder—don't do that here if you want to stay with us. Just click on the *Home* HTTP hyperlink and click Properties.

---

[6] For those who read ahead, we're making a distinction between System Roles that are assigned under Site Settings from roles that can be assigned on managed reports.

4. In our example, our User "TestUser" belongs to our INTERNAL Domain. This means you'll need to use your own Computer or Domain name here instead or create your own TestUser Domain name with which to experiment. In Figure 4.4, we can see that there are four out-of-the-box Roles from which to choose. Broadly speaking, the rights conferred correlate to their report descriptions as displayed:

- The *Content Manager* role sits at the "most trusted" end of the scale. This role provides full administrative ability for managed report infrastructure such as folders, reports, resources, shared Data Sources, and so on.

- The *Browser* role is more restricted in that it only permits navigation of the folder hierarchy, viewing reports and resources, and managing a user's own subscriptions. This is the role we're applying to our TestUser User account in Figure 4.4.

- The *Publisher* role is complementary to the Browser role—that is, it permits report definitions to be uploaded or "deployed" to the ReportServer database, along with the creation of linked reports and management of the report infrastructure. A User assigned to only the Publisher role on a managed report is not able to execute that report unless also assigned the Browser role.

- *My Reports* is a role almost as powerful as a Content Manager role. However, it's intended to be used only on each user's own special My Reports folder. This concept is very similar to the My Documents folder in the Windows file system. We'll show you how to configure My Reports in the "Managing Site Settings" section of this chapter.

5. Clicking OK returns us to the Properties page, as shown in Figure 4.5.

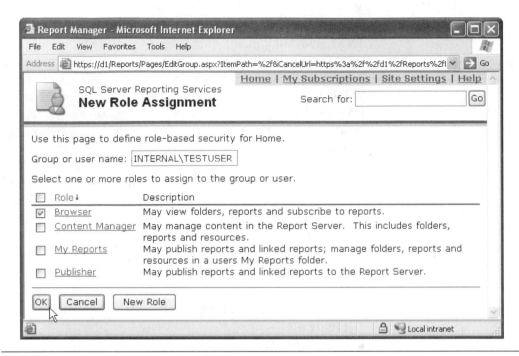

Figure 4.4 Applying the Browser Role to the Test User on the "Home" Folder

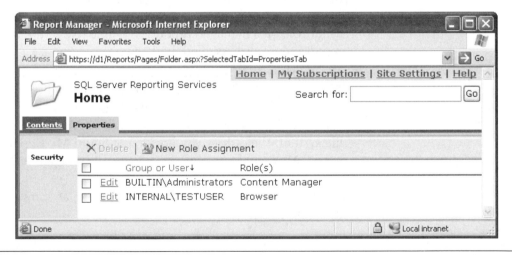

Figure 4.5 The Home Folder Properties Page After Applying the Browser Role to the TestUser Account.

At this point, return to the browser running under the TestUser credentials and refresh[7] or access the Report Manager again. Now you should be able to see that there is a folder named SampleReports in the root folder[8] (as shown in Figure 4.6). Any new folders or managed reports that are added under the root folder hierarchy provide the TestUser account with Browser role capabilities by default. Notice that when accessing Report Manager, the TestUser account's browser does not display many of the option links that are shown on the Administrators' browser. Closely compare Figures 4.6 and 4.1. The reason for the differences is that the Report Manager uses role-based security and the Administrator User has been assigned the Content Manager role, which provides additional (full) functionality. In contrast, the test user has only been given rights to browse—so far.

TestUser is assigned the Browser (only) role.

Guide me!

TIP *Can't Get a Sample Report to Work?* If you click into the SampleReports by clicking on its hyperlink and you can't get a sample managed report to work for your TestUser account, you probably also need to assign permissions on the AdventureWorks database to the TestUser account! This is most easily done by giving the TestUser account logon rights to the AdventureWorks database in SQL Enterprise Manager and assigning the db_datareader role on that database to your TestUser. To do this, follow the video clip. Just don't confuse SQL Server system or database roles with the Reporting Services roles.

If you select the *Show Details* hyperlink in the Report Manager, you'll be able to see a few more details about the user (as shown in Figure 4.7) who last modified the folder and when. You'll also find a nifty way to delete items. Before you panic, don't be concerned that a user with Browse-only permissions is about to trash your Report Server! The Report Server prevents changes attempted by users

---

[7] You might have to flush the cache to see the right page. To do so, press Control+F5.

[8] If your test user can't see the SampleReports folder and you've followed us religiously, perhaps you have specifically defined properties on the SampleReports folder that separate it from the hierarchy. If that's the case, return to the properties of the SampleReports folder as an Administrative user and choose "revert to parent permissions" if parent permissions are indeed what you want to be propagated.

who don't have permission to delete or move managed reports, and returns an appropriate message to the Report Manager. For a user with permission to delete, the Details view in Figure 4.7 provides a quick way to delete more than one item at a time.

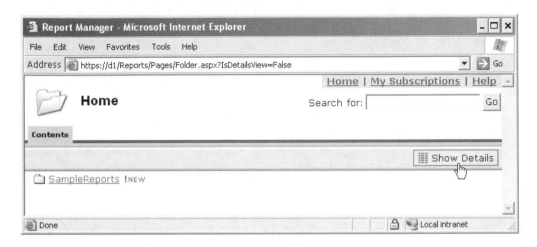

Figure 4.6   The Test User Should Now Be Able to Browse the SampleReports Folder

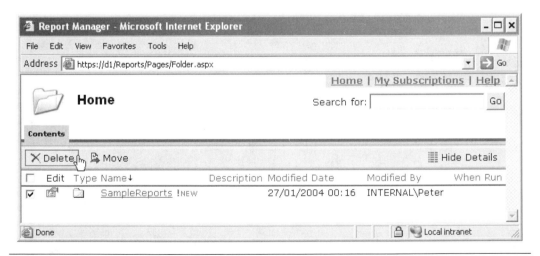

Figure 4.7   Trying to Delete the Sample Reports Folder in the Report Manager's Details View

You could try to delete the folder, *but you should not even attempt this if you are working on a production system, and especially not if the TestUser account already has delete rights*. What we want to show you is the error message in Figure 4.8. As you can see, the error message explains the problem, but it also displays a *Get Online Help* link. If you select this hyperlink, a new web browser window pops up, providing Help information directly from the Microsoft website. This can be helpful, but you may choose to disable the link. To do so, edit the RSWebApplication.config[9] file and change the DisplayErrorLink Key to False: `<Add Key="DisplayErrorLink" Value="False"/>`.

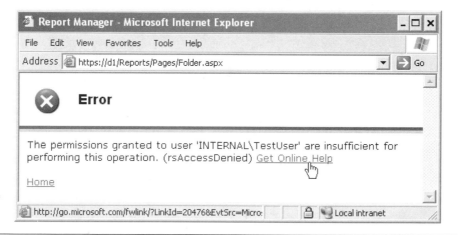

Figure 4.8 The Error Page Displayed When a User with Browser Role Rights Tries to Delete a Managed Report

Roles and Tasks

As we saw in Figure 4.4, four out-of-the-box roles are available to choose from: Browser, Content Manager, Publisher, and My Report.

---

[9] You'll find the RSWebApplication.config file in the *\Program Files\Microsoft SQL Server\MSSQL\Reporting Services\ReportManager* folder. While it looks like an XML file, it isn't—it doesn't have the XML header—so don't try inserting XML-like comments <!- - - ->.

It's possible to redefine these roles, delete them, or create entirely new roles. A role can be considered a collection of ***Tasks***—actions that a User (or Group) can be given permission to perform. There are presently 13 such fixed (non-extensible) Tasks, or actions, that can be aggregated into named ***Roles***. Although there are 8192 (2^13) possible distinct Roles that can be created, for the most part you'll probably find the four out-of-the-box roles sufficient.

Let's take a look at these various Tasks by creating a new Role called the "Hitchhiker's Test." In a minute, we'll assign this role to our TestUser account. Next, we'll provide a route map for adding more Tasks to that role, and we'll investigate the functionality that this role exposes.

Creating a New Role Assignment

1. With a web browser, return to the Report Manager as an Administrator, navigate to the Home folder, and select the Properties tab—just as we did earlier to arrive at Figure 4.3. If you followed the steps earlier and you have the Browser role assigned to your TestUser account, you can simply click the *Edit* hyperlink next to TestUser.

2. Next, uncheck the Browser role assigned to the TestUser, or if you are starting from scratch and don't have any role assignments for your TestUser, you can click the New Role button. At this point, we should be on the Edit Role assignment web page for the TestUser or on the New Role assignment web page, where you enter the TestUser account details. In any event, the New Role button is at the bottom of these pages, and that's what you need to click. This launches the New Role web page, as shown in Figure 4.9.

3. Create a Name and a Description for your new role (we call ours Hitchhiker's Test and refer to it throughout this chapter).

   Click the View Folders task to grant this permission to the role. Figure 4.9 shows that we've filled in the name and description.

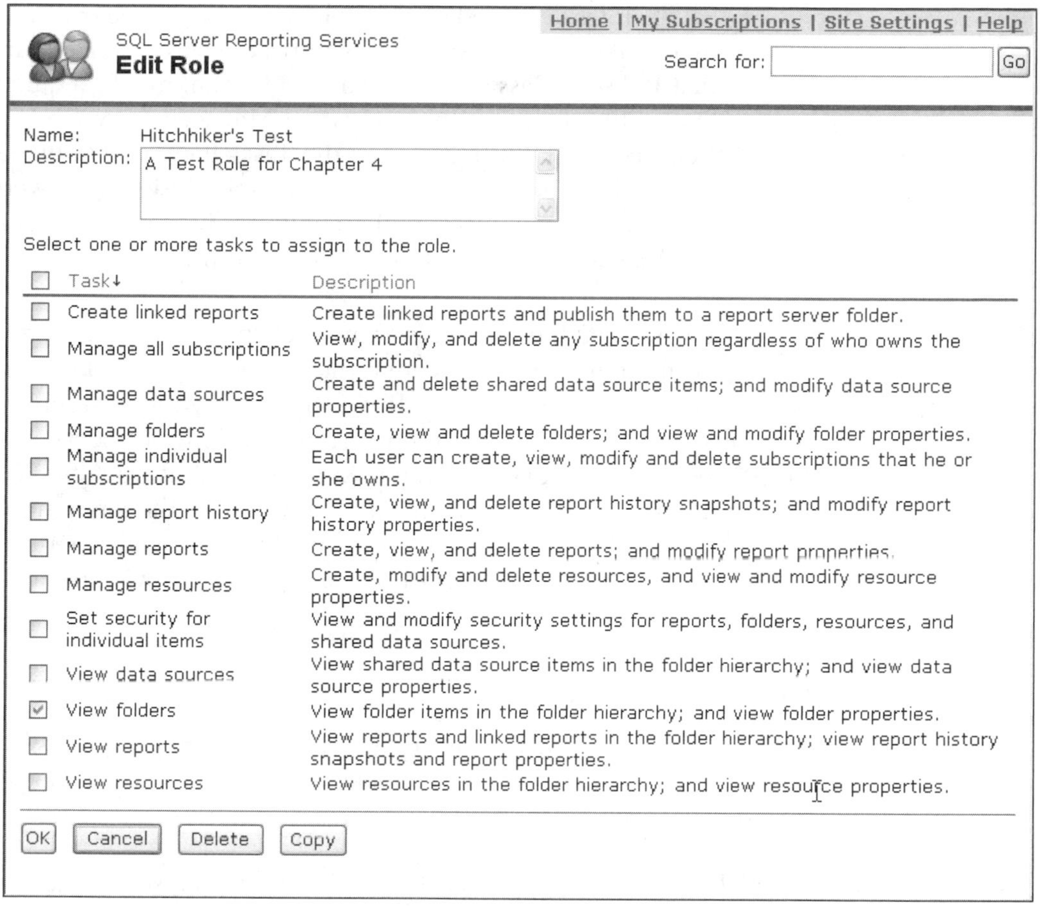

Figure 4.9 Creating a New Role

Assign View
Folders task to
the Hitchhiker's
Test role.

Just before we cruise off, take some time to scan through the 13 Tasks that can be assigned to a role (they're listed in Figure 4.9). We'll come back here another dozen times to add these Tasks one by one to the Hitchhiker's Test role to observe the effect.

4. Once you select OK, you'll be returned to a web form where you can complete the role assignments to your User (or Group). At this point, you'll notice the newly created Hitchhiker's Test role.

Assign TestUser to
the Hitchhiker's
Test role.

5. All the roles displayed on the Role Assignment web page are hyperlinks that take you to a web page where you can edit that Role's task assignments. You might want to take a quick look at the standard Roles (Content Manager, Browser, My Reports, and Publisher) to see the Tasks they permit. Once you've done fiddling, return to the Role Assignment web page and assign just the Hitchhiker's Test role to your TestUser account, and click the OK or Apply button.

Once you make these role assignment changes and open a web browser using your TestUser account, the SampleReports folder can be seen under the Home folder. If you try to view the contents of that folder, you won't see any reports, but you do have access to a Properties tab on the folder. If you're super-observant, you'll notice that a Search for textbox facility has also appeared in the top right of the web form. This hyperlink can be used to find managed reports in the Report Server that the User's Role Assignments provide permission to see.

Viewing Reports

Go back to the Hitchhiker's Test role and add View Reports to its list of Tasks. To return to the role and make this change, you can choose one of these two routes:

■ Use the route you've seen before: As Administrator, access the Report Manager. Click Home, select the Properties tab, select Edit on the TestUser User, select the *Hitchhiker's Test* hyperlink, check the View reports checkbox, and click OK.

Or

■ Try another route: As Administrator, access the Report Manager. Click the *Site Settings* hyperlink at the top of the page. Under the Security section (near the bottom of the page), click "Configure item-level role definitions." Next, select the *Hitchhiker's Test* hyperlink, check the View reports checkbox, and click OK.

Grant View Reports
rights to the
Hitchhiker's Test
role.

This enables TestUser to see managed reports in the SampleReports folder and execute them.

Search for (Managed Reports)

Once your TestUser account has sufficient permissions assigned by virtue of the Tasks assigned to the Role, or assigned to the TestUser on the Home folder, the person using this account can use the "Search for" feature. To try this, use the TestUser's browser to search for Catalog or Sales (if you have the AdventureWorks sample databases installed). Search is a great way to interrogate the Report Server to find all the managed reports whose Name or Description contains the search term regardless of the folder where the report resides. You should be aware of a few minor points and quirks:

- The searches respect the case sensitivity of the database.
- The + operator, or wildcard characters used by many search engines, are not yet implemented (we expect the Yukon build to implement this).
- The search string is restricted to 128 characters.
- You *must* click the Go button to the right of the Search For textbox. If you simply hit the Enter key with the cursor focus in the Search For textbox, the page code doesn't default to executing the search for you.
- If the results are viewed with Details showing, the results are tabulated with additional information such as the Folder location of each managed report.
- If the Item is a Report (depending on its Execution properties), it indicates when the report was last run. (We'll discuss this in more detail a bit later).
- In the Details view, the results are sortable by clicking on the headers. As you can see in Figure 4.10, the results of searching for "Product" are sorted by name in ascending order (note the small down arrow).

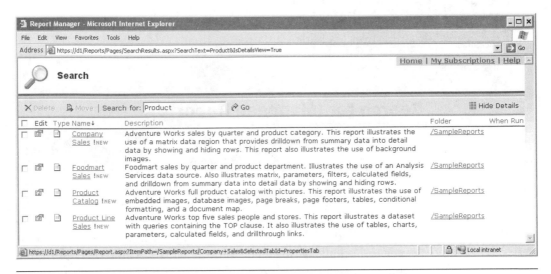

Figure 4.10 The Search Results Form in Details View Sorted by Name in Ascending Order

Drilling into the Search URL

NOTE *For Trainee Gurus* This section is not a formally published interface of the Report Manager. This means Microsoft could (is likely to) change things, but we thought that at least a couple of people would be interested in how to extend the search capabilities. Send us an e-mail if you have benefited from this extra insight on the technology behind the scenes—or have suggestions about how we might improve upon it.

Examine the URL in the web browser after executing a search—you'll see that the SearchResults page can be called directly. That's because the search term "SearchText" and the viewing mode, IsDetailsView, are passed as parameters. This has several ramifications—you could save your favorite searches to your web browser's Favorites list to re-execute later, transfer the URL by e-mail, incorporate the URL into a redirect, or incorporate it in a form on a web page. We'll talk a lot more about the programming aspects of the

Report Manager in Chapter 11. This section is designed to get you started. You might find it more convenient to change the order of the parameters, placing IsDetailsView before the SearchText, so that the search text can be concatenated to the end of the string. Here's a URL to search for all managed reports containing "Sales" in their Name or Description. To use it, replace the **<Server>** with your own Report Server's name:

```
https://<Server>/Reports/Pages/SearchResults.aspx?⏎
  IsDetailsView=True&SearchText=Sales
```

Try this URL while logged on as TestUser and as Administrator. Notice the difference in what's returned—only the content that a user has permission to see is returned to the browser.

Just before we leave this topic, consider that you can't search using a wildcard in the Report Manager as when you want to show all managed reports. No, you can't leave the search textbox empty because the Report Manager squeaks at you to enter one or more search terms. However, you can get the Report Manager to list all of its reports by using the URL—just leave the SearchText parameter blank, as in:

```
https://<Server>/Reports/Pages/SearchResults.aspx?⏎
  IsDetailsView=True&SearchText=
```

We predict that administrators will find this useful when they want to see all managed reports on one web page. We're hoping that for the Yukon release the Details view will also show the managed report's Creator and Creation Time. Administrators will find it particularly useful to see that in the Report Manager.

Adding Search to Your Own Website

We'll talk a lot more about programming and leveraging the Report Manager in Chapter 11, but for now here's something to try in your own web page. Add this code (shown in Listing 4.1) to the Body section of an HTML web page. As always, don't forget to substitute **<Server>** with the appropriate values.

Listing 4.1 Adding Search Capabilities to Your Own Website

```
<FORM id="SEARCH"
action="https://<Server>/Reports/Pages/SearchResults.aspx">
   <INPUT type="hidden" name="IsDetailsView" value="True">
   <INPUT name="SearchText" maxlength="128" size="35">
   <INPUT type="submit" value="Search">
</FORM>
```

And while we are gushing with extra-curricular tips, here's a Windows registry change you can make that enables you to search directly from an Internet Explorer browser window (if you are not familiar or comfortable with registry file changes, ask someone who is—like your system administrator).

1. Start RegEdit.
2. Next, create a new Windows registry key called "rs" in *HKCU\Software\Microsoft\Internet Explorer\SearchUrl.*
3. Edit the default value to be (substituting **<Server>** with your Report Server name):

```
https://<Server>/Reports/Pages/SearchResults.aspx?IsDetailsView=True&SearchText=%s
```

Once you make these registry changes, you'll be able to search your Report Server directly from the Internet Explorer Address bar by simply typing rs <SearchTerm>. No, don't put an HTTP or HTTPS or anything in front of the rs; leave a space and just replace <SearchTerm> with what you want to look for, and let Internet Explorer take over for you!

By the way, if you're wondering why it doesn't work for TestUser's browser, it's because the "HKCU" refers to the currently logged-in User's registry hive. To solve this, formally log on to your machine as the TestUser Domain User and make the registry change in the HKCU of that user. That entry is saved to the TestUser Domain User's profile.

Rendering Reports

At this point, we know how to locate reports based on a search criterion. Let's dissect some of the functionality provided by the Report Manager when viewing managed reports while logged on using the TestUser account. Open the SampleReports folder in Report Manager, and run the Product Catalog report by clicking on its link. Alternatively, if you have the Product Catalog report listed in a Search window, click its hyperlink from there. If the TestUser account has been assigned the task roles of View Folders and View Reports through the Hitchhiker's Test role (as just discussed in this chapter), when you run the report you should see three tabs: View, Properties, and History. The History tab won't have anything interesting at this point. The Properties tab only shows the report's auditing properties: size, when and who created it, and when and who last modified the report.

For now, we'll concentrate on the View tab. By default, the report should execute and render within the View tab. If for some reason you get an error, the most likely cause is that you have not added your TestUser Domain User to the db_datareader role in the AdventureWorks database—assuming that the report Data Source is using integrated security.[10]

Let's take a look at the rendered report when launched by the Report Manager. You'll see (as shown in Figure 4.11) that there's a double-decker toolbar. On the top line is a button to hide or show the top portion, or what we call the "Tabs" area.[11] On the bottom line, starting from the left, if the report has a Document Map, there is a button to show or hide it—followed by VCR-style buttons for navigating the report's pages, a dropdown scaling feature, an in-report forward-only text search, a dropdown list and button to Export the report to a selected format, a Refresh button, and a Help button.

---

[10] The sample report data sources use integrated security by default.

[11] Behind the scenes, this is called the "shaded" area. We think that "Tabs" area is more descriptive. I guess we're lucky they didn't call it the "XM54Z" area.

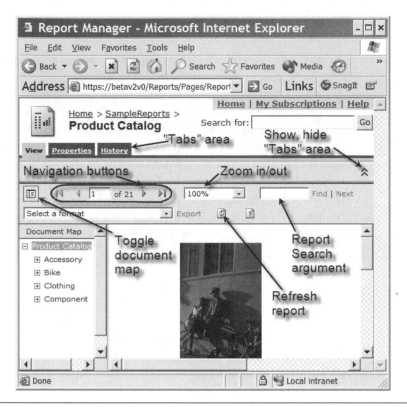

Figure 4.11 The Report Manager View Tab Rendering the Product Catalog Report

Exporting Managed Reports to Other Formats

While you're familiarizing yourself with these features, we want to draw your attention to a few issues relating to exporting managed reports to other formats. In Chapter 1, we mentioned that out-of-the-box Reporting Services can render reports to other formats, depending upon which Rendering extensions are installed. By default, the Report Manager provides the ability to export to seven formats: HTML, MHTML, TIFF, XML, CSV, EXCEL, and PDF. Each has its own caveats and limitations. By all means, go ahead and try them out. Note that if you export to Excel, you'll need Microsoft Excel 97 or above. To export to PDF you'll need Adobe Acrobat

Reader.[12] If you export to CSV, you'll get only the data—not the report formatting or any images.

Reporting Services Service Pack 1 made changes to the Excel Rendering and changed the format to BIFF (Binary Interchange File Format). This now enables rendering to Excel 97 and above, whereas before Excel 2002 was required.

TIP *Tuning the Export Formats List* For organizations that want to limit the number of entries displayed in the Export "Select a format" dropdown list, modify the RSReportServer.config[13] file. Change the <render> element by adding Visible=False to any entry you don't want to support. This is a great idea for organizations that don't want to answer a bunch of questions about versions of Excel. An example of this entry is shown below.

```
<Extension Name="EXCEL"
Type="Microsoft.ReportingServices.Rendering.ExcelRenderer.ExcelRenderer,⏎
Microsoft.ReportingServices.ExcelRendering" Visible="false"/>
```

If you have a version of Excel that predates Excel 97, you can choose to export the file from the Report Manager as a CSV (comma-delimited) file, and then from within Excel import the exported CSV file. This gets the raw data (but no pictures) into Excel for you, but it won't give you the rich export created when exporting to Excel 97. The CSV format leaves out the graphics and formatting information that visually makes an Excel 97 report a near clone of the report as rendered in a web browser.

The last Export format we'd like to mention is HTML with Office Web Components. To illustrate this feature and take advantage of the Office Web Components, export a report that contains a Matrix control—the "Company Sales" sample report can be used for

---

[12] You can download the Adobe PDF rendering program for free from www.adobe.com/products/acrobat/readstep2.html.

[13] *\Program Files\Microsoft SQL Server\MSSQL\Reporting Services\ReportServer\ RSReportServer.config*

this example. The web browser displays the Matrix control's portion of the report using an Office Web Components PivotTable ActiveX control. If the Office Web Components are not installed or cannot be loaded, a hyperlink is provided to a location containing the localized version of the Office Web Components, along with a hyperlink so you can view the report without Office Web Components.

If you haven't used the Office Web Components PivotTable before, you might like to see what happens when you click, drag, and drop the column and row headers around. You can morph columns to rows and rows to columns, change their ordering, or drag a header onto the Filter area. If you click on the down arrow on a header, you can even filter that row or column. There's a lot more functionality to a PivotTable, so go have fun with it. We'll wait here while you play.

Managing Folders

To enable TestUser and other members of the Hitchhiker's Test role to create, move, delete, and hide folders requires that we add the Manage Folders task to the Hitchhiker's Test role.

TIP   *Save Yourself Some Time*   If you need reminding on how to alter the Task list for a User, as Administrator access the Report Manager, click Site Settings, Item-level Role definitions, and select the *Hitchhiker's Test* hyperlink. Yes, this is a drag. Because we're going to be coming back here over and over to update the Hitchhiker's Test role, make life a little easier. Add this page to your web browser's Favorites. That way you can immediately get back here next time.

Grant Manage Folders to the Hitchhiker's Test role.

Once you've added the Manage Folders task, click OK. Then launch the Report Manager in your web browser as TestUser. You should notice immediately that this introduces a new item on the toolbar—New Folder, as shown in Figure 4.12.

Click on New Folder, and create a new folder called TestReports. You'll see that you can specify a folder description as well as whether or not the folder is to be hidden in List view. Sure, you can still see folders in Details view. Examine the Details view by clicking the

Show Details button, and experiment with moving your new folder to a subfolder within the SampleReports folder. You can do this by checking the checkbox next to your folder and selecting the Move button on the toolbar. No, drag and drop does not work (as Bill expected it to). Perhaps it'll be attended to in the next version.

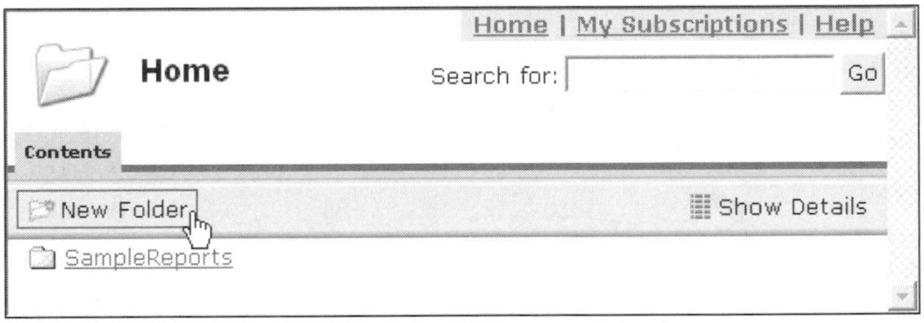

Figure 4.12 The Manage Folders Task Adds the New Folder Button to the Toolbar

You should be able to delete your TestReports folder, assuming you've been strictly following the instructions in this chapter. If you try to delete the SampleReports folder, you should get a message box informing you that you (TestUser) don't have permission to delete it. That's because the SampleReports folder contains several items—namely a shared DataSource and Reports. TestUser doesn't have permission to delete those managed reports because the TestUser account does not yet have rights through the Hitchhiker's Test role to manage those managed reports. Before you leave this section, just humor us—create a folder in the root Home folder and name it Searches.

View and Manage Resources

Reporting Services has the ability to retain resources in its folders—these can be literally any file under 4 MB in size. This feature was originally created with the intention to install and share graphics files between managed reports. However, you can store anything—even Word document files or Excel files—assuming that the IIS server is enabled to serve files of that type and they're not too large.

Grant Manage
Resources
rights to the
Hitchhiker's
Test role.

Unfortunately, the Microsoft Reporting Services samples don't have any "Resources" managed reports, so we are going to have to break with our trend of view rights before manage rights and give our Hitchhiker's Test role Manage Resources rights in order to upload a file. So, give TestUser Manage Resources rights—you did save the shortcut to your Favorites, didn't you?

Tips and Tricks

At this point, we thought it would be cool to show you some tricks, such as how you can customize the behavior of the Report Manager—through Resources Management. Earlier, we showed you a few tricks you can use by calling the Report Manager's Search URL directly, and we showed you how to create a web form that contains a Search Form. Well, we thought it would be cool to show another way to do this. This time, instead of the web form being hosted in a browser outside Report Manager, why not integrate the Search Form into Report Manager? The HTML that implements this feature is shown below (and on the file Searches.htm on the DVD). What we have here (Listing 4.2) is a very crude but effective web form that displays a couple of buttons and permits you to press one and search for "All" Report Objects—or to press another and Search for "Any" object—but it defaults to Report Objects containing the Term "Sales."

Listing 4.2 Searches.htm Can Be Used to Add Search Functionality to the Report Manager

```
<!DOCTYPE HTML PUBLIC "-//W3C//DTD HTML 4.0 Transitional//EN">
<HTML>
<HEAD></HEAD>
<BODY>
  <FORM action="https://<Server>/Reports/Pages/SearchResults.aspx" method="get"
  target="_top">
    <INPUT type="hidden" value="True" name="IsDetailsView">
    <INPUT type="hidden" value="" name="SearchText">
    <INPUT type="submit" value="ALL" >
  </FORM>
```

```
<HR>
  <FORM action="https://<Server>/Reports/Pages/SearchResults.aspx" method="get"
  target="_top">
    <INPUT type="hidden" value="True" name="IsDetailsView">
    <INPUT id="Text1" maxlength="128" size="35" value="Sales" name="SearchText">
    <INPUT type="submit" value="Search">
  </FORM>
</BODY>
</HTML>
```

Next, launch the Report Manager as TestUser. Because that user has been assigned Manage Resources rights, you should notice that the toolbar has a new feature, Upload File, as shown in Figure 4.13.[14]

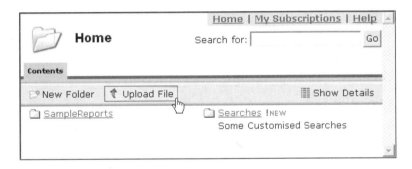

Figure 4.13 The Report Manager with Manage Resources Rights

Navigate into your Searches folder, and click Upload File on the toolbar. A form (as shown in Figure 4.14) opens in which you can select the Browse button. Look for your Searches.htm file, or just put the path directly into the textbox, change the name to Custom Searches as shown in Figure 4.14, and click OK.

---

[14] Please excuse our occasional use of British spelling. We're equally comfortable with either spelling of "customized."

Figure 4.14 Using the Custom HTML Search Form from Within Report Manager

This uploads the Searches.htm web form. As you view the form by clicking on its link—all you'll get are the properties. This is handy if you want to rename, move, delete, see the auditing details, or provide a description. Remember, without the View resources task in the Hitchhiker's Test role, the TestUser account can't view the resource.

Try to get the TestUser browser to upload an RDL or RDS file—you should find some in *\Program Files\Microsoft SQL Server\ MSSQL\Reporting Services\Samples\Reports* (if you installed the samples). You'll find that you can't upload these files because the Hitchhiker's Test role still does not have sufficient rights—we'll add them later. A JPG file or Word document can be uploaded—as long as it is under the 4-MB limit.

Viewing Resources

Next, we'll expand the permissions on the Hitchhiker's Test role with the View Resources task. Return to the Custom Searches folder with the TestUser account, and voilà, up comes your shiny new (crude but effective) Search Form, as shown in Figure 4.15. Take it for a spin, and try it out. Without a lot of trouble, you should be able to take this concept further and make your forms more visually appealing.

Grant View
Resources
rights to the
Hitchhiker's
Test role.

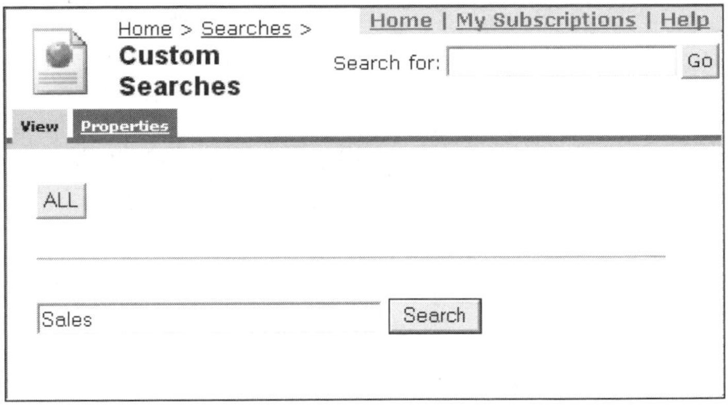

Figure 4.15 The Enhanced Report Manager with a Custom View

Enabling the Manage Reports Task

At this point, TestUser is unable to upload an RDL file, or delete or move any managed reports. Just before you add the Manage Reports task to the Hitchhiker's Test role, open up the TestUser's browser and open the Employee Sales Summary sample report to see how it operates. This is an example of a managed report that's dependent on user-provided parameters. In this case, you'll have to make sure that you've set a Month, Year, and Employee before you can execute the report by clicking the View Report button. Execute the report and examine the Properties tab. At the moment, only the auditing details are exposed. With your Administrator's browser, add the Manage Reports task to the Hitchhiker's Test role. Next, in the TestUser's browser, refresh the Properties tab on the Employee Sales Summary report. You should now see that in addition to the *General* link, you also have links for *Parameters*, *Data Sources*, and something called *Execution*, which we'll look at in a minute.

Once you add the Manage Reports rights, you'll notice that on the *General* hyperlink TestUser has now been granted the ability to rename a managed report, provide a description, and hide the report in the List view. These are all things we've seen before with folders. However, we also have the ability to edit or update the report definition. Clicking on the *Edit* hyperlink permits the user to download the RDL for the managed report, while clicking on Update permits uploading and overwriting the RDL. As you can see, with these few rights the user has been given the ability to change the ReportServer database.

Grant Manage Reports rights to the Hitchhiker's Test role.

Granting Rights to Manage Report Parameters

Parameters are used to limit the scope of a report and focus it on a targeted selection of rows from the database. Besides limiting the number of rows returned from the underlying query, parameters also permit users to customize the information being gathered to adapt the report to their own needs in real time.

It wasn't an accident that we had you open the Employee Sales Summary report, because we wanted to show you that managed reports that require parameters can be managed with the Report Manager after the User has been granted access via the Manage Reports task. Once enabled, the User can determine the parameter names, which have defaults, and the values of these defaults. It also determines which parameters are to be captured from the user through a prompting dialog. By setting the Prompt String, you can customize the prompt seen by the user. These options are useful when a managed report is run with preset default values that the user need not see or when only a few of the parameters need to be filled in by the user.

Figure 4.16 shows how this parameter information is gathered. For example, we provide a default value of 2004 for the ReportYear parameter. When the report is viewed, it's rendered immediately—although you can still adjust the parameters and render different reports for other employees by selecting another EmpID value.

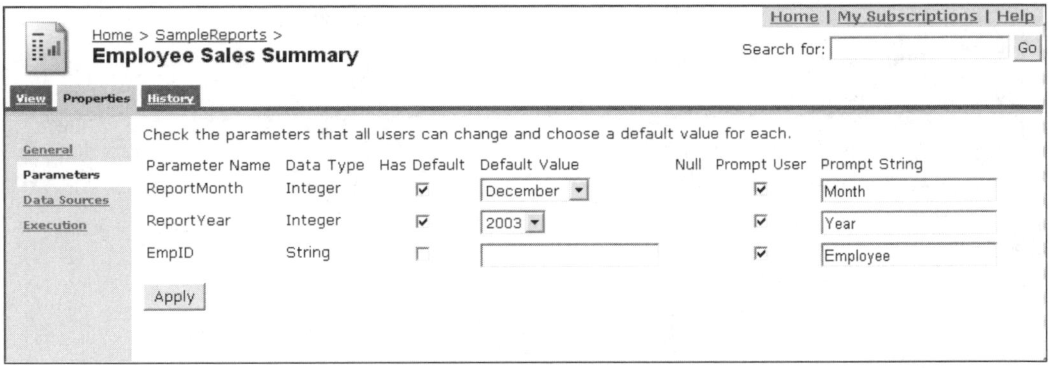

Figure 4.16 Setting Parameter Defaults Using the Report Manager

Report Data Sources

Let's move on to the Data Source link. So far, we've not given TestUser the Task rights to view or manage report Data Sources. This means that TestUser cannot see or manipulate any shared Data Sources (at the moment) and the Browse button in Figure 4.17 is superfluous—but try it out if you must. However, we can define a custom Data Source that can be used only by this report. Just remember our tip to include the Application Name so that you can more easily trace your work with the SQL Server Profiler.

Figure 4.17 shows that the Data Source for this report has been reconfigured to prompt the user for credentials, and to use Windows credentials as the credential passed. If you do this and run the report, you'll see that the system prompts the User for the credentials just as if the credentials are additional parameters. We'll be sending you back here in a minute, so press the Apply button and run the report.

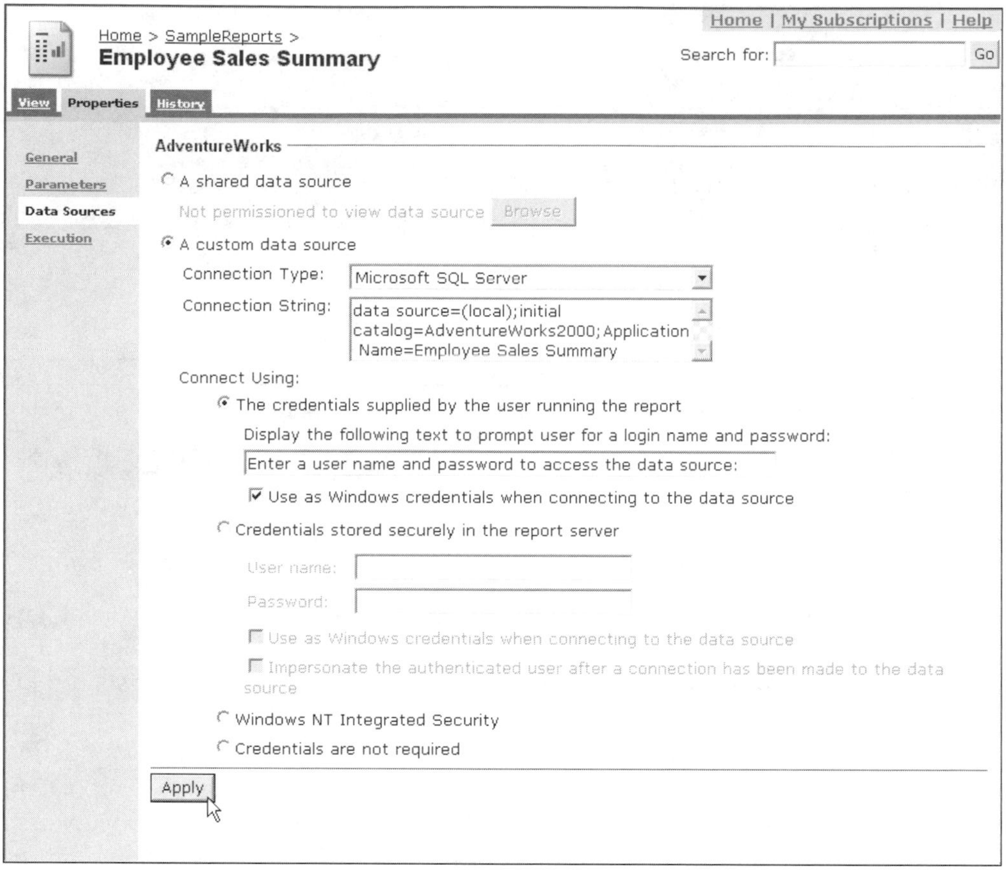

Figure 4.17 Configuring the Employee Sales Summary Report to Use a Custom Data Source

Granting Rights to the Execution Properties

Next, we're going to take a look at the Execution properties. These properties determine how a report should be rendered—from a snapshot or cached copy, or if it should always query the data source (the DBMS) each time it's rendered. Setting a report to execute from a cached copy instead of from querying data sources is a technique used to optimize performance. However, this performance gain is at the cost of the report having up-to-the-moment, "live" information. This is not a problem for reports on static data that is not subject to frequent changes or when up-to-the-second data is less important than performance.

To help you understand what's going on when setting Execution properties, we've created a test report called Sales People.rdl.[15] The most important characteristic of this report is that it displays the execution time and the User that executed the report. It also returns some relatively uninteresting data from the AdventureWorks2000 database concerning sales people. The report requires its own independent Data Source, and it's initially configured to use Windows NT integrated security (SSPI). If your Windows configuration won't permit you to run the report using integrated security, we suggest you modify the Data Source properties to use prompted credentials, as we discussed in the previous section.

Because TestUser now has Manage Reports task privileges, try uploading this report to your SampleReports folder. Navigate to the SampleReports folder, click the Upload button on the toolbar, find the Sales People.rdl file on the DVD, and click OK. It's important to click OK because if you just hit the Enter key, you'll return to the SampleReports folder without performing the upload. We expect a Service Pack or the Yukon version to be a little friendlier here. Execute this new managed report with both the Administrative web browser and the TestUser's web browser and notice the differences.

Idiosyncratic Refresh Buttons

There is a feature on the web browser's toolbar (not the report toolbar) that can be confusing: the Refresh button. What happens when you click on the web browser's Refresh button? Nothing, really; there might be a short repaint of the screen. But look closely at the report execution time—it doesn't change! That's probably not what you were expecting—at least it's not what we expected. Press the F5 function key (to refresh), press Ctrl+F5 (to flush the cache and refresh), and click on the View menu's Refresh button. Notice that the Report Executed At value *still* does not change when any of these actions are taken. We bring this to your attention because the report is *not* updating—not being rerendered—even though you

---

[15] This file is on the DVD in the Chapter 4 directory.

might be seeing an animated Report Processing icon appear. We also didn't want you to think the report was cached as a result of the Execution properties we're about to discuss.

However, if you click on the Refresh button on the *report's* toolbar, as shown in Figure 4.18, you'll see the report refreshes each time the button is pressed—updating the displayed execution time. That's because this button (which looks like the green squiggly Refresh button in Internet Explorer) is really a "re-execute" button. We were working late one evening and decided that perhaps a better icon would be a tiny guillotine—but we don't want to kill the report, just execute it. We hope you have a better suggestion.

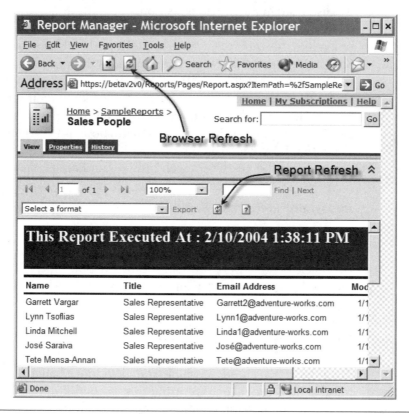

Figure 4.18 The Report Toolbar's Report Refresh Button

Caching Managed Reports

Now that we have the browser Refresh button idiosyncrasy tucked away in your subconscious, let's start adjusting some of the managed report's Execution properties. Caching is an important Reporting Services feature that permits the Report Server to save a pre-rendered report in the cache so that if it's requested again, it's easily (and quickly) retrieved and displayed. This feature is designed for reports that are generated using "point-in-time" data or for which the data changes infrequently.

Along the way, we've discovered a number of interesting Reporting Services quirks and strange lights in the predawn sky. One of these has to do with how managed reports are cached. To see this issue in action, let's tell the Report Manager that we want to cache the report on the server for one minute. Yes, we know that is a very short time to cache a report, but we figure you'd want to see this in action—sitting around for 30 minutes wondering if the property change made a difference in the report isn't much fun. Certainly, in a production environment you'll want to balance the need for having "live," up-to-the-moment data in a report against knowing that the report data is still valid "n" minutes later.

To illustrate, let's see what happens when we try to use the report Properties tab and the Execution page (as shown in Figure 4.19) to render a report with the most recent data, and then cache the report temporarily (for only one minute).

Try clicking Apply after having requested to "Cache a temporary copy of the report. Expire copy of the report after a number of minutes: [1]." We've actually deliberately led you down a blind alley, in this case, because chances are you won't see the warning to the right of the minutes textbox telling you that the Report Manager cannot comply with your request. To see this warning, you might have to horizontally scroll your browser or buy a bigger monitor. The problem is that in order to cache a copy of the report, the credentials used to run the report need to be stored in the report Data Source—you can't use SSPI security. By not using trusted credentials, the

Reporting Services engine can share the cached copy of the managed report across any number of users to optimize performance.

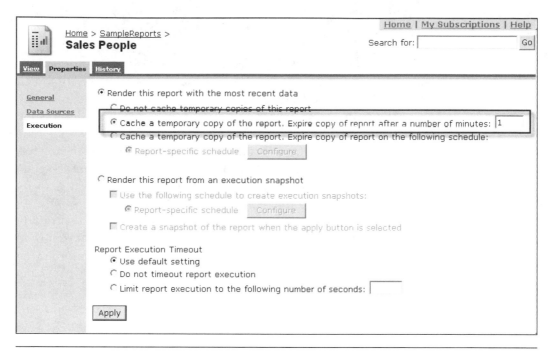

Figure 4.19 Setting the Report Cache Expiration Time to One Minute

To address this issue, return to the Data Source Properties (as shown in Figure 4.20) and explicitly indicate that you want to use a custom Data Source and *stored* credentials. For this example, use the TestUser account's name with the User's Domain name, as in MyDOMAIN\TESTUSER, and type the password (whatever you used as the password when you setup the account). You also need to check the box that says "Use as Windows credentials when connecting to the data source."

Now we're ready to return to the Execution properties and set the report to be cached for one minute, as shown in Figure 4.19.

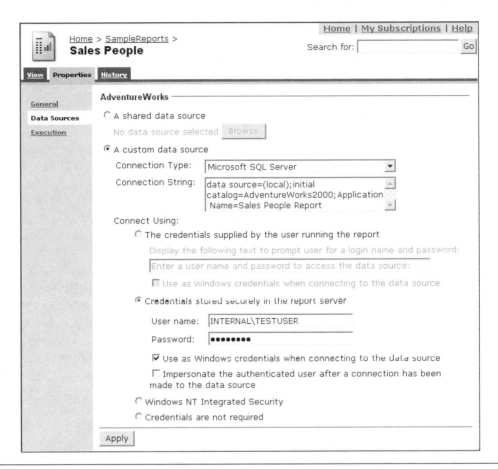

Figure 4.20 Changing the Report Properties Data Sources to Stored Credentials Security

To show how the report is rendered when it is cached, use the TestUser and Administrator web browser accounts to execute the Sales People report and compare what you see. Pay close attention to the Execution Time. Notice that they probably both say the reports were executed at the same point in time. If this is not the case, simply hit the Refresh button on the Report toolbar on both browsers and sit back for a minute. After that minute has expired, you can refresh again. Notice that the times have been updated. That's because the reports expired in the cache, and the next request (when you clicked on Refresh) caused the Report Server to rerender the report from the live data. It's also possible to have cached reports expire on a report-specific schedule, rather than every "n" minutes. We'll let you explore that option on your own because there isn't much to confuse you.

Managing Managed Report Snapshots

Rather than have Reporting Services create a cached managed report when first executed, it's possible to setup a schedule to create a **Snapshot** of a report and then update it manually if necessary. Suppose you have a large report that takes quite a while to query the data source (DBMS) and render the report. To improve performance, you can proactively configure the server to create Snapshots ahead of time and cache them based on your own schedule. This means when the reports are requested by the User, the Report Server simply has to route the rendered report to the browser.

Let's walk through the process of creating a Snapshot of the Sales People report. We'll start by navigating to the Sales People Properties tab and selecting Execution (as shown in Figure 4.19).[16] Click "Render this report from an execution snapshot." At this point, any temporary caching settings are disabled, and you can choose to either create a schedule to produce the Snapshot or simply create a *permanent* Snapshot that's built immediately after you click Apply on this form. In this example, we create a schedule for our Snapshot (as shown in Figure 4.21).

The arrow in Figure 4.21 points to the Configure button, which is used to define the schedule. This launches another form (as shown in Figure 4.22) that prompts you for the details of the schedule. For this example, we set the report to create the Snapshot every minute (despite the fact that this data is not changing at all), starting on 2/3/2004, and ending on 4/5/2004. To set a start and end date for the schedule, you'll have to click on each of the Calendar controls—they don't trust you to enter properly formatted dates.

---

[16] If you don't see *General*, *Data Sources*, and *Execution* hyperlinks under the Properties tab, you skipped a step when granting permissions to the Hitchhiker's Test role. Be sure "Manage reports" is checked in the task assignments.

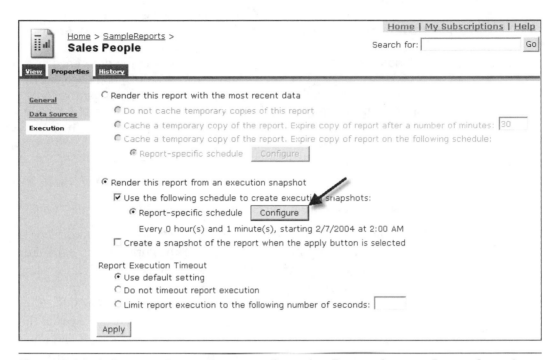

Figure 4.21 Setting the Report Properties Execution Form to Create a Report Snapshot

To commit your schedule, click OK and *wait*. If you don't give the Reporting Services engine time to post the change before you leave this form, your changes could be lost. You should be returned automatically to the Sales People Properties Execution form. At this point, you must click Apply. Again, you need to wait to give Reporting Services time to create the schedule. If you get an error message that complains about not having the SQL Server Agent program running, it's probably because it isn't—running, that is—on the Reporting Services server. Since the SQL Server Agent schedules these jobs, it's important that it start when the system boots and remain running. Use the SQL Server Service Manager to start the SQL Server Agent at boot time.

NOTE When the Report Manager shows dates in the Sample Reports, they are localized to the language setting on the user's browser. We talk about localization issues in Chapter 6. To see the difference in action, try changing this setting between English(US) and English(UK). In your web browser you'll find the Language Settings under the Tools | Internet Options menu, and then on a button on the General Tab page. After making the change, you might find you need to restart the web browser for the settings to take effect.

Snapshot Schedule Expiration Date Idiosyncrasies

We found some idiosyncratic web form behavior that can drive you completely nuts if you don't have a high-resolution video card. For example, suppose you try to set the cache expiration end dates using the Calendar controls (as we point out in Figure 4.22). If you have to scroll down the page, the screen redraws. When you scroll back up to edit a schedule's start and end dates, don't always expect the Calendar control to remain located on the selected date—and don't expect the Date controls to be editable. Also, take extreme care with the Start Time. This appears to default to start at 2:00 AM and most of the time that is not a problem. However, if you happen to be working in the twilight hours between midnight and 2:00 AM and you set a start date before the present day, you'll find that your schedule won't start running until 2:00 AM. These are all things that the development team knows about. Again, we expect that this issue will be addressed in a Service Pack, or hopefully in the next version. Functionality is not impaired; things still work. So if you're working in the twilight hours, you just need to wind the start time back to before the present time at the server—if you want the schedule to run before 2:00 AM, that is. These things will just work better in future (we hope).

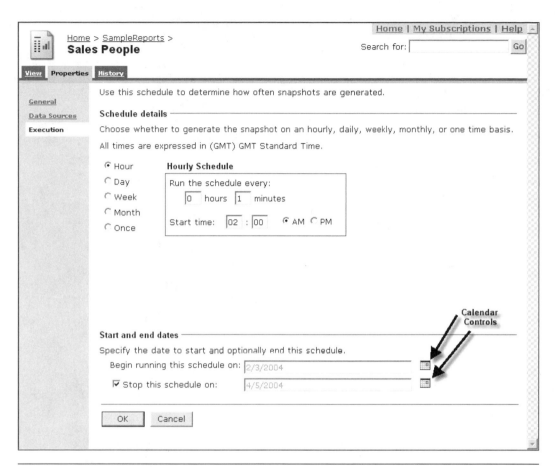

Figure 4.22 Configuring the Snapshot Schedule

Displaying the Last Run Time

When you configure a managed report to render from an execution Snapshot, the last run date and time are displayed alongside that report in the folder where the report is stored (as shown in Figure 4.23).

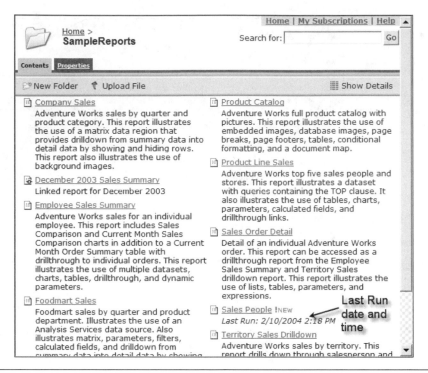

Figure 4.23 The SampleReports Directory Showing the Sales People Report Last Run Time

Limiting Managed Report Execution Time

To limit the amount of time that the Report Server spends trying to run a managed report query and render the report, you can change the Report Execution Timeout setting (as shown in Figure 4.21). Judging how long the Report Server should take to render a report can be fairly subjective. Many factors can affect performance, so reducing this value might mean that a heavily loaded server simply times out while trying to render a report—thus wasting the processing time consumed up to that point. If you suspect that the report creation queries might lock up waiting for resources, it might be wise to set this timeout value, but use a value that accounts for server load and other conditions that might hinder performance in the normal course of daily operations.

TIP *Clean Up After Yourself!* Finally, before you finish experimenting with the Execution properties, don't forget to remove schedules that might still be repeating every minute or so!

Managing Managed Report History Properties

Reporting Services also has the ability to create historical Snapshots that store a preprocessed report in the server using the data state at a "snapshot" point in time and make that Snapshot available on the Report Manager History tab to be rerendered at a later date and time. No, the Snapshots are not stored in their "rendered" format. Saving a report Snapshot means that a user might come back to a report long after it is initially generated and order a reprint. To use this facility (just as with execution caching), a report must use a Data Source that uses stored credentials (not SSPI). That Data Source can be a shared Data Source with stored credentials or a Data Source custom to the report.

Set Allow
history to
be created
manually in
the Sales
People Report
Properties |
History
properties.

To see History in the making (so to speak), access the Sales People report with the Report Manager as the Administrative User, and go to the History tab. On the toolbar, you should see a button called New Snapshot. If you don't see it, you'll need to go to the Properties tab and the History properties and ensure that Allow history to be created manually is checked. The Report Manager will flag you if the credentials are not stored when you try to check this, so if you haven't setup some stored credentials you'll have to do that before being able to make the History work.

Click the New Snapshot button on the History tab toolbar—you can click it several times. You'll see that links are added with a date and time that the Snapshot was taken each time you clicked (as shown in Figure 4.24).

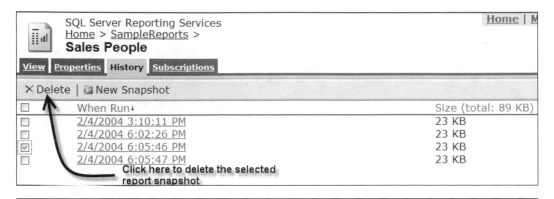

Figure 4.24 The Historical Snapshots Stored in the Report Database

Once the Snapshot is taken, you can click on each hyperlink, which renders the Snapshot based on data at that time. Select one of the links and see what happens. First you should notice that the report is rendered in a new web browser window outside the Report Manager. Take a close look at the URL in the Address bar of that browser:

```
https://d1/ReportServer?/SampleReports/⏎
    Sales+People&rs:Snapshot=2004-02-04T03:10:11
```

In Chapter 6, we'll be talking about the structure of direct URL access to the Report Server, but we thought we'd highlight this here so that you can start experimenting.

You'll appreciate why it is helpful to use the Sales People report definition for this demonstration—it shows the time the report was executed. As an experiment, you might change some of the underlying data being shown in the Sales People report. For example, change one of the sales people's last names, if for no other reason than to convince yourself that you're looking at a Snapshot.

To delete one or more Snapshots, simply click on the checkbox next to the report to be deleted, and click the Delete button (as shown in Figure 4.24).

Adding Manage Report History Rights to User Accounts

Before we grant Manage Report History rights to the TestUser account, take a look at the Report Manager with the TestUser's web browser. If you've been following along, the TestUser should have a History tab. If you've created some Snapshots, the TestUser can see those listed on the History tab page but there will not be any History toolbar. And on the Properties tab page the TestUser does not have a hyperlink to manage the History properties. So let's add the Manage Report History task to the Hitchhiker's Test role. Now TestUser can see and use the History link on the Properties tab shown in Figure 4.25. Let's discuss the History properties dialog a bit more deeply. Each of these options grants rights to the user to customize how report history is maintained:

Grant Manage Report History rights to the Hitchhiker's Test role.

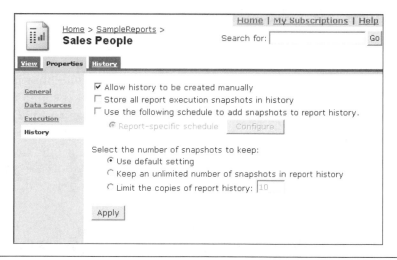

Figure 4.25 The Sales People History Properties Tab

- **Allow History to be Created Manually:** This determines whether the New Snapshot button is available on the History tab toolbar and governs whether the Report Server permits manual creation of historic Snapshots.
- **Store All Report Execution Snapshots in History:** In the previous section, we said it's possible to set reports to be created

on Execution schedules or when the Apply button is selected on a Snapshot. If this option is selected, Execution Snapshots are indexed in the History list and remain in the Report Server database catalog rather than expiring without a trace.

- **Use the Following Schedule to Add Snapshots to Report History:** This option creates a schedule that determines *when* report Snapshots are added to the History. If you compare what TestUser and the Administrator can see on the History properties at this point, you'll see that the Administrator can also choose to use a shared schedule rather than one that's specific to just the report in question. We'll show you a little later that this comes from system-wide role and task rights granted to the Administrator. These rights are independent of the Tasks and Roles we assign to the TestUser through the Hitchhiker's Test role.

- **Select the Number of Snapshots to Keep:** This option limits the number of Snapshots kept in the History. There are also other system-wide properties that we cover a little later in this chapter that enable the number of Snapshots stored in the History to be limited to a specific number on a site-wide basis. This site-wide value is used by default. You can set a limit on a report-specific basis to an unlimited or a specific number. If you choose unlimited, you might need to "manage" those Snapshots, because they consume more and more space on the ReportServer database as time passes.

Creating and Managing Managed Report Subscriptions[17]

One of the coolest Reporting Services features we've found is its facility for a user to subscribe to a managed report and have it delivered via e-mail or published to a file share location on a one-time or periodic

---

[17] We did encounter a few configuration issues that we hope will be ironed out by the time you are reading this, so if things don't work out as we're indicating here, be sure to check our website, www.SQLReportingServices.NET, for further information.

basis. Users can specify how managed reports are rendered as well as the parameters used to fetch and manipulate the report data.

Individual Subscriptions

Report subscriptions require that the subscribed report use stored credential Data Sources, because it is the Report Server Windows service that performs the actual report execution and delivery.

> Grant Manage Individual Subscription rights to the Hitchhiker's Test role.

To see how Subscriptions work using the Administrator's Report Manager, let's add the Manage Individual Subscription rights to the Hitchhiker's Test role. Then, with the TestUser's Report Manager, we'll take a look at the Sales People report. The TestUser's Report Manager now displays an additional Subscriptions tab. Click that tab, and on the toolbar you should see a new button, New Subscription—click it. At this point, you should see a configuration page similar to that shown in Figure 4.26.

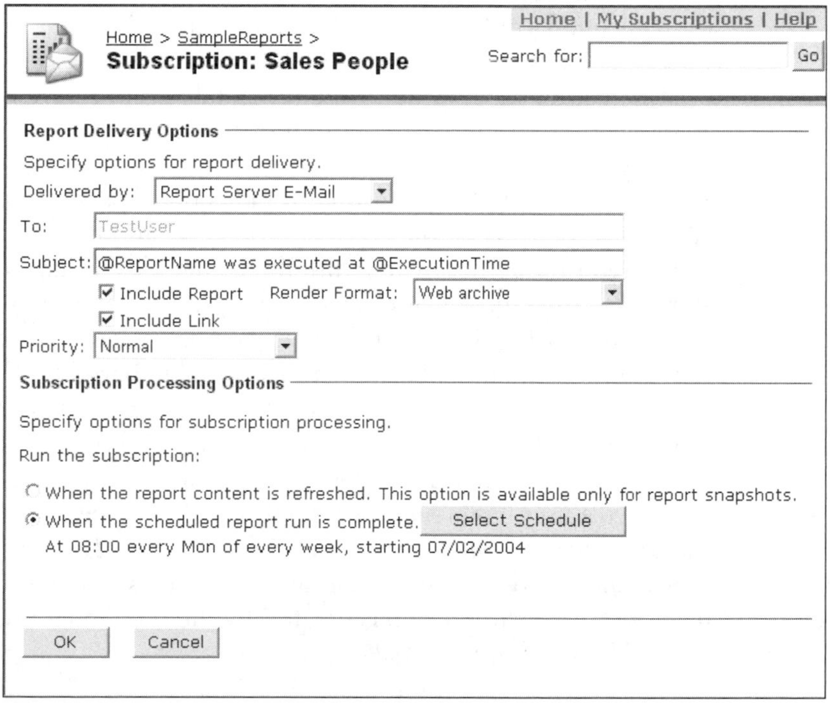

Figure 4.26 The Subscription Configuration Page for E-Mail Delivery

With Manage Individual Subscription task rights, the TestUser account cannot control whom a managed report is sent to—it's automatically routed to the individual user creating the subscription. If the user needs more control, the Administrator must assign the Manage All Subscriptions task to the role. Many users can subscribe to a single managed report by configuring their own individual subscriptions—subject, of course, to your having given at least Manage Individual Subscription task rights to a Reporting Services Item-level Role. This is assigned either directly or through inheritance to the user or group on the managed report to which they wish to subscribe.

If you've followed along with our discussions of History and Execution properties, you'll be familiar with setting up scheduling. Just as with History and Execution, the scheduler used is provided by the SQL Server Agent—so you'll need to ensure that it is up and running—and if you're reluctant to reboot, we suggest you set the SQL Server Agent to auto-start. As an alternative to using the E-Mail Delivery extension, you can elect that the managed report be delivered to a file share. In this case, there is a slightly different page for the collection configuration information, including the credentials to use to access the file share. If the filename is to overwrite preexisting copies or provide an incremental serial number, refer to Figure 4.27 to see what options to set.

If you've configured the managed report to render from an Execution Snapshot by adjusting the Execution properties, it's possible to tie delivery of the report to the generation of the Snapshot rather than trying to create a different schedule, which (hopefully) starts after the schedule for the new Snapshot generation. Under the covers, Reporting Services uses SQL Server Agent to create events that are subsequently placed in an Event table based on the schedule you provide. The Report Server Windows service polls the Event table and performs any required tasks. The service subsequently processes these events in no deterministic order.

Once a user has created subscriptions, they're managed through the *My Subscriptions* hyperlink at the top of the Report Manager, sandwiched between the *Home* and *Help* links (as shown in Figure 4.28). Only subscriptions created by the individual user appear under *My Subscriptions*.

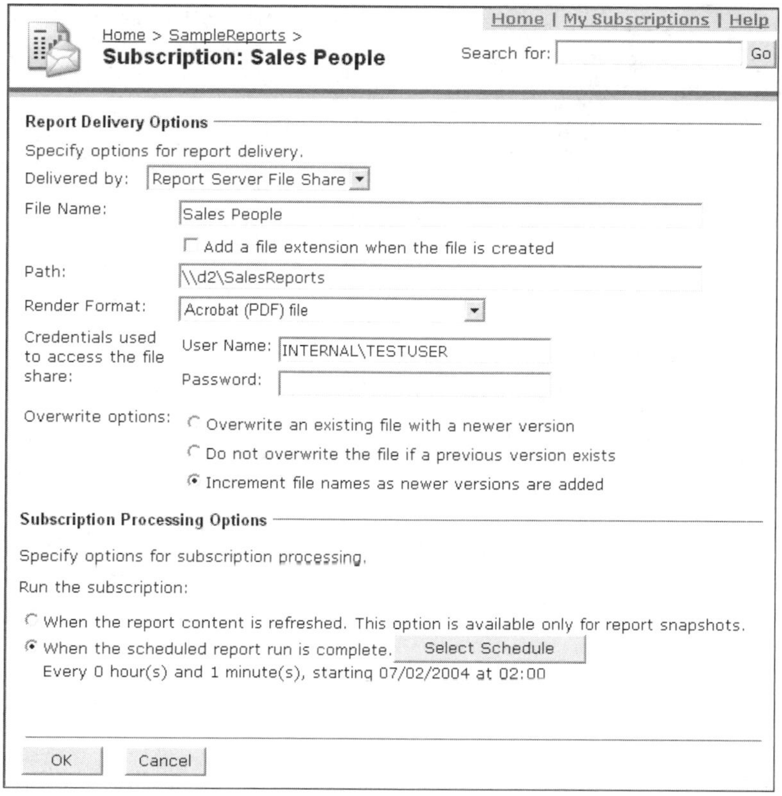

Figure 4.27 Setting Subscription Report Delivery and Processing Options

The Manage All Subscriptions Task Rights

Grant Manage
All Subscriptions
rights to the
Hitchhiker's
Test role.

Manage All Subscriptions is an additional Task level of permission relating to Subscriptions. If you give your TestUser those rights by assigning them to the Hitchhiker's Test role, the user is granted much more control on the To, Cc, Bcc, and Reply-To properties of the e-mail generated by a subscription, in addition to being able to embed comments in the body of the e-mail, as shown in Figure 4.28.

A user who has Manage All Subscriptions task rights can use the Subscriptions tab page of a managed report to see and manage all the individual subscriptions created by any and all users.

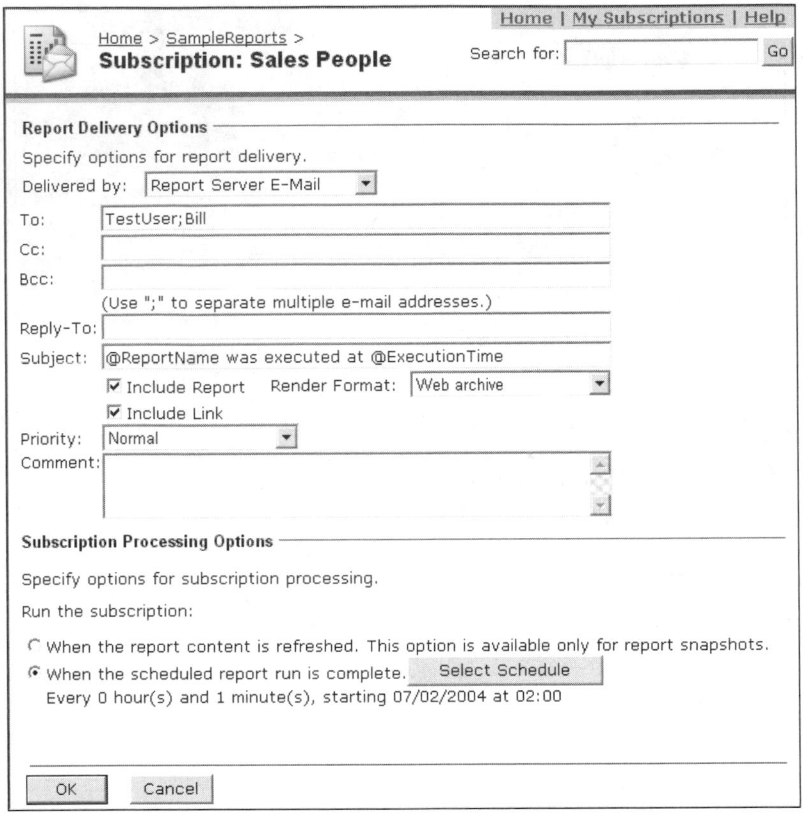

Figure 4.28 Expanded User Rights Expose the Subscription E-Mail Fields

Data-Driven Subscriptions

With the Manage All Subscriptions rights granted, specific users can easily modify all relevant e-mail fields. But suppose you have large distribution groups, and a humongous mailing list of executives and salespersons clamoring to be kept up to date with sales reports. The task of constantly updating a Subscription's To field can be full-time employment for a small team. You might mitigate this task by leveraging an existing mailing list on your mail server so that all you need do is send the report to the mail list alias and leave the mail system administrators with the headaches. On the other hand, if you have large database-managed e-mail lists, the data-driven subscription feature of Reporting Services can help you define a query that can be used to populate all the fields of a Subscription. Data-driven subscriptions are implemented in the Report Manager through a set of wizard pages, and they're designed to work with any Delivery extension, including custom Delivery extensions. You could use this approach to publish via NNTP or FTP. We'll take a look at this wizard from the perspective of driving the standard Report Server File Share Delivery extension—which is an out-of-the-box publishing feature usable with the Enterprise Edition. Don't confuse this with the File Share Data Processing Extension sample. It's concerned with Data Sources, not data subscriptions. Follow along as we create a data-driven subscription.

NOTE Data-driven subscriptions are only usable on the Enterprise Edition—not on the Standard version. While the feature can be evaluated on the Evaluation and Developer Editions, it can only be used in a production system with the Enterprise Edition.

In the TestUser account's Report Manager, select the Sales People report and navigate to the Subscriptions tab. You should be able to see a New Data-driven Subscription[18] button on the toolbar, as shown in Figure 4.29.

Figure 4.29 Creating New Data-Driven Subscriptions

---

[18] If you don't see the New Data-driven Subscription button, you need to add the Manage All Subscriptions role as mentioned earlier.

This takes you to Step 1 of the wizard, as shown in Figure 4.30. Here the subscription is named; you decide which Delivery extension to use and whether to use a shared or specific Data Source. For our example, we're going to use a specific Data Source.

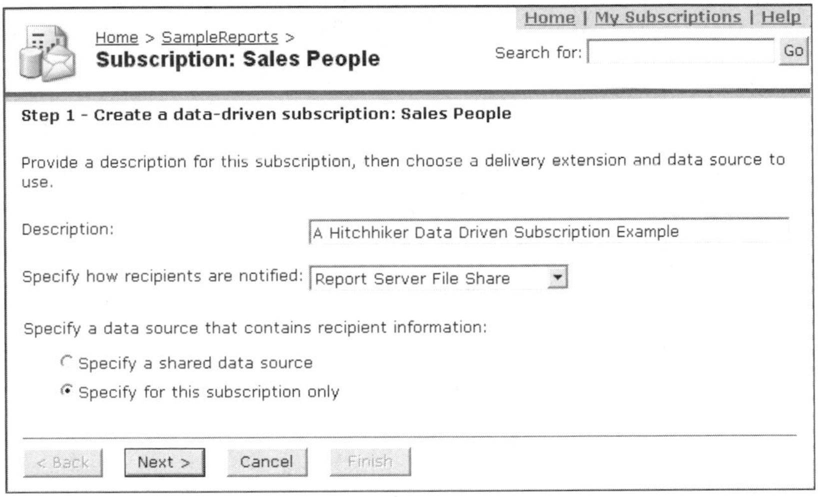

Figure 4.30 Describing the Properties of a Data-Driven Subscription

In Step 2 of the wizard (as shown in Figure 4.31), we define the Data Source. Note the options chosen. In this case, we specify Microsoft SQL Server as the Connection Type, and then we set some options in the Connection string to enhance security:

- **We Include the Clause "persist security info = false":** This prevents exposing the Connection string to any code that interrogates it. If this setting is set to "true" (which is the default if not specified), the user credentials are exposed whenever the Connection string is accessed.
- **We Include an "Application Name" Clause to Make It Considerably Easier to Trace Reporting Services Operations in the SQL Profiler:** We'd be able to trace this in the SQL Profiler by filtering on the application name of SalesPeopleSub.

If you edit an existing data-driven subscription, you'll be taken through these same six or seven steps. For example, in Step 2, if you're storing credentials you must always reenter the password, although the Report Manager won't complain to you that there are problems until you try to confirm it in Step 3. This is an argument for using a shared Data Source instead of stored credentials.

Another point that we cannot emphasize enough is that you should *never* store credentials in any Data Source that has more than read-only permissions to the specific data that you are targeting.

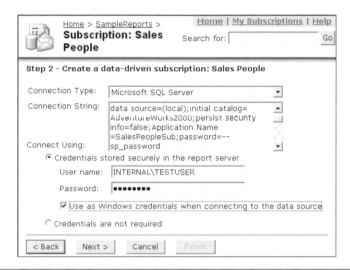

Figure 4.31 Step 2 of the Data-Driven Subscription Wizard—Specifying the Data Source Attributes

Having defined the Data Source, click Next and move on to Step 3, as shown in Figure 4.32. This step describes how Reporting Services queries the database for values used to set the Delivery Extension properties. We will show you how we created the DataDrivenFileShareExample table in just a moment. No, it doesn't matter what the fields are called because we map the fields (returned by the query in Step 4) to the Delivery Extension properties. Each row of the query resultset is processed as a separate report delivery. In production, we suggest that you use a stored procedure rather than dynamic SQL as we've done here—just code the stored procedure name and parameters in the query string. You can hit the Validate button and remain on the same Step 3. This simply tells you that the query you have written is declared by the underlying server to be well formed (i.e., its syntax is okay). If there is a problem with your credentials, as when you edit an existing data-driven subscription and forget to reenter your password, that exception is trapped here too. You can hit the Back button, enter the password again, and return to Step 3 without losing your query.

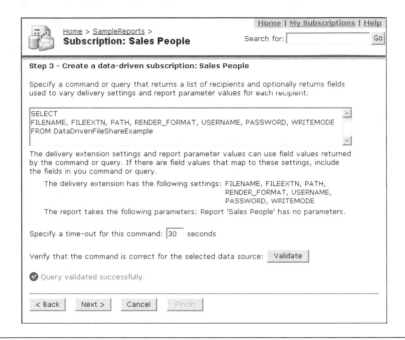

Figure 4.32 Step 3 of the Data-Driven Subscription Wizard—Specifying the Query

Listing 4.3 shows the DDL we used in the SQL QueryAnalyzer to create the table that stores the data-driven subscription e-mail list. This schema is based on trial-and-error tests we did in the lab, but we know it works.

Listing 4.3 Creating a Data-Driven Subscription Table

```
CREATE TABLE DataDrivenFileShareExample
(
   ID uniqueidentifier ROWGUIDCOL NOT NULL DEFAULT (newid()),
   FILENAME nvarchar (255) NOT NULL ,
   FILEEXTN bit NOT NULL ,
   PATH nvarchar (260)  NOT NULL ,
   RENDER_FORMAT nvarchar (10) NOT NULL ,
```

```
USERNAME sysname NOT NULL ,
PASSWORD sysname NOT NULL ,
WRITEMODE nvarchar (15) NOT NULL
)
```

Before we show you the DataDrivenFileShareExample table's sample data, and tell you about the "sleazy hack" we pulled, we need to show you Step 4 of the wizard, as shown in Figure 4.33. In this step, the field names returned from the Step 3 query are mapped to the Delivery Extension properties.

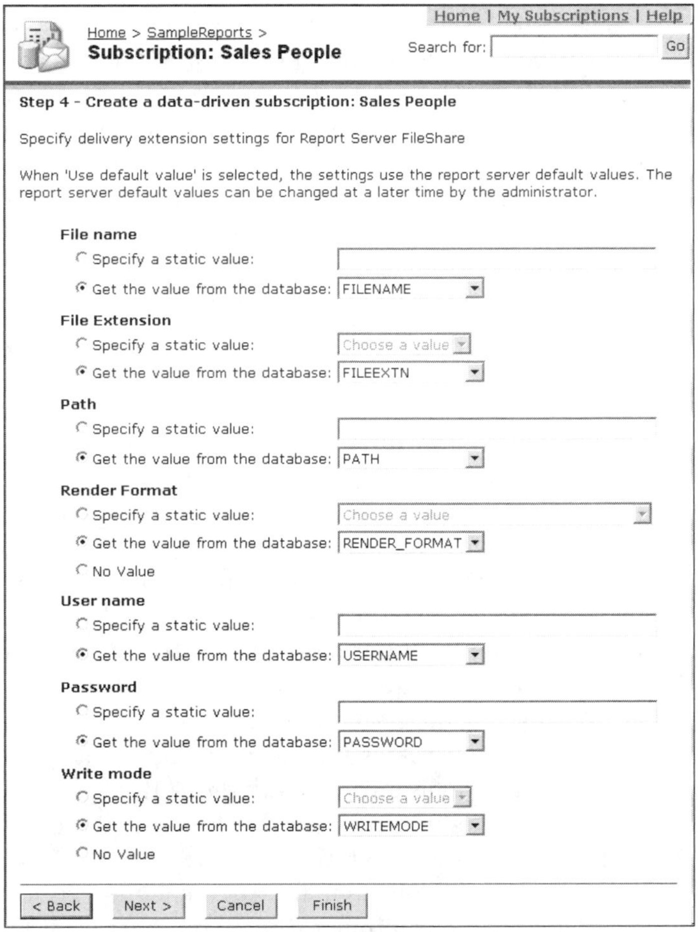

Figure 4.33 Step 4: Mapping the Query Fields to the Delivery Extension Properties

In Step 4, you can choose a static value, no value, or a value from the query. In our example, we bound all of the properties to columns from our query created in Step 3. But we had a bit of bother. You may find that it's more convenient to use fixed values for the User Name and Password properties. You see, Reporting Services' File Share Delivery extension is designed to be secure (of course), and therefore it expects the password and user name to be encrypted with your Reporting Services symmetric key. The Report Manager does this for you if you are using fixed values for the password and user name. However, you'll encounter a bit of an upward struggle if you are going to encrypt the credentials yourself with the symmetric key, because there is no exposed interface with which to do this. In most cases, you ought to be able to use a single user name and password for all the network shares you intend to use to save the managed reports. This can help if you have inter-domain trusts in place, and you want to save to shares on more than one domain. To get a copy of the credentials encrypted with the symmetric key (which is, of course, "unsupported" by Microsoft), we created a data-driven subscription and used a fixed account name and fixed password. At the same time, we used SQL Profiler to trace communication with the SQL Server, watching for the call made to the UpdateSubscription stored procedure. Once we had this statement trapped in the SQL Profiler, we looked for the UserName and Password values placed in the `@ExtensionSettings` parameter. These are the encrypted (with the symmetric key) form of the User Name and Password. We then snagged those values and saved them in our table. (If you miss them on the wire with the SQL Profiler, there is an easier way to grab them out of the extension settings column in the Subscriptions table in the ReportServer database). After that, we came back into the data-driven subscription and hooked up the Password and Username fields to come from our table rather than using fixed values, as we had originally indicated in the Connection string in Step 2.

As deviant (and secure) as this approach is, our advice is to simply use fixed values for the user name and password and only venture off into this territory with the SQL Profiler, or delve into the Subscriptions table if you absolutely must. We expect that this too will be addressed in a future version.

For example, you might have to create reports for a federation of companies on your intranet where you don't want to share the user credentials between the users, but you don't mind having a report DBA use all of these private credentials to setup the reports. Then again, there are ways to get the OS to grant permissions to specific shares and use ACLs to manage access to the reports.

Figure 4.34 shows a copy of our DataDrivenFileShareExample table. Notice the encrypted Usernames and Passwords.

FILENAME	FILEEXTN	PATH	RENDER_FORMAT	USERNAME	PASSWORD	WRITEMODE
Sales People	1	\\SalesServer1.boost.net\Sales	PDF	ZHve9dgeAjTPnJsF	/KgfoEk+uKhde3pC	AutoIncrement
Sales People	1	\\MarketingServer1.Betav.com\Contacts	MHTML	ZHve9dgeAjTPnJsF	/KgfoEk+uKhde3pC	AutoIncrement
Sales People	1	\\Web1\FTPSVC	PDF	ZHve9dgeAjTPnJsF	/KgfoEk+uKhde3pC	AutoIncrement
Sales People	1	\\d2\c$	PDF	ZHve9dgeAjTPnJsF	/KgfoEk+uKhde3pC	AutoIncrement

Figure 4.34 The DataDrivenFileShareExample Table Populated with Encrypted Credentials

If you examine the Data table in Figure 4.34, you'll notice that most of the columns are fairly intuitive. However, we need to examine the values in the FILEEXTN, RENDER_FORMAT, and WRITEMODE columns. Generally, these settings determine the path, filename, and extension as well as the user credentials of the generated report file being created.

- The WRITEMODE column should contain either None, Overwrite, or AutoIncrement. This attribute determines how Reporting Services deals with existing files (if any). None means that the filename remains the same, and Reporting Services does not overwrite an existing file should it already exist. Use Overwrite when you want the existing file (if present) to be replaced. Use AutoIncrement to append an incrementing number to the filename—this leaves all previous files on the drive.
- The FILEEXTN Boolean column should contain 1 to mean "append a file type extension corresponding to the RENDER_FORMAT selected" when building the filename from the PATH, or 0 to ignore it.
- The RENDER_FORMAT should be one of the rendering formats specified in the RSWebApplication.config file. It should contain either XML, CSV, IMAGE, PDF, HTML4.0, HTML3.2, MHTML, or EXCEL. However, by default this is excluded from the File Share Delivery extension because FILEEXTN defaults to 0.

Step 5 in the wizard (as shown in Figure 4.35) asks to configure any parameters that the report requires. However, our Sales People report doesn't take any parameters, so Step 5 is simply a click through for us.

Figure 4.35 Specifying the Report Query Parameters

Step 6 in the wizard (as shown in Figure 4.36) specifies when we'd like the Delivery extension to run. We can choose that the report is to run on a specific schedule or when the report data is changed on the ReportServer database. Later in this chapter, we'll show you how shared schedules are created and used. In production, shared schedules are much better for this kind of thing. For example, a shared schedule can be paused, resumed, and also shared by many other operations needing the scheduler.

Figure 4.36 Step 6 of the Wizard—Specifying When the Report Is to Be Scheduled

And finally, we arrive at Step 7 (as shown in Figure 4.37). At this point, we must remind you of the twilight foible. For some reason,[19] the Start Time is set to 02:00 AM by default. This caught us by surprise many times as we wrote this book and had us chasing ghost bugs that disappeared in the mist at 02:00 AM. Frankly, we thought the scheduler was haunted. Apparently, it doesn't matter even if you set the Start Date back to the day before—it still only starts running once the time is past 2:00 AM. So if you are working late (or should we say, early), don't let this Twilight Zone haunting puzzle you to distraction as it did us. Just be sure to wind the Start Time back to 00:00 (midnight).

Figure 4.37 Step 7 of the Wizard—Providing the Scheduling Parameters (Note the Start Time Defaults to 02:00 AM)

---

[19] It's probably one of the unsolved mysteries of the sea, like the Bermuda Triangle.

Delivery Extension Configuration Issues

When a user selects New Subscription, by default the Report Manager is configured to present the e-mail delivery provider rather than the file share delivery provider. If you would prefer your users to be presented with the file share delivery provider instead, you can edit the RSWebApplication.config[20] file and carefully move the

```
<DefaultDeliveryExtension>True</DefaultDeliveryExtension>
```

to immediately beneath the node that starts:

```
<Extension Name="Report Server FileShare" ….
```

You can also choose the default rendering format for each Delivery extension. This way you can change the <DefaultRenderingExtension> from MHTML to appropriate values for each extension. For example, the following XML ensures that the default rendering choice is an Adobe PDF file:

```
<DefaultRenderingExtension>PDF</DefaultRenderingExtension>
```

The list of possible Rendering extensions contains the following:

- XML
- CSV
- IMAGE
- PDF
- HTML4.0
- HTML3.2
- MHTML
- EXCEL
- HTMLOWC (but by default this is excluded from the File Share Delivery extension)

We noticed another issue in the released version (1.0) of Reporting Services that might get fixed in a Service Pack by the time

---

[20] RSWebApplication.config is located by default in the *\Program Files\Microsoft SQL Server\MSSQL\Reporting Services\ReportManager* folder.

you read this. It appears that the Default Rendering extension option was not working for the file share delivery provider. That's because under the <configuration> node, the node should be <FileShareConfiguration>, not <Fileshare>, so you might like to experiment "correcting" that to read as follows:

```
<FileShareConfiguration>
    <DefaultRenderingExtension>PDF</DefaultRenderingExtension>
</FileShareConfiguration>
```

But check our website for the latest information on this and other issues.

The RSReportServer.config[21] also has a number of configuration options relating to Delivery extensions. Locate the <extensions>, <delivery> sections in that file. The <ExcludedRenderFormats> nodes under each Delivery extension will be of particular interest if you would like to block one of the rendering formats—such as the Excel rendering format when your users have not yet upgraded to Excel 97. Other settings in this configuration file also specify how many times Reporting Services should retry delivery (<MaxRetries>) and the time it should wait before trying again (<SecondsBeforeRetry>).

Managed Report Item-Level Security Settings

Grant Set Security for Individual Items rights to the Hitchhiker's Test role.

At the beginning of this chapter (while using the Administrator's Report Manager), we assigned the TestUser with a Hitchhiker's Test role to the root Home folder hierarchy. If we now add the Set Security for Individual Items task rights to the Hitchhiker's Test role, TestUser can start assigning Users and Groups to pre-existing managed report roles to any item in the Report Server. Take a moment to appreciate that we are *not* talking about the ability to create new roles or to assign which tasks are aggregated in a role; that's a site-wide security setting that we'll discuss before the end of this chapter.

---

[21] RSReportServer.config is located by default in *\Program Files\Microsoft SQL Server\MSSQL\Reporting Services\ReportServer.*

Guide me!

This section is
illustrated by
a Guide me!
narrated screen
capture demon-
stration on
the DVD.

For everything we've done up to this point, the same rights have
existed throughout the folder hierarchy for our TestUser because,
by default, the assignments are inherited throughout the system.
However, rights can be assigned using much finer granularity, as
we're about to illustrate.

Once we've given our TestUser Set Security for Individual Items
task rights by adding this task to the Hitchhiker's Test role, we can
assign the Domain Users group to have Browser Role rights just on the
SampleReports folder. By now, we're going to assume that you're familiar with the assignment of the Task to the Role with the Administrator's
Report Manager. So after you're done, use the TestUser's Report
Manager browser to navigate to the SampleReports folder and select
the *Security* hyperlink on the Properties tab, as shown in Figure 4.38.

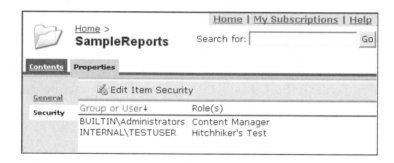

Figure 4.38 The TestUser's Browser Now Exposes the Security Tab

Now, if you have a good memory you'll remember that we
warned you to stay away from the Edit Item Security button at
the beginning of this chapter, and then we wanted you to assign the
TestUser Role against the Home folder. This time we *want* you to
click the Edit Item Security button and click OK in the warning dialog, as shown in Figure 4.39. It informs you that you're breaking the
inheritance from the parent.

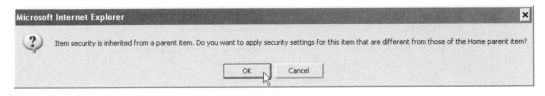

Figure 4.39 Clicking the Edit Item Security Button Triggers This Warning

At this point, you are presented with report toolbar options either to perform a New Role Assignment or to Revert to Parent Security. Here you should select the New Role Assignment option, as shown in Figure 4.40, and assign the User Group DOMAIN USERS from your Domain to the Browser role, as shown in Figure 4.41.

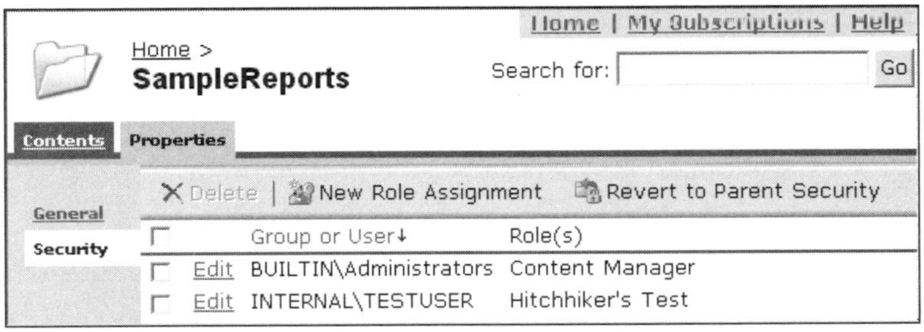

Figure 4.40 Setting Role Security

Yes, you can reassign the roles assigned to the TestUser or Administrator by selecting one of the *Edit* links. But we'll let you do that on your own.

You can then select OK. Yes, we know that we told you that you can't create new Roles or adjust the Tasks of any pre-existing roles. If you don't believe us, go ahead and try by clicking the New Role button in the TestUser's Report Manager. Yes, you'll be able to go a long way down the route of convincing yourself that we are not entirely honest, but at the end of the road when you try to save the new Role, the Report Server steps in, tells you that you don't have permissions, and gives you an rsAccessDenied message. Yes, we expect Microsoft will correct this at some point.

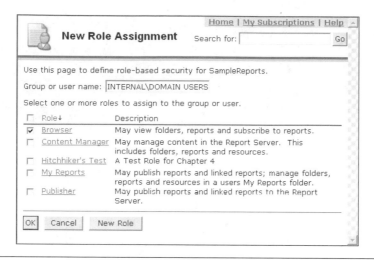

Figure 4.41 Enter the Group or User Name and Select the Role to Assign

We hope that you get back to a confirmation screen similar to Figure 4.42, showing that you have assigned Browser permissions to the Domain Users Group.

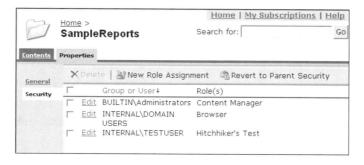

Figure 4.42 A New INTERNAL\DOMAIN USERS Role Has Been Added

At this point, we suggest that you access the Report Manager as a different user, not as TestUser, and not as the Administrative account you've been using, but as an ordinary user of your Domain. Perhaps you'll be surprised to see that when the Report Manager screen is rendered there is very little showing—basically, it looks just like Figure 4.2. Why? Well, the answer is simple. By default the

Report Manager tries to show the Home folder, but Domain Users don't have permissions on the Home folder. We only granted permissions to members of the Domain User Group on the SampleReports subfolder. Try the following URL with your Domain User's web browser:

```
https://<Server>/Reports/Pages/Folder.aspx?ItemPath=/SampleReports
```

Clearly, it's impractical to tell your Domain Users to enter this complicated URL into their web browsers. We brought you down this path to help you appreciate that, as a minimum, all users that need to have access to the Report Manager need to be provided with View Folders rights on the root Home folder. If you create a new role using the Administrator's web browser by going to the *Site Settings* hyperlink, click on Configure Item-level Role definitions. Next, create a new role called View Folders Role; assign the View Folders task right to that role, and assign that new role to the Home folder. Your Domain Users will then be able to navigate the folder hierarchy with ease. We'll let you decide how you are going to configure your Report Server folders. We just think that you'll probably want to restrict people's ability to create new items in the root Home folder.

Creating Linked Managed Reports

So far, we have seen that managed reports can have report parameters and that it's possible to configure default values for those parameters. We've also seen that reports can have specific execution and caching properties and that it's possible to create historical archives of reports. Well, it's also possible to create a *linked report*. The concept here is that a new managed report (called a linked report) can be created that points to and uses an original managed report. However, in this case the newly created linked report uses potentially different defaults bound to the report's parameters, Execution properties, History properties, Subscription properties, and possibly different Security properties as well. Sadly, there is no ability for a linked report to use a different Data Source in Reporting Services version 1.0, but there are strong indications that this feature will be provided in the next version. If you want to adjust linked report Execution, History, or Subscription properties, you'll still need to ensure that the underlying original report uses stored credentials in its Data Sources.

Let's walk through the process of creating a simple linked report using the Employee Sales Summary report. We'll run you into a little hole, so don't jump the gun by adding Create Linked Reports rights to the Hitchhiker's Test role just yet.

With the TestUser's Report Manager browser, select the Employee Sales Summary report in the samples. This managed report exemplifies how linked reports are used because we can create a linked report and choose default parameter values that are different from those in the original report. Once you select the Employee Sales Summary report, you select the Properties tab. We would suggest that you adjust the Data Sources property to use a shared Data Source that uses stored credentials, but we've not yet dealt with shared Data Sources. That's discussed in the next section. For this report, we're going to use a custom Data Source with stored credentials, as shown in Figure 4.43.

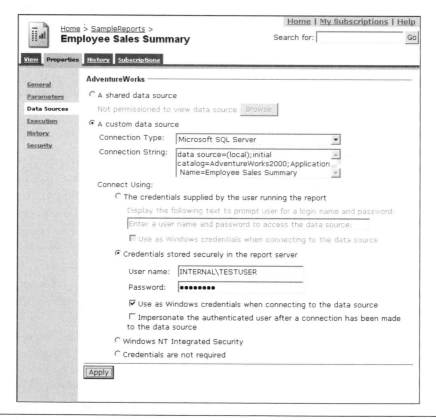

Figure 4.43 Changing the Employee Sales Summary Data Source Properties

After you reconfigure the Data Source Properties, click on the *General* hyperlink on the Properties tab and select the Create Linked Report button that we casually ignored earlier (as shown in Figure 4.44). (It's interesting to note that this button is displayed to our TestUser because we didn't give any rights to our TestUser to create linked reports.)

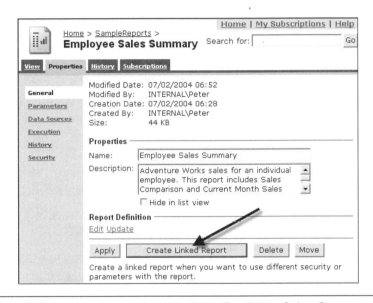

Figure 4.44 Creating a Linked Report Against the Employee Sales Summary Report

Apparently, this Create Linked Report button always appears on the General page even when a user doesn't have Task rights to create a linked report. Again, we think this is a minor oversight that might be fixed by the time you read this.

Grant Create Linked Reports rights to the Hitchhiker's Test role.

Although a user without permission can select the Create Linked Report button in the Report Manager, Report Server eventually catches the ball further down the line (actually, at the very end of the line, and complains with an error blocking an unauthorized user from creating a linked report). It's like standing in line for seven hours waiting to get tickets to the Stones concert, only to find out the ticket booth doesn't take debit cards. To address this problem, use the Administrative web browser to open your favorite hyperlink to the Hitchhiker's Test role and add the Create Linked Reports task. You should be able to handle that by now.

Once the task permission is established, we can return and create a linked report using the TestUser's browser. Select the Create Linked Report button again against the SampleReports Employee Sales Summary report. We're going to create a special version of the Employee Sales Summary report that only reports on a single month and year—December 2003. For this linked report, we'll "preset" the normal report parameters and not prompt the user for these values. We'll still have the user provide an employee ID.

1. Navigate to the Properties tab, and click the Create Linked Report button.
2. Next, name the linked report and set a description on the hyperlink (as shown in Figure 4.45). We used December 2003 Sales Summary, but you can call it anything you want, except "Worst December Sales in a Decade," which would probably offend your boss. Make up your own description with the same caveat, as these details are exposed in the report directory when you're done so that everyone can see them.

Figure 4.45 Creating a Linked Report to the Employee Sales Summary Report

3. You can choose an alternate location for the report, but the interface (as shown in Figure 4.46) does not permit you to add a new folder—you'll have to do that from the Home form. You can drill into the existing directory tree and click on a directory.
4. When you click OK, the Report Manager tries to execute the report—prompting you for the parameters.

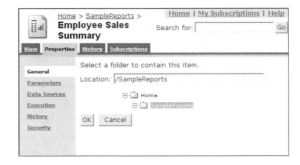

Figure 4.46 Selecting a Folder to Contain the Linked Report (or Any New Report)

> **5.** If you take a look at the SampleReports folder, you'll see that you can easily identify those reports that are "linked" because a little link symbol ▣ appears next to them, as shown in Figure 4.47.

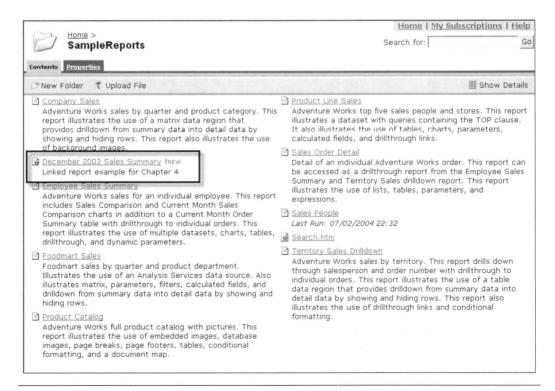

Figure 4.47 Linked Reports Listed in the SampleReports Folder

6. With the current set of Task rights assigned to the TestUser account, you should be able to set Parameter and Execution properties for the linked report. Clicking on the report properties parameters will take you to a form, as shown in Figure 4.48. Notice that we set the default values to December and 2003 but unchecked the Prompt User items for ReportMonth and ReportYear because we want Reporting Services to use the default values we set.

7. Click Apply and wait. Be sure to give Reporting Services enough time to process these changes before trying to do anything else with the browser.

8. Click on the View tab. The user should be prompted for the Employee name—but not the Year or Month. Choose your favorite employee, and click on View Report.

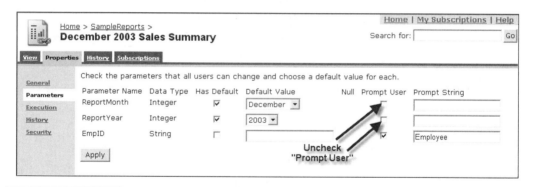

Figure 4.48 Setting Properties for a Linked Report

Once linked reports are defined, you can use them as "shortcuts" to regular managed reports by using their preset parameters to automatically focus the report on a particular subset of the report data.

Managing Data Sources

In Reporting Services, Data Sources link the report you're working on with the rows in the database that contain the data being displayed. As we've discussed in this and earlier chapters, a report

Data Source contains a Connection string (not unlike what you've used with ADO.NET), including the user credentials or "Integrated Security=SSPI" to request SSPI (domain-managed) security. It's up to the Reporting Services DBA to manage these Data Sources, even though the report developers might create them. This section describes how to create and maintain Data Sources, especially shared Data Sources.

Shared Data Sources—A Security Concern

A *shared Data Source* is designed to contain the information needed to connect to a specific data source (DBMS), but it's stored in the ReportServer database so that several managed reports can be tied to this common data source. This way if the data must move to a different server or the user credentials change, the Administrator can (theoretically) change the shared Data Source once and have it affect all of the managed reports linked to it.

In a general sense, using shared Data Sources is a good thing. Many reports in a system can have their DataSets associated with shared Data Sources. They provide an easily manageable unit, in which access credentials can be changed or Connection strings can be updated once instead of administrators having to visit potentially dozens, hundreds, or thousands of single reports. You'll find it a requirement to create report Data Sources that use stored credentials in reports that make use of Execution, History, or Subscription features—and opting to use shared Data Sources will make that management easier. But you must be made acutely aware of which accounts have which permissions to "see," modify, or use shared Data Sources. Think very hard about the permissions assigned to the accounts you embed into stored credentials. For the most part, you don't want to use accounts that have higher than read-only database privileges. Suppose you embed the SA credentials into a shared Data Source, and a malevolent person comes along. Initially, this person might only have rights to create a report. But consider that a report has to execute T-SQL on the server. What if the T-SQL executes using a shared Data Source with embedded SA credentials and happens to issue a DROP DATABASE command? What if it executes T-SQL commands to elevate the malevolent user's own privileges? We discuss these issues at length in Chapter 5.

Reporting Services provides you with some very sophisticated tools and also with the means to be safe—by your correct application of security. We encourage you to think about who can see, use, and manage your secure Data Sources. If you embed a super user account in a shared Data Source, we hope you have your résumé up to date. If you think you are so smart as to use Reporting Services security to hide the shared Data Source, someone might have been watching you save it (sniffing the wire).

Recovering Deleted Shared Data Sources

If you have a business of any size at all, you'll probably have thousands of reports being managed by Reporting Services. If the DBA (on his or her last day on the job) happens to delete a shared Data Source tied to a countless number of these reports, you're pooched (that's a technical term). Ordinarily, the published Reporting Services mechanism has no way to tell which reports are tied to which (now deleted) shared Data Sources. One way to prevent this from impacting your business is to follow a strict backup regimen. If you've done your homework, you might be able to recover the shared Data Source links through careful restoration from the backup database.

If this is not an option, there is another way. But be aware that the technique we're about to describe is not supported by Microsoft and you'll have to use it at your own risk. We can't guarantee that it will work past the first Service Pack, but it's the only easy way we know of to replace shared Data Sources once they've been deleted. Again, we hope that Microsoft will address this issue to make it very difficult to delete shared Data Sources (as it prevents you from deleting the parents of a parent/child data relationship), or (at least) provide a mechanism to tie these disconnected (and now useless) reports back to one or more shared Data Sources.

Okay, so you didn't listen, and you and one of your administrators deleted a shared Data Source that is used by a bazillion reports in your system. What can you do after calling your spouse to say you don't envisage being home for supper before the end of the next millennium? The "correct" and supported approach (if you don't have the time to do it all manually through the Report Manager) would be for you to write a small application against the Reporting Services'

SOAP interface, or download a utility from our website. Failing that, if you are not frightened, we'll tell you, but we give our usual caveat that this is not a supported Microsoft feature and things may very well change that will break this approach (okay, so you might use yesterday's backup tape, but you might lose today's data). So, an alternative is:

1. Back up the Reporting Services ReportServer database before you start. If you don't understand why this is important, step away from the keyboard.
2. Using Report Manger, re-create the shared Data Source—as best you can. It does not have to be exact, just functional and able to work with the reports it used to work with.
3. Using SQL Enterprise Manager, open the Catalog table in the ReportServer database and fetch the rows.
4. Examine the Catalog table data and locate your re-created Data Source in the Path column.
5. Once you've located your Data Source, copy the corresponding ItemID GUID value to the Clipboard.
6. Next, open the DataSource table in the ReportServer database and paste this ItemID into the Link column of each row that you need to relink. The value of the Link column is set to NULL for the disconnected shared Data Sources, so don't overwrite any non-NULL values. Consider that the relationship between the Catalog and DataSource table appears to be on the ItemID column. The name of the Data Source defined in the Report's uploaded RDL is listed in the Name column. Take care because it's only the name of the Data Source at upload time. Note that Data Sources in different folders can have the same name.
7. If you are in doubt what to do, contact us and for a modest consulting fee we'll do what we can to get you back up and running very quickly, or help you find a new job.

Again, we don't endorse direct access to the ReportServer database tables. However, until Microsoft comes up with a repair tool (or we do), this seems like the easiest (and safest) way to repair the damage. We also walk through a technique using SOAP to do this in Chapter 9¾—but this unsupported technique is far easier.

Using the Report Manager to Configure Data Sources

Let's get back to how you can use the Report Manager to create, change, and delete Data Sources—especially now that you know the dangers of deleting shared Data Sources. Once you provide the Hitchhiker's Test role with the Manage Data Sources task, the TestUser account browser exposes a new button on the Report Manager toolbar: New Data Source. Now the TestUser can create new report Data Sources and modify the properties of existing Data Sources. Likewise, if you provide the Hitchhiker's Test role with the View Data Sources task, the TestUser account can manage shared Data Sources and link Data Sources to specific reports.

Grant Manage Data Sources and View Data Sources rights to the Hitchhiker's Test role.

Understanding Shared Data Sources

Shared Data Sources have an Enable property that can be set through a checkbox, as shown in Figure 4.49. This is useful if you want to disable a shared Data Source, albeit temporarily. To do so, simply uncheck the box. *Do not delete a shared Data Source without fully understanding the impact.* If you delete a shared Data Source, you must visit each and every report that used the previous shared Data Source and manually hook it back up to a new shared Data Source. Instead, use the Enable/disable checkbox to temporarily disable a shared Data Source. Deleting shared Data Sources is one of the quickest ways of reducing a Report Server to a broken, quivering mess (and losing your job). No, you can't redeploy the shared Data Source from Visual Studio .NET again to fix things. Sure, Visual Studio .NET creates a new shared Data Source (it can even use the same name), but it won't relink the new shared Data Source to the reports that were using the old deleted version. Deleting all the reports using the deleted shared Data Source and redeploying them again with a new shared Data Source might get you a little closer, but of course you'll lose all your Subscriptions, Execution, and History property assignments. Take our word for it; deleting shared Data Sources is ugly—really ugly. Anyone with Manage Data Source Task rights is two clicks away from wrecking the Reporting Services database.

Do not delete a shared Data Source.

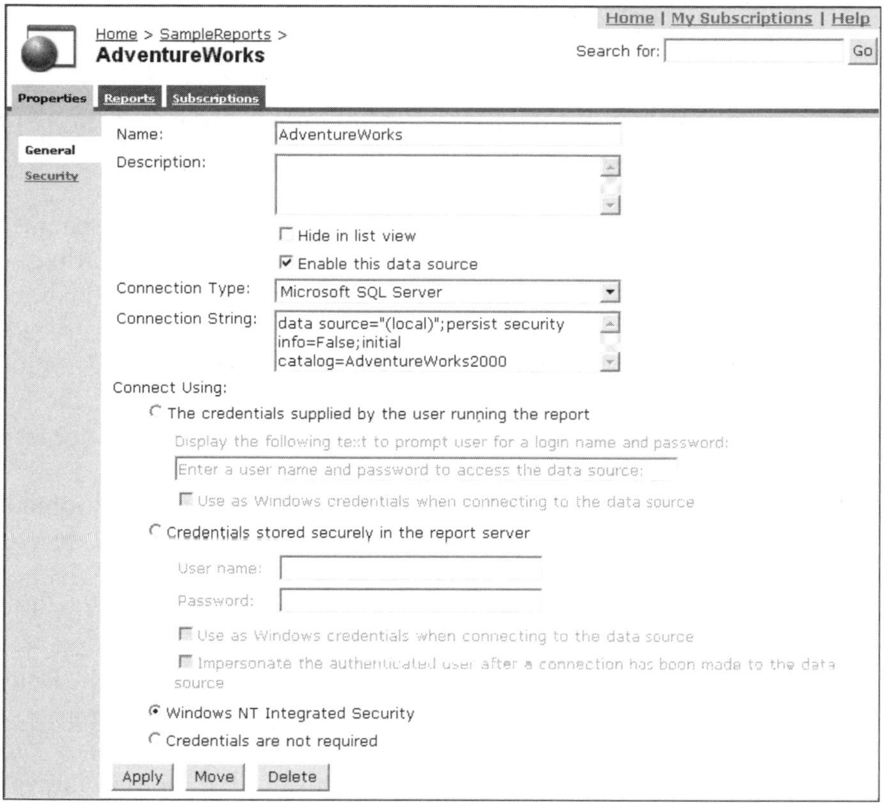

Figure 4.49 Enabling (or Disabling) a Data Source

Managing Site Settings

We're almost done with this adventure through the Report Manager. The last area for us to explore is the Site Settings. You'll notice if you look at the TestUser's Report Manager and compare it closely with the Administrator's Report Manager that the *Site Settings* hyperlink is missing even though we've given the Hitchhiker's Item-level Role all of the possible Item-level Tasks. That's because Item-level Tasks relate specifically to managed-report infrastructure, not to the Site or Report Server as a whole.

The Site Settings are features such as:

- Viewing and managing shared schedules
- Viewing and managing ReportServer database properties
- Managing roles, security, and jobs, and generating events

These features are controlled by a Role and Task scheme similar to what we have seen on report attributes. The only difference here is that these Roles and Tasks relate to *site-wide* functionality.

There are eight site-wide tasks that can be aggregated into named System Roles. However, in the default configuration these tasks are aggregated differently in two System Roles: the fully permissioned System Administrator role and the more restricted System User role.

Unless the configuration is changed, the BUILTIN\Administrators Group is assigned the default System Administrator role. Our TestUser presently has no System Role assignments, which explains the difference in the site-wide functionality between the TestUser's and the Administrator's Report Managers.

Yes, the infrastructure lets you create new System Roles using different aggregations of the System Tasks and permits you to redefine or even delete the out-of-the-box System Roles. You'll find that various steps are in place to ensure that there is always at least one System Role assignment in the system. However, no matter what you do, members of the BUILTIN\Administrators Group can always get to the Site Settings pages and redefine Site Security—regardless of any existent or nonexistent site-wide System Role membership assigned to a member of the BUILTIN\Administrators Group.

Let's explore these System Roles by creating a new role and assigning it to the TestUser account. In the Administrator's Report Manager, select the *Site Settings* hyperlink. In the Security section of the web page, select Configure system-level role definitions. You then arrive at a System Roles web page, where you can click the New Role button on the toolbar. Create a new System Role, called System Hitchhiker, and assign the View Report Server Properties task to the role, as shown in Figure 4.50. Don't forget to click the OK button!

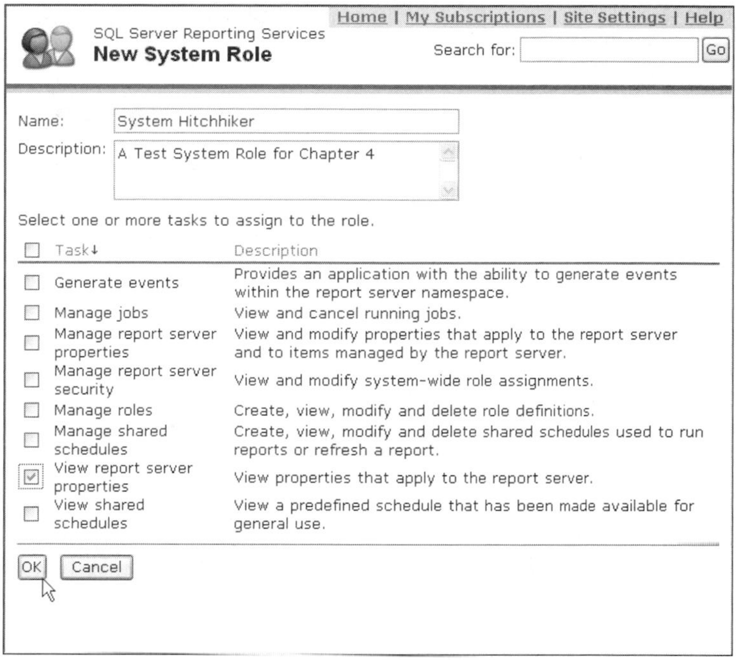

Figure 4.50 Assigning a New System Role

After a new System Role is defined, it should be assigned to a User or Group. In production, we'd suggest that you base things on Domain Groups with Item-level Roles, but for now let's just assign this new role directly against the TestUser account. So, while still using the Administrator's Report Manager browser, return to the *Site Settings* link, and select the *Configure site-wide security* hyperlink in the Security section of that web page. Once the System Role Assignments page renders, Select the New Role Assignment button from the toolbar, and then assign the System Hitchhiker role to the TestUser, as shown in Figure 4.51.

Return to the TestUser's Report Manager and refresh the web page. Look closely at the top left of the page. You'll see that the site name is now displayed. If the site name has not been changed from the default, SQL Server Reporting Services will be displayed.

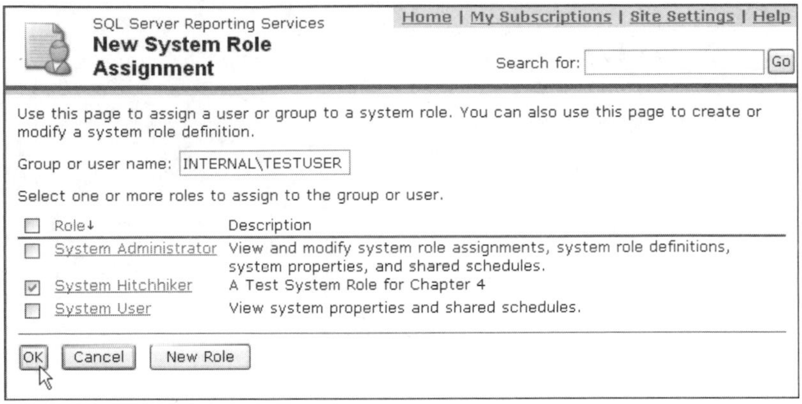

Figure 4.51 Making a New Role Assignment to TestUser

Grant Manage
Report Server
Properties rights
to the System
Hitchhiker role.

Let's have a look at all the Report Server properties once we add the Manage Report Server Properties rights to the System Hitchhiker role. In the Administrator's Report Manager click the *Site Settings* link and click Configure system-level role definitions, followed by the *System Hitchhiker* link. Once you add this and refresh your TestUser's Report Manager, you'll see that the *Site Settings* link now displays. If you select that hyperlink, you'll get to see something that looks like Figure 4.52.

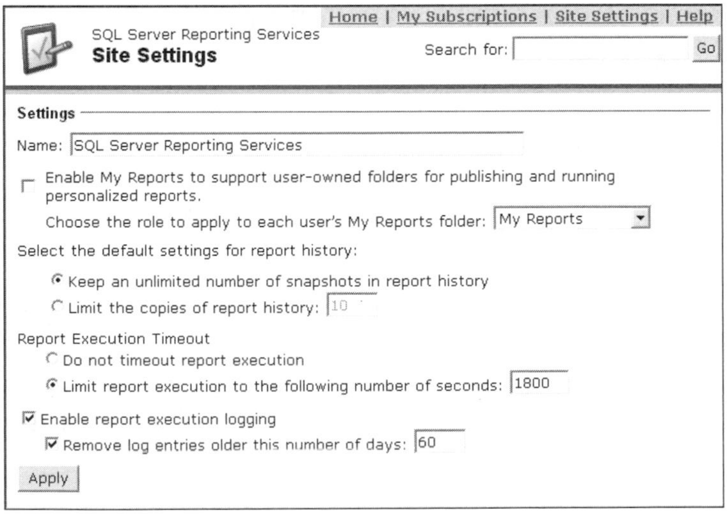

Figure 4.52 Configuring the Site Settings

Site Name

We've just talked about the Site Name, and once the Manage Report Server Properties rights have been granted, the TestUser can customize the Site Name. You might want to change the Site Name to something that makes more sense for either your company or department.

Managing the My Reports Folder

Each User can be provided with a My Reports folder in the Home folder (as shown in Figure 4.53). This folder is specific for each user—very much like the My Documents folder in Windows. You also need to set an Item-level Role that determines the permissions individual users have on their own My Reports folder. If you want your users to be able to upload/publish managed reports, that role needs to have Manage Reports task rights—It's a pretty powerful out-of-the-box role.

Figure 4.53 Configuring the My Reports Folder

Adding User Accounts to the BUILTIN\Administrators Group

Now, no matter which Item-level or System-level rights you give your TestUser account within Reporting Services, you can never get the last ounce of functionality out of the My Reports feature unless the TestUser account is also a member of the BUILTIN\Administrators Group. When looking at the Report Server's Home folder in the

Report Manager, it appears that only members of the BUILTIN\ Administrators Group have access to Users Folders (as shown in Figure 4.54). This is an aggregation of all of the My Reports folders from all of the users who have accessed the Report Manager once My Reports has been enabled in the System properties (as shown in Figure 4.55). You may recall that earlier in this chapter we discussed searching. Remember, you must be an Administrator if you want to be able to search all managed reports in *all* folders, including all the users' My Reports folders.

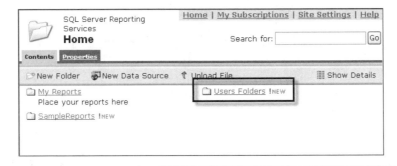

Figure 4.54 Using the Administrator's Browser to View My Reports Folders

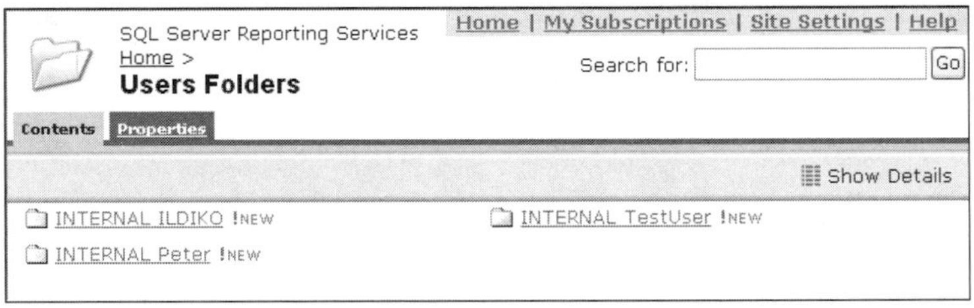

Figure 4.55 View of the Contents of the Users Folders

Suppose you change your mind about having My Reports, and you remove the My Reports System property. At this point, the Report Manager removes the My Reports folder from each user's Home folder view, but it won't remove the Users Folders from any member of the BUILTIN\Administrators Group view of the Home folder. It is quite difficult to delete the Users Folders. You must assign the Users Folders to a role that includes manage and view rights, and you have to delete each item separately. This was intentionally made difficult to prevent people from inadvertently deleting other users' private reports that administrators might not be able to see. However, we found it very difficult and frustrating, and we have to admit that we simply dug into the ReportServer database Catalog table and deleted the entries relating to objects in the Users Folders path. Of course, that technique is not supported, and it aggravates the designers at Microsoft a little. We suggest you plan to create a utility that does this using the approved SOAP interface—or perhaps we will. We'll make it available through our website at www.SQLReportingServices.NET.

Managing the History Snapshots Limit

You may recall when we were defining history Snapshots that we left the setting "Select the number of snapshots to keep" to "Use the default setting." This is the place where you can set the site-wide default value. In Figure 4.52, we have left this value at unlimited. This means that from time to time on a busy system, we might need to consider managing (purging) the history Snapshots.

Managing Report Execution Timeouts

Back in Figure 4.19, we similarly left the Report Execution Timeout to the default value. Here is the point where the site-wide default can be set. If a report execution takes longer than the specified timeout, and it's caught by the system, the report is aborted and a message is displayed to the user, as shown in Figure 4.56.

Figure 4.56 Message Displayed When the Report Times Out

Enable Execution Logging

This is a site setting that logs executions to the ExecutionLog table in the ReportServer database. The setting is enabled by checking the Enable report execution logging option in the Site Settings dialog (as shown in Figure 4.52). This table (like all other ReportServer database tables) should not be manipulated by hand without extreme care, unless you enjoy spending time on the unemployment line. A better (safer) approach is to use the Data Transformation Services (DTS) project provided by Microsoft that can safely interrogate the ExecutionLog table and create a catalog RSExecutionLog. This data can be examined offline with a host of sample reports based on this log.

It's a good idea to decide how much log data is retained by setting the aging period (again, see Figure 4.52). Unless you indicate some reasonable aging period, the volume of data will overflow onto the floor.

Shared Schedules

Casting your mind back to when we were dealing with Execution, History, and Subscriptions properties, you'll probably recall that we created various schedules on each item. What a drag! Well, fortunately you can setup a Schedule that can be shared across the system. If a user belongs to a System role that has the View shared schedules task assigned, anywhere a schedule is called for (anywhere in the system), such as in the Execution, History, and Subscriptions properties, users can see and select a shared schedule. Users who belong to System roles that have the Manage shared schedules task assigned are also able to configure these shared schedules.

Grant Manage Shared Schedules rights to the System Hitchhiker Test role.

Using the Administrator's Report Manager, add the Manage Shared Schedules rights to the System Hitchhiker role. When using the TestUser's Report Manager, a *Manage shared schedules* hyperlink is made visible in the Site Settings.

Shared schedules are useful because they can be centrally administered, but more importantly they can be paused and resumed from the same central management point. See Figure 4.57.

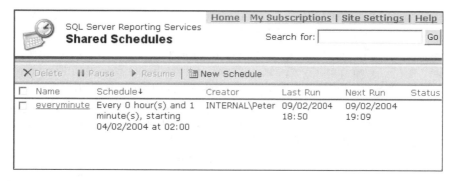

Figure 4.57 Managing Shared Schedules

In Figure 4.57, you can see that the shared schedule called *everyminute* is a hyperlink. This hyperlink takes us to property pages where the schedule can be edited. Additionally, the reports that make use of that schedule can be listed on that page too. Before editing a pre-existing shared schedule, it's probably a good idea to verify which reports may already be using it.

Managing Roles and Report Server Security

All the way through this chapter, the Administrator's Report Manager has been acting as Mission Control—enabling our TestUser's account to have more and more privileges by assigning Item-level Task roles. If you add the Manage Roles task to the System Hitchhiker role, at last our TestUser is elevated to a position that it can manage the Item-level Roles. And at the very last, if the Manage Report Server Security task is added to the System Hitchhiker role, the TestUser is able to manage the system-wide role definitions and assign users and groups to System Roles. At this point, our TestUser has now graduated to a fully fledged Reporting Services Administrator in all its glory. No, we don't expect or recommend that report DBAs create these super users/administrators if they want to keep the database (and their jobs) protected. Grant only those rights the user really needs—and no more.

Summary

This has been a very detailed journey through the Report Manager. If you followed with us from start to finish, you should give yourself a pat on the back as we've taken you through all the features of the Report Manager. If you dipped in and out, you probably had a little trouble following because this chapter was really designed as a walk-through tutorial.

While we worked through this chapter and assigned the TestUser account with roles, in practice we suggest that you don't do that. In production systems, assign your roles against security groups from your Active Directory Domain. This way, permissions can be centrally managed on the Active Directory rather than having to manage permissions in Reporting Services.

Be aware that IIS caches the security group memberships of users for up to 15 minutes. This means you'll encounter situations where a user who might initially access a Report Server doesn't have a particular right to perform some functionality because his or her user account has not been made a member of the correct Domain Group. Yes, you can update Domain Group memberships in the Active Directory, but (as we said) it might be 15 minutes before Reporting Services respects this change. You may be able to speed up this "respect" process by restarting IIS, but this might be a drastic step. Alternatively, you can switch IIS group credential caching off, but this is detrimental to performance because the IIS box constantly queries the Active Directory regarding every user's group memberships for each access to Reporting Services. A one-time 15-minute wait is not a long time after privilege elevation. However, be aware that 15 minutes could be a very long time if you are removing some delinquent (and possibly malicious) user from a group that has Report Server administrative privileges. Depending on the situation, you might want to restart IIS in this case.

Another note regarding shared Data Sources—we need to belabor this point: If you are going to make use of shared Data Sources (and we think you should because they make management much easier, and you in fact need to if you are going to use Subscriptions, History, and some Execution options), *never, ever, ever* store any credentials into a shared Data Source that has any more than read privileges to data (unless you really need a write-back facility, and in that case lock down the write privilege on the database server for the specific tables). Just remember that we've told you, and we want you to keep your job. Think "focus," and limit stored credentials to specific data. (If you store system administrator credentials in a shared Data Source, those credentials could be hijacked by any user who can see that shared Data Source and use it with a report that includes nefarious T-SQL. In the event that the hijacker cannot see the shared Data Source, if that user can deploy an ASP.NET application to the IIS machine upon which the Report Server is running, he or she can hijack those credentials directly in the SQL Server ReportServer database. It's not that such users can decrypt any stored credentials; it's just that they can "use" them as the credentials to execute their despicable code. (We'll talk a little more on security in Chapter 5.)

Don't forget to ensure that you also include `"persist security info=false"` in any Data Source Connection strings with stored credentials. This stops connection objects from revealing the user name and passwords. And finally, if you include an `"Application Name=<Report Name>"` clause when tracing with the SQL Profiler, the connections make a little more sense as they can be filtered out of the morass of connections.

CHAPTER 5

Report Security

Bill Baker
(General
Manager of
SQL Server
Business
Intelligence)
encourages
you to read
this chapter
twice! It's
extremely
important.

At this point, we hope that you're feeling confident as you deploy and work with Reporting Services. However, *so far we've shown you just enough for you to be inadvertently dangerous.* It's all too easy to stick one's head in the sand (or elsewhere) and overlook any inherent security risks when running a report before or after it's deployed. Reports by their very nature need to query data sources using a query language specific to the DBMS where the report's source data (and all other corporate data) is held. Many of these query languages (including Transact SQL [T-SQL], used in SQL Server) are very sophisticated and powerful languages in their own right, and in the hands of deviant or malevolent people can be (ab)used in ways that can compromise data or the database itself. Unfortunately, just as much damage can be done by well-intentioned folks who stumble around in ignorance. Administrators need to be acutely aware in *any* reporting system like this (not just Microsoft Reporting Services) that managed reports and their authorship should be afforded the same guarded respect as other executables. Managed reports, like executables, perform actions on behalf of a user by utilizing the ability to assume the rights assigned to the user or process executing the report. No responsible administrator would let any executable program run on systems under his or her custodianship without consideration having been made to establish the origin, authenticity, and security of those executables—the same should be true for managed reports.

Within organizations, report programmers need to be trusted and granted rights to the same extent afforded programmers creating executables. In Chapter 4, we discussed how to protect the data and reports by limiting the rights granted to users and developers, so you should have a reasonably good understanding of the problem. In this relatively short chapter, we look at some additional security considerations we suggest you implement. We'll also make a number of suggestions and, perhaps surprisingly for some, one of those suggestions is to remove certain execution rights from administrator accounts and to be very careful when using Integrated Security! You'll understand this before the chapter is done. Clearly, this is another "must-read" chapter for both report programmers and administrators.

NOTE After the Microsoft Reporting Services development team read the first draft of this chapter they took our feedback to heart and implemented some changes to enable Administrators to completely turn off Integrated Security for the Report Server. We reworked this chapter to explain the issues and still offer an alternative.

Motivation

Trying to answer the question of why someone would want to intentionally abuse or break into a system is something a criminologist or sociologist would do a better job of answering than we mere computer scientists. All we can do here is recognize that there are bad, corrupt, larcenous, malicious, immature, or simply ignorant people in the world, and to provide some real-world relevance for why you, your management, and your coworkers should be concerned with matters of security.

The motivations driving people who attack systems can vary from the extreme anarchist on the outside of an organization to the financial opportunist on the inside of an organization to the ignorant person or systems administrator just fumbling around. Unfortunately, in our five combined decades of experience in the industry, we've had direct experience with all of them. An anarchist may be driven to cause maximum damage, downtime, or embarrassment to your organization to make a political point, or could simply be driven by a desire to satisfy some juvenile hormones and show the world that they are worthy of some notoriety. Evil-minded perpetrators outside your organization have a somewhat tougher task, as they first must penetrate your network to have their code executed. However, perpetrators on the inside of an organization already have access to your network—they may be sitting right next to you in the staff meeting. Their motivation may be as simple as wanting to get some form of misplaced retribution for being passed over in promotion, served with their notice, or simply slighted in some other way. There are also those who seek pecuniary personal gain. Perhaps they can gain by accessing market-sensitive data to which they have no right. Recent high-profile court cases aside, consider that the executives of many organizations are prevented from publicly trading on inside market-sensitive knowledge, but people lower down in the organization's hierarchy who should not have access to such market-sensitive information are less regulated and less scrutinized and therefore might be tempted.

These malevolent people often utilize very sophisticated tactics and techniques when attacking systems—the most effective among them take technical steps to conceal their activities. However, in the systems we've reviewed over the years, all too often we've found the security door left unlocked or swinging open in the wind for anyone to walk in and take what they want.

The Microsoft Reporting Services development team took the design of the security model very seriously. For the most part, they appear to have provided secure software. This assumes that a special account for the web and Windows service to access the Reporting Services Catalog is defined after installation. In this case, only members of the BUILTIN\Administrators group can initially make any use of Reporting Services. Of course, any reporting system that can only be used by administrators is of limited value, so administrators need to make provisions for ordinary users to be able to use Reporting Services, as we discussed in Chapter 4. While there are a host of powerful features, administrators need to be aware of what those features provide (and enable) and consider the suitability of those features for each individual user or group.

Trojan Reports

You are probably already familiar with the concept of a "Trojan" program—it's a program that on the face does something useful or seemingly innocuous but causes some mischief behind the scenes using the credentials of the user executing it, invariably without the user knowing that anything malicious is going on. Many e-mail worms and viruses are based on the Trojan program principle. It really should not surprise you that it's entirely possible to create a Trojan report, although when we first mention this to developers, they are often a little shocked, which surprises us.

Wake up and smell the coffee! A Reporting Services report is dependent on a specific query program, or "script," written for the Reporting Services engine to execute, collect, and then present data in a more humanly readable form. In the case of querying a SQL Server database, this query script could be a dynamic program written and embedded in the report as a T-SQL string or stored procedure written in T-SQL, or perhaps even an extended stored procedure written in another high-level language such as C++.

This is neither new nor earth-shattering, but consider for a moment that it is also possible to write a T-SQL query, which, in addition to performing a SELECT, also quietly issues TRUNCATE TABLE or DROP DATABASE statements. More insidiously, the malicious query could alter underlying data, issue GRANT statements, create accounts, or add logins to the administrator group. Of course, if a report DataSet is based on such a query, the report would appear to make the SELECT resultset available to the report, and attempt to execute whatever malignant code has been slipped in. If you are a T-SQL guru, you'll immediately realize that the logic that can form part of such an evil query can be deviously complex. Such a query could execute the malevolent parts conditionally on any configurable criterion. For example, it might execute only if executed on a certain day, by a certain user from a certain machine, or only if Arnold Schwarzenegger gets elected president. Such a query could also take steps to cover its tracks after executing, simply by replacing itself in the Report Server Catalog with a pedestrian version of itself after having expunged its malevolent parts so as to hinder future forensic analysis.

NOTE *Prime Directive* Because reports are effectively programs, you must consider carefully to whom you grant the Manage Reports Task right. You need to appreciate that you are trusting the integrity and probity of these people, and entrusting *your* data (and possibly your job and your company's future) to their hands.

Data Sources—Custom or Shared, Stored Credentials, or Integrated Security (SSPI)

As we've seen, Data Sources are the connectoids that hold the Connection strings and credentials used by managed reports, thus enabling them to gain access to the underlying database management systems. When it comes to report Data Source credentials (basically, the keys to the security locks), you'll find there are a myriad of choices provided to permit you to specify and store credentials ahead of time, or prompt for credentials at runtime. Each technique has its own peculiarities. A general rule of thumb is if you use credentials with minimum privileges, the "damage" a Trojan report might perform is rather limited. For example, a managed report executed by a user account that has read-only rights to the source data cannot make changes to the data or anything else in the database.

Runtime Prompting

Runtime prompting of a user for credentials might appear to be the most secure, but this comes with the heavy burden of having to recall user names and passwords, which can be different for each report. Hopefully, these report-specific user names and passwords have no more than read-only privilege to the data. If these credentials are not the user's own (frequently used) user name and password, you'll find users writing down credential information on yellow sticky notes that they adhere to their monitors or to the undersides of their keyboards. We've also seen and reported to Microsoft that encrypted forms of prompted credentials are frequently left behind in the browser cache and can be replayed against other reports. Microsoft told us this will be addressed in Service Pack 2. Of course, this defeats the security intention and makes it easy to crack into the system—just ask David Lightman.[1] Users will also use your name in vain whenever they have to waste time reentering mistyped passwords—especially if they are the more complex, "strong"[2] variety. Don't forget that if you haven't installed SSL on the Report Server website, then user-provided

---

[1] In "War Games," Matthew Broderick's character finds the school's passwords taped to the secretary's desk.

[2] See this article for more information on how to create strong passwords: `www.microsoft.com/security/articles/password.asp`

credentials will traverse the network between the browser and the IIS server in an easily sniffable form, which is another security breach big enough to drive a truck through. While prompted credentials are okay for some situations, you can't use them for Snapshots or Subscriptions because the report is executed by the Reporting Services Windows service. This is because the service cannot respond to a prompt for credentials. For these (and several other specific cases), this means credentials must be provided when the report description is deployed.

Credentials Stored Securely in the Report Server

In the interest of convenience over security (and arguably more security as users are prone to write passwords down), and in the interest of usability in the case of Snapshots and Subscriptions and certain other situations, you'll tend more and more toward stored credentials. When using stored credentials, you'll also want to check that you've taken sensible steps to ensure your credentials are *really* secure. To appreciate the security implications, it helps to be aware of what goes on under the covers when the system validates the credentials. Credentials and Connection strings that you store with the Report Manager are encrypted with the Report Server's symmetric key, and stored in the DataSource table in the Report Server database in their encrypted form. The Reporting Services architects at Microsoft would rather that you didn't go poking around in the Report Server database—and we sympathize with them because the Report Server databases are "unsupported implementation details" that Microsoft can (and probably will) change at any time. However, attackers given half a chance will focus the full force of their attention (at least initially) on trying to directly manipulate and drill into the DataSource table. It's the most vulnerable portal to the database and the data jewels it contains. If an attacker can make direct changes to the DataSource table, the attacker can hijack or misappropriate *any* of the stored credentials, be they stored credentials associated with shared or custom Data Sources. An attacker *with access to this table* but no access to the symmetric key might not be able to easily decrypt the credentials. However, there is little need to have the symmetric key—it is a trivial exercise to copy encrypted credential rows in that table to new rows, and then link to other managed reports in the Report Server Catalog table. At this point, the attacker is effectively able to execute any T-SQL in the context of the user whose encrypted credentials are stored in the Data Source. If you are remiss and store your SA credentials in a Data Source, the attacker can get control of your Report Server SQL Server, lock you out, and watch as you furtively tap on the glass from the outside. Even if you have not stored SA credentials, the attacker still has access to all the data, and can make changes to any data that the credentials expose. So, a lot hinges on the security of the Report Server's DataSource table.

It's vital that you protect the DataSource table.

Security of the DataSource Table

In case you didn't get it by now, the DataSource table is where some of the Keys of the Kingdom are stored—hopefully only limited-access read-only keys. Only the Report Server and Windows and web services have any business directly interacting with the DataSource table. The User account that these processes use to access the Report Server databases is governed by one of the installation steps you may recall from Chapter 2. Prior to installation, we strongly suggest that you create a special Domain user account for these services to use. This user account is only used to (and should *only* be permitted to) access the Report Server database. It should not be used by any other user. (Alternatively, you can use a SQL Login credentials account, but if you do so, make sure you are using TLS Encryption with SQL Server). For our installation, we created an account called RSExec and used that account during Reporting Services installation, as shown in Figure 5.1.

Following this step, the installation wizard creates a SQL Server database role called RSExecRole. Note that this role name is fixed by the installation and has no relationship to the name of the Domain User Account or SQL Server Account that you might use—so if you call your execution account SQLRSExec instead of RSExec, the role created will still be called RSExecRole. This special role is created in the ReportServer, ReportServerTempDB, and msdb databases, and the execution account (in our case RSExec) is made a member. The RSExecRole is granted permissions on all user objects in the ReportServer and ReportServerTempDB databases, and on a handful of objects in the msdb database. What all this means is that members of the RSExecRole should be the only accounts that can directly access and manipulate the DataSource table.

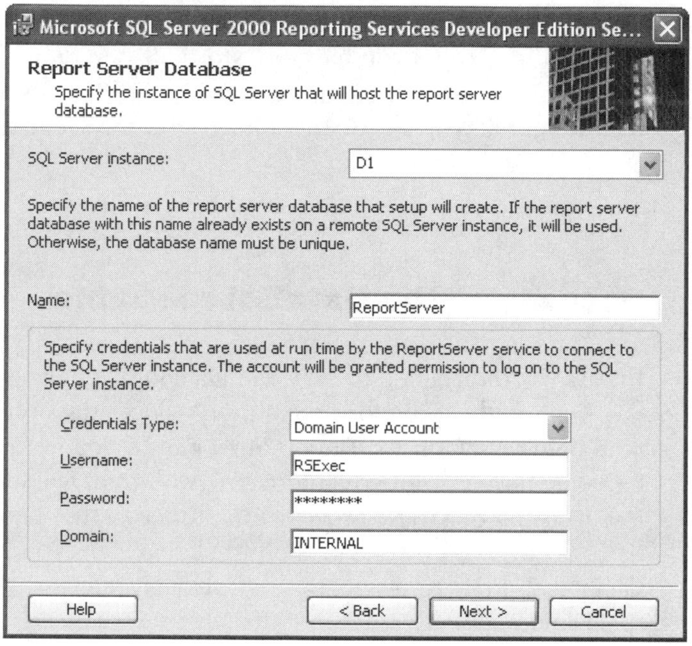

Figure 5.1 Specifying the Special RSExec User Account During Installation

Perhaps now is a good opportunity to take the Enterprise Manager for a spin and review the accounts that have direct permission to manipulate the DataSource table. By default, there should be no individual accounts or domain groups assigned. What you should have is just the Reporting Services' RSExecRole assigned with complete rights, as shown in Figure 5.2.

Assuming that you're still on the rails and only the RSExecRole is assigned, you need to check which User Accounts and Domain Groups are assigned to the RSExecRole—it's these accounts that have direct access to the Reporting Services Database tables.

In Figure 5.3, we can see that only the Domain Account INTERNAL\RSExec is a member of the RSExecRole. That's good.

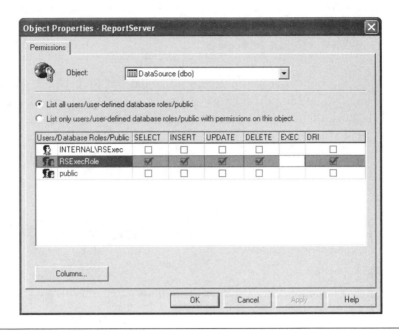

Figure 5.2 SQL Enterprise Manager Setting Access Rights to the RSExecRole

Figure 5.3 SQL Enterprise Manager Examining the RSExecRole Users

Possible Problem Membership for the RSExecRole

If you didn't listen to our installation advice and you've already installed Reporting Services before reading Chapter 2, or during the installation you selected to use the Service Account (as shown in Figure 5.4), when you look at the membership of the RSExecRole, you'll either see the ASPNET machine account or the NT AUTHORITY\Network Service Account. Not good.

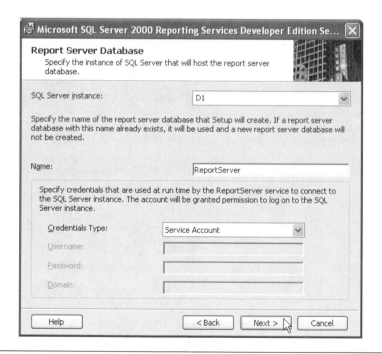

Figure 5.4 Reporting Services Installation Wizard Prompting for Credentials

The big deal here is that anyone you permit to deploy ASP.NET applications can also deploy a program that on their behalf can directly access the Report Server databases. In particular, this account can directly manipulate the DataSource table containing the Keys to the Kingdom. This might not be a problem to you at all—you might be in a situation where your ASP.NET developers are the same trusted folks who develop your reports. But if this is not the case, and you think that it's a problem, you can follow these steps to retrofit a Domain User Account to be used by Reporting Services:

1. Create a minimally privileged RSEXEC user account in your domain, set a strong password, and consider the policy for changing the password. Remember, if you don't set the "User cannot change password" option, that account will be subject to your domain policy and the password will eventually need to be changed.
2. Remove all accounts from the RSExecRoles in the ReportServer, ReportServerTempDB, and msdb databases. Note that the msdb database is used for the SQL Server Agent jobs—i.e., the scheduled report actions.
3. Remove all login accounts (other than the dbo account) from the ReportServer and the ReportServerTempDB databases. Be more careful about what you remove from the msdb database because there may be perfectly valid reasons for the ASPNET account or the NT AUTHORITY\Network Service Account to have permission to access the msdb database.
4. Using the Enterprise Manager's Security Logins, add the RSEXEC Domain Account to the ReportServer, ReportServerTempDB, and msdb databases and ensure that this is made a member of the RSExecRole in each of those databases.

We are now ready to hook up Reporting Services to use the new RSEXEC account by using the command-line tool RSCONFIG.EXE. You may recall from Chapter 2 that the RSCONFIG.EXE tool encrypts the credentials for the User Account and DSN Connection string that both the Reporting Services Windows and web services use, and stores the encrypted forms in RSReportServer.config file (located in *Program Files\Microsoft SQL Server\MSSQL \Reporting Services\ReportServer*). At the command line, a typical usage of RSCONFIG.EXE to set this reconfiguration would be:

```
rsconfig -c -s <Server> -d ReportServer -a Windows -u <Domain>\RSEXEC -p <Password>
```

Integrated Security

At this point, you've ensured that security is tightened down on the precious DataSource table, or at least think you know with whom you are sharing the information—you might think that you are in the clear. Not so fast. You yourself could be the next problem. If you are one of these folks who wander round networks with full Admin privileges and if you administer your Report Server with an account that belongs to the BUILTIN\Administrators group, your account is an ideal target for an attack. Consider that members of the BUILTIN\Administrators group are (by definition) capable of direct access to the tables in the ReportServer database—including the DataSource table. However, more importantly, members of the BUILTIN\Administrators group can usually do just about anything on a SQL Server through their implied membership in the SysAdmin SQL Server Role. The corollary of this is that should a Trojan report be written so that it's configured to use Integrated Security, and that if a report is executed by any member of the BUILTIN\Administrators group, bad T-SQL can be executed in the context of a sysadmin. Yipes!

The possibility that spurious or malicious T-SQL might be embedded in a managed report is even more dangerous if you consider that when you access a report with the Report Manager, it is immediately executed—while you stare at the animated spin wheel and the Generating Report message appears. However, if you always use the Report Manager in Show Details view, you get an opportunity to edit the properties without executing the report first. In everyday use of Reporting Services by users just accessing their reports, the default Hide Details view is more desirable. However, in the context of an administrator, you possibly don't want the report to execute immediately—especially if the report is a potential Trojan using Integrated Security just waiting for an administrator (or a user with elevated privileges) to come along. There is no way to view the T-SQL a report executes by using the Report Manager. As a conscientious administrator, you should, therefore, download any new report description and inspect its RDL before running it, or at the very least ensure that the report is not using a custom Data Source with Integrated Security.

While you could create your own application for Report Management, this is a bit extreme. A quicker workaround may be to revisit the Reporting Services Roles discussed in the last chapter and consider making the BUILTIN\Administrators group a member of a Role similar to the Content Manager role—just remove the View Reports task from that Role. That would mean that as an Administrator you would not be able to execute and view a report. In Chapter 4, we showed you how to execute a browser Report Manager session as a different user so that removing the rights for an Administrator to view reports should not overly inconvenience an Administrator. In addition, you possibly also need to think about which folders that role is assigned to, and which users or groups have the ability to adjust the security. You'll also need to think carefully about the permission set granted to the My Reports folder of each user.

Don't think that the potential risk of Integrated Security is restricted to administrators—a Trojan report targeting a user with read privileges higher than those of the author of the report could be the target. This enables the attacker to siphon off privileged information when the user with higher privileges runs the report.

In general, we like Integrated Security and use it extensively with ordinary data access applications; indeed, we will be showing you in Chapter 6 where Integrated Security is beneficial for developers in the Report Designer in Visual Studio .NET 2003, but we need to point out that there are potential issues with using Integrated Security in deployed report scenarios. Having worked in some extremely hostile and competitive environments, we'd be concerned about enabling Integrated Security in reports as a general rule. In Service Pack 1, Microsoft introduced a new Report Server system property called *EnableIntegratedSecurity*. For backward compatibility, this is defaulted to True, so by default Integrated Security will work with an installation, which means that by default the system is insecure. There is no Report Manager user interface for setting this property—you have to dive into either SOAP programming or into Report Script to set it. Microsoft also promised to supply a script file and some documentation about how to use it, but we didn't get to see that before we went to press. So Listing 5.1 shows our script to disable Integrated Security using the *EnableIntegratedSecurity* system property.

Listing 5.1 The Script File to Disable Integrated Security

```
Sub Main()
  Dim props(0) As [Property]
  props(0) = New   [Property]
  props(0).Name = "EnableIntegratedSecurity"
  props(0).Value = False
  rs.SetSystemProperties(props)
End Sub
```

If you create such a script in Notepad and save it as DisableISec.rss, you can execute the script from the command prompt:

```
rs.exe -i DisableISec.rss -s https://<YourServer>/ReportServer
```

You may also find that you need to restart IIS with a call to IISRESET from the command prompt to get the Report Server to take notice of the change.

This approach is all very well and good and does disable Integrated Security—for *all* Data Sources. If you implement a custom Data Processing extension of your own that you are convinced can safely use Integrated Security without fear of Trojan misuse, disabling Integrated Security across the whole Report Server could frustrate you and be quite problematic. The unsupported way of resolving this is to leave Integrated Security enabled but remove all Data Sources that use it and then put a trigger on the DataSource table in the ReportServer database. That calls ROLLBACK if the creation or update of an Integrated Security Data Source is attempted, unless it's being done for your custom Data Processing extension. Listing 5.2 show such a trigger, which disables Integrated Security for all Data Sources other than for Data Sources that use our custom Event Log Data Processing extension.

Listing 5.2 Our Unsupported Technique for Disabling Integrated Security on All Data Sources Apart from the Custom DataSource "EventLog"

```
CREATE TRIGGER DisableIntegratedSecurity
ON dbo.DataSource
FOR INSERT, UPDATE
AS
IF UPDATE(CredentialRetrieval)
BEGIN
   SELECT CredentialRetrieval
   FROM inserted
   WHERE (CredentialRetrieval = 3)
   AND (Extension <>'EVENTLOG')
   IF @@ROWCOUNT >0
   BEGIN
      RAISERROR ('Integrated Security is disabled for DataSource type', 18, 1)
      ROLLBACK TRANSACTION
   END
END
```

Transport Layer Security (TLS)

Using SSL (HTTPS) to communicate to a Report Server's IIS over the network is a great idea. As we've discussed, SSL encrypts the network traffic between browser and IIS server. If the SQL Server is on the same physical machine as the Reporting Services, there is less concern for someone intercepting the Reporting Services' interaction with the Report Server database. However, if the Report Server database and IIS components are on *different* machines, installing a server certificate for the SQL Server to use enables encrypted communication between the IIS and the SQL Server. This option takes advantage of Transport Layer Security—*TLS encryption*. You also need to consider that while you may secure the connection to the Report Server database, you might want to secure the connections made from the Reporting Services to *other* DBMSs—especially if the source data is not on the same DBMS as the Report Server databases. If you're querying data held in remote SQL Servers, those servers can also have server certificates installed. In this case, you can set the force protocol encryption option in the SQL Server network configuration settings. This encrypts *all* traffic between the server and all clients that support encryption. However, it also consumes extra CPU cycles and degrades performance (albeit slightly). On the other hand, a report can request encryption even though the force protocol encryption option is not set on the server. This is done by including "Encrypt=YES" in the Connection string of the Data Source. However, don't try to do this when building a Connection string in the Visual Studio .NET Report Designer. This can only be done when editing a Data Source's Connection string in the Report Manager. We suggest you consult our website for more details on how to configure TLS—in case you have trouble sleeping some night.

Auditing

Some organizations get quite paranoid about maintaining an audit trail of who accessed and changed data in their systems. While Reporting Services does include an ExecutionLog or a DTS project to interrogate the ExecutionLog, this log would not keep track of the actual T-SQL executed. If your customer or company has reached this level of paranoia, you might like to check out Lumigent's (www.lumigent.com) Integra and LogExplorer products. The LogExplorer is able to interrogate the Transaction Logs, revealing all T-SQL that resulted in a state change in the database—to which the Transaction Log belongs—along with on which connection (and thus which client machine) and under which user context the T-SQL was executed. The Integra product goes one step further and also enables SELECTS to be logged.

Summary

We took short a tour around the precipice of some security issues—you should be aware that by design managed reports need to execute custom and specific code right in the heart of your potentially business-critical information store. Ultimately, you need to consider whom you are going to trust to execute the reports and see the data. Reporting

Services provides you with the tools to have a secure deployment and to limit access to shared Data Sources and reports through a sophisticated role-based security model that we examined in Chapter 4. We also discussed locking down the Report Server database access to a specific Domain User Account, as we advised in Chapter 2. However, this time we hope that the content had some more poignant relevance and context. We also explained how you might retro-fit your security configuration using the `RSCONFIG.EXE` command-line tool if you didn't initially install Reporting Services to use a single account for Report Server database access. We also touched on the exposure that Integrated Security brings, and suggested various approaches you can take to deal with this issue. In addition we mentioned that we have at least one unsupported tool to disable Integrated Security, available for registered readers to download from our website. We finished the chapter with a short discussion of TLS, and how you can install and make use of it both for the Report Server databases and for any other remote SQL Server Report database.

CHAPTER 6

Building Data Sources and DataSets

This chapter is all about data—how to connect to it, how to fetch it, and how to manage it once it arrives and before you pass it to a report to display it. We'll also talk about security and performance as well as developer performance and productivity because these issues pertain to Data Sources and DataSets. We'll provide a lot of great tips and techniques here that can make your reports render more quickly and your Report Server scale to more users. We'll show you how to build efficient queries using dynamic SQL or by calling stored procedures; focus the queries with user-selectable parameters; sort the results (or sort the rowset before it arrives); and filter "in" the rows you need (or select just the rows and columns you need). In Chapter 7, we'll show you how to lay out your data in a report.

Data Sources and DataSets

As we discussed in Chapter 1, data can be extracted from any data source exposed by a .NET, OLE DB, and ODBC provider or driver. You point to the desired data source through one or more Reporting Services Data Sources. If you're familiar with ADO, DAO, RDO, ODBC, or OLE DB data access programming, you can think of a Data Source as simply a way to persist a Connection string—including the credentials and other key-value pairs. If you aren't a data access developer, don't worry; we provide all the guidance you'll need to build and deploy Data Sources and DataSets. Because we expect that our readers are working in a variety of disciplines, we want to make sure that you understand the terms and technology Reporting Services uses.

What Is a Data Source?

A Reporting Services RDS Data Source contains properties that determine what data provider is to be used when fetching the data. Data Sources can also address data providers that you can write yourself in addition to those built into Reporting Services. A Data Source includes a Connection string that contains a pointer to where the data is located (usually the name of the server and an initial catalog), any credentials needed to validate access to the data, and additional properties. All of the Data Source properties and settings are captured and managed through dialogs in the Visual Studio .NET Reporting Services Report Designer add-in, by directly manipulating the RDL file, through the Report Manager, or by using one of the third-party tools.[1] As we've discussed repeatedly, and we'll discuss again, it's also possible to create and manage "shared" data sources that several reports can use. But as we talked about in Chapter 5, there are distinct advantages and disadvantages to using shared data sources.

Data Sources can either be shared among all of the reports in a project, or attached directly to the report RDL file—embedded in the report. We'll discuss how to use both of these options later in this chapter. Clearly, shared Data Sources have an appeal in that it's far easier to change the source of your report data by altering a single shared Data Source than by visiting each report in a project to alter an embedded Data Source.

---

[1]   We provide links to various third-party tools on our website.

NOTE *Using SSPI Security* An important point we need to pound in before we begin in earnest is that although it's okay for developers to use SSPI (Integrated Security) and Shared Data Sources to create and tune their reports, SSPI should *only* be used during development in the Report Designer. We *do not* recommend that these SSPI shared Data Sources ever be deployed to the Report Server. To make this work correctly, we also recommend that you setup a suite of shared Data Sources beforehand that use Windows login security—whose credentials reference specific role-based logins. For example, you might create logins for specific departments or groups within the company that have different rights to the underlying data. If this security configuration is not familiar to you, go back to Chapter 5 and review the discussion there or talk it over with your DBA—assuming you're still on speaking terms. When developers deploy their reports, Reporting Services prevents the shared Data Source from being overwritten—unless the developer intentionally overrides this behavior. To ensure that this does not take place by accident and to prevent a Data Source that's being deployed from using Integrated Security, we provide a trigger to selectively disable Integrated Security. Service Pack 1 permits you to turn off Integrated Security, although by default it's permitted. We'll walk you through setting up your shared Data Sources in the next section of this chapter.

Chapter 5 also showed you how important it is to maintain data security and how the supplied Data Source credentials play a key role in many data-protection schemes. It's very important that credentials be managed correctly—we'll show you additional techniques in this chapter.

What Is a DataSet?

A DataSet is simply the object that holds the SQL query Command text used to return a one-dimensional set of rows to the Report Processor. The query's Command text can contain:

- A SQL query that returns a single rowset—usually a single SELECT.
- The name of a stored procedure that returns a single rowset.

- The name of a View.
- The name of a database table (when the provider supports this—as when working with JET databases).

DataSets also have a number of properties that you can alter using the Report Designer or by modifying the RDL directly. A report might define several DataSets—some used to provide query parameter lookup values, and others to provide the data to display in the reports. Each DataSet can target its own Data Source, which means reports can be generated from several disparate (or related) databases or other sources of data. The DataSet query can (and often does) contain one or more query parameters. DataSets can be designed in the Visual Studio .NET[2] Report Designer in the report's Data view or in your favorite SQL editor—even in Visual Notepad. DataSet objects define SQL queries using syntax specific to their data sources. This means the SQL might be different for SQL Server, Oracle, JET, or other data sources.

NOTE *DataSets Aren't DataSets* Reporting Services uses its own rendition of the "DataSet" to manage queries and retrieve rowsets from the Data Source. Microsoft documentation refers to the RDL DataSet element as a "Dataset," which only adds to the confusion. Reporting Services DataSets should not be confused with ADO.NET DataSet objects.[3]

Because the Reporting Services DataSet is different from the ADO.NET DataSet object, today you won't be able to take an existing DataSet or DataTable object and pass it to Reporting Services, without having to write your own or use a third-party Data Processing extension. However, it's not that hard to extract the query from a DataAdapter SelectCommand and use it to create a Reporting Services DataSet. In Chapter 13, we'll show you how to create your own Data Source extension that exposes an ADO.NET

---

[2] Remember, the Report Designer add-in requires Visual Studio .NET 2003 or Visual Basic .NET 2003.

[3] Apparently, Microsoft ran out of good names to use for this type of object—at the rate they're using them, we're not surprised.

DataReader to Reporting Services to give you more flexibility in data retrieval. We expect that in future versions (SQL Server 2005) this won't be as big a problem. By then we expect the two technologies to have merged.

Building DataSets from Stored Procedures

We've found the easiest way to create queries for reports is to start from basic SELECT statements. Yes, DBAs don't usually like to expose the base tables to users, and for good reason. It's usually much more secure and scalable to expose rights-protected views and stored procedures.

That said, you may find that some of the stored procedures that you use won't necessarily work as expected with Reporting Services if they return more than one rowset. That's because Reporting Services does not know how to deal with multiple resultset (in which multiple rowsets are returned) stored procedures—it uses only the first resultset that contains a rowset. If you try to execute a stored procedure that generates more than one resultset, the Reporting Services engine steps over any resultsets that don't contain a rowset (such as when an action query is executed) as it looks for the first resultset that has a rowset. If the stored procedure returns more than one rowset, subsequent rowsets are ignored and there is no easy way to get to them, and you might also waste processing resources on data that's never seen.

We've discussed (between ourselves) several strategies to pick off these additional rowsets, but the solutions all require considerable programming—mostly in the Data Processing extensions or using smoke and mirrors in T-SQL. You'll probably have much more success rewriting those stored procedures that return multiple resultsets into several procedures, each returning a single resultset (or possibly a set of views). Remember that these objects must be sewn into the database protection scheme in order for the report login "user" to access them. This means you'll often want to setup specific SQL Server roles to manage permissions for these query objects. Today, you'll have to use SQL Enterprise Manager to do this.

Preparing the Development Server and Workstation

How you build and deploy your reports is really up to you, but we suggest you take several configuration steps before starting to develop reports in earnest. These tips can make the process easier for you and the rest of your development team. They also ensure that you follow our guidelines in regard to using SSPI (Integrated Security) with shared Data Sources:

- Create a deployment folder and set specific permissions on it to keep users from interfering with your work as you try to configure a report. The general idea here is to create a "scratch pad" folder on a file server. This is where reports can be authored, tuned, and tested before the final report file is passed to the release folder.
- Create a suite of Data Sources. By spending a bit of time preparing your development workstation and production server to cooperate, you can save yourself (and those who consume your reports) a lot of trouble.
- Create mirrored SSPI (Integrated Security) shared Data Sources on the development workstation that have the same names in the scratch pad folder on the server. The development workstation Data Sources use Integrated Security and are almost identical to Data Sources on the server—of course, server Data Sources should (hopefully) use securely stored and encrypted credentials—and *never* Integrated Security.

Let's go over these configuration suggestions in more detail.

Creating a Deployment Folder

In Chapter 3, we saw that Reporting Services lends itself to deploying reports directly from the Report Designer into a folder in the Report Server where your users can select and execute them with the Report Manager. At first this might seem like a good idea, but many features of a report's configuration cannot be configured from or with the Report Designer (as we discussed in Chapter 4). For example, stored Windows credentials in Data Sources, or execution, history, and subscription properties require configuration with the Report Manager. This means that after a report has been deployed, the report developer or administrator may have a number of properties to configure with the Report Manager before releasing the report for general access.

To prevent users from seeing our works in progress, we find it useful to create a "development" folder—a kind of staging folder or scratch pad on the Report Server. We grant permissions on that folder such that only the report developers and administrators can see it in the Report Manager. This means that reports can be deployed to this staging post-development folder before the report is fully ready for users to execute. Here the report's properties can be fully configured in peace and quiet without users getting in the way, with those time-consuming telephone-support calls....

"Hey, Bob, do you know the new sales report isn't working?" To which an exasperated Bob screams to the nth caller since uploading the report two minutes earlier, *"Just give me a chance to finish it!"* Ring! Ring!

When all the properties on a report have been configured, you can use the Report Manager to move the report from the staging folder into its final production resting place—a folder in which the report can be seen and executed by users with sufficient rights. When you read Chapter 9¾ on SOAP, you'll see how to deploy reports and configure them without using the Report Manager— either with a .NET program that uses the SOAP interface or through the report scripting tool, rs.exe.

Yes, you might want to use the site-wide MyReports feature because it gives every user the ability to create reports. This feature also provides each user with a private folder in which reports can be deployed. The problem is that the MyReports feature is a site-wide feature and either everybody has it or nobody does. This can be a problem if you do not want all users to be able to create reports. Additionally, sharing MyReports folders among users can be problematic if you have a collaborative development environment.

Deploying Tuned Reports

But typically, mechanics don't own as much Microsoft stock given to them by their previous employers, Bill, and they also only get dirty in all that grime and oil. That said, I suppose I could turn your stomach with stories about what was in the keyboards of some of the people I've worked with. You needed to sterilize your hands after looking at their keyboards, let alone actually touching them, which would have probably required wearing a biohazard suit if Health and Safety ever learned of it.

–Peter

If you find that you need to make changes to the report once it's configured, you can move the report back from the production folder to the staging folder on the server. This is like checking the car in for service at the garage where the mechanics (who get paid more than most of us) tinker with and tune the car before returning it to the road. If you follow this route, all the report properties that you set with the Report Manager remain intact, even when you upload a *newer* version from the Report Designer that overwrites a previously uploaded report.

A rule of thumb in overwriting a report is that properties set by the Report Manager take precedence over properties set by the Report Designer. For example, if you set properties in the Data Source using the Report Manager, subsequently change the same Data Source in the Report Designer, and redeploy it and overwrite the deployed report, the properties originally set in the Report Manager are retained. This means the existing (modified) Data Source is left unchanged. We've seen that this behavior often surprises developers because the changes they've made in the Visual Studio .NET Report Designer don't propagate to the report—even when it is overwritten. We asked Microsoft about this behavior and were told that properties configured through the Report Manager are likely to have been configured by an administrator or DBA rather than a developer, and that administrator's configurations should always take priority. Our view is that eventually (perhaps in the next version) there should be the ability to configure all properties both in the Report Designer and Report Manager—and that the ability to configure certain properties ought to be controlled by specific (new) Task rights.

Creating a Suite of Data Sources

We've talked about Data Sources several times in earlier chapters. In this chapter, we show you how to integrate these into the reports at design time. Be aware that the Report Designer doesn't permit you to create Data Sources that use stored or prompted Windows credentials. If you've read Chapter 5, you'll know why we're not wildly enthusiastic about deploying shared or custom Data Sources that use Integrated (SSPI) Security. If there is very tight control over who can create reports, if those people can be completely trusted, and if those users never leave their terminals unattended, we would look the other way if you use SSPI Security.

Creating Mirrored Data Sources

We suggest that the best credentials management scheme is to create a suite of shared Data Sources that use stored Windows credentials, and that you place these shared Data Sources in the development staging folder. Their use should be limited to a set of accounts in the domain that have (for the most part) read-only access to specific database objects (databases, views, tables, stored procedures, or perhaps even down to column level) and no more. You must bear in mind the users who are permitted to view these shared Data Sources. Remember, anyone who can see these shared data sources and link a report to them can execute T-SQL on your server under the context of the user account stored in the data source. It's safer if the permissions applied to the development staging folder expose only these shared data sources to members of your developer group. Recall that if you are going to allow any data source in your system that uses Integrated Security, there is an opening for a Trojan report to harvest and/or use those stored credentials and worse! We've also heard of a variation on the Trojan report that uses a large wooden rabbit instead of a horse,[4] but this problem appears to be limited to remote mountainous regions that don't yet have electricity, let alone Internet access.

Returning to the suite of shared Data Sources, it's helpful to manually create the suite with the Report Manager in the development staging folder. That's because when a report is deployed from the Report Designer, Reporting Services tries to create any shared Data Sources that the report needs. That is, unless one or more shared Data Sources that have the same name are already present in that folder. In this case, the Report Designer won't try to overwrite the Data Source unless you've set the report project's deployment properties to *OverwriteDataSources*—the default is not to overwrite existing shared Data Sources.

---

[4] You might need to watch "Monty Python and the Holy Grail" to understand that. Search Google for *Holy+Grail+Wooden+Rabbit+Scene+8.*

For a number of reasons, we've found that it's much more convenient for developers to use shared Windows NT Integrated Security Data Sources in the Report Designer. As long as they don't deploy them to the Report Server, these developers can remain on our good side.[5] The problems we've identified with stored credentials in the Report Designer are:

- They can only be SQL credentials. To be secure would mean those SQL Servers unlocked by the credentials need to support Transport Layer Security (TLS). Basically, TLS encrypts the data being sent to and from SQL Server—it's like SSL for Tabular Data Stream (TDS). (See our website at www.SQLReportingServices.NET for details on setting up TLS.)
- The credentials are encrypted using the DPAPI libraries. There is nothing wrong with this approach, it's just that the credentials are linked to a specific user and machine. This means that it's not possible to copy a project folder created by one developer for another developer to work on without passing over the credentials in plaintext. Because the second developer works on another machine under a different user account, his or her machine won't be able to decrypt the credentials encrypted under the original user account on a different machine. To make matters more complex, given that the credentials are encrypted and stored in a project configuration file, if you copy or move the report definition RDL file to another project, you'll also have to re-create the credentials.
- Stored credentials are not persisted to Visual SourceSafe, which means developers must keep track of the credentials manually. Perhaps they should write them on the underside of their keyboards?

Basically, this means that your developer's user or group accounts will have to be given permissions on the DBMS objects the developer needs to access to create the report.

---

[5] There are tools on our website, www.SQLReportingServices.NET (in the premium area), that can prevent Integrated Security from being used in any data sources in the Report Server.

Building New Reports from Scratch

In Chapter 3, we used the Report wizard to walk through creating reports, so the concepts and process involved in developing a report using the wizard should be reasonably familiar to you. In this section, we're going to repeat the process of creating a report, but this time we're going to do it without the training wheels—without the Report wizard. This process might seem harder at first, but we've found that it's really easier to use this technique—especially after having created a custom Report Template, as we'll discuss in Chapter 9. These custom templates take all the drudgery out of creating standardized reports.

The visual aspects of a report are governed by how report controls are laid out and bound to the DataSet fields in the Layout view in the Report Designer. After previewing a report in Preview view, the report's project properties can be configured and the report can be deployed to a Report Server where, after final tweaking with the Report Manager, users can access it.

Creating a New Report Project

In Visual Studio .NET, you can create a new blank report project by selecting a new Business Intelligence Projects project (File | New Project) and then selecting the Report Project template (as shown in Figure 6.1), or by choosing the Report Project wizard, as we did in Chapter 3. If you don't have Business Intelligence Projects listed as an available Project Type, the Reporting Services Report Designer is not properly installed. Refer back to Chapter 2 to review how to install the Visual Studio .NET Report Designer add-in. We'll show you how to create your own Report Templates in Chapter 9.

It's a good idea to name your report project at this step to ensure you can find it later. It's tough to figure out which report you were working on if you use the default "ReportX" name. For this example, we named the report Development and placed it in the *C:\Company Reports* path.

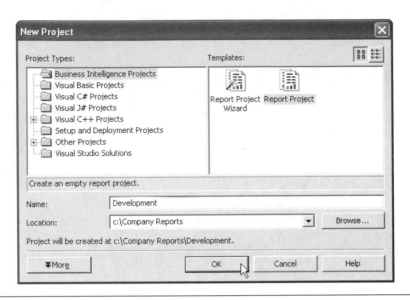

Figure 6.1   Starting the Report Designer with a Report Project Template

The Report Project template loads the Visual Studio .NET Report Designer and creates a blank report Visual Studio .NET project. At this point, you can add new, shared Data Sources and reports. Figure 6.2 shows the Solution Explorer configured with our new report project.

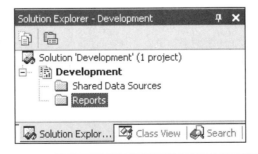

Figure 6.2   The Visual Studio .NET Solution Explorer with Our New Report

Once Visual Studio .NET has created the Business Intelligence Project, you're ready to add your first report to the project. Next, right-click on the Reports folder in the Solution Explorer and choose Add New Item (as shown in Figure 6.3) or press Ctrl+Shift+A. No, don't pick Add New Report from this menu unless you want to launch the Report wizard. Doing this tripped us up several times, so we suggest you create your own shortcut key or custom toolbar to permit creating a new report without having to click through three levels of menus.[6]

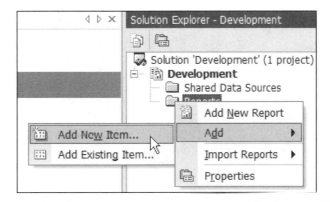

Figure 6.3 Adding a New Report Item Before Choosing a Report Template

The Add New Item dialog (shown in Figure 6.4) permits you to choose the base Report Template, choose a Report Template you created yourself (we'll show you how to create one in Chapter 9), or import an existing report. You should also use this dialog to name your report, but you can set this property later if you forget.

---

[6] To create such a custom toolbar in Visual Studio .NET, right-click on any toolbar in Visual Studio .NET, select Customize on the Toolbars tab, and click the New button. Give the new toolbar a name, and look over your screen for a new blank toolbar—it'll probably be to the right of the modal dialog box. Select the Commands tab on the dialog, from the Categories list select Project, and from the Commands list scroll down searching until you find Add New Item (the commands are not in alphabetical order). Then simply drag this command onto your new custom toolbar, and select Close on the dialog.

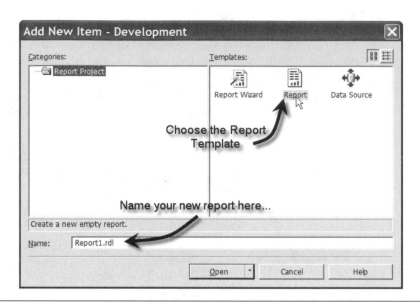

Figure 6.4 Choosing a Report Template and Naming the New Report

Once you choose a Report Template, the Report Designer is loaded and the familiar (at least it should be by now) Report IDE appears (as shown in Figure 6.5).

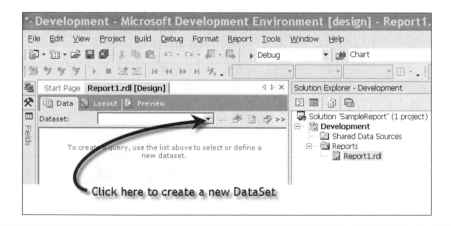

Figure 6.5 The Report Designer IDE Ready to Add a New DataSct

Guide me!

You can walk through this process with the Guide me! video.

If you click on the Dataset down arrow in Figure 6.5, the dialog shown in Figure 6.6 is displayed. If there aren't any shared Data Sources defined for the report, you're asked to define a new Data Link first, which builds a Connection string used by the report-specific Data Source and begins the process of creating an embedded report Data Source. We recommend use of shared Data Sources, so we won't go down that path. Instead, we encourage you to create a shared Data Source.

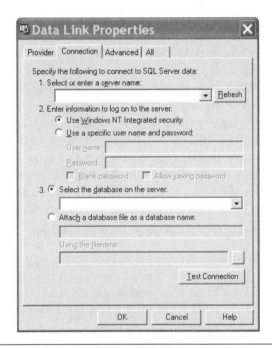

Figure 6.6 The Data Link Properties Dialog Ready to Build a New Connection String

Creating Shared Data Sources

Creating a new, shared Data Source is pretty intuitive, and we explained this in Chapter 3, so you shouldn't have any problems doing so at this point. Start by right-clicking the Shared Data Sources folder in the Solution Explorer and choosing Add New Data Source to pull up the Data Link Properties dialog that creates the shared Data Source Connection string (as shown in Figure 6.6). Shared Data Source Connection strings are named after the database referenced in the Connection string (if an initial catalog is specified) and are stored in the Report Server database. Yep, it's a great idea to specify an initial catalog when creating any Data Source. Otherwise, you'll get the default database specified by the DBA when the login is first created. Don't forget to set the *Application Name* property too. In time, you'll probably find it helpful to read Chapter 7 and create a set of Data Source templates that mirror the suite of Data Sources you've created for your Report Server's staging folder—that way you'll be able to choose a preconfigured Data Source.

If you add a shared Data Source to the project for use only in the Report Designer as we suggested (particularly if you are targeting a SQL Server), you'll find it helpful to use Windows NT Integrated Security (SSPI). As we described earlier in this chapter, we suggest you name the Data Source using the same name as a Data Source already configured in the target deployment folder in the Report Server, and that you do not overwrite Data Sources when deploying.

Choosing a Data Processing Extension

When initially creating a Data Source, you must first decide which Data Processing extension[7] the report is to use. If you right-click on the shared Data Source you just created, you'll see these extensions listed on the General tab on the Data Source dialog under Type as shown in Figure 6.7. Each of these Data Processing extensions uses its own Connection string, and the Report Designer does its best to construct one for you based on the Connection string returned from the Data Link Properties dialog launched when you click Edit....

---

[7] Data Processing extensions are .NET assemblies that form part of Reporting Services implementation under the hood. They implement a subset of interfaces exposed by the ADO.NET data provider. We take a brief look at custom Data Processing extensions in Chapter 7.

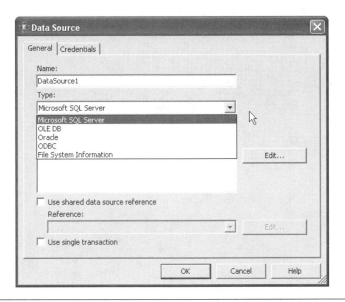

Figure 6.7 Choosing a Data Processing Extension for a Data Source

By default, the Report Designer assumes you're connecting to a SQL Server database, so if you're using JET or Analysis Services, you'll need to choose an appropriate OLE DB provider from the Data Link Properties dialog. Be sure to choose a provider that matches the version of the data source. You'll also need to use an OLE DB provider when accessing older versions of SQL Server (version 6.5 or earlier) or other data sources not supported by a .NET managed provider. Remember, each provider (especially the OLE DB providers) has its own peculiarities. For example, if you try to access a CSV (comma-delimited) file, you'll have to consider unique deployment and security issues that are dealt with automatically when you use SQL Server.

To choose a Reporting Services Data Processing extension (other than SQL Server, which is the default), use the Data Link Properties dialog to specify the server location, credentials, and initial catalog, as shown in Figure 6.8. It returns a Connection string adapted to match the Data Processing extension you've selected.

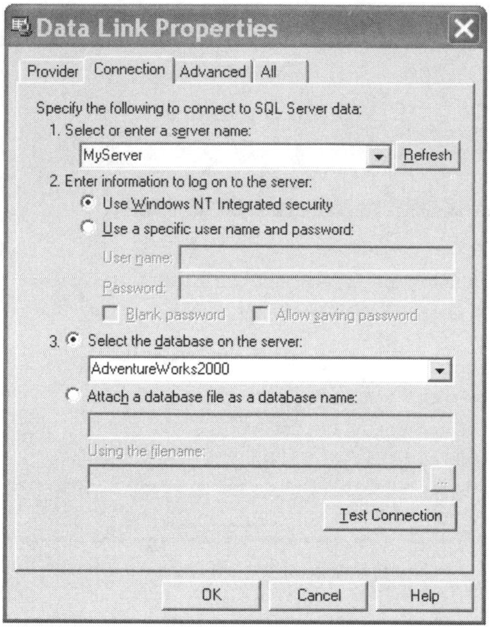

Figure 6.8 The Data Link Properties Dialog Used to Address Your Data Source

Once you click OK on the Data Link Properties dialog, you can right-click on the Shared Data Sources list in the Solution Explorer and choose Open. This exposes the Shared Data Source dialog, as shown in Figure 6.9. Use the dropdown list under Type to select the Data Processing extension you wish to use. If you choose OLE DB, your Connection string is morphed to the correct syntax; but if you choose ODBC, you'll have to enter your own ODBC Connection string or click Edit... to reopen the Data Link Properties dialog.

Data Processing extensions are based on ADO.NET technology and enable Reporting Services to connect to database servers or other data providers, run queries, and fetch rowsets. They serve as a bridge between the Data Source and the DataSet. Out of the box, Reporting Services exposes SQL Server, Oracle, OLE DB, and ODBC Data Processing extensions preconfigured for use with the Report Designer and with the Report Server. It's also possible (and not that difficult) to create and use a custom Data Processing extension—but we'll leave that discussion for Chapter 13.

TIP *Add Application Name* When using the SQL Server Data Processing extension, it's easy to forget to add the *Application Name* property to the Connection string. The trick here is to set an application name that can track the report's server-side operations to anyone tracing SQL Server network communications with SQL Profiler. By specifying a unique application name, this trace shows that the connection being made is from the development environment, rather than from a deployed report.

When creating a Data Source, the Data Link Dialog applet is leveraged but not all properties that can be set in a Connection string through the applet can be persisted. Apparently, some mangling and editing take place behind the scenes. Take care to inspect the actual Connection string persisted in a Data Source after you have saved it. Just reopen the Data Source and examine the properties, as shown in Figure 6.9

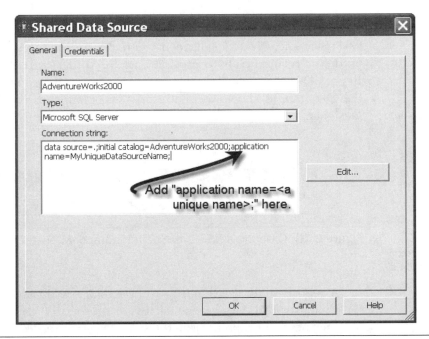

Figure 6.9 Setting the Application Name in the Data Source Connection String

When you click OK on the Shared Data Source configuration dialog, the Report Designer munges (that's a technical term) the string and removes anything it does not recognize or does not want you to use. Microsoft developers did this in an attempt to remove credentials being stored in the Connection string—at least that's what they told us. But we think they might have been a little overzealous because it's not possible to pass Connection string options such as *Encryption=True* or *Connection Pooling=False* in the Connection string in the Designer. They never told us which options are available and which aren't. This is yet another reason to originate Data Sources that you intend to use in deployed reports with the Report Manager instead of deploying Data Sources from the Report Designer where you are afforded a little more flexibility. Connection strings created with the Report Manager appear to take whatever literal string you give them—correct or not.

Designing Report DataSets

Peter calls this the "three-fingered-salute." I usually save that designation for especially worthy individuals.

–Bill

Bill, you don't mean developers who make awkwardly navigable menus, do you? Anyway, I think you are confusing things with the salute given by English and Welsh archers to the French after the Battle of Agincourt.

–Peter

Once you've created the shared Data Sources you expect to use, you can add a blank report to a project (using the keyboard shortcut Ctrl+Shift+A). Next, you'll need to create one or more DataSets used to return rowsets to provide data for your report. Using the Report Designer, click the down arrow on the dropdown list on the Data tab, as shown in Figure 6.10. This launches the DataSet Designer.

Figure 6.10 Creating a New DataSet in the Report Designer

A report might need and use more than one DataSet—especially if it uses DataSet-driven pick lists or subreports. Each DataSet need not necessarily come from the same Data Source. This means a report can include data from virtually any number of databases. Every DataSet must be linked to a Data Source—either a shared or custom Data Source. Custom Data Sources are designed for use only by a specific report.

TIP *Joining Tables from Different Servers* While it is possible to use data from different servers, having each returned to separate DataSets, if you need to combine them in one DataSet you'll find the best approach is to use the SQL Server Linked Server feature. That will permit you to perform JOIN operations in the query itself. The only other approach is to create a custom Data Processing extension. Joining or combining DataSets in Report Expressions is not possible.

Generally, DataSet query strings created and persisted by the Designer are passed to the Data Processing extension specified in the Data Source Connection string when the report is executed. These queries return a tabular resultset with a single rowset to the Report Processor. If you know ADO.NET programming, you'll understand what we mean when we tell you that the Data Processing extension returns data coerced into a DataReader. As we'll show in Chapter 13, they're not that hard to write. Actually, the Data Processing extension you have to implement is not a full System.Data.IdataReader, it's just a cut-down version: Microsoft.ReportingServices.DataProcessing.IDataReader.

When you create a new DataSet, a tabbed dialog is exposed (as shown in Figure 6.11), and by default the new DataSet references the first shared Data Source found in the report project. If there are no shared Data Sources in the project, you are forced to define a custom Data Source that's associated with the report (not shared). It's possible to return to this dialog to change other properties by selecting the ellipsis (…) button on the Data tab's toolbar. You can use this dialog to enter the SELECT query for the DataSet or use one of the two other designers that we'll describe next.

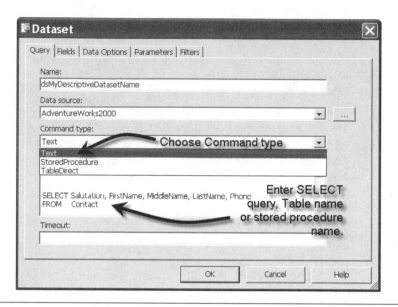

Figure 6.11 Creating a new DataSet and Specifying the Command Type and Query String

The initial Dataset[8] dialog provides the ability to set what type of query string you wish to present (Text, StoredProcedure, or, if a JET database, TableDirect). It also provides a place to enter the query string that sets the RDL CommandText element. However, you'll probably find it more helpful to define the query using one of the two query designers: either the generic or a graphical designer. To launch the default (generic) query designer, simply click the OK button. It's the Data Processing extension that interprets what each of these Command types means. If you select a Command type that's not supported, the extension throws an exception to warn you.

The Generic Query Designer

The **generic query designer** is the more powerful of the two because it supports all out-of-the-box and custom Data Processing extensions and can accept any SQL query, table,[9] or procedure

---

[8] Again, Microsoft's GUI designers, RDL designers, and doc team could not agree on the casing of the term we're calling a DataSet. We're hope you won't be confused by all of the variations.

name. It's configured to be the default designer for out-of-the-box Data Processing extensions. While we say it's more powerful, that doesn't mean it's the easiest for a novice to use. The generic query designer interface (shown in Figure 6.12) simply exposes a large text box where you enter the query command text, a dropdown menu to choose the Command type, and a grid to display any results that might be returned during the design and test phase. The generic designer doesn't try to preprocess any of the query text—it simply passes it to the Data Processing extension for execution and returns any rowset data to the grid or chokes on it and reports the error.

Using the TableDirect Command Type

If you're accessing a JET database through the OLE DB data provider (or another Data Processing extension that supports it), you can set the Command type to TableDirect. This simply builds a query behind the scenes that returns all rows and columns from the selected database table. This process isn't particularly efficient in databases where there are more than a few hundred rows to retrieve—it's a throwback to the days when JET developers simply performed SELECT * FROM MyTable queries. We don't recommend its use.

Executing Stored Procedures

If you need to execute a stored procedure using the generic query designer, simply choose StoredProcedure as the Command type (as shown in Figure 6.12) and enter the name of the stored procedure as the query string (the command text). If the stored procedure takes parameters (as most do), you can specify them later—we'll show you how in a minute.

---

[9] Each provider determines what these Command types mean. Most existing providers don't support direct table access, which is unique to JET. If you create your own Data Processing extension, you determine how each of the Command types are interpreted and processed.

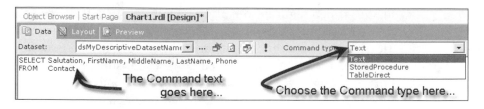

Figure 6.12 The Generic Query Designer Choosing the Command Type

The Graphical Query Designer

The alternative designer, dubbed the **Graphical Query Designer**, is simply a leveraged Visual Design Tools Query Designer that you may have used with Visual Studio .NET when supplying SQL for your queries. The Graphical Query Designer (GuiQD) has some benefits over the generic version in that it permits you to interrogate the data source to select Tables, Views, or Functions that return tabular result-sets (rowsets) and add them to the query. However, the downside is that GuiQD can't interpret and work with all types of queries or data sources. It also becomes confused if the query gets too complex.

Setting Up a Table-Based Query

Once you set the Command type to Text, you'll need to help the GuiQD build the SQL for your query. Once you choose one or more tables, you're ready to choose (just)[10] the columns needed for a report. You can also visually create and inter-table JOINs—but we recommend that you carefully validate these inter-table relationships.

However, note that the GuiQD is leveraged technology not specifically designed for Reporting Services. This means it has a few undesirable features as far as Reporting Services is concerned. Keep these GuiQD limitations in mind:

- It works only with simple queries. You can build `JOIN` queries using the GuiQD, but the queries have to be fairly simple. If queries get too complicated, the SQL to graphics interface breaks down and cries. It's best not to upset it. If you need to

---

[10] Don't select columns (or rows) you won't need for the report. This improves performance and scalability.

submit more sophisticated dynamic queries, consider using stored procedures and the generic query designer.

■ It's possible to get the query designer to change the query type—it permits creation of a Make Table query. This does not make much sense for a report DataSet!

■ The drag-and-drop routines don't always construct the appropriate JOINs—as we discuss next.

Executing Stored Procedures

The GuiQD can setup stored procedure–driven DataSets as well, and it's even easier than using the generic query designer. If you choose StoredProcedure as the Command type in the Dataset properties dialog as shown in Figure 6.13, you can (optionally) supply the stored procedure name as the Query string. You're then taken to the Data tab in the Report Designer where you can choose a named stored procedure from the dropdown list. The problem is that the Report wizard does not expose this dialog, so you might find it harder to setup a stored procedure–based DataSet. Don't worry about setting up the parameters—the Report Designer has done it for you, as you'll see in a minute. If your stored procedure returns a RETURN value or OUTPUT parameters, you can still use a DataSet to return them, but the technique is a bit different. We discuss processing the RETURN value and OUTPUT parameters after we go over Report Parameters later in this chapter.

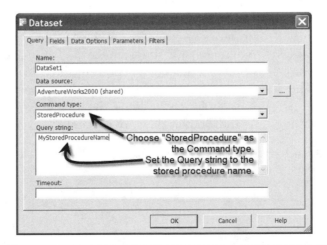

Figure 6.13 Setting Up a Stored Procedure Call Using the Dataset Properties Dialog

Watch Out for Improper JOINs

This "error" had slipped past me, and was pointed out to me by my wife. There I was writing this book while my wife was "assisting" by vacuuming around me. She stopped for an instant to watch what I was doing and said, "That query is wrong!" and then carried on vacuuming. I thought she was just winding me up, and at my peril I carried on writing. I hadn't noticed the circular JOIN. Later when I was being fed, she asked me if I'd corrected the query. I told her I thought she was just joking, at which time she pointed out what was wrong with it.

–Peter

Perhaps she could come do some housekeeping here. I have lots of code she can review. My wife serves a different role here—she tests my applications because she invariably breaks them.

–Bill

A much more insidious problem can be caused when the GuiQD attempts to infer inter-table relationships when adding a table to the query. That's because the designer examines *any* possible table JOINs between Primary Key columns of tables and any column of the same name and type in any other tables that could possibly be a Foreign Key. Sometimes this can be helpful, but at other times, you'll need to examine these auto-created JOINs under a microscope. For example, take a quick look at a query generated for the out-of-the-box sample report, Territory Sales Drilldown (as shown in Figure 6.14). This was clearly built with the Graphical Query Designer, but the developer forgot to verify the generated JOINs constructed as intended. As a result, the SalesTerritory table gets joined to both the SalesOrderHeader and SalesPerson tables. The report dutifully filters out sales data that a salesperson made while assigned to another territory. To see what we mean, if you execute the report you'll notice that there are no sales to the UK territory. If you edit the underlying DataSet, remove the link between SalesPerson and SalesTerritory, and re-execute the report, you'll see that more rows are returned—there *are* sales to the UK.

Another "challenge" attributed to the Graphical Query Designer is that it attempts to reparse the SQL statements. To be fair, the designer has little room to maneuver in. You are able to choose columns and criteria using a very visual point-and-click metaphor. By its very nature, the designer must translate your clicks, drags, and gestures[11] into SQL for you. This can create issues if you want to create UNION queries or pass SET statements before the main SELECT. Unless you provide fairly simple SQL, the Graphical Query Designer complains that it is unable to represent the SQL in a graphical way. The designer also has issues when executing some SQL with parameters. For example, try running the following query in both the generic and the Graphical Query Designers:

```
"SELECT @param1 AS MyParameter"
```

---

[11] You can guess what kind of gestures we give. ☺

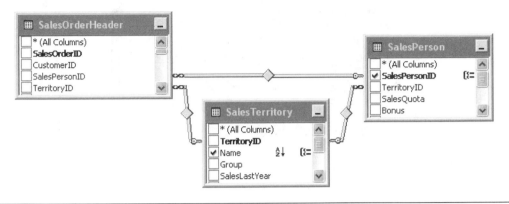

Figure 6.14 The Graphical Query Designer Gets a Bit Over-Enthusiastic at Times

However, the designer appears to handle parameters used in WHERE clause expressions reasonably well. When all is said and done, we find ourselves using the GuiQD to choose tables and organize the JOINs and then we switch to the generic query designer to tune up the query.

Single Transactions or Not?

If your report's underlying data is being queried from SQL Server and you have more than one DataSet in your report, the Report Processor can be programmed to wrap *all* calls for *all* DataSets in a report that uses a particular Data Source within a transaction. This option is tucked away out of sight and is quite awkward to locate. To find it you'll have to do a bit of deep diving. Click the ellipsis (…) on any Dataset toolbar in the report that uses the Data Source and calls through the Data Source you wish to wrap in a transaction. This launches the Dataset dialog, as shown in Figure 6.15.

Click on the ellipsis (…) button to the right of the Data source dropdown to launch the Data Source configuration dialog, as shown in Figure 6.16. The General tab exposes the "Use single transaction" checkbox.

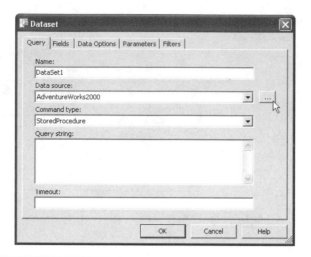

Figure 6.15 Configuring the DataSet to Support Transactions—Step 1

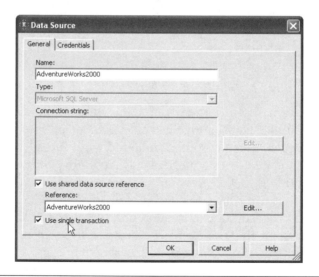

Figure 6.16 Specifying That the Query Should Be Wrapped in a Transaction

You could be forgiven for thinking that it's far easier to simply adjust the RDL directly to achieve this. All you'd need to do there is choose View Code on the report's context menu in the Solution Explorer, and slip in `<Transaction>true</Transaction>`.

```
<DataSources>
  <DataSource Name="AdventureWorks2000">
    <Transaction>true</Transaction>
```

The effect of this is to encapsulate the DataSet query into a transaction in which the ISOLATION Level is READ COMMITTED. However, before getting excited that this might permit some inter-communication between the query Command text strings from different DataSets, bear in mind that there is no formally defined order in which a DataSet's query commands are executed. For example, as part of one DataSet's query Command text you might try to create and populate a temporary table that is selected from a different DataSet's query Command text. Unfortunately, this won't work. Shown below is a copy of a SQL Profiler Trace that shows there is no *defined* and therefore no supported way of reordering the execution of StoredProcForDataset2 to occur before StoredProcForDataset1 is executed. You might be able to tune it by reordering elements in the RDL or renaming DataSets, but this approach is not sustainable.

```
SET TRANSACTION ISOLATION LEVEL READ COMMITTED;
BEGIN TRANSACTION
GO
SELECT DATABASEPROPERTYEX(DB_NAME(), 'Collation'),
COLLATIONPROPERTY(CONVERT(char, DATABASEPROPERTYEX(DB_NAME(),↵
'collation')), 'LCID')
GO
EXEC StoredProcForDataset1
GO
EXEC StoredProcForDataset2
GO
COMMIT TRANSACTION
```

Setting DataSet Query Options

Depending on the capability of your server, it's possible to configure your DataSet to use customizable Windows Collation Sorting Styles. These settings affect how data is sorted and are especially useful when you're working with different languages that require special collating sequences. These options can be configured by selecting the Data Options tab of the Dataset properties dialog, as shown in Figure 6.17. Most DBAs setup their servers to be case insensitive. That is, the server will consider "Fred" to be the same as "FRED" or "fred." However, through careful use of these settings as shown in Table 6.1, it's possible to create a DataSet that's case sensitive without having to reconfigure the entire server to be case sensitive.

By default, all of these options (except Collation) are set to Auto, which means that the Report Processor attempts to determine the option value from the Data Processing extension (the data provider) when the report is executed. Note that the Collation (localization) setting is determined from the browser settings unless you specify a value. We've included additional details about these settings in Table 6.1 and included how SQL Server's behavior is changed. For more information, see "SQL Server Collation Fundamentals" in SQL Server Books Online.

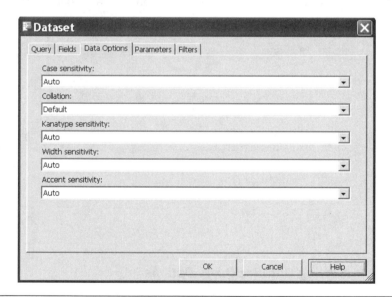

Figure 6.17 Customizing the Windows Collation Sorting Styles Using the Data Options Tab

Table 6.1 Data Options Settings to Configure Windows Collation Sorting Styles

Option	Settings	Description
Case sensitivity	True, False, **Auto**	Specifies that the data provider distinguish between uppercase and lowercase letters. If not selected, the provider considers the uppercase and lowercase versions of letters to be equal.
Collation (Locale)	Select Locale. See Figure 6.18.	Determines the collation sequence to be used for sorting data. If the value cannot be derived or left unchanged, the locale setting of the server is used.
Kanatype sensitivity	True, False, **Auto**	Specifies that the data provider distinguish between the two types of Japanese kana characters: Hiragana and Katakana. If set to False, SQL Server considers Hiragana and Katakana characters to be equal. If it cannot be derived from the provider, it's set to False.
Width (ANSI/Unicode) sensitivity	True, False, **Auto**	The data provider is to distinguish between a single-byte character (half-width or ANSI) and the same character when represented as a double-byte character (full-width or Unicode). If set to False, SQL Server considers the single-byte and double-byte representation of the same character to be equal.
Accent sensitivity	True, False, **Auto**	The data provider is to distinguish between accented and unaccented characters. For example, "a" is not equal to "á". If set to False, SQL Server considers the accented and unaccented versions of letters to be equal.

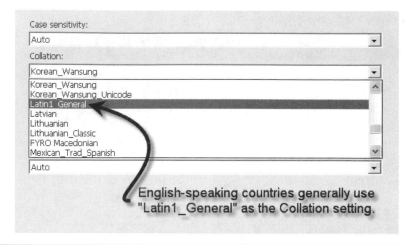

Figure 6.18 Choosing a Collation Setting from the List of Locales

Fields—Database or Calculated

Once you define a functional query that returns a suitable rowset, you can use the Report Designer to view and modify the returned columns. These are referred to as *Fields* in Reporting Services—we guess this makes it easier for the Access folks, those not working with relational databases, and a small group of EAM workers in Cleveland. The Report Designer exposes the DataSet Fields selector window, as shown in Figure 6.19. Once you switch to Layout view in the Report Designer, this Fields selector dialog appears on the right-hand side of the Designer. It can be made visible by clicking on Fields from the View menu or by using the Ctrl+Alt+D key sequence. The list of fields it displays is refreshed when you (re)select the DataSet in the combo box at the top of the Fields window.

This same dialog can be used to modify the name assigned to a particular Field, add a new Field, or delete an existing Field. This is not the way to delete fields from the DataSet—use the query editor for that. It's okay to add, edit, or delete fields that contain expressions you've created using this technique. Right-clicking on a specific Field exposes a context menu to permit these changes (as shown in Figure 6.20).

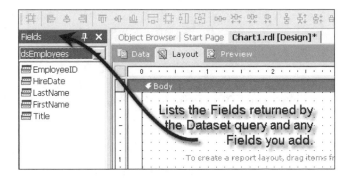

Figure 6.19 The Fields Selector Window

Figure 6.20 Editing the Query Fields

You probably already know how to use T-SQL to create calculated fields and provide them with a column name alias, or alias a field (column) in the query's command text. In this case, it'll be the underlying target DBMS, or perhaps your custom Data Processing extension that generates the calculated field or aliases the field name.

However, the Report Designer's Fields selector also can edit DataSet fields to alias their names, as well as create calculated fields. These functions are available on a context menu in the Fields window (as shown in Figure 6.20) and also on the Fields tab of the Dataset dialog, via the ellipsis button on the Dataset toolbar. These facilities are really most useful when your DataSet is populated from a stored procedure that you can't alter or from a source of data (a DBMS engine) that doesn't have a query language that supports alias names on the server. In many cases, we work with stored procedures that we don't have permission to see or alter. By using the Fields selector, we can specify more developer- (or user-) friendly field names on chosen columns or perhaps add a calculated field. Fields calculated in Reporting Services using the Fields selector instead of the DBMS (via SQL) can be based on calculations that utilize Visual Basic .NET expressions (or any .NET language if you create a custom assembly of library functions, which we'll show you in Chapter 9). Don't assume that calculated fields must be the result of complicated calculations. It's often useful to create a calculated field that is simply the concatenation of several other fields. For example, when creating an EmployeeName calculated field from the concatenation of the LastName and FirstName fields separated by a space, this "calculated" expression Field, once defined, is made available in the Fields selector to drag and drop onto the Report Layout surface when binding to report controls. Of course, there are other ways to do this. You could perform the concatenation in the report controls themselves, but if you plan on using the expression more than once in a report, it can simplify maintenance if you just add an expression-based Field.

Filtering Data Before It Arrives

Generally, it's best to filter or restrict the number of rows in a result-set used to populate a report DataSet at the source DBMS or in any custom Data Processing extension. That usually improves performance because the DBMS has access to the raw data as the query is processed along with indexes and caches that can optimize the query plan. Passing all the data through to another process that subsequently filters the query rowset is inefficient and problematic. Fetching large volumes of data puts more demand on precious network, RAM, server, and CPU resources.

Another issue that can complicate your attempts to filter data in a DataSet is caused by "nothing." That is, you'll discover (as we did) that the Filter expressions don't work very well and especially not when they have to deal with NULL (or Nothing) values. Every modern database supports NULL values, so it's not unusual to expect some columns to be returned as NULL. For example, "DateSold," "DateMarried," "NumberOfToes," or any other column might not be set to a specific value if the information is not known or cannot be determined without a strip search. In this case, instead of using a placeholder value (as we did in the olden days), we set these columns to NULL. The problem is, a NULL cannot be compared in an expression without special handling. Apparently, the Report Processor knows how to execute aggregates on columns that contain NULL values, but it stumbles if you try to filter a DataSet that contains NULLs. We think it's a lot easier to simply add SQL to your query to remove any rows that contain NULL values, but this could skew your report, so it's not always a viable option.

Even when you consider the aforementioned techniques, you might want to leave the filtering to the report on occasion—for instance, when you make Snapshots and use Report Parameters in the Filter expressions. So long as you manually mark those parameters in the RDL by inserting a `<UsedInQuery>False</UsedInQuery>` element, you'll be able to filter using those Report Parameters when rendering a Snapshot report.

Filtering Data in a DataSet

We know it's a real world we live in, and sometimes you can't restrict the rows returned to your DataSet. This may be the case if your report is based on a stored procedure that you can't or are not permitted to change. It might also be a problem if your report is using a custom data source that doesn't have the ability to filter or restrict its output. This can happen when you have to import data from mainframes or process control data sources, or when the Data Source is based on the custom File Share Information Data Processing extension.

Fortunately, you can apply .NET filters on a report DataSet when you can't restrict the rowset membership using SQL criteria. DataSet filters can be manipulated through the Filters tab on the Dataset properties dialog. This dialog can be launched from the ellipsis button on the Dataset toolbar (as shown in Figure 6.21).

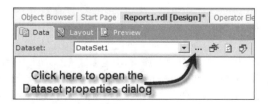

Figure 6.21 Opening the Dataset Properties Dialog

NOTE *Wildcards in Your SQL* The filters you specify for your reports are based on Visual Basic .NET 2003 syntax, so you'll find that the pattern matching with the `Like` operator uses * as a wildcard and not `%`, as you might use in SQL `LIKE` expressions.

Dealing with NULL Fields

As we made our way through the inner workings of the Report Processor's filtering mechanism, we got our hands pretty greasy and bruised trying to figure out how to deal with NULL values as well as how to get the Filter to work with non-string Fields. Let's talk about NULL filtering before we go on. This approach must be used whenever you want to filter non-string columns that might contain NULLs. Reporting Services seems to handle NULL values in string Field expressions without difficulty. So if you want to filter for decimal, integer, or any numeric value, you'll have to either strip the NULL rows from the DataSet (the preferred option, not always possible) or make sure your Filter expressions are written to account for NULLs. We'll show you a few easy techniques to deal with this issue when we get to setting the Filter expression.

Filtering String Fields

Figure 6.22 shows the Filters tab of the Dataset properties dialog. Here we set a DataSet filter used to test incoming rows and restrict DataSet rows as they are passed to the Report Renderer. In this example, the Filter is programmed to examine the DataSet and ensures that it contains only those rows with an "A" or an "a" somewhere in the Name field. Note that we said "...when passed to the Renderer" because the Filter is *not* applied when the DataSet is executed in the DataSet Designer. This means if you want to test a Filter, you should preview the report by going to the Preview tab in the Report Designer—but before you can preview it, you'll need to do some control layout first. Sure, you could add criteria to the SQL statement in the query designer or your handwritten SQL to prevent unneeded rows from reaching the Report Renderer. You could also use Views or stored procedures to do the same thing. We often use parameter-based queries to filter *in* those rows needed for the report. We'll discuss these other approaches later in this chapter.

Case-Sensitive Comparisons

And if you've been spoilt by using Visual Basic.

—Peter

If you're familiar with .NET filters such as the `Like` operator, you probably already know that the `Option Compare Text` or `Option Compare Binary` setting governs how .NET filters perform pattern matching. In the context of using Compare Text, an "A" is equivalent to an "a," but the two characters are different when using Compare Binary. However, it appears that there is no way to change the Report Processor's default setting of `Option Compare Text`. That's why we said that this filter restricts the DataSet to rows that contain either "A" or "a" somewhere in the Name field. However, if a binary comparison is crucial to you, keep the faith; there is indeed a way to do this by using a Report Expression and some custom code in the report. We'll show you how a little later.

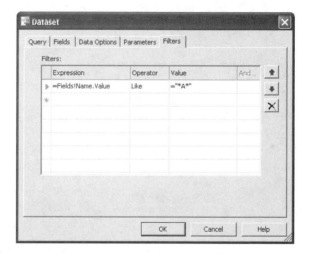

Figure 6.22 Specifying a DataSet Filter

When you examine the Expression and Value entries shown in Figure 6.22, note that the syntax uses an "=" sign at the beginning of each expression. Because the expression begins with an "=" sign, the Report Processor knows that the value is an expression and not a literal string. The Expression field in the Filter dialog Filters tab (or anywhere an expression is used) tells the Report Processor where to find the data, the Operator field specifies the operation to use, and the Value field specifies the Filter expression. As each row arrives, the specified Field's Filter expression is evaluated using the operator against the specified value. This "Expression Operator Value" expression must return True in order for the row to be accepted.

Choosing a Field

When setting up a Filter using the Dataset properties dialog, each of the Fields returned by your query are returned in a dropdown list under Expression in the Filters dialog. As we move through this chapter, you'll find that virtually everywhere that you're required to enter a Field name, the Report Designer provides a dropdown list of the DataSet Fields, as shown in Figure 6.23.

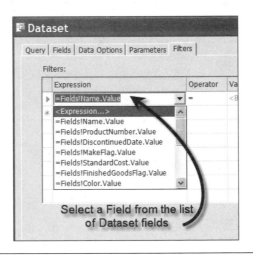

Figure 6.23 Field Names Derived from the DataSet Are Exposed in a Dropdown List

Another interesting (and important) point to note: Microsoft has resurrected the *!* operator (pronounced *bang* or *pling*). Visual Basic developers first saw this circa VB3 (IIRC), when it provided a simple collection addressing syntax. In this case, the expression `=Fields!Name.Value` uses the *!* operator to indicate that the named Field ("Name," in this case) is being addressed. The "." operator indicates that the *Value* property of the Name Field is being referenced. A useful alternative syntax is `=Fields("LastName").Value`. If you replace the string literal with a string variable, you have a form of dynamic addressing that you can't achieve with the ! syntax.

Choosing an Operator

Most of the RDL FilterValue operators are exposed in the dialog via a dropdown list, as shown in Figure 6.24. Other operators not shown in this figure are *Bottom N*, *Top %*, and *Bottom %*. A list of these operators and the number and type of elements they support is shown in Table 6.2.

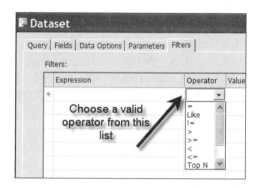

Figure 6.24 Choose an Operator from the Valid Operators List

Table 6.2 Valid Operators Used in DataSet Filters

Operator	Filter Value Must Contain
=, Like, !=, >, >=, <, <=	A single element
Top N, Bottom N	A single integer element
Top %, Bottom %	A single integer or float element
(*Between*)	Exactly two elements
(*In*)	Multiple filter elements

Although *Between* and *In* are supported RDL operators, they are not exposed in the Report Designer Dataset properties dialog Filters tab. You can try to modify the RDL manually to implement these operators, but they are displayed as multiple expressions in this dialog.

Setting a Value

Once you've chosen a Field and an operator, you'll have to decide what Value to assign—unless you've installed the new Read Programmer's Mind add-in, which fills in the value for you. Be sure to match the Value setting with the Field and operator type. When specifying any value, start with an "=" sign. If the operator and expression expect a string, use double quotes ("") around the value. As we said, if you use this approach with non-string values, you won't have much luck.

Handling Non-String Fields

If you need to filter numeric values, we recommend a subtly different approach. While there are several ways to work around how the Report Processor handles numeric filter values, we've found it easiest to enter an expression that resolves to True or False. Actually, we prefer this approach for all comparison filters (=, Like, !=, >, >=, <, <=, In, Between), whatever they are—it's just a lot cleaner, and perhaps Microsoft should have forced this implementation to be the only approach to be used for all filters. The expression used in Figure 6.25 illustrates this technique. We think this is far easier than trying to get the Report Processor to coerce the expression into a string (another approach) so that it matches the Operator and Value entries. It turns out that this technique also deals with NULL values without extra help.

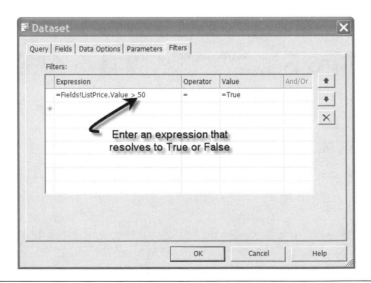

Figure 6.25 Using a Boolean Expression to Handle Numeric Types

If you find a situation where it's necessary to include NULL values in the Fields being filtered, you can add an expression to the Filter to ignore any rows containing NULL field values. Use the following code as the expression—just substitute your own field name.

```
=IIF(Fields!ListPrice.Value IS Nothing,↵
    0,Fields!ListPrice.Value)
```

Additional Filter expressions can follow this expression because the Filters are executed serially. This prevents rows containing NULL values from being tested. To create compound Filters, simply add more Filter expressions to the list, as shown in Figure 6.26.

Another approach is to convert the Field Value to a string or the Value to the same type as the named Field Value. With this technique, you can use the Operator and Value Filter properties to construct the filter. An example of this approach is shown in Figure 6.26.

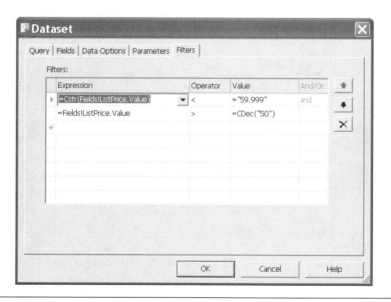

Figure 6.26 Using Coercion to Filter Numeric Fields

In case you didn't notice, the Report Designer adds the *and* or *or* operator to the dialog as you add additional expressions. If two sequential expressions match, the *or* operator is used, otherwise the *and* operator is used. If you use our preferred filtering suggestion of creating expressions that simply evaluate to True or False, you can create expressions that take advantage of parentheses in the Boolean logic.

Testing for NULL

If you need an expression to test for NULL columns, consider that the variables used behind the scenes can't be NULL, but they can't be Nothing either. Assuming you understand, this means you can write an expression to filter on NULL or simply convert the value to a more appropriate string. The first line of code shown below illustrates an expression used to return True if the field is Nothing and False if it's "something" (not Nothing). This approach can also be used to change the value returned from Nothing to "something"— the second line of code does this by converting a Nothing to "Fred." Not that Fred is nothing, she's really something…but that's another story. According to the developers at Microsoft, using Nothing to mean NULL is specific to Reporting Services. They used to (pre-beta 2, we think) just follow the VB convention of DBNull and IsDBNull(), which evolved to Nothing and IsNothing(). However, Nothing had some other rules in Visual Basic (mostly regarding objects), but they repurposed Nothing to mean null. This is another source of confusion among users, who may know about NULL (SQL) and DBNull (VB) but would never think to use Nothing. Confused? We're sorry, but we just try to explain what we can. This is one of the great mysteries of life—and in this case the answer is not 42.

```
=IIF (Fields!ListPrice.Value IS Nothing, True, False)
=IIF (Fields!ListPrice.Value IS Nothing, "Fred",↵
 Fields!ListPrice.Value)
```

Fred is my daughter's nickname. She's pretty well known on my speaker circuit.

–Bill

Bill does his best to embarrass her on the speaker circuit in front of thousands of people. Like announcing from the stage to 5,000 developers on Valentine's Day that Fred (who was sitting in the back of the room) was very upset because she hadn't gotten a Valentine's card, and asking if someone would be kind enough to organize one for her. Bill, Fred is keeping score. From what I hear, "shock and awe" revenge has been in the planning for several years.

–Peter

It was only 850 people, and she had already IM'ed me in the middle of my session. We're even (I hope).

–Bill

Specifying and Capturing Parameters

Parameters, when associated with queries, are simply those values passed to the query that focus it on the items in the database you want to retrieve. For example, if we asked you to find a doctor, you would start looking in the phone book and discover that there are more doctors than anyone ever imagined. You would immediately ask for a "parameter" to thin out the number of doctors you had to search. You would want to know the medical specialty, location, and whether or not they treat humans or are simply Ph.D.s.

Virtually all of the queries we execute take parameters. We pass them to dynamic SQL queries and stored procedures alike. Reporting Services includes considerable built-in infrastructure to capture, manage, and insert parameter values into the queries you write. Parameters play a vital role in any application architecture because they help the database engine focus its work on a limited subset of the data. Parameters can be linked to table indexes to further assist the query processor in optimizing the query plan and returning rows more efficiently.

NOTE *Warning: SQL Injection* Do not permit your users to "fill in" parameter values—it's very dangerous. As we've said before, this allows users to "inject" SQL commands directly into the server using the report's credentials. SQL injection attacks are very common but are not hard to prevent, as long as you populate your parameter values and permit only your report users to select from one of the items in the parameter list.

As we work through this section, you'll see that there's a subtle but important difference between "query" parameters and "report" parameters. *Query parameters* are the values the Data Processing extension inserts into the query Command text when executing the DataSet query. *Report Parameters* are typically the values captured from the user or provided as default values but do not have to be included in the DataSet query—they could be values used in Report Expressions such as filters. Likewise, a query parameter does not have to have a corresponding Report Parameter because it can get its value elsewhere. For example, the locale global parameter used in the Product Catalog report comes to mind. Just be aware that query parameters and Report Parameters are completely separate. Sure, query parameters driven by Report Parameters is a (if not *the*) primary use of parameters in reports, which is why Microsoft made the linking transparent (to the chagrin of anyone wanting to delete their parameters without knowing they are indeed separate).

Query Parameters

Not all Data Processing extensions support query parameters (especially if you've installed custom DPEs), so you might not be afforded the option to pass parameters into the query. Each provider has its own SQL syntax and rules that determine how parameters are marked, managed, or supported. Table 6.3 lists several common DPEs and the parameter syntax they require. For those of us who understand ADO or ADO.NET, we quickly recognize these parameter prefix characters and how they help mark "named" and positional parameters in SQL statements. For those non-programmers out there, just remember to prefix your query parameters appropriately.

Table 6.3 Parameter Identification for Typical Data Processing Extensions

Data Processing Extension	Parameter Rules	Example
SQL Server	Named, prefixed with "@"	WHERE X = @MyParm
Oracle	Named, prefixed with ":"	WHERE X = :MyParm
JET (OleDb), ODBC	Marked with "?"	WHERE X = ?

From this point forward, when we discuss this topic we'll assume that we're working with the SQL Server Data Processing extension.

If you code your DataSet query with correctly marked parameters, the Report Designer automatically constructs a Report Parameter to capture the value at runtime. For example, we inserted the parameter @HireDate in the following query:

```
SELECT     FirstName, LastName, HireDate, EmployeeID
FROM       Employee
WHERE      (HireDate < @HireDate)
```

If you execute the query in the DataSet Designer, a dialog pops up asking you to provide a value for the parameter (as shown in Figure 6.27). The DPE is responsible for parameter formatting, so you won't have to quote string parameters or use special date framing. You do have to pay attention to localization settings to ensure your users know how to enter dates, as we discuss in a minute.

Figure 6.27 Design-Time Query Parameter Testing Using the Query Designer

If the DataSet query names a stored procedure to execute and you've set the Command type to "Stored Procedure" as we did in Figure 6.15 several sections ago, the DataSet Designer queries SQL Server for the stored procedure fields and the parameters and populates the query parameters for you in Figure 6.28. However, we noticed that there is no place in the DataSet Designer to define the query parameter datatypes. If you trace this "discovery" process with the SQL Profiler, you'll see that when using the generic query designer these parameters are passed as nvarchar(4000) and that coercion into other types is left to the SQL Server.[12] Using coercion like this might be problematic in certain circumstances, but runtime-type coercion is handled by Report Parameters.

---

[12] The Graphical Query Designer executes the same SQL code differently too—use the SQL Profiler to see what we mean.

One frustration for Europeans and our Antipodean cousins with the RTM version was the apparent insistence of the Report Previewer and DataSet Designer upon American date formatting of the style mm/dd/yy when entering date parameters. Fortunately, Service Pack 1 addresses these issues and takes the date formatting style from the System Locale. Take a look at the Parameters tab on the Dataset dialog shown in Figure 6.28:

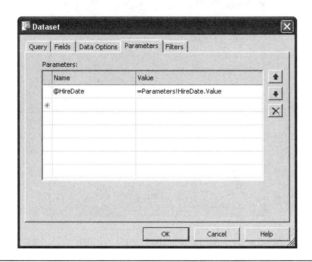

Figure 6.28 Viewing or Defining a Query Parameter

You'll notice that our `@HireDate` parameter has a value of `=Parameters!HireDate.Value`. This dialog is all about binding our query parameter to a Report Parameter. Yes, behind the scenes the DataSet Designer helped out by creating a Report Parameter of the same name. The point we're trying to make here is that you don't need to accept the default binding of a query parameter to a Report Parameter. You could, for example, decide that you wish to bind a query parameter to one of the following:

- Fixed value = `"1 JAN 2002"`
- Function = `Now()`
- Report Expression =
  `Code.MyDateFunction(Globals!ExecutionTime)`

By the way, depending on where in your SQL statements you are trying to use a query parameter, we think you'll probably find the generic query designer more satisfying and productive than the Graphical one.

Report Parameters

Report Parameters provide a mechanism for collecting parameter information from defaults configured by the user or administrator, or by prompting for parameter values from the person executing the report. In Chapter 4, we saw how to administer a report, configure Report Parameter default values, and adjust the Prompt String for the Report Parameters whose values are queried from the user.

TIP If you need to create a report that extracts data from different databases (on the same SQL Server), you can parameterize the name of the database in the query. Just concatenate the database name and owner in the `SELECT`. For example: `"=SELECT Col1, Col2 FROM " & Parameters!DatabaseName.Value & ".dbo.MyTable..."` We discuss dynamic queries near the end of this chapter.

As we've just seen, Report Parameters are closely linked with query parameters. We also mentioned that as you create query parameters in the Query Designer, the Report DataSet Designer creates Report Parameters for you. However, if you delete a query parameter, the Report DataSet Designer *doesn't* remove the Report Parameter it created for you. If you subsequently rename a query parameter, it'll create another Report Parameter rather than rename an existing parameter. This is probably the best approach, though—despite the fact that it creates orphaned parameters. Given the number of properties that you've configured on Report Parameters, there's a chance the parameter could be used elsewhere. To be sure everything works as planned, you should make a point of cleaning up any parameters that you decide are not needed.

NOTE Sure, we understand that you often don't want users entering values for parameters—you want them to choose from a list of valid parameter values. We'll discuss this aspect of Report Parameter management later in this chapter.

Using the Report Parameters Dialog

The Report Parameters dialog manages the query parameters to be used when your report is executed. This dialog can be launched in several ways:

- In Visual Studio .NET 2003, select the report and then on the Report menu select Report Parameters.... This option works even if no parameters are defined for your report, but it is available only in Data or Layout view.
- In the Layout view, select Report in the Properties pane, and then select *ReportParameters* in the properties list.
- In the Layout view, right-click the box in the top left "origin" between the vertical and horizontal rulers, and select Report Parameters from the context menu.

If you open the Report Parameters dialog but don't see a parameter that you defined in your SQL query, make sure you marked it correctly. See Table 6.3 for correct parameter marking conventions. When working with dynamic queries (as we discuss later), the Designer can't populate the Fields list or parameters. That is, when you switch to Layout view, the Report Designer tries to fetch the schema and derive the Fields list and input parameters. If it can't find them for some reason—as when the functionality is not supported or your credentials have insufficient privileges—you can click the Refresh Fields button to run the query internally and fetch the Fields and parameters. If that doesn't work, you must manually update Fields and parameters. Nope, the Report Designer never tries to fetch Fields and parameters for a dynamic query. We'll show you a way to get around this problem later in this chapter.

Figure 6.29 shows the HireDate Report Parameter as created by the Report Data Designer when it created the @HireDate query parameter. Note the parameter type is set to String. We'll set the correct datatype next.

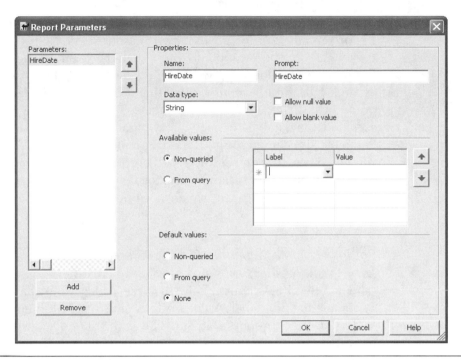

Figure 6.29 The Report Parameters Dialog Used to Configure Report Parameters

Setting Report Parameter Datatypes

The first thing to note is that Report Parameters can only be assigned datatypes of Boolean, DateTime, Integer, Float, or String. Sure, your DPE might return different types such as Decimal, Money, NVarChar, Char, or others, but you have to map the Reporting Services type to the type expected by your DPE. Generally, if you use String for the string types, DateTime for the date types, Float for the decimal type, and Boolean for the bit types, the DPE and Reporting Services should work out the coercion details.

If the Report Parameters are created as a result of a DataSet query that calls a parameterized stored procedure, the parameter's datatype information is interrogated from the SQL Server. These datatypes are used when the Query Designer creates the corresponding Report Parameters. On the other hand, if your DataSet is based on a dynamic SQL string that includes parameters, the Query Designer simply assigns String datatypes.

You will want to pay attention to the datatypes assigned to your Report Parameters for at least two reasons. First, if the Report Parameter is to be prompted from the user executing the report, the parameter value supplied can be validated at that stage. For example, the browser can ensure that DateTime parameters are properly formatted date and time values. Secondly, when a report is executed, the datatype of each query parameter bound to a Report Parameter is coerced to the Report Parameter datatype. That way, you can explicitly control any type coercions. In some cases, you may wish to flag Report Parameters to allow nulls and/or blanks and the report's user interface, which becomes part of the parameter validation.

Setting Available Values for Report Parameters

As we shall see shortly, it's also possible to create pick lists of pre-validated Report Parameter values. These values can be hardcoded by completing the Label / Value grid (as shown back in Figure 6.29) or derived from a report DataSet. This is the *only* place where the Report Parameter value lists can be manipulated because there is no user interface to configure a Report Parameter's available values in the Report Manager.

Setting Default Values for Report Parameters

Default values for a Report Parameter can be based on Report Expressions or a DataSet or they can have no default at all. It is possible to override these in the Report Parameters Properties page in the Report Manager with a fixed value, but it appears that the values set in the Report Designer are visible only for the initial deployment of the report definition. After initial deployment, you'll need to use the Report Manager or the SOAP interface to update the properties; you can't update them in the Report Designer and redeploy—it just doesn't work that way. These are more of the now notorious "write-once" properties we discussed earlier in this chapter.

Setting Report Parameter Prompt Strings

This string is presented to the user when executing the report to prompt for the parameter to be completed. It can be a very long string indeed—it is unlimited—or rather *limited* by the fact that the total size of a report's RDL file is about 4 MB, so the Prompt String can take up as much space as is left in the Report's RDL file to keep the total size less than 4 MB. It is somewhat frustrating that this of all properties cannot be bound to a Report Expression because that would enable language localization of Prompt Strings within the report. You can override the Prompt String in the Report Manager Report Parameters Properties page—but that's not the same thing as being able to make the prompt specific to the language setting of the browser that is executing the report. It's our understanding and hope that this will be addressed in the SQL Server 2005 version of Reporting Services.

Let's walk through an example that illustrates use of pick lists and default parameters.

1. Create a report using the Report wizard that executes the query shown in Figure 6.30. This query returns quite a bit of data, so we added (quite) a few parameters to help focus the query on just the information the user needs:

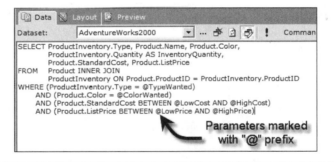

Figure 6.30 Creating a Query Containing Marked Parameters

2. We don't want the user to have to guess what types or colors are currently available, so we need to provide dropdown lists for this parameter. To do this, we'll run another query to extract a list of known colors—we'll hardcode the known Product Type values because these are not likely to change. Add another DataSet to your report to return all valid colors, as shown in Figure 6.31.

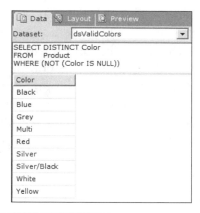

Figure 6.31 Create a DataSet to Return a List of Valid Colors

3. Return to the Report Layout view, and click on Report |
Report Parameters…. You should see the dialog shown in
Figure 6.32.

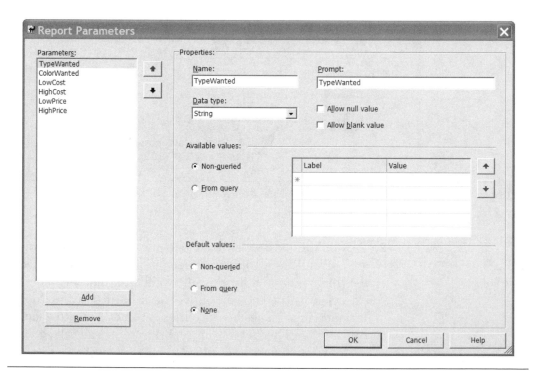

Figure 6.32 Managing the Report Parameters

For the TypeWanted parameter, since we're all too familiar with the AdventureWorks2000 database, we know that there are only two valid types: "I" and "W" (Inventory and Warehouse). To make it easy for the user (who should not have to remember what the codes mean), we'll set up non-queried parameters that have friendly prompt Label text and the appropriate Value text to pass into the query at runtime. Sure, you can have as many Label/Value pairs here as makes sense. Remember, this approach is used only for situations where you know the data is not going to change from day to day. Figure 6.33 shows how the TypeWanted parameter is configured.

Figure 6.33 Setting a Non-Queried Parameter Label and Value

4. Next, we need to setup the parameter dropdown list for the ColorWanted parameter. Choose the ColorWanted parameter from the list of parameters on the left of the dialog shown in Figure 6.32 This time we'll choose to configure the parameter to use the "From query" option, as shown in Figure 6.34.

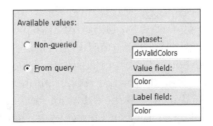

Figure 6.34 Configuring the ColorWanted Parameter to Use a Query Pick List

5. Next, we need to setup the four cost and price parameters. In this case, all we need to do is set the datatype for each parameter. We'll let the user provide any value for these parameters. Select the LowCost, HighCost, LowPrice, and HighPrice parameters in turn and choose Float from the Data type drop-down list.

6. When we preview the report, the user is prompted for all six parameters, as shown in Figure 6.35.

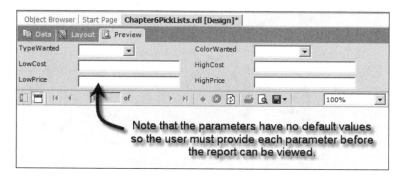

Figure 6.35 The User Is Prompted for All Parameters That Don't Have Default Settings

Setting Parameter Default Values

We're of two minds when it comes to providing Report Parameter default values. If you pre-stuff all of the parameters with default values, the report will render immediately after you click Preview, View Report, or however the report is launched. But this means users might be presented with data that they don't really want or need (after the system goes to the trouble of running the query and rendering the report). You should think about this issue and consider providing defaults for some of the parameters, but not all. This makes it easier for the user to run the report, but does not mean the report is executed without correctly specified parameters.

To set defaults for the six parameters in our report, we need to revisit the Report | Report Parameters… menu option and set the default behavior for each parameter that needs a default. Click on Layout in the Report Designer, and open the Report Parameters dialog. Notice at the bottom of the dialog you have the option to set the Default values to either a non-queried constant, a value from a query, or (the default) no value at all.

We'll start with the `TypeWanted` parameter, as shown in Figure 6.36. In this case, we set the default to a non-queried (constant) value of "I." The Report Processor knows that this is to display as Inventory, so that's what's shown in the dropdown for the `TypeWanted` parameter.

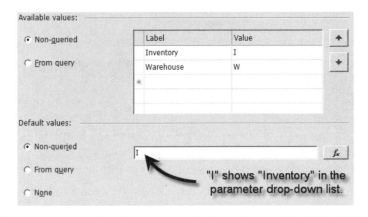

Figure 6.36 Setting the Default Value for the `TypeWanted` Parameter

We repeated this process and set the default parameter for the `ColorWanted` parameter to Black. For the cost and price parameters, we wanted to let the user choose from a range of values based on the current database values. To do this, we created another DataSet that uses SQL aggregates to determine these minimum and maximum values. The query is shown in Figure 6.37.

Figure 6.37 Using SQL Aggregates to Return the Minimum and Maximum Cost and Price

Returning to the Report Parameters dialog, we can set the `LowCost`, `HighCost`, `LowPrice`, and `HighPrice` parameters to the named Value field returned from the dsMinMaxCostPrice DataSet query. The HighPrice configuration is shown in Figure 6.38.

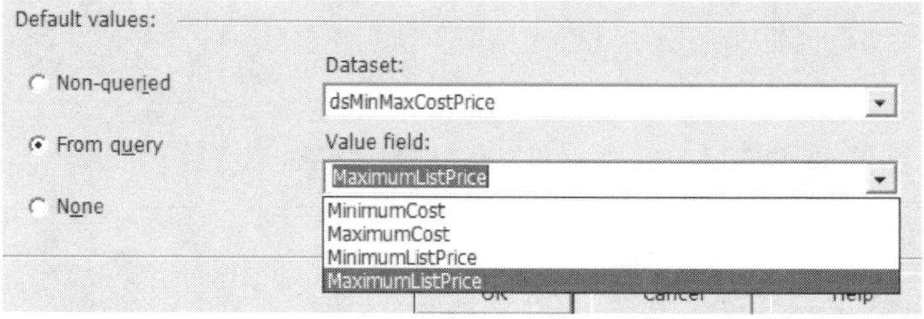

Figure 6.38 Selecting the MaximumListPrice from the Value Field for the `HighPrice` Parameter

Once all of the parameters have been supplied with default parameters, clicking Preview from the Report Designer causes the report to be rendered immediately, as shown in Figure 6.39. Because we used minimum and maximum values for the cost and price parameters, all data was returned to the Report Renderer—which is probably not a good idea for production reports that have to work against large databases.

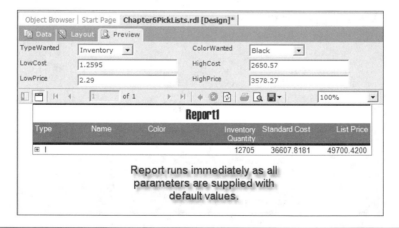

Figure 6.39 The Parameter-Driven Report in Which All Parameters Are Supplied with Default Values

Report Expressions

We've seen many situations in which the value needed in a report cell is not a fixed value fetched from a column in a rowset but rather is generated as a composite of several columns (Fields) or by some sort of mathematical expression. We use expressions to concatenate a person's first and last name or build up a formatted phone number from its component parts. We also use expressions to compute aggregates or to incorporate business rules or custom filtering into our reports.

Before long, you'll discover that "<Expression…>" is a selectable option for many properties on items throughout Reporting Services. This provides the ability for a developer to bind that particular property to a Visual Basic .NET expression that's evaluated when the report is executed. As a rule of thumb, if you can get the expression syntax to work in Visual Basic .NET, it should also work in an expression. Expressions can also contain custom code, which becomes handy as the complexity of the expression starts to challenge your ability to express what you want done—we discuss this later in this chapter.

Selecting the <Expression…> or *fx* option (Figure 6.36) launches the Edit Expression dialog shown in Figure 6.40. This provides a simple user interface to edit the expression. Depending on which property you are editing, this dialog has a selectable list of Constants, Globals (such as page number, execution time, report server, and so on), Parameters, Fields, and aggregates of Fields. There isn't any Intellisense performed as you create and manipulate the expression, but some syntax errors are detected when you try to save the expression. Just be aware that some Globals (such as PageNumber and TotalPages) can be used only in expressions that are used with controls placed in a report's PageHeader or PageFooter—we'll mention these report sections in just a moment.

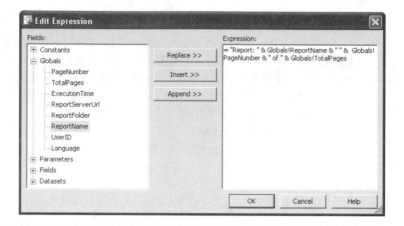

Figure 6.40 Using the Edit Expression Dialog

Managing Cascading Parameters

We noticed that the documentation for the Cascading Parameters feature needs a bit more work. For some reason, Microsoft chose to illustrate this technique using a fictitious database—not AdventureWorks2000, as in the other examples. That's a shame because it's an important feature that can be very useful as well as a bit tricky to implement.

Cascading Parameters change a Report Parameter's available values dynamically—based on a "primary" parameter. If you examine Figure 6.32, you'll notice that the parameters are ordered. You can change the order by pressing the up-arrow or down-arrow keys. If the Report Designer discovers that the query you're executing to populate a Report Parameter's available items requires a parameter higher in the list, the "secondary" parameter is grayed out (disabled) until the primary parameter is supplied.

Let's walk through a short demonstration to see how this works.

1. Start with a new report and add a DataSet with the query that follows. All of these queries can be executed against the

AdventureWorks2000 sample database. First, find all of the valid ProductLine values from the Product table. We'll call this dsValidProductLines.

```
SELECT DISTINCT ProductLine
FROM Product
WHERE (NOT (ProductLine IS NULL))
```

2. Next, create a DataSet to find all of the valid styles for a selected ProductLine. Note that this query requires a parameter named @ProductLineWanted. We'll call this dsValidStyles.

```
SELECT DISTINCT Style FROM Product
WHERE (ProductLine = @ProductLineWanted)
AND (NOT (Style IS NULL))
```

3. Next, create a DataSet with a query to return details from the Product table using the two parameters we just captured. Note that we're using the @ProductLineWanted parameter twice—once in the preceding query (Step 2) and here. We'll call this dsProducts.

```
SELECT ProductID, Name, StandardCost, ListPrice, Size,
  Weight, ProductLine, DealerPrice, Style,
  SellStartDate, SellEndDate, FinishedGoodsFlag
FROM   Product
WHERE (ProductLine = @ProductLineWanted)
AND (Style = @StyleWanted)
```

4. Now you're ready to configure the Report Parameters. Click on the Report menu and choose Report Parameters.... Note that both the ProductLineWanted and the StyleWanted Report Parameters are shown in the Report Parameters dialog on the left (see Figure 6.41).

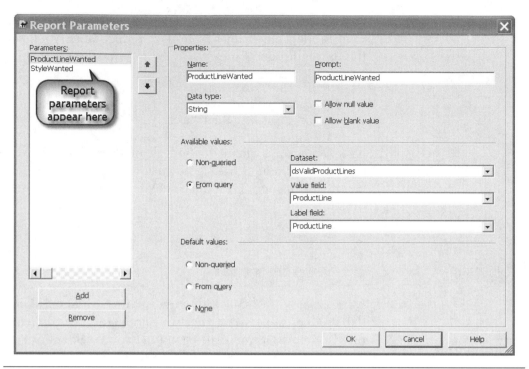

Figure 6.41 Managing Cascading Parameters

5. Select the `ProductLineWanted` parameter from the list on the left. In the Available values pane, point to the dsValidProductLines DataSet to populate the parameter dropdown menu that appears on the report when it's executed.

6. Next, select the `StyleWanted` parameter from the list on the left. In the Available values pane, point to the dsValidStyles DataSet to populate the parameter dropdown menu that appears on the report when it's executed. Note that this query requires an input parameter—`ProductLineWanted`. That will be provided automatically when the report is executed.

7. Lay out the report using a Table control as you see fit, and click on the Preview button to observe how the Report Parameters are handled. Figure 6.42 shows how the parameters are handled. Until the user chooses the primary parameter, the secondary parameter(s) are disabled.

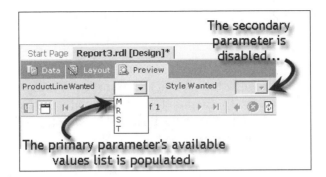

Figure 6.42 The Secondary Parameter Is Disabled Until the Primary Parameter(s) Are Chosen

Cascading Parameters let you refine your parameter pick lists by reducing the choices available to the user who applies intelligent parameter-driven queries. The tricky part of this approach comes up if a parameter high in the chain must be changed. In this case, it can be a bit difficult to put the chain back together again.

Advanced Techniques

We want to provide a few extra tips to handle some of the less ordinary problems associated with handling stored procedures and more exotic ways to build SQL queries.

Managing RETURN or OUTPUT Parameters

If your stored procedure returns needed RETURN value or OUTPUT parameters from SQL Server, you're going to have to take a slightly different approach to retrieve them because there's no built-in mechanism to capture these types of parameters. But it's not that hard to do. Basically, you need to create an EXEC query that captures the values using a SELECT statement. For example, to retrieve the RETURN value from a stored procedure:

1. Create a Report Parameter and remove its Prompt String completely so that the user is not prompted.
2. Give the parameter a default value and set its datatype. For the RETURN value it should be an integer. In the example, we name the parameter "retval."
3. Use the generic query designer and enter the following command text that executes the stored procedure and captures the RETURN value:

```
EXEC @retval = myStoredprocwithReturnValue
SELECT @retval as retval
```

4. Once the stored procedure has been executed, you can access the RETURN value through the Report Parameter *Value* property.

You can use a similar approach to execute stored procedures that return OUTPUT parameters. In this case, follow the same steps, but create a separate Report Parameter for each OUTPUT parameter you wish to capture. Each must be typed according to the datatype returned by the specific OUTPUT parameter. The following SQL executes the stored procedure and captures an OUTPUT parameter.

```
EXEC @retval = MyDB.dbo.myOutput @myinparm, @myoutparm OUTPUT
SELECT @retval as retval,@myinparm as MyInparm,@myoutparm as MyOutParm
```

Executing "Dynamic" SQL Queries

We often see situations in which the query we need to execute varies by factors that can't be handled by simply substituting a parameter into the WHERE clause of a SQL query. For example, you might want to limit the number of rows returned during testing or use dummy parameters to implement more complex variations in the SQL being executed. As we're about to show you, you can take several approaches to this challenge. The first simply uses an expression instead of the SQL. These expressions can be in several forms. The two most common forms are:

- Provide an expression that resolves to a properly formatted SQL query based on Report Parameters or other values used or concatenated into the logic of the expression.
- Use the "custom code" approach. In this case, you provide the logic to construct the SQL in a Visual Basic function that returns a string.

We'll discuss both strategies in this section, but let's get started by walking through an example of building an expression that returns a SQL query string.

1. Start a report project, and when it comes time to provide the SQL for your DataSet query, enter an expression in the dialog, as shown in Figure 6.43. This expression changes the SQL to include a value for a TOP clause that's driven from a Report Parameter. This is another way to limit the number of rows returned by your DataSet. To support this approach, we created the Report Parameter MaxRows, which defaults to 500.

2. Using the Report | Report Parameters menu, add a new Report Parameter named MaxRows and set the default to 500. Yes, this approach is fraught with danger because it permits users to enter destructive SQL and inject it directly into your SQL. That's why we test the inbound parameter within the expression to be a numeric value and within a reasonable range. Another approach to this Report Parameter would be to create a list of valid values.

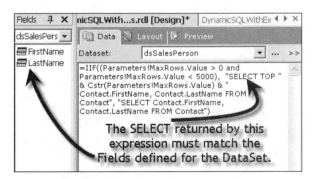

Figure 6.43 Building an Expression to Generate a SQL SELECT

In this case, we had to populate the DataSet Properties Fields manually because the design-time query editors were not used. Sure, you can shortcut this by creating a prototype SQL query with one of the query editors to populate the *Fields* collection. Otherwise, you'll have to enter the SELECT Fields yourself, as shown in Figure 6.44.

3. Use the Preview tab to test the expression. We tend to stay away from adding extra CRLF (return key) lines to the expression because it seems to confuse the expression evaluator. It would be nice if this dialog implemented the usual expression builder dialog we see everywhere else. It would also be nice if the designer gave you the ability to populate the Fields collection without having to resort to a pseudo query.

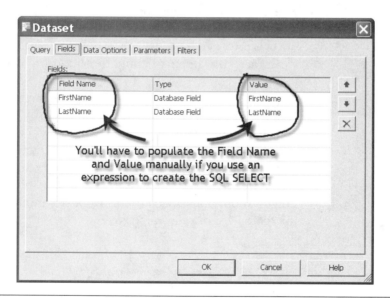

Figure 6.44 Populating the DataSet Fields Manually When Using an Expression

Conceptually, this approach seems compelling, but we had some difficulty getting the objects to link together. For example, we had to hard-cast the Parameter object to a string and be especially careful as we concatenated the lines together. No, you can't (and shouldn't) use the Visual Basic line continuation character for expressions. Generally, object coercion is handled for you in Visual Basic. It's also easy to imagine that if the query gets too complex, you'll have to spend quite a bit of time filling in the *Fields* collection. Sure, in this case we would certainly fall back on the pseudo query approach.

Creating a Custom Code Function

It might be a lot easier for Visual Basic .NET programmers to use the approach we mentioned a bit earlier—a code function. In this case, you'll (again) have to pre-populate the *DataSet Fields* collection, but the "expression" code is kept in a custom code function. Functions are simply blocks of Visual Basic code that accept 0 to N input parameters and return a value or object—usually a string or number. These functions are written just like any other Visual Basic function and can use most .NET Framework classes. Sure, the existing Visual Basic functions are also suitable for use in an expression. For example, you can use the Today function (coded as =Today()) or the Date, string, or decision functions (such as IIF or PctComplete)—and there are many more. But this section talks about creating your own functions.[13]

So, for those of you who aren't familiar with writing Visual Basic functions (but are familiar with Visual Basic), the Visual Basic .NET function is coded about the same but uses the *Return* operator to pass back the value from the function. Visual Basic .NET requires far more enumerations, and you have to spell everything out more than you do in Visual Basic "classic." But if you use the Visual Basic .NET code window, you won't have many problems that can't be overcome by a good glass of wine and a walk around the block. The following steps walk you through the process of creating and testing functions.

1. Create a report in the usual way. It might be easier to create a SQL query to populate the Fields collection unless you don't have that many Fields to define if your function is designed to replace a SELECT statement in the DataSet. Sure, you can reference your custom code function in any expression.
2. Open the Layout tab, and right-click on the upper-left corner of the report layout area, as shown in Figure 6.45.

---

[13] This example is saved on the DVD as "CodeBehind.RDL."

Figure 6.45 Opening the Report Properties Dialog

3. Click on the Code tab to expose the custom code dialog. Here's where you type in your Visual Basic function code. No, we don't, but you can if you want to. What we do is add a Visual Basic class or Windows Form project to our project and use the developer-friendly Visual Basic code editor to code and debug the Visual Basic function code. We're really pretty spoiled because without this help, we find it a lot harder to write the code and make reasonably sure it's right. The code we created and tested is shown in Listing 6.1.

Listing 6.1 Coding a Shared Function to Return a Formatted SQL String

```
Shared Function GetCustomerSQL(ByVal strInParm As String, _
 ByVal strDebug As String, ByVal intMaxRows As Integer)↲
   As String
' Set to production report path if production
Dim strSELECTView As String
If strDebug = "" Then
   strSELECTView = "SELECT TOP " & CStr(intMaxRows) & ↲
     " * FROM AddressesByLocation "
Else  ' Production
   strSELECTView = "SELECT * FROM AddressesByLocation "
End If
Dim strWHERE As String = _
   "WHERE (CountryRegionCode = '" & strInParm & "') "
Dim strORDERBY As String = _
   " ORDER BY CountryRegionCode, City, PostalCode"
```

```
If UCase(strInParm) = "ALL" Then
    ' Use View without WHERE clause
    Return strSELECTView & strORDERBY
Else
    ' Use View with WHERE clause
    Return strSELECTView & strWHERE & strORDERBY
End If
End Function
```

4. The coded (and tested) Visual Basic function as pasted into the code dialog is shown in Figure 6.46. Note that this dialog does not care one snit about Visual Basic syntax. That won't be checked until you try to execute the code. That's why we suggest that you test the code in a separate project.

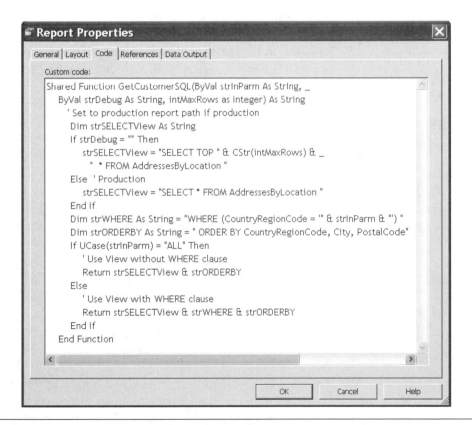

Figure 6.46 The Report Properties Code Dialog

Note that this custom code function (`GetCustomerSQL`) accepts three input parameters:

- A string (`strInParm`) that's used as an ordinary query parameter to feed the `WHERE` clause (the Country RegionCode). This parameter is also used to determine if the `WHERE` clause is used at all—in cases when all rows are wanted.
- A string (`strDebug`) that's used to indicate whether or not the report is running in the Report Designer (as it's being debugged) or in Internet Explorer (in production).
- An integer (`intMaxRows`) used to pass the value into a `TOP` expression should be inserted into the SQL `SELECT`.

Let's see how our custom function is invoked and its input parameters are populated.

5. Navigate to the Data tab and create a new DataSet—we named it dsCustomersByCountry in this example. Instead of using a `SELECT` statement, we provided a custom code function, as shown in Figure 6.47. Note how the three input function parameters are populated:

- The `strInputParm` parameter is collected from the `CountryCodeWanted` Report Parameter. You'll need to use the Report Parameters dialog to create this parameter. It's populated from another DataSet that simply returns all of the valid CountryCode values. We'll show you how that's done in a minute.
- The `strDebug` input parameter is fed from the `Globals!ReportFolder`, which returns an empty string while in the Report Designer and a full path when running in the Internet Explorer browser.
- The `intMaxRows` parameter is fed from the `MaxRows` Report Parameter we defined earlier in the project.

We also need to build another DataSet to populate the Report Parameter used to choose the desired country. Because we want only rows from the Addresses table where there are customers, we write a query to that effect, as shown in the DataSet query definition in Figure 6.48.

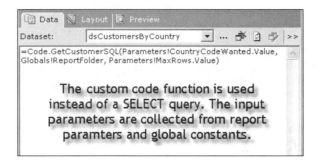

Figure 6.47 Using a Custom Code Function Instead of a `SELECT` Query in a DataSet

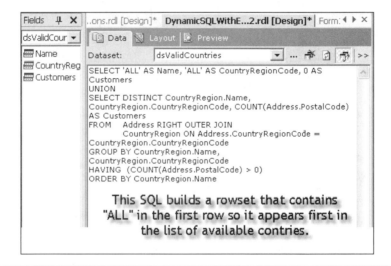

Figure 6.48 A `SELECT` with a `UNION` and a Second `SELECT` to Populate the Valid Countries Report Parameter Pick List

This query uses a `UNION` to concatenate a row to the front of the rowset, so the first element of the parameter pick list is ALL. This permits the user to return rows from all of the countries. We pass this parameter to the custom code function that uses it to determine whether or not a `WHERE` clause is concatenated to the `SELECT` query.

As we said, custom code functions can be used virtually anywhere an expression can be used. This means you can change the behavior of many report or control properties programmatically. Another nuance—we changed the report's *BackgroundImage* property to a "Testing in progress" image if the `Globals!ReportFolder` returns an empty string—to indicate that the report is in a test mode. The following expression does the job: `=iif( Globals!ReportFolder = "","testmode","")`.

Sharing Code Between Reports by Creating Class Libraries

When you find yourself placing the same function in several report code blocks, you're better off creating a shared function, compiling it as a class library DLL, and calling it from all of the reports that need it. Leaving these code snippets in the reports creates a maintenance nightmare should you need to update the code. When your code makes tax or business rule calculations, performs custom formatting, or aggregates using the `RunningValue` function, the functions are probably best created as a library assembly that can be referenced in and shared by the reports that need them. When it comes time to change the logic to accommodate changes in tax law or your business rules, for example, it's a simple matter to redeploy updated class library DLLs. This approach has many other benefits, including the ability to create the library in a programming language such as C#, Managed C++, or Visual Basic .NET, which provide all the richness of IntelliSense in the Visual Studio .NET 2003 IDE— features you probably missed from the crude Visual Basic .NET code-behind block. If the code you want to implement is straightforward and needs only execution permissions (which means that the code doesn't need to do anything like read from a database, file system, registry, network, the event log, or anything else beyond an execution-only sandbox), you can implement the class library without having to concern yourself with code access security. That's because by default Reporting Services is configured to provide execution-only permissions to referenced library assemblies. On the other hand, if you need to step outside the restricted execution-only sandbox through your library, refer to Chapter 9 where we explain code access security in more depth.

NOTE *Don't Click on the Preview Tab* Whenever a report process (such as the Report Processor or the Report Designer) loads a referenced assembly, it is loaded into and remains locked in memory until the process is terminated. This means you should not use the Preview tab in the Report Designer while testing the code in assemblies referenced by a report. You need to "run" your reports in LocalDebug mode to permit them to be launched in a separate process space that is completely torn down when you close the RSReportHost.exe previewer, which removes the locks on any referenced assemblies that process created.

This next exercise illustrates how to build a CLR project that exposes a class and its functions. We'll use this CLR-based function just as we did in the previous example to generate a SQL string, but you can make it do almost anything that needs execution-only permissions.

Let's step through the process of creating a shared function in a class. We'll start with the Visual Studio .NET project we used for the previous exercise.

1. Add a new project to your solution to contain our CLR class and choose Class Library—we call this class prjBuildSQL. Note that we prefix each name with a three-letter code to help identify the object later when it comes time to reference the namespace, class, and function.
2. Copy the shared function code used in the previous example (see Figure 6.46) into the Class prototype. Your class should look something like Figure 6.49.
3. Once you code the class, we've found it helpful to hardcode the version number in the class while we're testing to make it unnecessary to synchronize the reference string in the RDL each time we refine the function code. Open the prjBuildSQL AssemblyInfo.VB file, and edit the version number, as shown in Figure 6.50. If you don't do this, each time the project is built, the AssemblyVersion value is incremented and you'll need to revisit the References dialog (as we'll show you in a minute).

TIP *Testing* Sure, it's a good idea to test your function before using it in a report. We often create a test harness to call the function with expected (typical) parameters and see what it returns. We'll leave that part of the exercise up to you to work out.

```
Start Page  clsBuildSQL.vb*

(General)                                          (Declarations)

 1    Option Strict On
 2    Public Class clsBuildSQL
 3        Shared Function GetCustomerSQL(ByVal strInParm As String, _
 4            ByVal strDebug As String, ByVal intMaxRows As Integer) As String
 5            ' Set to production report path if production
 6            Dim strSELECTView As String
 7            If strDebug = "" Then
 8                strSELECTView = "SELECT TOP " & CStr(intMaxRows) & _
 9                    " * FROM AddressesByLocation "
10            Else  ' Production
11                strSELECTView = "SELECT * FROM AddressesByLocation "
12            End If
13            Dim strWHERE As String = "WHERE (CountryRegionCode = '" _
14                & strInParm & "') "
15            Dim strORDERBY As String = " ORDER BY CountryRegionCode," _
16                & " City, PostalCode"
17            If UCase(strInParm) = "ALL" Then
18                ' Use View without WHERE clause
19                Return strSELECTView & strORDERBY
20            Else
21                ' Use View with WHERE clause
22                Return strSELECTView & strWHERE & strORDERBY
23            End If
24        End Function
25    End Class
```

Figure 6.49 The clsBuildSQL Class and GetCustomerSQL Shared Function Code

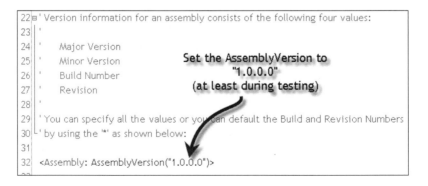

```
22    ' Version information for an assembly consists of the following four values:
23    '
24    '       Major Version
25    '       Minor Version                 Set the AssemblyVersion to
26    '       Build Number                          "1.0.0.0"
27    '       Revision                      (at least during testing)
28    '
29    ' You can specify all the values or you can default the Build and Revision Numbers
30    ' by using the '*' as shown below:
31
32    <Assembly: AssemblyVersion("1.0.0.0")>
```

Figure 6.50 Setting the AssemblyVersion to 1.0.0.0

4. Now you're ready to build the class. Right-click on the prjBuildSQL class and choose Build. This compiles the code and builds a DLL in the project Bin directory.

5. Neither the Report Processor nor the Report Designer can find the DLL you've just created (prjBuildSQL.DLL) unless you copy the DLLs to the appropriate directories. We found the process of building and manually deploying the DLLs to be fairly time-consuming, so we created a batch file to move the DLL to the appropriate locations. Your batch file must also deal with the fact that the Report Server might be on another system. We saved the batch file (deploy.bat), shown in Listing 6.2, into the project directory and added it to the project so that it's easy to find and execute (directly from the Visual Studio .NET IDE).

Listing 6.2 The Deploy.bat File That Deploys the Compiled DLL Class

```
copy "C:\Company Reports\CLR Shared ↵
Functions\prjBuildSQL\bin\prjBuildSQL.DLL"↵
  "C:\Program Files\Microsoft SQL Server\80\Tools\↵
   Report Designer\prjBuildSQL.DLL"
copy "C:\Company Reports\CLR Shared Functions\↵
   prjBuildSQL\bin\prjBuildSQL.DLL" ↵
   "C:\Program Files\Microsoft SQL Server\MSSQL\↵
   Reporting Services\ReportServer\bin\prjBuildSQL.DLL"
```

6. Once you've built the project and the deployment batch file, run the batch to move the DLL to the appropriate directories.

7. Next, we need to reference the DLL in our report. As with the previous example, we'll use the CLR function to return a parameter-generated SQL statement. Copy the existing example (CodeBehind.RDL) file to the same project directory and rename it CLRSharedFunction.RDL.

8. Add this existing RDL to the working Reports project.

9. Navigate to the CLRSharedFunction.RDL Data tab and drill down to the dsCustomersByCountry DataSet. Replace the command text with a reference to the new CLR function. Note that we reference the function by =<project>.<class>.<function> notation, as shown in Figure 6.51.

Figure 6.51 Addressing the Project, (Assembly) Class and Function in an Expression

NOTE *Warning...Don't Click Preview* You still have another few steps to take before you can view the report. But don't get antsy. Do *not* click the Preview tab. If you have, it's too late—you're pooched and you won't be able to work through the issues without restarting Visual Studio. NET. If you click on the Preview tab, the shared assembly is loaded (and locked) in memory and it's locked in place. At this point, you can change the source, rebuild, and deploy the new DLL, but when you execute the report, the in-memory (locked) version is used—not your newly created version. This can be most confusing when you think you're fixing problems and nothing seems to change. In this case, you'll need to save everything, exit Visual Studio .NET, and restart.

10. Open the Report Properties page and visit the Code tab. Make sure it's cleared out. We won't be using a code-behind function in this case.

11. Click on the References tab and navigate to the prjBuildSQL.DLL using the ellipsis button, as shown in Figure 6.52. This populates the Assembly name string, which points to the DLL by name and indicates the Version, Culture, and PublicKeyToken. No, the DLL binary is not added to the RDL—only a pointer to the DLL is added. Don't worry about the Class name and Instance name values for now. We'll show you how to set those in a minute.

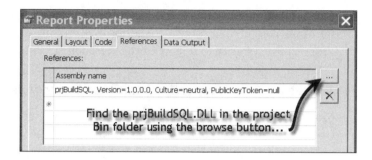

Figure 6.52 Setting the Assembly Name String by Browsing to the CLR Function DLL

12. Now you're ready to test the report from the Report Designer. No, keep away from the Preview tab. If you hit it by accident, read the note before Step 10 to undo the damage. You will find it helpful to put a sticky note label over the Preview tab to keep you from clicking it by mistake. To test the report safely, switch the solution configuration to DebugLocal. Be sure that the Project configuration properties for the DebugLocal configuration have not set a TargetServerURL.

13. Right-click the CLRSharedFunction.RDL report, and choose Run to test the report and the CLR function. This compiles the report and launches a separate Internet Explorer process to test it. On our systems, this process can take some time (10 to 30 seconds on occasion) to launch the first time, so be patient. Eventually, a new browser window appears and you can test the report—assuming you hooked it up correctly.

14. The final step is to test the report in a "deployed" environment. In this case, the CLR DLL is not drawn from the Report Designer directory but from the Report Server\bin directory. Remember our deploy.bat file? It copies the newly created DLL to both the Report Designer directory and to the ReportServer\bin directory. This means you should be able switch to Debug or Production, click on Deploy, and use your Report Manager to launch and test the CLRSharedFunction report.

If your code tries to access memory or functionality outside the sandbox, you'll trip a security exception. We'll talk about how to use code access security to deal with these issues in Chapter 9.

Accessing Class Properties and Other Instance Issues

Many classes expose shared properties that you might want to access from your reports. As we're about to illustrate, these properties are not difficult to implement in code or reference from your report definition. Starting from the previous example, we can add a block of code to add two "constructors" to the class, so any code (such as the Report Designer or Report Processor) that wishes to create an instance of the class can do so. Next, we'll add a Public (read-only) property that can be referenced by a Report Expression. Let's get started:

1. Open the clsBuildSQL.vb file with Visual Studio .NET, and append the code in Listing 6.3:

Listing 6.3 Exposing Properties for Shared Classes

```
Option Strict On
Public Class clsBuildSQL
    Private lngCreationTime As Long
    Sub New()
        lngCreationTime = Now.Ticks
    End Sub
    Sub New(ByVal lngParmCreationTime As Long)
        lngCreationTime = lngParmCreationTime
    End Sub
    Public ReadOnly Property CreationTime() As String
        Get
            Return lngCreationTime.ToString
        End Get
    End Property
```

This code creates a local instance variable *lngCreationTime* and exposes two new constructors—one with no arguments that sets the *lngCreationTime* variable to the current "tick" count and another constructor that accepts an argument to set the *lngCreationTime* instance variable. The code also exposes a public read-only property to return the *lngCreationTime* as a string. Sure, this is a pretty simple implementation (at least we think so), but you can take this as a starting point for your own classes, properties, and functions.

2. To reference the function and its instance property, we add a bit more information to the Report Properties References tab, as shown in Figure 6.53.

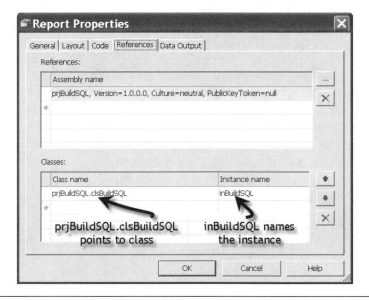

Figure 6.53 Adding the Class Name and Instance Name to the Report Properties References

3. Once the References tab is setup correctly, we can now reference our class using the instance name (*inBuildSQL*). Note that the class name (clsBuildSQL) must be fully qualified with the project (assembly) name (prjBuildSQL).

4. Return to the report definition and add a Textbox control, as shown in Figure 6.54. We'll use this control to display the TickCount value returned from the class instance variable. Remember, the *CreationTime* property routine returned the string representation of the TickCount value, so we don't have to reformat it.

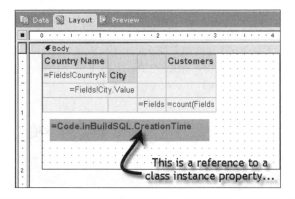

Figure 6.54 Adding a Textbox That Returns a Value from the CLR Class Instance Variable

As you have seen, it's possible to add quite a bit of functionality to your reports using a variety of techniques that leverage Visual Basic .NET as well as other CLR-language classes and the functions and properties they expose. We'll talk about this again in Chapter 9 as we get into using similar functions to access code outside the sandbox.

Summary

We've covered a lot of ground in this chapter. We spent quite a bit of time discussing how to access your data sources efficiently and safely and how to build queries to return the data for your reports. We talked about pre- and post-query filtering and sorting as well as how to manage expressions used to get the most out of these properties. We also showed you a number of advanced functions so that you can incorporate more sophisticated expressions in your reports—including custom Visual Basic code. Next, we'll take the DataSets you've created and lay out reports that display the data they return.

CHAPTER 7

Report Layout and Design

Once you've created your report's Data Sources and DataSets and defined any parameters you need, you're ready to start defining and laying out the visual presentation elements of the report. This chapter focuses on the visual aspects of report design—what your report "consumers" see. More than any other factor, what your report looks like can make or break its success. We walk through a (perhaps not so) typical scenario of a developer being asked to create and then refine a report for an all-too-typical client. As we go, the report gets more complex and illustrates more Reporting Services features. We'll show you how to add details, drill into those details, and add graphics and subreports to your base reports and controls.

Previewing and Deploying Reports

Before we get started designing and laying out your reports, we want to visit another topic—how to preview your report and, once you're ready, how to deploy it to the Report Server so your users can see it too. One interesting point we've discovered is that for the most part the Preview tab in the designer is WYSIWYG—well, almost. Sure, in several situations what renders in the Preview "browser" won't render exactly the same way once deployed. We'll discuss these differences in a moment. Just keep in mind that before you tell your users to view your report with a browser, you should actually *test* it with a browser.

To start with, let's touch on performing a quick check of how your report can be executed and viewed in the Preview window. During the development cycle of a report, you're going to want to see what the rendered version of it looks like. This process opens the connection, validates the credentials, runs the query, returns the rowset(s) to populate your DataSet(s), and renders the report—all based on the RDL file you're working with in the Report Designer or the compiled report stored in the server.

You can preview your report in three ways:

- **In the Report Designer:** Click on the Preview tab. While this is the fastest and easiest way to preview your report, this approach has some big drawbacks if you're developing custom assemblies (we'll deal with those in Chapter 9). Keep in mind that it's not always a good idea to deploy untested software or reports. Using the Preview tab does not deploy anything to the server—in fact, the Report Server is not used to render the report.

- **In the RSReportHost:** Right-click on the Solution Explorer and choose Run. If you want to use this technique, you need to choose the DebugLocal configuration from the Solution Configurations, as shown in Figure 7.1. This enables a different set of project properties. The key to this technique is that the *TargetServerURL* property is *blank*. If you now select the report definition in the Solution Explorer and choose Run, the report is launched in the RSReportHost program. Yes, this is very similar to the look and feel of previewing in the Report Designer. It is, in fact, the same program that is used, but the crucial difference is that this program is launched in its *own* process space, not in the Visual Studio .NET 2003 process space. If you're doing any custom assembly work, this is the preview route of choice because when you close it, the report process is completely ripped out of memory. As discussed in Chapter 6, when you use the Preview tab within Visual Studio .NET 2003, any custom assemblies that your report accesses are loaded into the Visual Studio process space. These custom assemblies remain in memory until you completely close Visual Studio .NET 2003, so you can't do any further editing or compilation work on the custom assembly.

So, when you want to debug custom assemblies used by your reports, you'll only want to use the RSReportHost, unless you're paid by the hour and want to complain that Visual Studio .NET 2003 has locked your assembly in memory again.

Figure 7.1 Setting the Project "DebugLocal" Option from the Solution Configurations Dropdown

- **Previewing (Viewing) in the Web Browser:** If you set the Project Solution configurations to a profile that has a valid *TargetServerURL* property, when you select a report in the Solution Explorer and choose Run, the report definition is deployed and launched in a web browser. (If you only select Deploy, the report definition will be deployed but is not opened in a browser.) Rendering in a web browser is actually the best test of what the user is most likely to see because it's subject to the localization issues of web browser language. We'll get to localization and other issues a little later in this chapter. This is the only situation in which the Report Server does the rendering. Both of the other techniques use RSReportHost.exe. Some of the issues we've seen when previewing reports in the browser include how controls (especially graphics and the Rectangle control) are placed and how color gradients are rendered. Other issues came up when we used Netscape to view the report—another issue we discuss later in the chapter. Service Pack 1 fixed many of the RSReportHost issues, but still, nothing beats the real thing, does it?[1]

---

[1] Unless we want the Pepsi versus Coca-Cola debate…again!

Data Caching for the Designer's Preview

Once you've installed Service Pack 1 and previewed the rendered report using the Visual Studio .NET 2003 Preview tab, the underlying report data (the rowset(s) returned by your queries) is cached in the project folder with the file extension .data. This cached data is indexed by Data Source credentials and Report Parameters. If your subsequent preview requests use the same parameter values and credentials, the previewer uses data directly from the cached file instead of querying the underlying database(s) again. At first blush, you might think that this is handy, as it certainly improves performance. However, be aware that the cache file is *not* encrypted. This is a concern if the file contains sensitive data because even if it's deleted, it can be harvested from the hard drive quite easily. If you want to switch this feature off for any reason, you need to edit the RSReportDesigner.config file in the \Program Files\Microsoft SQL Server\80\Tools\Report Designer folder by adding the entry <Add Key="CacheDataForPreview" Value="false" /> in the configuration section, as shown in Listing 7.1.

Listing 7.1 Overriding the CacheDataForPreview Data Caching Feature

```
<Configuration>
  <Add Key="SecureConnectionLevel" Value="0" />
  <Add Key="InstanceName" Value="Microsoft.ReportingServices.PreviewServer" />
  <Add Key="SessionCookies" Value="true" />
  <Add Key="SessionTimeoutMinutes" Value="3" />
  <Add Key="PolicyLevel" Value="rspreviewpolicy.config" />
  <Add Key="CacheDataForPreview" Value="false" />
  <Extensions>
    . . .
  </Extensions>
</Configuration>
```

If you make changes to the RSReportDesigner.config file, be sure to restart Visual Studio .NET 2003 after the changes are made. Also, from our testing it appears that preview caching works only for previewing reports *inside* the Report Designer. It does not appear to work for reports previewed in the RSReportHost.exe previewer. If security of cached data is an issue for you, don't forget that you can encrypt the project folders and contents with EFS (Encrypting File System). To implement this, right-click on the project folder to launch the Properties dialog, select the Advanced button on the General tab to show the advanced properties, and check the "Encrypt contents to secure data" checkbox.

Laying Out Your Report

Conceptually, building reports with the Visual Studio .NET Report Designer is very much like designing a web page or a Windows form. Unless you use the Report wizard, you start out with a blank report work surface and a toolbox of nine Report Items controls to choose from, as shown in Figure 7.2. If you use the Report wizard, the process is far more automated and a good starting point for those new to Reporting Services. We've already shown you how to use the wizard in earlier chapters, but if you need more control over the report layout, follow along here to get a better grip on how the individual report controls work and interact—with each other and with the DataSet(s) you use with them.

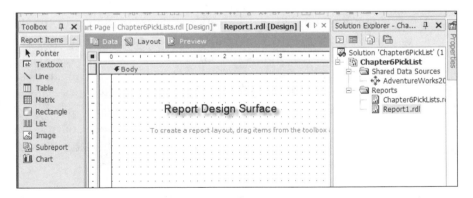

Figure 7.2 The Report Designer Toolbox and Report Design Surface

The rest of this chapter discusses the Toolbox Report Items controls, including the Textbox, List, Rectangle, Image, and Subreport controls. We'll show you how to use each of them to construct your own custom reports. These are the same controls used by the Report wizard and by the custom templates you'll be learning how to create in Chapter 9. We discuss the Chart control in Chapter 8, as it requires a somewhat different approach to building DataSets and user interaction.

Data Binding and the *Value* Property

Once these controls are dragged from the toolbox onto the design surface, their various properties can be configured and bound to literals or expressions. When you "bind" a control, Reporting Services automatically fills in the *Value* property of the control. The data is extracted from the control's assigned DataSet (DataSetName) or by setting the *Value* property to a literal string (such as "My Report Title"). The *Value* property can also contain an expression that resolves to a Field in the control's DataSet. Because each row of the DataSet is processed at runtime, the controls are scanned for references to the current row and their *Value* properties are filled in.

It may surprise you to know that only Textbox and Image controls formally have a *Value* property that can be bound to expressions based on DataSet Fields. However, many control properties can be bound to expressions that can be based on DataSet Fields. Right away, you'll notice a glaring restriction: you can't bind positional layout information to expressions. All positional information must be bound to literal fixed values. We've discussed this with the development team and the problem as they explain it is that they are faced with the difficulty of reconciling expression-based positioning when controls move because of other items growing or shrinking. We understand that this is a tricky problem to solve (especially without full control over the UI, as you would have in a Windows Forms application), but we would still like to have more control—perhaps by being able to write custom code that repositions controls after the rendering code runs.

Working with SQL Queries

Our approach in this chapter will be to develop a number of reports. As we do, we'll discuss the challenges you'll face as you lay out the controls and program their interaction with the DataSets, other controls, and the Report Processor itself. Of course, if we were developing reports for a production environment, the T-SQL in these

DataSets would address views or stored procedures. However, bear with us as we work with dynamic SQL instead. We expect many of you will simply use T-SQL as well until you get the queries solidified.

Have you (as a developer) ever been working away in your office and had a client call up and ask:

Client: *"I need a report of the AdventureWorks Product Inventory and List Price Valuation."*

Developer: *"Sure, no problem. Do you have anything particular in mind that you want to show on this report?"*

Client: *"Oh, you know, the usual product details."*

The phone line goes dead. You sit there shaking your head, thinking you need better clients.

Like virtually all of the software projects we've been involved with, clients never seem to know exactly what they want—until they don't get it. In those few cases when you and the customer write project specifications, they're usually so loose that what appears to be straightforward turns out to be a heuristic budget-balancing report for the combined countries of the United Nations. We often end up working (or more accurately, wedging) in new requirements as the client changes his or her mind, or argues that you misunderstood the project requirements in the first place.

It's never a waste of time to write a detailed project specification—before getting started.

Building a Product Inventory and Valuation Report

Since this is a good customer, we'll help you out this time. Let's launch out on our new project to build a "usual" (whatever that means) product inventory and valuation report. We start by creating a new project, following the guidelines we laid out in Chapter 6.

1. With the Report Manager, create a target folder and an AdventureWorks shared data source that uses stored credentials from a user account with read-only permissions on the data.
2. In the Report Designer, set the report project's *TargetFolder* and *TargetServer* properties.
3. Create an Integrated Security data source named AdventureWorks for use in the Designer.
4. Create a new report (Ctrl+Shift+A) and name it Product List.

5. Create a new DataSet, name it dsProduct, wire it up to the shared AdventureWorks data source, and ensure that the underlying T-SQL is based on the code shown in Listing 7.2.

Listing 7.2 T-SQL Query to Fetch Fields from the Product and ProductInventory Tables

```
SELECT    Product.Name, Product.ProductNumber, Product.Color,
          Product.ListPrice, SUM(ProductInventory.Quantity) AS Qty,
          SUM(ProductInventory.Quantity * Product.ListPrice)
          AS StockValue
FROM    Product INNER JOIN
          ProductInventory ON Product.ProductID =
                              ProductInventory.ProductID
WHERE    Product.FinishedGoodsFlag = 1
GROUP BY Product.Name, Product.ProductNumber, Product.Color,Product.ListPrice
```

Choose Portrait or Landscape layout first—before you add your controls.

(If you're a real professional, you'll do that by making a stored procedure—if not at first then once you're satisfied that the SQL does the right job.)

6. Select the Layout view in the Report Designer. Now we're ready for our first pit stop.

Page Sizing—Landscape or Portrait

We know you're itching to put some controls on the report, but one of the important things to consider before laying out too many controls on a report is the size and layout of the report pages. This is especially true if your report might be printed at some stage. You'll be kicking yourself later if you don't pay attention to these points early on. You might find that your report, which rendered beautifully when viewed online in a browser, bleeds into the next logical page horizontally when exported in preparation for printing to TIF or PDF formats. Figure 7.3 shows each area of the report and how it's defined, along with the property names that define each region.

While placing controls on the report design surface, you need to bear in mind the maximum width for the Body area of the report (again, use Figure 7.3 as a reference). The maximum depends upon the combination of a report's *PageSize* and *Margins* properties and the report body's *Columns* and *ColumnSpacing* properties.

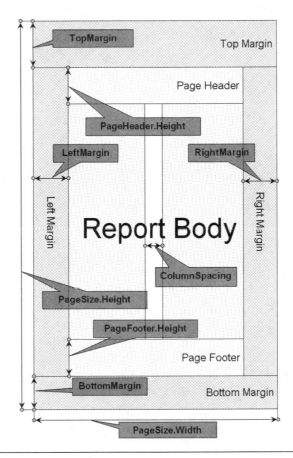

Figure 7.3 The Properties Used to Determine Page Layout

It's more convenient (and easier) to configure these properties using the Report Properties dialog Layout tab. This dialog (shown in Figure 7.4) can be launched from the Report menu. Once you've set the properties and done the math,[2] you'll be able to set the report body's *Width* property. Once it's set, try to ensure that your placement of any controls doesn't accidentally enlarge the width when you're dragging controls to the design surface—it's not that hard to do, so be careful.

---

[2] Body width = (PageSize.Width – (Margin.Left + Margin.Right)) – ((Columns -1) * ColumnSpacing)

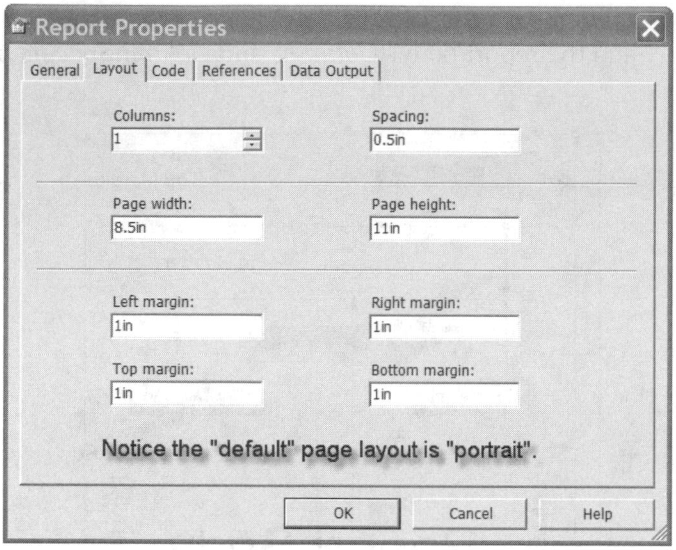

Figure 7.4 The Report Properties Dialog Layout Tab

One question we're frequently asked is how to configure Landscape or Portrait orientations. There isn't any specific configuration; it's simply a matter of the ratio of the *PageSize.Width* property to the *PageSize.Height* property. If the width is greater than the height, you'll have a landscape report and portrait otherwise. The default Report Template uses a Portrait layout, but you could change this. We show you how in Chapter 9. The RTM version exhibited some problems with the PDF renderer in relation to landscape/portrait issues, but our tests on Service Pack 1 show that this has been addressed.

As you work on setting up the customer report, you find that you need more information from the client. He's in a good mood, but busy, and open "for output only," as usual.

Developer: *"For the Product List report you want me to create, you didn't say if you might want to print it? If you do, do you want it landscape or portrait, and what paper size will you be using?"*

Client: *"Well, you'd better make it landscape when it prints. Oh, and by the way when it prints can you include the page number, report name, and total number of pages?"*

Developer: *"Okay, but what paper size: U.S. or European?"*

The phone line has already gone dead—you're speaking to the dial tone. You decide to SPAM the client with anonymous mail about a listening course you heard about last week, taking care not to use your default SMTP Server or IP Address.

So, if you are working from the default template, swap the PageSize's *Width* and *Height* properties to get a landscape orientation. If you are using a custom user interface, as you would if you were using the SOAP interface, you also have some control in overriding the *Width* and *Height* properties when the renderer is called through the deviceinfo attribute.

Introducing the Page Header and Page Footer

As we mentioned earlier, a report can have an optional page header and page footer. These special report areas are not data regions, so they're not capable of hosting controls that depend on data from the DataSet(s). The default Report Template doesn't have either the page header or page footer enabled. To enable them, you can toggle Page Header and/or Page Footer from the Report menu—but only if you're in Layout view. If the Report menu isn't visible, first click on the body to give it the focus and the menu should appear. To display the report page number and total pages on each page of your report, you can write an expression that includes the *PageNumber* and *TotalPages* global variables in the *Value* property of a Textbox control.

NOTE By default, the page header and footer are shown on every page of the report. You can, however, suppress printing these areas on the very first and very last pages by setting the report *PrintOnFirstPage* or *PrintOnLastPage* properties to False.

The header and footer are special areas of a report, and they only support the parenting of the Textbox, Rectangle, Line, and Image controls. When these controls are placed in the header or footer, they cannot have *any* of their properties bound to data that originates from any of a report's DataSets. That can be most inconvenient. We'll tell you a little later what you can do about it when you absolutely must bind these controls to data—the process does involve a bit of sorcery and chicken gizzards, but it works pretty well. However, you can create expressions that can be bound to a control's properties and can make use of global variables. As it happens, the PageNumber and TotalPages global variables can be used only in expressions within controls in the header or footer.

Using Global Variables

Global variables are values set and managed internally by the Report Processor. These values can be used in expressions or by themselves in report cells. There are eight global variables, as listed and detailed in Table 7.1.

Table 7.1 The Global Variables

Variable	Header	Body	Footer	Datatype	Notes
PageNumber	Y		Y	Integer	The current page number.
TotalPages	Y		Y	Integer	Total number of rendered pages in a report.
ExecutionTime	Y	Y	Y	DateTime	The date and time that the report was first executed. If the report is being rendered from a Snapshot or a cached version, this is the original execution time.
ReportServerUrl	Y	Y	Y	String	The URL of the Report Server. Excludes the folder path and report name.
ReportFolder	Y	Y	Y	String	The report folder path. Excludes the Report Server URL and report name.
ReportName	Y	Y	Y	String	The report name.

Table 7.1 The Global Variables, *continued*

Variable	Header	Body	Footer	Datatype	Notes
UserID	Y	Y	Y	String	The User ID of the person rendering the report. This changes even when rendering from a cached or Snapshot report. While all the other global variables are addressed Globals!<variable>, UserID is addressed USER!UserID.
Language	Y	Y	Y	String	The language setting of the user's web browser.

Let's get back to our example report and continue tuning it to meet these new requirements.

1. Enable the Page Footer and drag a Textbox control from the Toolbox palette into the Page Footer area.
2. Construct an expression for this Textbox control's *Value* property that concatenates some of the global variables. Because we're in the Page Footer area, we're permitted to use the PageNumber and TotalPages global variables. You may find it helpful to launch the Expression Editor by right-clicking on this textbox and selecting the "Expression…" option.

Avoid situations where the controls expand beyond the Body area.

3. Within the Expression Editor, concatenate the two global variables using Visual Basic .NET syntax:

```
= Globals!PageNumber & " of " & Globals!TotalPages
```

You *might* want to stretch this textbox to extend over the whole width of the report, especially if you want to select alignment to center the text. Take care, because the body expands automatically if you drag too far to the right. If you do, you'll be bleeding to the right when printing, and Mr. Client will be back on your case in no time. We'll let you decide which fonts, colors, and text alignment you want to use for the report. Look at our sample report, 001 Product List, to see an implementation of the header and footer for the report. Figure 7.5 illustrates how this could look when you're done.

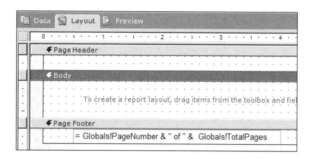

Figure 7.5 Adding a Textbox Control Containing an Expression to the Page Footer

TIP *Place at Least One Control up Against the Report's Right Margin* It is very easy to stretch the body over the right margin area when placing controls, adding columns to a table, or just temporarily moving controls out of the way. If you have one control that you know is positioned against the right margin, after repositioning the offending controls, you can quickly drag the right-hand side of the body back up against the control that's positioned as the anchor point on the right margin.

Make the development and maintenance tasks easier—choose intelligent names for your Textbox and other controls.

You'll probably find it much easier to directly adjust the *Size* properties of the controls you need to position against the right-hand margin by manipulating the properties in the Properties pane instead of dragging or stretching.

Naming Textbox Controls

Notice that the Textbox controls you add to a report and then don't bind to data from any DataSets are named serially using incrementing string literals such as Textbox1, Textbox2, and so on. Those controls you simply bind to data automagically rename themselves to serially incrementing string literals based on the name of the Field to which they are bound. With this naming convention in mind, think about renaming those Textbox controls whose *Value* properties are bound to expressions. Use names that might be more helpful when you're working late at night, frantically looking through dialog options and wondering which textbox you want to use.

Editing Textbox Controls

Those familiar with Microsoft Access will be used to editing Textbox controls in situ—that is, they can be edited in the layout designer by typing expressions directly into the textbox. Thankfully, you can also set control properties using the Properties dialog. Both techniques are supported in the Report Designer. Perhaps one day, the Visual Studio development team will realize the usefulness of in-place expression and property editing and add them into Visual Studio!

If you want to create a literal string label for a Field, you have two options. You can make the literal string into an expression, as in =My Literal Label. If there is no expression to evaluate, you can enter the text for the label directly in the textbox without the "=" prefix or quotes. There isn't a Label control as such—just use a textbox.

Layout—Snapping to the Grid

If you want controls to snap to the grid as you place, size, and adjust them, you may find it helpful to adjust the alignment grid on the Layout view. These grid properties can be adjusted from the Report Properties dialog General tab, or by adjusting the design properties of the report, in the Properties window.

Displaying Controls Bound to Data

If you've come from a Microsoft Access background, you're possibly used to grabbing a Field from the Field list and dragging it directly to the report layout design surface. Once dropped, Access creates Textbox and Label controls and binds the Textbox control to the Field. When you execute the Microsoft Access report, the Field displays repetitively—once for each row.

You can try this approach in Reporting Services, but it won't work in the same way. To illustrate this, drag the Name Field from the Fields list directly onto the report's body, as shown in Figure 7.6. Look closely at the binding as displayed in the Textbox control:

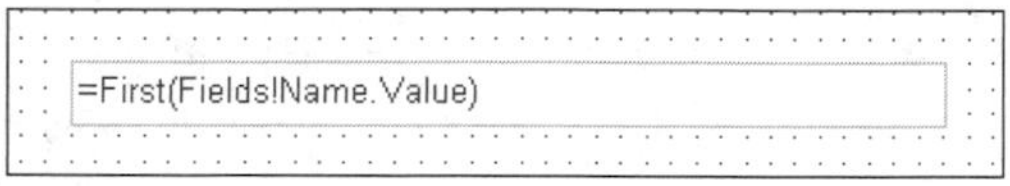

```
=First(Fields!Name.Value)
```

Figure 7.6 Default Binding to a Textbox Control

The Textbox control serves double-duty as a report label—there is no "Label" control.

In this case, the Textbox control is bound to the default aggregate of First() on the Name Field. If you happened to pick a Field with a numeric datatype, you may get a Sum() aggregate instead. If you preview the report by selecting the Preview tab, you'll see only one element and only the first row, or Sum aggregate result. That's probably not what our client had in mind, so let's remove the Textbox control by selecting it and deleting it.

If you want to display data for each row, the big secret is that you need to use a Data Region control to host the Field instead of placing the Field directly in the body. For our purposes, we need either a List or a Table control. We've already worked extensively with the Table control in Chapter 3, so drag a List control from the toolbox (see Figure 7.7) onto the body while we tell you all about Data Region controls.

Data Region Controls

There are four Data Region controls: List, Table, Matrix, and Chart. All Data Region controls have a *DataSetName* property that determines the DataSet they work with. Each has its own unique way of manipulating data, iterating through, and processing each row in the single DataSet to which it is bound. After placing a Data Region control in the report body and sizing it, you'll be able to start selecting Fields from the Fields list. Each of these Fields can be dragged and dropped onto the selected Data Region control. If you have a report with more than one DataSet, you need to take a little care about the first field you drag onto each Data Region control, as this automagically determines the Data Region control's *DataSetName* property setting. Yes, you can change this property manually—you'll need to if you initially drag the wrong Field from a DataSet that you did not intend to bind to the Data Region control. The magic doesn't appear to work in reverse. By the way, Data Region controls can only be used in the Body section of a report, not in the header or footer.

NOTE Remember that the Report Designer is simply capturing properties that are translated into a Unicode RDL XML data file. As such, these properties all contain strings or resolve to strings. Unlike Visual Basic .NET, where some properties are set to binary pointers to objects, all of these properties are human-readable. It's entirely possible to examine the RDL file directly and even make changes there.

Using the List Control

Returning to our example, we're ready to make some additional changes.

1. As described previously, drag a List control to the report Body area.
2. Drag the Name Field from the Fields list, and drop it onto the List control, as shown in Figure 7.7.

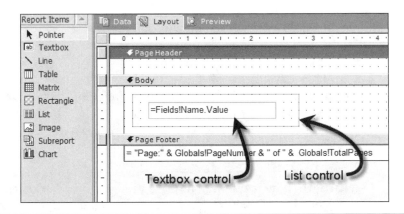

Figure 7.7 A List Control Hosting a Textbox Control

3. Preview the report by clicking on the Preview tab. The List control will repeat once for each row. Notice that the binding is as expected. You're not bound to some aggregate function. Your report should look something like Figure 7.8 at this point.

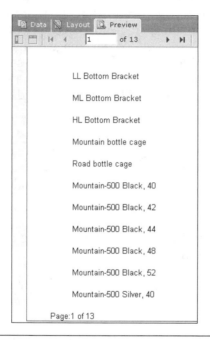

Figure 7.8 Previewing the List Control with the PageFooter Value

The "advantage" of a List control is that it permits free-form hosting of any of the other controls, including other Data Region controls. By *free form*, what we mean is that the controls can be positioned anywhere inside the List control—think of these Data Region controls as "containers" in the Visual Basic sense.

NOTE Over the last few months we've seen a number of innovative applications of Reporting Services, including reports laid out to match paper forms. The List control is ideal for this type of report, where you need free-form layout flexibility. The trick here is to switch off the *CanGrow* and *CanShrink* properties to prevent the controls from moving from their assigned locations.

Using the Table Control as an Alternative

The Table control that we demonstrated in Chapter 3 is very powerful and is perhaps the optimal control to use in many applications. Remember that the Table control can merge adjacent column cells (but not rows). This means many layouts that can be achieved with List controls can be achieved easily with judicious merging of Table control cells. However, it would be problematic to use a Table control if you wanted the report to have vertically offset fields, as shown in Figure 7.9. Yes, you could use the padding properties, but if you also wanted a solid border around each Textbox control, you've got some thinking to do. We'll straighten up these fields, and accept that we can probably achieve the desired effect better by using a Table control. The Table control also supports sorting, grouping, and built-in placeholders for headers and footers at group levels. Bear with us and we'll show you how to use a List control, but know that in practice we've found so very few situations where we couldn't use a Table control instead. In the AdventureWorks sample reports supplied by Microsoft, a Table control could have been used instead of a List.

> The Table control is the "control of choice" for many reports.

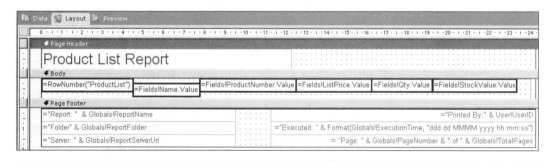

Figure 7.9 Laying Out List Controls with Vertical Offsets

Using the RowNumber() and RunningValue() Aggregate Functions

If you look closely at Figure 7.9 or if you load the 002 Product List sample report, you'll see that we made use of the RowNumber(*Scope*) running aggregate function. This is a built-in function that returns an incrementing integer counter for each row in the scope passed to the function as a parameter. It's possible to pass Nothing, in which case the scope becomes the outermost data region.

As an alternative, you can use the RunningValue aggregate, which is another built-in function that permits a running value to be created by aggregating an expression function.

Client: *"Gee, that 002 Product List report is just darn right ugly!"*

Developer: *"Yes, I'm still working on it. It wasn't ready for you to run yet."*

Client: *"Well, I'm just letting you know it's real ugly, okay? Heidi, the CFO, says you obviously don't know that you should be using Table controls!"*

You quietly wish that you'd listened to the advice we gave in Chapter 6 and created a staging folder for reports under development. Perhaps for the next project. You'd only been experimenting after all. But then you distract yourself with thoughts of, *"Ha...ugly! Ugly? He's got room to talk—he can't own a mirror!"* Anyway, Heidi was right, you should have been using a Table control for this report and you'd intended to do so; but now this is a NIHS[3] matter—even though you know that doing this with a List control is going to be making a lot of trouble for yourself, you plod on.

Using the RepeatWith *Property*

Your client thought the 002 Product List sample report looked ugly with its unaligned Textbox controls and borders. Because you still want to keep this client happy, we aligned everything and removed the borders. However, testing the report shows there's still something missing. Labels! Don't confuse the report's *Label* property (we'll get to that—the *Label* property is used with Document Maps) with Label controls, which simply enable developers to identify the Fields on the report. When working with a Table control, the labels can be filled in for us in the header; but with the List control, we're on our own.

---

[3] NIHS (noun): Not Invented Here Syndrome. Occurs when developers know they can code better than anyone else and are resistant to change or adopting anyone else's ideas. Usually appears in shops where politics matter more than performance or productivity.

We create labels by dragging Textbox controls into the Body and assigning their *Value* property with a literal string or expression. Of course, if we positioned these Textbox controls inside the List control, the label text would repeat for each row. Ideally, we want the labels outside and above the List control. If you run up the report at this point, the new labels display just fine on the first page, but not thereafter. Take a look at 003 Product List in the Report Manager, and browse a few pages of the report to see what we mean.

Don't forget to update the Name property of these Textbox controls to make them easier to identify.

The solution to this problem is to set the *RepeatWith* property on the Textbox controls (the ones we place outside the List control) to *RepeatWith* the List control. This means when the List control splits over a page boundary, the Textbox controls are repeated. While this works for the report when it is rendered to the browser, don't expect it to work in the Report Designer. (We hope this irritation will be addressed in an upcoming Service Pack.)

The 004 Product List report shown in Figure 7.10 is probably ready to show to the client for some feedback.

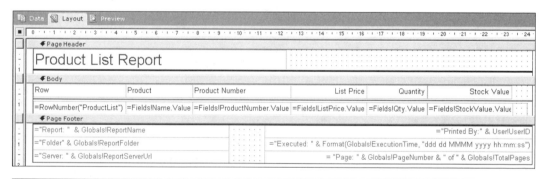

Figure 7.10 The 004 Product List Report

Developer: *"Have you got a moment to take a look at where we are with your Product List report? It's ready for you to review, and we'd just like to check that this is the sort of thing you had in mind."*

Client, in a rare moment of gratitude: *"Oh, thank you for that lovely poster-sized mirror you sent me! I've placed it on my office wall opposite the window and I can see right across now into your office without having to get up from my desk! Let me take a look at the report. Hmmm, where's the company logo? The money columns need to show that they are currency, and the report needs sorting by Product Name."*

The phone line goes dead…. Apparently, the little hints you've been sending the client about his communication skills are not sinking in—in fact, they're backfiring. Why didn't you think of what he'd do with the mirror? D'oh! You look up and realize he's watching you. As you ponder something more drastic, you go back to refining the report.

Let's forget the logo for a while and concentrate on the currency fields and sorting.

Currency and Internationalization

We need to ensure that the Textbox controls displaying currency fields show as U.S. dollars. That's because the data we're retrieving from the database is stored in U.S. dollars. Let's get started by binding a Textbox control's *Value* property to an expression that formats the value, such as: =Format(Fields!StockValue.Value,"$#,#.00"). The advantage of using this approach is consistency—irrespective of which browser or Rendering extension is used to render the report. No matter where the report is viewed, it always shows $.

Consider that there is another way of getting a currency symbol to be displayed in a Textbox—set the Textbox's *Format* property to "c" for currency. However, the currency symbol that you as a developer see can be different from the symbol your report's user might see. That could be very embarrassing for your client if the report is an invoice that says the price of your product is £240 instead of $240, or vice versa. By default, the currency symbol displayed when the report is rendered is governed by the language setting of the user's browser! You can override the default by remembering to set the *Language* property on the Textbox displaying the Field to the appropriate language—in our case, "English (United States)."

Our concern with this approach is that it's all too easy to forget to set the *Language* property. When you preview your report, you won't necessarily be immediately alerted that there is anything untoward within it. The other issue with marking the *Format* property with "c" is, what happens if at some future date the local currency setting changes? For example, say the UK joins the €uro—do you really want all your historical reports showing the € symbol against transactions that took place in £?

Be aware that your reports might be viewed by users in other countries.

Of course, the simplest solution is for Great Britain to never join the €uro. Indeed, forget European integration. The U.S. could benefit from rejoining the British Empire and swapping the $ for the £.

–Peter

It might be easier if the UK just adopted the U.S. dollar, our "unique" date formatting, baseball, American football and…well, perhaps not.

–Bill

Yes, it's best you keep the Jacksons safely under lock and key.

–Peter

BTW, Bill, that c is the currency format c, not the wonderful programming languages that were derived from Dr. Martin Richard's seminal work on BCPL.

–Peter

Another approach to this issue might be to create a custom assembly implementing a method that takes a currency field and other configuration information such as the transaction date, and properly formats the currency field. That way, should the dreaded conversion ever happen when the UK starts using the €, the bazillion financial reports you've written for A.N.OTHER UK Bank can still work without modification. All you'd need to do is update the custom assembly. Such an assembly could also do parameterized currency conversions for your report. (We'll tell you about that in Chapter 9.) In the meantime, take it from us and avoid the problematic use of "c."

Report Language, TextBox Language, and Browser Language

By default, the report language inherits the browser language set by the user accessing a report. All expressions are evaluated using the report language setting (Report.Language). It's possible to force a report to use any of the recognized languages by setting the *Report.Language* property. As a result, all expressions are evaluated subject to that selected language.

Textbox controls also have a *Language* property. By default, they use the language set in the report's *Language* property as their default. This means that if the report language is set to default, the controls use the user's browser language. Again, it's possible to override the *Language* property on a Textbox control to use a particular language. But take care—this doesn't apply to any expression evaluations during evaluation. It only uses the language for the *Format* property used after the expression has been evaluated.

Sorting in a List Control

When we experimented with the Table control in Chapter 3, we said that for the most part you'll probably want to offset as much of the sorting as possible to the DBMS rather than have Reporting Services do any post-query sorting for you. Now we're going to tell you how you can get Reporting Services to do sorting for you in the List control. At its simplest, it's easy—just select the List control, right-click, and select Properties. This launches the Properties dialog. On the Sorting tab, you can specify a sorting expression that

It's often better to filter and sort data before it arrives in the DataSet.

applies to the List control. Figure 7.11 sets the first sort expression on the selected List control to sort by Name using Ascending sequence. Sure, you can add as many sort expressions as you wish.

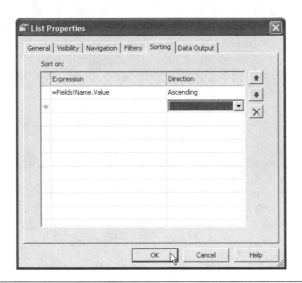

Figure 7.11 Setting the Sort Expression on a List Control

We're ready to take the newly revised 005 Product List report back to the client.

You call the client and find he's in and already in a good mood, and you wonder who let him win at golf again. You can see him in his office prancing about with his imaginary golf club.

Developer: *"I've ensured that the currency fields are taking on the correct $ symbol, and I've got the report sorting on Product Name. We'll do your company logo later on."*

Client: *"I said it needed to sort by Product Category"*

Developer: *"Sort the whole report by Product Category?"*

Client: *"No, sort that by Descending Stock Value."*

Developer: *"How about I give you the choice about how to sort the report when you run it?"*

Client: *"That's what I asked for."*

The phone line goes dead as you ponder what was just said. You decide to read that article on writing specifications you saw last month but discarded. There has to be a better way.

Given that the client is always right, we need to go back and take another look at sorting. We could create a Report Parameter called SortField and define it as shown in Figure 7.12.

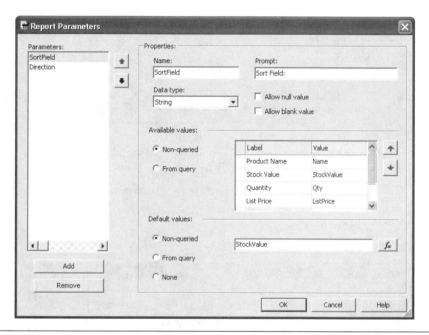

Figure 7.12 Defining a Sort Report Parameter

The first thing to note is that because we are binding to literal values we don't need to encapsulate the Label and Value settings in quotes or prefix them with =. Now we can return to the sorting properties on the List control and use a sneaky expression of =Fields(Parameters!SortField.Value).Value, as shown in Figure 7.13. The result is that our user can choose the Field by which to sort the report.

Figure 7.13 Binding the Sorting Expression to a Report Parameter

If you want to go a little further and permit the user to manage the sort direction, or in other words choose between an ascending or descending sort, you'll need to create a Report Parameter for Direction, as shown in Figure 7.14.

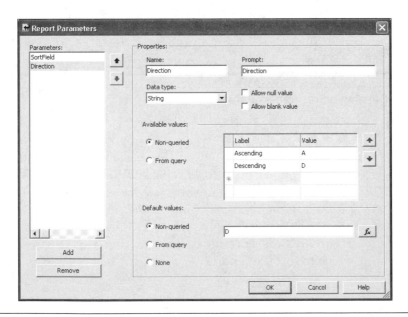

Figure 7.14 Creating Another Report Parameter to Manage Sort Direction

In the List's sorting properties, use this clever inline if (IIF) statement using two expression entries—one for ascending and one for descending, as shown in Figure 7.15.

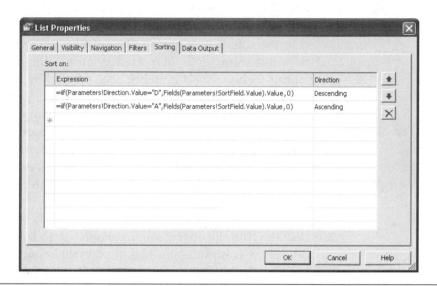

Figure 7.15 Sorting Conditionally Based on the Direction Report Parameter

Oh, by the way, this same technique can work for you with sorting in Table controls too. The 005 Product List report shows this sorting technique in action.

Sorting Optimizations for Snapshot and Historical Reports

In Chapter 4, we mentioned that by adjusting a report's execution properties it's possible to configure a report to be rendered from an execution Snapshot. Recall that this has certain performance benefits at the "cost" of having a report that uses aged data. When data is relatively static (as in a monthly sales report in which data does not change often), rendering from a historical Snapshot might be a great performance enhancement. This saves the Report Server the burden and resource expense of having to re-query data source DBMSs. But by default if your report uses Report Parameters in the underlying DataSet, queries, or complex expressions (e.g., IIF() expressions), when you run that Snapshot you'll find that all those parameters are disabled and grayed out. That means that you can't create an interactive user experience where the user re-sorts columns (or uses filters) based on expressions that use Report Parameters in Snapshots.

However, you can use a trick that isn't particularly well known. It turns out that you can mark certain Report Parameters as not being used in the underlying query. This enables editing on these selected Report Parameters when used against a Snapshot. The downside of this technique is that there is no user interface to mark the parameters, so you must manually edit the RDL by placing a `<UsedInQuery>False</UsedInQuery>` element into the RDL code against each Report Parameter that you wish to make updatable when the report is rendered from a Snapshot. Remember, these parameters can't be used in the query when it's executed.

To see an example of this technique, follow these steps:

1. Load the 005 Product List report.
2. Select the RDL file in the Solution Explorer, and choose View Code on the context menu. This displays the report's RDL.
3. Look through the RDL for the Report Parameters node, and then look under that for the particular Report Parameter you wish to mark.
4. Insert the `<UsedInQuery>False</UsedInQuery>` RDL element immediately under that node (as shown in Figure 7.16).

Take care when placing the `<UsedInQuery>` element, as each Report Parameter can have only zero or one `<UsedInQuery>` elements. When you flip over into the report's Design tabs, the `<UsedInQuery>` element is relocated to the position just before the `</ReportParameters>` element close in the RDL. Why didn't we put this element at that location to start with? We could have, but it's so easy to put the `<UsedInQuery>` element in the wrong place against a different Report Parameter. Placing it directly under the Report Parameter Name attribute helps you know you're placing it against the correct parameter.

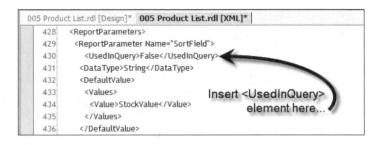

Figure 7.16 Inserting the `<UsedInQuery>` Element

Once the RDL has been modified to mark the parameter as not being used in a query, you can deploy the report. Next use the Report Manager to configure the report to render from a Snapshot. As you change the sorting Report Parameters and re-render the report, you'll see that the Executed Date we placed in the footer is not changing. This way, you can be confident that the report is not being reprocessed or making calls to the underlying data source DBMS. (We've already marked the parameters in 006 Product List as not being used in the query.) Use the SQL Profiler to convince yourself if you want to be sure!

Unfortunately, in version 1 of Reporting Services this technique doesn't work to optimize cached reports. However, this feature might be added to a Service Pack. We'll let you know through our website if we hear that this feature has been added.

Grouping with List Controls

List controls can be grouped by an expression and can contain other List controls as well. We'll find this very useful here as we tune our report to better approximate what the client thinks he wants. Remember that our client asked for sorting by product category, but he probably meant for the report to group by product category instead. When we look at the underlying query, we notice that Product Category is not immediately available. That's because it's off in the Product Category table. This table is linked through to the Product table via a Product SubCategory table. So let's add these tables and redefine the query (shown in Listing 7.3).

Listing 7.3 Expanding the T-SQL Query to Expose More Fields

```
SELECT   ProductCategory.Name AS Category,
         ProductSubCategory.Name AS SubCategory,
         Product.Name, Product.ProductNumber, Product.Color,
         Product.ListPrice, SUM(ProductInventory.Quantity) AS Qty,
         SUM(ProductInventory.Quantity * Product.ListPrice) AS StockValue
FROM   Product
INNER JOIN
     ProductInventory ON Product.ProductID = ProductInventory.ProductID INNER JOIN
   ProductSubCategory ON Product.ProductSubCategoryID =
       ProductSubCategory.ProductSubCategoryID
INNER JOIN
   ProductCategory ON ProductSubCategory.ProductCategoryID =
       ProductCategory.ProductCategoryID
WHERE (Product.FinishedGoodsFlag = 1)
GROUP BY Product.Name, Product.ProductNumber, Product.Color,
       Product.ListPrice, ProductCategory.Name, Product.SubCategory.Name
```

Using a Rectangle Control as a Temporary Container

Let's go back and work on the report again. We need to make some additional changes to the layout. We're going to use a Rectangle control to host the LstProducts control and the Label Textbox controls temporarily while we work elsewhere.

1. To give yourself more working room, increase the height of the Body section.
2. Drop a Rectangle control onto the report beneath the LstProducts List control.
3. Set the *Visibility* property of this rectangle to Hidden.
4. Cut and paste all the controls in the Body into this rectangle. We like to identify temporarily hidden controls like this rectangle by setting their back color to a vivid color. This makes the rectangle easy to see and identify in the designer, but not when previewing. It is also more convenient if controls are within Rectangle controls when trying to move them around—you only need to select and move the rectangle.

5. Now we can add a new List control at the top of the Body above the hidden rectangle and name it LstCategory.
6. Drag the Category Field from the Fields list into the top of this List control.
7. Configure any display properties you'd like for this text control. For example, configure the font, font size, color, and so on.
8. Select the LstCategory and bring up its properties from the context menu. On the General tab, ensure that the *Data set name*[4] property has been set for the LstCategory.
9. Click on the "Edit details group" button, as shown in Figure 7.17.

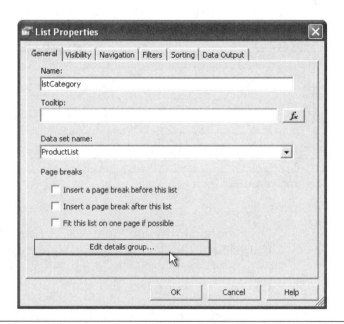

Figure 7.17 Setting the List Control's *Data set name* Property

---

[4] Yes, we noticed the space in the property name "Data set name." Strange.

10. Name the grouping and choose the Category Field to group on in the Group on Expression, as shown in Figure 7.18. At this point, given that the LstCategory List control is grouping by category, any Fields that you drag from the Fields list automatically take an aggregate function.

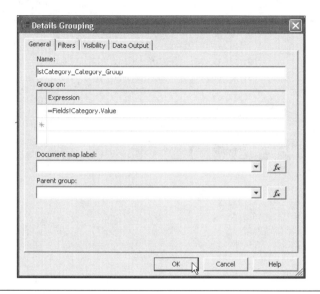

Figure 7.18 Choosing the Grouping Details

11. Drag in the StockValue Field, set its *Language* property to United States, and set its *Format* property to "c" to properly format the StockValue Field as containing U.S. currency. Figure 7.19 shows how this should look on the rendered report in the Preview tab.

12. Drop another List control within the LstCategory and call it LstSubCategory.

13. Check that its *Data set name* property is set to ProductList and that it's grouping on SubCategory. If you haven't noticed, we're building a report that's grouped by Category and then SubCategory.

14. Similarly, drag the SubCategory Field and the StockValue Field into the LstSubCategory Field.

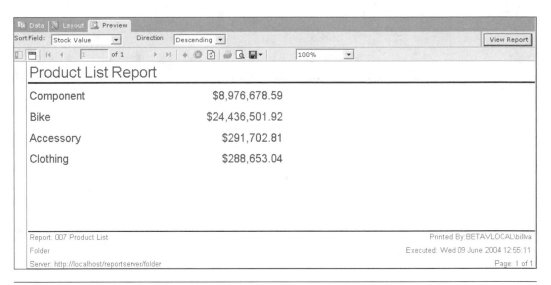

Figure 7.19 The Previewed 007 Product List Report

15. Set the language properties, currency formatting, and font styling properties for these Fields. The result is that our report is closer to what (we think) our client wants. Figure 7.20 is a layout version of this report.

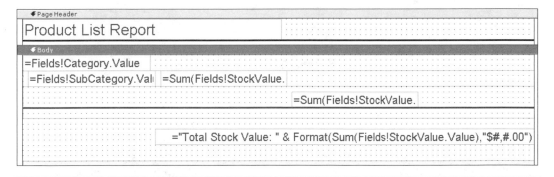

Figure 7.20 The Layout View of the 008 Product List Report

Figure 7.21 shows the report as rendered in the Preview tab.

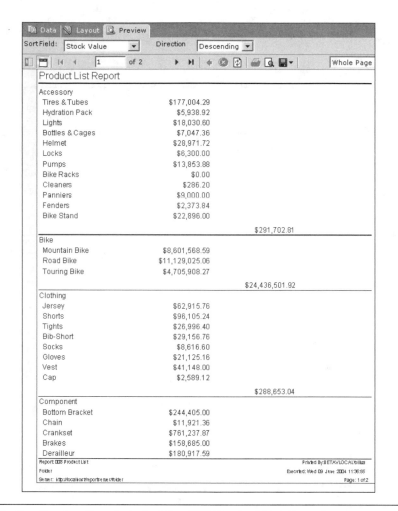

Figure 7.21 The Preview Rendering of the 008 Product List Report

As you develop your report, have someone else review the control layout. We developers often aren't much good at user interface layouts.

NOTE At this point, we thought that we should be able to cut and paste or move the rectangle to make it reside within the LstSubCategory list. However, when we created the 009 Product List report, we received rendering exceptions—but only some of the time, and only on some of the pages when deployed. While a solution appeared to be to jiggle the controls around a little and try to make sure they didn't overlap or even touch one other, the results (or lack thereof) were inconsistent at best. We discussed this with the

Reporting Services development team, who quickly identified the issue. They said that this will be addressed in the first Service Pack (SP1). In the meantime, they suggest a workaround—put a grouping on the inner list, but be careful to ensure the grouping is unique. Otherwise you'll get less than you bargained for. So we grouped on `=Fields!ProductNumber.Value` because this is unique and appeared to work in our testing. So, the 009 Product List report will probably fail on version 1 of Reporting Services, but will work post SP1. However, the 010 Product List report, which differs only in that it has a grouping on the inner list, works on both the current version and should work on the SP1 version (as shown in Figure 7.22).

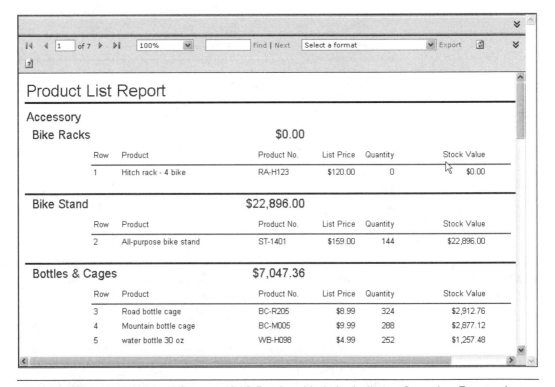

Figure 7.22 The "Working" Report (010 Product List), Including a Grouping Expression on the Innermost List Control

Working with Images

This section discusses use of the Image control as well as how to work with controls that accept graphic images as property settings. For example, you can change the *BackgroundImage* property of the Chart, Rectangle, Textbox, Table, Matrix, and List controls as well as the *BackgroundImage* of the report body. These graphics can dramatically change the visual impact of your report, as shown in Figure 7.23. In this case, we used a bitmap editor to change the transparency of a stock graphic.

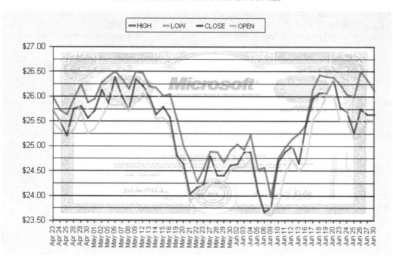

Figure 7.23 Using a "Watermarked" Graphic as a Chart Control *BackgroundImage* Property

Remember, our client asked for a company logo to be added to our report, so it's time to start thinking about strategies that work with the way that Reporting Services handles images. Images come in many shapes and sizes, file types, resolutions, and color depths. They can also be stored in the database as Binary Large Objects (BLOBs) in image columns, in files on disk, or simply as referenced by URL.[5] We found that Reporting Services can deal with images

---

[5]   URL image referencing is only supported once SP1 is installed.

from a variety of sources and in many formats, but each has its own challenges. If you want to include an image in the report body, we think it's easiest if the BLOB (the picture image) is stored in the database. We are pretty adamant about not storing images in the database for a litany of reasons, but to make it simpler for these reports, we're going to have to compromise our principles. Don't necessarily think that URL referencing is a panacea. As we'll see, it's not the user's web browser that *initially* references and fetches the image source but the Report Server itself when you're not using one of the RSReportHost previewers. This can lead to double buffering, network latency, and accessibility issues that require you to specify the unattended execution account. Another issue you need to be aware of is how Microsoft Access stores images (and other binary objects). It turns out that Access prefixes its images with an OLE header. If you don't strip off this header, you won't be able to render the picture. Next, we'll talk about some techniques that deal with these and other issues.

Setting the *BackgroundImage* Property

Because it's so widely supported by the report controls, we expect you'll be using this approach in a number of situations. No, the *BackgroundImage* property does not have the flexibility of the Image control—you can't set the *sizing* (as we'll discuss later). The background image property also asks you to set the following "sub" properties:

- *Source*: This indicates where the graphic is sourced.
- *Value*: A string indicating the path to the external graphic file or an expression that resolves to the database field that contains the graphic to render.
- *MIMEType*: Describes the type of graphic. Valid types are *image/bmp*, *image/jpeg*, *image/gif*, *image/png*, and *image/x-png*. This property is only important when accessing images from a database (and when *Source* is *Database*).
- *BackgroundRepeat*: Used when the image is smaller than the target control's size. The *BackgroundRepeat* subproperty has many sub-subproperties:
    - *Repeat* (the default setting): In this case, the image placed in the *BackgroundImage* property is "repeated" to fill the

control's space—maintaining the size and aspect ratio of the original graphic.

- *NoRepeat*: In this case, the image is stretched to fill the control background (as with the Chart control) or simply rendered starting at the top left corner of the control. However, if the graphic is too large for the space, only the top left is shown—bounded by the size of the control.
- *RepeatX*: In this case, the image is repeated as with *Repeat*, but on the X-axis of the control (from left to right).
- *RepeatY*: In this case, the image is repeated as with *Repeat*, but on the Y-axis of the control (from top to bottom).

Figure 7.24 shows how *BackgroundRepeat* options change the way the controls are rendered. Note that if the graphic is larger than the control (as in the second and third rows of this example), it's simply docked in the upper-left corner. The graphic coloring and "transparency" can obscure the text placed in the control, so it's a good idea to use low-density graphics for background images and contrasting text colors.

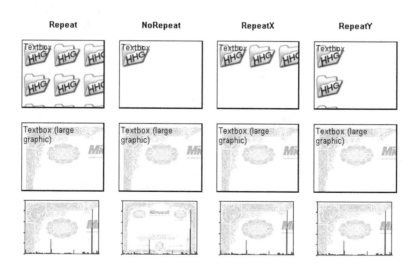

Figure 7.24 Using the Preview Tab to Render Images in Textbox and Chart Controls

Adding Images to a Report

Regardless of how you display an image in a report, you need to choose one of the supported techniques that set the *Source* property:

- **Embedded:** The binary image is stored directly in the RDL of the report. Since the RDL is limited to 4096 Kb or less, this means that embedded images can't be very large. Each image you embed in the RDL can be found on the report's Embedded Images Properties dialog.
- **Project:** The binary image is stored within the project and uploaded as a resource file type when the project is deployed. The maximum size of such an image is 4096 Kb. This is the ASP.NET default maximum upload size.
- **Database:** The binary image is retrieved from a database using a DataSet query.
- **Web**[6]**:** The binary image is stored on a server accessed through a URL—using the unattended execution account.

If you aren't using the Image control (and its wizard) and you want to embed images into your report, you'll need to use the Report | Embedded Images menu to add graphics to the report definition (as shown in Figure 7.25). In this case, we've added two graphics to the report—a GIF file and a JPEG file. Once you add these embedded images to the report, they appear in the pick lists when you set the *BackgroundImage* property. This dialog is also used to remove the images from your report. It's a great idea to remove unused graphics because this prevents having to move unneeded graphics images over the wire between the database and Rendering extension.

---

[6] There's a bit of confusion here. URL referenced graphics are also called "External" graphics in some cases.

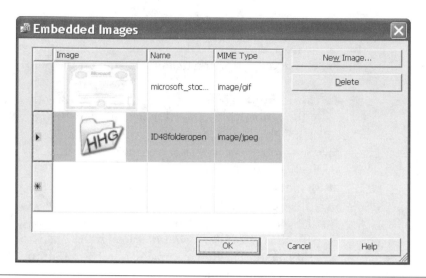

Figure 7.25 The Report Embedded Images Dialog

Adding Images to Reports Using the Image Control

Another way to display an image on a report is use the Image control. When you drop this control on the report, you are confronted with the Image wizard, which attempts to help you configure the image source and MIME format. The Image wizard permits you to select from the four image sources described earlier. Your selection populates the Image control's *Source* property.

The wizard is self-explanatory when you're dealing with embedded and project images. For our Product List report logo, we simply dragged an Image control into the page header, and followed the wizard's guidance to embed the image, locating the AdventureWorks logo on the disk.

We're lucky that our client hasn't asked us for a logo in the header that's bound to a report DataSet—because that just wouldn't work (without some sorcery that we'll tell you about in a moment). Remember that we can't have any DataSet Fields in the page header or page footer.

External Images, AKA Web Images

Although the Image wizard calls an external image a ***web image*** and directs you to construct a URL to access the image, the *Source* property is described as "External" in the Visual Studio .NET 2003 Designer in the Properties window. Be aware that the HTML Rendering extension doesn't send the image source URL to the web browser so that it can request the image from the source. Instead, the Rendering extension attempts to fetch the image. If the image is on a password-protected website, the Rendering extension tries to use the Unattended Execution Account credentials. Then it passes a URL for the image to the web browser. The web browser can subsequently request the image from the Report Server. This is a little convoluted, and it means that you can have only one set of credentials for all images. To configure credentials for the Unattended Execution Account, you'll need to use the rsconfig.exe command-line utility with the –e switch:

```
rsconfig.exe -e -u DOMAIN\USER  -p PASSWORD
```

You've built up your courage, and you're ready to show off the new report to the client. You send him to version 11 of the Product List report and hope he likes it—and does not come up with more changes.

Developer: *"The Product List report is ready for you to take another look."*

Client: *"It's looking good, but can you include a picture of each product?"*

Developer: *"Hmm!"* You hesitate, but before you can answer or ask about that raise…the phone line goes dead. You weren't disappointed. He did manage to get in a request for another feature. Even though you know he'll not like the result. You think to yourself that you really must iron out a complete specification before you go through this with another client—even if he isn't your father-in-law.

Back to the Drawing Board

Hmm, indeed! We can't just add the ProductPhoto table to our query and return the LargePhoto column, because we're using a GROUP BY query. Consider that the LargePhoto column is an image datatype and grouping by image datatypes on SQL Server is not supported.

One solution might be to lose all the performance benefits of having the DBMS do the GROUP BY and have all the grouping and aggregate functions performed by Reporting Services in a List or Table Data Region control instead. However, another approach to keep the performance of the grouping and aggregation on the DBMS is to use the T-SQL of our query as the basis for a SQL Server view—perhaps an indexed view for even better performance. To implement this approach, we need to make a few more changes:

1. Using the current SELECT statement, add the ProductPhotoID Field, and create a view with the Server Explorer, Enterprise Manager, or Query Analyzer (as shown in Listing 7.4):

Listing 7.4 Creating a View to Handle Our DataSet Query

```
CREATE VIEW vwProductList
AS
SELECT    ProductCategory.Name AS Category,
          ProductSubCategory.Name AS SubCategory, Product.Name,
          Product.ProductNumber, Product.Color,
          Product.ListPrice, SUM(ProductInventory.Quantity) AS Qty,
        SUM(ProductInventory.Quantity * Product.ListPrice) AS StockValue,
          Product.ProductPhotoID
FROM      Product
INNER JOIN
   ProductInventory ON Product.ProductID = ProductInventory.ProductID INNER JOIN
   ProductSubCategory ON Product.ProductSubCategoryID =
         ProductSubCategory.ProductSubCategoryID
INNER JOIN
   ProductCategory ON ProductSubCategory.ProductCategoryID =
         ProductCategory.ProductCategoryID
WHERE     (Product.FinishedGoodsFlag = 1)
GROUP BY
   Product.Name, Product.ProductNumber, Product.Color,
   Product.ListPrice, ProductCategory.Name, ProductSubCategory.Name,
   Product.ProductPhotoID
```

2. This view can be joined to the ProductPhoto table and the LargePhoto Field. Here's the latest T-SQL for the DataSet's query string (as shown in Listing 7.5). We can also create an index on this view on the ProductPhotoID column, but we'll leave that as an exercise for you. We suggest that you test the performance differences with and without the index.

Listing 7.5 Fetching Graphic Images from the ProductPhoto Table

```
SELECT    ProductPhoto.LargePhoto, vwProductList.Category,
          vwProductList.SubCategory, vwProductList.Name,
          vwProductList.ProductNumber,
          vwProductList.ListPrice, vwProductList.Qty,
          vwProductList.StockValue
FROM      ProductPhoto
RIGHT OUTER JOIN
          vwProductList ON ProductPhoto.ProductPhotoID =
vwProductList.ProductPhotoID
```

3. Select an Image control, drop it into the LstProducts List control on the report, and follow the wizard to bind it to the DataSet's LargePhoto Field.
4. Examine the sample 012 Product List report. However, if you want to run it, you'll first need to execute the 012 Product List.SQL script in the AdventureWorks database to create the required view, and you'll also need to ensure you have the right permissions.

You like the way the new report looks, and you're anxious to see what the client thinks about the changes. It wasn't that hard to add the images after all, but you would like to move on to other work.

Developer: *"Okay, I think we're getting there. What do you think?"*

Client: *"Those pictures ruin a good report, don't they? Can you make them display optionally, perhaps? Also, I don't really want all the detail all the time. Can that be optional too?"*

This time the client makes a lot of sense. He's right; too much clutter on a report detracts from its usefulness.

Adding User-Enabled Fields

To enable users to choose whether they want to view the report with or without images, we need to make a few more changes:

1. Create a Boolean Report Parameter called ShowPhotos.
2. Use that parameter in an expression for the image's *VisibilityHidden* property using the following expression:

```
=Not(Parameters!ShowPhotos.Value)
```

3. Examine the 013 Product List report to see this in action. Alternatively, providing our user with some drilldown features might fit the bill as well. We'll discuss that next.

Formatting the Image

In many cases, you have no idea at design time how large an image is likely to be. Performance issues notwithstanding, it's important that you design your reporting system to preformat any images you expect to use. Users usually care more about performance than image clarity, so it's a good idea to choose a lower-resolution image format. When we take digital pictures, they can be very large (over a megabyte) and render at 1600 x 1280 or larger—far too large for a report picture. There are a host of picture processors out there. One of our favorites is SnagIt[7] (which we used to manage the screenshots in this book). SnagIt can do bulk reformatting—taking a directory full of pictures and resizing them to a more usable resolution before they're uploaded to the database.

Reporting Services also defines several image formatting options that you should be aware of before you slap an Image control on a report. If you don't choose the right settings, your pictures can be hard to see or even overlay other controls on the form.

---

[7] www.techsmith.com/products/snagit/

Setting the Sizing Property

The *Sizing* property dictates how the Image control is resized if the image data does not conform to the specified size. Figure 7.26 shows how the *Sizing* property affects how the picture is displayed relative to the size of the Image control itself. The default *Sizing* property setting is Fit, which in our opinion is rarely the right choice. Pictures are often crunched or otherwise distorted when you use this setting. However, the alternatives are a bit more dangerous to use, as we'll see in a minute. The captions on the Textbox controls refer to the *Sizing* property assigned and the image source: Tn = thumbnail, and LP = large picture (from the AdventureWorks database ProductPhoto table). Note how the various settings affect the clarity and graphic proportions. The AutoSize setting seems appealing, but when you preview the report….

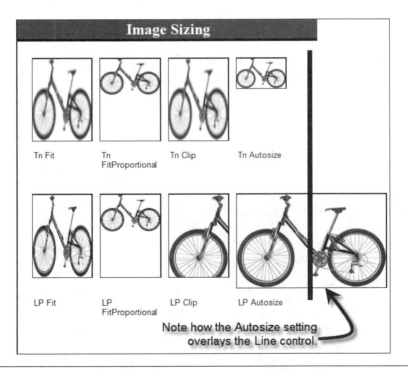

Figure 7.26 The *Sizing* Property Affects How the Image Control Displays

Oops! Now you're in trouble. Hmm, looks like your picture is going to bleed off your page to the right. So setting the *Sizing* property value to AutoSize is an approach that needs to be treated with respect and tested. It's probably best not to use AutoSize when you don't know the sizes of all the possible images. We'll let you make adjustments to the Product List report. The *Sizing* property is bindable to an expression, so you might get clever about auto-sizing.

NOTE *Rendering Issues* We tried to render the report shown in Figure 7.26 in a variety of formats. Each and every one rendered the images and the lines differently. In some cases, the line was virtually missing; in other cases, it rendered as shown in the browser (even in SP1). The point? YMMV (your mileage may vary).

Padding

You can make sure the report provides space between the Image control and an adjacent control by setting the *Padding* property. You can add 1 or more points (a point is $\frac{1}{72}$ of an inch) of space around each edge of a picture.

MIME Type

The *MIMEtype* property informs Reporting Services of the format of the image data returned from the database query. This helps it decide how to process the image when it's sourced from a database. You can choose between JPG, BMP, GIF, PNG, and X-PNG. Frankly, we haven't seen any issues when this property does not match the binary image data, but it's probably a good idea to make sure it matches the image format you're using. We would have liked to see a JET/OLE DB type to automatically and transparently deal with Access data sources, because without it, handling these images is a PIA, as we discuss next.

Dealing with Special Image Issues

As we touched on earlier, you might find there is a problem if you need to use images that have been added to SQL Server through Microsoft Access or drawn directly from an Access/JET database or another similar tool. If you've run the Image wizard and bound the images to the DataSet and they still don't appear to render, the image data might be corrupted or simply prefixed with an OLE header. The 030 Northwind Employees report (as shown in Figure 7.27) is an example of a report with this issue—red error boxes appear in the Image controls.

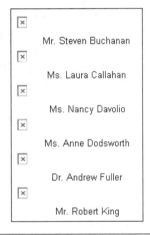

Figure 7.27 Corrupted Image Data or Images with OLE Headers Won't Render

The reason for this could be that the image data is corrupted or simply has an OLE header at the beginning of the binary image data. Once this header is removed or bypassed, the image displays correctly. The typical OLE header is 105 bytes long and can be stepped over by editing the image control's *Value* property to the following expression:

```
=System.Convert.FromBase64String(Mid(System.Convert.ToBase64String(
Fields!Photo.Value ),105))
```

Figure 7.28 shows how this report should look—with a properly formatted Image control. We can't help with the quality of the photo. We'll bet that Steve regrets having his picture cast in silicon.

Mr. Steven Buchanan

Figure 7.28 The 031 Northwind Employees Report Using the Step-Over Technique

Using Custom Code to Transform Images

Reports have the ability to share code used in expressions, so we could create a ***shared function*** (that's a static to our C# friends) that we can use with all images bound to DataSets. This way, if the OLE header is detected, the header is stripped out—otherwise, the stream is passed untouched. That would permit standard images and OLE images to be stored in the same table and to display in the same Image control.

To insert a custom code routine to the report, open the Report Properties dialog (as shown in Figure 7.29). Here you'll find a Code tab. Visual Basic shared functions can be pasted in there as a block. Because there's no IntelliSense, you'll need to ensure that your code functions properly in a Visual Basic .NET project first before pasting it into the report code block.

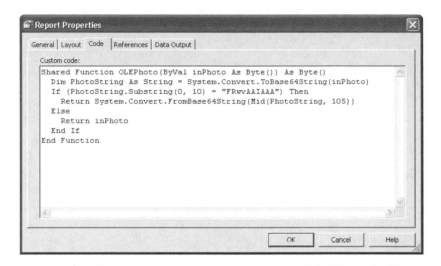

Figure 7.29 A Custom Code Function to Strip Out the OLE Header

These custom code shared functions can be used in virtually any expression. For example, the image's *Value* property can contain an expression that calls this shared code function using the following syntax. When using a shared function in an expression, the function is preceded with "Code."

```
=Code.OlePhoto(Fields!Photo.Value)
```

The sample report 032 Photo Album demonstrates use of custom code functions and also shows the way in which you can use explicit addressing in the DataSet's query to return data from more than one database.

Drilling Down into Report Data

It's often a good idea to reduce the amount of data a user has to deal with initially. That's what drilldown is all about.

Drilldown in Reporting Services is really very easy. When you think about drilldown on a conceptual level, consider that it simply hides the visibility of items that you want your report's users to drill into, and re-enables that visibility when they click on a selected report item.

Parenting the LstProducts List control inside a Rectangle control as we have done enables us to toggle the visibility of the rectangle in order to provide drilldown. We just need to mark the rectangle's *Hidden* property to True and decide which report item (ToggleItem) to wire up that can toggle the *Hidden* property when it is clicked on. Let's make the SubCategory textbox the ToggleItem. Take a look at the 014 Product List report (in Figure 7.30) to see this in action. We take this one step further in the 015 Product List report (see Figure 7.31), where we also set the LstSubCategory to be initially hidden and set its ToggleItem to Category. (By the way, ToggleItems don't have to be nested.)

Product List Report	ADVENTURE WORKS cycles
Accessory	
ᶠ Bottles & Cages	$4,170.24
ᶠ Lights	$18,030.60
ᶠ Locks	$6,300.00
ᶠ Pumps	$12,052.00

Figure 7.30 The 014 Product List Report Showing an Example of Drilldown

Product List Report	ADVENTURE WORKS cycles
ᶠ Accessory	
	Accessory $194,862.46
ᶠ Bike	
	Bike $23,555,257.86
ᶠ Clothing	
	Clothing $159,021.00
ᶠ Component	
	Component $1,203,648.95

Figure 7.31 The 015 Product List Report Showing Another Example of Drilldown

Implementing a Document Map

Another approach that can make sense when you want to let users navigate through long reports using drilldown is to create a *Document Map*. This is a hierarchical tree grouping that appears in a panel on the left of an online report (as shown in Figure 7.32). The entries displayed in the Document Map are controlled by setting the *Label* property on one or more report items to a literal string or expression. The 016 Product List report illustrates a Document Map. Notice that we set expressions for the *Label* properties of the LstSubCategory List control and the SubCategory Textbox control. The Document Map thus produced is navigable. As the user selects the nodes in the map, the report navigates to the point selected. The document map itself can be concealed by clicking the toolbar button, as shown in Figure 7.32.

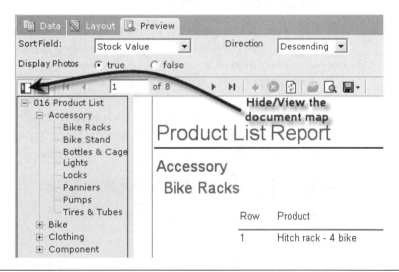

Figure 7.32 A Document Map for the 016 Product List Report

When the report is exported to PDF format, the report's Document Map is translated into PDF bookmarks. When exported to Excel (XP), the Document Map is translated into an equivalent navigable paradigm.

You might think that you can create a Report Parameter that uses expressions to enable your user to choose a Document Map or drilldown functionality. The 017 Product List report shows how far we took this approach—it gets us about 95 percent of the way there by ensuring that the labels and the hidden properties use the Report Parameter as it is passed in. However, the stumbling block turns out to be that the *ToggleItem* property just won't take an expression for the ToggleItem. Even when you show the Document Map, your users can collapse content by clicking on the ToggleItem. Experiment with the 017 Product List report to see what we mean.

Setting the Bookmark *Property*

Just as the *Label* properties provide the ability to navigate a report through the Document Map, there is another approach—use the *Bookmark* property on report items. **Bookmark referencing** permits reports to be navigated using the report URL.

Setting the Action *Property*

The full name of this property ought to be *Hyperlink Action*, which would really tell what it's all about. The *Action* property is just a simple mechanism for creating and associating a hyperlink to a Textbox or Image control. To set the property, access the Textbox control's Property page and look for "Action." Or access the Image control's Property page and look for "Action." The Action dialog shown in Figure 7.33 can help create three types of links, as shown in Table 7.2.

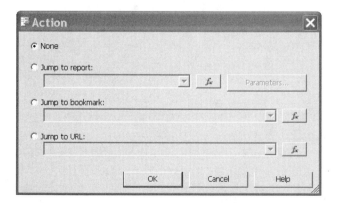

Figure 7.33 Setting the *Action* Property

Table 7.2 *Action* Property Settings

Action Property Setting	Description
Bookmark	Redirects the user's browser to a bookmark in the current report. Remember, any report item can be bookmarked—simply assign a string to the *Bookmark* property.
Jump to Report	Redirects the focus to another report on the same Report Server. Yes, you can jump to the current report, and you might even want to do so for good reason. The dialog will help you define defaults for the target report's parameters. So you could call the current report again with different parameter values.
	By default, there is a dropdown list that helps you choose any of the reports in the current project. Don't let that restrict you. You can provide paths to other reports in the Report Server as long as you start the path with a "/" to effectively address the report from the Home folder. No "/" implies that the report is in the current folder.
Jump to URL	Redirects the focus to any other URL. Using this option, you can link to your website or any other resource that can be accessed with a URL. This is the technique to use if you want to redirect to a report held on another Report Server. You can resolve the URL for the target Report Server and report, along with the parameters, by cutting and pasting the URL out of the web browser when addressing the Report Manager as it's rendering the target report. You can create an expression that configures the parameters as you want, but you are limited by the maximum URL length.
	The Jump to URL Action setting simply needs to evaluate to any valid URL including the protocol such as http://, https://, file://, ftp://, mailto:, or news: etc.

Using the Table Control

We built the report without the Table control, but let's take a look at how the same report can be written (or should have been written) using a Table control. We can do this by leveraging what we already have and taking some shortcuts by converting the list-based report instead of starting from scratch.

1. Copy the RDL file for 014 Product List.rdl to 001 Product Table.rdl.
2. Select Add Existing Item, and add 001 Product Table.rdl to your project.
3. Make the Body area bigger, and drag all the contents of the body down to give yourself more working room.
4. We're going to not use the page header, so cut and paste the contents of the page header to the Body area and switch the page header off through the Report menu. Remember to drag the contents against the left margin.
5. Now drag a Table control onto the report and name it tblCategory.
6. If you look at the List control version of the report, you'll see that we needed about seven columns, so add columns to the table by selecting a column, and add four more columns.
7. Resize the Table control columns and resize the report width.
8. At this point, the Table control probably isn't associated with any DataSet, so set its *DataSetName* property.
9. Select the Detail row, and let's add a Table grouping by selecting Insert Group. Name the group GrpCategory, and then select "=Fields!Category.Value" from the expression. If it's not there, you need to go back to the previous step and associate the *DataSetName* property.
10. Drag the Textbox control containing "=Fields!Category.Value" (this textbox was named "Category" when we created it earlier) from the list and drop it into the first cell of the grouping header. Then, similarly, drag the two Footer Textbox controls into the Group Footer Textbox controls.
11. Select the group footer as a whole and change its border properties to give us the horizontal blue line (BorderStyle.Top = Solid, BorderColor = Blue, BorderWidth = 2pt).
12. Select the Detail row and insert another group. Call this one "GrpSubCategory," and set the expression to group on "=Fields!SubCategory.Value". We don't need a group footer for this grouping level, so you could switch that off on the dialog, or delete it later by selecting the Group Footer for SubCategory and selecting Delete Row.

13. Select the group header for the SubCategory and insert a row. Drag all the Textbox controls we'd created called lbl*, Row, Product, Product No, List Price, Quantity, and Stock Value into the Textbox controls on that header.

14. Select that row and set the following border properties: BorderStyle.Bottom = Solid, BorderWidth = 1.5pt.

15. Populate the Detail section with the expressions, and then you can finally delete the List controls.

16. At this point, the report won't preview because all the lbl* Textbox controls still have their *RepeatWith* properties set. To fix this, remove *RepeatWith* properties from the Row, Product, Product No, List Price, Quantity, and Stock Value, and then preview.

17. You probably want to do a little tidying up by merging table cells and setting the cell padding properties to move text to where you want it.

18. You might want the report header to appear on each page, so you could set the *RepeatWith* property on the lnRptHd, image1, and txtRptHdTitle report items to repeat with tblCategory. Another approach is to place the image and the txtRptHdTitle Field into the table header and set the table header's *RepeatOnNewPage* property to True.

19. You can then delete the lnRptHd and set a bottom border on the Table Header row. You might also like to move the txtTotalStockValue into the Table Footer Field.

So there we have it, the report in a table. You can similarly play around with setting the visibility on table rows, as we did back in Chapter 3, in order to get drilldown. You can also set label properties on the table rows to get a Document Map. We'll leave that for you to experiment with.

Your client is finally happy with the Product List report, so you make the mistake of calling him to talk about a rate increase.

Developer: *"Well, since you really liked the Product Report I thought we might discuss…"*

Client, breaks in with: *"I was just thinking of you. I need a new director."*

You're startled at first, your heart excitedly skips a beat, you feel dizzy. At last the Board Room beckons…only then you're crushed by the rest of the sentence: *"….ry report of employees."*

Developer: *"Okay,"* and the client hangs up again. Perhaps he's upset that you forgot his wife's birthday yesterday, while working on the earlier reports. Oh, no! What will *your* wife say? You know what your mother-in-law is like. It will be all over town that you forgot. You decide to impress him and get the report done more quickly. You want to stop off at the mall on the way home—just a little insurance in case it was the dreaded birthday—but hang on, didn't you just send a mirror?

Customizing and Annotating the Table Control

Let's also build this report with the Table control instead of using the List control. Report 050 Employee illustrates this approach. There are quite a few things for you to take away from this report.

- We did not use page headers or footers, although we achieved First Page Header, Every Page Headers, Every Page Footers, and Last Page Footer. If you look closely at those controls, you'll see that their *RepeatWith* property makes the difference. They are also positioned outside the outermost data region of the table. But to see the footers rendered properly, you may need to deploy the report and view it in a browser—we've seen a number of issues when using the Preview window.

- We have included two Report Parameters: one to determine how the Table control should be grouped, and another to provide a filter on the employee names. We manually marked these parameters as not being used in the query. This means that if the report is run from a Snapshot, the grouping and filtering do not create any further stress on the underlying data source's DBMS.

- Notice also that the visibility of some columns is set to an expression based on the selected grouping.

- We've even created a calculated Field of YearHired. This performs a formatting expression on the HireDate Field.
- We've also set the Table control's sort order (Sorting tab in the properties) to be the same as the grouping order.
- We've used an expression on the *BackColor* property of the Detail row to give an alternating GreenBar background. This is accomplished by using the `RowNumber()` function as follows:

```
=IIF(RowNumber(Nothing) mod 2=1,"PaleGreen",Nothing)
```

TIP *Transparent Is Not a Color* You may notice that here we are assigning a color of `Nothing` to achieve transparency. Although the Designer user interface would have you believe that "Transparent" is a selectable color option, actually what happens behind the scenes is that the backcolor rdl element is not created at all when set to Transparent. This has the same effect as setting it to Nothing. If you try to set the *Backcolor* property to an expression that evaluates to Transparent, you'll get an error telling you that Transparent is not a valid background color.

- Similarly, we've used an expression to set the *FontWeight* property of the Detail row conditionally. If the employee HireDate is before a given parameter date, we change the *FontWeight* property to Bold. This expression is very simple:

```
=IIF(Fields!HireDate.Value < Parameters!HireDate.Value ,"Bold","Normal")
```

But we brought you here to talk about the filtering. As we said earlier, filtering is subject to .NET-"like" rather than SQL-"like" rules. This means that the only accepted wildcard is *. Take a look at the Filter expression on the table. If you or your users are from a SQL background, you'll possibly find this a little irksome. However, you can build a solution to this problem by using an expression with the .NET `Replace` method:

```
= Parameters!FilterEmployeeNames.Value.Replace("%","*")
```

Report 051 Employee implements this enhancement, but it still doesn't get us around the case-sensitivity issue. As it is, Filter expressions appear to be evaluated using case-insensitive rules. That said, report code functions are evaluated using case-sensitive rules. Given this dichotomy, if you created a report function such as

```
Shared Function BinaryLike(ByVal name As String, ByVal filter As String) As Boolean
       Return (name Like filter)
End Function
```

you can place this in the report's code block in places where you might need a case-sensitive Like clause. In this case, you can substitute the Filter expression shown below in the Table control's Properties Filters tab. The operator for this Filter expression is "=" and the value is "=True." The 052 Employee report implements this technique. Remember that we prefix the function name with "code" when referencing code in the report's code block in expressions.

```
=code.BinaryLike(Fields!Employee.Value, ⏎
Parameters!FilterEmployeeNames.Value.Replace("%","*"))
```

Recursive Data Structure Handling in Tables

Client: *"I also want a GreenBar employee report that can show off the hierarchical structure of the company with me on top. Do you think you can do that?"*

Developer: *"Let me see what I can do."*

If you take a close look at the AdventureWorks employee table, you'll notice that there is a recursive reference back to the table itself. This is because all managers are also employees—even if they don't seem so to some of the employees. Reporting Services has the ability to cope with recursive structures, and to keep track of how deep you are within the recursion by calling the Level() function.

Take a look at the 053 Employee Hierarchy report. In this case, the DataSet query was set to:

```
SELECT   Employee.FirstName + N' ' + ISNULL(Employee.MiddleName, N'') +
         N' ' + Employee.LastName AS EmployeeName,
         EmployeeDept.Name AS Department,
         Employee.Title AS EmployeeTitle,
         Employee.EmployeeID,
         Employee.ManagerID
FROM   Employee
LEFT OUTER JOIN   Department EmployeeDept
     ON Employee.DepartmentID = EmployeeDept.DepartmentID
```

To illustrate an implementation of recursive data handling in a table, we made these changes to the report.

1. In the Layout view, we created a table with four columns, and dragged EmployeeName, EmployeeTitle, and Department to cells in the Detail row of the table.

2. We then bound the remaining empty Detail cells to =Level() so that we could show you the current recursion level.

3. We further prettified the report such that the Detail row *BackColor* was bound to

```
=IIF(RowNumber(Nothing) mod 2=1,"PaleGreen",Nothing)
```

You'll recall this gives us the "GreenBar" effect.

4. At this point, we executed the report to see that change result in nothing special. It just returns all the rows, and the Level column is set to zero.

5. The magic to specify to Reporting Services is that this is a recursive table. We selected the Detail row and selected to edit the group, as shown in Figure 7.34. At this point, we need to set the Detail row to be grouped by the EmployeeID, but to mark that the EmployeeID Field is effectively a child of the ManagerID by setting the Parent Group to ManagerID, as shown in Figure 7.35. Make sure when doing this that you don't confuse this with inserting a new group into the table—you need to be working with the Detail row.

Figure 7.34 Editing the Group Properties for a Detail Row

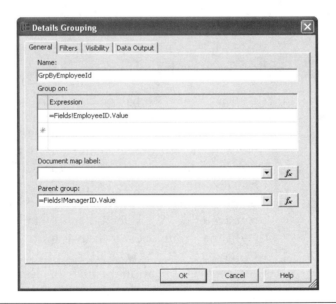

Figure 7.35 Configuring the Detail Grouping

When we executed the report again, like magic the Level() showed much more interesting content than "0," demonstrating how deep into the recursive structure we were at each Detail row. This report gets even more interesting if we adjust the left padding of the cells in the Detail row by a function based on the depth of recursion. For example, set the Left Padding of the Detail row to:

```
=2 + (Level()*10) & "pt"
```

The result? A stair-stepped GreenBar report (shown in Figure 7.36) that's a lot easier to read and more clearly shows the relationships of the employees on the corporate ladder.

Employee Name	Employee Title	Department	Level
Ken J Sanchez	Chief Executive Officer	Executive	0
Brian S Welcker	VP Sales	Sales	1
Stephen Y Jiang	North American Sales Manager	Sales	2
Pamela O Ansman-Wolfe	Sales Representative	Sales	3
David R Campbell	Sales Representative	Sales	3
Fernando O Caro	Sales Representative	Sales	3
Shu K Ito	Sales Representative	Sales	3
Linda C Mitchell	Sales Representative	Sales	3
Tsvi M Reiter	Sales Representative	Sales	3
José E Saraiva	Sales Representative	Sales	3
Garrett R Vargar	Sales Representative	Sales	3
Michael G Blythe	Sales Representative	Sales	3
Tete A Mensa-Annan	Sales Representative	Sales	3
Syed E Abbas	Pacific Sales Manager	Sales	2
Lynn N Tsoflias	Sales Representative	Sales	3
Amy E Alberts	European Sales Manager	Sales	2
Ranjit R Varkey Chudukatil	Sales Representative	Sales	3
Rachel B Valdez	Sales Representative	Sales	3

Figure 7.36 The Final Employee List Report Showing the Employee Hierarchy

Advanced Tips and Techniques

While exploring the inner recesses of Reporting Services, we found a few hidden niches. We want to show you a few of these techniques to help you through some of the roadblocks you've encountered so far.

Doing the "Impossible" with Page Headers and Footers

We said earlier that controls displayed in the header or footer cannot be bound directly to Fields from a report DataSet. While this might be true, you just knew that we'd be able to tell you some inside tricks to get around this limitation, didn't you? In reality, there is only one instance when displaying DataSet Fields in the header or footer is compelling: when you need to show such DataSet Fields in the same vertical space as the Page Numbers and Total Pages global parameter values, because those global parameters can only immutably be displayed in the header or footer. The following techniques document a couple of ways to solve this problem. Note that these techniques appear to be case sensitive.

Technique 1: Manipulating the *ReportItems* Collection

This approach can be applied to Textbox or Image controls. Suppose you want to position a bound Textbox control in the report header or footer, and you already have a Textbox control in the body that is bound to a DataSet Field or to an expression. You can reference that Textbox control through the *ReportItems* collection in the *Value* property of a textbox placed in the header/footer:

```
=ReportItems!MyBodyTextbox.Value
```

Aggregate functions can also be used on *ReportItems* in the header/footer areas but not in the body:

```
=First(ReportItems!MyBodyTextbox.Value)
```

For example, this might come in handy if you were creating a telephone directory and wanted to show the first names in the header.

You can also use this technique with Image controls, but you have to modify the approach slightly. First, you can't reference the *Value* property on another Image control in the body—it simply won't work. In this case, you need to bind a Textbox control to the image data coming from the database. Because the image data is contained in a binary byte array stream, you need to convert it to a string. This way, the "proxy" image textbox would typically have its *Value* property bound using the following expression:

```
=System.Convert.ToBase64String(Fields!LargePhoto.Value)
```

Typically, you want to set the visibility of the textbox to Hidden, as it's not really meant to be displayed. The tricky part comes in placing an Image control within the header, binding its *Value* property back to the "proxy" image Textbox control, and converting the stream back to a byte array in the process. You then reference the proxy image textbox through the *ReportItems* collection:

```
=System.Convert.FromBase64String(ReportItems!HiddenProxyImageTextbox.Value)
```

Figure 7.37 shows how the 040 Header DataSet report illustrates this technique.

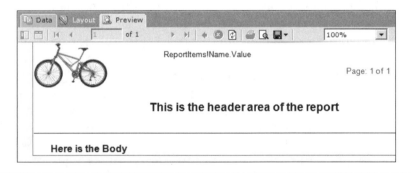

Figure 7.37 Placing Bound Image Controls and Textbox Controls in the Report Header

Technique 2: Using Report Parameters as Proxy Controls

Rather than using Textbox controls in the body as a proxy control, you can pass these values by using Report Parameters. We like this approach better because the "hidden textbox" approach is a little ugly—especially if the textboxes are there only to support data binding for header images and textboxes.

An alternative technique is to create Report Parameters and to completely remove the Prompt String. This prevents the Report

Parameter from being queried for values from the user. The sample report 041 Header DataSet illustrates this technique. Examine the bindings in the *Value* property for the Image control in the header and the Textbox control. You should also examine the Report Parameters to see how these are bound to values derived from the DataSet. The final part of the magic is to appreciate that the DataSet includes a calculated field to convert the binary image stream to a string so that it can sit in a Report Parameter that has a datatype of String.

How to Do Away with Page Headers and Page Footers

If your report doesn't need page numbers or total pages being rendered in the header or footer, you don't actually need these report regions to render content that appears at the top or bottom of each page or only on the first and last pages. If you want things to appear only on the first page, simply place those controls at the top of the page above any of the outermost Data Region controls. Similarly, if you need content only on the last page, place that underneath the outermost Data Region control. If you want the content to appear at the top/bottom of each page, set the *RepeatWith* property on those controls to repeat with the outermost Data Region control. The only thing that you need to watch out for is that it would appear that the *RepeatWith* property doesn't work for previewing in the Designer.

Alternatively, if your outer Data Region control is a Table control, you'll be able to put things into the Table control's Header row and set the *RepeatOnNewPage* property to True. We demonstrate this in the 050 Employee report.

Converting Reports from Microsoft Access

Reports written using Microsoft Access can be converted (at least partially) using the Import wizard. The wizard takes a lot of the hard work out of the conversion process and leaves you with tasks it doesn't know how to convert such as charts and built-in Access functions. The wizard doesn't make intelligent use of the Table control—it simply uses the List control. As a result, you may find you have a bunch of ugly alignment issues to cope with, especially if the Access report made use of Line controls and the report author let the controls overlap. Access can cope with overlapping controls, but the HTML browsers called on to render reports from Reporting Services and some of the other Rendering extensions involve certain challenges when it comes to overlapping display elements. This means you'll have to deal with these issues manually on a case-by-case basis. It might be best to convert the report to use a Table control instead of free-form list layouts. To use the wizard, you need to have Access installed on the same machine as your Reporting Services Visual Studio .NET Report Designer. Create a new Reporting Services project, and select the Access project in the Solution Explorer. On the right mouse context menu, you'll see Import Reports. If you don't see Import Reports, you either don't have Microsoft Access installed or the version you've installed is not a version from which you can import reports. It couldn't be much simpler—you navigate to your MDB or ADP file, which contains the reports to convert, and import. You'll get all the reports from the container file imported into a Reporting Services project. This is why we suggest you import into a blank project and choose which reports are needed.

Creating Subreports

A subreport is simply a pointer to a managed report or a report definition in your project. To add a subreport to an existing report, drag a Subreport control onto the layout area of a report definition and set its *ReportName* property. Sure, it's a good idea to create the subreport first. You'll be able to choose from reports in the current project folder (apart from the report you are working on). Alternatively, you can manually enter a path and report name into the *ReportName* property.

As you are probably aware, reports can take parameters, and you'll be relieved to know it's possible to configure the parameters of a Subreport control to be linked to expressions in the parent report. Those expressions in the parent report can be derived from DataSet Fields or from Report Parameters in the parent report. To setup these parameters, right-click on the Subreport control and choose

Properties. Click on the Parameters tab, as shown in Figure 7.38, and fill in an expression to pass to the subreport. Sure, if you reference the DataSet Fields, the values supplied are synced with the parent report context. (The parent report contains the Subreport control.)

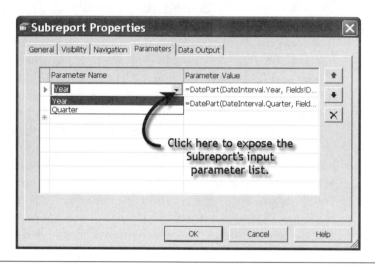

Figure 7.38 Setting the Parameter Value Property of the Subreport Input Parameters

Subreports can be hosted within Data Region controls, including all cells in a Table control, or simply launched by setting the navigation properties. But think carefully before blindly creating reports that use subreports. Each time the Subreport control is rendered, the Report Server re-executes the DataSet query against its data sources. This means if you place a Subreport control in the Detail row of a table that has 300 rows, your subreport queries its data sources 300 times. This can be a performance issue leading to the DBA squad arriving to introduce you forcibly to the end of "Vanilla Sky,"[8] so keep your base-jumping kit strapped to your back if you are going to test this on a live server.

---

[8] At the end of "Vanilla Sky," Tom Cruise jumps backward off the top of a sky-scraper—or does he?

Hiding and Launching Subreports

One technique we've used and seen demonstrated quite effectively is to use subreports to provide additional drilldown data—but in an entirely different format. In this case, set the *Visibility.Hidden* property of the Subreport control to True and set the ToggleItem to point to a Textbox control. Clicking on the contents of this control either navigates to the subreport or makes it visible. But what if you don't have a "spare" Textbox control to click on? Well, in that case you can use the graphic elements in a Chart control to view the subreport, as shown in Figure 7.39.

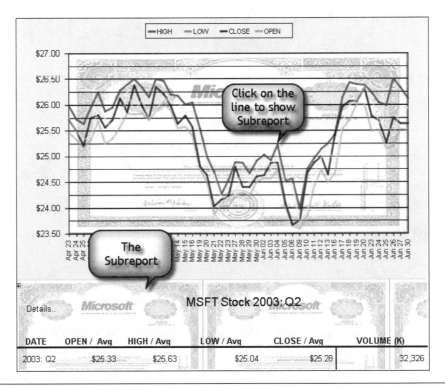

Figure 7.39 A Subreport Control Made Visible by Clicking on a Line in the Chart Control

We discuss the Chart control in Chapter 8, but it's important to note here that you can also use the Chart control properties to set an Action on each graphic element being rendered. This approach is similar to the navigation behavior discussed next. Drill into this "Jump to report" setting by opening the Chart control's Property page and clicking on Data and Edit for one of the values. In this case, we simply address our subreport as shown in Figure 7.40.

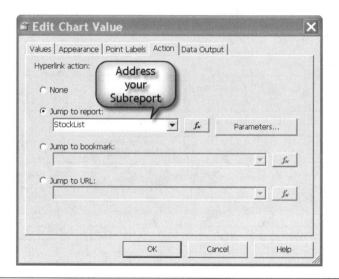

Figure 7.40 Using the *Action* Property to Address a Subreport Control

You can also setup a "Jump to report" in many controls if you dig deep enough. This approach does not require use of a Subreport control—it simply navigates the browser to another report, as we discussed earlier. The Textbox, Matrix, and Table controls all sport a Navigation tab that permits you to use these controls (or their cells) to navigate to another report. Click on Advanced from the Properties dialog, choose Navigation, and you'll see the dialog shown in Figure 7.41. Once you set this Navigation tab and the report is rendered, watch for the mouse icon to change shape as you hover over the text in a control. When it changes to a pointing finger, you can to click to navigate to your subreport.

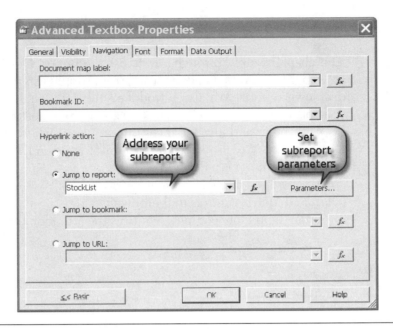

Figure 7.41 Using the Navigation Tab to Setup a Pointer to a Subreport

Getting Back to the Parent

Now that the browser focus has changed to a subreport (when not using the Subreport control), you might be able to navigate back to the parent report by simply clicking on the Back arrow in the Report Designer. However, we've seen a few cases in which this Navigation button is disabled or missing—in that case, just use the browser's Back button.

Subreport Tips and Techniques

Caching tricks and Snapshots might enable you to prepare the data in off-peak times when you are thinking about really big reports. The other point to consider is that given how powerful data regions are, such as the Table control, many reports that require subreports in products such as Microsoft Access don't need them in Reporting Services. They're awfully expensive, so be judicious in their use.

Summary

This chapter walked through how to use the Report Designer to create reports that varied in complexity from simple lists to multitiered drilldown reports. We also introduced the List, Table, and Image controls and showed how to use these controls most effectively to display tabular and image data—even in places where it's not ordinarily shown. We also showed you how to add graphics and subreports to your managed reports.

Wait, we've left off a few things. Good catch. We're deferring the Chart and Matrix controls to their own chapter so we can give these important (and more complex) controls the attention they deserve.

CHAPTER 8

The Chart and Matrix Controls

They say that a picture is worth a thousand words. Does that mean a chart is worth 32,768 bits? Perhaps, but perhaps it's worth more because in many situations you can't really express the information you're trying to convey in seemingly endless lists, tables, or hierarchical dumps of data. When you find that the number of rows to display in an ordinary report exhausts your users' brain capacity to assimilate, you'll find that a Chart control can summarize the data and help your users to visualize the data quite effectively. We postponed discussing the Chart and the Matrix controls until now so that we could spend more time helping you understand the way they work and how to leverage them in your reports.

One of Bill's favorite college courses was "How to Lie with Statistics." It emphasized the plethora of ways to portray information to sell, influence, inform, or mislead. We're not suggesting that you strive to deceive your report consumers, even though people with an agenda to forward do this all too often. However, we do think there's nothing wrong with using your data to prove or disprove an assertion. We also think that the Reporting Services Chart control can make that task a lot easier and more effective.

A Brief History of the Chart Control

If you worked with the early betas of Reporting Services, you probably came across the *Microsoft Office Chart control*. Close to the end of the development cycle, Microsoft replaced this control with the ***Dundas***[1] ***Chart control***. The Microsoft team tried to keep the Office Chart's look and feel in the Reporting Services Chart property pages, but this resulted in an occasional disconnect between terms as the transition was made to the Dundas Chart control.

We understand that Microsoft changed to the Dundas Chart control to improve performance and scalability. Consider that the Chart control has to run on the Report Server and "serve" many report requests simultaneously, so it's under considerable pressure to be fast, light, and efficient. Microsoft felt that the Dundas Chart control was better suited for .NET and shared application use within Reporting Services. By using a .NET-managed, code-packaged component, Microsoft was able to integrate it with its existing .NET Reporting Services code fairly quickly—in a matter of a few weeks. The Dundas Chart control supports the output formats exposed by the Rendering extensions in Reporting Services, it has a small memory footprint, and it is highly scalable. As far as we're concerned, this was the right choice.

That said, Microsoft did not have time to implement several of the more sophisticated features of the Dundas control as integrated into Reporting Services, and it left off a number of important extensibility features that make it impossible to access the Chart control directly. This also means customers can't upgrade to any third-party Chart control. This feature is supposed to be implemented in the SQL Server 2005 version. The program managers at Dundas tell us that the SQL Server 2005 betas scheduled to ship this fall expose more features of the "Professional" version of the Dundas control and implement a number of extensibility features. Features you might expect to see (but are missing in the Reporting Services implementation) include many chart types and sub-types, along with drilldown, mouse-over, fly-by, and additional background properties. To get a feel for what the Dundas control can do, but doesn't within Reporting Services (at least not yet), see www.dundas.com. A few more features afforded by the Dundas Chart control *are* enabled in SP1, and we'll point them out as we go. From this point forward, it's best if we simply accept the fact that Microsoft adapted the Dundas

---

[1] Dundas is a third-party controls vendor located in Toronto.

Guide me!
Check out the
DVD, where we
provide several
Guide me!
narrated screen
capture demon-
strations of the
Chart control.

Chart control to implement the Reporting Services Chart control. You need not be concerned with how the Chart control is implemented behind the scenes.

We realize that several examples are included with the Reporting Services sample reports that demonstrate use of the Chart control. We're not going to repeat those examples here. Rather, we will create a few of our own so that you can see the different challenges you'll face as you integrate the Chart control into your reports.

Fetching Chart Data

The mechanisms used to pass data into the Chart control are basically the same as those we discussed in Chapter 7, which are used in populating the List, Table, and Matrix controls. Ideally, the data returned by DataSets feeding the Chart control should be structured to clearly identify those rowset field values used in the Chart control's X- and Y-axes. There is no Z-axis in the Chart control, although it's capable of simulating a third dimension when you request 3D rendering.

A chart can plot as many sets of data as desired. For example, a DataSet can return Sales and SalesLastYear Fields and plot them on the same chart. Generally, you'll be using one or more sets of data Fields from each row, along with category or series Fields that label and group the data shown in the chart. As we work through the various chart types, you'll see how each type of chart uses the Fields in different ways. While you can have as many Chart controls in your report as you need, each can refer to only one DataSet.

As with any other report item, the data passed to the Chart control is a function of the scope of the data region where it's placed—that's because it's another "data region" control. This means that if the Chart control is placed on the report surface or in a report header or footer, its data is drawn from the entire DataSet. However, if the Chart control is placed in a Table control group header or footer, the data passed to the control is restricted to the subset of data that constitutes that group. As with any data region control (such as the List, Table, or Matrix), the Chart control cannot be placed in the Detail row of a Table control in which only one row of data points is referenced.

NOTE As you work with the Chart control, you'll notice an occasional "disconnect" between the Chart control properties as exposed in the Report Designer property pages, the properties used in the RDL file, and the properties as exposed by the underlying Chart control property pages. We'll highlight those differences along the way.

Using "Too Much" Data

As you construct your charts using the Report Designer, one of the issues you'll have to deal with is over-filling. As we said earlier, each chart type can support several data series. We expect the upper limit is a function of how presentable the chart will be once your data density gets beyond a certain point, given a particular chart size. An easy mistake is to cram too much data into a small chart. As you'll soon discover, if you try to use too much data, the result in most chart types is a jumble of confused bars, lines, or dots on the report—useless to your report consumer. In some cases, the data is simply too dense to display, and the Chart control seems to give up and not render anything. Sure, you can capture Report Parameters to limit the focus of the Chart control's DataSet query, and we encourage this approach. We'll also have to deal with scaling when the number of plotted rows varies from group to group. As the volume of data increases beyond the capacity of the space allocated to the Chart control, we've seen a perfectly formatted chart look like it went through the Starship Enterprise transporter in "disperse to space" mode. Unfortunately, the Reporting Services implementation of the Dundas Chart control exposes very few ways to dynamically adjust for varying data volumes to help smooth out these issues. You simply have to use Filters or Report Parameters to focus the data on fewer rows.

In the late '70s, when working on my master's degree, I took a course entitled "Air," which discussed atmospheric environmental issues. I noticed that one southern state seemed to rank low—below all the rest—in the number of airborne pollutants its air contained. I queried the instructor, who smiled and said, "That's because that state does not have any monitoring stations." It's not that their datapoints were zero—they were missing altogether.

–Bill

Something About Nothing

We think it would be wise to touch on this nothing issue; that is, what should the Chart control do if there is no data? You can set the *NoData* property on the Chart control to display a string if your DataSet returns no rows. You'll also discover that if a column returns NULL values, the Chart control either skips over the value or (as we'll see later in this chapter) substitutes a value on its own. One way to control this behavior is to add NOT IS NULL to the criteria on those columns where we suspect data won't be returned. You can also replace the auto-generated series labels by specifying group label expressions. However, the Chart control always replaces label values that are NULL or contain empty strings with the auto-generated labels.

Customization of empty point handling is something that the Dundas Chart upgrade will eventually provide. Microsoft recognizes that handling NULL values is important in that sometimes your chart should interpret NULL as zero. But NULL often needs to be identified as data that is simply missing. A company might have sales on a given day, but showing a value as zero is wrong and spoils the trend line of a chart. Showing data as missing lets the user know that the data exists but is not present when the chart is rendered.

Understanding the Chart Control's User Interface

For those of us who don't spend a lot of time making charts, the Chart control UI presents us with a few initial challenges. I guess the folks who spend most of their day using Excel or Access to build charts won't have a problem with these concepts, but to make things clear for the novitiates, let's walk through the basic Chart control user interface.

When you drag the Chart control to the report layout design surface, the Chart control exposes three or more areas that we call *landing zones (LZs)*, shown in Figure 8.1. Each of these can be targeted by Fields dragged and dropped from the Fields list, and the specified DataSet *Fields* can be linked to the Chart control. You'll start by dropping one or more DataSet Fields to the "Drop data fields here" area. Basically, these Fields specify the data points the Chart control is to plot. You must provide at least one Field for this LZ. Figure 8.1 shows the three LZs on the chart exposed by the vertical bar-type chart.

Sure, in some cases you'll want to drop more than one Field into the same LZ. Dropping more Fields into the top (primary) "Drop data fields here" LZ programs the Chart control to plot an additional set of points—one for each Field you place in this LZ.

When you drop a Field on "Drop series fields here," the Chart groups the primary Fields into separate series and labels the groups using the values in the Field(s) provided. The Legend (shown in Figure 8.1) is populated with these series names.

In a similar way, when you drop one or more Fields on the "Drop category fields here" LZ, the chart groups the primary Fields into separate categories and labels the categories along the X-axis. The easiest way to understand these drag-and-drop interfaces is to create a few charts and try it out for yourself. We'll revisit this topic again after we add a Chart control to our sample report.

TIP If you return to the Layout view and the LZs are hidden, they can be shown again if you double-click on the control. They're exposed automatically as you drag Fields onto the chart.

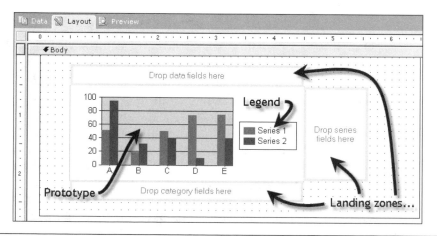

Figure 8.1 The Landing Zones, Legend, and Prototype Pane Shown in the Layout Tab

These LZs are designed to make it easy to specify the sources for the X-axis and Y-axis data Fields for column-style reports as well as the data Fields passed to non-linear charts such as the pie and doughnut. Figure 8.2 shows how the LZs are mapped to the X-axis and Y-axis of a typical report.

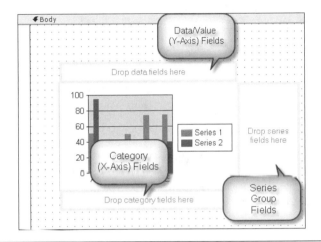

Figure 8.2 How the LZs Are Mapped to the X-Axis and Y-Axis of the Chart Control

These three Chart control LZs are mapped to corresponding Chart control properties that can be also be programmed and managed using the Chart Properties dialog Data tab that we'll discuss later in this chapter. You can use this properties dialog to specify many of the minute details that make your chart more readable and informative.

Some chart types expose more LZs than others because their charts display data in special ways. This means you'll want to customize your DataSets to match what the chart type expects to consume. For example, the Stock type Chart can be configured to expose LZs for High, Low, Open, and Close data Fields that correspond to stock price fluctuations, as shown in Figure 8.3. Sure, these LZ properties can be programmed to contain expressions as well, but before we jump ahead to properties, let's make sure we understand the basics.

Once you drag Fields to the LZs, the Chart control renders a ***prototype*** of the chart as it might appear when it's rendered in the Preview tab or from a browser. It uses made-up data, but this gives you immediate visual feedback to help you decide which options are best. Sure, the prototype can be a poor representation of "reality" because the actual data can radically change how the chart is rendered. How your report renders is a function of what data is actually passed to the control through your DataSet(s) and how the Rendering extension displays the report.

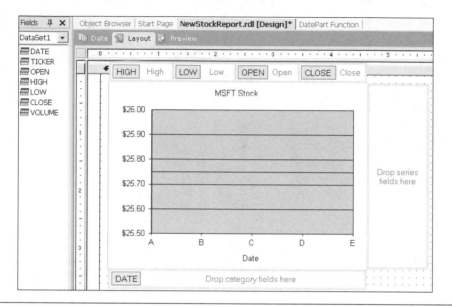

Figure 8.3 Using the Landing Zones to Address Fields in the DataSet

What Should Be Placed in the Landing Zones?

As we described briefly a bit earlier, when you select a chart type, the Chart control morphs itself to display three or more LZs designed to help you capture appropriate DataSet Fields. Once you drop one or more Fields onto an LZ, the Chart control maps these Fields into appropriate Data tab properties behind the scenes and renders its prototype pane. Let's discuss these LZs, which are exposed by the most common control types: Data Fields, Category Fields, and Series Group Fields.

What Are Data Fields?

The **Data Fields LZ** is used to pass one or more sets of data point values to the Chart control. Each value supplied is represented by a graphic element (based on the chart *Type* and *SubType* properties). This LZ is used to set the required *Value* property. Data points are ordered based on the order of the DataSet rowset but grouped based on the Category and Series Fields.

NOTE When you drag a Field from the Fields list to an LZ, camel-case names are broken up into separate words. For example, "ProductsInLine" becomes "Products In Line."

For column and bar chart types (as well as many others), the Chart control positions graphic objects (bars, columns, lines, or points) on the chart using the Data Field value. This value (positive or negative) determines the height of the graphic object above or below the X-axis. Its position on the X-axis (from left to right) is determined automatically by the Chart control.

Each column, bar, or point is plotted on the X-axis based on the number of Category Fields or Series Fields the Chart control is asked to plot in a given space. You define the space available by sizing the chart in the Layout view or setting the Chart control size properties. As more points are added to the set of Data Fields, the width of each graphic element is reduced in an attempt to plot all of the graphic elements and labels in the available space. Accommodations are made for the text width of the Category Field names, along with any tick marks or other graphic elements that consume space. When you add additional sets of points (another set of Data Fields) to a chart, they are plotted with the existing series and share space on the X-axis. In 3D charts, the graphic elements are rendered as three-dimensional objects and can be plotted in front of one another.

NOTE While it's also possible to provide several Data Fields for a chart, the Chart control does not permit you to place Data Fields on the chart that are from different DataSets.

What Are Category Fields?

As data points are plotted on the X-axis, the category group provides one alternative to determine how the data is grouped and labeled. For example, as shown in Figure 8.4, the values seen below the chart (the

Territory Names) on the X-axis are drawn from the TerritoryName Field of the DataSet. These are used to group the data by Territory Name. Without a category group, the Chart control assumes that all Data Fields are in the same (unnamed) Category. However, once you define a category group by dropping a Field in the "Drop category fields here" LZ, the Chart control groups the data values and creates a new graphic element for each group. As a result, the number of groups in the rendered chart dictates the number of graphic elements on the X-axis. As the Chart control constructs the columns for each X-axis position, it labels the column by plotting the matching category field value. It makes sense to provide meaningful values for the Category Fields—values that make good labels. For example, if you're plotting Sales over time, placing a corresponding date Field in the Category Field would make sense.

It's possible to provide more than one Category Field. Based on the order in which you drop them on the LZ, the Chart control further groups the data into subgroups. Figure 8.4 also shows how the report is "prototyped" while in the Layout tab of the Report Designer after we dragged two Fields to the Category Fields LZ— ProductLine and CategoryName. Each group is labeled in the chart using the horizontal brackets, as shown. Notice how the camelcased Field names are morphed to separate the words of the labels.

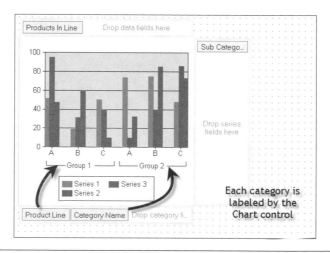

Figure 8.4 Using the Layout View, a Prototype of the Report Is Displayed

What Are Series Group Fields?

The Series Fields provide another way to group (and label) the X-axis data points. As shown in Figure 8.5, if you drag a DataSet Field to the Series Fields LZ, the Chart control creates a "series" for each group. It also populates the chart Legend with the values in the Series Fields and colors each group differently. As with the other LZs, you can provide more than one Series Field. This instructs the Chart control to further subdivide the series into sub-series.

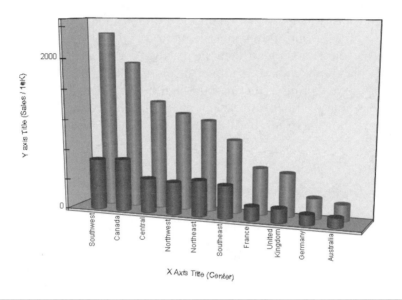

Figure 8.5 Plotting More Than One Series on the Same Chart

All of these charts are available on the DVD. Search under Chapter 8 in the DVD report directory for a complete list.

How Do I Maintain Order?

In the chart shown in Figure 8.5, the order in which the series were placed on the "Drop Data Fields here" target is significant. In this case, we knew that the unit sales figures were smaller than the sales dollar figures, so we placed these (smaller) values last. This positions the columns (in this case) in front of the taller columns. The particular chart is a Column type with several three-dimensional

(3D) effects enabled, including Clustered and Cylinder. We also adjusted the other 3D properties to adjust the Horizontal Rotation, Perspective, Wall thickness, and Vertical rotation. We'll let you experiment with these options.

What Are the X- and Y-Axes?

I did.

–Bill

I'm self-taught, so I didn't.

–Peter

If you slept through basic geometry, you might have missed the part where the teacher droned on about the **X- *and Y-axes***. No, these are not wood-chopping tools—they're the way we refer to the logical plane where data is displayed or plotted. Figure 8.6 reminds you how values are plotted on a two-dimensional plane. The point where the X- and Y-axes meet is plotted with values of (0, 0). Generally, your charts plot data in the positive X, Y area (upper right) portion of a graph or chart. However, if you're plotting negative values (like last year's profits), these are plotted below the X-axis. But this is really only of much use when you're plotting vectors—continuous lines showing trends or dynamically changing data values over time.

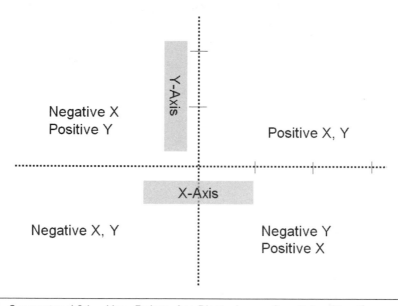

Figure 8.6 Geometry 101—How Points Are Plotted on a Graph (or Chart)

Choosing the Chart Type

By setting the Chart control's *Type* and *SubType* properties, you alter the fundamental appearance and behavior of the rendered chart. These properties can be changed in Layout mode using any one of three techniques:

1. Right-click the Chart control, and choose Chart Type and Subtype from the menu.
2. After selecting the Chart control, change Type and Subtype in the Visual Studio object properties dialog.
3. Right-click on the chart, choose Properties, and set the chart type and sub-type from the General tab in the Chart Properties dialog, as shown in Figure 8.7.

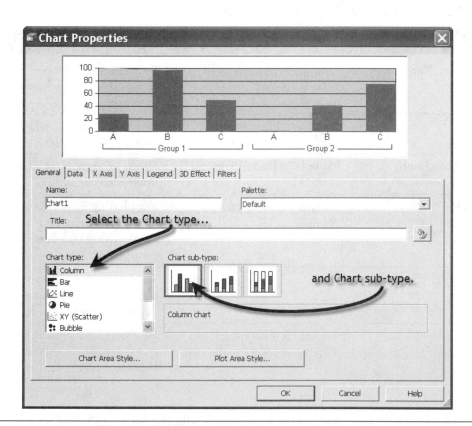

Figure 8.7 Choosing the Chart Type and Sub-Type from the Chart Properties Dialog

There are nine possible settings for the chart *Type* property. Each *Type* has a number of *SubTypes* that vary the basic chart type to accommodate special artistic, data, or presentation requirements. Table 8.1 shows the selectable chart types exposed by Reporting Services[2] and the valid sub-types. Generally, once you choose a type, it's easy to switch sub-types or even choose another type from the same family without having to reset the other properties. If you choose an invalid type/sub-type combination, the chart fails to render—it might seem to work in the prototype pane, but it won't compile. Note that the object properties dialog uses Plain, but the control dialogs use Simple. The remaining variations in the spelling of the *Type* and *SubType* properties are intuitive. The valid Chart control *Type* and *SubType* properties are shown in Table 8.1.

Table 8.1 Valid Chart *Type* and *SubType* Property Options

Chart *Type*	*SubType*	Description and Notes
Column, Bar, Area	"Simple":: Plain, Stacked, "100% Stacked" :: PercentStacked	Best suited for comparing groups of series such as territories.
Line	"Simple":: Plain, Smooth	Best suited for data where time is shown on the X-axis.
Pie, Doughnut	"Simple" :: Plain, Exploded	Shows percentage of whole fractional relationships.
Scatter	"Simple" :: Plain, Line, Smooth	For plotting points to show data distribution. Plots points by specifying both X and Y coordinates.
Bubble	Plain	To plot points by specifying both X and Y coordinates and size of the plotted point.
Stock	HighLowCloseOpen, HighLowClose, Candlestick	Best suited for stock charts showing highs, lows, and change in value over time.

---

[2] Many other chart types are available in the Dundas control, but only those shown in Table 8.1 are exposed.

Creating a Chart

The bulk of the work of programming the Chart control is done through the Chart control properties dialog, as we saw in Figure 8.7. Once you've built a DataSet to display in a chart, the process of adding one or more charts to your report is fairly simple:

1. Drag the Chart control to a suitable place on the report. The Chart control is generally placed in any group area. This means it can't be placed in the Detail row of a Table or Matrix control or in a Textbox control. Remember, the location of the Chart control determines what subset of the data is used to plot its graphics.

2. Drag one or more DataSet Fields to the top Data Fields LZ. When working with the linear chart types, these data points define the size (height or width) of the Chart control's graphic elements—one for each data value. When working with pie or doughnut charts, the points defined by the *Field Value* property are aggregated, and the size of the slice is a function of the percentage of the summed total of all Field values. For bubble and scatter charts, Field values are used to directly control the position of the point or bubble on the X- and Y-axis. For bubble charts, you can also supply a "size" Field to control the size of the plotted bubbles. See the discussion of these special chart types later in this chapter.

3. Drag one or more appropriate Category Fields from the Fields list to the bottom Category Fields LZ. This groups the data values based on the set of category values and labels the elements on the X-axis. Figure 8.8 illustrates a Chart control rendered using the Category Field to group the data. Notice that all columns are the same color. Yes, this book is in black and white—just take our word for it, they're all the same color.

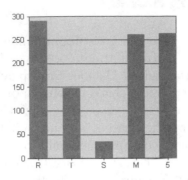

Figure 8.8 Using the Category Fields to Group the Data Fields

    4. An alternative to Step 3 is to drag one or more Fields to the Series Fields LZ. This groups the data values based on the set of series values and labels the elements in the Series legend. In this case, instead of grouping the data all into the same series, the Chart control groups the data into "N" series— one for each category (as shown in Figure 8.9). Each column is colored differently (again, you'll have to take our word for it). For this chart, we moved the Legend to the bottom.

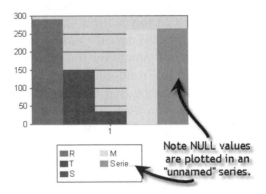

Figure 8.9 Using the Series Fields to Define Data Grouping

Programming the Chart Using the Data Tab

As you drag DataSet Fields to the LZs, the designer performs several tasks behind the scenes. First, it maps the Fields specified in the LZs to appropriate properties. The <DataValue> RDL element is set and exposed in the Chart control's properties dialog in the Data tab. This means that another way to setup your chart is to navigate directly to the Data tab from the Chart control's Properties dialog. See Figure 8.10 and Figure 8.11.

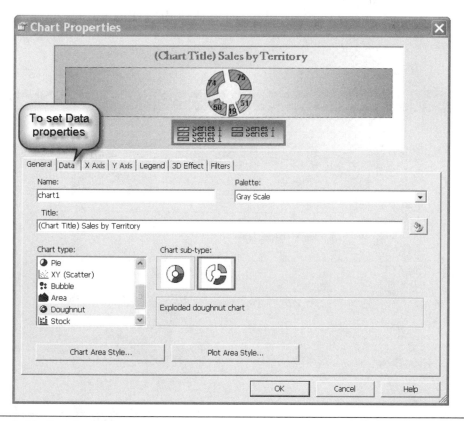

Figure 8.10 The Chart Control Properties Page

The puzzling part of the Data tab is the inconsistency between the properties shown in the Chart control Properties dialog, the RDL properties, and the property names exposed by the Report Designer property dialogs. We're not going to obsess about this, but it would be nice if these matched to avoid confusion. For example, in the Data tab, a dialog labeled Values corresponds to the Data Fields LZ. We highlighted this in Figure 8.11. The DataSet name is shown here, but the dialog labeled Category Groups corresponds to the Category Fields LZ. Fortunately, the Series Groups are labeled the same in both dialogs. Each of these dialogs can be edited and programmed with expressions. For example, you can alter the Series Label, provide an expression for the Value, or change the appearance of each of these Fields using the Edit Chart Value dialog. We discuss this later in the section "Annotating Charts."

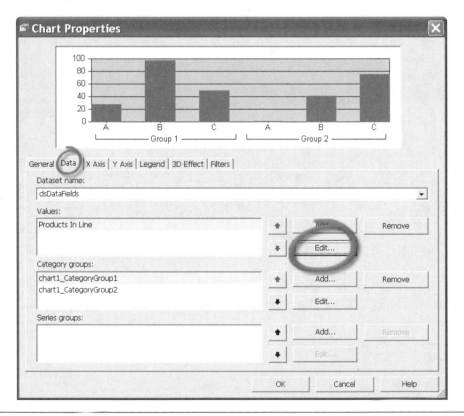

Figure 8.11 The Chart Control Data Properties Tab

> **NOTE** Many (but not all) of these properties permit you to provide an expression. Anywhere you see the *fx* icon, you can provide an expression, as discussed earlier.

Working with Pie and Doughnut Charts

This type of carbo-rich chart requires a somewhat different approach to the data. No, not the Atkins Diet—it assumes that the data is expressed as a percentage of the whole. That is, the size of the "slice" in these charts is a function of the value supplied in the Data Fields/*Value* property. The angle used to determine the slice "size" is computed using the following formula: 360 * (Value ÷ Sum(Values)); that is, if the total of all values is 500 and the Field Value in question is 250, the slice would take up 180°, or ½ of the pie or doughnut. This means that if any individual slice would be less than about 5 percent of the total, its slice will be increasingly hard to see. By "exploding" the pie or doughnut, as shown in Figure 8.12, you can make smaller pieces easier to see. In some cases, using "flat" instead of three-dimensional (3D) rendering can help make smaller segments easier to identify.

The charts in the following examples were created using a query (shown in Listing 8.1) that groups sales data by Territory and adds the Territory Name to the Fields returned to label the chart segments.

Listing 8.1 Query to Return Sales Information from AdventureWorks2000

```
SELECT SalesOrderHeader.TerritoryID, SalesTerritory.Name
AS TerritoryName, SUM(SalesOrderHeader.TotalDue) AS TotalSales
FROM    SalesOrderHeader INNER JOIN SalesTerritory
ON SalesOrderHeader.TerritoryID = SalesTerritory.TerritoryID
GROUP BY SalesOrderHeader.TerritoryID, SalesTerritory.Name
```

NOTE SP1 added the ability to place labels for pie charts outside the chart.

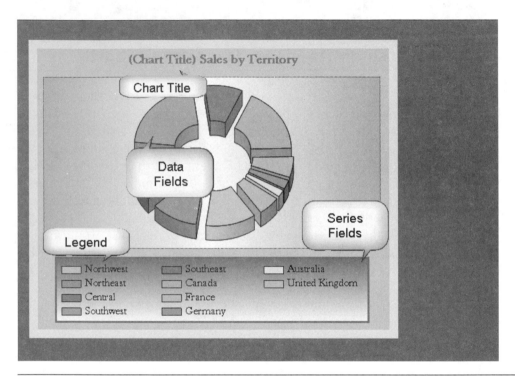

Figure 8.12 A Fully Configured "3D Exploded Doughnut" Chart

You can also rotate the pie and doughnut charts (if they are rendered in 3D mode) to put more emphasis on a specific segment or to make it appear at the top or in any chosen quadrant of the chart. To do this, right-click on the chart, open the Properties page, and click on the 3D Effect tab (as shown in Figure 8.13). Alter the Horizontal rotation, Perspective, Wall thickness, or Vertical rotation to gain the desired effect. We'll let you experiment with these settings.

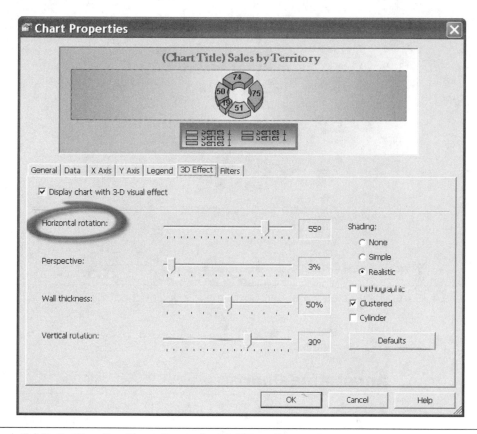

Figure 8.13 Setting the Chart Control's 3D Effect Properties

Another approach to managing the slice distribution is to sort the data series. This places the largest segment first and the smallest last, as shown in Figure 8.14. To do this, we merely added an ORDER BY clause to the query:

```
ORDER BY SUM(SalesOrderHeader.TotalDue)
```

As a rule, we prefer to perform this type of manipulation as data is being fetched (on the server) instead of while the report is rendered. This shifts the processing load to the query, which might not have to be run again, and also leverages the ability of the server to use appropriate database indexes to do the sorting.

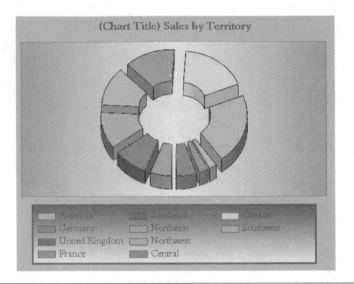

Figure 8.14 Sorting the Sales Data Also Sorts the Pie or Doughnut Slices

Annotating Charts

When the chart does not appear to show what it's supposed to show, it's time to add additional annotation. As we'll see, most of the Chart control properties can be set by using the Chart control properties dialog, as shown in Figure 8.15. However, you must use the Visual Studio .NET IDE property page to change other global properties such as *BackgroundImage*, padding, and others. The following discussion is intended to familiarize you with the mechanics of the Chart control properties dialog and show you how to set a variety of "annotation" properties to enhance the look and feel of your charts—and your reports in general.

Adding Labels to Chart Elements

One approach to enhancing your chart (and a good idea) is to label the segments in the chart—all charts include this option in one form or another. Again, if you have too many segments or data points, you'll find the labels run together. SP1 enhanced the ability to annotate charts by permitting pie chart labels to be outside the pie segments, which helps alleviate this problem. Let's step through the process of adding labels to chart segments:

1. In Layout view, right-click on the Chart control. If the "landing zones" appear, click away from the control and right-click again. This should open a menu—choose Properties.
2. From the properties dialog, as shown in Figure 8.15, you can set the Chart *Name*, *Palette*, *Title*, *Type*, and *Sub-type*, and then navigate to other property pages. In this case, we need to navigate to the Data tab, as shown. We talk about the *Palette* property later in this chapter.

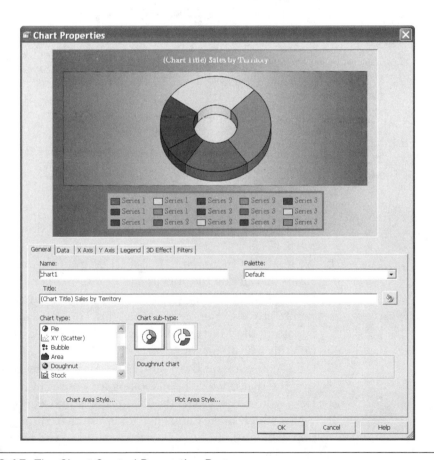

Figure 8.15 The Chart Control Properties Page

3. From the Data tab (as shown in Figure 8.16), click on the Edit... button for the Values, Category Groups, or Series Groups sections of the chart.

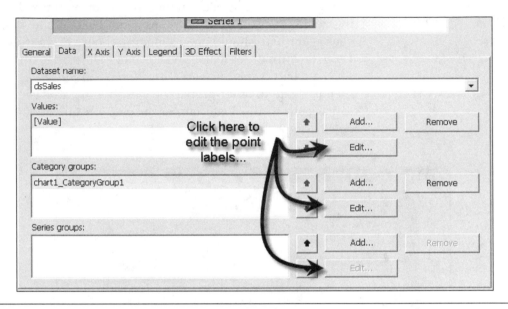

Figure 8.16 The Chart Control Data Properties Tab

4. This navigates you to yet another dialog (shown in Figure 8.17).

5. We're almost there. Note that a bit later (in Figures 8.26 and 8.27) you can edit the appearance of the "markers," which can be used to annotate a chart with shapes such as squares, circles, crosses, diamonds, or triangles. You determine the size by setting the Marker size property. We'll let you experiment with this feature on your own.

6. Once you click on the Point Labels tab, you're confronted with the dialog we've been looking for, shown in Figure 8.18. Here you can activate the point labels and choose a fixed value (which makes no sense for most charts) or an expression, which might be necessary to shorten the length of the label. To move the labels outside the segments (such as pie slices), uncheck the Auto button and choose one of the alternate locations for the segment labels. Figure 8.19 shows the final result.

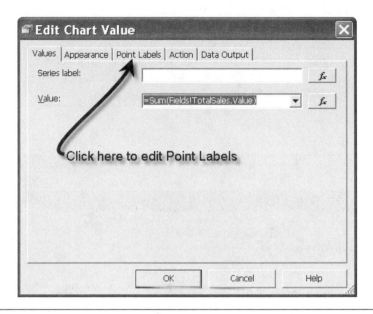

Figure 8.17 The Edit Chart Value Dialog—Navigating to the Point Labels

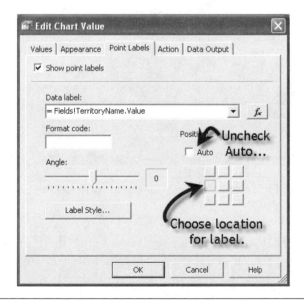

Figure 8.18 Positioning the Labels Outside the Segment or Graphic Object

NOTE Using "Auto" label positioning in chart types other than pie and doughnut ensures that labels never overlap. When Auto is checked, the Chart control tries to find an empty space in which to draw the label. If there is not enough space to draw all labels, it removes data point labels that don't fit.

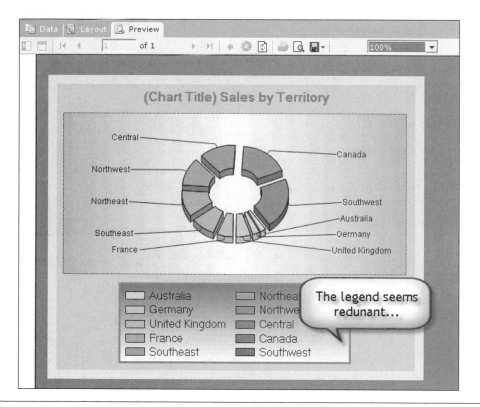

Figure 8.19 SP1 Permits Pie Segment Labels to Appear Outside the Segment

7. If you think it's necessary to alter the font or appearance of the label, simply click Label Style... from the Edit Chart Value dialog, and the Style Properties dialog is exposed, as shown in Figure 8.20.

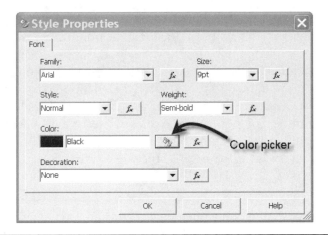

Figure 8.20 Setting the Style Properties for the Chosen Label

8. If necessary (and it often is), choose an appropriate font size and style that won't overwhelm the chart display. You can also choose another color for the text using the color picker, as highlighted in Figure 8.20. Once you're done here, you can return up two levels (to the Data tab shown in Figure 8.16) and repeat the process for the other groups and Values.

SP1 Chart Style Enhancements

In the RTM version of Reporting Services, the report items controls (including the Chart control) did not support expressions on the *Style* property. SP1 fixed that. This means you can drill down into the *Style* properties (as we have just described) and write your own expression to change the *Style* properties as needed. This means you can use expressions to determine your own colors, gradient and gradient end colors, as well as border and line style, width, and color.

Using the Stock Charts

Another specialized variation of the control configuration types is *stock*. This chart type exposes three or four target areas to help set up Chart controls intended to display stock sales data. As shown in

Figure 8.21, the chart exposes High, Low, Open, and Close price LZs where you can drop appropriate Fields. To generate the example for this report, we included a CSV (comma-delimited) text file that has stock quote data (for Microsoft, of course). We had originally planned to use an ODBC Data Source to access this file using the Text File driver, but this was a significant challenge as we found a number of permissions issues while trying to work with this non-standard provider—but that's fodder for another article or book. Let's walk through the process of setting up and testing the stock type chart.

NOTE One of the other challenges here is changing the scale of the chart to better match the data range—to zoom in on the data so that the details can be seen. Unfortunately, the RDS does not support an expression on the X- or Y-axis scale Minimum or Maximum property settings.

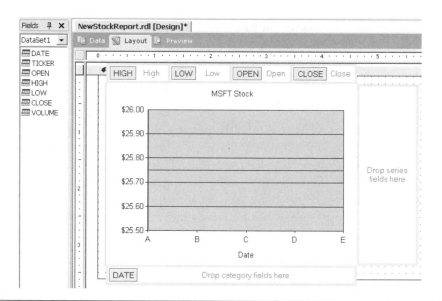

Figure 8.21 A Configured Stock Type Chart Control

Once the report is rendered, as shown in Figure 8.22, the stock-type Chart control displays its unique variation of the chart. Well, yes, we did add a few extras to illustrate how to further annotate the chart. For this chart, we set the *Background image* property to a "watermarked" graphic, added another Chart control to the bottom of the chart to show stock volume, and added a subreport that's launched by clicking on the main chart.

Figure 8.22 The Rendered Stock Report After a Bit of Annotation

---

TIP If you expect that no data will be returned by your query, you can set the *NoRows* property of the Chart control to any string you choose. "Nope, no data today" would work....

A Touch of Color

When it comes time to choose a color from the list of available colors, remember that Transparent really means "no color"—it's not a color. It also means the chart elements are displayed using the automatic color assignment drawn from the chart palette. In other words, you can't use Transparent in an expression in the same way as you could use "nothing." You can use White, but it might not match the background color (which is what Transparent does). The Chart control exposes the *Palette* property that permits you to choose from a set of color combinations that deal with special situations or personal taste. You can choose Default, Earthtones, Excel, Grayscale, Light, Pastel, or SemiTransparent. Most of these are self-explanatory. For example, we expect those of us on the West Coast would prefer Earthtones, and the folks in the UK would use Pastel. We have no clue what the people in Cleveland would use.

NOTE The properties exposed from *within* the Chart control's property page are not the same. They are not spelled with camel-case. For example, Grayscale becomes "Gray scale," Earthtones becomes "Earth tones," and so forth. We expect this to get sorted out eventually.

Chart and Plot Area Styles

To change the background color of the Chart or the Plot area, you can use the Visual Studio .NET object property dialog or visit the Chart Properties dialog (see Figure 8.15) and choose Chart Area Style.... This takes you to the Style Properties page (see Figure 8.20) where you can customize the *Border* and *Line* properties as well as define a Fill with the Fill tab, as shown in Figure 8.23. Again, be conservative with your choice of colors as they can tend to obscure the labels and other content that have to be plotted over them.

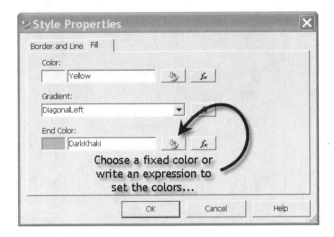

Figure 8.23 The Style Properties Fill Tab

Shades of Gray or Hashing?

Let's touch on the Grayscale palette because it has other implications and is undergoing change for SP1. As you might expect, the Grayscale palette is designed for use with black and white (B/W) printers (there are a few still out there). Grayscale dithering makes it easier to differentiate between the graphic elements used in your chart, as shown in Figure 8.24. However, this feature is disabled when you enable 3D rendering (as shown in the chart on the top in Figure 8.24)—all you get are shades of gray that are increasingly hard to differentiate.

Color fills and gradients can add considerable eye appeal to your chart or report, but they can also obscure text captions that have to be written over them. Be sure to view the report on the target browser or renderer to make sure you can still read the text. You should also try printing the reports if that's the way you expect to disperse the information. Because there is no facility to add an overriding background color to the text cells in a chart, you'll have to choose the fill colors carefully. We've found that using less radical gradients is best—not black to white or red to green.

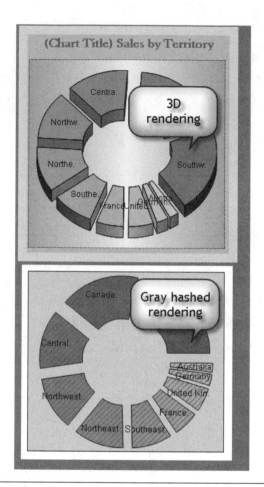

Figure 8.24 Dithering Appears When Using 3D and Grayscale Palette

SemiTransparent Shading

SemiTransparent is simply another color palette to choose from. In this case, the graphics objects are rendered, so they permit any background color or object to "show through" the object. This is easier to show than it is to describe. Figure 8.25 illustrates a chart rendered using the SemiTransparent palette. Notice how the colors of the rear wall and floor of the chart can be seen through the columns.

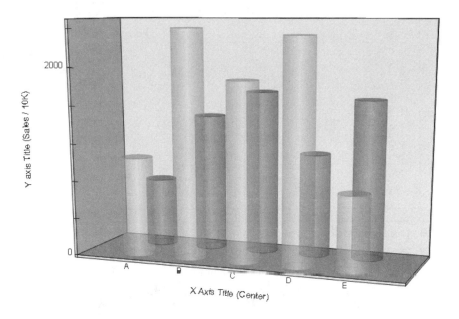

Figure 8.25 A 3D Chart Rendered with the SemiTransparent Palette

Using the Bubble and Scatter Charts

The bubble and scatter charts are different from other chart types in a number of respects. In typical charts, the X value is derived from the category grouping, but the scatter and bubble charts have an explicit X value. For these charts, the category grouping only defines the color encoding for the legend. When you request the bubble or scatter chart types, the chart exposes several new LZs, as shown in Figure 8.26. This permits you to plot points (or "bubbles") at specific X and Y locations on the chart.

Actually, you don't have to plot "bubbles" for the bubble or scatter chart types—you can choose the type of point to plot (the marker) using the Edit Chart Value dialog. This dialog can be reached by navigating to Properties, Data tab, Edit Values and then clicking on the Appearance tab. As shown in Figure 8.27, you can choose from a variety of marker types.

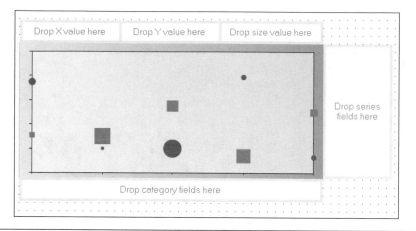

Figure 8.26 The Bubble Chart Type Exposes X, Y, and Size LZs

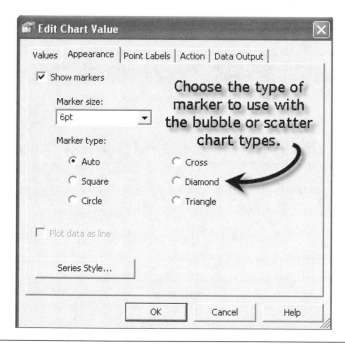

Figure 8.27 Select the Type of Marker to Use for Bubble and Scatter Chart Types

However, setting up a bubble or scatter type chart is not all that simple. If you don't specify category and series groupings in a scatter/bubble chart, everything collapses into one data cell and gets aggregated. It's like a matrix with no groupings and just one cell. To get around this problem, follow these steps:

1. Visit the Chart control property page, navigate to the Data table, and change the Values, as shown in Figure 8.28. In SP1, the Chart control uses Count() aggregates. In the RTM version, the Sum() aggregate is used. Both of these should be removed as shown.

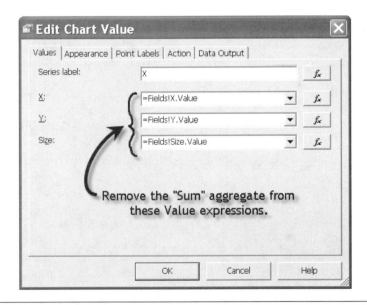

Figure 8.28 Resetting the Value Property for the Bubble Chart

2. Next, add a category grouping to the "Drop category fields here" LZ. You can just use the same expression as for the X values: =Fields!X.Value.
3. Finally, go to the X-axis tab and set Numeric or time-scale data.

NOTE In some scatter/bubble charts you still might want to use the aggregates—for the same reasons you typically use aggregates in matrix cells. This is especially true if your chart series/category grouping doesn't guarantee that every "cell" contains only one data point at runtime. For example, aggregates make sense when plotting sales (Y-axis) versus cost (X-axis) in a scatter plot.

4. To demonstrate use of the bubble chart, we built a program to generate points for a circle and added a little trigonometry to generate a "size" value. Once plotted by the Chart control, the result is shown in Figure 8.29.

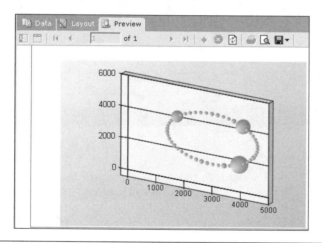

Figure 8.29 The Bubble Chart Plotting a Circle Using Varying Size Settings

Note that the aspect ratio (height to width) is a bit off. This can be corrected by making sure the Chart control is as square as possible after having removed the Legend or by placing the Legend at the bottom to prevent it from stealing space from the width.

No, you won't be able to set a gradient on the bubble chart in 3D. The implementation does not support this feature.

The Scatter Chart

The scatter chart is very similar to the bubble chart except that it does not have a "bubble" size parameter to set. In other respects, the results are about the same, but the points generated are of a fixed size.

NOTE For the scatter chart type to work when rendered in the 3D mode, you must ensure that the points are pre-sorted.

The Matrix Control

In Chapter 3, we created a report containing a *Matrix control* with the Report wizard, and we saw that the Matrix control provides a tabular mechanism to display data in a cross-tab or pivot format. Conceptually, you can think of the Matrix control as a Table control where column headings and row headings are dynamically driven by data, and where the tabular content is derived from aggregated data values. The Matrix control has a lot in common with the PivotTable, which you or your users may have already seen and used in Excel or Office Web Components. The PivotTable is distantly related to the kind of data presentation available with Microsoft Access crosstab queries. Pivot or cross-table data transformations are incredibly powerful analysis tools and are especially loved by those with financial responsibilities within organizations. The Matrix control doesn't offer the same level and richness of end-user interaction that a PivotTable does, although much of the functionality can be faked if you have the inclination, patience, and time. Fortunately, none of these is needed if you recognize that reports using the Matrix control can usually be rendered to HTML with the Office Web Components PivotTable, and from there can be exported into Excel itself. We say "usually" because there are a few exceptions to this, as we describe later in this chapter.

Taken from "The Sound of Music." Now, presumably we didn't quote more of the song here because clearly Homer Simpson got involved with a "D'oh!" or is that a different pronunciation?

–Peter

Yes, I like Ms. Andrews, but I think her glass-shattering performance in "Victor Victoria" was more to my taste.

–Bill

Getting Started with the Matrix Control

In the words once uttered by Bill's singing heroine of all time, Julie Andrews, "Let's start at the very beginning…." The Matrix control can seem a bit daunting at first, but we'll take you through it a step at a time. We expect that somewhere in the chapter you'll say "Oh! I get it!" and understand what the Matrix control is all about. We start with a simple query and build up from there. We'll show how the Matrix control is a lot like the chart in that it has landing zones and unique (and sometimes irksome) drag-drop functionality. Later on, we'll tune up the report and show how to make your Matrix control reports really shine. In our first simple query against the AdventureWorks SalesOrderHeader table (shown in Figure 8.30), we'll just pick four columns.

Column	Alias	Table	Output	Sort Type
SalesPersonID		SalesOrderHeader	✓	
CurrencyCode		SalesOrderHeader	✓	
TotalDue		SalesOrderHeader	✓	
OrderDate		SalesOrderHeader	✓	

```
SELECT    SalesPersonID, CurrencyCode, TotalDue, OrderDate
FROM      SalesOrderHeader
```

SalesPersonID	CurrencyCode	TotalDue	OrderDate
31	GBP	25.8283	01/09/2003
302	USD	2435.091	01/09/2003
27	USD	972.785	01/06/2003
29	USD	92.0444	01/03/2003
302	USD	2313.1346	01/06/2004

Figure 8.30 Raw Data in the AdventureWorks SalesOrderHeader Table

Joining Other Tables

For this report, we include the sales person's name instead of just the ID, so we need to JOIN the Employee table. We previewed the data, and we notice that there are rows in the SalesOrderHeader table where the SalesPersonID column is NULL. Presumably, this is where sales have taken place without being attributable to a sales person—under-the-table payoffs, we suppose. For this report, we'd really like to return all rows—not just those that have a non-NULL SalesPersonID column—so we have to use a LEFT OUTER JOIN, as shown in Listing 8.2. This ensures that our data has all rows returned from the SalesOrderHeader table—NULLs and all.

Listing 8.2 Joining the Employee Table

```
SELECT ISNULL(ISNULL(emp.FirstName + ' ' + emp.LastName,
       ISNULL(emp.FirstName, emp.LastName)), 'UNKNOWN') AS SalesPerson,
     soh.CurrencyCode,
     soh.TotalDue,
     soh.OrderDate
FROM SalesOrderHeader soh
LEFT OUTER JOIN Employee emp
ON soh.SalesPersonID = emp.EmployeeID
```

One of the other things to learn about from Listing 8.2 is the ISNULL hierarchy that we are using when concatenating the FirstName and LastName. When any SalesPerson value evaluates to NULL we use this SQL to coerce the column to "UNKNOWN." These sales took place without being attributable to a sales person. We've also taken this a little further to show the ISNULL hierarchy to allow one of the columns (either FirstName or LastName) to be NULL and to ensure that they are safe to concatenate. (In AdventureWorks there are table-level constraints on the Employee table to ensure that NULL values are not allowed in FirstName or LastName columns, so we didn't really need these extra checks, but on real data you might need them.)

Breaking Out the Date

The query returns an OrderDate field, but for this report we are only interested in seeing this as a Year and a Month. Because of this, we remove OrderDate and substitute three calculated fields using T-SQL functions—Year, MonthNumber, and MonthName, as shown in Listing 8.3. Don't forget to check Listing 8.4 for a more optimal query for the Matrix control, and an explanation of what makes it perform better.

Listing 8.3 Breaking Out the Date in T-SQL

```
SELECT      ISNULL(ISNULL(emp.FirstName + ' ' + emp.LastName,
  ISNULL(emp.FirstName, emp.LastName)), 'UNKNOWN') AS SalesPerson,
              soh.CurrencyCode,
              soh.TotalDue,
              {fn YEAR(soh.OrderDate)} as Year,
              {fn MONTH(soh.OrderDate)} as MonthNumber,
              {fn MONTHNAME(soh.OrderDate)} as MonthName
FROM        SalesOrderHeader soh
LEFT OUTER JOIN  Employee emp
ON soh.SalesPersonID = emp.EmployeeID
```

Creating a Report with a Matrix Control

The query shown in Listing 8.3 is sufficient for use with a Matrix control, but it's by no means optimal. If the Data Processing extension you are using supports grouping and aggregation functions, you can optimize performance by performing the grouping in the DBMS itself where there is access to underlying indexes. Sure, Reporting Services is capable of performing all of the necessary grouping and aggregation, but doing so can be expensive. Let's take a look (again, be sure to check the end of this chapter where we talk about optimal queries and studying the performance metrics of reports).

1. In Visual Studio .NET 2003, create a new report project and add a new blank report.
2. Create a DataSet that uses a Data Source that connects to the AdventureWorks2000 database, and use the T-SQL from Listing 8.3.
3. Once you have the DataSet created, turn to the Layout tab and drag a Matrix control from the toolbar onto the design surface. Figure 8.31 shows a Matrix control with its awaiting landing zones (LZs) into which you can drag and drop fields from the Fields list.

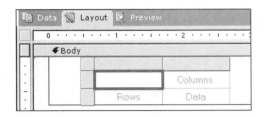

Figure 8.31 A Matrix Control Awaiting Fields to Be Dropped into the Landing Zones

4. One way of choosing the Fields is to drag and drop them. That is, select a Field from the Fields list and drag it to the appropriate LZ. The very first Field that is dropped associates the Matrix with that Field's DataSet and sets the Matrix's *DataSetName* property.

   Most of the time, that's what you want, but if you happen to have more than one DataSet in your report and you make a mistake (like dropping a Field from the wrong DataSet), you'll find that you need to select the Matrix and reassign its *DataSetName* property directly in the Properties window. Perhaps a greater challenge is removing the grouping for a "wrongly" added field. In this case, the Matrix complains bitterly that it needs at least one column and one row grouping. You'll find that you need to add the intended Fields before being able to delete any mistakes. It's not as forgiving as the Chart control.

   You can drag as many fields as you want to the Rows and Columns landing zones. Reorder the grouping priorities by dragging the Fields with the mouse.

TIP *Use the Extended Properties Dialog* We've found this approach awkward to use, and even more awkward to explain. If you are trying to show this to someone who is mouse-challenged, you'll probably find it easier to edit the *Matrix* properties using the Extended properties dialog. This dialog is exposed when you right-click on the Matrix itself (as shown in Figure 8.32) or click the Property Pages button at the top of the Properties window.

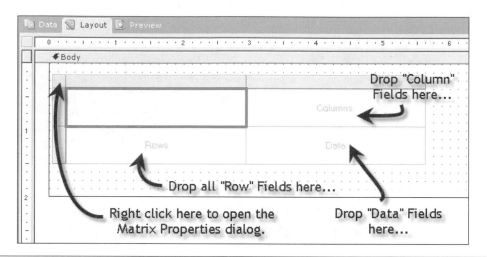

Figure 8.32 Opening the Extended Properties Dialog on the Matrix Control and Its Landing Zones

Figure 8.32 shows the initial Fields selected and dragged to the landing zones of the Matrix control. What might not be obvious is that the SalesPerson, CurrencyCode, and MonthName Fields were all dragged to the same Rows LZ. The Matrix control automatically adds additional columns to the control as we drag and drop each additional Field.

5. Next, drag the TotalDue Field to the Data LZ and Year to the Columns LZ. Notice that an aggregate function of Sum is generated by default for the Data landing zone. You can change the aggregate function if necessary. We selected all the cells in the Matrix and gave them a solid border to make it easier to see the groupings, as shown in Figure 8.33.

			=Fields!Year.Value
=Fields!SalesPerson.Value	=Fields!CurrencyCode.Value	=Fields!MonthName.Value	=Sum(Fields!TotalDue.Value)

Figure 8.33 Add the Fields to the Matrix Landing Zones

If you inspect the Matrix Properties dialog Groups tab, you can see how the Rows and Columns groups have been configured (as shown in Figure 8.34). Sure, you could have simply entered these Field references here using the Edit . . . button.

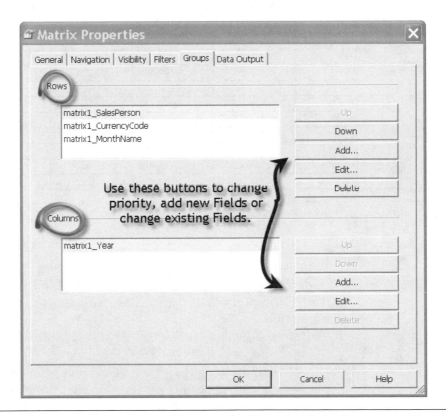

Figure 8.34 The Matrix Properties Dialog as Configured with the Rows and Columns References

Figure 8.35 shows how the Matrix now appears when rendered in the Preview tab. We can see here that we have columns derived from the data values from Fields!Year.Value. We also see the rows derived from the data and grouped by

Fields!SalesPerson.Value, by Fields!CurrencyCode.Value, and finally by Fields!MonthName.Value.

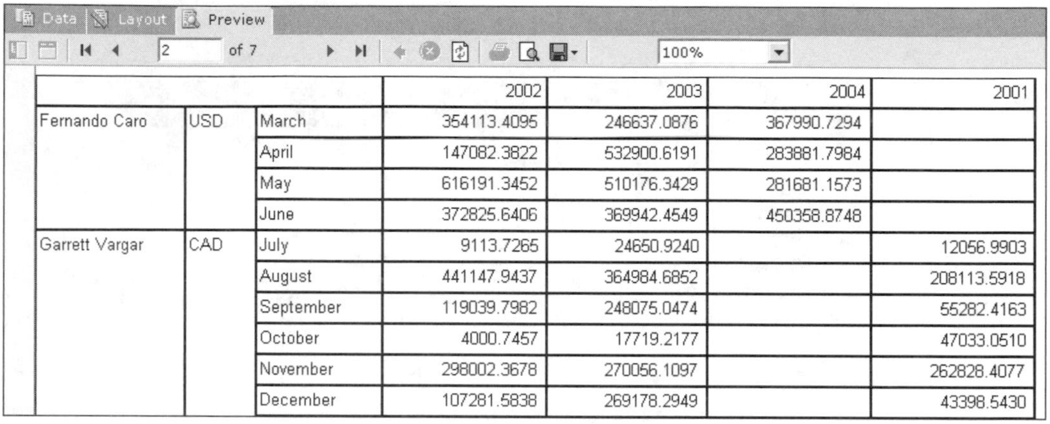

			2002	2003	2004	2001
Fernando Caro	USD	March	354113.4095	246637.0876	367990.7294	
		April	147082.3822	532900.6191	283881.7984	
		May	616191.3452	510176.3429	281681.1573	
		June	372825.6406	369942.4549	450358.8748	
Garrett Vargar	CAD	July	9113.7265	24650.9240		12056.9903
		August	441147.9437	364984.6852		208113.5918
		September	119039.7982	248075.0474		55282.4163
		October	4000.7457	17719.2177		47033.0510
		November	298002.3678	270056.1097		262828.4077
		December	107281.5838	269178.2949		43398.5430

Figure 8.35 Previewing the Rendered Matrix

While our groupings may be what we intended, the sort orders within those groupings could do with improvement, and the report would look better with the financial data formatted.

6. Select the TotalDue data cell in the Matrix control and set its *Format* property to "#,###.00," as shown in Figure 8.36. Nope, don't be tempted to use "Currency" formatting, as these values are not all in the same currency.

It might be an interesting exercise to prefix each TotalDue and the Sum(TotalDue) value cells with the appropriate currency figure. However, this would entail quite a bit of processing that's really beyond the scope of this book. We hear from a trusted source that the financial community usually does not like to see currency symbols anyway.

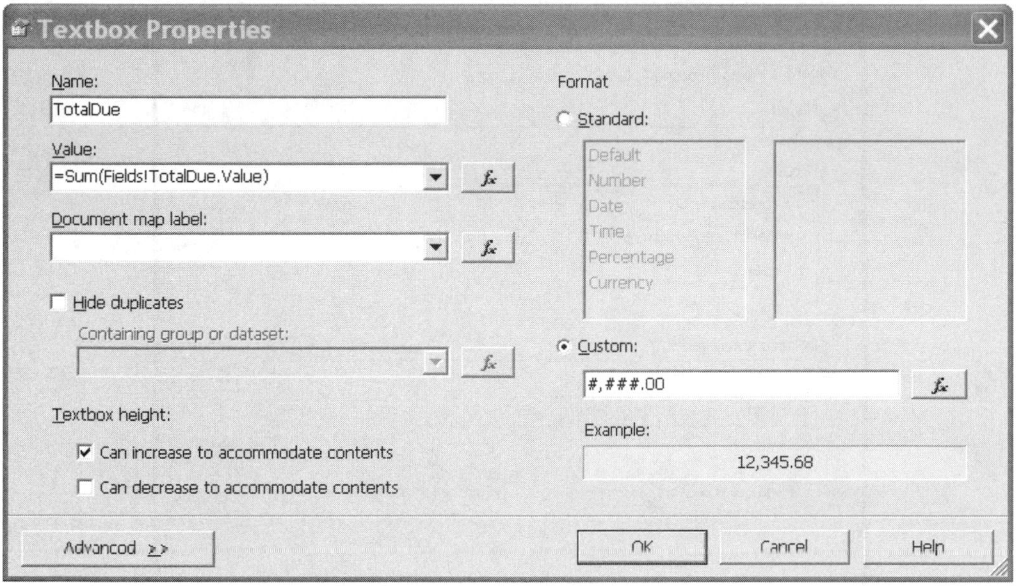

Figure 8.36 Setting the *TotalDue Format* Property in the Textbox Properties Dialog

Sorting and Naming the Groups

If you call up the Extended properties dialog on the Matrix by clicking on the Property Pages button in the Properties window when the Matrix is selected or by contorting your mouse standing on one leg and clicking in the magic area on the Matrix itself, you can get to the Groups properties tab, as we showed you in Figure 8.34. Here you can re-order the row and column groupings and set the sort expressions—just select a group and click the Edit... button. This displays the Grouping and Sorting Properties dialog, as shown in Figure 8.37.

We suggest that you name the groups with the end user in mind. The point is that when the Matrix is rendered to a PivotTable control in Office Web Components, it uses the grouping names as headers, which are then visible to users as columns and headers.

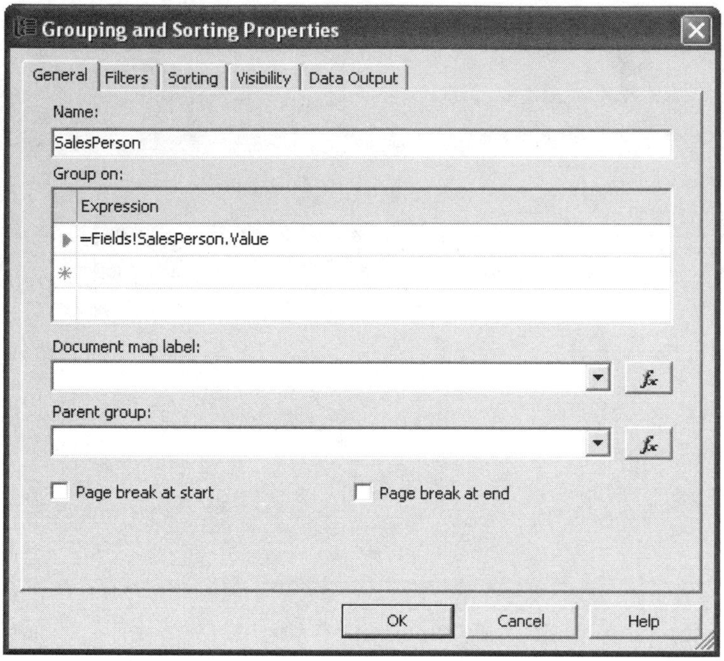

Figure 8.37 The Grouping and Sorting Properties for a Matrix Group

Through this Grouping and Sorting Properties dialog, you can set expressions for Filters, determine Sorting, and control the Visibility. Yes, these can use expressions (as we discussed in Chapter 6) and those expressions can use Report Parameters. If those Report Parameters are not used in the underlying query (and are marked in the RDL as <UsedInQuery>False</UsedInQuery>), the parameters are available to be changed by a user at runtime when rendering a snapshot report.

Sure, it's possible to group by expressions based on Report Parameters, and to bind the columns and rows to expression-based fields. By so doing, you can "fake" the ability (as you can in a PivotTable) to exchange rows for columns and vice versa. Okay, so *fake* is a bit of an overstatement because you *can* make it work, it's just that you don't have the real snazzy drag-and-drop functionality directly in the browser unless you go deep into creating htc behavior files. This entails so much work that it's easier to simply render to HTML with Office Web Components.

Figure 8.38 shows the state of our example now. At this point, we renamed all of our row and column groupings, and sorted them by their respective fields. As for the Month names, we sorted those by the MonthNumber, and provided a format string on the financial values.

			2001	2002	2003	2004
Fernando Caro	USD	September	187,326.34	608,216.81	567,272.27	
		October	123,986.90	443,614.82	321,553.36	
		November	526,398.49	486,879.14	299,402.98	
		December	401,366.18	465,991.40	432,576.66	
Garrett Vargar	CAD	January		36,757.23	3,783.71	22,883.42
		February		150,450.00	159,026.73	154,432.30
		March		113,340.69	91,130.39	147,114.16
		April		51,925.50	10,737.13	6,332.93
		May		229,317.00	285,179.93	231,334.78
		June		44,377.96	107,106.24	193,495.70
		July	12,058.99	9,113.73	24,850.92	
		August	208,113.59	441,147.94	364,984.69	
		September	55,282.42	119,030.80	248,075.05	

Figure 8.38 The Example After We Have Sorted the Groupings and Formatted the Financial Values

Putting GreenBars in Matrixes Using `RunningValue` and `CountDistinct`

One thing that often confuses people is how to alternate background row colors in a Matrix, and having seen the trick with tables using the `RowCount` function they set about trying to use that in a Matrix. At this point, folks are pretty confused when instead of alternately colored rows they get more of a patchwork quilt effect. Well, the trick with the Matrix control is to use the `CountDistinct` and `RunningValue` functions in a Textbox control's cell whose *Value* property can be queried with `ReportItems!<Textbox>.Value`.

The best way to see this is to see it in practice:

1. Select the Matrix, and from the context menu choose to add a Row Group. In the dialog that comes up, call it RowColor and give it a grouping expression of "=1", as shown in Figure 8.39.

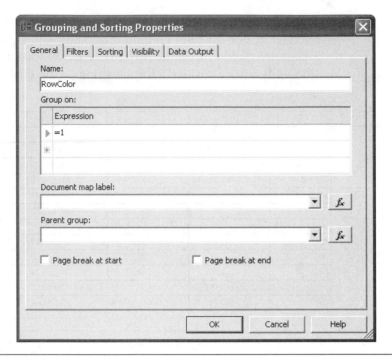

Figure 8.39 Creating a Grouping to Use with Background Row Colors

2. Find the textbox created for the RowColor in the Layout view, and enter the expression:

```
=RunningValue(Fields!SalesPerson.Value & ↵
Fields!CurrencyCode.Value & Fields!MonthName.Value ↵
,CountDistinct, Nothing).
```

This creates a running value count of distinct values of the string made from

```
Fields!SalesPerson.Value & Fields!CurrencyCode.Value & ↵
Fields!MonthName.Value.
```

3. Click on the Preview tab to see the effect, shown in Figure 8.40.

				2001	2002	2003	2004
Garrett Vargar	CAD	June	53		44,377.96	107,106.24	193,495.70
		July	54	12,056.99	9,113.73	24,650.92	
		August	55	208,113.59	441,147.94	364,984.69	
		September	56	55,282.42	119,039.80	248,075.05	
		October	57	47,033.05	4,000.75	17,719.22	
		November	58	262,828.41	298,002.37	270,056.11	
		December	59	43,398.54	107,281.58	269,178.29	
Jae Pak	CAD	January	60			343,155.70	291,643.66
		February	61			310,176.51	272,052.13
		March	62			431,485.85	469,144.82

Figure 8.40 Previewing the Report Using the RunningValue of CountDistinct

4. Given that we have an effective counter on the distinct groupings, we can now take the modulus over 2 (mod 2) and use that in an IIF expression to return a color value:

```
=IIF(RunningValue(Fields!SalesPerson.Value & Fields!CurrencyCode.Value
 & Fields!MonthName.Value ,CountDistinct, Nothing ) mod 2,"LightBlue",
"White").
```

This alternates the textbox background value between "LightBlue" and "White."

5. Because we can get to the *Value* property of the RowColor textbox only from other Textbox controls contained within its grouping level, and the RowColor textbox itself must remain visible, at this point you need to use several non-intuitive techniques. The trick is to set the Textbox control's *BackGroundColor* and *Color* properties to the *Value* property (=Value), and then fiddle around with the borders to remove the left-hand edge. By removing the right-hand edge of the border around the Month textbox, we faked a bigger cell for the Month, and our RowColor textbox won't be noticed. The TotalDue textbox placed in the Data landing zone can have its *BackGroundColor* property set to ReportItems!RowColor.Value. This gives it an alternating-color background.

6. As the MonthName textbox is outside the grouping level for the RowColor, set the MonthName's *BackGroundColor* property to the same IIF expression used for the RowColor.

7. Finally, to ensure that the RowColor textbox is big enough for the text that it must contain, set the FontSize to 1pt (1 point).

8. Click the Preview button again to see the results of our labor. It should look something like Figure 8.41.

			2001	2002	2003	2004
Garrett Vargar	CAD	June		44,377.96	107,106.24	193,495.70
		July	12,056.99	9,113.73	24,650.92	
		August	208,113.59	441,147.94	364,984.69	
		September	55,282.42	119,039.80	248,075.05	
		October	47,033.05	4,000.75	17,719.22	
		November	262,828.41	298,002.37	270,056.11	
		December	43,398.54	107,281.58	269,178.29	
Jae Pak	CAD	January			343,155.70	291,643.66
		February			310,176.51	272,052.13
		March			431,485.85	469,144.82
		April			574,107.98	494,501.82
		May			335,994.10	293,013.24
		June			480,865.14	590,749.49

Figure 8.41 A Matrix with Alternating Background Colors

Summing Columns and Rows

It's also possible to create subtotals on one or several of the row or column level groupings. In the Layout tab, choose Subtotal from the context menu, and a Total will appear, as shown in Figure 8.42. The formatting properties for the subtotals are available if you select the tiny green triangle that appears in the top right of a SubTotal textbox.

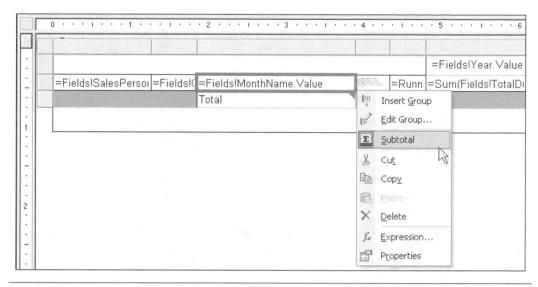

Figure 8.42 Adding a Subtotal to the Matrix Report

WARNING If you're also performing alternately colored backgrounds, expect some spurious results. There appears to be a bug in RunningValue when there are Subtotals on groupings. We reported this bug to Microsoft, and we hope that this issue can be fixed soon, but at this point in time we expect the fix to be after SP1 rather than part of it.

Understanding and Tuning Matrix Performance

Remember that we based this Matrix report on the query in Listing 8.3 and that it is a sub-optimal T-SQL query for the Matrix because it returns more than 31,000 rows and forces heavy processing to take place in the Report Server to perform grouping and aggregation. If the Data Processing extension being used supports server-side Grouping and Aggregation (and SQL Server does), it's a good idea to use it. In this case, we saw a performance increase of about 300 percent by grouping in the SQL Server. In the process, we significantly reduced the number of rows returned to the Report Processor. The query in Listing 8.4 shows how we optimized the T-SQL to include server-side Grouping and Aggregation.

Listing 8.4 An Optimal Query for the Matrix Where Much of the Grouping Is Done in the DBMS

```
SELECT ISNULL(ISNULL(emp.FirstName + ' ' + emp.LastName,
 ISNULL(emp.FirstName, emp.LastName)), 'UNKNOWN') AS SalesPerson,
                soh.CurrencyCode,
                SUM(soh.TotalDue),
                {fn YEAR(soh.OrderDate)} AS Year,
                {fn MONTH(soh.OrderDate)} AS MonthNumber,
                {fn MONTHNAME(soh.OrderDate)} AS MonthName
FROM SalesOrderHeader soh
LEFT OUTER JOIN  Employee emp
ON soh.SalesPersonID = emp.EmployeeID
GROUP BY ISNULL(ISNULL(emp.FirstName + ' ' + emp.LastName,
        ISNULL(emp.FirstName, emp.LastName)), 'UNKNOWN'),
           soh.CurrencyCode,
           { fn YEAR(soh.OrderDate) },
           { fn MONTH(soh.OrderDate) },
           { fn MONTHNAME(soh.OrderDate) }
```

Exporting to Office Web Components

One of our reviewers at Microsoft reminded us to include a few words on exporting a report to a Microsoft Office Web Component (OWC). **OWC** is a set of ActiveX controls that are supported in Microsoft Office 2000 and later. Reports containing a Matrix control can (sometimes) be exported to OWC so that the user can perform far more sophisticated data manipulation than is possible with the Reporting Services Matrix control. We say *sometimes* because if the report does not meet the requirements listed below, the Matrix control is not rendered in the OWC PivotTable. The following requirements must be met to render in the OWC:

■ The web browser used to display reports must support ActiveX.

■ The web browser must permit execution of ActiveX controls by changing the device information setting to False.

■ OWC must be installed on the client, or the client must be able to download OWC.

In addition, the OWC PivotTable control cannot display all items that can appear in a Matrix. A Matrix control that includes any of the following does not display as a PivotTable:

■ Any data region (table, chart, matrix, or list)

■ An Image control

■ A subreport

■ More than one group expression in a grouping

■ Both static columns and static rows

■ Dynamic columns or rows nested inside static columns or rows

■ A data size larger than 262,144 rows

If your Matrix is simple enough but your web browser cannot load the OWC, the user is given the option to download the OWC from a language-specific Microsoft website or to view the report without OWC. To alter the download location of OWC, change the OWCDownloadLocation element in the RSReportServer.config file.

When a report is rendered to HTML with OWC, data in a Matrix renders as an OWC PivotTable (as shown in Figure 8.43). At this point, the user can manipulate the data as necessary. There are enough features here to make any accountant or financial analyst ecstatic. This manipulation does not re-execute the query—all of the data is contained within the OWC PivotTable. Users can also export this PivotTable to an Excel spreadsheet by clicking on the toolbar button as indicated in Figure 8.43.

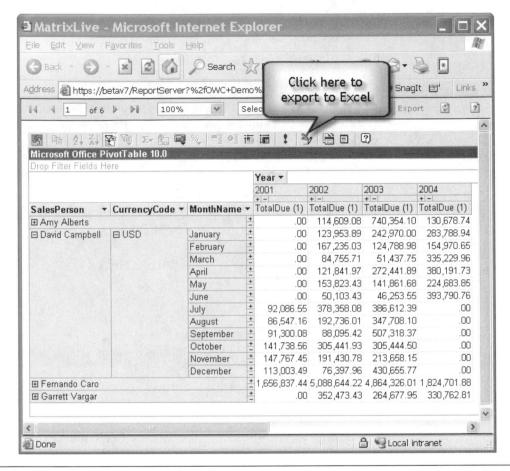

Figure 8.43 The Matrix Control as Exported to "HTML with Office Web Components"

Monitoring the Report Processor

We often have to determine how to optimize a report (as we illustrated in the last section). However, without the proper statistics, you have to use less scientific means to improve performance. Fortunately, Reporting Services exposes these statistics. When reports are executed, the report's performance metrics are written to the ExecutionLog table in the ReportServer database. These logs include information such as:

- Who executed the report?
- When was the report processed?
- How many rows were returned by the report queries?
- What parameters were presented?
- What was the total processing time?
- How long did the data retrieval take?
- How long did the rendering take?
- How many rows were returned?
- What report rendering format was used?

This information is very useful when diagnosing report performance, but don't try to interact directly with the ExecutionLog table. This isn't supported, and it easily can get in the way of the Report Processor. Remember, while you're running a report against the ExecutionLog table, additional entries are being added by your own report. Instead, create a new SQL Server database called RSExecutionLog, and execute the CreateTables.SQL T-SQL that you'll find in *\Program Files\Microsoft SQL Server\80\Tools\ Reporting Services\ExecutionLog*. This creates a set of tables that you can populate with the DTS package RSExecutionLog_Update.dts found in the same folder. This DTS package safely interrogates the ExecutionLog and creates a set of tables that are safe for you to query and create reports against.

We show you how to set this up on the DVD and demonstrate these performance metrics.

Summary

This chapter provided a brief overview of the Reporting Services Chart and Matrix controls. We saw how to pass DataSet Fields to these controls as well as how to group and format the data as it's rendered. We saw how to setup the Chart control to display typical bar-type charts, as well as how to use the more specialized pie, doughnut, stock, bubble, and scatter chart types. We also showed how to annotate a chart using fixed property settings as well as expressions. At the end of the chapter, we provided an in-depth study of the Matrix control and how to make the best use of this control, including ways to provide GreenBar and other enhancements.

CHAPTER 9

Customizing Reports—Report Templates and Styles

Or, How We Came to Love Code Access Security

I once had a life before I started dissecting Reporting Services.

–Peter

And I had a life until Peter talked me into this! But then I would not know as much as I do about Reporting Services.

–Bill

This chapter is full of tips, techniques, and technology innovations that you won't find in the Reporting Services documentation or (we suspect) anywhere else, with the possible exception of our website.[1] We've spent countless hours researching and developing these techniques, which we reveal here for the first time. Some of the techniques illustrate ways to increase report developer productivity and security— many address widely reported issues with Reporting Services. We'll show you how to build custom report formatting styles as well as templates to use for your own company's reports. This can save you and your team countless hours in setting up reports that share a common appearance.

In the back half of this chapter, we get into some serious configuration tuning issues. We'll show you how to call your own functions and other code from your reports and how to configure Reporting Services so it does not croak or complain when you do. We'll also show you how to write your own style sheets—just as you can with websites to customize your reports.

---

[1] www.SQLReportingServices.NET

When you launch the Report wizard (whether you intend to or not), you're given several choices when it comes time to automatically format the report: the Bold, Casual, Compact, Corporate, and Plain report styles. We've often been asked if it's possible to create custom report styles in addition to these out-of-the-box styles used by the Report wizard. Immediately thereafter, this question is usually followed by another asking if it's possible to create custom Report and Data Source Templates for the Add New Item dialog. You'll be pleased to hear that the answers to both questions are a definite "Yes!" and "It's real easy when you know how." At this moment, what we're about to show you is not formally documented. We worked this out on our own so you and your report design team can be more productive—and more secure.

It turns out that it's also possible to apply report styles dynamically as the report is rendered—in a similar way that CSS files are applied to HTML pages as they are rendered in a web browser. So, we'll also show you how to bind a ReportItem's style to values in an external style file. This custom style file can then be used by each of your reports. When changes are made to the common style file, these changes are applied to all reports that reference it. This way, you can efficiently change your report rendering at runtime. But there's a catch. (Isn't there always?) Well, okay, to use these cool techniques, we need to show you some hardcore .NET topics. We'll start by explaining Reporting Services' implementation of code access security (CAS). In the process, we'll take away any mystique about CAS that you might perceive, and we'll cover Strong Naming and policy permission files. We'll even explain XML XPath and why that's important. It's not really too difficult, so don't get frightened. Once you've worked through this chapter, you'll think it's ever so easy and you'll be the champion Reporting Services guru in your company—unless someone else has also read your copy of the book!

Building Report Wizard Style Templates

If you worked through Chapter 3, you used the Report wizard to create Table and Matrix reports. Recall the choice of styles that the wizard can apply: Bold, Casual, Compact, Corporate, and Plain. These built-in styles can be modified to represent your own custom styles simply by editing the XML file named StyleTemplates.xml (even with Visual Notepad). This sounds easy because it is; the XML file is human-readable. The challenge is editing the "correct" version of the StyleTemplates.xml file. If you dig into the folder *Program Files\Microsoft SQL Server\80\Tools\Report Designer\ Business Intelligence Wizards\Reports\Styles*, you'll see a StyleTemplates.xml file. You'll also see a bunch of folders with names based on culture; see Figure 9.1.

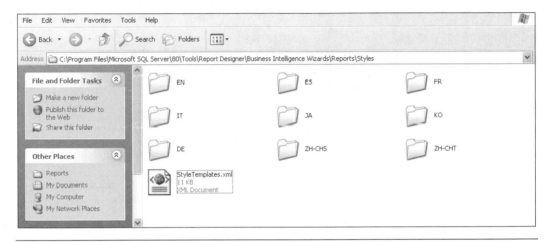

Figure 9.1 Source Folder for StyleTemplates.xml Showing Localization Folders

Each of those folders contains a localized version of StyleTemplates.xml. The one you edit depends on the Visual Studio .NET User Interface (UI) culture being used to design reports (in other words, the language the UI is using). When it comes time to display the list of report styles, the wizard initially looks for a copy of StyleTemplates.xml in the language culture folder being used. For example, if you're using French (for some reason), the wizard looks in the FR folder. If a StyleTemplates.xml file exists in the culture-specific directory, the wizard uses that copy. So, for the United States, the wizard first looks to see if there is a folder named EN-US (the English-United States culture designation). In the default Report Designer installation, there is no EN-US folder, so when the wizard fails to find this folder, it looks for the StyleTemplates.xml file in the folder of the parent culture of EN. Again, if there is no EN folder at all, the wizard continues to navigate back and tries to use the generic version in the root of *\Program Files\Microsoft SQL Server\80\Tools\Report Designer\ Business Intelligence Wizards\Reports\Styles*.

As we said, there isn't an EN-US folder in the default Report Designer installation, so you can copy your own custom styles definition file into the wizard's search path by creating an "EN-US" or other culture-specific folder and placing the StyleTemplates.xml file therein. If you're wondering which culture your Visual Studio uses, look in the Tools | Options dialog under Environment | International Settings, as shown in Figure 9.2.

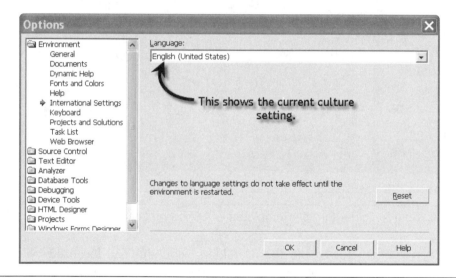

Figure 9.2 Using the Tools | Options Dialog to Inspect the Current Culture Setting

Before you get started manipulating StyleTemplates.xml files, we want to issue a word of caution. Make a backup copy of any StyleTemplates.xml files that you intend to change *before* you start. We also suggest that you back up your own copy of StyleTemplates.xml to another location so that a future Service Pack or reinstall does not overwrite your custom version of the file. We suggest that you save the file outside the \Program Files hierarchy to prevent this eventuality.

As you modify styles in the StyleTemplates.xml file (a subset of this file is shown in Listing 9.1), feel free to change the `<Label>` element to identify your style. This label element can be virtually anything—in the example in Listing 9.1, we called our style Boost Bold.

However, you *must* make sure that the Name attribute of the <StyleTemplate> element that you are modifying is one of the standard Bold, Casual, Compact, Corporate, or Plain names (as shown).

Listing 9.1 A Truncated Snippet of the Boost Bold Style in StyleTemplates.xml

```
<StyleTemplate Name="Bold">
   <Label>Boost Bold</Label>
   <Styles>
      <Style Name="Title">
         <BackgroundColor>Blue</BackgroundColor>
            <FontFamily>Times New Roman</FontFamily>
            <FontSize>18pt</FontSize>
            <Color>White</Color>
            <FontWeight>700</FontWeight>
            <TextAlign>Center</TextAlign>
            <BorderStyle>
               <Bottom>Solid</Bottom>
            </BorderStyle>
            <BorderWidth>
               <Bottom>3pt</Bottom>
            </BorderWidth>
            <BorderColor>
               <Bottom>Black</Bottom>
            </BorderColor>
      </Style>
...
   </Styles>
</StyleTemplate>
```

The wizard uses the Name element to index the greeked[2] graphic on the right-hand side of the wizard dialog, and if you change the Name attribute and the DLL does not recognize it as one of the known style graphics, you'll probably get an exception. The downside here is that those folks using your custom style will see one of the standard greeked graphics. Just choose one that most closely approximates your own custom style.

---

[2] "Greeked" text or graphics are intentionally blurred. They are provided to show the layout—not the actual text.

Figure 9.3 shows the Report wizard dialog after you've added a custom style by modifying the StyleTemplates.xml file. Note that the greeked graphic is for the standard Bold built-in style and doesn't necessarily represent your style in terms of color scheme, font choices, and so on.

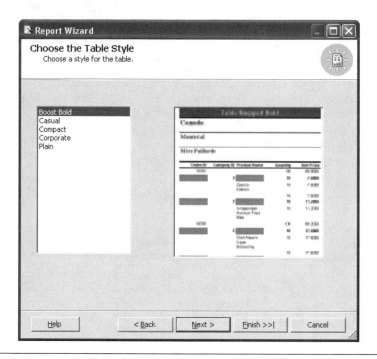

Figure 9.3 A Custom Template of "Boost Bold" in the Report Wizard with the "Compact" Graphic

The ***Style Templates*** are only designed to expose the Style elements linked to certain properties of the report—just the Textbox controls are exposed, so only the following properties can be set through StyleTemplates.xml:

- *BackgroundColor*
- *BackgroundImage*
- *BorderColor*
- *BorderStyle*
- *BorderWidth*

- *Calendar*
- *Color*
- *Direction*
- *FontStyle*
- *FontFamily*
- *FontSize*
- *FontWeight*
- *Format*
- *LineHeight*
- *Language*
- *NumeralLanguage*
- *NumeralVariant*
- *PaddingLeft*
- *PaddingRight*
- *PaddingTop*
- *PaddingBottom*
- *TextDecoration*
- *TextAlign*
- *VerticalAlign*
- *UnicodeBiDi*
- *WritingMode*

The Books Online (BOL) topic "Style Element" in the Report Definition Language Reference lists the valid values and subelements for these properties. Make sure you watch for case-sensitivity issues.

Using Gradient Fills for Textbox Controls

Don't think that just because *BackgroundGradientType* and *BackgroundGradientEndColor* are listed as valid Style elements in the "Style Element" BOL topic that they are supported in a StyleTemplates.xml file. If you read the BOL small print, you'll see that they only apply to Chart controls—not Textbox controls. However, don't be disheartened. If you really want a background gradient, you can create a background image using your own graphics program. Simply create a graphic of an appropriate size and apply a gradient fill. You can place this image into the project folder, and the Style Template can be marked up as shown in Listing 9.2.

Listing 9.2 Addressing a Custom Background Image in the Style Template

```
<BackgroundImage>
    <MIMEType>image/bmp</MIMEType>
    <BackgroundRepeat>NoRepeat</BackgroundRepeat>
    <Source>External</Source>
    <Value>MyGradientFill.bmp</Value>
</BackgroundImage>
```

This approach requires that any projects using this custom Style Template need to have the image loaded separately in the project and deployed to the Report Server. You can mitigate this if you embed these images into the Report.RDL standard template. Alternatively, you can place the image in the special location for the Add New Items dialog to make it much easier to add to new projects. We'll uncover the Report.RDL hiding place in just a minute.

Customizing Headers and Footers

The Report wizard creates a "Title" that's almost like a Page Header, although this doesn't appear on every page of the report. It would be nice if you could set the *RepeatWith* property in the Style sheet. We expect that the Reporting Services developers had to draw a line in the sand somewhere when finalizing the feature set for version 1— better to ship an incomplete but functional product than a feature-rich albeit buggy product.

One solution to adding a custom Page Header is to put up with manually setting the *RepeatWith* property after the wizard has done its magic. However, another possibly more elegant solution is to adjust the standard template Report.RDL to have formal Page Headers and Footers. To do this,

1. Place a Textbox control into the Page Header.
2. Size and style the Textbox control so that it mimics the Title Textbox control that the Report wizard places in the Body section of the report layout.
3. Ensure that its name is different from that of Textbox1. This way it won't clash with the Title Textbox control created by the wizard.

4. Next, set the *Value* property of your Textbox control to be "=ReportItems!Textbox1.Value."
5. Set the Header property *PrintOnFirstPage* to False since the Title, AKA Textbox1, ordinarily appears on the first page but not on any subsequent pages.

Perhaps the best (and far easier) solution is to cut and paste the Query and Body elements built with the Report wizard into a new report based on one of your own Report Templates.

Customizing Report and Data Source Templates

As we've mentioned, the whole point of this chapter is extending and customizing your reports. The trick is to figure out how to do this once and have the changes apply to all subsequent reports that you produce. We've shown you how to customize the wizard, but now it's time to customize Report Templates. That way you can build custom Report and Data Source Templates that reflect your own company logos or custom styles and layouts. Okay, it's time to tell you where the templates are and how to customize them to speed up or simply beautify the reports you generate.

Customizing Report Templates

The templates available to the Report Designer's **Add New Item dialog** (as shown in Figure 9.4) are governed by the contents of the *\Program Files\Microsoft SQL Server\80\Tools\Report Designer \ProjectItems\ReportProject* folder. Initially, you'll find the RDL for the default report in this folder is aptly named Report.RDL. By default, you'll find two wizards in this folder as well—the Data Source wizard and the Report wizard. The Report.RDL file that you see in this folder is the one (and only) template used for the Report wizard. It's also used as the template when adding a new report.

You can add your own items to this folder—they appear automatically in the Add New Item dialog. In addition to template reports (RDL files) and data sources (RDS files), you can also place resources such as .bmp/.gif/.jpeg graphics or the search form HTML that we showed you in Chapter 4 into this same templates folder.

NOTE *Back Up the Existing and Custom Files* Be sure to make backup copies of anything that you place into this template location because it is likely to be overlaid by any subsequent Reporting Services Service Pack.

You might be tempted to save a Report RDL or Data Source RDS file directly into the Templates folder. But before you do, we suggest that you make a few changes to the RDL, RDS and configuration files. This affects how the Add New Item dialog displays the items.

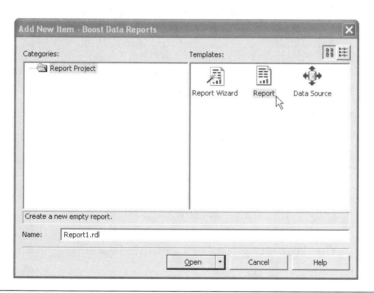

Figure 9.4 The Base Installation Report Templates

If you examine the default raw Report.RDL template (shown in Listing 9.3), you'll see that it contains only a few lines of XML code. Most of this code sets up the localization for your Report Designer's measurement system and default paper size. (Notice that all the "rd:" elements are in the *ReportDesigner XML* namespace). As you know, ***report geometries*** are provided in either metric or U.S. measurements (equivalent to Imperial as long as we're talking lengths and not gallons!). These settings are applied in the Report Designer to any property or expression that accepts a report geometry measurement. The specific default measurement system is determined by the system's language and regional customization settings. Don't blink when you create a new report because these <rd: properties> exist for only a brief time. As soon as the Report Designer needs to write anything to the RDL file, they're consumed, acted on, and removed.

Listing 9.3 The Report.RDL Template

```
<?xml version="1.0" encoding="utf-8"?>
<Report xmlns="http://schemas.microsoft.com/sqlserver
  /reporting/2003/10/reportdefinition" xmlns:rd="http://schemas.microsoft.com/
  SQLServer/reporting/reportdesigner">
<Width>6.5in</Width>
<Body>
   <Height>2in</Height>
</Body>
<rd:InitialLanguage>true</rd:InitialLanguage>
<rd:InitialDimensions>
   <rd:UnitType>Inch</rd:UnitType>
   <rd:LeftMargin>1in</rd:LeftMargin>
   <rd:RightMargin>1in</rd:RightMargin>
   <rd:TopMargin>1in</rd:TopMargin>
   <rd:BottomMargin>1in</rd:BottomMargin>
   <rd:PageWidth>8.5in</rd:PageWidth>
   <rd:PageHeight>11in</rd:PageHeight>
   <rd:ColumnSpacing>0.5in</rd:ColumnSpacing>
</rd:InitialDimensions>
<rd:InitialDimensions>
   <rd:UnitType>Cm</rd:UnitType>
   <rd:Width>16cm</rd:Width>
   <rd:Height>5cm</rd:Height>
   <rd:LeftMargin>2.5cm</rd:LeftMargin>
   <rd:RightMargin>2.5cm</rd:RightMargin>
   <rd:TopMargin>2.5cm</rd:TopMargin>
   <rd:BottomMargin>2.5cm</rd:BottomMargin>
   <rd:GridSpacing>0.25cm</rd:GridSpacing>
   <rd:PageWidth>21cm</rd:PageWidth>
   <rd:PageHeight>29.7cm</rd:PageHeight>
   <rd:ColumnSpacing>1cm</rd:ColumnSpacing>
</rd:InitialDimensions>
</Report>
```

Apart from the `<rd:InitialDimensions>` element, other sibling elements can be set. For example, to enable or disable the layout grid or the snap-to-grid feature you can set the appropriate attributes, as shown here:

```
<rd:DrawGrid>false</rd:DrawGrid>
<rd:SnapToGrid>false</rd:SnapToGrid>
```

Designing a suite of Report Template RDL files is simply a matter of using the Report Designer to configure a report to use its RDL as a template or editing RDL by hand. It's fine to embed images and include code-behind and DataSet definitions. Another approach is to start from a final report you may have already built. While you can take the RDL of a report you've already created and use it as a template, you might want to insert the `<rd: ... >` elements from the standard template. This enables your template to be sensitive to both U.S. and metric measurements. When a new report is based on this custom Template, the Report Designer can by default be sensitive to U.S. or metric measurements.

If the RDL contains a `<rd:ReportID>` GUID `</rd:ReportID>` make sure you remove it from the template.

Once you have a functional custom Template, you can name it using the RDL file extension and save it directly into the template folder: *Program Files\Microsoft SQL Server\80\Tools\Report Designer\ProjectItems\ReportProject*.

Before you rush off to show this to your coworkers and your boss, pause a second. You're within a cat's whisker of having a professional finish. At this point:

- The Template appears when you select Add New Item in the Report Designer.
- You can select the Template from the dialog.
- The Template successfully loads into the Report Designer IDE.

However, the icons, the descriptions, and the default names won't be there. This is the spit and polish that makes the Template more usable. You'll want to hook them up by editing the ReportProjectItems.vsdir file you'll find in the Report Designer's templates folder. Take our advice and back up the ReportProjectItems.vsdir file before tinkering with it, but don't let it frighten you away with its GUIDs and other strange numbers. Each line is just a configuration line of nine fields delimited by the pipe character, "|". Each line is terminated with a carriage return. If you use Notepad to view the file, use the Format menu to disable word wrap so you can breathe a little easier. This is the structure of a line in the VSDir file (note that all the characters are on the same line):

```
RelativePathName|{clsid}|Name|SortPriority|Description|↵
    IconDll|IconResId|Flags|BaseName
```

Let's walk through the steps needed to edit or customize the ReportProjectItems.vsdir file.

1. Start by adding a new line of eight pipe (|) characters into the ReportProjectItems.vsdir file as field delimiters.
2. Terminate each line with exactly one carriage return.
3. Add each field in turn, as described below.

Setting the RelativePathName Element

This is the relative pathname, including the filename to your Template RDL or RDS file from the Report Designer templates folder. If you're putting your Templates in this folder, you won't need the path, just the filename. Be careful if you're going to put your own Templates in the same folder with the Microsoft Templates; consider that the next Service Pack, upgrade, or uninstall might just wipe that folder away—taking your Templates with it. It might be best to create a custom templates folder somewhere out of the way. To make it easy, we use the same folder as Microsoft and ensure that we have our custom Templates and VSDir file backed up. For example, if the Template file is named Boost Table Report.RDL and is located in the same folder as the VSDir folder, our edited line looks like this:

```
Boost Table Report.rdl|  | | | | | | | |
```

Setting the {clsid} Element

This is the **class identifier (clsid)** of an installed package surrounded in curly braces. For the default Microsoft Templates, this is the clsid GUID for the installed Reporting Services package. This enables Microsoft to use Resource String Identifiers for the Name and Description parameters in the VSDir file and enables localization of those strings. We suggest that you leave this blank—just leave a single space in the second parameter position, as it's not required.

Setting the Name Element

This determines the text that appears beneath your custom Template icon in the Add New Item dialog. If you create a resource file and install a package (like Microsoft did) you'd be able to use an index in the String Resource table, and take the benefits of having that name localized. However, we suggest you simply enter your name in plain text. At this point, our edited line should look like this—we used Boost Table Report for the Name element:

```
Boost Table Report.rdl|    |Boost Table Report| | | | | |
```

The SortPriority Element

If you inspect the values for the other entries, you'll see that this is an integer number that determines the order in which the IDE shows the icons when displaying the Add New Item dialog. The lower the number, the higher in the list the icon will be displayed. You'll need to adjust the other entries to get the desired sort order. Because we want this entry at the top, we're going to give it a sort priority of 0. If you include two entries with the same sort order, the Earth will stop in its rotation—but only briefly. Your edited line should now look something like this:

```
Boost Table Report.rdl|    |Boost Table Report|0| | | | |
```

The Description Element

When an item is selected in the Add New Item dialog, a line of text is displayed in the dialog that describes the item. You might use this to explain what the Template is for or whom to complain to if it needs work. In our example, we're creating a standard template for reports using a Table control, so we'll put some text in to explain that. (Of course, if we create and install an installation package and put the clsid in the second field, we can use a string resource id.) Your edited line should now look something like this (remember, this should all be on the same line):

```
Boost Table Report.rdl|    |Boost Table Report|0|↵
    Creates a Standard Boost Table Report|  |  |
```

Because I am comfortable with C++ IDE in Visual Studio .NET, I simply knocked together a C++ resource DLL, including the icons that I want to use for my templates as I'm confident that the Visual Studio shell can consume these. There is probably a way to do this with Visual Basic .NET or C#, but I haven't invested the time. If someone knows a way, e-mail me ☺ and we'll post the solution on our website for the book. We're reliably informed that this will be much easier to do in the next version of Visual Studio .NET.
–Peter

Setting the IconDLL Element

This is the complete path and the filename of a DLL that contains at least one icon resource (or a clsid of an installed package). However, if you are happy with icons that Reporting Services uses from Microsoft.ReportingServices.Designer.dll, you can point to this DLL. While this works, if you use this DLL you're creating a dependency upon an unsupported feature. Of course, Microsoft might change the icon and/or the index to that icon in a future release or Service Pack. If the file Microsoft.ReportingServices.Designer.dll is copied to another location and that path is used instead, it might work, but you'll probably need to read the EULA small print to be legal.

We've found that it's incredibly awkward to use the .NET Framework when creating icon resources in Visual Basic .NET or C# in a form that can be easily consumed by the Visual Studio shell. Another approach would be to use the Visual Basic 6.0 resource editor and create icons in DLLs that the Visual Studio shell itself can consume. So, to conclude here: If you can make do with the standard icons, you'll save yourself a lot of time, or you can hunt around in other resource DLLs for the icon you want. (By the way, icons can be extracted from assemblies with ILDASM /out.)

Your edited line should now look something like this:

```
Boost Table Report.RDL|    |Boost Table Report|0|Creates a Standard Boost Table
Report| C:\Program Files\Microsoft SQL Server\80\Tools\Report
Designer\Microsoft.ReportingServices.Designer.dll|  |  |
```

Setting the Icon Resource Id (IconResId) Element

This element is the index to the Icon resource in the **Icon DLL**. If you are using the Report Designer\ Microsoft.ReportingServices.Designer.dll, just copy one of the indexes from the other entries to choose the desired icon. We used Icon ID 201. (Again, this should be on a single line).

```
Boost Table Report.RDL|    |Boost Table Report|0|↵
 Creates a Standard Boost Table Report|↵
 C:\Program Files\Microsoft SQL Server\80↵
 \Tools\Report Designer\Microsoft.↵
 ReportingServices.Designer.dll|201|  |
```

The Flags Element

If set to 8192, this Field blocks off the Base name field so that you have no choice what the item is called when added to the project. You can set this element to a blank space or 8192. You'll see that on a default VSDir file the Data Source wizard entry blocks off the name field. This is because when the Data Source wizard is executed, it chooses a default name based on the Data Source you select. So, if you set this Field to 8192, it indicates that you want to force the Base name. For our example, we set this element to a blank space. Your edited line should now look something like this:

```
Boost Table Report.rdl|    |Boost Table Report|0|↵
 Creates a Standard Boost Table Report|↵
 C:\Program Files\Microsoft SQL Server\↵
 80\Tools\Report Designer\Microsoft.ReportingServices.↵
 Designer.dll|201|   |
```

The Base Name Element

This element specifies the Base name to be used. As long as you haven't closed it off by setting the Flags element to 8192, the user can change the name in the dialog. However, even if you do disable the Base name in the dialog, the user can still rename the item in the

Visual Studio .NET IDE. In this case, we set the Base name to Boost Table. Your edited line should now look something like this:

```
Boost Table Report.rdl|    |Boost Table Report|0|↵
Creates a Standard Boost Table Report|↵
 C:\Program Files\Microsoft SQL Server\↵
 80\Tools\Report Designer\Microsoft.ReportingServices.↵
 Designer.dll|↵
 201|    |Boost Table
```

Repeat this process for each of the custom Templates you wish to expose in the Report Designer dialogs. As a final point, don't forget to archive your custom Report Templates and the ReportProjectItems.vsdir files. This protects you in case you need to do surgery after a Service Pack install or upgrade. If you choose to research this subject on your own and manage to get wizard templates working based on a VSZ wizard file, be sure to let us know! Figure 9.5 shows how the Add New Item dialog appears after you tune up the ReportProjectItems.vsdir file.

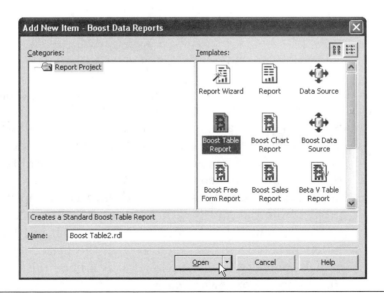

Figure 9.5 Once You Add Your Custom Templates, They'll Appear Here in the Add New Item Dialog

Creating Custom Data Source Templates

It can be a lot of work creating Data Sources for use in the Designer. In Chapter 6, we discussed how it helps to have a staging deployment folder on the Report Server. This folder should contain a suite of Data Sources configured to use embedded credentials. We also mentioned that it helps to have Data Sources with the same names, but configured to use Integrated Security for use in the Designer. Above all, we suggested that you try to be friendly to your DBAs by setting an application name in the Connection string. This way they can monitor their databases with the SQL Profiler and know which reports are causing problems—and which are guiltless. The "pain" is that each time you create a new reporting project, you need to run the Data Source wizard. Each time, you must remember the incantations used to create these Data Sources—which server, which initial catalog, and so on. It can help productivity slightly if you copy the Data Source RDS files that you've already created into the templates folder: *\Program Files\Microsoft SQL Server\80\Tools\ Report Designer\ProjectItems\ReportProject.*

Just before you do so, you might want to remove the following element from the Data Source's RDS file.

```
<DataSourceID> GUID </DataSourceID>
```

This GUID is used as an index to select the appropriate set of encrypted credentials stored in the user options file. A new element is created if a value is not supplied. You may recall when we discussed using Data Sources in the Designer in Chapter 5 that any embedded credentials are encrypted using the DPAPI libraries and that these are restricted to Machine and User.

You'll notice that when you add the RDS Template file to the project from the Add New Item dialog, the RDS file opens up in text/code view. If this happens, just close it. If you try to open it in the Report Designer, you'll see that the Data Source Designer applet launches. We didn't find any way around this behavior other than to create your own wizard.

Using Code Access Security

This section discusses how to use the *.NET Framework's code access security (CAS) functionality* to permit your reports to execute code that they would ordinarily be prohibited from executing. By default, reports and the code they execute cannot reach beyond the process in which they are executing. It's only by specifically requesting permission that you can execute code that ventures out of the "sandbox." This section starts with a discussion of custom report Style sheets, which can require permission configurations that involve CAS.

Creating Custom Report Style Sheets

If you create reports for an organization that changes its name or branding on a whim each day of the week (whichever comes sooner) or is constantly being merged or taken over, you are acutely aware of the tedious frustrations addressed in this section. We know you have to rework existing reports just to change the color, size, font family, and logos (and other visual aspects) to be in sync with the new edict-style-de-jour-from-on-high that you know might change again before you can finish the first set of changes.

In the world of HTML web pages, you may have encountered cascading style sheets (CSS). If you have, you know how easy it is to change the visual effect of a website to suit some new style simply by changing a CSS file—as long as that website was designed to use CSS files in the first place. Reporting Services Version 1 doesn't have an indigenous style sheet mechanism such as CSS, but nevertheless you can quite easily create your own. We're about to show you how.

When a report is deployed to the Report Server, a Visual Basic .NET class is created and compiled to generate accessor "get" expressions for all *ReportItems* properties set in the report. Each formatting property on each control and each value binding is coerced into these compiled expressions. Once the report is deployed, you can't change these expressions without editing and redeploying the report.

The trick is to ensure those expressions look up their values from an *external* source like a StyleTemplates file. This way, to adjust the styles of all reports, you simply need to change an external source file bound to the reports. This enables reports and their expressions to remain the same indefinitely, while still permitting the visual style resulting from those expressions to be altered by changing the external source. Of course, that external source can be applied to the litany of your dependent reports.

Configuring a Code Block

You might expect that this can be implemented by putting Expression code in the report's code block. In fact, you may even completely convince yourself that this can work when you try it out in the Designer. However, you'll find that when you deploy the report, it just doesn't work. Let's try this approach, and we'll explain why it doesn't work once deployed. For an example concept test of this, you might:

There is a solution file for this example containing the Report Project and the Custom Assembly Project on the DVD in a folder named 001 StyleSheet.

1. Create a text file, c:\RSSSTest.txt, and edit it to contain the single word "Red." Make sure that there is no space or new line character in that file. If you look at the system properties for this file, its size should be exactly 3 characters.

2. Create a new report, and enter the code in Listing 9.4 into a report's code block, as shown in Figure 9.6. Don't try to be clever and include exception handling as you would and should do if creating commercial quality code. We want to show you an issue that can be masked by an exception handler.

Listing 9.4 The CodeBehindBackGroundColor "Code Behind" Function

```
Shared Function CodeBehindBackGroundColor() As String
    Dim sr As System.IO.StreamReader = New _
        System.IO.StreamReader("c:\RSSSTest.txt")
    Dim retval As String= sr.ReadToEnd()
    sr.Close()
    Return retval
End Function
```

This shared function simply opens a StreamReader object to read in the text from a file and returns the contents of the file as a string.

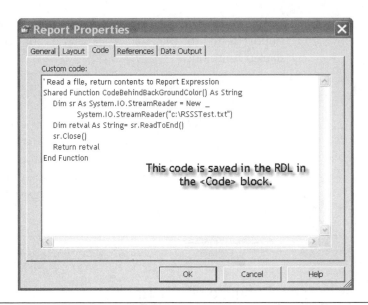

Figure 9.6 Entering Code into the Report Properties Code Tab (`<Code>` Block)

This code is placed in the Report RDL file in the `<Code>` block, as shown in Figure 9.7.

> **TIP** *Caution!* We don't recommend use of static field variables in reports or in any custom assemblies accessed by reports. That's because as multiple instances of the code are loaded, the static variables can be altered by other instances—not good and tough to debug. We don't do that here, but we thought we should tell you why we don't.

```
Start Page    Report1.rdl [XML]*    Report1.rdl [Design]*
26    <TopMargin>1in</TopMargin>
27    <Code>' Read a file, return contents to Report Expression
28    Shared Function CodeBehindBackGroundColor() As String
29        Dim sr As System.IO.StreamReader = New _
30        System.IO.StreamReader("c:\RSSSTest.txt")
31        Dim retval As String= sr.ReadToEnd()
32        sr.Close()
33        Return retval
34    End Function
35    </Code>
```

Figure 9.7 The Function Is Saved in the RDL Code Block

3. Next, bind the *BackGroundColor* property of some ReportItems to the following expression that calls the shared function:

```
=Code.CodeBehindBackGroundColor().
```

4. It's a good idea to also bind the *Value* property of a Textbox control to this expression to see the string that it returns. We've implemented this in our example report 001 StyleSheet.rdl. If you try this out, you'll see that it works fine in the Report Preview tab, as shown in Figure 9.8.

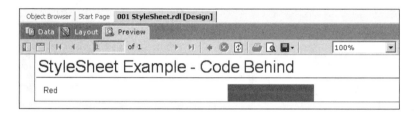

Figure 9.8 Previewing the Report Calling the Shared Function

5. Now set the Solution Configuration dropdown to DebugLocal mode, as shown in Figure 9.9.

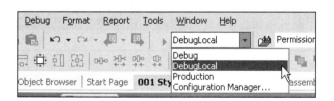

Figure 9.9 Set DebugLocal Mode

6. Select the report in the Solution Explorer, and execute it in the RSReportHost.exe by choosing Run from the right mouse button context menu.

7. What is returned is "#Error" (as shown in Figure 9.10) or perhaps nothing at all. This is not terribly helpful in itself, but what's interesting is the Output window of Visual Studio .NET.

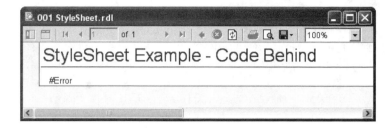

Figure 9.10 DebugLocal Execution of the Report Containing the Shared Function

The text returned in Visual Studio .NET 2003 (as shown in Listing 9.5) tells us:

Listing 9.5 Text Exception Message Returned by Visual Studio .NET

```
The background color expression for the rectangle 'rectangle1' contains an error:
Request for the permission of type System.Security.Permissions.FileIOPermission,
mscorlib, Version=1.0.5000.0, Culture=neutral, PublicKeyToken=b77a5c561934e089
failed.
The value expression for the Textbox control 'Textbox control1' contains an error:
Request for the permission of type System.Security.Permissions.FileIOPermission,
mscorlib, Version=1.0.5000.0, Culture=neutral, PublicKeyToken=b77a5c561934e089
failed.
```

If you deploy to a Report Server instead, and run the deployed report, it still fails but you won't get an error reported to Visual Studio .NET 2003. Errors that happen after the report is published on the server are reported to the Report Server logs. No, there are no logs for the Report Designer.

Let's discuss what is going on and why. The error that we're seeing here is caused by a permissions violation—in particular, a FileIOPermission error. Well, we know what it means—we tried to execute some code that tried to access the file system, and our code is not permitted to do so. By default, a report's expression code (including the code in the code block) is only given *execution* permissions—that is, "execute in a rarefied sandbox." It does not have permission to access the file system, databases, network, DNS, printers, registry, or, hopefully, your little black book of addresses. Actually, we should be pleased that these security measures are in place. If they weren't, nefarious people would plant all kinds of evil expressions that would destroy the file system, corrupt the registry, or just steal confidential document files. Without these safeguards, it could see the entire network. If you recall Chapter 5, if the report is executed with Integrated Security, this reach could be very far when an administrator runs a report. So you can write your thank you letters to Microsoft for not leaving that door open.

That said, let's investigate ways to manage these permissions so that they work in our favor. These execution permissions are controlled by policy configuration files.

Configuring Policy Configuration Files

Three policy files are in use in Reporting Services, as shown in Table 9.1.

Table 9.1 The Policy Configuration Files

rspreviewpolicy.config	*C:\Program Files\ Microsoft SQL Server\ 80\Tools\Report Designer*	Security Policy for the RSReportHost.exe Report previewer.
rssrvpolicy.config	*C:\Program Files\ Microsoft SQL Server\ MSSQL\Reporting Services\ ReportServer*	Security Policy for the Report Server.
rsmgrpolicy.config	*C:\Program Files\ Microsoft SQL Server\MSSQL\ Reporting Services\ ReportManager*	Security Policy for the Report Manager.

Before we go any further, let us emphasize two points. First, take a backup of these files before editing them—they are very fragile. We always copy these files into Visual SourceSafe before editing them each time. If you don't have a source control system in place, copy the file to a safe place before editing it and rename it by appending the current date and time. Keep those backups around for some time—there's no telling when you'll need them.

TIP *Caution: Back Up These Policy Files Before Any Edits!* This is meant to be a little more than the standard "don't play with the registry" warning before backing it up that everyone ignores; we've burnt our fingers several times with these files simply as a result of not realizing how fragile they are.

One thing that is just sitting there like an alligator disguised as a log waiting to grab you as you pass by is that you might think that these are XML files. Technically, they are what XML people (who know the jargon) call "well formed." But these files don't have an XML header, and they choke up if you try to include XML style comments <!-- -->. All the more frustrating is that if you do add comments or bollix up the syntax, when it does choke up it invariably dies elsewhere—with very cryptic clues that don't immediately lead you back to these (delicate) config files. It's like playing with the tiny little gears in your grandfather's watch. They never seem to go back into place as easily as they were taken out.

Returning to the problem at hand, we can (carefully) adjust the policy files, rssrvpolicy.config and rspreviewpolicy.config, to enable Expression code to break out of the Execution sandbox and read the file system. But that's the wrong approach, and it opens the door to an insecure system—don't do this. A more secure approach is to create an assembly that can contain our file IO code and that we can specifically permission. This approach uses .NET technology as it should be used to gate access to the code and the objects it manages. Let's step through the process:

1. Create a new class library project in Visual Basic .NET. We called ours RSStyleSheet, and the resulting assembly is named RSStylesheet.dll.
2. Enter the code as shown in Listing 9.6.

Listing 9.6 The Shared Functions We'll Be Calling from Report Expressions

```
Option Explicit On
Option Strict On

Public Class Style

    Shared Function BackGroundColor() As String
        Dim sr As System.IO.StreamReader = New _
                System.IO.StreamReader("c:\RSSSTest.txt")
        Dim retval As String = sr.ReadToEnd()
        sr.Close()
        Return retval
    End Function

    Shared Function BackGroundColor( _
        ByVal icolor As Integer) As String
        If (icolor >= 5) Or (icolor < 1) Then icolor = 1
        Return CStr(Choose(icolor, "Blue", "Yellow", _
        "Green", "Pink"))
    End Function

End Class
```

This code implements a very simple class with a single shared method, `BackGroundColor`, that has two signatures—one of which has no arguments and takes its value from a file. In simple terms, this is the same code that we used for the earlier `CodeBehindBackGroundColor()` function. The other shared function accepts an argument and returns a string literal.

3. The resulting assembly needs to be copied to two file locations—one for the Report Server to use: *C:\Program Files\ Microsoft SQL Server\MSSQL\Reporting Services\ ReportServer\bin* and the other for the RSReportHost.exe (and the Preview tab) to use: *C:\Program Files\Microsoft SQL Server 80\Tools\Report Designer*.

4. We find it helpful when developing custom assemblies to put a batch file in the project folder that can copy the resulting output assembly to the locations required. Figure 9.11 shows an example of such a batch file.

```
COPY bin\RSStyleSheet.dll "C:\Program Files\Microsoft SQL Server\MSSQL\Reporting Services\ReportServer\bin"
COPY bin\RSStyleSheet.dll "C:\Program Files\Microsoft SQL Server\80\Tools\Report Designer"
PAUSE
```

Figure 9.11 A Batch File Used to Copy the RSStylesheet.dll to Appropriate Locations

NOTE At one point during our testing, we ran into difficulties because (for some reason) the file system permissions applied to these files after they were copied were not as we expected. We recommend that you reassure yourself that the files are inheriting their permissions from the parent folders after they are copied into place.

5. Create another report, and provide the report with a reference to the new RSStylesheet assembly. To do this, select the report in the Designer, and launch the References dialog from the References properties (under Misc) or from the Report Properties dialog References tab (as shown in Figure 9.12). You'll probably need to browse to find the assembly.

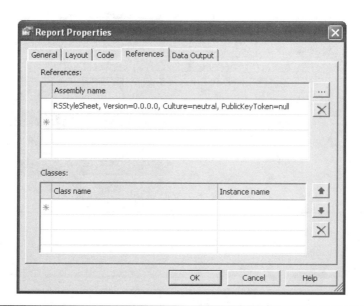

Figure 9.12 The Report Properties Dialog References Tab

6. Create five text controls on the report, and bind their *Value* properties to the following expressions:

```
=RSStyleSheet.Style.BackGroundColor()
=RSStyleSheet.Style.BackGroundColor(1)
=RSStyleSheet.Style.BackGroundColor(2)
=RSStyleSheet.Style.BackGroundColor(3)
=RSStyleSheet.Style.BackGroundColor(4)
```

7. Create five rectangles and bind their *BackGroundColor* properties to the same five expressions.
8. Notice that instead of "Code" our functions are now prefixed with "RSStyleSheet.Style"—that is, we're using the namespace.class.method() naming convention. As these methods are shared methods, we didn't need to instantiate any classes. We'll show you how to do that later in this chapter.
9. Execute the report (002 StyleSheet.rdl) in the RSReportHost.exe previewer and you should see a rendered report (albeit with errors), as shown in Figure 9.13.

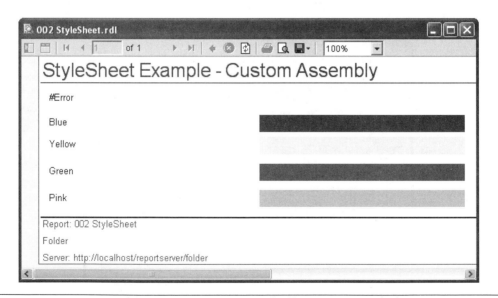

Figure 9.13 The StyleSheet Example Phase II

Again, if we look in the Output window of Visual Studio .NET, we'll see the same old permissions problem is thwarting us. At least it's partially working. We're still getting "#Error," but that's to be expected as we haven't configured permissions that permit this assembly to make calls to the file system. However, as you can see, the assembly does have execution permissions—that's why we're seeing results for the calls that don't access the file system. When you preview a report in the Report Designer's Preview window, any custom assemblies that are used are loaded and locked in process space. These assemblies remain locked until you close the Visual Studio 2003 development environment holding the lock. However, reports previewed in the Report Designer are executed with FullTrust, so that explains why it apparently works in the Report Designer. In contrast, the RSReportHost.exe previewer runs in its own process space and checks the security permissions. Because RSReportHost.exe tears down its process space when it is closed, any locks placed on custom assemblies are released during the tear-down. Again, this is why debugging with the RSReportHost.exe is useful—and essential—when working with custom assemblies.

Asserting Permissions in Code

To make this work, we need to resolve two issues. First we have to "assert" within our code that we want and need the FileIOPermission using the System.Security.Permissions class in our .NET executable code. This is because the Report Server runs with FullTrust, but in order to execute the report expressions, the Report Server needs to call the expression host, which executes the expressions with ExecutionOnly. Because ultimately it is a report expression that makes the call to the custom assembly, the custom assembly will run with ExecutionOnly unless it asserts for any additional permissions it has been granted through the config file. Behind the scenes, this is implemented using code access security. Unless you specifically assert in your code before you make calls to privileged resources, .NET denies access and raises a security exception.

The second issue to resolve requires us to provide a permission level for the assembly itself, which is set in the policy files. So, when your code asserts that it wants to make a privileged call, the .NET Framework can verify that your particular assembly has been granted permission to the resource. Don't fall asleep at this point.

Go get some strong tea and pay attention. Yes, you *must* assert permissions in code that uses a privilege and is executed from a report expression, even if the assembly is given FullTrust permissions in the policy files. It's a good idea to revert the permission assertion when you have used the permission. (Actually, in this case it makes no difference because we are falling out of scope when we return). Let's show you how to code the assert for these permissions first.

Returning to our code, add the following shared function. It might be easier to simply edit the `BackGroundColor()` method (as shown in bold in Listing 9.7) to include the assertion—but either technique will work.

Listing 9.7 Adding Code Access Security FileIOPermission Assertion

```
Shared Function AssertedBackGroundColor() As String
    Dim FileIOperm As New _
        System.Security.Permissions.FileIOPermission( _
        System.Security.Permissions.FileIOPermissionAccess.Read, _
        "c:\RSSSTest.txt")
    FileIOperm.Assert()
    Dim sr As System.IO.StreamReader = New
System.IO.StreamReader("c:\RSSSTest.txt")
    Dim retval As String = sr.ReadToEnd()
    sr.Close()
    FileIOperm.RevertAssert()
    Return retval
End Function
```

Notice that we're trying to practice safe computing here. Because of this, we're going to the trouble to assert that (specifically) we want read-only permission on a very specific file—but no other permissions. You might wonder why it's necessary to assert permissions with this granularity. We're doing this because we're following the best practice of using the least permissions required to do the job. Regardless of what this code might do or how it's abused, it should (hopefully) be able to read only the specifically permissioned file and no others. If a system administrator comes along to clamp down on the policy file, your custom assembly will continue to work until FileIO read permissions are denied to the assembly. At that point, it will be a lot easier to argue for the administrator to just open up the policy file permission settings to permit your assembly to read that one file.

Assigning the Policy File Permissions

Neither Peter nor I are barristers, attorneys, or lawyers (but I have played one on TV). Nevertheless, I expect we would provide expert testimony that suggests that granting FullTrust to your custom assemblies coupled with over-asserting unnecessary permissions is foolhardy at best.

–Bill

Let's put it like this: If you were the office facilities manager at a bank, you'd probably need to give your cleaning contractors a key to gain access to the bank so they could clean it in the early morning hours before anyone else arrives. But it would be ludicrous for the facilities manager to provide the cleaning contractors with a master key, especially one that opened all the safe-deposit boxes of all customers. That would be giving a privilege that is just not required. Clearly, once the cleaning contractors had cleaned up (so to speak) and disappeared to the Bahamas, the facilities manager would have a lot of questions to answer.

–Peter

The policy file is all about letting the .NET Framework know how it can identify your assembly (called *evidence* in .NET jargon), and then letting the .NET Framework know what level of permissions your assembly is to be granted. The sledgehammer approach is to tell the .NET Framework that you want your assembly to have FullTrust permissions—that is, complete unrestricted access to the machine and network. If you develop applications for use by others and you always take the FullTrust approach (perhaps because it's marginally easier), we hope you have good lawyers and understanding insurers, you know what you are doing, and you never, ever make any coding errors. EULAs not withstanding, enabling FullTrust when FullTrust is not really required, and then making coding mistakes in your assembly probably constitutes professional negligence—especially when your client has had confidential information sucked off its network by an assembly with FullTrust being abused, or its mail system has crashed through malevolent misuse of an assembly.

Defining NamedPermissionSets for Code Access Security

The following is a list of the levels of permission that can be granted to assemblies. Examine the rspreviewpolicy.config file[3] `<NamedPermissionSets>` section. If this file is in its default state, it has three named permission sets (as shown in Figure 9.14):

- FullTrust: This permission set grants full rights to all resources on the local machine.
- Nothing: This set denies access to all resources, including the right to execute.
- Execution: This set defines a very limited, supposedly safe sandbox. Expressions typically run under this permission level.

---

[3] By default, you should find it in *C:\Program Files\Microsoft SQL Server\80\Tools\ Report Designer.*

```
      <SecurityClass Name="ZoneMembershipCondition" Description="System.Security
   </SecurityClasses>
   <NamedPermissionSets>
      <PermissionSet
            class="NamedPermissionSet"
            version="1"
            Unrestricted="true"
            Name="FullTrust"
            Description="Allows full access to all resources"
      />
      <PermissionSet
            class="NamedPermissionSet"
            version="1"
            Name="Nothing"
            Description="Denies all resources, including the right to execute"
      />
      <PermissionSet
            class="NamedPermissionSet"
            version="1"
            Name="Execution">
         <IPermission
               class="SecurityPermission"
               version="1"
               Flags="Execution"
         />
      </PermissionSet>
   </NamedPermissionSets>
   <CodeGroup
         class="FirstMatchCodeGroup"
         version="1"
```

Insert your custom PermissionSet here…

Figure 9.14 The rspreviewpolicy.config File `<NamedPermissionsSet>` Section

Let's add a new permission set that provides the ability to read our StyleSheet file. Locate the last closing `</PermissionSet>` tag in the policy file. It's located just before the closing `</NamedPermissionSets>` tag. Insert the code from Listing 9.8:

Listing 9.8 Adding a PermissionSet Element to the rspreviewpolicy.config File

```
<PermissionSet class="NamedPermissionSet"
   version="1"
   Name="ReportStyleSheetPermission"
```

```
   Description="Grants read access to specified report style file">
    <IPermission class="FileIOPermission"
       version="1"
       Read="C:\RSSSTest.txt"/>
      <IPermission class="SecurityPermission"
         version="1"
         Flags="Assertion"/>
</PermissionSet>
```

> **NOTE** We've included a set of text files (e.g., 00n Permission.txt) in the accompanying project folders to make it easier for you to cut and paste. The above PermissionSet is 001 Permission.txt.

Adding this PermissionSet is not enough—we still need to assign it to a CodeGroup. Defining a PermissionSet is like the office facilities manager deciding which keys can open which doors. Just because the manager has decided that one key should open three particular doors doesn't mean that anyone can open those doors—not until they've been given the keys. That's what CodeGroups are all about. It's about granting permissions to the assemblies you've created.

Configuring a CodeGroup

Examine the CodeGroup hierarchy in the rspreviewpolicy.config file. Notice that the defined CodeGroups are hierarchical and nested. CodeGroups provide information (called evidence) that enables the .NET Framework to identify your assembly and assign a particular PermissionSet against it.

Evidence that enables an assembly to be identified can be provided in a number of ways, each with its own benefits or quirks. For example, you can provide matching conditions. The jargon evidence just makes it harder to understand. We suggest that you think of using evidence to identify an assembly, just as the *CSI* people on TV use fingerprints, DNA, blood type, voice print, or body odor to identify a victim or perpetrator. Table 9.2 describes some of the bits of evidence .NET can use to identify the target assembly.[4]

---

[4] See the .NET documentation for more details.

Table 9.2 Evidence Used to Identify an Assembly and How It's Defined

Evidence	Class Name	Description
Url	UrlMembershipCondition	"Evidences" assemblies by their location. This can be a particular network or file location. If network, then must include the protocol, e.g., ftp://, http://; if a file then it can be just the path. This can also make use of wildcards such as * at the end of the URL. This is only as secure as ACLs on the locations. If an assembly can be replaced in that location with one of a same name, Reporting Services would accept the replacement as valid. A malevolent person who can switch assemblies on you can own the machine.
StrongName	StrongNameMembershipCondition	Evidences an assembly by its strongname public key (assuming it's signed). Assemblies that have been signed with a key expose the key's public key BLOB. This is a very secure mechanism because it is thought to be practically impossible to forge a signature. It is possible to further restrict the matching to names and versions of assemblies or simply match all assemblies that have been signed with that key. If you look in the policy files, you'll see that this is the technique Microsoft uses to evidence its own assemblies to Reporting Services.

Table 9.2 Evidence Used to Identify an Assembly and How It's Defined, *continued*

Evidence	Class Name	Description
Publisher	PublisherMembershipCondition	Matches assemblies that have been signed with an Authenticode signature. This is as secure as strong-names, but usually a lot slower.
Site	SiteMembershipCondition	This is a special class of URL that permits assemblies to be evidenced by network site, but excludes FILE://.
Zone	ZoneMembershipCondition	This permits assemblies coming from sites that belong to different Zones. You'll be familiar with these security zones through Internet Explorer: Internet, My Computer, Local Intranet, Trusted Sites, and Untrusted Sites.
Hash	HashMembershipCondition	No, these are not those assemblies created while the programmers were smoking a variety of marijuana. Hash evidences those assemblies that match an assembly's hash calculated by MD5 or SHA1 algorithms.
Application Directory	ApplicationDirectoryMembershipCondition	Evidences assemblies in the running application's directory or subdirectories
AllCode	AllCodeMembershipCondition	Matches all assemblies.

Having confused and frightened (and possibly bored) you with all these evidence conditions, we're only going to concentrate on two, the Url and StrongName conditions, because they are the most commonly used. Take a look at the documentation for System.Security.Policy if you really want more information on this subject. Be sure to bring that cup of hot coffee.

URL Evidence

Let's just recap where we are at the moment. So far, we've:

- Written our assembly, which asserts that it wants read FileIOPermissions.
- Deployed the assembly to the location on disk where the Report Server will run it.
- Created a permission set, ReportStyleSheetPermission, in the rspreviewpolicy.config file that specifies read-only access to a specific file.
- Saved the target file to the designated place on disk.

All we need to do now is assign the permission set to our assembly and provide Reporting Services with information that it can use to evidence our assembly. This way, the assembly can assert that it wants to break out of the Execution-only sandbox and the .NET Framework can determine whether it's okay to read the file based on the evidence provided.

Listing 9.9 shows the incantation that you'll need to insert (carefully) into the rspreviewpolicy.config file:

Listing 9.9   Inserting a CodeGroup Section into the rspreviewpolicy.config File

```
<CodeGroup class="UnionCodeGroup"
    version="1"
    PermissionSetName="ReportStyleSheetPermission"
    Name="ReportStyleSheetGroup"
    Description="Report Style Sheet Custom Assembly">
    <IMembershipCondition class="UrlMembershipCondition"
        version="1"
        Url="C:\Program Files\Microsoft SQL Server\80\Tools\Report
Designer\RSStyleSheet.dll"/>
</CodeGroup>
```

The preceding
CodeGroup
is 002
Permission.txt in
the supporting
files for this
chapter.

Where you place this CodeGroup in the rspreviewpolicy.config file is crucial. Locate the point in the file where the CodeGroup hierarchy starts (as shown in Figure 9.15).

```
                    Url="C:\Program Files\Microsoft SQL Server\80\Tools\Report Designer\BoostSt
        />
    </CodeGroup>
    <CodeGroup
        class="FirstMatchCodeGroup"
        version="1"
        PermissionSetName="Execution"
        Description="This code group grants MyComputer code Execution permission. ">
    <IMembershipCondition
            class="ZoneMembershipCondition"
            version="1"
            Zone="MyComputer" />
    <CodeGroup
            class="UnionCodeGroup"
            version="1"                              Insert the new
            PermissionSetName="FullTrust"            CodeGroup here...
            Name="Microsoft_Strong_Name"
            Description="This code group grants code signed with the Microsoft strong na
        <IMembershipCondition
```

Figure 9.15 The Point in the rspreviewpolicy.config File to Insert the New CodeGroup

Look for the *first* FirstMatchCodeGroup class. Insert the CodeGroup shown in Figure 9.15 immediately after this CodeGroup is closed with a "/>". Take exceptional care that the URL path is perfect and contains no typographical errors. We spent many hours tracking down problems with typos in URL paths.[5]

Now that we've made the changes to the rspreviewpolicy.config file, we're ready to try this out. We modified our sample report and saved it as 003 StyleSheet.rdl so that it calls the AssertedBackGroundColor() method, which asserts that it wants to access the text file. We should now be able to run that report in the RSReportHost.exe previewer, and we should be able to see that it is reading the file (as shown in Figure 9.16).

---

[5] In particular, if you try out the File System Information Data Processing extension sample, the CodeGroup shown in the accompanying readme has such a typo that prevents it from working. In Chapter 13, we show you how to get this working.

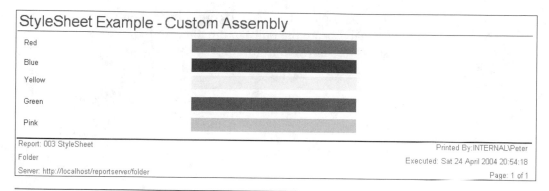

Figure 9.16 The Completed Example That Reads from a File

You might try putting the names of different colors into the file (c:\RSSSTest.txt). As this is only a proof of concept, you'll need to be aware that the color names should not have any trailing spaces or carriage returns. Of course, you can expand upon this concept to intelligently interrogate the file and make it more resilient and robust. We'll give you some ideas about this in a little while, because we'll ultimately leverage the XML StyleTemplate file. For now, we want to help get you through the difficult bits without making this task overcomplicated.

If we want this report to work when deployed to a Report Server (given that we've copied the assembly to *C:\Program Files\ Microsoft SQL Server\MSSQL\Reporting Services\ReportServer\ bin*), we need to edit the rssrvpolicy.config file to contain the same ReportStyleSheetPermission set that we created earlier. Don't confuse the server version of this config file with the "preview" config file we worked with earlier. You'll find the rssrvpolicy.config file in *C:\Program Files\Microsoft SQL Server\MSSQL\ Reporting Services\ReportServer*. Cut and paste the CodeGroup from the 003 Permission.txt file we've given you on the DVD (as shown in Listing 9.10), and add a corresponding CodeGroup. Again, you need to place this within the first CodeGroup nesting immediately under the closing `</CodeGroup>` tag of the Report_Expression_Default_Permissions CodeGroup, as shown in Figure 9.17.

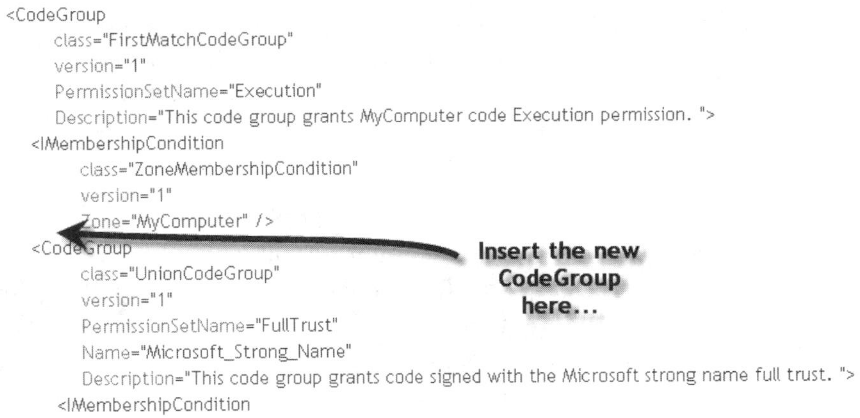

```
<CodeGroup
    class="FirstMatchCodeGroup"
    version="1"
    PermissionSetName="Execution"
    Description="This code group grants MyComputer code Execution permission. ">
  <IMembershipCondition
      class="ZoneMembershipCondition"
      version="1"
      Zone="MyComputer" />
  <CodeGroup
      class="UnionCodeGroup"
      version="1"
      PermissionSetName="FullTrust"
      Name="Microsoft_Strong_Name"
      Description="This code group grants code signed with the Microsoft strong name full trust. ">
    <IMembershipCondition
```

Insert the new
CodeGroup
here...

Figure 9.17 Insert the 003 Permission.txt File into the rssrvpolicy.config File

Listing 9.10 The 003 Permission.txt File CodeGroup Declaration

```
<CodeGroup class="UnionCodeGroup"
    version="1"
    PermissionSetName="ReportStyleSheetPermission"
    Name="ReportStyleSheetGroup"
    Description="Report Style Sheet Custom Assembly">
    <IMembershipCondition class="UrlMembershipCondition"
        version="1"
        Url="C:\Program Files\Microsoft SQL Server\MSSQL\Reporting⏎
        Services\ReportServer\bin\RSStyleSheet.dll"/>
</CodeGroup>
```

Again, pay very close attention to the URL. It's different from the URL used for the rspreviewpolicy.config file. We've given you a file named 003 Permissions.txt on the DVD that you can use to cut and paste.

At this point, you should now be able to execute the 003 StyleSheet.rdl report on the Report Server, and it should be able to read the RSSSTest.txt file.

NOTE A solution file containing the Report Project and the Custom Assembly Project on the DVD located in a folder named 002 StrongName StyleSheet deals with the next part of this chapter.

StrongName Membership Condition

The URL Membership condition is all well and good for many in-house projects in which someone has control over the folders (via the ACL[6]) where the assemblies and policy files are kept. When you introduce a new custom assembly, and if it needs more than execute permissions, you need to edit the policy config files. You can update the assembly as needed, and as long as the name is unchanged, it can continue to work—that is, as long as the permissions asserted continue to be within the PermissionSets it has been granted. This means if you update your assembly (perhaps adding functionality to query a database), you'll need to grant the database permissions in the code. In addition, the permissions granted to the assembly also need to include permissions that enable it to reference a database.

Strong Naming is closely related to cryptography involving a public and private key pair paradigm. This permits the public key to be embedded in assemblies and to have the assembly signed with the private key. This enables the CLR to detect whether the assembly has been tampered with post signing. The private key is kept very secret and is not distributed with the assembly. A properly signed assembly can have the *public* key extracted by the .NET Framework at runtime. This key can be used to verify that the assembly has not been changed since it was signed, because if the assembly has been dinked with manually, the checksum is not going to verify with the public key. If the assembly has been changed, the .NET Framework can drop the assembly like a hot brick—but with a lot less noise and screaming. It's currently believed that this approach makes it extremely difficult[7] to tinker around with the binary of a signed

---

[6] ACL: Access Control Lists. This is not the list of developers allowed to use JET. It's the formal permissions enforced on the file system.

[7] Folks, we all know that some kid out there is spending his free time trying to figure this out instead of going out on dates. Nothing is ever guaranteed, but this should take quite a bit of computing power to crack. Who knows, he might crack the problem before puberty makes girls more interesting than computers.

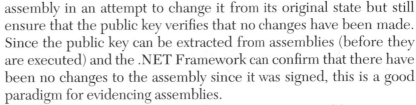

Be sure to keep production private keys secure—say, on a floppy disk or other removable medium.

assembly in an attempt to change it from its original state but still ensure that the public key verifies that no changes have been made. Since the public key can be extracted from assemblies (before they are executed) and the .NET Framework can confirm that there have been no changes to the assembly since it was signed, this is a good paradigm for evidencing assemblies.

If you use Strong Naming with your custom assemblies, you can create entries in your policy file that evidence *any* assemblies signed with the private key. The policy file contains a copy of the public key BLOB to compare against the public key BLOBs it extracts from assemblies as they load. Strong Naming an assembly involves signing it with a private key of a private/public key pair that provides a digital signature to the assembly and embeds the public key of the signature into the assembly. Let's take a look at the mechanics of using Strong Naming.

Create Your StrongName Key

First, you are going to need to generate a Strong Name key using the sn.exe command-line tool.

Peter had to lead me to this utility. It's installed with the .NET Framework but best launched from the Visual Studio .NET command prompt. See Start | All Programs | Visual Studio .NET 2003 | Visual Studio .NET Tools | Visual Studio .NET 2003 Command Prompt.

–Bill

1. Open up the Visual Studio .NET 2003 command prompt and type `sn -k TestStrongNameKey.snk`. This creates the public and private key pair and stores the pair in the specified file. The folder where this file is created should be either on the removable medium (as mentioned earlier) or in an encrypted folder to prevent malevolent access from disk-harvesting utilities when you think you've deleted it.

2. Return to your assembly source code (see Listing 9.11) and locate the Assembly information file (AssemblyInfo1.vb for a Visual Basic .NET project).

3. For Strong Naming to work, you need to be concerned with three entries in the Assembly information file. We suggest that you simply load the completed project and follow along (solution 002 StrongName StyleSheet.sln). Add the following text (as shown in Listing 9.11) to your project.

Listing 9.11 Add This Text to the RSStrongNameStyleSheet Project's AssemblyInfo1.vb File

```
<Assembly: System.Security.AllowPartiallyTrustedCallersAttribute()>
<Assembly: System.Reflection.AssemblyKeyFile("<full path to snk file>")>
<Assembly: System.Reflection.AssemblyVersion("<Version>")>
```

We used "1.0.0" as the version number in the completed solution and c:\TestStrongName.snk for the SNK file path. This is the file we created in Step 1. We also included the full class names, including their namespaces, in these references. That makes it easy to see where they're coming from, but you can further optimize using *Imports* in Visual Basic .NET and *using* in C#. Figure 9.18 shows the Edit References Dialog and shows the Assembly Version and the PublicKeyToken of the RSStyleSheet assembly.

Figure 9.18 The Edit References Dialog

Setting the AllowPartiallyTrustedCallersAttribute Attribute

This assembly attribute indicates the assembly is a Strong Named assembly that can be called by other assemblies not executing under the unlimited FullTrust permission set. If you didn't include the AllowPartiallyTrustedCallersAttribute, your assembly could be called only from assemblies that themselves were fully trusted. We know that we're calling our custom assembly from Expression code, which runs only under the Execution PermissionSet.

Setting the AssemblyKeyFile Attribute

Here is where you should embed the path to your TestStrongNameKey.snk file. Remember that this file contains highly classified information, so ideally you don't want to copy it to your hard disk unless you can hide it in an encrypted directory. Ideally, you want it made available only temporarily on a floppy disk while you compile. You might find it useful to look through the MSDN documentation for information on "delayed signing"—especially if you're working as part of a large team and want to delay the signing of an assembly until the very last minute.

Setting the AssemblyVersion Attribute

The reason we mention the AssemblyVersion attribute is that if you leave it in its default state of 1.0.*, each time you compile the assembly, Visual Studio .NET will automatically increment the version number in the compiled assembly. When you reference the assembly from the report, note that, by default, it will reference a particular assembly Version number.

Should you ever recompile and redeploy the assembly, you may find that your report no longer works as it tries to bind to the previous version. As always, you have several choices: You could determine that you don't care about auto-incrementing versioning. In this case, you can remove the version in the Edit References dialog. At that point, the report uses whatever version of the assembly is found. This approach has its drawbacks. If you want more control over things, taking control of the version numbering at compile time and binding the reports directly to a numbered version is a good idea. When it comes time to upgrade the custom assembly, you can make choices about whether it is backwardly compatible with a previous version, and if it is you can make use of .NET's <bindingRedirect> functionality.

Briefly, assume that you create and deploy a Strongly Named assembly versioned as 1.0.0.0. You subsequently create a bazillion reports that reference that numbered version of the assembly. Sometime later, you come along and want to replace the assembly with a later version—say, 2.0.0.0. You convince yourself that this new assembly is backwardly compatible with version 1.0.0.0. If this is the case, you can edit and re-reference all dependent reports to point to the new assembly. Sure, when you initially reference the assembly in your report, you can rip out the version number and the report will try to bind to any assembly version that has the same name. Binding to a specific version enables you to have side-by-side versions, which is sometimes quite useful. Another approach would be to tell the .NET Framework to redirect the binding to bind to a later version when asked to locate the earlier version. You can implement this approach in a number of ways by editing a configuration section of some config files. That's what we're going to show you in this section.

This is the section you need to create the `<configuration>` element, as shown in Listing 9.12.

NOTE (Warning) Do not append the .DLL file extension to the assemblyIdentity name attribute.

Listing 9.12 The `<Configuration>` Element in the web.config File

```
<configuration>
   <runtime>
      <assemblyBinding xmlns="urn:schemas-microsoft-com:asm.v1">
         <dependentAssembly>
            <assemblyIdentity name="<Your AssemblyName without .dll>"
                               publicKeyToken="<PublicKey>"
                               culture="neutral" />
            <bindingRedirect oldVersion="1.0.0.0"
                             newVersion="2.0.0.0"/>
         </dependentAssembly>
      </assemblyBinding>
   </runtime>
</configuration>
```

This customized element should be inserted into the following three files:

- The Report Server's web.config file in *C:\Program Files\ Microsoft SQL Server\MSSQL\Reporting Services\ReportServer*.
- The ReportingServicesService.exe.config file in *C:\Program Files\Microsoft SQL Server\MSSQL\Reporting Services\ ReportServer\bin*.
- The Devenv.exe.config file in *C:\Program Files\Microsoft Visual Studio .NET 2003\Common7\IDE*.

For more information on this, look up BindingRedirect in the Visual Studio .NET MSDN help.

Setting StrongNameMembershipCondition in Policy Files

The policy files rspreviewpolicy.config and rssrvpolicy.config hold CodeGroup blocks, as shown in Listing 9.13, instead of the CodeGroup blocks used with the URL Membership conditions. Again, you need to place these immediately under the closing `</CodeGroup>` tag of the Report_Expressions_Default_Permissions CodeGroup:

Listing 9.13 A Customized `<CodeGroup>` Element in the Config Files

```
<CodeGroup
      class="UnionCodeGroup"
      version="1"
      PermissionSetName="ReportStyleSheetPermission"
    Name="ReportStyleSheetGroupStrongNAme"
      Description="Report Style Sheet Custom Assembly">
   <IMembershipCondition
          class="StrongNameMembershipCondition"
          version="1"
PublicKeyBlob="00240000004800000940000000602000000240000525341310004000001000100017
7012c91e89ea93359ca8b82655a02ab2e7c0f3dc001e35763a12dfaec5327cafdbdbcfb68e6a580ab
d34836a6f36c98b7f307191f2d3da57c01b5f9ce9019eb11a3f9fb768cbccdd9de8f3cb78af7d45dc
2fd779216fc9fe48ce7ac3a8f06a998a2ce4c770ee9a136d2df5f5333b3fecd74ce637790e8923464
6aeb97f09ec"/>
</CodeGroup>
```

Okay, so we didn't tell you how to get *your* PublicKeyBlob bit, did we? Here are two ways to do this using sn.exe:

- `sn.exe -tp TestStrongNameKey.snk` This will extract the Public Key Blob and Public Key Token from the public/private pair Strong Name key itself.
- `sn.exe -Tp <`**StrongNamed Assembly**`>` This will extract the Public Key Blob and Public Key Token from a Strong Named assembly.

1. To return to our example: We assume that you have already created the PermissionSet used to permit read access to

the file. If not, you'll find the code block to cut and paste into place in 004 Permission.txt. Paste this into the NamedPermissionsets node in the following files: *C:\Program Files\Microsoft SQL Server\80\Tools\Report Designer\ rspreviewpolicy.config and C:\Program Files\Microsoft SQL Server\MSSQL\Reporting Services\ReportServer\ rssrvpolicy.config*.

2. Then take 005 Permission.txt, extract your own Public Key Blob as we just described using sn.exe, and paste that blob in. Then paste the whole CodeGroup into the same two config files immediately under the closing `</CodeGroup>` tag of the Report_Expressions_Default_Permissions CodeGroup.

3. Build the RSStrongNameStyleSheet assembly, and deploy it to both the *C:\Program Files\Microsoft SQL Server\ MSSQL\Reporting Services\ReportServer\bin* folder and the *C:\Program Files\Microsoft SQL Server\80\Tools\ Report Designer* folder.

4. Report 004 Stylesheet uses the Strong Named assembly you've created. Go to that Report's *References* property, remove the reference to our assembly, and then browse for your compiled version of RSStrongNameStyleSheet.dll to reference that.

Creating the Final StyleSheet

Let's wrap up this chapter with a flourish of style. At this point, we've covered all the real hard parts. At the start of the chapter, we showed you the StyleSheet.xml file, and we've seen that the Report wizard uses the localized version of that file when it builds reports. But the wizard only applies those styles statically at design time. If you change the style definition later, it won't have any effect on the reports written previously. Well, wouldn't it be cool if we could use that StyleSheet.xml file and apply the styles at report runtime? What we'd want is a way of creating an expression that could query the StyleSheet.xml file for the element style property we need. Thankfully, the .NET Framework provides us with a very easy way of doing just that. This means that we can create a custom assembly for our reports and bind our properties to expressions such as this for the BackGroundColor of an item:

```
=Code.Style.Use("Corporate.Title.BackGroundColor#Yellow")
```

Or, for the Title element's font family:

```
=Code.Style.Use("Corporate.Title.FontFamily#Arial")
```

Expressing this more generically, we have:

```
=Code.Style.Use("<Template Name>.<Style Name>.<Property>#<Default>")
```

In our first example, the syntax that we are using provides our own `Use()` method with an argument it can parse. It can then use this argument to search the StyleTemplates.xml file hierarchically to find the Corporate StyleTemplate, the Title StyleName, and the *BackGroundColor* property. Finally, we also provide a default of Yellow. This is our safety net in case anything goes wrong when searching the StyleTemplates.xml file. If the search fails, we have a default BackGroundColor.

You might be wondering what "Code." is doing back here. No, we've not implemented any code in the report's code block, but we did instantiate an instance of the assembly's `StyleSheet.Style` class with an instance name of *Style*. To use the instantiated class in expressions, we need to reference it as `Code.Style`, as shown in Figure 9.19.

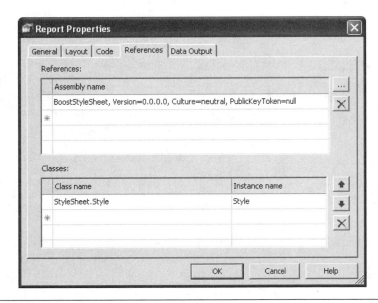

Figure 9.19 Report Properties Dialog Adding a Reference to Our Custom XML Style Sheet

This project is named 003 Boost Stylesheet on the DVD. Let's give you brief instructions on what to do to build it and then be able to experiment with it. To implement this example, follow these steps:

1. Copy the StyleTemplate.xml file into the *C:\Program Files\ Microsoft SQL Server\MSSQL\Reporting Services\ ReportServer* folder. (This assumes you are running the Report Server on your local workstation. If you're not, copy the file to the system where the Report Server is being hosted.)

2. Name this file BoostStyleTemplates.xml (or whatever you want, but the names need to match everywhere they're referenced). We are going to want these templates separate from the StyleTemplates.xml file.

3. Create a NamedPermissionSet to grant read access to the BoostStyleTemplates.xml file in the rssrvpolicy.config file and in the rspreviewpolicy.config file. This should be as shown in Listing 9.14:

Listing 9.14 Create a NamedPermissionSet to Grant Access to the BoostStyleTemplates.xml File

```
<PermissionSet class="NamedPermissionSet"
   version="1"
  Name="BoostReportStyleSheetPermission"
  Description="Grants read access to Report StyleFile">
   <IPermission class="FileIOPermission"
      version="1"
     Read="C:\Program Files\Microsoft SQL↲
     Server\MSSQL\Reporting Services\ReportServer\BoostStyleTemplates.xml"/>
    <IPermission class="SecurityPermission"
       version="1"
      Flags="Execution, Assertion"/>
</PermissionSet>
```

The file 006 Permissions.txt in the project folder contains this extract.

You can create more complex PermissionSets and roll up several different permissions into a single PermissionSet. Trying to do this manually is like weaving barbed wire by hand, so if you find that you must do it, we recommend that you carefully leverage the .NET Framework Configuration Tool (Mscorcfg.msc). This utility is on the Administrative Tools menu, but we tend to start it directly from the Visual Studio .NET command prompt by typing `mscorcfg.msc` into the prompt. Give the tool a few seconds to load and navigate down to the Runtime Security Policy. Expand Machine, expand Permission Sets, and create a New Permission Set. (It's not a good idea to change any of the pre-existing ones). Take care—this tool actually affects the whole .NET platform on the machine—not just Reporting Services. When you launch the New Permission Set, there is a dialog to help you create all the permissions and properties you want. Choose a name for your PermissionSet that is easy to find. Once you've created it, you'll have to dig deep into *C:\WINDOWS\Microsoft.NET\Framework\v1.1.4322\ CONFIG\security.config* and search there for your PermissionSet. *Don't* change anything in the security.config file with a text editor—it won't work. You can copy your PermissionSet to the Clipboard so that it's ready to be pasted into your Reporting Services policy config files. If you want to delete the PermissionSet from the security.config file, do it with the mscorcfg.msc tool—it's the only way. Take care because you are venturing "where angels fear to tread" when you play with the security.config file. It's another one of those brain surgery in the bathroom mirror experiments.

4. Next, you need to create a CodeGroup. We're not going to strongname the assembly, but you could. In this example, we're going to use the UrlMembershipCondition. This means we'll need two different CodeGroups—one for each of the rssrvpolicy.config and rspreviewpolicy.config files.

Here's the CodeGroup for the rspreviewpolicy.config file (see Listing 9.15). This file is 007 permissions.txt in the solution.

Listing 9.15 The CodeGroup File for Our XML BoostStyleSheet Implementation

```
<CodeGroup
        class="UnionCodeGroup"
        version="1"
        PermissionSetName="BoostReportStyleSheetPermission"
        Name="BoostReportStyleSheet"
            Description="Report Style Sheet Custom Assembly">
    <IMembershipCondition
            class="UrlMembershipCondition"
            version="1"
            Url="C:\Program Files\Microsoft SQL Server\80\Tools\Report⏎
            Designer\BoostStyleSheet.dll"/>
    />
</CodeGroup>
```

Listing 9.16 shows the CodeGroup for the rssrvpolicy.config file. This file is 008 permissions.txt in the solution.

Listing 9.16 CodeGroup for the rssrvpolicy.config File

```
<CodeGroup
        class="UnionCodeGroup"
        version="1"
        PermissionSetName="BoostReportStyleSheetPermission"
        Name="BoostReportStyleSheet"
            Description="Report Style Sheet Custom Assembly">
    <IMembershipCondition
            class="UrlMembershipCondition"
            version="1"
            Url="C:\Program Files\Microsoft SQL Server\MSSQL\Reporting⏎
            Services\ReportServer\bin\BoostStyleSheet.dll"/>
    />
</CodeGroup>
```

5. Next, build the BoostStyleSheet.dll and copy it to the following path on your Report Server host system: *C:\Program Files\Microsoft SQL Server\MSSQL\Reporting Services\ReportServer\bin* folder, and *C:\Program Files\ Microsoft SQL Server\80\Tools\Report Designer* folder.

Now, we really didn't want you to think that the coding is difficult—it really isn't. Quite literally, the BoostStyleSheet.dll consists of 39 lines of code. We could have reduced that further, but at the cost of clarity. We'll let you walk through the code on your own to help you better understand what it does. We've provided lots of comments so that you can see what's going on. We use the cool `split()` method on the delimited string passed through to the `Use` method to parse the argument into a `String` array, and then make use of the strings in a simple XPath Query, which is really very simple. For example, when passing Bold.Table.BorderWidth/ Top#3pt into `Use()`, the resulting XPath Query is just:

```
descendant::StyleTemplate[Label='Bold']/Styles/Style[@Name='Table']/BorderWidth/Top
```

At this point, you are ready to use your new report. You can edit the BoostStyleTemplates.xml to add more Templates, as well as more items and properties. On our website www.SQLReportingServices.NET (for registered readers), we'll have a few more techniques and ideas you can use with Style Templates.

Summary

In this chapter, we've shown you how to create your own default styles that anyone on your team can use with the Report wizard. We've also shown you how you can make your own Report Templates and Data Sources, as well as making them available to the Add New Item dialog. These are the easy groundwork topics that should help set you up to become more productive.

In the second half of the chapter we ventured out into the land of custom assemblies where the "real" programmers play hardball. We took you through some real hardcore .NET by showing you how you can safely create a custom assembly for your reports. And then just to show off, we ended the chapter with a project that you can use to implement a runtime Style against your reports so that you can update reports by simply changing a StyleTemplate file.

CHAPTER 10

Accessing the Report Server via URL

From time to time, report administrators, DBAs, and selected users need to launch reports without using the Report Manager. This chapter discusses the simplest of these techniques—using the browser Address bar and a URL—as well as more sophisticated techniques that use HTML forms and POST. Of course, when you create web pages or other documents, you can include URLs that address reports. These URLs can specify the name, input parameters, and a host of other options that we're going to show you in this chapter.

Using a URL to access managed reports mimics the techniques used by the Report Manager when it addresses reports from the Report Server and enables them to be displayed in a web browser, given that all the Report Manager does is calculate the URL and give that URL to an HTML IFRAME in the Report Manager. Yes, you can also use SOAP API calls to launch and manage reports—that's the interface used by the Report Designer and the Report Manager to deploy and manage reports, and it's the supported interface you'll need to use if you are going to develop programs that manage reports. This chapter will touch lightly on the use of SOAP when we show you how to use the `rs.exe` scripting utility—we'll cover SOAP in more detail in Chapter 9¾.

It turns out that all of a managed report's configurable options, such as rendering format, size, toolbar toggles, and other options, can be passed in the **URL Request String**,[1] including any credentials and parameters that might be required or otherwise prompted for. Another approach passes these configurable options to the Report Server as part of an HTTP Postback. We'll take a look at both of these techniques in action and discuss the security implications of prompted credentials.

Simple URL Addressing the Report Server

This first section discusses the fundamentals of launching reports using a browser and a simple URL. If you directly address your Report Server from your web browser with https:// <Your Server>/ReportServer/, you'll get a sparse HTML web page (see Figure 10.1). This page simply lists CatalogItems in the Home root folder, with hyperlinks that can launch CatalogItems or drill into other folders. **CatalogItems** are all those objects stored in the Report Server's notional folders,[2] and they include managed reports, graphics, HTML files, or other files deployed to the Report Server. What you see and can do here depends on what permissions you've been granted in regard to those items. When you've got no permission to browse these items, they won't display at all.

To investigate what's going on under the covers, we suggest that you view the HTML source of these rendered pages. Drill into the Sample Reports folder, right-click on the page, and select the View Source option from the context menu.

Figure 10.2 shows the underlying hyperlinks.

---

[1] The Request String is what you see in the Address bar of a web browser.

[2] Notational folders are the server-side directory folders you create to organize your reports.

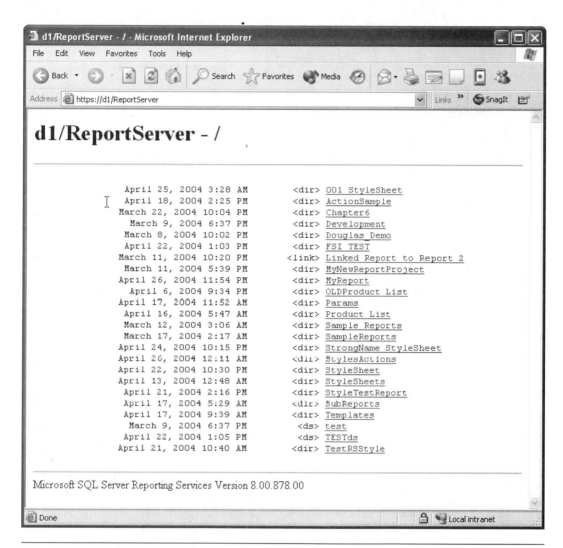

Figure 10.1 The Sparse HTML Web Page Generated by Navigating to the ReportServer

```
<html>
  <head>
    <meta name="Generator" content="Microsoft SQL Server Reporting Services Version 8.00.878.00">
    <title>xpvs2003/ReportServer - /SampleReports</title>
  </head>
  <body><H1>xpvs2003/ReportServer - /SampleReports</H1><hr>
```
Command=ListChildren
```
<pre><A HREF="/ReportServer?&amp;rs%3aCommand=ListChildren">[To Parent Directory]</A>
           21 March 2004 21:20       17318 <A HREF="?%2fSampleReports%2fCompany+Sales&amp;r
           21 March 2004 21:20       &lt;ds&gt; <A HREF="?%2fSampleReports%2fAdventurework
           21 March 2004 21:20      460830 <A HREF="?%2fSampleReports%2fAdventureworks.jpg&
</pre><hr>
Microsoft SQL Server Reporting Services Version 8.00.878.00

  </body>
</html>
```

Figure 10.2 The HTML Source Code Behind the SampleReports Directory

What's interesting here are the `<A HREF= ...>` attributes, because they contain the hyperlinks. If you look, for example, at the hyperlink for `[To Parent Directory]`, you'll see that the HREF is `/ReportServer?&amp;rs%3aCommand=ListChildren`. This can be appended to `https://<your server>/` in a browser's Address bar as

```
http://<your server> ↵
/ReportServer?&amp;rs%3aCommand=ListChildren.
```

I just dig out my IBM 360 "green card" and look them up. It's a bit tattered after 35 years of use, but it always comes in handy.

–Bill

However, if you hover the mouse over the rendered link, you'll see that `&amp;` and `%3a` are **decoded** to & and :, respectively. What is going on here is that certain characters are **escaped** when used in the HTML so as to *try* not to confuse the browser; however, this is not always consistent in Reporting Services. Sometimes if you look at the source you'll see some parts of the URLs have escaped characters and others do not. You'll also see inconsistencies in uppercase or lowercase for characters used in hexadecimal. Table 10.1 lists some of the encodings we encountered in our delving, so that you can convert the text back to a slightly more readable human form. If you encounter others that we didn't list, you can search the MSDN help files for "ISO Latin-1 Character Set" and convert the hexadecimal to decimal.

Table 10.1 What Some of the Typical HTML Escape Sequences Mean

Encoding	Character	Description
&amp;	&	Ampersand
%20	<space>	Space character
%2b	+	Plus sign
%2f	/	Forward slash
%3a	:	Colon

Exposing the Reporting Services URL Commands

If you return to the source and mentally decode the escape sequences, you'll see that we effectively have the following URLs embedded for the hyperlinks in Figure 10.2. We did the mental conversion for you, as shown in Figure 10.3.

```
https://<Your Server>/ReportServer?&rs:Command=ListChildren
https://<Your Server>/ReportServer?/Sample+Reports/Company+Sales&rs:Command=Render
https://<Your Server>/ReportServer?/Sample+Reports/AdventureWorks&rs:Command=GetDataSourceContents
https://<Your Server>/ReportServer?/Sample+Reports/Adventureworks.jpg&rs:Command=GetResourceContents
```

Figure 10.3 A Decoded Set of URLs Showing the Reporting Services Commands

You'll find these four documented commands for rs:Command in the Reporting Services Books Online under "Using the Command Parameter" topic:

- ListChildren: Lists the ReportItems in the selected directory.
- Render: Launches and displays the report.
- GetDataSourceContents: Examines the contents of the selected Data Source.
- GetResourceContents: Examines the contents of the selected resource (like a JPG or file).

If you look closely at the source code we've been studying, you'll see these rs:Command expressions are embedded in the source, as shown in Figure 10.4.

Command=GetDataSourceContents

rs:Command=Render

```
</A>
rts%2fAdventure  ks&amp;rs:Command=GetDataSourceContents":
Company+Sales&amp;rs:Command=Render">Company Sales</A>
Employee+Sales+Summary&amp;rs:Command=Render">Employee Sal
Foodmart+Sales&amp;rs:Command=Render">Foodmart Sales</A>
microsoft+stock+certificate.gif&amp;rs:Command=GetResource
Product+Catalog&amp;rs:Command=Render">Produc  Catalog</A>
Product+Line+Sales&amp;rs:Command=Render">Pr  uct Line Sal
Sales+Order+Detail&amp;rs:Command=Render">Sa es Order Deta
Sales+People&amp;rs:Command=Render">Sal  People</A>
Stock&amp;rs:Command=Render">Stock</
Territory+Sales+Drilldown&amp;rs:  mmand=Render">Territory
```

Command=GetResourceContents

Figure 10.4 Zooming In on the rs:Command Expressions in the URL

However, if you dig a bit deeper and examine the source when the Report Manager is interacting and rendering reports from the Report Server, you'll see some additional "undocumented" rs:Commands:

- `?rs:Command=Blank` This returns a blank page similar to `about:blank`.
- `?rs:Command=Get` This is an internal call that Microsoft uses to pull resources such as JavaScript files, cascading style sheets, and images out of their own resource DLLs.

URL Syntax and Parameter Prefixes

The formal syntax for the URL interface per the documentation is as follows:[3]

```
http://server/virtualroot?[/pathinfo]&prefix:param=value⏎
    [&prefix:param=value]...n]
```

Technically, this might be misleading because it indicates that all parameters should have a prefix and ":"; this is not the case, as we shall see in just a moment. The more correct formal syntax actually is:

```
http://server/virtualroot?[/pathinfo]&prefix:param=value⏎
    [&[prefix:]param=value]...n]
```

---

[3] Note that these URLs should be on a single line. We've used the ⏎ symbol to indicate where we broke the line to fit it on this page.

But hey, what are a colon and prefix among friends?
These are the acceptable prefixes:

- `rs:` Indicates that the parameter addresses the Report Server.
- `rc:` Indicates that the parameter is for the Renderer.
- `dsu:` Indicates that the parameter is for the Report Data Source user name.
- `dsp:` Indicates that the parameter is for the Report Data Source user password.
- `dspe:` Indicates that the parameter is for the Report Data Source encrypted password (undocumented).

We should mention another variation: the empty prefix without a colon. This is used to reference exposed report parameters.

Handling `rs:` Parameters—Sending Instructions to the Report Server

We suggest that you load up a URL for a report with no parameters in your browser's Address bar—say, the Product Catalog Sample that Microsoft supplies, as shown here—and work through it with us.

```
https://<server>/Reportserver?/Sample+Reports/Product+Catalog↲
    &rs:Command=Render
```

We saw `rs:Command` a little earlier, but there are other `rs:` parameters to show you—namely, `rs:Format` and `rs:Snapshot`.

The `rs:Format` Parameter

The `rs:Format` parameter instructs the Report Server to use a specified Rendering extension. If it's not specified in the URL, the browser detection logic determines which HTML version should be used.

The supported Format parameters are:

- `&rs:Format=XML`
- `&rs:Format=NULL`
- `&rs:Format=CSV`
- `&rs:Format=IMAGE`

- &rs:Format=PDF
- &rs:Format=HTML4.0
- &rs:Format=HTML3.2
- &rs:Format=MHTML
- &rs:Format=EXCEL
- &rs:Format=HTMLOWC

You could try appending those to the URL and see how they influence the stream that comes back from the Report Server. For example, you'll see that if you call

```
https://<server>/Reportserver?/Sample+⏎
Reports/Product+Catalog&rs:Command=Render&rs:Format=XML
```

you'll get back a report rendered as XML.

Working with the rs.exe Report Scripting Utility

Let's take a minute to show off the command-line report scripting utility (rs.exe). We can use it to create a simple script to call the ListExtensions() SOAP exposed method on the server to show all the supported format types. Okay, well, we know you might be able to look at the server's rsreportserver.config file sitting in the *C:\ Program Files\Microsoft SQL Server\MSSQL\Reporting Services\ ReportServer* folder, but we need to show you that the rs.exe scripting utility is *so* easy to use.

Open Notepad, type in the code shown in Listing 10.1, and save it to a file named ListFormatExtensions.rss. If you fancy yourself a guru, try the shortcut guru's way, shown in Figure 10.5.

Listing 10.1 A Script to Be Executed by rs.exe

```
Sub Main()
For Each Ext As Extension In rs.ListExtensions(ExtensionTypeEnum.Render)
Console.WriteLine(Ext.Name)
Next
End Sub
```

If you're a bit lazy or a bad typist, you'll find a file on the DVD named ListFormatExtensions.rss. Note that you don't have to worry about any OO silliness. The `rs` object referred to in this code is a `ReportingService` object created for you behind the scenes when you run the following script from the Visual Studio .NET command prompt.[4]

```
rs.exe -i ListFormatExtensions.rss -s ↵
    "https://<your server>/ReportServer"
```

The `-i` indicates the input file, and `-s` indicates the server on which to run the script. (Yes, you can specify other command-line arguments to explicitly indicate the user, password, and other options.)

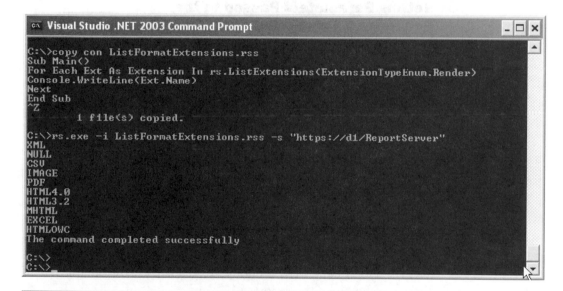

Figure 10.5 Peter Showing Off That He Can Type a Script Straight off and Run It.... These Are the Formats You Can Use with `rs:Format=`

---

[4] Remember, you can find the Visual Studio .NET command prompt (if you installed it) from the Start menu under Visual Studio .NET 2003 | Visual Studio .NET Tools.

Setting the `rs:Snapshot` Parameter

We'll leave `rs:Snapshot` for you to experiment with. First you'll need to create a report Snapshot with the Report Manager. Once it's created, you can render that Snapshot using the `rs:Snapshot` command. Just make sure that you give the Snapshot time in the correct syntax, as shown in Listing 10.2.

Listing 10.2   Using the Snapshot Parameter to Indicate Snapshot Time

```
https://<your server>/ReportServer?/↵
  <Path to your Report>&rs:Command=Render↵
  &rs:Snapshot=YYYY-MM-ddThh:mm:ss
```

Setting Parameters Passed to the Rendering Extension

The parameters to pass to the Rendering extension (`rc:`) depend (for the most part) on the Rendering extension. For example, if we request the HTML Rendering extension, the values discussed next are of interest (the defaults are in bold). Their effect or the functionality exhibited is also browser dependent. This means if you're going to be using anything other than Internet Explorer 6.0, you'll have to experiment to see what is supported. We have heard tales that in at least one case Netscape browsers did not render reports or the Report Manager as expected.

Rendering Extension Parameters: Visible Areas of a Report

These parameters dictate whether the toolbar, the parameters area, and the Document Map sections are displayed. By default, all of these are shown on the report.

- `rc:Toolbar=true|false` Indicates whether to display the toolbar on an HTML rendered report.
- `rc:Parameters=true|false` Indicates whether to display the parameters collection area.
- `rc:DocMap=true|false` Displays the DocMap if there are any label properties set.

Here are some examples you can try out:

```
https://<server>/Reportserver?/Sample+Reports/Product+Catalog↵
    &rs:Command=Render&rc:Toolbar=false
https://<server>/Reportserver?/Sample+Reports/Product+Catalog↵
    &rs:Command=Render&rc:Toolbar=false&rc:DocMap=false
```

Rendering Extension Parameters: Sizing and Navigation

Two main parameters can be used to determine how much the web browser window should be magnified (the zoom percentage), and which page or section of the rendered report should be the initial navigated target:

- `rc:Zoom=100|<% zoom as integer>|Page Width| Whole Page` Determines the level of Zoom for the rendered report.
- `rc:Section=1|<integer>` Navigates to the section or page.
- `rc:DocMapID=<integer id>` Scrolls the report to the indicated ID.

This last navigation parameter is used in conjunction with the Document Map, although we believe it's probably not that useful because we've not been able to find any documentation on how to determine the IDs to use with the DocMapID. We had to render a report with a Document Map in a web browser, navigate to the required page, and then display that page's HTML source. There we found a JavaScript declaration for DocMapIds.

```
var docMapIds = ["1669", "1943"];
```

We found that we could use any of the values in the URL when setting the `rc:DocMapID` parameter, but we just don't know how these ID values are derived in the first place, or whether and how they change when a report is edited. We're reliably informed, though, that a future version will address this very issue.

However, a far more useful parameter is:

```
rc:LinkTarget=<window/frame name>
```

This parameter controls which window is the target recipient of HTML Postbacks when clicking on drill-through links in the rendered report. This can take any of the special built-in names such as:

- `rc:LinkTarget=_top`
- `rc:LinkTarget=_self`
- `rc:LinkTarget=_search`
- `rc:LinkTarget=_parent`
- `rc:LinkTarget=_blank`

These parameters can also be set to any window that you have specifically named. For example, try using the following URL:

```
https://<server>/Reportserver?/Sample+Reports/Product+Catalog↵
  &rs:Command=Render&rc:Section=2&rc:LinkTarget=_search
```

If you subsequently scroll to the bottom of the page (we're on page 2) and click on the link to www.adventureworks.com, you'll see that this opens up in the Search pane of the browser. Of course, www.adventureworks.com is not a real trading company, so the URL resolves to the Microsoft website.

Setting the Rendering Extension Parameters: Searching

Four parameters are used to launch a Reporting Services search:

- `rc:FindString` The string to search for.
- `rc:StartFind` The starting page for the search.
- `rc:EndFind` The ending page for the search.
- `rc:FallbackPage` The page to navigate to when the search fails.

Each of these parameters can be passed in a URL in connection with using the built-in search options. You might have already used the search option from the toolbar. In fact, this is really just a URL hook into the same toolbar functionality with a few extra bells and whistles. For example, you can set a range of pages or sections in which the search is to be performed and also set a page or section to display if the search doesn't return a value.

Let's start at the beginning and try this out against the Sample Catalog report. We'll search for "Bike" using `rc:FindString=<String to Find>`.

```
https://<server>/Reportserver?/Sample+Reports/Product+Catalog↵
    &rs:Command=Render&rc:FindString=Bike
```

Notice that there are no quotes around "Bike" in the command, and there shouldn't be any. Also notice that if you try this out against the Product Catalog report, it will load up the toolbar's Find textbox with the search string, but it won't be successful in finding and navigating to "Bike." The reason is that, by default, a search run from the URL only searches the current page or section. This means you'll need to add the `rc:StartFind` and `rc:EndFind` parameters for it to work properly.

```
https://<server>/Reportserver?/Sample+Reports/Product+Catalog&↵
    rs:Command=Render&rc:FindString=Bike&rc:StartFind=1&rc:EndFind=1000
```

Now, let's assume that we're searching for something that isn't found in the Product Catalog report—such as "humor." In this case, we can set the `rc:FallbackPage` to the page or section *in the report* that we'd like users to see, after they've acknowledged on the pop-up dialog that the search text was not found. The following URL attempts in vain to search for "humor" in the Product Catalog and displays page 3 when no humor is found, keeping at least the British programmers smiling. Actually, American programmers don't think the Product Catalog is a bit funny either.

```
https://<server>/Reportserver?/Sample+Reports/Product+Catalog↵
        &rs:Command=Render&rc:FindString=humor&rc:StartFind=1↵
    &rc:EndFind=1000&rc:FallbackPage=3
```

Managing Report Server Sessions

You may have noticed that once a large report has been processed, navigating pages in an Internet Explorer 6.0 web browser is usually quite fast. If you've enabled a SQL Profiler trace against the DBMS where the Report Processor collects its underlying data, you'll see that there is *usually* no traffic (after the initial preparation of the report) as you navigate between each report page in the web browser. This is because the entire rendered report is not simply dumped onto the browser—unless it all fits on one page/section. Instead, the report Intermediate Format is cached in its entirety into a ***session*** maintained in the Report Server's TempDB database. Or, if you have installed SP1 you can configure the session to be cached to the file system instead.

This caching is indexed by a SessionID variable and provided to the client (web browser). It's used whenever the client returns to manipulate that report. If the client returns before the session has expired, the content will be taken out of the session cache. The default session timeout is set to 10 minutes. It's measured starting from the last call the client made on that session. If, however, the returning call occurs *after* the content has expired, you'll get a new session and the report will be re-created, so it takes a little longer to move to the next page. Note that it's the Report Server that chooses the SessionID string as soon as the `Render()` method is called. Don't worry if this sounds complicated—we have an example you can work through that makes it seem simple.

1. On a *test* system, *not on a production system*, launch the SQL Enterprise Manager, navigate to the ReportServerTempDB tables, and open up the SessionData table. You don't want to do this on a busy system. Ideally, do it on a test development system that you can afford to pooch.[5]
2. Leaving the SessionData table open, open a web browser and launch the Sample Reports Territory Sales Drilldown report by entering the following URL in the Address bar:

```
https://<Server>/ReportServer?↵
/Sample+Reports/Territory+Sales+Drilldown
```

---

[5] A technical term. A "pooched" system often needs FDISK, reformat, and a new keyboard, depending on the level of pooch.

We're deliberately choosing a report that doesn't have a Document Map—because a report with a Document Map will complicate this testing. (Document Maps are treated as their own separate requests and appear to have their own sessions for each report.)

3. After the report has rendered, refresh the SessionData table in the Enterprise Manager and locate the newly added row. If you have trouble finding it, look closely at the ReportPath and the Expiration and CreationTime columns.

4. Close that web browser session, and open a new one. It's important to follow us here in terms of closing and opening a new web browser. In the new web browser, enter the URL for the Sample Territory Sales Drilldown report again.

```
https://<Server>/ReportServer?/Sample+Reports/↵
Territory+Sales+Drilldown
```

You should notice that a new row is created in the SessionData table. You can create new rows by starting new web browsers and navigating to the Sample Territory Sales Drilldown.

5. Alternatively, launch a new web browser, and copy and paste the SessionID from the SessionData table for one of the previous sessions that targeted the Territory Sales Drilldown report. For example, the URL looks like this:

```
https://d1/ReportServer?/Sample%20Reports/↵
Territory%20Sales%20Drilldown↵
&rs:SessionID=pbivskaern5ghibtm01npgec
```

Note that you need to replace the actual ID string for the SessionID with one from your own server. Before clicking Go on the web browser, take a close look at the Expiration column in the SessionData table. You see the report render as expected, but because you specified a SessionID that already exists, and that report is in the SessionData table, Report Server uses the existing session instead of creating a new one. The Expiration time is also reset for another 10 minutes.

You're probably wondering what all of this means. First, we need to warn you not to interfere with the SessionData table in production systems. We also don't recommend building solutions that query the SessionData table directly in an attempt to use a pre-existing session. That's because this technique is not supported, and it's an implementation detail that's subject to change on a whim. However, when you're using the SOAP interface, you can call the Render() method on the ReportingService object and then inspect the SessionHeaderValue.SessionId to return an ID that you can use in a URL. This means that if you have a report that you're working with in code that takes a considerable time to process, you can make use of a version in session rather than having to take the processing hit all over again. Your SOAP program would shell-execute to a browser with the URL containing the SessionID or would provide that URL to an IFRAME or web browser control.

The example shown in Listing 10.3 illustrates an rs.exe script that uses the SOAP interface to render the Territory Sales Drilldown report, both as a PDF and as a CSV file. It uses the same session and writes the SessionID to the console. Copy the SessionID to an rs:SessionID parameter, and use it in a web browser URL. Watch the SessionData table. You'll see that the same session gets reused as long as it has not expired by the time you use it. As a result, the underlying database is not requeried.

Listing 10.3 An rs.exe Script to Render the Territory Sales Drilldown Report in PDF and CSV Formats

```
Const strReport As String = "/Sample Reports/Territory Sales Drilldown"

Sub Main()
  Dim result As Byte() = Nothing
  rs.SessionHeaderValue = New SessionHeader
  Dim strOutType As String = "PDF"

  For i As Integer = 1 To 2
    Console.WriteLine("Call {0} to Render.", i)
    result = rs.Render(strReport, strOutType, Nothing, "", Nothing, _
                Nothing, Nothing, "", "", Nothing, Nothing, Nothing)
```

```
    Console.WriteLine("SessionID after call to Render: {0}",_
                      rs.SessionHeaderValue.SessionId)
    Console.WriteLine(("Execution date and time: " & _
                      rs.SessionHeaderValue.ExecutionDateTime))
    Console.WriteLine(("Is new execution: " & _
                      rs.SessionHeaderValue.IsNewExecution))

    Dim outFile As New System.IO.FileStream("c:\TerritorySales." & _
                            strOutType, IO.FileMode.Create)
    outFile.Write(result, 0, result.Length)
    outFile.Close()

    strOutType = "CSV"
  Next
End Sub
```

Here are the Report Server parameters that you can use to manipulate sessions in a URL:

- rs:SessionID=<SessionIDString>
- rs:Command=ResetSessionTimeout
- rs:ClearSession=true

Passing Data Source Passwords as URL Parameters

If any of the report or shared Data Sources in the target report require prompted credentials, it's possible to provide these in the URL as parameters. Say you have a Data Source named "AdventureWorks" that is setup for prompted credentials. You can specify the UserName in the URL as:

dsu:AdventureWorks=<UserName>

and provide the password in plain text as:

dsp:AdventureWorks=<plaintext password>

We're not convinced this is such a good idea. Let's think about security here, you certainly wouldn't want to be doing this over an http:// connection for a start. But is an https:// connection that much better? Well, perhaps while in transit over the network, but not from a browser cache point of view. For example, consider a scenario where you are the report administrator for a Reporting Services installation, and a user is complaining that a report with prompted credentials is not working on his or her system. This report could be accessed through the Report Manager, or one that your application calls directly from the Report Server. You go over to the machine, and you see the user able to demonstrate that it's not working. So you try it out on the machine with your super user or SA credentials, and either it works or it doesn't. Let's not worry too much about the report working. Just go and take a look in the browser cache (in Internet Explorer 6.0, Tools | Internet Options | Settings | View Files). There you will see the URL with the user name and an encrypted form of the password:

```
dspe:AdventureWorks=<encrypted password>
```

It is not the initial request from the Report Manager that's spilling the beans because that uses a POST, as we'll discuss in a minute, and so the credentials are passed there in the HTTP header. It's all the requests for resources like report images and charts that the report will request with GET, and that's where the password is exposed in the URL. Well, at least the password in the URL is encrypted! But here's the stinger. The *encrypted* form of the password and the plaintext user ID can be harvested and rerun against other reports that require prompted credentials. Oops. What's worse is if your friendly users with a problem have the ability to publish reports to, say, a My Reports folder and also happen to be of malevolent intent, or let people of malevolent intent use their machine. In this case, they can easily create a report that executes any T-SQL using prompted credentials. They can also use the harvested encrypted form of the super user credentials you kindly left for them in their browser cache. This is Trojan Reports all over again. So, beware that prompted credentials are only as secure as the Access Control Lists guarding the browser caches as well as others' physical access to those machines! We discussed this with the development team. While they are addressing this, it can't be fixed in a stored procedure. However, they have placed it high on the list of things to be attended to in SP2. We hope this problem will eventually go away.

Passing Report Parameters in a URL

If the report that you want to launch has Report Parameters, you can simply pass them in the URL. Here is an example of passing the EmpID, ReportMonth, and ReportYear Report Parameters into the Employee Sales Summary sample report:

```
https://<Server>/ReportServer?/Sample+Reports/Employeeø
+Sales+Summary&rs:Command=Render&EmpID=31&ReportMonth=5&ReportYear=2004
```

There are a number of things to note about Report Parameters passing in the URL:

- They do not take a prefix.
- They are case sensitive.
- You don't have to pass all the parameters, but if there are no default values assigned for the missing parameters the report pre-populates the parameter collection frame with the values you have supplied, but the report won't be viewable until the user has completed all the required parameters.
- If you pass illegal types to parameters, the Report Server chokes. For example, the EmpID is an integer type, so if you were to pass it a string, the server would return an appropriate error message.
- Similarly, if you pass more parameters than are required, the Report Server will cough and also give you an error message. You might wonder why one would supply more parameters than necessary. Well, when creating HTML forms, you might inadvertently do that by naming a control. We'll illustrate that in a minute.

HTML Forms—HTTP Postback

Report Parameters can be sent to the server as the result of an HTTP Postback from an HTML web form instead of in the URL. The documentation tells you that the advantage of this approach is that the URL is limited to about 2 KB in length. Using the Post method gets around this issue by placing the parameters into the Postback Header and not in the URL. This is correct but misleading. That's because despite the initial request hitting the server in that way, the subsequent interactivity with the server when rendering the report involves putting some of those parameters back into URLs, which get recorded into the browser's cache. So, don't think that just because you aren't passing the parameters in the URL that they are completely concealed. In addition, if the length of all your Report Parameters takes up more than 2 KB, expect problems.

Try this out: Open Visual Notepad and create the web form shown in Listing 10.4 to call the Territory Sales Drilldown report. We've included this file, named TerritorySalesDrilldown.htm, in the chapter's supporting folder. Don't forget that you will need to change the <server> to your own server.

Listing 10.4 A Web Page to Call the Territory Sales Drilldown Report

```
<!DOCTYPE HTML PUBLIC "-//W3C//DTD HTML 4.0 Transitional//EN">
<HTML>
<HEAD>
<TITLE>Territory Sales Drilldown</TITLE>
</HEAD>
<BODY>
 <FORM id="frmRender" action= "https://<server>/reportserver↵
  ?/Sample Reports/Territory Sales Drilldown"
      method="post" target="_self">
  <INPUT type="hidden" name="rs:Command" value="Render">
  <INPUT type="hidden" name="rs:Format" value="HTML4.0">
  <INPUT type="submit" value="View Report">
 </FORM>
</HTML>
```

Before viewing this in a web browser, take a moment to clear your web browser's cache. Use Tools | Internet Options, and then select to clear the History and also to Delete Files. Okay, so you might not want to do that with your main account—especially if you know you have interesting things in your history or cache that you want to keep. In this case, start your web browser with a Test

User account, as we showed you in Chapter 4. Use this web browser session, and clear its cache and history.

At this point, open the TerritorySalesDrilldown.htm file with the web browser. All you will see is a single button labeled View Report. Click that button, and note what gets placed in the URL (as shown in Figure 10.6):

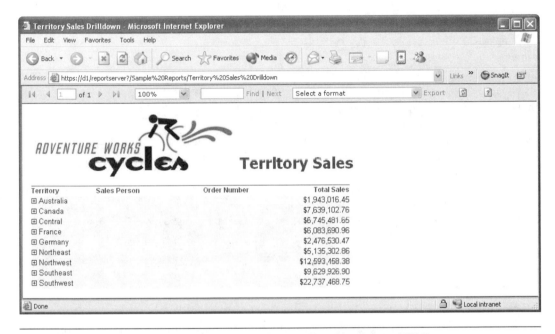

Figure 10.6 The Territory Sales Drilldown Report Rendered from HTML

There appears to be no `&rs:Command=Render` and no `&rs:Format=HTML4.0` in the URL. Indeed, these are passed to the server in the Header, but take a look at the cache. You'll see that some of the subsequent calls for images and other items construct long URLs with many of the parameters put back in. Sigh.

If you look closely at the HTML in Listing 10.4 and Listing 10.5, you'll see that parameters are passed by giving the names of the HTML elements of the parameters that they target. If we wanted to create an HTML form that launched the Employee Sales Summary report that takes parameters of EmpID, ReportMonth, and ReportYear, we need to create HTML elements named EmpID, ReportMonth, and

ReportYear and place them inside the HTML form that targets the report URL, as shown in Listing 10.5.

Listing 10.5 A Web Page to Launch the Employee Sales Summary Report with Hidden Parameters

```
<!DOCTYPE HTML PUBLIC "-//W3C//DTD HTML 4.0 Transitional//EN">
<HTML>
<HEAD>
<TITLE>Employee Sales Summary</TITLE>
</HEAD>
<BODY>
<FORM id="frmRender" action=
"https://<Server>/reportserver?/Sample Reports/Employee Sales Summary"
        method="post" target="_self">
<INPUT type="hidden" name="rs:Command" value="Render">
<INPUT type="hidden" name="rs:Format" value="HTML4.0">
<INPUT type="hidden" name="rc:Toolbar" value="false">
Employee <INPUT type="text" name="EmpID" value="35"><BR>
Month <INPUT type="text" name="ReportMonth" value="5"><BR>
Year <INPUT type="text" name="ReportYear" value="2004"><BR>
<INPUT type="submit" value="View Report">
</FORM>
</BODY>
</HTML>
```

In passing, we would like to make another point—which old hands at HMTL are aware of—regarding the FORM element's target attribute. We've targeted _self but you could instead use a named child window or IFRAME element, or just for fun you could set this to _search.

Prompted Credentials in HTML Postbacks

The story here is much nicer than that of raw URL access. In our testing, we've not seen the credentials encrypted or left behind in the browser cache when passed to the Report Server in an HTML Postback. To check this out, you could change the Employee Sales Summary report to use a DataSource that has prompted credentials. At this point, you can add two HTML elements for the user name and the password. Assuming that the DataSource for the report is named AdventureWorks, you would put this in an HTML form, as shown in Listing 10.6:

Listing 10.6 A Web Page to Launch the Employee Sales Summary Report with Prompted Credentials

```
<!DOCTYPE HTML PUBLIC "-//W3C//DTD HTML 4.0 Transitional//EN">
<HTML>
<HEAD>
<TITLE>Employee Sales Summary Prompted Credentials</TITLE>
</HEAD>
<BODY>
<FORM id="frmRender" action=
"https://<Server>/reportserver?/Sample Reports/Employee Sales Summary"
        method="post" target="_self">
<INPUT type="hidden" name="rs:Command" value="Render">
<INPUT type="hidden" name="rs:Format" value="HTML4.0">
<INPUT type="hidden" name="rc:Toolbar" value="false">
Employee <INPUT type="text" name="EmpID" value="35"><BR>
Month <INPUT type="text" name="ReportMonth" value="5"><BR>
Year <INPUT type="text" name="ReportYear" value="2004"><BR>
User Name <INPUT type="text" name="dsu:AdventureWorks"><BR>
Password <INPUT type="password" name="dsp:AdventureWorks">
<INPUT type="submit" value="View Report">
</FORM>
</BODY>
</HTML>
```

Service Pack 1

Service Pack 1 introduces three new URL parameters:

- `rs:ParameterLanguage`
- `rc:Parameters`
- `rc:StyleSheet`

The `rs:ParameterLanguage` parameter specifies the culture used to interpret the parameters passed. Before SP1 (and if you don't include this URL parameter), the Report Server interprets the parameters using the the web browser language setting. This occasionally causes problems when passing dates. After SP1, you can pass parameters containing dates, specifying the format. The `rs:ParameterLanguage` parameter informs the Report Server of how it should interpret the dates. Within a URL, `rs:ParameterLanguage` takes values such as

`&rs:ParameterLanguage=en-us`

or

`&rs:ParameterLanguage=en-gb`

etc.

The new URL `rc:Parameters` parameter directs the Report Server in how it should treat the parameters area on a report. It can take three values:

- `&rc:Parameters=true` This is the default and enables the parameters area to be visible.
- `&rc:Parameters=false` The parameters area is not sent to the browser, and cannot be expanded.
- `&rc:Parameters=Collapsed` The parameters area is sent to the browser, but is displayed collapsed so the user must expand the parameters area to see the parameters.

The new URL `rc:StyleSheet` parameter permits a customized Style sheet to be used by the browser when rendering a report inside the HTML viewer. SP1 puts a sample Style sheet called HTMLViewer.css in the *Program Files\Microsoft SQL Server\ MSSQL\Reporting Services\ReportServer\Styles* folder. You can use this Style sheet as a template for your own styles, which must be saved in the same folder. For example, to address "MyCustomStyle" you would code: `&rc:StyleSheet=MyCustomStyle`. It's important to note that although the Style sheet is assigned the extension .css, you don't specify .css in the URL parameter.

Final Thoughts

Given that you know how to extract the encrypted form of the credentials out of the cache, you can change the password parameter used in Listing 10.6 to work with `dspe:AdventureWorks`. But you need to put the long encrypted form of the password into the value programmatically. Beware that a user would be able to select View Source and extract the encrypted credentials, and we're off into the land of the Trojans again. You might recall from Chapter 4 that we uploaded an HTML form into the Report Server. You can upload these pages into your Report Server and use them to collect parameters in a more controllable way than the Parameter's dialog supports—give it a try, by all means.

If you then look at the HTML page with the Report Manager, you'll find that the Report Manager considers it to be a resource and wraps an inconvenient border around it. Take heart—the next chapter is all about customizing the Report Manager, and we'll tell you what you can do about that border.

Summary

This chapter ventured into the back alleys and narrow streets behind the scenes of the Report Server URL interface. We talked about how to launch reports using URL access as well as how to use the rs.exe script tool. We saw how easy it is to harvest encrypted connections, and (hopefully) you understand now how to avoid situations in which your credentials can be compromised.

CHAPTER 11

Customizing the Report Manager

Report developers the world over have been literally frantic to know whether they can customize the Report Manager. These folks are motivated by the end users, DBAs, and others who use the out-of-the-box Report Manager and just want more. Some are used to working with rich-client applications or custom-written (or control-rich) ASP applications. Sure, we think the Report Manager is indeed a superb ASP.NET application, but some things about it could use a bit more polish. Microsoft isn't deaf, so we expect that many of these issues are on the short list to be addressed in the next version.

An example of an area that needs a bit of help is that in Reporting Services, one of the most often bemoaned problems is Report Manager's inability to expose a multi-select list box to collect Report Parameter values. This has led to a bit of picketing outside Building 35 on the Microsoft Campus—report developers are desperate for Microsoft to release the source code to the Report Manager. This would allow them to customize the code to add their own tweaks, bells, and whistles. The good news is the official word from Microsoft is that the Report Manager source code *will* be made available to everyone and anyone who wants it—as soon as the sun starts sinking in the East. We're not sure if that means Sun stock, but we don't expect Microsoft to release any source before our book goes to press. Unfortunately, if you go poking around the assemblies you'll see that they've been obfuscated to protect intellectual property.

The *real* official word is that if the Report Manager doesn't handle all your needs, you should create your own Report Manager application from scratch, building on the formally supported SOAP interface. To make this "easy," Microsoft provides a starter sample application—all you need to do is add a bit of flour, an egg, and a cup of water. Building your own application against the SOAP interface has its benefits. That's because these SOAP interfaces will be supported long into the future—kinda like ADO classic has been supported for many years. We think that building (testing, debugging, and supporting) your own Report Manager with all the richness of the current Report Manager won't be a trivial undertaking, especially when all you wanted was to have a mechanism for supporting, say, multiselect list boxes in parameter collections. We figure you'll need six months or so to do this in C++, a few weeks in C#, and a few days in Visual Basic .NET to build a Report Manager as fully functional as the one true Report Manager. After you finish, you'll have to keep others from stealing the code. You'll also bear the burden of keeping it current and your users supported when stuff changes—and it always does.

Yeah, yeah, Bill. Yawn. I guess you want to gloss over that Voldemort Basic's SOAP proxy class wizard you'd have to use puts an Option Strict Off in the proxy class. But then the followers of Voldemort have not really understood performance. (Check out Chapter 9¾ for the scoop on SOAP).

–Peter

We'll show you in this chapter how to do things with the Report Manager that the accepted wisdom says can't be done. Let us know how well we did with the information by posting on our website, www.SQLReportingServices.NET, and let us know any additional tricks you find.

Bear in mind, though, that the tricks and interface hooks that we show you here are not all formally supported and might not work in the next version. However, the upside is that for the effort required (just a few minutes) you can short-circuit several days, if not months, of development time.

Simple Customizations—Tuning the CSS File and Graphics Objects

The Report Manager is simply an ASP.NET application. This means there are some easily accessible places where you can quickly (and safely) change its look and feel. Navigate to the subfolders under *C:\Program Files\Microsoft SQL Server\MSSQL\Reporting Services\ ReportManager*—in particular, look at the Images and Styles subfolders. Microsoft deliberately ensured that these files were external to the Report Manager's assemblies so that there could be a degree of end-user customization. The next few sections discuss how to customize the Report Manager using the custom images and cascading style sheets found in these folders.

The Images Folder

All the image icons used in the Report Manager come from graphics files stored in the *C:\Program Files\Microsoft SQL Server\MSSQL\ Reporting Services\ReportManager\images* folder. Substituting your own images with the same names works pretty well. Would you want to? Well, that is up to you—perhaps you might want to use animated GIF files to add a little more user interactivity. However, while we said all image icons used in the Report Manager come from this folder, understand that the image files used by the Report Server are extracted from the ReportingServicesWebServer.DLL, and you can't change those as easily. In addition, Report Manager "hosts" certain pages from the Report Server in IFRAMES. On systems using lower resolution, this IFRAME border takes up quite a bit of screen space.

The Report Manager Cascading Style Sheet

When the Report Manager transmits a web page over the network, the user's browser also links in a cascading style sheet named ReportingServices.CSS. If you view the source of a Report Manager page, you'll see that in the beginning of the page (see Listing 11.1):

Listing 11.1 A Snippet from the ReportingServices.CSS File

```
<!DOCTYPE HTML PUBLIC "-//W3C//DTD HTML 4.0 Transitional//EN" >
<HTML>
<HEAD>
<script language="JScript" type="text/Javascript"
src="/Reports/js/ReportingServices.js"></script>

<TITLE>Report Manager</TITLE>
<link href="/Reports/styles/ReportingServices.css"type="text/css" rel="stylesheet">
....
```

You can edit the ReportingServices.CSS file in Visual Studio .NET 2003, but before you do, do yourself a big favor and make a backup of the file. Don't complain to us that you had to reinstall Reporting Services 'cause you pooched this file.

Many of the HTML elements that the Report Manager sends to the web browser have class attributes associated with them. Listing 11.2 shows a snippet from a web page of the Report Manager's Home folder, where it displays "! NEW" next to a new report item in a folder.

Listing 11.2 A Couple of Class Attributes from the ReportingServices.CSS File

```
<font class="msrs-newPunc">!</font>
<font class="msrs-newText">NEW</font></td>
```

(We have a new subfolder in our Home folder, and as you might have noticed new report items are flagged by default with green "! NEW" text.) The web browser looks up these classes in the cascading style sheet and applies the styles it finds when displaying these elements. Take a look in the ReportingServices.CSS file. If you open it in Visual Studio, you can search for the classes shown in Listing 11.3 either in the file or in the CSS outline.

Listing 11.3 The Attributes in the CSS File That Control How New Items Are Marked

```
.msrs-newPunc
{
    font-family: Verdana, Sans-Serif;
    font-size: x-small;
    font-weight: bold;
    color: Green;
}

.msrs-newText
{
    font-family: Verdana, Sans-Serif;
    font-size: xx-small;
    color: Green;
}
```

If you right-click on .msrs-newText, you can launch the Style Builder, as shown in Figure 11.1 from the Build Style… option. This gives you a visual interface on which to edit the selected entry in the CSS file. You can change other attributes from this dialog as well, but we'll get to that in a minute.

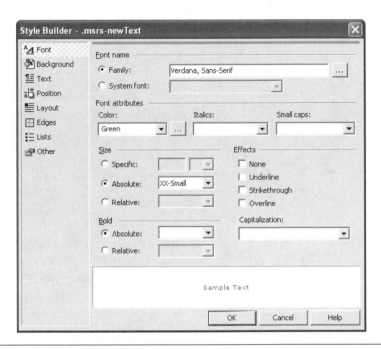

Figure 11.1 The Style Builder Dialog

We'll let you experiment with adjusting styles to see the effect. Just save the CSS file back to the *C:\Program Files\ Microsoft SQL Server\MSSQL\Reporting Services\ReportManager\ Styles* folder as ReportingServices.CSS, and launch the Report Manager to see your changes. Ah, did we tell you to do this on your own test server? If you don't, as you experiment the whole report user community gets to share the results—in real time. Just take your phone off the hook.

Adding Your Company Logo in the Report Manager

You might like to put your company or department's logo into the Report Manager. One way to do this would be to place your custom logo image file—say, logo.gif—in *C:\Program Files\ MicrosoftSQLServer\MSSQL\ReportingServices\ReportManager\ images* and adjust the BODY element in the CSS file to read as shown in Listing 11.4:

Listing 11.4 Adding a Custom Company Logo to the Report Manager

```
body {
    background-position: center 30px;
    background-image: url(..\images\logo.gif);
    background-repeat: no-repeat;
    margin: 0;
    font-size: x-small;
    font-family: Comic Sans MS, Sans-Serif;
}
```

If you use the Style Builder to help you locate your logo, be careful to edit the Background image to use a relative path, as shown in Figure 11.2, rather than an absolute one involving file:///. If you don't do that, you're likely to find that it doesn't work, and if you have SSL installed you'll start to see messages telling you that there is insecure content on the page when it is rendered.

If you put your own images into the folder at *C:\Program Files\ Microsoft SQL Server\MSSQL\Reporting Services\ReportManager\ images*, make sure you back up the CSS file to a different location so that the inevitable Service Pack that breaks your toys can be corrected.

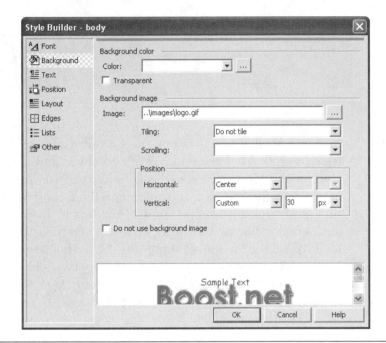

Figure 11.2 Using the Style Builder to Set the Background Image Attribute

Who said JavaScript was just the prototype for C#? I bet no one at Microsoft who still works for the company! By the way, Bill Vaughn is presently tied to his chair, duct tape over his mouth, and electrodes appropriately placed. Bill, this JavaScript won't hurt. Honest!

–Peter

<mmmmfs!>

–Bill

Adding Behavior

We want to work up to how you get to the hidden jewels of customizing the parameter collection area, but first we need to show you some JavaScript. JavaScript is code that runs in the client's web browser. We know that those curly braces {} are going to scare some, but there's no need to start hyperventilating (yet). We're going to make it look easy, and if your ultimate goal is to have your own custom parameter areas, we'll be giving you a working framework so that you don't have that much JavaScript to learn. Let's start with some simple JavaScript—a HelloWorld() MessageBox implemented by the code in Listing 11.5. Note that in JavaScript, MessageBoxes are called ***alert boxes***.

Listing 11.5 A Java Code Alert Box

```
function HelloWorld(){
   alert('Hello Bill');
}
```

Our first task shows how to wire this function up to the Report Manager. Well, it turns out that the CSS file can help us, along with what are called **behavior** files. Let's go ahead and incorporate this alert (ahem, MessageBox) to display when the user passes his or her mouse over the ! NEW text displayed in the Report Manager alongside newly uploaded report items. First, open Notepad and create the behavior file, as shown in Listing 11.6. Next, save the file as HelloWorld.htc in the *C:\Program Files\Microsoft SQL Server\ MSSQL\Reporting Services\ReportManager\js* folder, or create an htc subfolder in *C:\Program Files\Microsoft SQL Server\MSSQL\ Reporting Services\ReportManager*. This file is included in the chapter's supporting files.

Listing 11.6 The HelloWorld.htc Behavior File

```
<?XML version="1.0"?>
<COMPONENT id="bvrScriptlet1">
<REGISTRATION progid="BehaviorScriptlet"/>
<IMPLEMENTS type="Behavior">
   <ATTACH event="onmouseover" handler="HelloWorld"/>
</IMPLEMENTS>

[CDATA[[
   <SCRIPT language="javascript">
   function HelloWorld(){
      alert('HELLO Bill');
   }
</SCRIPT>
]]>

</COMPONENT>
```

As you can see, an htc behavior file is just an XML file that specifies the event(s) to which the behavior attaches, and which function

handles the event. One of the events to which we are attaching is
`onmouseover`, and that is handled by our `HelloWorld()` function.
Another point to note is that the function is encapsulated inside a
`[CDATA[[ ... ]]>`. If you read the MSDN examples as we did, we
found that there were issues concerning the placement of the `CDATA`
in relation to the embedded script. The MSDN examples need some
updating, but the example we give you here works. Once the
Microsoft folks read our book, we expect this to be corrected. What
a `CDATA` actually does is escape the containing text so that it won't be
confused as XML. Actually, you can place the function into the
ReportingServices.js file. In this case, you wouldn't need the `CDATA`
or the `SCRIPT`, but you would then be hostage when Microsoft
updates the ReportingServices.js file in a Service Pack.

So far we have a function, and we've described in the behavior
file which events it is to handle. However, we have not attached this
behavior to any HTML elements. The ! NEW is styled by two
entries in the CSS file: .msrs-newPunc and .msrs-newText. Locate
the .msrs-newPunc and .msrs-newText in the CSS file, and make the
changes shown in Listing 11.7. In this case, we change the color to
red, but the key to this is putting in the behavior with a relative URL
to the htc file.

Listing 11.7 The Modified .CSS File to Change the New Message to Red

```
.msrs-newPunc {
    padding-left: 5px;
    font-weight: bold;
    font-size: x-small;
    behavior: url(../js/HelloWorld.htc);
    color: red;
}

.msrs-newText {
    padding-left: 5px;
    font-weight: bold;
    font-size: x-small;
    behavior: url(../js/HelloWorld.htc);
    color: red;
}
```

If you save the CSS file at this point and open a new session of the Report Manager in a web browser, as you pass your mouse over any report items that have ! NEW displayed next to them the browser will deploy a MessageBox, as shown in Figure 11.3. Not particularly useful unless you want to bother Bill (and everyone else), but we have at least shown you how you can attach to events.

Figure 11.3   The JavaScript Alert Fired as We Hover over the ! New Notation

Customizing the Parameters Area

At long last—we're going to tell you how to manage Report Parameters. To solve this problem, you can take a number of approaches—one is to customize the Report Manager report parameter area displayed when a report has parameters that need to be collected from the user. There are two approaches: server side and client side. In this chapter, we'll take a look at the client-side approach. The server-side approach is far more complex because it requires some advanced techniques, and we would rather not go into that level of detail in this book.

To illustrate the approach, open a report that collects parameters from the user (the Employee Sales Summary is a good example). Right-click in the parameters area, and select View Source from the context menu. If you look closely at the HTML, as shown in Listing 11.8, you'll see an HTML form that is very similar to the HTML forms we were creating at the end of Chapter 10.

Listing 11.8 Snippet of a Parameter's Collection Form in the Report Manager

```
<form action=
"https://d1/ReportServer?%2fSample+Reports%2fEmployee+Sales+Summary"
onsubmit="javascript:return(ValidateParams())" method="post" id="oParamsForm">

<input name="rc:Area" type="hidden" value="Params" />
<input name="rc:LinkTarget" type="hidden" value="_top" />
<input name="rc:JavaScript" type="hidden" value="True" />
<input name="rc:Toolbar" type="hidden" value="True" />
<input name="rc:ReplacementRoot" type="hidden"
value="https://d1/Reports/Pages/Report.aspx?ServerUrl=" />
<input name="rc:AutoPostBack" type="hidden" value="" />
<input name="rs:ClearSession" type="hidden" value="true" />
<input name="rs:Format" type="hidden" value="HTML4.0" />
<input name="rs:Command" type="hidden" value="Render" />
<table id="oParamsGrid" cellpadding="0" cellspacing="0"
class="MenuBarBkGnd MaxSize ParamsGrid">
```

The first thing that this source code tells you is that the parameter's collection area is just a simple HTML web form—plain and simple. If you right-click in the top of the web page in the Report Manager and select View Source, you'll see that the report parameter area is being loaded into an IFRAME. If we can attach a behavior file to that IFRAME, we can attach our own function that handles the IFRAME `onload` event. That event handler can replace the contents of the frame with our own custom page. Because this is an IFRAME, we can get it to point off to any URL, including an ASP.NET page or some simple HTML page. In fact, these HTML pages can be stored inside the Report Server as resources. Let's see this in practice.

1. Ah, we didn't tell you the secret. The IFRAME doesn't have a class name of its own that the CSS file has already configured, so these next lines of code are worth their weight in gold. In the ReportingServices.CSS file, add the following lines of code (as shown in Listing 11.9), replacing <Server> with your Report Server.

Listing 11.9 The Key to the Puzzle—Addressing a Custom Behavior File on the IFRAME

```
table.msrs-contentFrame IFRAME {
    behavior: url(https://<Server>/Reports/js/CustomParameters.htc)
}
```

As if that's going to happen. Why can't one do this in Visual Basic Script? Okay, so it won't work in Netscape. That means 4.6 percent of the folks out there won't be able to use this feature.

–Bill

Sure, you can use Visual Basic Script, but the standard has been JavaScript and that's what Microsoft itself uses for its client-side scripting in Reporting Services.

–Peter

Yeah, there are a lot of Delphi and Java heads there too.

–Bill

This permits us to create an htc behavior file that implements our CustomParameters behavior whenever an IFRAME is rendered within a table that has the class of `msrs-contentFrame`. We're in by the back door!

2. Let's now take a look at the behavior file. This we configure to attach a function to the `onload` event. All our function has to do is examine the IFRAME URL, and if it's the URL of a parameter-driven report that we'd like to intercept, the IFRAME URL is replaced with our chosen code. Very crudely, we have done this by matching the entire URL and using a JavaScript `switch` statement. If it matches, we call our own function, `replaceUrl()`, that replaces the URL. The `replaceUrl()` does a little dancing as it writes a blank space to the screen. This has the effect of blanking out anything that might have been momentarily displayed from the location of the previous page. Next we manipulate the history before finally replacing the IFRAME URL. Oh, one other thing. When we replace the IFRAME URL, its `onload` fires again. To deal with this, we maintain a variable `_custParamsLoaded` as a flag to determine whether we have already changed the URL. This prevents an endless loop. Once you become proficient at JavaScript, you should be able to optimize this. Listing 11.10 implements the custom behavior.

Listing 11.10 The CustomParameters.htc Behavior File

```
<?XML version="1.0"?>
<COMPONENT id="bvrScriptlet1">
<REGISTRATION progid="BehaviorScriptlet"/>
<IMPLEMENTS type="Behavior">
    <ATTACH event="onload" handler="CustomParameters"/>
</IMPLEMENTS>
```

```
[CDATA[
<SCRIPT language="javascript">
var _custParamsLoaded = 0;

function CustomParameters(){
  if ( _custParamsLoaded == 0) {
  _custParamsLoaded = 1;
  switch ( window.frames.item(0).location.href ){
    case 'https://d1/ReportServer?%2fParams%2fEmployees↵
    &rs:Command=Render↵
    &rc:ReplacementRoot=https://d1/Reports/Pages/Report.aspx↵
    ?ServerUrl=' :
                replaceUrl('https://d1/RSParameters/Parameters.aspx');
                break;
    case  'https://d1/ReportServer?%2fParams%2fStatesSales&rs:Command=Render↵
    &rc:ReplacementRoot=https://d1/Reports/Pages/Report.aspx↵
    ?ServerUrl=' :
                replaceUrl('https://d1/RSParameters/USA_StateMap.htm');
                break;
  }
  }
}

function replaceUrl(target)
{
  window.frames.item(0).document.writeln(' ');
  window.frames.item(0).history.go(-1);
  window.frames.item(0).location.replace(target);
}
</SCRIPT>
]]>

</COMPONENT>
```

If you're going to work with the CustomParameters.htc file that we supply in this chapter's supporting files, you need to remove the `case` statements that target our server and replace them with `case` statements that target your own servers:

```
case '<Requested URL for your Report>':
    replaceUrl('<URL of your Custom Parameters>');
break;
```

Let's take a look at this in practice with a report that provides the much-requested multiple-select functionality with custom parameters.

Multiple-Value Select Report Example

Before we plough into hooking up a multiple-value select, we want to take a step back and consider the underlying query string for the DataSet. We want to discourage you from executing SQL strings containing Report Parameters. That's because this (very common) approach provides an opportunity for SQL injection. Consider the following query:

```
SELECT EmployeeID, FirstName, LastName, MiddleName, NameStyle, Title FROM Employee
WHERE EmployeeID IN (1,2,3,4,5)
```

Wouldn't it be cool if you could replace (1,2,3,4,5) with a parameter like:

```
SELECT EmployeeID, FirstName, LastName, MiddleName, NameStyle, Title FROM Employee
WHERE EmployeeID IN (@parameter)
```

Well, this SQL syntax won't work unless the @parameter happens to be an integer. You have to change the SELECT to be something like this:

```
EXECUTE ('SELECT EmployeeID, FirstName, LastName, MiddleName,⏎
         NameStyle, Title
         FROM Employee
         WHERE EmployeeID IN (' + @parameter + ')')
```

This works by creating a string for SQL Server to execute, and you can supply the @parameter as a string of "1,2,3,4,n".

But what if someone provides the @parameter as:

```
4);INSERT INTO Employee(FirstName,LastName)VALUES(1,2)--
```

That's called **SQL injection**, and although it only adds an entry to a table (subject, of course, to the permissions granted by the Data Source object), the injected SQL could be much more damaging— and it has been. We can't emphasize how serious SQL injection attacks have become. Whenever you accept parameters from a user or another application, you must make *sure* that the values supplied are within the range and datatype expected.

Let's show you a much more secure way to do this, by using a Table-valued function, as shown in Listing 11.11. ParamParserFn.sql is included in the supporting files for the chapter.

Listing 11.11 ParamParserFn.sql

```
CREATE FUNCTION ParamParserFn( @delimString varchar(255) )
RETURNS @paramtable
TABLE ( Id int )
AS BEGIN

DECLARE @len int,
        @index int,
        @nextindex int

SET @len = DATALENGTH(@delimString)
SET @index = 0
SET @nextindex = 0



WHILE (@len > @index )
BEGIN

SET @nextindex = CHARINDEX(';', @delimString, @index)

if (@nextindex = 0 ) SET @nextindex = @len + 2

 INSERT @paramtable
 SELECT SUBSTRING( @delimString, @index, @nextindex - @index )


SET @index = @nextindex + 1

END
 RETURN
END
```

This function takes a delimited string such as "3;4;5;6;" and returns a SQL table with a column named "Id" and one row for each of the delimited values, as shown in Figure 11.4.

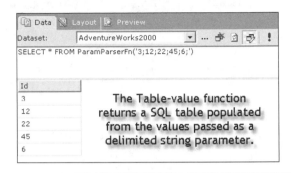

Figure 11.4 Testing the Table-Value Function ParamParserFn

This means that we can use this function as if it were a table in our DataSet query using parameters, as shown in Listing 11.12:

Listing 11.12 A SQL Query That Accepts a Parameter Argument Passed to the ParamParserFn Function

```
SELECT   Employee.EmployeeID, Employee.FirstName, Employee.LastName,
         Employee.MiddleName
FROM     Employee
INNER JOIN ParamParserFn(@Param) ParamParserFn
ON Employee.EmployeeID = ParamParserFn.Id
```

TIP *Caution* A word of caution about the Query Designers. While the GUI Query Designer can help you find tables and functions, it is a little challenged when it comes to dealing with parameters being passed into functions. Be prepared to flip over into the generic query designer before trying to execute a query that includes a Table-valued function.

Okay, so after that security briefing, we've covered the background for dealing with a multiple-value select. Next we'll need a way of coercing multiple values into a single parameter to use in a query. Let's build a report that uses the query we showed you in Listing 11.12 for its Data Source and populates a Table control. We've included the report definition in the supporting files. You need to upload it into the Sample Reports folder, and run the ParamParseFn.sql so that it's installed in the AdventureWorks2000 database. Figure 11.5 shows this test report in the Visual Studio .NET Report Designer. Once the report is working in the designer, deploy it to the Sample Reports folder on the Report Server.

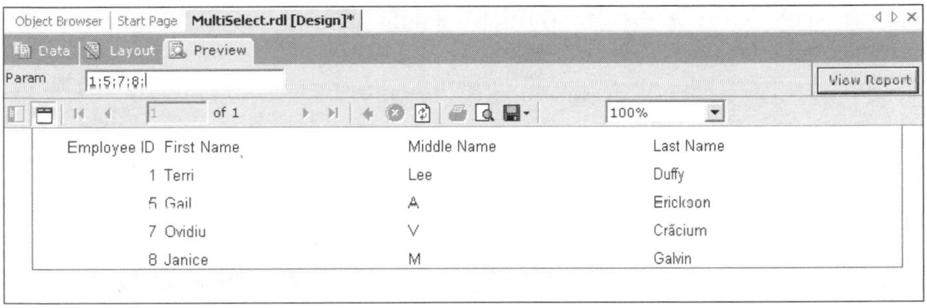

Figure 11.5 A Preview of Our Report Populated from a Parameterized-Like Expression

The next step is to build a simple HTML web page that calls the managed report in a Postback. For now, we'll just get things hooked up to a simple textbox. Listing 11.13 shows the HTML you'll need to get started.

Listing 11.13 HTML Source for MultipleSelects1.htm

```
<!DOCTYPE HTML PUBLIC "-//W3C//DTD HTML 4.0 Transitional//EN">
<HTML>
<HEAD>
<TITLE>Multiple Value Selects Part 1</TITLE>
</HEAD>
```
continues

```
<BODY>
  <FORM id="frmExample" action=
    "https://<Server>/Reportserver?/Sample+Reports/MultiSelect"
     method="post" target="_self">
    <INPUT type="hidden" value="Render" name="rs:Command">
    <INPUT type="hidden" value="main" name="rc:LinkTarget">
    <INPUT type="hidden" value="HTML4.0" name="rs:Format">
    <INPUT type="hidden" value="false" name="rc:Parameters">
    <INPUT id="Param" type="text" name="Param">
    <INPUT id="Button1" type="submit" value="View Report">
  </FORM>
</BODY>
</HTML>
```

If you've been following along, you should be able to enter a set of semicolon-delimited values and click View Report to get the managed report to launch, as shown in Figure 11.6.

Figure 11.6 MultipleSelects1.htm as Rendered in a Web Browser

Before we go on, let's take a closer look at Listing 11.13. We just talked about passing the `rs:` and `rc:` parameters and why we've hidden them. Note that we're using an ordinary HTML INPUT element of type Text named Param. We'll be changing the type of this INPUT element to hidden in just a moment after we've introduced a list box (a SELECT element) that enables us to implement multiple-value selects. Also note that the Submit button doesn't have a name—if you add the Submit button with the Visual Studio .NET designer, it will probably give it a name. In this case, the name is passed to the Report Server, which looks for a parameter of that name. Reporting Services chokes if it doesn't find one, so don't forget to remove the name attribute on the Submit button.

We're ready to try something a bit more sophisticated by adding an HTML SELECT to the page and hardcode some OPTION values into this SELECT. We'll have a few comments to make about getting dynamic content for the OPTION values later on, but let's get the basics out of the way first. Listing 11.14 shows the HTML for the form. Just replace the <FORM... block in Listing 11.13 with the <FORM... block in Listing 11.14.

Listing 11.14 The <FORM... Block to Add a SELECT List to Our Web Page

```
<FORM id="frmExample" action=
  "https://<server>/Reportserver?/Sample+Reports/MultiSelect"
    method="post" target="_self">
  <INPUT type="hidden" value="Render" name="rs:Command">
  <INPUT type="hidden" value="main" name="rc:LinkTarget">
  <INPUT type="hidden" value="HTML4.0" name="rs:Format">
  <INPUT type="hidden" value="false" name="rc:Parameters">
  <INPUT id="Param" type="text" name="Param">
  <SELECT id="Select1" multiple size="10">
    <OPTION value="1">Employee 1</OPTION>
    <OPTION value="2">Employee 2</OPTION>
    <OPTION value="3">Employee 3</OPTION>
    <OPTION value="4">Employee 4</OPTION>
    <OPTION value="5">Employee 5</OPTION>
    <OPTION value="6">Employee 6</OPTION>
    <OPTION value="7">Employee 7</OPTION>
  </SELECT>
<INPUT id="Button1" type="submit"
onclick="Submitting(frmExample)" value="View Report">
</FORM>
```

Stop hyperventilating,
Bill. There aren't too
many curly braces!
–Peter

I'm still peeling tape
off my mouth....
–Bill

Take note of these issues in Listing 11.14: First, we introduce an HTML SELECT that has been marked for "multiple" so that it permits the user to hold down the Ctrl key while selecting several items using the mouse. It has no name attribute for reasons we just discussed. We also slip in a call to a JavaScript function named `Submitting()`, which accepts the form object as a parameter.

The `Submitting()` function shown in Listing 11.15 populates the HTML INPUT element Param with the delimited string of the selected values. This code block needs to be inserted in the HTML in Listing 11.14 below the BODY and above the FORM elements.

Listing 11.15 A JavaScript Code Block to Populate the Delimited-String Parameter List

```
<BODY>
<SCRIPT language="javascript">
<!--
var _submitted = 0

function Submitting(frm)
{
  var allvals='';

  for (var Current=0;Current < frm.Select1.length;Current++){
    var value = eval('frm.currentValue' + Current);
    if (frm.Select1[Current].selected) {
      value = frm.Select1[Current].value;
      allvals=allvals + value + ';' ;
    }
    else {
      value = '';
    }
  }
  frm.Param.value = allvals;
  _submitted=_submitted+1;
}
-->
</SCRIPT>
<FORM ...
```

Update the URL for the form's *Action* property to point to your own Report Server if you haven't already done that. Save the new HTML to a file named MultipleSelects2.htm. Yes, you'll find a version of MultipleSelects2.htm in the supporting files. Open this new file with a web browser. Figure 11.7 shows what you'll see momentarily when you click the View Report button.

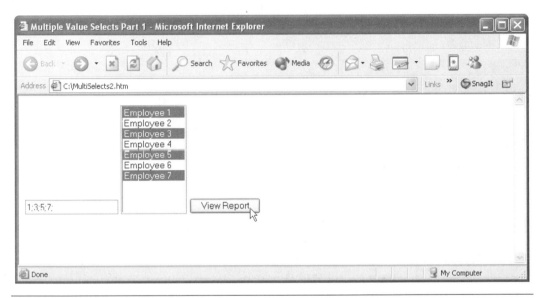

Figure 11.7 The `MultiSelect` Web Page to Feed the ParamParserFn

After you choose one or more employees from the SELECT list and click View Report, the Submitting JavaScript function fires and populates the Param INPUT element, submits that delimited string to the Report Server in a Post, and waits for the response shown in Figure 11.8. If you get an error that talks about button1, it means you forgot to remove the Name attribute from the button1 element. Go back three squares and try again.

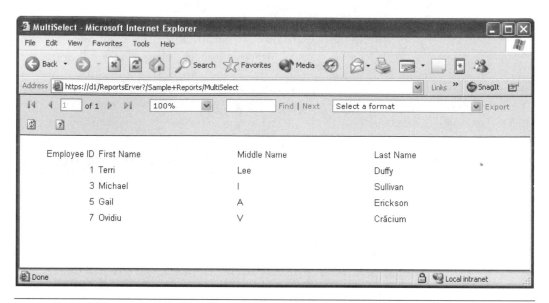

Figure 11.8 The Report Generated from Our Multiple-Parameter Pick List

Now that the Param INPUT box is working, we can change its type from "text" to "hidden." Look at the file MultiSelects3.htm in the supporting files to see how this change is applied. At this point, we have an HTML web form that we can store anywhere. It could be on a file share, or we could even place it in a folder on a web server and access it by URL—anywhere our users can get to it and launch the report. Ideally, we'd like the web form to take advantage of our Reporting Services security scheme, so that it can't be seen by users who don't have permissions to see it. The best approach is to upload the HTML form to the Report Server as a resource (as shown in Figure 11.9) to be available in the Report Manager.

And "yes," the MultiSelects3.htm file can be launched directly in the Report Manager, but aesthetically you'll have a problem because the Report Manager considers this to be a resource and frames it differently. When your user launches the HTM page in the Report Manager, the View and Properties tabs think that the content is a resource rather than a report. As a result, a white border is placed around the content area. That makes the report look a bit detached, as shown in Figure 11.10 and Figure 11.11.

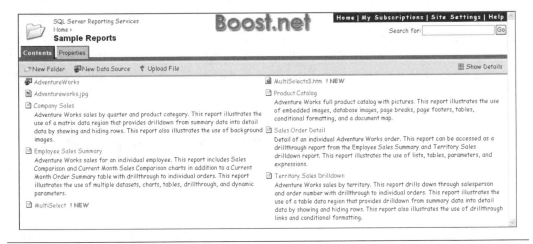

Figure 11.9 The MultiSelects3 Web Page After Uploading to the Sample Reports Folder

Figure 11.10 Launching the MultiSelects3.htm Page in the Report Manager

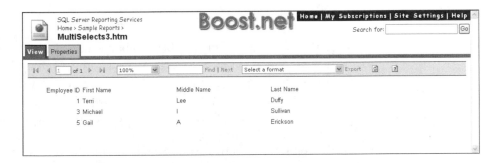

Figure 11.11 The Report Generated from the MultiSelects3.htm Page

When you launch the real report in the browser, you'll still get the real report's parameter collection—but at least the report won't be framed with a large white border. However, let's try it because we need to snag a URL. Launch the real MultiSelect report, as shown in Figure 11.12.

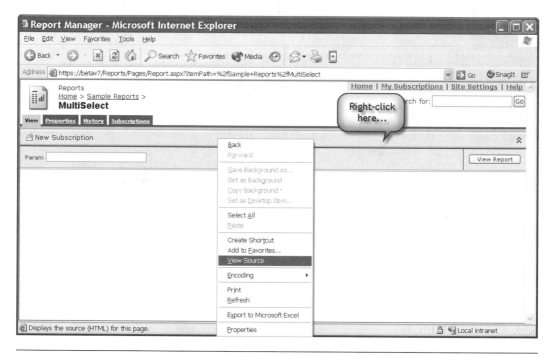

Figure 11.12 The Real MultiSelect Report as Rendered in the Report Manager

It's important to right-click in the toolbar area (as shown in Figure 11.12) and choose View Source from that context menu. The web page source you'll see has different IFRAMES, and we want to address the src URL of the present content area frame. Search the HTML source for "IFRAME" where the call is made to the ReportServer for the Report. We've extracted that section (and reformatted it to fit in the book), as shown in Listing 11.16.

Listing 11.16 Snippet of the HTML Source for the MultiSelect Report When Displayed in the Report Manager

```
<tr>
  <td valign="top" height="100%">↵
    <IFRAME SRC="https://betav7/ReportServer?↵
      %2fSample+Reports%2fMultiSelect&amp;↵
      rs:Command=Render&amp;↵
      rc:ReplacementRoot=https://betav7/Reports/Pages/Report.aspx↵
      ?ServerUrl=" frameBorder="none" width="100%" height="100%"↵
      scrolling="auto">
    </IFRAME>
  </td>
</tr>
```

If you cut the URL of the IFRAME's src attribute, you should be able to paste it directly into the Address bar of a web browser. This verifies that it calls your report. This is the URL that we need to transfer back to the behavior file we created earlier by adding another case statement to the JavaScript. Before you do so, be sure to make one tiny edit—it's crucial to replace the "&" with just an "&" in the URL. Don't change anything else! Next, you'll need the URL of the custom parameter page, given that it's stored in the Report Server. The best way to find that is to navigate to https://<server>/ReportServer and search through the folder hierarchy until you find the custom parameter page you need. Cut and paste the URL from the Address bar into the replaceURL() function. The case statement that you should be adding to the CustomParameters.htc behavior file should look something like Listing 11.17. Be sure to substitute your paths and server names.

Listing 11.17 The JavaScript case Statement

```
case 'https://<your server>/ReportServer↵
?%2fSample+Reports%2fMultiSelect↵
  &rs:Command=Render↵
  &rc:ReplacementRoot=https://<your server>/Reports/Pages/Report.aspx↵
    ?ServerUrl=':replaceUrl('https:// <your server>/ReportServer?↵
      %2fSample+Reports%2fMultiSelects3.htm');
break;
```

That's more or less all there is to it. When you browse to the report with the Report Manager, it replaces the parameters area with your custom parameters collection area. It then displays the report correctly without the big white borders. One word of advice, though—your browser cache initially has the old version of the report and its parameter area loaded. Once you update the CustomParameters.htc file, be sure to flush your browser cache (Ctrl+F5) to load the latest version of CustomParameters.htc into your cache.

Using ASP.NET Web Forms for Parameter Collection

We've seen how we can use HTML web forms and an HTTP Post to the Report Server. This technique is good for static data in our multiple selects or custom parameter web forms where we don't need to do any complicated validation. It's also suitable when the initial option values for the HTML SELECT element are fixed. If, however, you would like to do complex parameters validation, and perhaps query a database for those option values, ASP.NET can provide the answer. We'll be posting some examples of that technique to our website, www.SQLReportingServices.NET. In principle, the technique is very much the same. We put a case in the htc behavior file that caches a custom parameters report that substitutes the ASP.NET web form URL. That form can interact with the user. If you provide the user with a View Report button that can target the Report Server with the final URL for the report with all the parameters configured, you're done.

Okay, so we told you all that you need to do to get custom parameter pages up and running, but it's a bit of a management nightmare. We'll be providing an integration tool on our website soon after publication that does all this manipulation for you while keeping all the gory details to itself.

Summary

This chapter showed you how to manipulate underlying HTML to change the way the Report Manager looks and behaves so that you can build custom versions of this tool for your own company. We also walked through an innovative (albeit convoluted) way to capture multiple parameters and use them to launch reports.

Managing Reports Using SOAP

As we've said many times in the preceding chapters, the Report Server is controlled through an XML web service. All web services communicate with the outside world through the Service Oriented Architecture Protocol (SOAP). SOAP is not that new. It evolved at Microsoft in early 1998 and was exposed to Visual Basic developers, along with the SOAP SDK, in the years that followed. Since then, it has been implemented as a way to create a remote-control mechanism for software running under IIS. Reporting Services is a fairly sophisticated example of this technology. As we'll see in this chapter, SOAP makes it easy to access some parts of the Report Processor to perform typical Reporting Services operations but difficult (and painfully slow) to perform others. But this chapter is not about SOAP—it's about how Reporting Services exposes its functionality through SOAP. We'll see how to use a Windows Forms application and SOAP to expose the reports, Data Sources, and other objects managed by the Report Server, all using SOAP. We'll also show you how to setup an ASP page to launch reports, and if you're smart you'll see the missing link—how to implement server-side printing.

If you're new to SOAP, you'll soon be able to stop wondering why. Hitherto, people kept a good distance from you, holding their breath and communicating only through gestures when sharing the same elevator space if you didn't maintain a close enough relationship to SOAP and a bit of water. But don't despair, a new world is about to open up for you. It's really quite easy—in fact it's as easy as hurtling full stride into a brick column with a school year's worth of luggage in tow (assuming you're heading for the right train platform). There should not be too much to worry about once you understand the references and incantations.

Like many things in the world of technology, it's the acronyms and buzzwords that make the simplest of things scary and frighten people away when really there is no need. We have to admit, though, when we first heard people talking of needing a ***Whizzdle***[1] file, we thought it was the new more grown-up and politically correct term for a ***Piddle*** file.[2] Ahem! We understand the need for hydrolysis of this subject and the alchemy of tallow of goat and ash of beech. If you are still groping for understanding, take a look at www.deancoleman.com/whatissoap.htm, and then forget everything you read there because the real story and wizardry you'll be interested in starts here.

We've already explored the Report Server's URL interface and worked with it in Chapters 10 and 11. As we've said before, Report Server exposes a SOAP interface, and perhaps surprisingly for some, we've already been making use of it. The Report Manager and the Report Scripting Utility (rs.exe) make extensive use of the Report Server's SOAP interface. So, what is it? In its simplest terms, you can think of SOAP as yet another way that one program can make a second program do things for it, and be able to pass arguments and return values between the two. What makes SOAP powerful is that both programs do not need to be on the same machine, they just need to be able to communicate with each other over a network using HTTP or HTTPS. Visual Studio .NET 2003 and the .NET Framework make all of the implementation details easy, and for the most part once you've established a web reference to the Report Server's SOAP interface, it looks like any other class library that your program references. That's because that's precisely what you reference: a .NET proxy class library that the environment creates for you.

---

[1]   The real acronym is WSDL, and people pronounce it "wizzdle." And it is an XML file that describes the interface of web methods that can be called on an object.

[2]   Piddle files are used with Python. Piddle stands for Plug In Drawing Does Little Else: http://piddle.sourceforge.net/.

Prior to Adding a Web Reference—McGonagall's Strict Admonition

No, we're not talking about giving naughty students a good caning, but that's not a universally bad idea for a number of people I can think of.

–Bill

[waving his wand in a puff of smoke]: C#-no-more-is.

–Bill

Okay, Dumbledore Vaughn, we'll play your game, but it's going to need more than a magic spell to make Voldemort Basic .NET as fast as C# beyond make believe. Perhaps for the Whidbey, or is that the would-be, release?

–Peter

Before we add a web reference, let's take a short lesson on being strict. Open Visual Studio .NET 2003 and start a new Windows Forms project. Let's call the solution Example 9.75. To determine whether we should show you a C# project or a Voldemort Basic .NET Forms project, the area between Redmond and Huntington, England, witnessed lightning, thunder, several Nimbus 2000s flying, and a violent game of Quiditch, or was it Cobra attack helicopters and 7.62-mm miniguns at 50 paces? As a result, we didn't choose C# because we agreed that the C# folks are smart enough to put the semicolons and curly braces back in, and because we wanted to ensure that certain pacemaker batteries wouldn't need to be replaced before the book was complete.

Seriously, folks, there is a point to be made here. When it comes to Visual Basic .NET programming, there is a "go slow" switch—it's the Option Strict compiler directive. By default, Microsoft set this in Visual Basic .NET programs as "Off." This has the effect of making Visual Basic .NET slower, and also permits a plethora of errors that could otherwise be caught. If `Option Strict On` is set at compile time, many issues are exposed and the compiled code runs faster because it does not have to perform as much Visual Basic "handholding." Even in the Reporting Services BOL and samples, Voldemort has his impact. Several examples have clearly been translated from C# but (clearly) have never been executed. These transmogrifications apparently compile, but they have runtime problems that `Option Strict On` would have caught. We've let our friends at Microsoft know, and they plan to fix those examples. The point to repeat as a mantra is that you should *always*[3] set `Option Strict On`.

---

[3] `Option Strict Off` provides maximum backward source code compatibility with Visual Basic 6.0 legacy code at the cost of runtime performance and trapping many runtime problems at design time.

Before we get started building our SOAP examples, let's ensure that the project properties are set for `Option Strict On`, as shown in Figure 9¾.1. Select the project on the context menu by right-clicking on the project and selecting Properties, on the dialog.

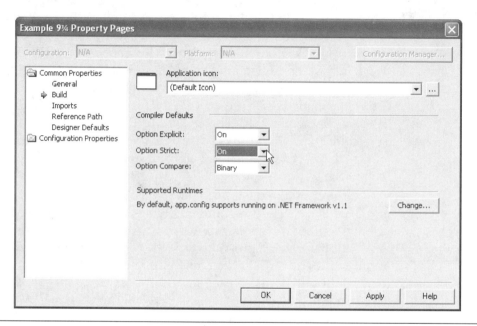

Figure 9¾.1 Setting `Option Strict On` at the Project Level

Adding a Web Reference

To address an XML web service, you need to add a "web reference" to the service. Launch the dialog to add a web reference to either a Visual Basic .NET 2003 or C# project:

- Through the Project menu's Add Web Reference...
- From the right-click context menu on the project in the Solution Explorer window

Use either of these approaches to launch the Add Web Reference dialog, as shown in Figure 9¾.2.

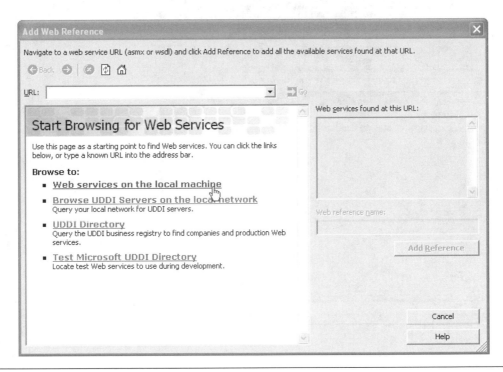

Figure 9¾.2 Adding a Web Reference

If you have everything installed on one development machine, you'll probably be drawn into browsing the web services on the local machine. Yes, you'll even find the Reporting Services web service there, as shown in Figure 9¾.3. But look closely and you'll see that the URL embeds "localhost." This is problematic, and Voldemort and his minions left behind a few gremlins and spider webs there to trip you up.

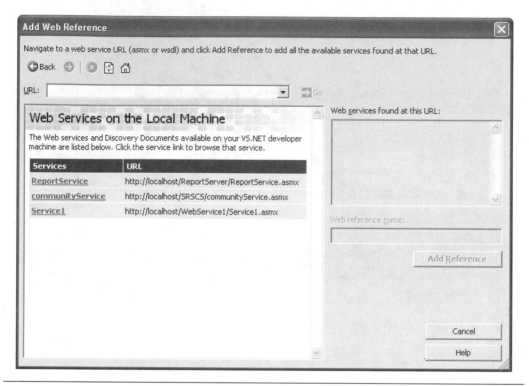

Figure 9¾.3 Browsing the Local Machine for Web Services

You see, all you have to do to spring the trap is click on the ReportService link in the Add Web Reference dialog, as shown in Figure 9¾.3. This displays all the Reporting Services interface's methods, as shown in Figure 9¾.4.

The trap that you just sprung is insidious and catches many folks unawares—even the folks at Microsoft were surprised. What happens is that a web request is sent to http://localhost/ReportServer/ReportService.asmx. That request returns the WSDL interface definition file. Visual Studio .NET 2003 subsequently passes this file over to the WSDL.exe program, which makes a proxy class that is included with the project. The underlying class constructor includes information from the WSDL file (as shown in Listing 9¾.1).

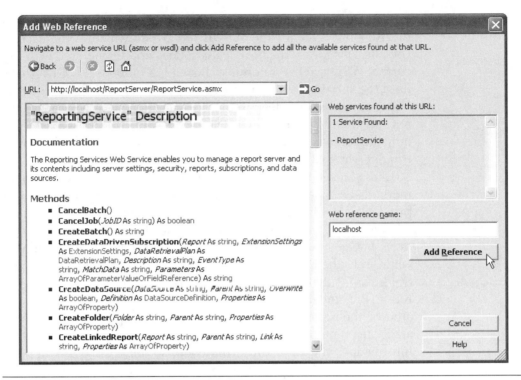

Figure 9¾.4 Springing the Trap—By Just Looking at the ReportService Interface

Listing 9¾.1 The Constructor Built (in Reference.VB) Contains the WSDL SOAP Address Location Attribute

```
Public Sub New()
    MyBase.New
    Me.Url = "http://localhost/ReportServer/ReportService.asmx"
End Sub
```

The problem is (until Microsoft fixes it) that the Report Server embeds an attribute <soap:address location= URL> into the WSDL file, and it embeds this URL string the first time it is asked for it, as shown in Listing 9¾.1. Then, any subsequent requests to the Report Server for the WSDL file are drawn from the cached version. This means the proxy class code is not regenerated with the correct WSDL SOAP reference. Instead, it embeds the URL that's used the very first time it was called. Ultimately, this location attribute gets embedded deep in the proxy class in areas where you are not supposed to go meddling. The WSDL SOAP address location is only flushed when the aspnet_wp.exe process is cycled. You might wonder why that would make a difference? Well, if you've installed SSL (as you should), the ReportService ASP code insists that some methods be called over HTTPS. When you realize that there is a problem, you might try to solve it by deleting the web reference and adding a new one—this time addressing the web service directly over https://<server>/ReportServer/ReportService.asmx. Indeed, when you then look at the new web reference in the Visual Studio .NET 2003 IDE you'll think that it setup the reference correctly. But under the covers in the proxy class constructor generated by the aspnet_wp.exe, it still has the <soap:address location> attribute pointing to the first URL. So, once you're armed with this information, you can fix it in the code, so don't worry if you have been browsing the Report Service addressing via http://localhost.

The next step is to choose a name for your web reference. In this case, we're using the BetaV7 server and we're going to name our reference AppReportService. Add the web reference by clicking on the Add Reference button, as shown in Figure 9¾.5. If you've been smart, you added the reference manually by selecting https://<yourserver>/ReportServer/ReportService.asmx after restarting IIS or recycling the aspnet_wp.exe process. This way, any residual web service reference is flushed before the URL that addresses your server is embedded.

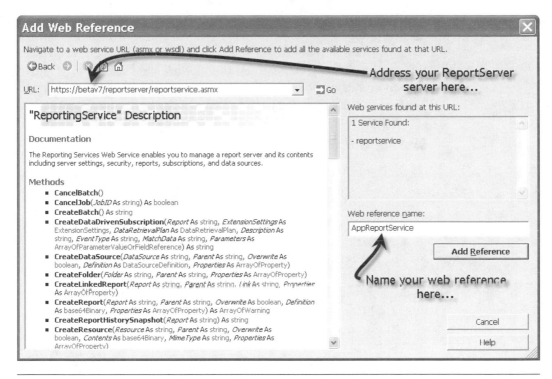

Figure 9¾.5 Providing a Name and Finally Adding the Reference

Once you click Add Reference, Visual Studio .NET 2003 works its magic and creates the proxy class. If you're curious what the 52 classes and 15 enums are, you can launch the Class Viewer (Ctrl+Shift+C) and browse around.

Before getting started, we need to add a global constant to the application to make it easier to reference the addressed Report Server. To this end, add the following two lines of code in the form's global address space (just above the Windows Form Designer-generated code block):

```
Public Const strReportServerURL As String =⏎
    https://<Your Report Server>/ReportServer/ReportService.asmx
```

This constant must be modified to address your Report Server. To setup our test application, we need to drag a mainmenu control from the toolbar onto the form in our Windows Forms project. Edit the top-level menu to read "Action." Next, add a Textbox control named txtResult, set the *Multiline* property to True, *Scrollbars* to Vertical, and *Text* property to "".

Listing the Secure Methods

As we mentioned, some methods on the Report Service can be called only over an HTTPS (secure) connection. Which methods are exposed by HTTP or HTTPS depends on whether the value of <Add Key="SecureConnectionLevel" Value= n /> is in the RSReportServer.config file. You'll find this file in the *C:\ Program Files\Microsoft SQL Server\MSSQL\Reporting Services\ ReportServer* folder. If you have not installed SSL and the SecureConnectionLevel is set to 0, all methods are callable over HTTP.

To dump a list of the secure methods, let's enter List Secure Methods in the first MenuItem and provide a name of MenuListSecureMethods. Next, double-click on this menu item to open the event handler, and add the code shown in Listing 9¾.2.

Listing 9¾.2 Example Calling ListSecureMethods

```
Private Sub MenuListSecureMethods_Click(ByVal sender As System.Object,
    ByVal e As System.EventArgs) Handles MenuListSecureMethods.Click

    Dim rs As New AppReportService.ReportingService
    rs.Credentials = System.Net.CredentialCache.DefaultCredentials
    rs.Url = strDirectIPReportServer
    Dim strSecureMethods As String() = rs.ListSecureMethods()

    Array.Sort(strSecureMethods)
    txtResult.Lines = strSecureMethods

    MessageBox.Show(String.Format("There are {0} SecureMethods ",
    strSecureMethods.Length.ToString))

End Sub
```

The most important parts of Listing 9¾.2 are in bold. Let's go through them:

I don't like to use Imports in Visual Basic .NET, or Using in C# and prefer to give the full namespace referencing because it enables familiarity with the class libraries and prevents any confusion.

–Peter

And one of us must be paid by the hour. I find it great to be able to speed up the process of writing code by placing an Imports statement or two in my code.

–Bill

- **ReportingService:** First of all, the code creates a new ReportingService class object and names the local instance `rs`. You might recall when we used the Report Scripting Utility (rs.exe) that an `rs` object is already in scope. That's the very same ReportingService object we're using here. We'll take another look at the Report Scripting Utility in a moment. As you can see, `rs` is derived from our proxy class, which we named AppReportService. Yours might be something different. Yes, we could have used the Visual Basic .NET Imports directive and not had to prefix ReportingService with AppReportService.
- **URL:** We mentioned earlier and created some hullabaloo concerning the WSDL file and the address it embeds in the <soap:address location=..> attribute. This is where you have an opportunity to overwrite the embedded location. Given the problematic WSDL file issue, we always try to include an `rs.URL`.
- **Credentials:** When your program calls methods on the SOAP interface, you are effectively making calls to the ReportService.asmx that resides in the Report Server's IIS virtual directory. Your program must authenticate itself against the virtual directory in accordance with the authentication methods set up in IIS on the ReportServer virtual directory, as shown in Figure 9¾.6. However, note that Reporting Services only supports Basic authentication and Integrated Windows authentication. It doesn't support Digest authentication. And while Anonymous access can be made to work, you should only be using that with a custom security extension. Reporting Services leverages its knowledge of the authenticated user when applying the underlying Reporting Services Role-based security system as it's applied to many calls. For example, if the account doesn't have task permissions to View Reports, you may be able to execute certain methods but they won't return any data. We'll show an example of that later in this chapter.

- **Exception handling:** Sure, exception handling should be built into the design—not tacked on like tarpaper covering a hole worn in the roof. This routine has no exception handling, but it's enough to get started. We'll also touch on exception handling a bit later in the chapter.

Figure 9¾.6 The Authentication Methods on the ReportServer Virtual Directory in IIS

We're using the credentials of the user running the program extracted from System.Net.CredentialCache.DefaultCredentials. Yes, this is Integrated Windows Security, which raises similar concerns that using Integrated Security in deployed Data Sources raises. The slight difference is that your programs will usually be ones you designed and for which you defined the content. These programs can also be secured through .NET code access security, and it's a little more difficult for those credentials to be hijacked to do things that have not been enabled in a code access security policy. Rather than use Integrated Windows Security, you can use specific credentials of a specific Windows user account. In this case, you'd code something like Listing 9¾.3:

Listing 9¾.3 This Is a "Bad" Way to Embed Credentials

```
rs.Credentials =
  New System.Net.NetworkCredential("TestUser", "password", "Domain")
```

But just before you do, you should take several important considerations into account:

- If you are not using SSL (and remember, we told you that you should) and are thus communicating with your Report Service over HTTP, the credentials you pass are not going to be secure while in transit over the network. Again, we suggest you use HTTPS.
- It is a *very* bad idea to embed literal credentials, such as those in Listing 9¾.3, into a program. Given the plethora of decompilation and reverse engineering tools floating around, the passwords and user account details can be extracted from your program quite easily. So if you are going to use alternative credentials, either collect the user name and password from the user at runtime, or use a technique that encrypts the value and stores it outside the application. If you want to cache those credentials for use next time the user runs the program, consider encrypting them before caching using the DPAPI encryption libraries.
- The final point to note is that it's difficult to connect to the local machine's Report Server. That's because Windows complains about already being connected to the local machine under another context. This means if you are going to try out specific credentials, try them against a remote Report Server to which you are not already connected in some context.

Exception Handling

When calling methods on the SOAP interface, there can always be *exceptions*. Think about it—the Report Server is usually located on another machine. In this case, any number of things can happen to break the connection, or disrupt processing—most of which are out of your control. With this in mind, it's always a good idea to use a try/catch block to trap specific exceptions and handle them in your code, rather than permitting the .NET Framework to catch them for you and scare your users silly. Listing 9¾.4 shows a typical exception handler routine that you can use. SOAP exceptions can be trapped into a variable of SoapException type, which exposes the *System.Web.Services.Protocols* namespace.

Listing 9¾.4 Pro Forma for All Examples

```
Try

  'Report Service Connection set up
  'In the examples the Proxy class Namespace is "AppReportService"
  Dim rs As New <Your Proxy class Namespace>.ReportingService

  rs.Credentials = <Your Credential Scheme>
  rs.Url = strReportServer ' As defined in the Form globals

'Meat of your Method
<Insert your code here >

'Handle the exception

Catch se As System.Web.Services.Protocols.SoapException

  System.Diagnostics.Debug.Assert(False, se.Detail.InnerXml.ToString())

  < Exception handling code to handle Release builds ..Console, Debug, Messagebox
etc>
End Try
```

Throughout the rest of the examples in this chapter, we'll expect you to implement exception handling in your code, so we won't say much more about it after this section. We would, however, like to draw your attention to the magic of Blackburn's Stone, the `System.Diagnostics.Debug.Assert` method, and the supernatural Vaughn's Rock, the `System.Diagnostics.Debugger.Break` method. If you have not used either of these in your .NET programming, let us tell you why you should add them to your skill set.

Using Debug.Assert

`System.Diagnostics.Debug.Assert` is useful in Windows Forms applications and .NET client applications alike. The call is only compiled into a Debug build and is not included in Release builds. This means that when you release your product you don't have to go through and "manage" where you switch on or off Messagebox.Shows or Console.Writelines that are used in crude exception handlers.

The real magic happens with Debug builds. If a `System.Diagnostics.Debug.Assert` is encountered in the flow of execution and you've set the suppression parameter flag to False, a message dialog is displayed on the screen. That dialog is a bit scarier (as shown in Figure 9¾.7) for untrained end users, so don't give your mother-in-law Release builds until you've trained her to expect them (or you want to give her a conniption). However, the dialog provides three options: Abort, Retry, and Ignore, along with a call stack. Big deal? Well, Abort kills your program, and Ignore attempts to continue and ignore the exception. It's Retry that's really exciting (if you're into exception handlers). If you're running your application from Visual Studio .NET 2003, when the Debug.Assert is executed, you'll drop into the IDE where you can begin stepping through the code interactively. But this is by far the most useful if you have provided Debug builds of your application to testers. When the application is run outside Visual Studio .NET 2003 and the code encounters such an exception (depending on your access privileges to debug a particular machine), you can load the project in Visual Studio .NET 2003. At this point, you can connect remotely to the development machine and ask the hapless tester to hit the Retry button. Here you'll be dropped into the IDE in break mode right on the point where the Assert was triggered. You'll have the ability to inspect all the variables in scope and step through the code. It's a bit involved to get that running for remote debugging, so when you start to experiment try it out by working with a project on your own machine. We think it is cool, anyway, and we've been able to run a Debug build on a laptop in Redmond, Wash., USA, while the source code and development project are in England. In this case, an Assert was triggered and we were able to get back to the development system in England through the VPN, attach Visual Studio .NET 2003, and successfully start debugging and stepping through the code right where the exception occurred.

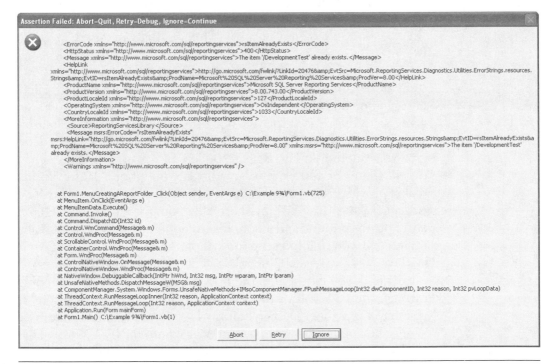

Figure 9¾.7 A Debug.Assert Dialog Showing the Voluminous Detail.InternalXML.ToString for a SOAP Exception

Using Debugger.Break

`System.Diagnostics.Debugger.Break` is a method that's similar to Debug.Assert in that it's only compiled in Debug builds. A problem with `System.Diagnostics.Debug.Assert()` is that in ASP.NET applications it's simply ignored, so it's not particularly useful. However, you'll need to think very carefully about using `System.Diagnostics.Debugger.Break` in ASP.NET applications. That's because it forces the aspnet_wp.exe worker process to stop execution in its tracks. This prevents it from servicing any other ASP.NET program and launches a dialog on the *server* console. This is not much help if your application's user is on the other side of the planet and can't see the server's console monitor when Debugger.Break is executed. All the user sees is an unresponsive frozen application, just like all other users connected to your server. Nevertheless, it *is* a useful tool to use in certain *development* circumstances when debugging, but only when you have the server's console *in sight* to see the Assert dialog (as shown in Figure 9¾.8). In this case, you can attach the debugger to the aspnet_wp.exe process and get into scope with all the variables and ViewState made available for that web page.

Figure 9¾.8 The Message Deployed on the Server Console

It's up to you to correctly handle exceptions in your code. For brevity in the rest of this chapter, we won't be clouding the examples with a lot of exception handling code, but that doesn't mean that you should follow this pattern when programming commercial applications.

Listing Report Items in Folders

Listing all the Report Items is simply a matter of calling the `ListChildren` method on a ReportingService object. This method (shown in Listing 9¾.5) takes two arguments: the first is the path to the folder that lists the child objects and the second is a Boolean value to indicate if this is a recursive listing into all subfolders that may be encountered.

Listing 9¾.5 Example Calling `ListChildren`

```
Dim rs As New AppReportService.ReportingService
rs.Credentials = System.Net.CredentialCache.DefaultCredentials
rs.Url = strReportServerURL

Dim strResult As String
Dim lCatalogItems As AppReportService.CatalogItem()
lCatalogItems = rs.ListChildren("/", True)

For Each CatItem As AppReportService.CatalogItem In lCatalogItems
  strResult &= CatItem.Path & vbCrLf
Next

txtResult.Text = strResult
```

Notice that `ListChildren()` returns an array of CatalogItem objects, as shown in Figure 9¾.9.

Figure 9¾.9 An Array of CatalogItem Objects

Each object stored in Reporting Services notional folders can be represented by a CatalogItem. If you're only interested in a selection of types, such as reports or linked reports, you need to filter on *CatalogItem.Type*. To make this easier, there is an *ItemTypeEnum* exposed in an autocomplete dialog (as shown in Figure 9¾.10.) This enum uses integer values such as 0,1,2,3,4,5, rather than values that can be used in binary *or* filters like 0,1,2,4,8,16, so you'll have a bit more typing to do.

Figure 9¾.10 The *ItemTypeEnum*

Using the `FindItems` Method

You can search a Report Server recursively from any notional folder (including the root folder) with the `FindItems()` method, using a combination of search conditions with the following properties:

- *Name*
- *Description*
- *CreatedBy*
- *CreationDate*
- *ModifiedBy*
- *ModifiedDate*

To use the `FindItems` method, you need to construct an array of SearchCondition objects. This array supports only one condition per property, so you can't set up two search conditions in the array against the same property. You'll soon find that `FindItems` is very crude, but Microsoft tells us it's therefore safe from SQL injection. There is no current support for wildcards mid-string, although you do have the opportunity to set if the match condition is a *ConditionEnum.Equals*, which specifies a case-insensitive search, or a *ConditionEnum.Contains*, in which case wildcards are prefixed and appended to the search term.

Let's look at some code that searches from the root folder for all report items whose *Name* property contains *Sales*. You can see in Listing 9¾.6 that we first create an array of type `SearchCondition` and pass this into the `FindItems` method.

Listing 9¾.6 Example Calling `FindItems`

```
Dim rs As New AppReportService.ReportingService
rs.Credentials = System.Net.CredentialCache.DefaultCredentials
rs.Url = strReportServerURL
Dim strResult As String
Dim lCatalogItems  As AppReportService.CatalogItem()

Dim srccond(0) As AppReportService.SearchCondition
srccond(0) = New AppReportService.SearchCondition
srccond(0).Condition = AppReportService.ConditionEnum.Contains
srccond(0).ConditionSpecified = True
srccond(0).Name = "Name"
srccond(0).Value = "Sales"

lCatalogItems  = rs.FindItems("/", _
   AppReportService.BooleanOperatorEnum.And, srccond)

For Each CatItem As AppReportService.CatalogItem In lCatalogItems
   strResult += CatItem.Path & vbCrLf
Next

txtResult.Text = strResult
```

Suppose you want to search for all reports created within the last two months, containing the word "sales" in their names. In this case, you can replace the iterating code in Listing 9¾.6 with the code in Listing 9¾.7. We can perform further matching once we have the array of `CatalogItems`.

Listing 9¾.7 Filtering for Those Reports in the `CatalogItems` Array That Were Created in the Last Two Months

```
For Each CatItem As AppReportService.CatalogItem In lCatalogItems
  If (CatItem.Type = AppReportService.ItemTypeEnum.Report) And _
     (CatItem.CreationDate > Now.AddMonths(-2)) Then
    strResult += CatItem.CreationDate.ToLongDateString & "    " &_
                 CatItem.Path & vbCrLf
  End If
Next
```

Creating a Schedule

We looked at creating shared schedules through the Report Manager in Chapter 4, and we mentioned that ultimately Schedules are passed to SQL Server Agent jobs. Don't forget to ensure that the SQL Server Agent is running before trying to create Schedules. To create a Schedule with the SOAP classes and methods, you must follow these steps:

1. Instantiate and configure a `RecurrencePattern` class.
2. Instantiate a `ScheduleDefinition` class, assign to it the `RecurrencePattern`, and set the start and end dates.
3. Call `CreateSchedule`, passing it a name for the Schedule, and the Schedule definition.

We agree that this should work—in theory. In practice, we found issues and deficiencies that we hope Microsoft attends to in a Service Pack.

Setting a `RecurrencePattern`

`RecurrencePattern` is simply a class that describes a timing pattern over which you'd like the SQL Server Agent to trigger the created job. Five classes inherit from `RecurrencePattern`, and you *must* use one of those. It won't work if you try to create your own class and inherit from `RecurrencePattern`. The five options you have are:

- `MinuteRecurrence`
- `DailyRecurrence`
- `WeeklyRecurrence`
- `MonthlyRecurrence`
- `MonthlyDOWRecurrence`

First, let's look at a simple example of a Schedule that fires every minute (as shown in Listing 9¾.8.)

Listing 9¾.8 Creating a Test Schedule to Fire Every Minute

```
Dim rs As New AppReportService.ReportingService
rs.Credentials = System.Net.CredentialCache.DefaultCredentials
rs.Url = strReportServerURL

Dim strResult As String

Dim recurpattern As New AppReportService.MinuteRecurrence
recurpattern.MinutesInterval = 1

Dim ScheduleDef As New AppReportService.ScheduleDefinition
ScheduleDef.Item = recurpattern
ScheduleDef.StartDateTime = Now

strResult = rs.CreateSchedule("Every Minute Test", ScheduleDef)
txtResult.Text = "Schedule Created with ID " & strResult
```

In Listing 9¾.8, you can see that we first create an instance of the `MinuteRecurrence` class. Next, we assign its *MinutesInterval* property to 1 and create a `ScheduleDefinition` class, assign the `MinuteRecurrence` to its *Item* property, and set the `ScheduleDefinition` instance's *StartDateTime* property. Finally, we called the `CreateSchedule` method on the Report Server, providing the name of "Every Minute Test" along with the Schedule definition.

For example, suppose you want to prepare financial reports to be executed on the first three days of each new quarter at 5 AM. This can be coded using a Schedule, as shown in Listing 9¾.9.

Listing 9¾.9 Creating a Test Schedule to Fire on the First Three Days of Each Quarter

```
Dim rs As New AppReportService.ReportingService
rs.Credentials = System.Net.CredentialCache.DefaultCredentials
rs.Url = strReportServerURL

Dim strResult As String

Dim recurpattern As New AppReportService.MonthlyRecurrence

Dim MonthsOfYear As AppReportService.MonthsOfYearSelector = _
        New AppReportService.MonthsOfYearSelector

MonthsOfYear.January = True
MonthsOfYear.March = True
MonthsOfYear.June = True
MonthsOfYear.September = True

recurpattern.MonthsOfYear = MonthsOfYear
recurpattern.Days = "1-3"

Dim ScheduleDef As New AppReportService.ScheduleDefinition
ScheduleDef.Item = recurpattern
ScheduleDef.StartDateTime = Date.Today.AddHours(5)

strResult = rs.CreateSchedule("5 AM on first 3 days of each quarter", _
        ScheduleDef)

txtResult.Text = "Schedule Created with ID" & strResult
```

Issues We Encountered with Schedules

When you inspect the ScheduleDefinition class, you'll see two other properties that you can set to specify an *EndDate*, which is the date the Schedule expires and can be no longer triggered. If you set the *EndDate*, you also need to set a Boolean flag in the

EndDateSpecified property to indicate that a specific *EndDate* has been set.

```
ScheduleDef.EndDate = Now.AddDays(1)
ScheduleDef.EndDateSpecified = True
```

However, although the documentation suggests that the *EndDate* property can take a time as well, it doesn't work. We investigated the underlying calls being made into stored procedures in SQL Server, and those stored procedures do support an end time value. The problem is that Reporting Services doesn't call them properly. This has been added to our growing list of things to get fixed. What it means is that presently you cannot setup a Schedule that (for example) fires every hour next Monday between 9 AM and 5 PM—at least not with SOAP. In some of our tests, we found that by setting a time on an *EndDate*, Reporting Services pushed an *EndDate* time to a time *before* the *StartDateTime*. This means that the scheduled task never ran—it's effectively created as expired. Of course, you can carefully manipulate entries in the ReportServer system tables where the SQL Server Agent keeps its configuration tables—something that isn't supported but which we have had some success in doing.

Another frustration is that the scheduling part of the SOAP interface could have been better named. For instance, if the various `Recurrence` classes had been named `RecurrenceXXXX`, they would have grouped together more naturally in the IDE's IntelliSense. We hope that the next version's SOAP interface addresses some of these basic issues—but we're not that hopeful when it comes to renaming things. Still, our developer friends at Microsoft tell us that they're open to input and that they will consider renaming parts of the interface—while at the same time goading us, tongue in cheek, that if they did attend to this, our book would be wrong. It's another Catch-22.

Listing Schedules

You can query the Report Server for a list of shared Schedules by calling the `ListSchedules` method on the Report Service, as shown in Listing 9¾.10.

Listing 9¾.10 Example Calling the `ListSchedules` Method

```
Dim rs As New AppReportService.ReportingService
 rs.Credentials = System.Net.CredentialCache.DefaultCredentials
rs.Url = strReportServerURL

Dim strResult As String

Dim lSchedules() As AppReportService.Schedule
lSchedules = rs.ListSchedules()

For Each sched As AppReportService.Schedule In lSchedules
    strResult += sched.ScheduleID & "      " & sched.Name & vbCrLf &↵
    sched.Description & vbCrLf & vbCrLf
Next

txtResult.Text = strResult
```

By the way, the `ScheduleID` returned from the `CreateSchedule` or on the *Schedule.ScheduleID* property is the same GUID that identifies the SQL Server Agent job in the Enterprise Manager. This means if you know what you are doing you can manipulate the SQL Server Agent job. Figure 9¾.11 shows such a job.

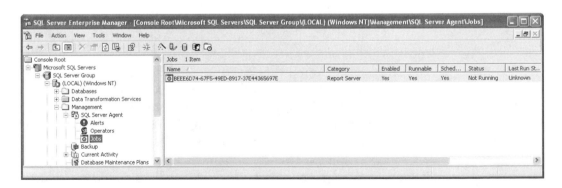

Figure 9¾.11 A SQL Server Agent Job for a Report Server Schedule

However, you might want to initialize certain options on SQL Server Agent jobs. For example, you can specify that the operator be notified when the job executes, given that there is no way to do that from the Report Manager or the Reporting Services SOAP interface— at least not yet. Beware that if you change things, you should also consider the impact of these changes on the Schedule table in the Report-Server database. Naturally, if you do go hiking into that territory you are pretty much on your own, unsupported, and perhaps up the creek without a canoe (or a paddle), especially because Reporting Services will re-sync with the SQL Server Agent jobs if any are found "missing."

Repairing Deleted Data Sources the Hard Way— With SOAP Calls

Hey, I'm glad we managed to get good old Humpty in this book—now we just have to find a way to get Mary Mary, Polly Flinders, Jack Horner, and Goldilocks, not to mention the Three Bears....

–Peter

Yeah, but they were too busy helping the MVPs out to get a mention.

–Bill

Mary had a little lamb. She thought it rather silly, so she threw....

–Peter

As we have said repeatedly (because it's easy to do), if a shared Data Source is deleted from the Report Manager, it breaks all the dependent reports. Not only that, deleting a shared Data Source breaks the ReportServer database so much so that even if you re-create a clone of the deleted shared Data Source and place it in the same folder with the Report Manager or even redeploy it from Visual Studio .NET 2003, the pieces just won't go back and all the reports will remain broken. Humpty Dumpty Data Sources or what? Oh yes, you can delete the reports and redeploy them along with their shared Data Sources. Yes, that works, but you'll lose all the other things that you may have setup on those reports with the Report Manager—things like the execution properties, subscriptions, and more. This can make a bad problem worse. In Chapter 4, we discussed an unsupported (but easy) way to manipulate tables in the ReportServer database to put the pieces back—but we promised to show you a supported way using the SOAP interface.

A good starting place to see this problem in action is to take the Microsoft-supplied Sample Report examples and deploy them to your Report Server. Convince yourself that they are working by launching one or more reports. Next, delete the shared Data Source and verify that the reports are broken. Now let's begin.

Listing Reports with Broken Data Sources

Our first step in the repair process is to examine the reports in the Report Server to verify whether they have Data Sources. We already know that we can call `ListChildren` on the root folder "/" to get an array of `CatalogItems` returned to us. That array can then be filtered on its type by iterating through the array. Once we know that we have a report `CatalogItem` type, we need a way of getting back an array of all the Data Sources used by the report. Perhaps you wonder why we mention *all*? Well, each DataSet in a report definition has its own Data Source definition or a reference to a shared Data Source. Because a report definition can have more than one DataSet, it can also have more than one Data Source definition or reference. Given the full path to a report, we can query the Report Server's `GetReportDataSources` method and pass it the path to the report. This returns our array of Data Source definitions or references, as shown in Listing 9¾.11.

Listing 9¾.11 Finding the "Broken" Data Sources Using `GetReportDataSources`

```
Dim rs As New APPReportService.ReportingService
rs.Credentials = System.Net.CredentialCache.DefaultCredentials()
rs.Url = strReportServer

Dim strResult As String
For Each CatItem As APPReportService.CatalogItem In _
            rs.ListChildren("/", True)

 If CatItem.Type = APPReportService.ItemTypeEnum.Report Then
  Dim rds() As APPReportService.DataSource = _
          rs.GetReportDataSources(CatItem.Path)
 For Each rd As APPReportService.DataSource In rds

 If TypeOf (rd.Item) Is APPReportService.InvalidDataSourceReference Then
   strResult += CatItem.Path & vbCrLf
   strResult += "Report Definitions Data Source Name: " & _
     rd.Name & vbCrLf & vbCrLf
 End If
Next rd

End If
Next CatItem

txtResult.Text = strResult
```

In C# or Voldemort Basic .NET, it still takes a relatively long time to iterate through all reports. And it's very expensive having to iterate through each `CatalogItem`, pull back a Data Source array for each report, and finally test each Data Source in that array. We really (really) hope that in the next SOAP interface there will be some cleaner methods of getting the job done in a supported way.

Finding reports with invalid Data Source references can be done simply and extremely efficiently by executing T-SQL at Listing 9³⁄₄.12 in the ReportServer database. But this approach is not supported.

Listing 9³⁄₄.12 The Simple and Efficient (but Unsupported) T-SQL Query to Find Reports with Broken Data Sources

```
SELECT c.path FROM dbo.DataSource ds
JOIN dbo.Catalog c ON ds.ItemID = c.ItemID
WHERE ds.Flags=1
```

Creating a Data Source Through SOAP Methods

Once you identify the reports with "broken" Data Sources, the next step is to create, or update, an existing shared Data Source. This is a no-fuss affair, as shown in Listing 9³⁄₄.13. Here we instantiate a new `DataSourceDefinition`, populate its properties, and call `CreateDataSource` on the Report Service—passing the name of the Data Source, the notional folder, a Boolean-enabled flag, and the `DataSourceDefinition`, along with any properties.

Listing 9³⁄₄.13 Creating or Updating a Shared Data Source

```
Dim rs As New AppReportService.ReportingService
rs.Credentials = System.Net.CredentialCache.DefaultCredentials
rs.Url = "https://<Your Server>/ReportServer/ReportService.asmx"

Dim dsd As New AppReportService.DataSourceDefinition
dsd.ConnectString = "initial catalog=AdventureWorks2000;↵
  Application Name=SOAP Repair;data source=."
dsd.CredentialRetrieval = AppReportService.CredentialRetrievalEnum.Store
dsd.Password = "SecurePassword#"
```

```
dsd.UserName = "DOMAIN\ReportUser"
dsd.WindowsCredentials = True
dsd.Enabled = True
dsd.EnabledSpecified = True
dsd.Extension = "SQL"

rs.CreateDataSource("AdventureWorksSOAPRepair", _
"/Sample Reports", True, dsd, Nothing)
```

NOTE In the process of testing this on the RTM version, we discovered a major issue with how the Reporting Services mechanism failed to update the last modified date when updating a Data Source. This affected any program (including the Report Manager) that uses SOAP. We reported this to Microsoft and after some debate, the problem has been purportedly fixed in SP1.

Well, so far in our plan we've been able to locate the reports that have invalid references to shared Data Sources, and we're able to create a new shared Data Source. What remains for us to do now is update the invalid references to the new Data Source, as shown in Listing 9¾.14:

Listing 9¾.14 Updating or Repairing the Reports with Broken Data Source References to Use New Data Source References

```
Dim rs As New APPReportService.ReportingService
rs.Credentials = System.Net.CredentialCache.DefaultCredentials()
rs.Url = strReportServer

Dim DSref As New APPReportService.DataSourceReference
DSref.Reference = "/Sample Reports/AdventureWorksSOAPRepair"

Dim strResult As String
For Each CatItem As APPReportService.CatalogItem In _
        rs.ListChildren("/", True)
If CatItem.Type = APPReportService.ItemTypeEnum.Report Then
```

continues

```
    Dim rds() As APPReportService.DataSource = _
            rs.GetReportDataSources(CatItem.Path)
    Dim bflag As Boolean = False

    For i As Integer = 0 To rds.Length - 1

     If TypeOf rds(i).Item Is↵
  APPReportService.InvalidDataSourceReference Then
       rds(i).Item = CType(DSref,↵
  APPReportService.DataSourceDefinitionOrReference)
       bflag = True
       strResult += "Report: " & CatItem.Path & "  Data Source: " & _
       rds(i).Name & " has been linked to: " & DSref.Reference & vbCrLf
     End If
    Next i

    If (bflag) Then
    rs.SetReportDataSources(CatItem.Path, rds)
    strResult += vbCrLf

    End If
End If
Next CatItem

txtResult.Text = strResult
```

Creating an Item-Level Role Definition

In Chapter 4, we discussed using the Report Manager to create both
site-wide and Item-level Roles and methodically worked through
steadily increasing the rights aggregated in those roles. Role
Definitions, in themselves, don't assign any rights, they simply provide a name, description, and selection of Tasks. It's only when they
are assigned to a report item such as a folder and given a Group or
user name that they have any effect. In a few moments, we're going
to need a Developer Role Definition that can have *all* the Tasks

enabled. When we looked around the class library, we were disappointed to find that some seemingly obvious components are missing—such as a helper class with which to define different Tasks. It seems that the interface expects you to call the `ListTasks` method on the Report Server. This returns an array of all tasks. It then expects you to build a new array, copying the individual Tasks you might want into the new array using a string match on the *Task* name. Yuck! We can't do that because of the issues regarding localized strings, code pages, and other string-comparison issues, so we created our own helper class that provides a much more elegant solution than the one in the Reporting Services Books Online (BOL). Take a look at the `CreateRole` method in BOL to see what we mean. Anyway, enough said. Voldemort obviously had his wand in there too. Figure 9¾.12 shows our helper class.

```
Public Class ItemTasks
    Public Const SetSecurity As String = "E96A7928-F3A5-409d-A6AA-0808172B28CB"
    Public Const CreateLinkedReports As String = "3246FDF7-16FB-4802-ABFA-76D4F4A8AD62"
    Public Const ViewReports As String = "E2723F22-E29C-496b-B981-1D775F45FC09"
    Public Const ManageReports As String = "88552A24-99BA-46ab-9UCD-EF66FD3E444D"
    Public Const ViewResources As String = "993C580B-3FBF-444b-B85E-A8DA50ADF40F"
    Public Const ManageResources As String = "1D574E69-B01D-4278-A25A-DEE6B3790F81"
    Public Const ViewFolders As String = "2FBF7AE5-0DB6-46f2-B9BB-480794FBC97E"
    Public Const ManageFolders As String = "683665AB-EE4B-4026-99AE-68A9899F8B6E "
    Public Const ManageReportHistory As String = "75D856B8-2FC1-41c9-8DFA-FE0FF6153C20"
    Public Const ManageIndividual As String = "F95F31D0-834A-4c0e-B290-E3E4477908CA "
    Public Const ManageAllSubscriptions As String = "7813C99B-3F84-4d02-930F-72FA3B86024A"
    Public Const ViewDataSources As String = "B96D28BB-23D0-4a32-B57A-7C12EBDD0704"
    Public Const ManageDataSources As String = "AD4523AD-09B6-46ab-A7F0-AD1F52449FE1"
End Class
```

Figure 9¾.12   Our `ItemTasks` Helper Class

In Listing 9¾.15, we first call the `ListRoles` method to obtain an array of Item-level Roles. Then we iterate through that array to see if we already have a role created with that name. If we do, we set a flag to use later. If the Role exists, we don't want to create it again with `CreateRole` because that causes an exception. We just want to update the Role's Tasks and properties with `SetRoleProperties`. We need to create an array of "N" tasks that we're going to associate with the role. We use our `ItemTasks` helper class to do that.

Listing 9¾.15   Creating a Role and Assigning Tasks to It

```
Dim rs As New AppReportService.ReportingService
rs.Credentials = System.Net.CredentialCache.DefaultCredentials
rs.Url = strReportServerURL

'Create a Developer Role
Dim bRoleExists As Boolean = False
For Each rle As AppReportService.Role In rs.ListRoles()
  If rle.Name = "Developer" Then
    bRoleExists = True
    Exit For
  End If
Next


Dim tsks(12) As AppReportService.Task

For i As Integer = 0 To tsks.GetUpperBound(0)
  tsks(i) = New AppReportService.Task
Next i

tsks(0).TaskID = ItemTasks.CreateLinkedReports
tsks(1).TaskID = ItemTasks.ManageAllSubscriptions
tsks(2).TaskID = ItemTasks.ManageDataSources
tsks(3).TaskID = ItemTasks.ManageFolders
tsks(4).TaskID = ItemTasks.ManageIndividual
tsks(5).TaskID = ItemTasks.ManageReportHistory
tsks(6).TaskID = ItemTasks.ManageReports
tsks(7).TaskID = ItemTasks.ManageResources
tsks(8).TaskID = ItemTasks.SetSecurity
tsks(9).TaskID = ItemTasks.ViewDataSources
tsks(10).TaskID = ItemTasks.ViewFolders
tsks(11).TaskID = ItemTasks.ViewReports
tsks(12).TaskID = ItemTasks.ViewResources

If bRoleExists Then
  rs.SetRoleProperties("Developer", "The Developer Role", tsks)
Else
  rs.CreateRole("Developer", "The Developer Role", tsks)
End If
```

Creating a Report Folder and Assigning a Role...
Within a Batch

We mentioned in Chapter 6 that it would be a really good idea to have a deployment folder in which you deploy your reports before configuring them. This folder is out of the view and reach of your users until you are ready to move reports into production folders. These production folders have been assigned a security role, which has at least View Reports Task rights so that the users can access them and the reports they contain.

Creating a folder programmatically is as simple and straightforward as calling the `CreateFolder` method on the Report Server, and passing it the folder name and the parent folder, along with a populated `Property` class for the *Description*. When a folder is created, it inherits the security policies assigned to its parent. You might have good reason to want to create a folder but remove the permissions inherited from the parent and set your own custom permissions. This can all be done in a batch that can be executed within a SQL Server transaction and cancelled if things don't go as planned. This leaves the Report Server in the same state as before you started executing the batch. That's the idea, anyway.

Listing 9¾.16 shows that we first jump through hoops to create a batch. Next we create the Folder properties array for the folder description and call the `CreateFolder` method. Note at this stage all that is happening is that an entry is placed in the ReportServer database's batch table. At this point, there still is no newly created folder in the ReportServer database. Before we call the `SetPolicies` method, we need to do some preparation, namely:

- Create an array of Role objects.
- Create an array of Policy objects assigning the Computer or Domain Group or User Account and Role objects array into the `Policy` array.
- Call `SetPolicies`.

Again, all that has happened in the SQL Server's ReportServer database is that an additional entry has been made in the batch table for the `SetPolicies` call. Eventually, the `ExecuteBatch` method is called and the contents of the batch table with the identified batch header are executed on the SQL Server within a T-SQL transaction.

Listing 9¾.16 Creating a Report Folder and Assigning a Role Within a Batch

```
Dim rs As New AppReportService.ReportingService
 rs.Credentials = System.Net.CredentialCache.DefaultCredentials
 rs.Url = strReportServerURL

 'Set the batch up
Dim batchHd As New AppReportService.BatchHeader
batchHd.BatchID = rs.CreateBatch()
rs.BatchHeaderValue = batchHd

 'Create the Report Folder
Dim props(0) As AppReportService.Property
props(0) = New AppReportService.Property
props(0).Name = "Description"
props(0).Value = "This is a Development Folder"

rs.CreateFolder("DevelopmentTest", "/", props)

 'Create a Roles Array

Dim rls(0) As AppReportService.Role
rls(0) = New AppReportService.Role
rls(0).Name = "Developer"

 'Create a Policy object assigning the Group to a Role(s)

Dim pol(0) As AppReportService.Policy
pol(0) = New AppReportService.Policy
pol(0).GroupUserName = "DOMAIN\GROUPORUSER"
pol(0).Roles = rls

 'Assign the Developer Role to the Folder

rs.SetPolicies("/DevelopmentTest", pol)

 'execute the batch
Try
  rs.ExecuteBatch()
Catch se As System.Web.Services.Protocols.SoapException
  System.Diagnostics.Debug.Assert(False, se.Detail.InnerXml.ToString())
Finally
  rs.BatchHeaderValue = Nothing
End Try
```

Manipulating Report RDL Files Through the SOAP Interface

Calling `rs.GetReportDefinition(<path to report>)` returns a particular report's raw RDL definition in a byte array for the notional path supplied—that is, the initially deployed RDL. If any properties have been promoted through the SOAP API (or through the Report Manager that uses the SOAP API), you should note that those properties are not folded back into the RDL. For example, if you have updated which Data Sources a report's DataSets use so as to apply different DataSets through the Report Manager, the RDL that you get back from the server does *not* reflect those changes. Listing 9¾.17 shows `GetReportDefinition` in some sample code that downloads all the reports found in a Report Server that the person executing the code has permission to manage. It then downloads the RDL definitions to a disk folder hierarchy mapping the notional folders.

Listing 9¾.17 Using `GetReportDefinition` to Copy All Reports to a Local Disk Folder Hierarchy

```
Dim rs As New AppReportService.ReportingService
rs.Credentials = System.Net.CredentialCache.DefaultCredentials
rs.Url = strReportServerURL

Dim strLocalDevFolder As String = "C:/DevReports"
Dim strLocalPath As String

Dim strResult As String
Dim lCatalogItems  As AppReportService.CatalogItem()
lCatalogItems  = rs.ListChildren("/", True)

For Each CatItem As AppReportService.CatalogItem In lCatalogItems

  If CatItem.Type = AppReportService.ItemTypeEnum.Report Then
    strLocalPath = strLocalDevFolder & CatItem.Path.Substring(0, ↵
    CatItem.Path.LastIndexOf("/")).Substring(0, ↵
    CatItem.Path.LastIndexOf("/"))
    If Not (System.IO.Directory.Exists(strLocalPath)) Then
System.IO.Directory.CreateDirectory(strLocalPath)
    End If
```

continues

```
   Dim fsReport As New System.IO.FileStream(strLocalDevFolder &⏎
      CatItem.Path & ".rdl", IO.FileMode.Create)
   Dim RepDef() As Byte
   RepDef = rs.GetReportDefinition(CatItem.Path)
   fsReport.Write(RepDef, 0, RepDef.Length)
   fsReport.Close()
 End If

Next CatItem
```

Creating a report in the Report Server is just a matter of:

- Calling the CreateReport method.
- Passing the report name and the notional parent folder.
- Passing a flag that indicates that if a report is present, it's to be overwritten.
- Creating a byte array representing the report itself (as we extracted in Listing 9¾.18).
- Creating an array of Property objects similar to the one in Listing 9¾.16 created with the CreateFolder method.

On the DVD, you'll find quite an involved sample that uses CreateReport to upload all the reports downloaded in Listing 9.¾.17. It uses recursion to step through the directory hierarchy to install the reports to a new notional root folder. Listing 9¾.18 is a simpler example. Notice that problems during the call to CreateReport are returned to an array of Warning objects. We need to iterate through that array to inspect any issues that occur. The most typical problem you are likely to see concerns Data Sources that the report requires but which are not present on the Report Server.

Listing 9¾.18 Example Using the CreateReport Method

```
Dim fsReport As System.IO.FileStream = New _
    System.IO.FileStream("c:\MyReport.rdl", io.FileMode.Open)
Dim Repdef(Convert.ToInt32(fsReport.Length)) As Byte
fsReport.Read(Repdef, 0, Convert.ToInt32(fsReport.Length))
fsReport.Close()
```

```
Dim warnings() As AppReportService.Warning


'Create the Report Properties
 Dim props(0) As AppReportService.Property
 props(0) = New AppReportService.Property
 props(0).Name = "Description"
 props(0).Value = "This is a My Uploaded Report "

warnings = rs.CreateReport("MyReport", "/", False, Repdef, props)

If Not (warnings Is Nothing) Then
For Each wa As AppReportService.Warning In warnings
    strResult += String.Format("Code: {0} Severity {1} Message {2} {3}", _
    wa.code, wa.Severity, wa.Message, Environment.NewLine)
Next
Else
  strResult =("MyReport was deployed successfully")
End If


txtResult.Text = strResult
```

Creating History

Now that we've seen how to handle a `Warning` we can create Snapshots, because the `rs.CreateReportHistorySnapshot` method generates warnings too. However, you have to recall that Snapshots can be taken only if the credentials for the Data Sources are stored securely in the Data Source itself, and if all parameters have default values, and so on. If you attempt to call `CreateReportHistorySnapshot` on a report that is not prepared to be rendered as a Snapshot, that raises a `System.Web.Services.Protocols.SoapException`, rather than creating a `Warning`. However, we found that a crude `Try/Catch` can come to our rescue, as we show in Listing 9¾.19.

Listing 9¾.19 Example Calling `CreateReportHistorySnapshot` to Create Snapshots of All Reports in the Report Server

```
Dim rs As New AppReportService.ReportingService
rs.Credentials = System.Net.CredentialCache.DefaultCredentials
rs.Url = strReportServerURL

Dim strResult As String
Dim warnings() As AppReportService.Warning

For Each CatItem As AppReportService.CatalogItem↵
  In rs.ListChildren("/", True)
    If CatItem.Type = AppReportService.ItemTypeEnum.Report Then

    Try
        rs.CreateReportHistorySnapshot(CatItem.Path, warnings)

        If Not (warnings Is Nothing) Then
        For Each wa As AppReportService.Warning In warnings
            strResult += String.Format(↵
  "Failure Snapshoting {0} Code: {1} Severity {2} Message {3} {4}",
  CatItem.Path, wa.Code, wa.Severity, wa.Message, Environment.NewLine)
        Next wa
        Else
        strResult += String.Format("Successful Snapshot of {0}{1}",↵
          CatItem.Path, Environment.NewLine)
        End If
    Catch se As System.Web.Services.Protocols.SoapException
        strResult += String.Format("Snapshot Failed on {0}{1}",↵
          CatItem.Path, Environment.NewLine)
    End Try
    End If
Next CatItem

txtResult.Text = strResult
```

Listing History

It's easy to list report Snapshots with a call to `ListReportHistory`. This SOAP method returns an array of `ReportHistorySnapshots`, which detail the Size, Date, and HistoryID of each generated Snapshot on that report, as shown in Listing 9¾.20.

Listing 9¾.20 Example Calling `ListReportHistory`

```
Dim rs As New AppReportService.ReportingService
rs.Credentials = System.Net.CredentialCache.DefaultCredentials
rs.Url = strReportServerURL

Dim strResult As String
For Each CatItem As AppReportService.CatalogItem↵
   In rs.ListChildren("/", True)
If CatItem.Type = AppReportService.ItemTypeEnum.Report Then

    Dim snaps() As AppReportService.ReportHistorySnapshot
    snaps = rs.ListReportHistory(CatItem.Path)

    If Not (snaps.Length = 0) Then
    strResult += String.Format("Snapshot: {0}{1}", CatItem.Path,↵
     Environment.NewLine)

    For Each SnapShot As AppReportService.ReportHistorySnapshot↵
     In snaps
        strResult += String.Format("  Date {0}, Size {1}, ID {2}{3}",↵
        SnapShot.CreationDate, SnapShot.Size, SnapShot.HistoryID,↵
        Environment.NewLine)
    Next SnapShot
    End If
End If
Next CatItem

txtResult.Text = strResult
```

NOTE We saw in Chapter 10 how it's possible to use the Report Scripting Utility (rs.exe) to capture rendered streams and save them as files. By now, having seen the examples in this chapter, you've probably gotten the idea that you can take many of these examples and convert them to run with the Report Script without much modification. Basically, all you need to do is strip out the `Dim` calls that instantiate the Reporting Service SOAP reference—"rs" is already in scope in the Report Scripting Utility, and it references the same object. By default, the `rs.Credentials` will be using `System.Net.CredentialCache.DefaultCredentials`, so you'd only need to override that if you must use specific credentials. Think carefully about that approach in terms of security. The `rs.Url` is also setup on the rs.exe command line, so again you only need to override it if you have to point off to a different server.

Rendering Reports with SOAP

The `Render` method on the Report Server can seem to be quite a monster with all the arguments that it can possibly take as input and those that it passes out by reference. We saw in Chapter 10 that we're able to get away with just passing the notional path to the report and specifying an output format. That outputs a single byte array stream that can be persisted to a file. We were a little sneaky back then because we deliberately chose rendering formats that use only a single stream—for example, PDF, IMAGE, MHTML, CSV, EXCEL, and XML.

HTML by its nature doesn't use a single stream. When you view any HTML web page with a browser, especially those that contain other resources like pictures, or pages that contain CSS and behavior files, the browser doesn't get bombarded with all of the resources in a single stream.

When rendering HTML, the browser is first sent a page definition from the web server. Sure, it contains the text parts, but the other resources are only referenced by pointers to their URL address. To render the page, the browser has to actively request each image and each resource file separately. Browsers often cache these resources (given that the files can be quite large) to eliminate the need to refetch them when a page containing the same resource is requested.

When requesting HTML in the context of Reporting Services, a call to the Render method returns a byte array stream containing the page definition without any embedded resources, which means no image data has to be processed (yet). All the resources in the page definition need to be requested separately. To optimize performance and save the client from having to interrogate the first stream received to see what other resources it needs to request, the Render method also passes back a string array of StreamIDs. Each StreamID is a GUID referenced in the first stream. The Report Server uses the RenderStream method to request those streams. Before we see this in action in an ASP.NET application, let's take a simplified look at the Render method itself, shown in Listing 9¾.21:

Listing 9¾.21 The Render Method's Signature

```
Public Function Render( _

  ByVal ReportPath As String _
  ByVal RequestedFormat As String _

  ByVal HistoryID As String _
  ByVal DeviceInfo As String _

  ByVal Parameters() As [Namespace].ParameterValue _
  ByVal Credentials() As [Namespace].DataSourceCredentials _

  ByVal ShowHideToggle As String _

  ByRef Encoding As String _
  ByRef MimeType As String _
  ByRef ParametersUsed() As [Namespace].ParameterValue _
  ByRef Warnings() As [Namespace].Warning _
  ByRef StreamIds() As String _
) As Byte()
```

As you can see, the Render method's arguments need a bit of explaining.

Understanding the `Render` Method's Input Parameters

The `Render` method returns several input parameters:

- `Report   Path`: The full notional path to the report in the Report Server. For example, `/Sample   Reports/ Product Catalog`.
- `RequestedFormat`: This string determines the Rendering extension to use. You can choose from HTML4.0, HTML3.2, HTMLOWC, PDF, IMAGE, MHTML, CSV, XML, EXCEL, or even NULL.
- `HistoryID` (optional): A History ID string taken from a `ReportHistorySnapshot` *HistoryID* property after calling `ListReportHistory` to establish the valid values. This parameter is sent only if it's a `ReportSnapshot` that we want to render, otherwise we can just use `Nothing`.
- `DeviceInfo`: A string formatted as an XML fragment like the various parameters that target the Report Server. Recall the `rc:` parameter settings from Chapter 10 that can be passed in the URL. You can pass those same values here, but without the `rc:`. For example, if you want to set the toolbar off and zoom to 200 percent in the rendered report, using a URL you append the following `rc:` parameters: `&rc:Toolbar=false&rc:Zoom=200`. When building the DeviceInfo XML string, you pass them as:

```
<DeviceInfo>
  <Toolbar>false</Toolbar><Zoom>200</Zoom>
</DeviceInfo>
```

  Check out the Reporting Services BOL topic "Device Information Settings" for a complete list of `DeviceInfo` parameters for each Rendering extension.

- `Parameters`: If the report doesn't have defaults for all its Report Parameters, before it can render you'll need to instantiate and pre-populate a `ParameterValue` array. We'll show you how to do this in just a minute.

- `DataSourceCredentials`: If the Data Source credentials are not stored in the Report Server, you may need to instantiate and pre-populate a `DataSourceCredentials` array.
- `ShowHideToggle`: This is a string parameter that determines which drilldowns are visible or hidden. The problem is that it's a toggle, so you're never quite sure whether the selected drilldown is visible or hidden without inspecting the HTML. To make matters tougher, you can't establish the IDs you need to pass into the `ShowHideToggle` string without inspecting the HTML.

The `Render` Method's Output Parameters

The `Render` method also returns a number of parameters, as we describe below:

- `Encoding`: A string that indicates the encoding used by the Report Server when rendering the report.
- `MimeType`: This is the Multipurpose Internet Mail Extensions (MIME) Type. Gee, aren't you glad to know that? This simply tells you the report stream return format.
- `ParametersUsed`: This parameter is an array of Report Parameters returned only if rendering a Snapshot report. These are the query parameters that were used to create the Snapshot. While you can't change these parameters, you can use them to show your user what parameters were used in the query to create the Snapshot.
- `Warnings`: An array of warnings the Report Server encountered during report processing.
- `StreamIds`: An array of StreamIds for the resources. These can be used with the `RenderStream` method.

Let's take another look at the `Render` and `RenderStream` methods being used in practice in an ASP.NET application. Nope, we can't teach you everything about ASP.NET, but we'll show you enough to make you dangerous and give you an idea of what's going on. The following steps walk you through the creation of a simple ASP application that obtains an HTML-rendered stream and the associated resource streams from the Report Server and returns them to a user browsing your ASPX web page.

1. Start a new project in Visual Studio .NET 2003, making sure you choose ASP.NET Web Application from the Project Templates, as shown in Figure 9¾.13. We named our project ReportOwl and created it on the Boost d1 server. Yes, we're using HTTP here, and we intend to expose our project on HTTP. While we won't be sending any credentials to our ReportOwl application, it does mean that returned content like the report and its images are transmitted using HTTP. Unless we take additional steps to apply security on the virtual directory for our application in IIS, this means these transmissions are insecure, so wire-tapping snoopers can see the report content.

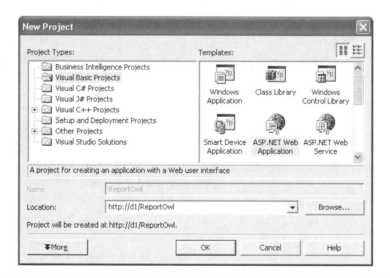

Figure 9¾.13 For This Example, You'll Need to Choose the ASP.NET Web Application Template

2. Make sure that Option Strict is set to On in the Project properties on the Build tab.
3. Once in the project, give the WebForm1.aspx page a more appropriate name. To remain true to our chapter theme, we

chose BarnOwl.aspx. Next, delete (yes, *delete*) all the HTML content from the page—except the first line, the one that starts `<%@ Page Language...`, as shown in Figure 9¾.14.

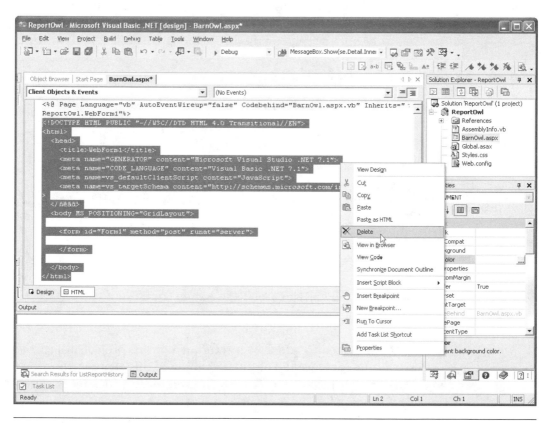

Figure 9¾.14 Delete All HTML in the New Page Except for the Top Line

4. The line that starts `<%@Page Language...` has an attribute Inherits="ReportOwl.WebForm1." Change that to Inherits="ReportOwl.BarnOwl. The web form inherits its methods from this class.

5. In the context menu shown in Figure 9¾.14, you can select View Code (two lines down from the highlighted Delete), or you can select Code from the View menu. Change the `Public Class` to "BarnOwl" or the name from which to

inherit. That brings up the Code behind the dialog, as shown in Figure 9¾.15. Because we removed the HTML, we need to add code to the `Page_Load` event to generate the HTML to be displayed on that web page. This is done by calling either `Response.Write` or `Response.BinaryWrite` with information we obtain from the Report Server's `Render` and `RenderStream` methods.

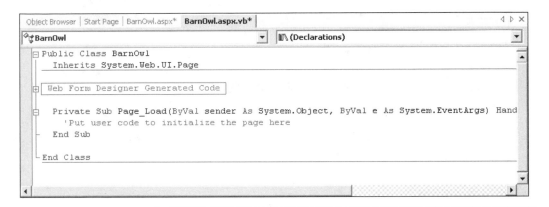

Figure 9¾.15 The Raw Stub of the ASP.NET Web Page `Page_Load` Event

6. We need to add a web reference to our project in just the same way we did at the beginning of this chapter. Just don't forget the WSDL issues. The reference you want is something like:

```
https://<your server>/ReportServer/ReportService.asmx
```

7. You'll need to choose an appropriate name for it—we chose AppReportServer.
8. Listing 9¾.22 shows the code that is used in the `Page_Load` event handler. There's lots to take home from it, so don't hurry through studying it. Before you try to run it, you'll need to configure a few things, which we discuss in a minute.

Listing 9¾.22 ASP.NET `Page_Load` Event Handler

```
Private Sub Page_Load(ByVal sender As System.Object, ByVal e As
System.EventArgs) Handles MyBase.Load
  Try
    'Create the rs object
    Dim rs As New AppReportServer.ReportingService
    'don't embed passwords like this in production code. (use DPAPI)!
    rs.Credentials = New System.Net.NetworkCredential("TestUser", _
                        "password", "YOURDOMAIN")
    rs.Url = "https://d1/ReportServer/ReportService.asmx"

    'Prepare the variables
    Dim RenderedRptArr As Byte()
    Dim RenderedResArr As Byte()
    Dim ResStreamIDs As String()

    Dim reportpath As String = "/Sample Reports/Product Catalog"
    Dim deviceinfo As String = "<DeviceInfo><StreamRoot>" _
      & "/ReportOwl/resources/" _
      & "</StreamRoot><StyleStream>True</StyleStream>" _
      & "</DeviceInfo>"
    Dim format As String = "HTML4.0"

    Dim warnings() As AppReportServer.Warning

    'Call Render -
    RenderedRptArr = rs.Render(reportpath, format, Nothing,↵
     deviceinfo, Nothing, Nothing, Nothing, Nothing, Nothing,↵
     Nothing, warnings, ResStreamIDs)

    ' call RenderStream for each resource
    ' write it to the resources folder.
    For Each streamid As String In ResStreamIDs
      Dim resourcefilepath As String = Server.MapPath(String.Format↵
      ("{0}{1}{2}", Request.ApplicationPath, "/resources/", streamid))
      Dim fsResource As System.IO.FileStream = _
            System.IO.File.Create(resourcefilepath)

        RenderedResArr = rs.RenderStream(reportpath, _
          format, streamid, Nothing, Nothing, Nothing, Nothing, Nothing)
```

continues

```
        fsResource.Write(RenderedResArr, 0, RenderedResArr.Length)
        fsResource.Close()

   Next streamid

   'Write the Report out to the User's Browser
   Response.BinaryWrite(RenderedRptArr)

 Catch se As System.Web.Services.Protocols.SoapException

#If DEBUG Then
    Response.WriteFile("DebugProblemPage.htm")
    Response.Flush()
    System.Diagnostics.Debugger.Break()
#Else
    'Your Production build exception handling code
#End If

   End Try

End Sub
```

The following points summarize the important features from this code sample:

- First, create the `rs` object. Note that we are using embedded credentials of a Domain User account called TestUser. It's a bad idea to embed user credentials in assemblies, especially those that you release into production. We suggest that after you've got this working in development you learn how to use the DPAPI encryption libraries. This way you can encrypt the credentials and load them from the registry or file. We expect that the new version of Visual Studio .NET will support this directly.
- The `DeviceInfo` string (as shown in the following code) is particularly crucial. This sets the `<StreamRoot>` and `<StyleStream>` parameters that we discussed earlier.

```
<DeviceInfo>
  <StreamRoot>/ReportOwl/resources/</StreamRoot>
  <StyleStream>True</StyleStream>
</DeviceInfo>"
```

The `StreamRoot` element addresses the virtual directory to be used to reference the image files and other resources as the Report Server's HTML renderer processes the page. In this case, we point to `http:<server>/ReportOwl/resources`. Here's an example:

```
http://d1/ReportOwl/resources/155
```

The `StyleStream` parameter determines if the report styles should be embedded inline as is the default or if you want to create a separate CSS style sheet resource. One advantage of setting the `Stylesheet` parameter is that you can write code to dynamically edit the styles, assuming you separate the styles out to a style sheet. As we discussed when customizing the Report Manager, you can add behavior (htc) files to the CSS style sheets. This way you can include JavaScript to customize your report's appearance.

- When we call the `Render` method, this returns a byte array that we can squirt at the user's browser simply by calling `Response.BinaryWrite`—that is, once we iterate through the resource `StreamIDs` and write any resources out to disk that have not already been received.
- The final point to take home is Vaughn's Rock. `System.Diagnostics.Debugger.Break` is a very powerful tool in Debug builds, but it's something that you'll want to use carefully—as with any incantation. The point of this magic is that *sometimes* when you or your fellow developers are testing, you don't run the application within Visual Studio .NET with the debugger attached. Up to now, you may get runtime error pages, so you pore over the logs and scratch your head, wondering what was really going on when the exception occurred. This code deploys a `Messagebox` on the IIS server console. Yes, it has to be the console. It cannot be a terminal server or remote desktop sharing console that mentions that it tried to attach a JIT debugger and failed. At this point, the IIS server is virtually hung and very unresponsive to other users.

This is why it's not a good idea to include Debug builds that contain calls to `System.Diagnostics.Debugger.Break` in a *production* environment. However, if you look carefully at the code you'll see that before we made the call we wrote a file out to the user's browser and flushed it from the response object. So, at least this user knows that there's a problem— even if no one is monitoring the server console. At this point, you can open Visual Studio .NET 2003 and navigate to the same project used to build the ASP.NET web application. Next, select the Tools menu and Debug Processes. You then need to find and attach to the aspnet_wp.exe or the w3wp.exe process on Windows 2003 Server, as shown in Figure 9³/₄.16.

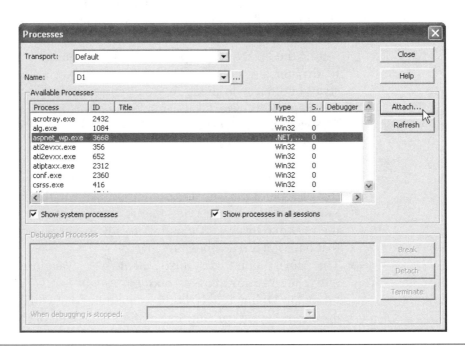

Figure 9³/₄.16 Attaching to the aspnet_wp.exe Process

Once you attach to the executing process with Visual Studio .NET, you can close the dialog and start stepping through the code with access to all in-scope variables. This is a debugging tool that you can add to your kit bag, and on many occasions you'll be glad you did. Just remember, don't use this technique for your production builds. Now, we're ready to continue the process of building our SOAP example.

9. Now that you understand a bit more of what's going on in the background, we're ready to get the samples to work. First, you'll need to do a few things:

■ Create a folder named "resources" in the application's directory at *C:\Inetpub\wwwroot\ReportOwl\resources.*

■ Ensure that the User Account under which ASP.NET runs has Write permissions on the resources folder. This is where ASP.NET caches the resources. If you are not sure which user name your ASP.NET is running under, you can find it by looking at the Task Manager (as shown in Figure 9¾.17).

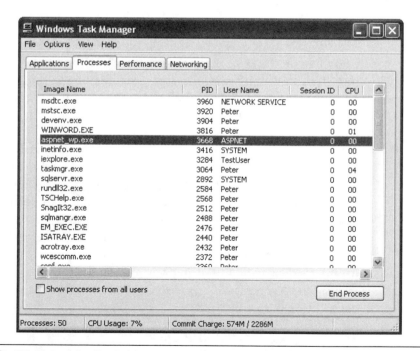

Figure 9¾.17 Using the Task Manager to Identify the User Executing the aspnet_wp.exe Process

10. Next, you should also make sure that your TestUser account has permissions to run the target report. As you can see in our example, we are targeting the /Sample Reports/Product Catalog report, so it's a good idea to follow the instructions that we gave you in Chapter 4 to start a browser as the TestUser. Using this browser instance, check that you can get to the report through the Report Manager URL interface and the Report Server URL interface before compiling and running the project.

11. Finally, you're ready to compile the project, so run it!

Thoughts on the ASP.NET IFrameless Approach

The approach just discussed can effectively provide a lot of flexibility, undoubtedly. For a start, it means that you can incorporate report content in your own ASP.NET web pages. It also means that users do not need to be able to directly see and connect to the IIS Report Server on the network—your web site can effectively act as "proxy." However, you'd need to do more leg work. For example, if you change the `reportpath` to the Territory Sales Drilldown report, run the application, and start drilling down, you'll see that as soon as you hit a drilldown link the browser gets redirected to the Report Server. That's because when requesting the rendering there is no way to tell the Report Server that the drilldowns should be mapped to your own application. We understand that the next version should have improvements in this area. At this point, it gets a little complicated because the drilldowns are toggling the showhidetoggles attributes as well. When it comes to drilldowns, the best solution that we've found is to dink around with the rendered `RenderedRptArr` byte array (carefully) before pushing it out to the user's browser and replacing the links. That's why we find it useful to deal with the string version of the rendered page and replace the `Response.BinaryWrite(RenderedRptArr)` with the code shown in Listing 9¾.23.

Listing 9¾.23 Code Snippet Showing Converting the Byte Array to a String for Manipulation and Then Pushing Out with a `Reponse.Write` Instead of a `Response.BinaryWrite`

```
Dim enc As System.Text.ASCIIEncoding = New System.Text.ASCIIEncoding
Dim strPage As String = enc.GetString(RenderedRptArr)


'    Manipulate the str Page with the String classes to replace references to the
Report Server


Response.Write(strPage)
```

In terms of ease of development, there is a Microsoft-supplied ASP.NET Report Server control that we'll discuss a little further in Chapter 13. That control implements an IFRAME that leaves you capable of interacting with the Report Server via the URL interface.

Using the `Render` Methods with a Windows Forms Application

The methods we have just used with the ASP.NET application can also be used in a Windows Forms application. Eventually, there will be a native Windows Forms Report control—you'll just have to wait a little for the next version of Reporting Services and Visual Studio .NET to use it. You can, of course, embed a web browser control into your Windows Forms application, and have that control communicate with the Report Server via the URL interface. That provides an interactive experience for your users, and we discuss the Microsoft-supplied sample of that in the next chapter. Alternatively you could use a System.Windows.Forms.PictureBox control and call `Render` methods on the SOAP interface to render a selected report as an IMAGE that you feed into the PictureBox. Listing 9¾.24 illustrates a way to do just this by creating a `MemoryStream` from the rendered report array and then dropping that into the *Image* property of the PictureBox control.

Listing 9¾.24 Using a Windows Forms PictureBox Control to Receive a Report Rendered as an Image

```
Dim rs As New AppReportService.ReportingService
rs.Credentials = System.Net.CredentialCache.DefaultCredentials
rs.Url = Form1.strReportServer

'Prepare the variables
Dim RenderedRptArr As Byte()
Dim RenderedResArr As Byte()
Dim ResStreamIDs As String()

Dim reportpath As String = Me.cmbReport.Text
Dim deviceinfo As String =
"<DeviceInfo><StartPage>1</StartPage><EndPage>1</EndPage></DeviceInfo>"
Dim format As String = "IMAGE"

Dim warnings() As AppReportService.Warning

'Call Render
RenderedRptArr = rs.Render(reportpath, format, Nothing, deviceinfo,Nothing, _
  Nothing, Nothing, Nothing, Nothing, Nothing, warnings, ResStreamIDs)

Dim ImageMemStream As New System.IO.MemoryStream(RenderedRptArr)

Me.PictureBox1.Image = System.Drawing.Image.FromStream(ImageMemStream)

ImageMemStream.Close()
```

Understanding the Session

In Chapter 10, we discussed interaction with the Report Server via the URL. We said that it's possible to specify a SessionID in the URL, and we mentioned that there can only be one report in a session at any one time. When you call a `Render` method on an instantiated ReportingService object, a session is created and all the details associated with that report are placed into that session. You can fetch the *SessionID* by querying the `rs.SessionHeaderValue.SessionID` property. If you have a session hosting a report, you can use the

SessionID when creating a URL to pass to a browser to enable it to use the report in the session. This can help optimize the process—especially if it takes a considerable amount of time to process the underlying report. However, this approach presumes that the user credentials creating the report through the ReportingService object are the same as the user credentials using the browser. If they aren't the same, you're pooched from a supported point of view because the Report Server creates a new session. This is a security issue, and we would be more critical of the approach if it were possible to snoop on sessions belonging to other users just by hitting a URL that included the SessionID of another user account.

That said, perhaps there are occasions when you might want to hand over a session created by a call to the Render method by one user to someone else to use in a browser session. There are unsupported ways of optimizing this. If you take a look at the SessionData table, you'll see that there is an OwnerID column that maps to the SID of the user that owns that session through the User table in the ReportServer database. We've found that we can change the OwnerID to the OwnerID of another user and copy the rows. Here we create a new SessionID string, but only if we manipulate the SessionData table directly.

Implementing Server-Side Printing

We suspect server-side printing is most valuable when you have a web application that uses the web rendering control (or IFRAME) to render a report. Perhaps you know the SessionID because you initially created the session with the report by calling Render before handing over the URL with the SessionID. If you're handing that over to a different user, you'll need to update the OwnerID on the SessionData table to the user that then interacts with the report, or copy it to a new row in the SessionData table. If your web page also has a custom toolbar on it, the page could have a server-side Print button that you placed there. When the user clicked it your program could take the SessionID back and then get on with routing that session's data to a printer.

The documentation says that SessionHeaderValue.SessionId is read-only, but we've found that the code showing in Listing 9¾.25 works to pass in a pre-existing session, before calling the Render method. We understand that the official documentation will be updated. You just need to make sure that you call the `Render` method under the same user context as reflected in the SessionData table, and if there are any parameters they need to be passed in too—and it is important that the same order for those parameters be used.

Listing 9¾.25 Setting the `SessionHeader.Value` and `.SessionID` to Use a Pre-Existing Session

```
'Use a Pre Existing Session
rs.SessionHeaderValue = New APPReportService.SessionHeader
rs.SessionHeaderValue.SessionId = "<PreExistingSession>"
```

Why the fuss? Well, it takes time to prepare reports and for the report processor to optimize things. When printing a report users have been browsing, folks are more likely to want a printed copy of the report they viewed on screen rather than waiting for a potentially different version if the underlying data has changed.

Summary

This chapter introduced a number of new techniques to manage the ReportServer database. Yes, SOAP is the recommended way to manage the reports, Data Sources, and other resources managed by the Report Server—but usually only when the Report Manager can't do the trick. We showed you several ways to repair a "broken" database using both SOAP and some unsupported (albeit far easier) methods. We also showed you how to create an ASP-driven application to capture parameters and launch reports. As we closed, we also showed you how to implement server-side printing—again using an unsupported technique.

Writing a Custom Data Processing Extension

Throughout this book we've mentioned how you can return data for your reports from non-standard data sources by writing your own custom Data Processing extension. Well, now we're going to tell you how to do it. When writing this chapter, we started with the Microsoft examples provided in the documentation (as we expect you would as well) and discovered a few issues. We'll lead you through that briar patch and get you back on solid ground. No, this chapter is not really meant for the DBA who's never written more Visual Basic than it takes to build a simple function—but you might want to try anyway to see what's going on behind the scenes in a Data Processing extension. You'll see that writing a custom Data Processing extension is relatively easy. Basically, we'll step you through:

- Using Visual Studio .NET to code a class library that implements a few (seven) interfaces
- Building the assembly
- Storing a copy of the assembly in three different places
- Configuring policy permission files in two places
- Making a few entries in the RSReportServer.config file and the RSReportDesigner.config file

That sounds easy, doesn't it? Oh, and along the way we'll also be careful to watch out for case-sensitivity issues in the XML configuration files. Let's get started.

Building a Data Processing Extension Using the Microsoft Sample

Microsoft supplies a sample Data Processing extension that queries the file system using Universal Naming Convention (which you know as UNC) file shares. This way, you can build reports that draw their data from the file system to show information on files and directories. For example, you can report on files' size, name, or other attributes. It is a great place to start when you are trying to write your first Data Processing extension. You'll find C# and Visual Basic .NET 2003 versions in the *Program Files\ Microsoft SQL Server\MSSQL\Reporting Services\Samples\ Extensions\FsiDataExtension* folder.

We thought it would be helpful to walk you through some of the issues that we encountered with the Data Processing extension sample. We make some suggestions about security, and point out a few typos in the Microsoft Readme.htm file that accompanies the projects. These typos prevent the sample from working for you if you blindly cut and paste code groups from the Readme.htm file to the policy files. These have not been fixed in SP1, but we expect the documentation team to catch up before long.[1] Some of these issues are mentioned in the SP1 readme—after we pointed them out.

Given these issues, let's give you our version of how the Microsoft sample *should* be installed.

1. Use Visual Studio .NET to load either the C# or the Visual Basic version of the File System Information sample project that you'll find in subfolders in *Program Files\Microsoft SQL Server\MSSQL\Reporting Services\Samples\Extensions\ FsiDataExtension*.

2. Locate the Microsoft.ReportingServices.Interfaces.dll. It's located on the Report Server system in the *Program Files\ Microsoft SQL Server\MSSQL\Reporting Services\ ReportServer\bin* folder. It's also on your development system in the *Program Files\Microsoft SQL Server\80*

---

[1] We've heard that this topic is to be covered in Microsoft Knowledge Base article Q842855.

Tools\Report Designer directory. Add a reference to the aforementioned DLL in your sample File System Data extension project.

3. Compile the project. This creates a compiled assembly DLL.
4. Locate the compiled assembly DLL: Microsoft.Samples.ReportingServices.FsiDataExtension.dll. You'll find it in the project's bin folder.

NOTE *A Security Matter* Whenever you install components on your server, you expose the system to possible abuse by nefarious people. In the native-code C++ development, there was no built-in way of setting permissions to restrict what components could do. In the managed code world of .NET, there is—it's called code access security. We strongly encourage you to read Chapter 9, where we explain how to protect your systems using code access security. The general principle that you should try to follow is to grant your code only the minimum number of privileges required.

---

5. Copy the FsiDataExtension.dll to the following three folders:

- The Report Server's bin folder:
  \Program Files\Microsoft SQL Server\MSSQL\ ReportingServices\ReportServer\bin.
  This enables the Report Server to use the Data Processing extension within Data Sources while running a report.
- The Report Manager's bin folder:
  \Program Files\Microsoft SQL Server\MSSQL\ ReportingServices\ReportManager\bin.
  This will enable you to configure both shared and custom Data Sources in the Report Manager. If you don't install it in the Report Manager's folder, you'll get errors when you try to manage Data Sources that use your custom Data Processing extension.
- The Report Designer's folder:
  \Program Files\Microsoft SQL Server\80\Tools\ ReportDesigner.

This enables Visual Studio .NET 2003 to make use of the Data Processing extension in its previewer and also in the RSReportHost.exe previewer.

CAUTION *Don't Copy the Prototype DLL to the Server* It's not a good idea to load a prototype extension to a production server until it's finalized. This prevents having to restart the Report Server to get it to release locks on the DLL when you want to install the next iterative build.

We automated the copy process by creating a batch file, as shown in Figure 13.1. Note that in this case the Report Server is on another system, but we run tests from that server as well, so the batch file copies the DLL into the Report Designer on that system too.

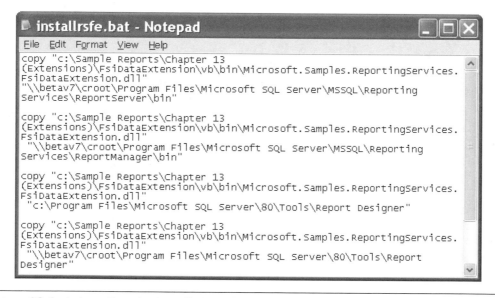

Figure 13.1 Automating the Installation of the Compiled File System Data Processing Extension DLL

NOTE As you iterate through building new versions of the extension and attempting to copy the resulting assembly to the destinations, you may find that you can't replace the file when it is in use. This means that you may need to stop the Report Server Windows service as well as IIS. Insidiously, if you have opened Visual Studio .NET and opened a report project, chances are you have also locked your custom Data Processing extensions in its process space. In this case, you'll need to close those Visual Studio .NET 2003 environments—completely.

6. Now the fun and games start. At this point, you need to insert a few entries into the policy config files to ensure that the assembly has permission to run.

   The example in the documentation illustrates giving the assembly FullTrust. Actually, the formal specifications state that extensions require FullTrust. However, we found that in this case it's not actually needed, and we were able to clamp the privileges down to just those that *are* needed. Our view is that always granting FullTrust is like running all your stored procedures in SQL Server with the SA account because it's easier to get them to work.

NOTE *Don't Default to FullTrust* We feel that using FullTrust in these samples is a fundamental mistake. We have seen samples like this used as prototypes and deployed into production after developers add their custom features—without an adequate understanding of what they're doing.

   Our approach is to create a PermissionSet for inclusion in the NamedPermissionSets locked down (as shown in Listing 13.1) to limit access to certain file shares. Note that you'd need to put your own paths in there and delimit by a semicolon—you'll also find that you need to set Read and PathDiscovery attributes.

Listing 13.1 A PermissionSet to Limit Folders the FSI Data Processing Extension Can "See"

```
<PermissionSet class="NamedPermissionSet"
    version="1" Name="FileShareInfoPermissionSet">
    Description="Limits Shares the FSI Extension can 'See'">
    <IPermission class="FileIOPermission" version="1"
        Read="\\<YourServer>\d$;\\<AnotherServer>\<YourPath>"
        PathDiscovery="\\<YourServer>\d$;\\<AnotherServer>\<YourPath>" />
</PermissionSet>
```

Alternatively, if you wanted the FSI Data Processing extension to have the ability to "see" anywhere on the network, rather than FullTrust we suggest that Unrestricted access be given on the FileIOPermission, as shown in Listing 13.2.

Listing 13.2 A PermissionSet to Provide the FSI Data Processing Extension with Unlimited FileIOPermissions

```
<PermissionSet class="NamedPermissionSet"
    version="1" Name="FileShareInfoPermissionSet">
    <IPermission class="FileIOPermission"
        version="1"
        Unrestricted="true"/>
</PermissionSet>
```

Sure, it's a great idea to back up these files before tinkering with them.

7. Copy whichever PermissionSet strategy you choose (Listing 13.1 or Listing 13.2) into the NamedPermissionSets section in the Report Server rssrvpolicy.config file that you'll find in the *Program Files\Microsoft SQL Server\ MSSQL\Reporting Services\ReportServer* folder—remember, this directory is on the Report Server.

NOTE Remember that these configuration files might look like well-formed XML files, but the programs that use them do not understand XML comment blocks.

8. Copy the same block of XML into the `NamedPermissionSets` section in the Report Designer rspreviewpolicy.config file that you'll find in the *\Program Files\Microsoft SQL Server\ 80\Tools\Report Designer* folder. You don't need to copy the PermissionSet into the Report Manager's policy file.

After our feedback, the SP1 Readme.htm documentation mentions some of these issues.

9. Next, create a `CodeGroup` section in the rssrvpolicy.config file. Pay close attention to spelling and case in the PermissionSetName and the URL path—it must be exactly correct. The examples in the Microsoft documentation show incorrect paths, so don't cut and paste without checking them.

The other crucial point: When inserting this `CodeGroup`, be sure to create the `CodeGroup` in the correct section. As we explained in Chapter 9, code groups are hierarchical and in this case you need to create the `CodeGroup` (as shown in Listing 13.3) within the MyComputer Zone.

Listing 13.3 The CodeGroup for the rssrvpolicy.config File

```
<CodeGroup class="UnionCodeGroup"
    version="1" PermissionSetName="FileShareInfoPermissionSet"
    Name="FSICodeGroup"
    Description="Code group for my FSI data processing extension">
        <IMembershipCondition class="UrlMembershipCondition"
            version="1"
        Url="C:\Program Files\Microsoft SQL Server\MSSQL\Reporting
  Services\ReportServer\bin\Microsoft.Samples.ReportingServices.⌐
        FsiDataExtension.dll" />
</CodeGroup>
```

We show where to place this block of XML in the rssrvpolicy.config file in Figure 13.2.

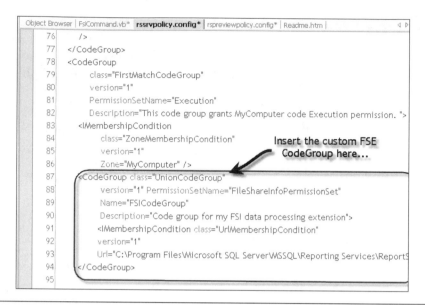

Figure 13.2 Insertion Point for the Custom File System Data Processing Extension CodeGroup

10. It's also necessary to create a code group to include in the rspreviewpolicy.config file. This CodeGroup XML element is the same as the rssrvpolicy.config file—except for one big difference: the Url element is different. It *must* point to the version of the DLL in the Report Designer folder, *not* the DLL in the Report Server folder. This entry (shown in Listing 13.4) must also be placed in the MyComputer CodeGroup hierarchy. The subtle difference is shown in bold.

Listing 13.4 The CodeGroup for the rssrvpolicy.config File

```
<CodeGroup class="UnionCodeGroup"
    version="1" PermissionSetName="FileShareInfoPermissionSet"
    Name="FSICodeGroup"
    Description="Code group for my FSI data processing extension">
        <IMembershipCondition class="UrlMembershipCondition"
            version="1"
        Url="C:\Program Files\Microsoft SQL Server\80\Tools\Report⏎
        Designer\Microsoft.Samples.ReportingServices.FsiDataExtension.dll" />
</CodeGroup>
```

11. Next, we need to make some changes to the RSReportServer.config. This file is in *Program Files\Microsoft SQL Server\MSSQL\Reporting Services\ReportServer*. This change "registers" the Data Processing assembly with the Report Server. Locate the `<Data>` section in that file and add the extension entry in Listing 13.5. Make sure to place this entire entry on one line and match the text case as shown. If you don't get the case and spelling right, the Data Processing extension simply won't work correctly.

> In case you didn't know, these XML files are case sensitive.

Listing 13.5 Registering the Data Extension

```
<Extension Name="FSI"↵
Type="Microsoft.Samples.ReportingServices.FsiDataExtension.↵
   FsiConnection,Microsoft.Samples.ReportingServices.FsiDataExtension"/>
```

12. The same block of XML in Listing 13.5 is used to register the Data extension in the `<Data>` section. Place the code into the RSReportDesigner.config file located in *Program Files\Microsoft SQL Server\80\Tools\Report Designer*. This registers your custom Data Processing extension to work with the Designer.

13. Finally, you'll also need to create an entry in the `<Designer>` section of the RSReportDesigner.config file. This entry (shown in Listing 13.6) specifies which query designer the extension should use. It makes sense in this case to limit this to the generic query designer.

Listing 13.6 Registering the Data Extension for Use by the Report Designer

```
<Extension Name="FSI"↵
Type="Microsoft.ReportDesigner.Design.GenericQueryDesigner,↵
   Microsoft.ReportingServices.Designer"/>
```

Once you're finished patching the configuration files pointing to your sample Data Processing extension, you should be able to create reports using it. You'll see the custom extension appear whenever you create a Data Source, as shown in Figure 13.3.

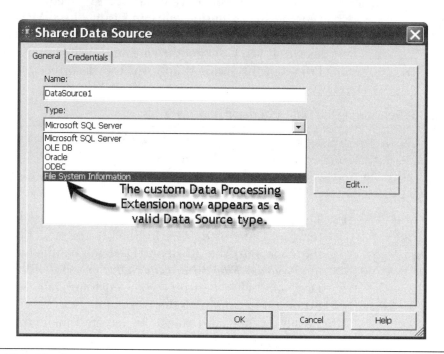

Figure 13.3 The Newly Registered Custom Data Processing Extension Appears as a Valid Data Source Type

Writing a Report Using the File System Data Processing Extension

To begin using the custom Data Processing extension, simply follow the normal procedure to create a report and a new DataSet. Create a Data Source and set the type to File System Information (as shown in Figure 13.3). Set the credentials to Windows Authentication or enter an appropriate user name and password for the UNC path used in the query. Sure, you can prompt for credentials as well by choosing the appropriate option in the Credentials tab.

The DataSet query CommandText is set to a UNC path such as `\\MyServer\MyShare`. When you click the Run button (!) in the query designer, the custom Data Processing extension you just installed runs and returns directory information from the specified path. No, the custom extension as implemented does not support using the local drive or network shared drives as the query CommandText. But with a little effort you can add this functionality to the extension. One other shortcoming is the lack of any example of how to create and manage input parameters. Fortunately, we've solved that less than intuitive problem, and we show you how to accomplish these tasks in our example. We suggest that you just start from scratch and build your own Data Processing extension.

Building a Data Processing Extension from Scratch

Let's take a step back and explain how to build our own Data Processing extension from the ground up. In essence, we'll see a custom Data Processing extension simply returns an ADO.NET DataReader. The example that we're about to create enables Reporting Services to return information from the Windows event log system on any machine within the local domain.

Designing the Custom Data Processing Extension

For our Windows event Data Processing extension, we'll use the Data Source's *ConnectionString* property to specify which machine we're interested in. Because accessing the event logs could require Domain User credentials when in the DataSet Designer, we'll show you how you can use the Data Source's embedded credentials to impersonate the user. Pay particularly close attention to our discussion concerning credentials because there are certain vulnerabilities, especially when you embed super-user credentials in a Data Source. Consider situations in which the Data Processing extension extracts passwords in plaintext, as it clearly needs to. For our example, we'll use the DataSet *QueryString* to specify which event log we want. Typically this is "System," "Security," "Application," or perhaps your own custom event log. Finally we'll show how parameters can be used to filter the returned information. Yes, Reporting Services can filter in the DataSet on its own, but event logs (especially on our systems) can be very large. As we've said before, if you are able to perform filtering in the Data Processing extension or on the DBMS itself, you can cut down on the size of the DataSet that Reporting Services has to manipulate and increase overall performance.

We've mentioned that creating a custom Data Processing extension is very similar to creating an ADO.NET data provider, but fortunately you don't have to implement *all* the ADO.NET data provider interfaces. However, you must implement six[2] cut-down interfaces. These interface definitions are found in the Microsoft.ReportingServices.Interfaces.dll file, which is scattered around the Report Server and report development systems and can be found in each of the Reporting Services bin folders.[3] You'll need to reference that DLL in your project, as we discussed earlier. We found that the official Microsoft documentation is hard to follow. Well, in building this sample we hope that by leading you along in cookbook fashion we can obviate countless hours and sleepless nights, and make writing a Data Processing extension seem like a walk in the park. Of course, some parks aren't nice to walk in without a gunship escort.

Understanding the Data Processing Extension Class

The Data Processing extension is a class library that provides connection, command, parameter, transaction, and data reader classes. It also exposes a tiny extension name and configuration class, through the implementation of the following interfaces:

---

[2] Yes, we said seven interfaces earlier—but one of them, Iextension, is a base interface to IDbConnection.

[3] The Report Manager, Report Designer, and Report Server all have copies of Microsoft.ReportingServices.Interfaces.dll in their bin folders. The Report Server's copy is *C:\Program Files\Microsoft SQL Server\MSSQL\Reporting Services\ReportServer\bin*.

- **Connection (required):** Here you need to implement the *IDbConnection* or its superset *IDbConnectionExtension* interface.
- **Extension (required as a part of the Connection interface):** Implemented through *Iextension*, but this is a base interface for the *IDbConnection* and *IDbConnectionExtension*.
- **Command (required):** Here you implement *IDbCommand*. If you want to integrate your custom Data Processing extension so that it can work cooperatively with parameters in the IDE, you should also implement the GetParameters method in *IDbCommandAnalysis*.
- **Parameters (required):** There are two interfaces, *IDataParameter* and *IDataParameterCollection*. These are small interfaces and are required even if it's just the raw stubs that return nothing when your Data Processing extension doesn't need to use parameters.
- **DataReader (required):** Either the *IDataReader* or its superset *IDataReaderExtension* interface must be implemented. The *IDataReaderExtension* provides additional methods for aggregation, and for reading more than one forward-only result set.
- **Transaction (optional):** If you need to support transactions, implement the *IDbTransaction* or its superset *IDbTransactionExtension*.

Coding the Custom Data Processing Extension

Okay, we're ready to build our custom Data Processing extension. The following steps walk you through the process of creating the class and coding the required interfaces.

1. Create a New Visual Basic .NET class library project named EventLogDataExtension.
2. Ensure that Option Strict On is set at the Project level.
3. On the project, add a reference to *Program Files\Microsoft SQL Server\MSSQL\Reporting Services\ReportServer\bin\Microsoft.ReportingServices.Interfaces.dll* to implement the interfaces.

NOTE *Watch Out for Duplicate Names* One of the things that you might find confusing is that the interfaces you need to create are named the same as interfaces in *System.Data*. It helps considerably if you include the full namespaces on all object references to ensure you're dealing with the correct object. Be very careful when coding the interfaces—especially when you're pointing to objects in *Microsoft.ReportingServices.Interfaces.dll* rather than those identically named in *System.Data*.

---

4. The default class library project creates a file named Class.vb (or Class.cs if you're creating a C# extension).

NOTE Typically, we delete this file and add five new EventLog class files, one for each class to implement. This makes the project easier to manage because it permits easier swapping and sharing among projects. See Figure 13.4 for suggested names.

Yes, we did say there are six interfaces to implement, but remember the *IExtension* interface is a base interface for *IDbConnection*.

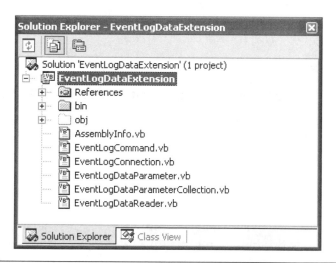

Figure 13.4 The Five EventLog Class Files in the EventLogDataExtension Project

Let's now go through and create each class one by one and implement their interfaces.

Coding the *EventLogConnection* Class

When implementing the EventLogConnection class, you have to make a choice whether to implement the class based on the simple *IDbConnection* interface (shown in Figure 13.5) or the slightly larger *IDbConnectionExtension* interface (shown in Figure 13.6), which is a superset of *IDbConnection*. If you choose to implement the *IDbConnectionExtension* interface, there are a few additional properties that support the user context under which the connection is to be made. This approach is required when you need to pass user credentials that are encrypted and embedded in a report-specific Data Source to the DBMS to which your Data Processing extension connects. For example, if your Data Processing extension needs to log on to a website or a file share that requires credentials, you would want to implement the *IDbConnectionExtension*. Note that the *IDbConnection* interface is a superset of the *IExtension* interface that includes the *LocalizedName* property and a SetConfiguration method called on object instantiation. This satisfies the requirement to implement the *IExtension* interface, because it's a base interface in *IDbConnection*.

Figure 13.5 *IDbConnection* Interface

Figure 13.6 *IDbConnectionExtension* Interface—Note That It's Based on *IDbConnection*

Follow these steps to code the `EventLogConnection` class:

1. To flesh out the interfaces, try to get the Visual Studio .NET IDE to do most of the work. Start by opening the blank class file EventLogConnection.vb you just created. We'll step you through how to implement the *IDbConnectionExtension* interface code.

2. Enter the *Implements* reference shown in Figure 13.7. As you type, statement completion should fill in the references as you go. If this is not happening, you have not added the correct references to your project, as we discussed in Step 3 of the previous exercise. When you hit the Return key at the end of the *Implements* line, Visual Studio .NET 2003 creates all the interface stubs for you for the required properties and methods.

```
Public Class EventLogConnection
    Implements Microsoft.ReportingServices.DataProcessing.IDbConnectionExtension
End Class
```

Figure 13.7 Creating the Connection Class Stubs

3. Given that we now have a set of property stubs, we can create some instance variables to support them. Add an instance variable to the class for each property generated, as shown in Figure 13.8.

> **NOTE** *Tip* We like to prefix the instance variable names that support properties with an underscore (_) character. This way we can more easily map these variables to the name of the class property that the instance variable supports in case and datatype. We also ensure that all the instance variables have default values. Yes, perhaps we should have put all the default values in the New() class constructor methods, but we left that for the compiler to do for us.

```
Public Class EventLogConnection
  Implements Microsoft.ReportingServices.DataProcessing.IDbConnectionExtension

  Private _LocalizedName As String = "Event Log Information"
  Private _ConnectionString As String = ""
  Private _ConnectionTimeout As Integer = 0
  Private _Impersonate As String = ""
  Private _IntegratedSecurity As Boolean = False
  Private _Password As String = ""
  Private _Username As String = ""
  Private _ConnectionState As System.Data.ConnectionState = System.Data.ConnectionState.Closed
```

Figure 13.8 The Instance Variables to Support the `EventLogConnection` Class Properties

It's not hard to get these instance variables wired up to the properties' Get and Set accessors (as shown in Figure 13.9 for the *ConnectionString* and *ConnectionTimeout* properties)—you'll have to do the rest on your own. Sure, you might want to add more functionality to these Get and Set accessors to deal with special situations in your custom Data Processing extension.

4. Step through each of the other property stubs and add appropriate code, as shown in Figure 13.9.

The Username and Password credentials are passed in as WriteOnly in an effort to protect them from being extracted.

> **NOTE** *The IDE Builds Most of the Code for You* There is nothing special about most of the `EventLogConnection` class properties— some properties are coded as ReadOnly, so they only have Get accessors; and some are coded as WriteOnly, so they only have Set accessors. The *Implements* operator takes care of that for you when the stubs are created.

```
Public Property ConnectionString() As String Implements Microsoft.ReportingServices.
   Get
      Return _ConnectionString
   End Get
   Set(ByVal Value As String)
      _ConnectionString = Value
   End Set
End Property
```

We added code to return or set the local variable as needed...

```
Public ReadOnly Property ConnectionTimeout() As Integer Implements Microsoft.Repo
   Get
      Return _ConnectionTimeout
   End Get
End Property
```

Figure 13.9 Wiring Up the Private Instance Variables to the Public Class Properties

Coding the `Open` and `Close` Methods

We don't really have a "connection" for our Data Processing extension, so we'll access the event logs directly in code. However, if your Data Processing extension needs to open or close a connection to your data source, this is where you implement the code. For our example, set the local variable to indicate that the connection state is "open" and "closed," as shown in Figure 13.10.

```
Public Sub Open() Implements Microsoft.ReportingServices.DataProcessing.IDbConnection.Open
   _ConnectionState = ConnectionState.Open
End Sub
```

```
Public Sub Close() Implements Microsoft.ReportingServices.DataProcessing.IDbConnection.Close
   _ConnectionState = ConnectionState.Closed
End Sub
```

Figure 13.10 Implementing the EventLogConnection `Open` Method

Coding the `SetConfiguration` Method

The `SetConfiguration` method comes from the *IExtension* interface. It's called after the `EventLogConnection` class has been instantiated—after any constructors. The Report Server calls this method and passes any XML-like fragment that is found under a <Configuration> element for the extension in the config file.

In the Report Designer, the XML string is taken from the RSReportDesigner.config file, or if we're in a deployed environment, from the RSReportServer.config file. The `<Data>` sections of both config files should create an entry for the *EventLogDataExtension*. We'll talk more about the config files later on in this chapter. Listing 13.7 shows (in bold) the part that's passed into the `SetConfiguration` method. In our example, we don't actually have a use for this, but we could have used it to provide a system-wide mechanism to externally configure which server's event logs can be queried, or who can query them. To implement this feature, we have to parse and process the XML passed into the Data Processing extension.

Listing 13.7 The Custom Configuration Data That Is Passed to the `SetConfiguration` Method

```
<Extension Name="EVENTLOG"
Type="EventLogDataExtension.EventLogConnection,EventLogDataExtension">
  <Configuration>
      <MyExtensionConfigurationData>
        <MyExtensionData1>Value</MyExtensionData1>
        <MyExtensionData2>Value</MyExtensionData2>
      </MyExtensionConfigurationData>
    </Configuration>
</Extension>
```

Coding the LocalizedName Property

This is the other part of the *IExtension* interface. Its sole purpose is to provide Reporting Services with a string name for the extension. In this case, this is the name that you see in the Data Source type in the Report Manager and in the Report Designer.

Coding the ConnectionTimeout Property

We set this property initially to 0 to use an infinite connection timeout by default. We can add code to the *ConnectionString* property handler to set this to another value.

Coding the State Property

To support functionality elsewhere in our custom Data Processing extension, we add a new read-only *State* property to the EventLogConnection class, as shown in Figure 13.11. Yes, this could have been implemented as a read-write property and we could have added code to permit external code to inspect the "state" of the connection (Open, Closed, Busy, or whatever).

```
Public ReadOnly Property State() As System.Data.ConnectionState
    ' This is a new ReadOnly property added to support functionality
    ' in the EventLogCommand class.
    Get
        Return _ConnectionState
    End Get
End Property
```

Figure 13.11 The *State* Property Implementation

Coding the *CreateCommand* Method

This is the real meat in the Connection class. All it needs to do is return an instantiated class based on *IDbCommand*. Figure 13.12 shows our one-line implementation.

NOTE *Compiler Warnings* The project won't compile (and you'll get a compile warning) until we have built the New constructor that accepts the current EventLogConnection, which is referenced by "Me" (in this case).

Before we code the EventLogCommand class, we're going to code the classes that handle the query parameters.

```
Public Function CreateCommand() As Microsoft.ReportingServices.DataProcessing.IDbCommand _
    Implements Microsoft.ReportingServices.DataProcessing.IDbConnection.CreateCommand
    Return New EventLogCommand(Me)
End Function
```

Figure 13.12 The EventLogConnection.CreateCommand Method

Understanding How Parameters Are Created

The `Parameter` and `ParameterCollection` classes are used to manage the query parameters passed to our Data Processing extension. To get a better understanding about how the Report Designer and the Report Processor pass Report Parameters to your custom Data Processing extension, we thought that this brief explanation is in order. The `GetParameters` method on the *IDbCommandAnalysis* interface is called by the Report Designer to return a *Parameters* collection from the Data Processing extension, but only at design time. The Data Processing extension (our code) then creates and populates a new `ParameterCollection` class, either from hard-coded values or by parsing the query string to locate parameters. Next, the `ParameterCollection` class is passed back to the Report Designer, which subsequently creates the necessary report and query parameters.

During runtime or preview (as opposed to design time), when the `EventLogCommand` class is instantiated, our Data Processing extension builds our new (empty) `ParameterCollection`. The Report Server obtains a reference to this empty `ParameterCollection` by calling the ReadOnly *Parameters* property on the *IDbCommand* interface of our `EventLogCommand` class. Once the Report Server's Report Processor has the reference, it's able to populate the `ParameterCollection` and the Data Processing extension is able to inspect the Parameter objects. The parameter population code is in the Report Server, so don't worry yourself that you can't see the parameters being populated anywhere in code.

Coding the `Parameter` and `ParameterCollection` Classes

At this point, we want to get the `Parameter` and the `ParameterCollection` classes out of the way because they are simple to implement. Figure 13.13 shows the `IDataParameter` class is simply two properties and a couple of constructors.

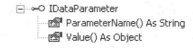

Figure 13.13 The `IDataParameter` Class

1. Continuing with our programming, open the `EventLogDataParameter` class, and then code the *Microsoft.ReportingServices.DataProcessing.IDataParameter* interface, as shown in Figure 13.14. This coding adds a couple of New constructors and fleshes out the public properties skeleton, as we did for the *IDbConnection* interface. Note that the *_ParameterValue* private property is defined as an object.

```
Public Class EventLogDataParameter
    Implements Microsoft.ReportingServices.DataProcessing.IDataParameter
    Private _ParameterName As String
    Private _ParameterValue As Object
    Public Sub New()
        Me.New(Nothing, Nothing)
    End Sub
    Public Sub New(ByVal parameterName As String, ByVal parameterValue As Object)
        _ParameterName = parameterName
        _ParameterValue = parameterValue
    End Sub
    Public Property ParameterName() As String _
        Implements Microsoft.ReportingServices.DataProcessing.IDataParameter.ParameterName
        Get
            Return _ParameterName
        End Get
        Set(ByVal Value As String)
            _ParameterName = Value
        End Set
    End Property
    Public Property Value() As Object _
        Implements Microsoft.ReportingServices.DataProcessing.IDataParameter.Value
        Get
            Return _ParameterValue
        End Get
        Set(ByVal Value As Object)
            _ParameterValue = Value
        End Set
    End Property
End Class
```

Figure 13.14 The `EventLogDataParameter` Class

The `IDataParameterCollection` class is shown in Figure 13.15. It implements two methods, `GetEnumerator` and `Add`, as we described earlier in this chapter.

Figure 13.15 The `IDataParameterCollection` Class

Next, we need to code the `EventLogDataParameter` class. We implement this from the *IDataParameter* collection, as shown in Figure 13.15. In our implementation (shown in Figure 13.16), we instantiate a private *ArrayList* collection and coerce its `Add` and `GetEnumerator` methods to the interface. We also create an *Item* property to extract entries from the *ArrayList* by a string name instead of by ordinal. We know that there won't be many parameters passed to our Data Processing extension. Otherwise, we might have chosen a more efficient technique to manage the parameter collection.

Recapping, when building a report with the Report Designer, the IDE asks for a list of parameters by calling the `GetParameters` method on the *EventLogCommandClass* interface. Our implementation of the `GetParameters` method parses the CommandText string and picks out the parameters by looking for @ as a parameter marker. You can implement this any way you see fit or simply have one or more fixed-name parameters that don't need to be dependent on the CommandText. The `GetParameters` method constructs and populates the ParameterCollection object and passes it back to the IDE. When the report is being previewed or rendered by whatever means, the RDL has already mapped the Report Parameters to the query parameters, so the report processor queries our Data Processing extension and asks for a reference to its internal parameters collection by calling the ReadOnly *Parameters* property.

2. To code the *EventLogDataParameterCollection* interface, open the corresponding Visual Basic class and implement it as shown in Figure 13.16.

```
Public Class EventLogDataParameterCollection
    Implements Microsoft.ReportingServices.DataProcessing.IDataParameterCollection
    Private m_Parameters As New System.Collections.ArrayList

    Default Public Overloads ReadOnly Property Item(ByVal index As String) As EventLogDataParameter
        Get
            For Each evntlgParam As EventLogDataParameter In m_Parameters
                If evntlgParam.ParameterName = index Then
                    Return evntlgParam
                End If
            Next evntlgParam
            ' No parameters are found, we simply return nothing.
            Return Nothing
        End Get
    End Property

    Public Function Add(ByVal parameter As Microsoft.ReportingServices.DataProcessing.IDataParameter) As Integer _
        Implements Microsoft.ReportingServices.DataProcessing.IDataParameterCollection.Add
        Return m_Parameters.Add(parameter)
    End Function

    Public Function GetEnumerator() As System.Collections.IEnumerator _
        Implements System.Collections.IEnumerable.GetEnumerator
        Return m_Parameters.GetEnumerator()
    End Function

End Class
```

Figure 13.16 The Implemented `ParameterCollection` Class

That's enough about parameters for now, but we'll have more to say about them because you'll need to make a few changes to the Command classes' `GetParameters` and `Parameters` methods to make things work.

Coding the IDbCommand and IDbCommandAnalysis Interfaces

These classes manage the query passed to the Data Processing extension. Here we'll pick off the Report Parameters and execute the query needed to return the DataReader.

1. To code these classes, open the `EventLogCommand` class and implement both the *IDbCommand* and the *IDbCommandAnalysis* interfaces, as shown in Figure 13.17.

```
Public Class EventLogCommand
    Implements Microsoft.ReportingServices.DataProcessing.IDbCommand
    Implements Microsoft.ReportingServices.DataProcessing.IDbCommandAnalysis
```

Figure 13.17 Creating the `EventLogCommand` Class

This stubs out the properties and methods shown in the object browser dump in Figure 13.18.

- ⟳O IDbCommand
  - ⊟ ⟳ Bases and Interfaces
    - ⊟ ⟳O IDisposable
      - ⟳ Dispose()
  - ⟳ Cancel()
  - ⟳ CreateParameter() As Microsoft.ReportingServices.DataProcessing.IDataParameter
  - ⟳ ExecuteReader(ByVal Microsoft.ReportingServices.DataProcessing.CommandBehavior) As Microsoft.ReportingServices.DataProcessing.IDataReader
  - ⟳ CommandText() As String
  - ⟳ CommandTimeout() As Integer
  - ⟳ CommandType() As Microsoft.ReportingServices.DataProcessing.CommandType
  - ⟳ Parameters() As Microsoft.ReportingServices.DataProcessing.IDataParameterCollection
  - ⟳ Transaction() As Microsoft.ReportingServices.DataProcessing.IDbTransaction
- ⟳O IDbCommandAnalysis
  - ⟳ GetParameters() As Microsoft.ReportingServices.DataProcessing.IDataParameterCollection

Figure 13.18 IDbCommand and IDbCommand Analysis Object Model

The properties on the IDbCommand object map to properties that you see in the DataSet Designer. You're already familiar with the *CommandText* property in the DataSet Designer as the query string—that's what we're implementing here.

2. To flesh out these interfaces, create the instance variables to support the properties, just as you have done before. Figure 13.19 shows how we coded these instance variables and the constructors. It looks like a lot of typing, but statement completion helps quite a bit. Notice the commented-out call to *System.Diagnostics.Debugger.Break()*. This is the easiest way to debug the Data Processing extension while using the Report Designer. When this Break is hit, a dialog is exposed that permits you to attach the debugger. Just remember to remove the debug code for the Release builds because you won't want that holding up a production Report Server. Sure, you could use conditional compile switches to bypass this code for production builds.

```
Private _EventLogConnection As EventLogConnection
Private _CommandText As String
Private _CommandTimeout As Integer = 0
Private _CommandType As _
  Microsoft.ReportingServices.DataProcessing.CommandType = _
  Microsoft.ReportingServices.DataProcessing.CommandType.Text
Private _Parameters As EventLogDataParameterCollection
Sub New()
    Me.New("", Nothing)
End Sub
Sub New(ByVal Connection As EventLogConnection)
    Me.New("", Connection)
End Sub
Public Sub New(ByVal cmdText As String, _
    ByVal connection As EventLogConnection)
    'System.Diagnostics.Debugger.Break()
    _CommandText = cmdText
    _EventLogConnection = connection
    _Parameters = New EventLogDataParameterCollection
End Sub
```

Figure 13.19 The Instance Variables and Constructors for the Command Class

3. Next, you need to wire up the properties for the instance variables. The *CommandText* and *CommandTimeout* properties are simply provided from the DataSet's *CommandText* (the query string) and *Timeout* properties. These are passed into these properties by the Report Server in a deployed report, and by the Report Designer in a report under development in Visual Studio .NET 2003.

Coding the CommandType Property

Reporting Services supports three values for the *CommandType* property:

- Text
- TableDirect
- StoredProcedure

These *CommandType* settings influence the way in which the Report Designer can choose to process the *CommandText*. For our custom Data Processing extension, we're only going to let our users use the Text type—we throw a NotSupportedException if they attempt to use TableDirect or Stored Procedure.

> **NOTE** There is a minor inconsistency between the Data Designer's generic query designer command types. All three command types are in the list of available types (as shown in Figure 13.20).

Figure 13.20 The Generic Query Designer Appears to Always Show All Command Types

However, notice that the Dataset dialog lists only the types that the Data Processing extension says it supports, as shown in Figure 13.21.

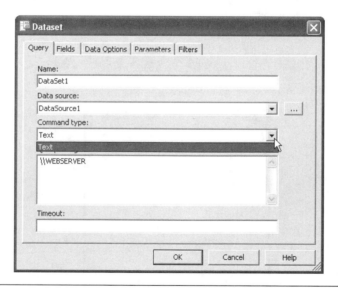

Figure 13.21 The Dataset Dialog Shows Only the Supported Command Types

What Text, StoredProcedure, or TableDirect means to your Data Processing extension is determined by your implementation. Figure 13.22 shows the code we used to ensure that only the Text *CommandType* is supported.

```
Public Property CommandType() As Microsoft.ReportingServices.DataProcessing.CommandType _
    Implements Microsoft.ReportingServices.DataProcessing.IDbCommand.CommandType
  Get
    Return _CommandType
  End Get
  Set(ByVal Value As Microsoft.ReportingServices.DataProcessing.CommandType)
    If Value <> Microsoft.ReportingServices.DataProcessing.CommandType.Text Then
      Throw New NotSupportedException
    End If
  End Set
End Property
```

Figure 13.22 Ensuring That the *CommandType* Supports Only Text

Coding the *GetParameters* Method

The Report Designer uses the `GetParameters` method on the *IDbCommandAnalysis* interface to generate the Parameters dialog, as shown in Figure 13.23. This also enables the Report Designer to map query parameters to corresponding Report Parameters.

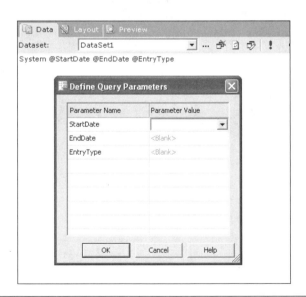

Figure 13.23 The Report Designer Creating the Parameters Dialog Generated from the CommandString

Because we decided to use the @ character to mark our query parameters, we can create a simple command syntax, which could be described as:

```
<EventLogName> [[@<ParameterName>] .. [@<ParameterName>]]
```

Code the `GetParameters` method, as shown in Figure 13.24. Within this method, our code parses the *CommandText* property to locate the parameters. Note that we create a new *EventLogDataParameterCollection*, populate it, and return it to the caller. No, the code *does not retain* a copy of this in the Command class. This might seem like a minor point, but we wasted many hours before we understood that the parameters are just used for the DataSet Designer.

```
Public Function GetParameters() As _
    Microsoft.ReportingServices.DataProcessing.IDataParameterCollection _
    Implements Microsoft.ReportingServices.DataProcessing.IDbCommandAnalysis.GetParameters
    ' We implemented this method by parsing the CommandText for the "@" symbol prefix
    ' and returns a EventLogDataParameterCollection object filled with any parameters found.
    Dim parameterNames As String() = Me.CommandText.Split("@".ToCharArray)

    If parameterNames.Length > 0 Then
        Dim DesignerParameters As New EventLogDataParameterCollection
        For i As Int32 = 1 To parameterNames.Length - 1
            DesignerParameters.Add(New EventLogDataParameter(Trim(parameterNames(i)), ""))
        Next

        Return DesignerParameters
    Else
        Return Nothing
    End If
End Function
```

Figure 13.24 Parsing the CommandText to Find Parameters for the Report Designer

Alternatively, instead of parsing the *CommandText* to locate parameters, we could have hard-coded the parameters returned to the *DesignerParameters* property.

Coding the Parameters Property

Take a look at Figure 13.25. It shows the implementation of the *IDbCommand.Parameters* property. The approach Microsoft takes here is a bit sneaky. Yes, this is a read-only property, but that's how the Data Processing extension passes back a reference to the Report

Designer and the Report Server. Yes, we said it's just a reference! To our classes, it's the instantiated *Parameters* collection. Because it's a reference that's passed out, the caller is able to add values to the collection and the Data Processing extension is able to use them. So don't get confused because the property is marked as read-only, or because there is no "Set" or other mechanism to pass parameter values in.

```
Public ReadOnly Property Parameters() _
   As Microsoft.ReportingServices.DataProcessing.IDataParameterCollection _
    Implements Microsoft.ReportingServices.DataProcessing.IDbCommand.Parameters
  Get
    Return _Parameters
  End Get
End Property
```

Figure 13.25 Implementing the *IDbCommand.Parameters()* Property

Coding the `CreateParameter` Method

When the IDE needs our Data Processing extension to build a new query parameter, it calls the `CreateParameter` method. This method simply returns a new EventLogDataParameter object.

Code the `CreateParameter` method as shown in Figure 13.26.

```
Public Function CreateParameter() As Microsoft.ReportingServices.DataProcessing.IDataParameter _
   Implements Microsoft.ReportingServices.DataProcessing.IDbCommand.CreateParameter
   Return New EventLogDataParameter
End Function
```

Figure 13.26 Coding the `CreateParameter` Method

Coding the Transactions Property

Our Data Processing extension does not need to support transactions, so all we need to do is make sure that the *Transaction* property Get accessor returns Nothing.

Code the *Transaction* property as shown in Figure 13.27.

```
Public Property Transaction() As Microsoft.ReportingServices.DataProcessing.IDbTransaction _
   Implements Microsoft.ReportingServices.DataProcessing.IDbCommand.Transaction
    Get
       Return Nothing
    End Get
    Set(ByVal Value As Microsoft.ReportingServices.DataProcessing.IDbTransaction)
       Throw New NotSupportedException("Transactions are not supported.")
    End Set
End Property
```

Figure 13.27 Returning Nothing for the Command Class's *Transaction* Property

Coding the `ExecuteReader` Class

Relax, this is not where we make use of the guillotine to execute our loyal readers, it's simply the method that's called to return a DataReader. For those of you who aren't familiar with ADO.NET, the DataReader object is a connected data stream returned when you execute the ADO.NET Command object's `ExecuteReader` method, which is responsible for executing the query in the *CommandText* against the open connection specified in the Command object.

For our Data Processing extension's implementation of the `ExecuteReader` class, we first check that the Connection is Open. However, in our case we don't really have a connection resource being held open, as in the case of a typical database or web connection. We added some code to illustrate how to test for a valid connection—but it's not really needed in this case. Next, we instantiate our `EventLogDataReader` and call our `GetEventLogEntries` method. This returns the DataReader to the Report Designer or Report Server. Figure 13.28 shows our implementation of the `ExecuteReader` method.

If your DPE needs connection pooling, it's up to you to implement it.

```
Public Function ExecuteReader _
  (ByVal behavior As Microsoft.ReportingServices.DataProcessing.CommandBehavior) _
    As Microsoft.ReportingServices.DataProcessing.IDataReader _
     Implements Microsoft.ReportingServices.DataProcessing.IDbCommand.ExecuteReader

    ' must have a valid and open connection
    If _EventLogConnection Is Nothing _
       OrElse _EventLogConnection.State <> System.Data.ConnectionState.Open Then
       Throw New InvalidOperationException("Connection must be valid and open.")
    End If
    ' Execute the command.
    Dim eventlog As String
    If Me.CommandText.IndexOf(" ") > 0 Then
       eventlog = Me.CommandText.Substring(0, Me.CommandText.IndexOf(" "))
    Else
       eventlog = Me.CommandText
    End If
    Dim reader As New EventLogDataReader(Me.Connection, _
       CType(Me.Parameters, EventLogDataParameterCollection))
    reader.GetEventLogEntries(eventlog)
    Return reader
End Function
```

Figure 13.28 Our Implementation of `ExecuteReader`

Coding the `EventLogDataReader` Class

We implemented the *IDataReader* (as shown in Figure 13.29) interface in the `EventLogDataReader` class. This is a much more streamlined version of the *System.Data.IDataReader* interface with only five methods and one property.

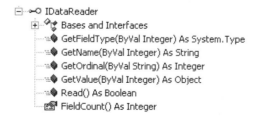

Figure 13.29 The *IDataReader* Interface

The *IDataReaderExtension* interface (as shown in Figure 13.30) inherits from the *IDataReader* interface and exposes additional methods for aggregation—which we don't need for our example Data Processing extension.

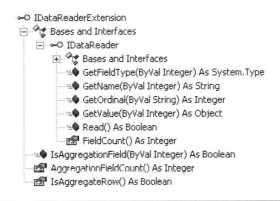

Figure 13.30 The *IDataReaderExtension* Interface

Reading Data from the EventLog

We read data from the selected Windows EventLog by accessing the .NET base class *System.Diagnostics* namespace. Here you'll find an EventLog class and methods that we can use. We can test to see whether a certain event log exists by calling the System.Diagnostics.EventLog.Exists method. To fetch the contents of a named EventLog on a specific machine, we can call System.Diagnostics.EventLog(EventLogName, machineName). The data returned contains a collection of all of the entries in the particular EventLog. Figure 13.31 shows our implementation.

The GetEventLogEntries method accepts the *CommandText* (*cmdText*) and stores the resulting EventLog entries in a private collection (*m_LogEntries*). We keep track of the entries using our own enumerator (*m_ie*).

```
Friend Sub GetEventLogEntries(ByVal cmdText As String)
  '  If Not Me.m_Connection._UserIdentity Is Nothing Then Me.m_Connection._UserIdentity.Impersonate()
  Dim machine As String = IIf(m_Connection.ConnectionString.Length = 0, ".", m_Connection.ConnectionString)
  ValidateCommandText(cmdText, machine)
  m_LogEntries = New System.Diagnostics.EventLog(cmdText, machine).Entries
  m_currentRow = -1
  m_ie = m_LogEntries.GetEnumerator()
  ' If Not Me.m_Connection._UserIdentity Is Nothing Then Me.m_Connection._UserIdentity.Impersonate.Undo()
End Sub


Private Sub ValidateCommandText(ByVal LogName As String, ByVal machine As String)
  Dim isValidCmd As Boolean = System.Diagnostics.EventLog.Exists(LogName, machine)
  If Not isValidCmd Then
    Throw New InvalidOperationException("The Selected EventLog does not exist.")
  End If
End Sub
```

Figure 13.31 The Call to Return the Collection of Event Log Entries and Validate the Existence of the Event Log

---

NOTE *Impersonating the User* Within the GetEventLogEntries call in Figure 13.31, you'll also see some commented-out calls that enable us to impersonate a Windows domain user during testing in the Report Designer. We'll talk more about that in just a moment.

When we instantiate the new EventLogDataReader class (as shown in Figure 13.32), we pass in the connection details that contain the EventLog desired and the *EventLogParameters* collection. Within the constructor, we instantiate class variables to hold the parameters so that when we read entries we can quickly filter them without having to do expensive searches on our parameter ArrayList.

No, this is not nearly all of the code used to implement the EventLogDataReader class. It's much too large to list here and well beyond the scope of this book to walk you through how it's done. The full implementation of the EventLogDataReader class is provided on the DVD.

```
Sub New(ByVal Connection As EventLogConnection, _
  ByVal Parameters As EventLogDataParameterCollection)
  m_Connection = Connection

  m_FilterEntryType = Convert.ToString(Parameters("EntryType").Value)

  If m_FilterEntryType = "%" OrElse m_FilterEntryType.Length = 0 Then
      m_FilterEntryType = "*"
  End If

  Dim startDate As String = Convert.ToString(Parameters("StartDate").Value)
  If startDate.Length = 0 Then
      m_FilterStartDate = System.DateTime.MinValue
  Else
      m_FilterStartDate = Convert.ToDateTime(startDate, _
      System.Globalization.CultureInfo.CurrentCulture)
  End If

  Dim endDate As String = Convert.ToString(Parameters("EndDate").Value)
  If endDate.Length = 0 Then
      m_FilterEndDate = System.DateTime.MaxValue
  Else
      m_FilterEndDate = Convert.ToDateTime(endDate, _
      System.Globalization.CultureInfo.CurrentCulture)
  End If

End Sub
```

Figure 13.32 The `EventLogDataReader` Constructor Class

Impersonation

When a deployed report connects to a Data Source through the
Data Processing extension, the Report Server is capable of imper-
sonating the authenticated user or impersonating the user whose
credentials are stored semi-securely in a custom or shared Data
Source. (The authenticated user accesses the Report Server [or
Report Manager] via the URL or SOAP interfaces.)

Alternatively, a deployed Data Source can:

- Prompt for credentials
- Use Integrated Security
- Impersonate the authenticated user after a connection
- Not use credentials at all

On the other hand, choices in the Data Designer are much more limited. By default, there is no intrinsic ability to impersonate a Domain user or indeed the Domain Name. (The User Name if represented as "DomainName\UserName" appears to get stripped down to just the User Name.) It is possible to get impersonation to work in the Data Designer, but you have to code the calls and come up with a delimiter other than "\". During testing of our custom Data Processing extension in the Data Designer, we modified the Connection class's `CreateCommand` method to parse a UserName that used an "@" for the delimiter. We also created a *System.Security.Principal.WindowsIdentity* from it. Take a look at the code commented out in the `CreateCommand` for an example. You'll also have to uncomment the instance variable *_UserIdentity* to support this. In Figure 13.31, look in the GetEvents call in the `Data Reader` class. There we commented out the code to impersonate and revert. The only other thing you'd need to do is add our Impersonation wrappers around the API calls to the project that we've supplied in Impersonate.vb. Perhaps Microsoft will give some attention to the impersonation in the Report Designer in a Service Pack after Service Pack 1.

Deploying and Configuring

Once you've compiled the custom Data Processing extension and have successfully built the project, you need to attend to a few housekeeping chores so that you can test, debug, and deploy your shiny new custom Data Processing extension.

Deploying the New DLL

First, you need to copy the DLL you just built to each of the three folders: for the Report Manager, Report Designer, and Report Server, as we did for the Microsoft FSI example. Take note that you may need to stop IIS and the Windows Report Server Service if you are replacing a DLL with a later version. You'll also need to close any open Visual Studio .NET 2003 development environments that contain report projects. This tedium is all about unlocking assemblies locked in the process space.

Figure 13.33 shows a Deploy.bat batch file that we use to simplify copying the compiled assembly to the correct folders. Note that we also copy the file to the Report Designer folder on the server (which is used to view reports from time to time as well).

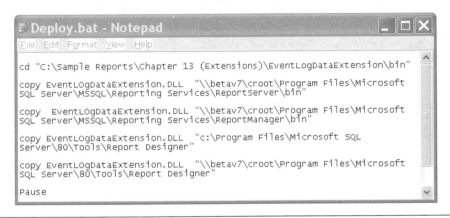

Figure 13.33 The Deploy.bat File We Place in the Bin Folder

Tuning the Config Files

As with the Microsoft FSI example we showed you early in this chapter, you'll have to tune the configuration files so that the Report Designer and the Report Server can "see" your custom Data Processing extension.

1. In *C:\Program Files\Microsoft SQL Server\MSSQL\ Reporting Services\ReportServer* locate the rssrvpolicy.config file and create the CodeGroup for the assembly, as shown in Figure 13.34. Yes, we're using URL evidencing, and we have to assign FullTrust. We'd have liked to have given just the EventLog permission, but it turns out that the System.Diagnostics assembly has a FullTrust Link demand, and that forces us to give FullTrust to our Data Processing extension <sigh>. In the Support Files folder in our sample project, you'll find a text file that you can use to cut and paste the required CodeGroup.

```
<CodeGroup class="UnionCodeGroup"
    version="1" PermissionSetName="FullTrust"
    Name="EventLogCodeGroup"
    Description="Code group for the HHG Event Log data processing extension">
    <IMembershipCondition class="UrlMembershipCondition"
    version="1"
    Url="C:\Program Files\Microsoft SQL Server\MSSQL\Reporting Services\ReportServer\bin\EventLogDataExtension.dll" />
</CodeGroup>
```

Figure 13.34 The CodeGroup for the rssrvpolicy.config File

Adjusting the Report Designer and RSPreviewHost.exe Config Files

2. You also need to edit the rspreviewpolicy.config file that you'll find in *C:\Program Files\Microsoft SQL Server\80\ Tools\Report Designer* to include a CodeGroup (as shown in Figure 13.35) similar to the one we used in Step 1. Take care that you are referencing the correct URL. Again, look in the Support Files folder in our sample project where we've provided a text file to cut and paste. This element must be placed in the MyComputer CodeGroup hierarchy, as we illustrated in Figure 13.2.

```
<CodeGroup class="UnionCodeGroup"
    version="1" PermissionSetName="FullTrust"
    Name="EventLogCodeGroup"
    Description="Code group for the Event Log Information data processing extension">
    <IMembershipCondition class="UrlMembershipCondition"
    version="1"
    Url="c:\Program Files\Microsoft SQL Server\80\Tools\Report Designer\EventLogDataExtension.dll" />
</CodeGroup>
```

Figure 13.35 The CodeGroup for the rspreviewpolicy.config File

3. We also need to update the RSReportServer.config file to link in the Data Processing extension. It's really important to edit this file correctly to introduce a new entry in the

<Data> section and ensure that the Type attribute is carefully typed, because it's case sensitive. The Data Processing extension Name is used in the DataSource table in the ReportServer database, as shown in Figure 13.36. Note that if you have configuration information to pick up from the SetConfiguration method (as we discussed earlier), the extension needs a <Configuration> element, as we show in Listing 13.7.

```
<Data>
  <Extension Name="SQL"
    Type="Microsoft.ReportingServices.DataExtensions.SqlConnectionWrapper,Microsoft.ReportingServices.DataExtensions"/>
  <Extension Name="OLEDB"
    Type="Microsoft.ReportingServices.DataExtensions.OleDbConnectionWrapper,Microsoft.ReportingServices.DataExtensions"/>
  <Extension Name="ORACLE"
    Type="Microsoft.ReportingServices.DataExtensions.OracleClientConnectionWrapper,Microsoft.ReportingServices.DataExtensions"/>
  <Extension Name="ODBC"
    Type="Microsoft.ReportingServices.DataExtensions.OdbcConnectionWrapper,Microsoft.ReportingServices.DataExtensions"/>
  <Extension Name="FSI"
    Type="Microsoft.Samples.ReportingServices.FsiDataExtension.FsiConnection,Microsoft.Samples.ReportingServices.FsiDataExtension"/>
  <Extension Name="EVENTLOG"
    Type="EventLogDataExtension.EventLogConnection,EventLogDataExtension"/>
</Data>
```

Don't try to add comments to these XML configuration files.
If you do they won't work.

Figure 13.36 The "EVENTLOG" Entry in the Data Element of RSReportServer.config

Adjusting the RSReportDesigner.config File

Finally, we also need to add two entries into the RSReportDesigner.config file that you'll find in the *C:\Program Files\ Microsoft SQL Server\80\Tools\Report Designer* folder. The first is an addition to the <Data> section to enable us to create Data Sources within the Visual Studio .NET 2003 environment, and the second is a change to the <Designer> section to force the DataSets to be designable only with the generic query designer. These entries (as shown in Figure 13.37) are also case sensitive.

```
<Data>
 <Extension Name="SQL"
   Type="Microsoft.ReportingServices.DataExtensions.SqlConnectionWrapper,Microsoft.ReportingServices.DataExtensions" />
 <Extension Name="OLEDB"
   Type="Microsoft.ReportingServices.DataExtensions.OleDbConnectionWrapper,Microsoft.ReportingServices.DataExtensions"/>
 <Extension Name="ORACLE"
   Type="Microsoft.ReportingServices.DataExtensions.OracleClientConnectionWrapper,Microsoft.ReportingServices.DataExtensions"/>
 <Extension Name="ODBC"
   Type="Microsoft.ReportingServices.DataExtensions.OdbcConnectionWrapper,Microsoft.ReportingServices.DataExtensions"/>
 <Extension Name="FSI"
   Type="Microsoft.Samples.ReportingServices.FsiDataExtension.FsiConnection,Microsoft.Samples.ReportingServices.FsiDataExtension"/>
 <Extension Name="EVENTLOG"
   Type="EventLogDataExtension.EventLogConnection,EventLogDataExtension"/>
</Data>
<Designer>
 <Extension Name="SQL"
   Type="Microsoft.ReportDesigner.Design.VDTQueryDesigner,Microsoft.ReportingServices.Designer"/>
 <Extension Name="OLEDB"
   Type="Microsoft.ReportDesigner.Design.VDTQueryDesigner,Microsoft.ReportingServices.Designer"/>
 <Extension Name="ORACLE"
   Type="Microsoft.ReportDesigner.Design.VDTQueryDesigner,Microsoft.ReportingServices.Designer"/>
 <Extension Name="ODBC"
   Type="Microsoft.ReportDesigner.Design.VDTQueryDesigner,Microsoft.ReportingServices.Designer"/>
 <Extension Name="FSI"
   Type="Microsoft.ReportDesigner.Design.GenericQueryDesigner,Microsoft.ReportingServices.Designer"/>
 <Extension Name="EVENTLOG"
   Type="Microsoft.ReportDesigner.Design.GenericQueryDesigner,Microsoft.ReportingServices.Designer"/>
</Designer>
```

Figure 13.37 The Amended RSReportDesigner.config File

Building a Report with the EventLog Data Processing Extension

Now that our custom EventLog Data Processing extension is ready to go, it's time to show it off. Let's build a sample report to see how it works.

1. Start a new report project—we call ours EventLogReport.
2. Create a DataSet and Data Source. Notice that the Data Source Type drop-down list now contains our custom Data Processing extension. Select the Event Log Information type.
3. In the Connection string dialog, enter the name of the system against which you wish to view the event logs. In this case we used "." (as shown in Figure 13.38) to indicate the

current system. To point to system "\\Fred," simply use "Fred" or the IP address of the machine you are targeting.

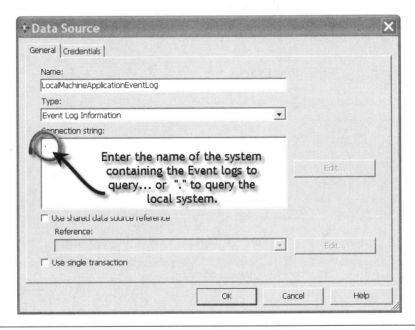

Figure 13.38 "Event Log Information" Now Appears as a Valid Data Source Type

4. On the Credentials tab, choose Use Windows Authentication (Integrated Security) and click OK.
5. Create a new report (manually) and open the Data tab. Enter the query shown in Figure 13.39 into the generic query designer dialog. This query returns information from the "application" event log and accepts the Report Parameters of @StartDate, @EndDate, and @EntryType.

Figure 13.39 Setting the CommandText in the Data Tab

6. Open the Fields list and notice the fields returned by this query to our custom Data Processing extension (as shown in Figure 13.40). We created some calculated fields here for MonthNumber:

```
(=Fields!TimeGenerated.Value.Month),
```

MonthName:

```
(=Format(Fields!TimeGenerated.Value,"MMMM")),
```

and Year:

```
(=Format(Fields!TimeGenerated.Value,"yyyy")).
```

Perhaps we could have built these expressions into the Data Processing extension and returned them as Fields from there. But because we only need these for a matrix-style report so that we can group and sort, perhaps it's better that we calculate them here.

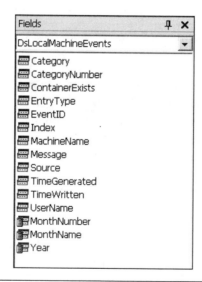

Figure 13.40 The Fields Returned by a Query Against the "Application" Event Log

We used some of these fields to create a SimpleMatrix EventLog report (as shown in Figure 13.41) using the Matrix control.

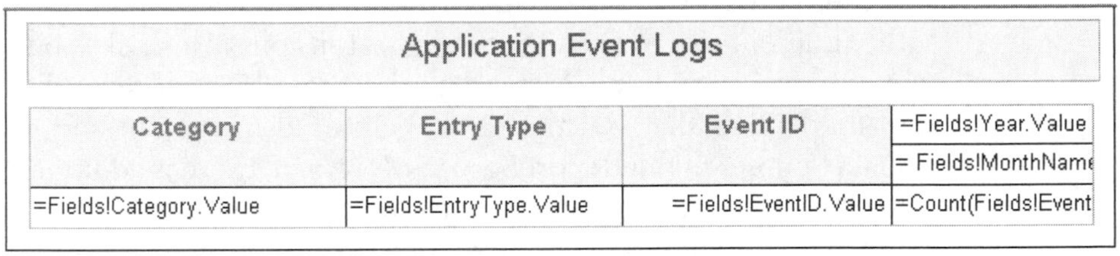

Application Event Logs			
Category	Entry Type	Event ID	=Fields!Year.Value
			= Fields!MonthName
=Fields!Category.Value	=Fields!EntryType.Value	=Fields!EventID.Value	=Count(Fields!Event

Figure 13.41 The SimpleEventLog Matrix Report in the Layout Tab

The completed version of this report is provided on the Premium Content Area of our website, along with a more sophisticated version that creates a Report Parameter to help construct the query CommandText. The rendered version of this report is shown in Figure 13.42. Note that the Preview tab does not render this report correctly—the Table control embedded in the Matrix control is hidden.

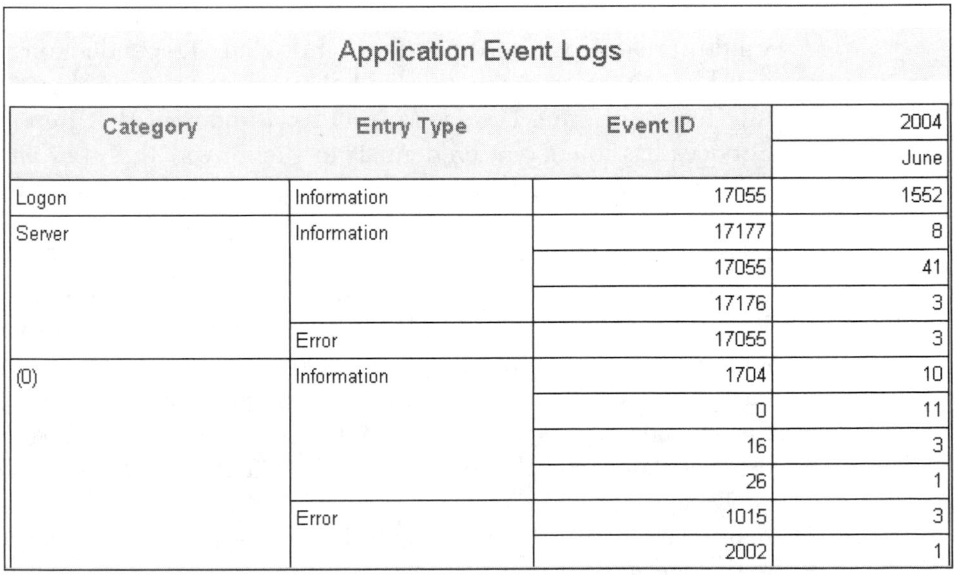

Application Event Logs			
Category	Entry Type	Event ID	2004
			June
Logon	Information	17055	1552
Server	Information	17177	8
		17055	41
		17176	3
	Error	17055	3
(0)	Information	1704	10
		0	11
		16	3
		26	1
	Error	1015	3
		2002	1

Figure 13.42 The Event Log Report Rendered in the Browser by the Report Manager

Security Considerations for Stored Credentials

At this point, we find it necessary to provide a warning to you about the inherent risk of Data Processing extensions. This risk is one that should make you think long and hard. Primarily, it concerns the level of credentials that you permit to be stored in custom and shared Data Sources in the Report Server. Moreover, there is additional risk in the implicit trust that you place in your programmers—namely, the rights granted to those programmers permitted to create and install Data Processing extensions.

Consider for a moment that in the Windows environment, passwords are stored by encrypting and hashing in such a way as to make them very difficult to reverse into the original plaintext password. Consequently, most attacks against operating system passwords by people with system administrator privileges are brute-force attacks. In this case, the hacker takes the hash table of passwords and the encryption key and using brute force tries to match the encrypted forms of the password against encrypted forms of words from dictionaries, lists of commonly used passwords, or just sequentially incrementing binary arrays. This is repeated by serially incrementing the values in an attempt to see if there's a match on the encrypted hash. A hacker with a match knows that he or she has a valid username/password pair for that domain. Depending on password length and strength, this kind of attack can take an almost infinite length of time. However, recall for a moment that Reporting Services has to encrypt credentials in such a way that they can be quickly and easily unencrypted back to their original plaintext forms so that they can be used to impersonate a specific user when connecting to data sources. Herein lies the risk. That is, Data Processing extensions may need to use those credentials that the Report Processor dutifully passes in plaintext into the *Password*, *UserName*, and *Impersonate* properties on the *IDbConnectionExtension* interface. It doesn't take long for the malevolent hacker to realize that this is a possible security vulnerability to exchange Data Processing extensions for ones that can harvest the plaintext credentials. What is perhaps a little more concerning is that it is trivial at this point to manipulate the DataSource table in the Report Server and get it to divulge *all* the stored user passwords in plaintext.

So we complete this book again with security in mind, imploring you to guard and control access to the DataSource table in the Report Server. Guard and control who can write and install Data Processing extensions for you and what they implement in those Data Processing extensions—especially if there is a need to implement the *IDbConnectionExtension* interface. So, in summary, to protect your system we highly recommend the following safeguards:

- Protect the DataSource table in the Report Server. This contains the keys to the kingdom. Be sure to follow our instructions in Chapter 2 (installation), in which we recommend that you use only a special Domain User account (that you have created for this purpose) for the Reporting Services to access the Report database. This is especially targeted at the ASP.NET user account—it should not have access to the DataSource table. No other account needs access to the DataSource table.
- Carefully consider the Access Control List (ACL) on the policy and config files to limit the ability to change the Reporting Services configuration files (as we have discussed in this chapter).
- Control the accounts with rights to deploy a Data Processing extension.
- Consider use of strongnames with code access security instead of URL evidencing to access the Data Processing extension DLL, as we illustrated in Chapter 9.

Summary

This chapter walked you through two Data Processing extensions—one to access the file system and another somewhat more sophisticated extension that makes use of parameters to access the system event logs. Given these two examples, we're sure you'll be able to adapt them to whatever data source you need to access for your reports.

Installing SSL on a Web Server

This appendix is intended for readers who need a bit more hand-holding when it comes to installing Secure Sockets Layer (SSL) on your web server. We discuss the importance of SSL security in Chapters 1 and 2. Here we'll walk you through the process of using the Internet Information Services (IIS) MMC snap-in to install SSL for your Default website. This certificate applies to all of the websites your server hosts, so you should inform your DBA before proceeding.

Installing SSL on Your Web Server

As we said in Chapter 2, if you're familiar with assigning an SSL web server certificate and already have one assigned to your Default website, you can probably skip this section. You don't have to install Reporting Services onto the machine hosting the SQL Server Report Server database catalog (but the machine will need a SQL Server license). Remember, all you need for Reporting Services is a machine running IIS server, ASP.NET 1.1, and a Default website with an SSL web server certificate. This can be a Windows 2000 Server or a Windows 2003 Server configured as an application server. It can even be a Windows XP system if you install IIS. The Reporting Services Setup program will check to make sure most of these requirements are in place when it is first started—all except the SSL certificate. Because you might not have an SSL web server certificate, we'd better tell you what you need to know about SSL.

Installing a Certificate Authority on Your Domain Controller

If you've already installed Certificate Authority services within your Domain, you can skip the following discussion that walks you through the process of installing a Certificate Authority. Yes, the service needs to run on a Windows 2000 or Windows Server 2003 system—Windows XP can't host this service. And, of course, this requires that you have access to the Administrator account or Administrative rights.

NOTE *Guide me! Demonstrations* To help make installing the Certificate Authority easy, we've included a Guide me! demonstration on the DVD that walks you through installation and configuration of an Active Directory integrated enterprise root Certificate Authority Server, and shows how we installed a certificate to the Default website. Take a look at this short demonstration—it will make it easy to setup this service.

Guide me!

Choosing a Certificate Authority

Apart from the network name to use in the certificate, some thought needs to be given to *which* Certificate Authority (CA) you're going to use to request the certificate. If you're on a Windows Active Directory Domain and all your users are members of the Domain, there may already be a CA for the Active Directory Domain. This is implemented by having Certificate Services installed on one of the domain servers configured in "Enterprise" mode. These cryptographic digital signatures are designed to be incredibly difficult to forge, even with all the computing power in the world, lots of time, and oceans of coffee. If you're installing Reporting Services on a Windows XP system, you'll have to obtain your web certificate from either an integrated domain CA (AKA enterprise Certificate Authority) or a stand-alone CA. By the way, Windows XP and Windows 2000 Professional cannot host Microsoft's Certificate Authority service.

If you request a web certificate from an Active Directory integrated Authority, that certificate will automatically be trusted by all client members of the Active Directory Domain. Trusted? Well, this is the whole point of SSL because software clients are able to inspect the public part of the certificate and perform various checks on it. These checks include:

- Verifying that the network name in the certificate agrees with the name the software client is using to access a site. In some cases, this can be an irritating case-sensitive comparison.
- Verifying that the current date is within the certificate's valid date range.
- Verifying the digital signature in the certificate against an internal database list of digital signatures that it already trusts.

It's also possible for a software client to check that a certificate was issued by a CA that it has decided to trust without having to contact the CA. However, there is also a mechanism for CAs to revoke certificates that have been issued. This means the CA maintains a Certificate Revocation List (CRL) that software clients can periodically download, and perform an additional check. Within each certificate, there is a property that indicates where the CRL can be accessed by the operating system when updating its copies of CRLs.

Permitting Access to Your Reporting Services Web Site from Outside Your Domain

It is also possible to sign your website with a certificate from an Active Directory integrated enterprise Certificate Authority and permit people outside your Active Directory Domain to securely access the website. However, each time these "outsiders" access the site (as when requesting a report), a dialog is exposed telling them that the website they are accessing is signed by a Certificate Authority that they have chosen not to trust. However, this dialog provides users with the ability to choose to trust that Authority for the future—subject to having sufficient rights to install certificates on their machine. You've seen other applications expose this dialog as you've wandered around on the web—Microsoft uses many of them to protect you and its own sites. If you have control over the installation of client software, you can mitigate this entirely by installing your Certificate Authorities public root certificate on the client machine so as to be trusted automatically.

All Windows operating systems contain an initial database of root CAs, whose certificates Microsoft has decided those operating systems will trust, and the Windows Update Service keeps this database up to date. This database includes commercial organizations such as Verisign (www.verisign.com), who happily provide you with a certificate for your website and lighten your bank account by a few dollars for the privilege—once you've convinced them that you are who you say you are. Of course, if you have a signed web server certificate, users who access your website with Microsoft Internet Explorer will trust you automatically and won't be scared away by a dialog asking if they really want to trust you.

Installing SSL on Your Website

Once the CA has been installed, or you've verified that it's already in place, you can use the IIS MMC snap-in to run the web server certificate wizard to create a new SSL certificate for your website—unless you already have a certificate installed.

To install SSL on a website, *all* you need is a web server certificate created and issued by a CA. The web server certificate is specifically created in response to a carefully crafted and encrypted request for that website from the IIS web server certificate wizard. Among other things, the wizard embeds details of the network DNS or NetBIOS name into the encrypted certificate request that will be used to address the website (this is referred to in the certificate as the *common name*). That sounds real easy, doesn't it? Sometimes it *is* easy, but to the uninitiated this can be fraught with a number of idiosyncratic problems out there just to make your day longer than it has to be.

To run this wizard, you should be logged into your system as a Domain Administrator or with an account that's a member of the Domain Administrator's group. For more details on this requirement, see "A Few Idiosyncratic Gotchas—SSL Web Certificates" later in this section.

The IIS certificate wizard can be invoked by selecting properties on the website in the IIS MMC snap-in, and clicking the Server Certificate... button on the Directory Security tab, as shown in Figures A.1 and A.2.

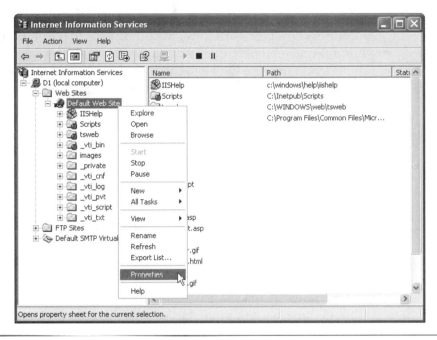

Figure A.1 Navigating to Your Website in the IIS MMC Snap-In

Figure A.2 The Default Website Properties Directory Security Dialog

For those who need more step-by-step guidance, you get to the web server certificate wizard by starting All Programs | Administrative Tools | Internet Information Services and selecting the target computer. Drill into the Web Sites list and choose the target Web Site. Next, right-click, choose Properties, and click on the Directory Security tab.

Here are a few step-by-step guidelines to help get you through the IIS certificate wizard if you have an enterprise Certificate Authority registered in your Domain.

1. Make sure you're running the wizard as a member of the Domain Administrators group. If not, don't bother.

2. When the wizard first starts, it asks if you want to create a new certificate. Click Create a New Certificate, and then click Next.

3. When prompted to delay the request, select "Send the request immediately…" and click Next.

4. Provide a descriptive name for the website SSL certificate—this name is used so that you can refer to the certificate in the Certificate Services database and also within IIS when managing the certificate. Choose something that identifies the website, "Default Website on Departmental Server X," for example.

5. Leave the bit length of the encryption at 1024 unless you need more durable encryption. This depends (in part) on your level of paranoia, but consider that more encryption means poorer performance. This is something you're going to have to decide on your own.

6. Leave the SGC and CSP boxes unchecked (for now).[1]

7. For the Organization Information, fill in your company and department name. This information will be presented to users when they're asked to trust you, so it's not a good idea to put something silly here.

---

[1] See the following website for more information on encryption and SGC/CSP: www.microsoft.com/technet/treeview/default.asp?url=/ technet/prodtechnol/windowsserver2003/proddocs/standard/ sec_encryp_aboutencryp.asp.

Okay, now you're ready to provide the network name. This is a bit complicated and very important, so we've dedicated an entire section to it.

Choosing the Right Network Common Name

The **network common name** is used to point to the Report Server and your reports on a network. You'll need to specify this name, as shown in Figure A.3. The Setup program uses the NetBIOS name no matter what you put here, but if you want to have your reports visible on the WWW, you're going to want to use a DNS name. However, Reporting Services was not really designed to deploy its reports to the Internet, and you'll face a number of security and other issues if you take this route. But we've not had any insurmountable problems accessing reports over the Internet—and you shouldn't either if you hold your mouth just right.

Putting the correct network name into the IIS certificate wizard is probably the most important part of the SSL installation because this name points to your Reporting Services website system. Don't bother using a NetBIOS name such as "OfficeSystem5" if the software clients connecting to the web server don't use NetBIOS names in the HTTPS URL used to access the website. For the same reason, it's pretty pointless to request a certificate with a network name of "localhost." Although you'll be able to access your local machine's IIS server with `https://localhost`, people on other machines won't be accessing your IIS server with that URL. If they tried, they would be addressing their local machine's IIS server, not yours!

Resolving NetBIOS or even DNS common names can be problematic. In many situations, a particular name might not be resolvable within or across trusted and non-trusted domains or across the room on a single server connection. There are a dozen dependencies that can make the decision to use a NetBIOS or DNS name for the common name particularly complicated. One way to cut through the morass, especially during testing, is to simply use the TCP/IP address for the common name in the certificate—this approach means side-stepping name resolution and case issues but does then mean that you'd have to reference the server along the lines of `https://<ip address>/Reports`. It's beyond the scope of this book to discuss the intricacies and sorcery behind your domain's network name resolution. We suggest you work with your Domain Administrator and figure out the best approach to use here.

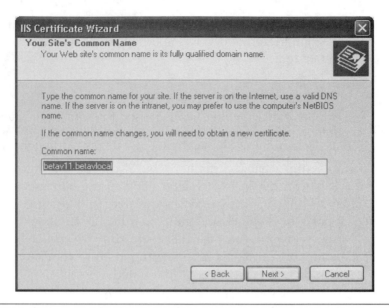

Figure A.3   Specifying a Common Name with Domain Specifically Referenced

The next steps of the IIS certificate wizard are pretty clear. The next dialog asks for your Country/region, State/province, and City/locality. If you don't know what these are or where you are, step away from the computer and get some rest or ask a grownup.

Next, you're asked to specify a Certification Authority. By default, if your domain already has a CA service running, choose the CA you want to use, click Next, and return to the Reporting Services installation dialog.

Guide me!

Creating a Certificate Request File Instead

We've included alternate instructions in Appendix B and discussion for getting a certificate through creating a certificate request file, and have included Guide me! narrated demonstrations on the DVD.

A Few Idiosyncratic Gotchas—SSL Web Certificates

When using the IIS web server certificate wizard to get a web certificate online from an Active Directory integrated enterprise Certificate Authority, you need to do this from an account with Domain Administration privileges, or more accurately an account that has been given sufficient permissions. First, you'll need a Domain Administrator's password and either use the Run as... option when launching the IIS MMC snap-in, or log in to the machine as a Domain Administrator. On a "server," you'll probably log in as a Domain Administrator, but if you are on your local development machine, which is a member of a domain, as a good practitioner of secure computing you should usually log in with an account that has at most Domain User privileges. Although, if you are a developer, that Domain User might indeed have Administrative rights over your own workstation.

If you are creating a request file to send in a browser to a Windows 2000–based stand-alone Certificate Server through the web interface, for example, by using http://<windows 2000 Domain Server with CA>/certsrv, make sure that the "certsrv" part and the network name in the certificate request are all lowercase. We've had lots of frustrating issues with the stand-alone Certificate Server, which have been "fixed" in the Windows Server 2003 version.

Using Secure Sockets Layer for Reporting Services

Creating an SSL Certificate to Ensure Your Confidential Reports Remain Confidential

We (Peter Blackburn and Bill Vaughn) are in the middle of writing our new book on Microsoft SQL Server Reporting Services, *Hitchhiker's Guide to SQL Server 2000 Reporting Services* (Addison-Wesley). While doing research for the book, the text of this article was left out on the table. We thought it was a good candidate for MSDN.[1]

One of our primary concerns as we write this book is security. It seems to be on everyone's mind nowadays. Security can mean a variety of things, including the ability to keep confidential information confidential. This is an expansive topic that could range from server physical security to network security to restricting access to login names and passwords and beyond. All the locks in the Pentagon won't protect your data if you're not vigilant about how the new Microsoft Reporting Services is installed—and that's the reason for this article.

---

[1] This appendix is based on an article published by MSDN (Microsoft Developer Network) and is provided here with permission from Microsoft Corporation.

Security can be a very large and daunting topic. It's often difficult to understand and more difficult to get right; in our experience developers sometimes feel that they're out of their depth when people start discussing Public Key Infrastructure (PKI), root Certificate Authorities, Trusts, certificates, Secure Sockets Layer (SSL), and the like. What we want to do here is give you some easily digestible information that can lower the access bar to your understanding. We provide several experiments that you can try in your development environments before implementing the code or configuration on production environments, which will enable you to secure the website where you intend to install Reporting Services.

In particular, we'll show you how you can install a root Certificate Authority and request certificates to secure a website. We'll also discuss when it is appropriate (if not just convenient) to shell out $500 a year for the benefit of a web server certificate, instead of one from a publicly trusted Certificate Authority.

We'll discuss securing an IIS server website, so you'll need Administrative rights to the IIS server. In addition, if you're going to install and then issue certificates from your own domain enterprise root Certificate Authority, you'll also need Domain Administrative rights. This means that if these server and network rights elude you, go and talk to those within your organization who manage your company domain and scare them silly. Tell them that you're planning to tear down the production network and shred the Active Directory to implement a PKI solution. They'll politely thank you for the warning, and help you clear your desk as the security guards manhandle you to the exit or nearest window. Seriously, though, in a production environment your organization may already have a PKI plan (and if it doesn't it probably would benefit from one). You'll likely want to be part of that, rather than paddling your own canoe. Network administrators have the ultimate power to chop you off by removing your network access, so don't get on their wrong side in a production environment when you're experimenting with the configurations we're going to show you here.

What Is SSL and Why Is It Important?

SSL is the acronym for *Secure Sockets Layer*. We all use it—every time we go to a secure website to order memory, books, or an airline ticket.

When the URL starts with https://, you're using SSL. In Internet Explorer, when you are viewing https:// web pages that are protected by SSL, you'll see the little lock symbol on the status bar.

Basically, the web server encrypts the raw HTTPS data being moved over the network (the WWW) so that "evil doers" out there can't sniff the wire and extract important information. The https:// pages use keys embedded in the web server's SSL certificate and encrypt the network traffic between browser and server; http:// pages don't—they leave everything in plaintext while in transit on the network. This makes the data about as hard to read as this article.

SSL and Reporting Services

When you install Reporting Services on a system, one of the first things the Setup dialog asks is should it use SSL to gate access to the Reporting Services and encrypt the data and credentials being moved over the wire. Your answer had better be yes. If it isn't, you might have a lot of explaining to do to your boss or the stockholders when important company information is compromised.

> ☑ Use SSL (Secure Sockets Layer) connections when retrieving data on these virtual directories.

The Setup program even warns you if you uncheck the box (as shown in Figure B.1). We encourage all of our readers and customers to enable SSL in virtually all cases. Sure, it means that the reports run a bit slower because the web server must decrypt and encrypt data being sent to and from the browser, but this is a small price to pay for better data security.

Figure B.1 If You Don't Check "Use SSL" in the Setup Dialog, You Get a Final Warning

To enable SSL on your Reporting Services website, you simply need to install an SSL *web site certificate*. This certificate contains information about your website such as who owns it and when it is valid. Figure B.2 shows the certificate we created to the website where we installed Reporting Services to use SSL within the closed world of our development Active Directory Domain, betavlocal.

Figure B.2 SSL Website Certificate Created for Our Reporting Services Website

How Does Reporting Services Use SSL?

Reporting Services executes queries against specified data sources as it generates the reports—this means it's going to need login credentials (Login ID and Password). These credentials can be referenced in several ways, including:

- Specifying the credentials explicitly within a report itself.
- Storing the credentials within a shared data source.
- Using the credentials of the user running the report (SSPI).
- Querying the user for appropriate credentials.
- Passing credentials to use in the URL.
- Extracting credentials via the POST verb of an http:// command.

These last few are particular risky because if the credentials are passed from the browser over http:// (effectively in plaintext) they might be intercepted and harvested with relative ease. To raise the security bar, you'll want to be able to ensure that login credentials should be transmitted only while accessing the Report Server over an https:// connection where the web server takes steps to encrypt the traffic.

The Report Server exposes Reporting Services' SOAP endpoint, and Visual Studio .NET deploys the report by simply making calls to public SOAP methods. At some point in time, you might want to create client software to utilize the SOAP web methods on the Report Server other than using the URL-based interface. The SOAP interface is the primary interface to Reporting Services—these web methods expose everything Reporting Services can do. A custom application written against these methods could create and launch reports or lots of other custom operations such as create and manage report schedules, adjust management group permissions, and more. Yes, many of these SOAP web methods can be used and accessed directly via HTTP, but more than a baker's dozen of these methods insist on the connection being secure in order to call them. This means if you don't have Secure Sockets Layer (SSL) installed on your web server (IIS), you just won't be able to call them.

Getting an SSL Certificate

Hopefully, you've been convinced that you need an SSL certificate, but now you need to know how to get one. Well, you can take one of two approaches: use your own Certificate Authority (CA), by way of installing Microsoft Certificate services, or use a public root Certificate Authority such as Verisign (www.verisign.com) or Thawte (www.thawte.com). The route you choose probably depends on whom you want to trust you (or more accurately, trust your website) by default.

When your users browse to a website that has an SSL web server certificate provided by an untrusted CA, the dialog shown in Figure B.3 greets them (or, more likely, scares them away).

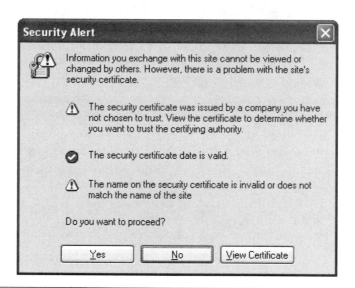

Figure B.3 A Security Alert Dialog Exposed When an HTTPS Site Is Not Trusted

"Trust" is at the heart of the issue here, as certificates are issued from CAs and the operating system has to make a decision—whether or not to trust that a particular certificate has been cryptographically signed by who the certificate *says* signed it. By default, all Microsoft Windows operating systems maintain an internal database (which is updated by the Windows Update Service) of all public root Certificate Authorities whose certificate signatures will be trusted by all Windows computers (which are kept current via Windows Update).

Windows computers that are members of a particular Active Directory Domain will also by default trust any certificates issued by any enterprise Certificate Authorities installed and registered within that particular Active Directory Domain.

Obtaining a web server SSL certificate from a public root Certificate Authority can cost $500 per year. In addition, the organization that sells you the certificate will most probably take steps to ensure that you are who you say you are, and that you have the legal right to have the certificate for which you are applying. They are the well-paid guardians of security.

While you are learning and testing, you are unlikely to want to fork out $500 a throw just for a certificate that you're going to throw away and not use in production. You might like to follow the steps we discuss here to setup your own Certificate Authority—even if only temporarily during the development phase.

Installing Your Own Certificate Authority

Generally, you can setup two configurations for the out-of-the-box Windows Server Certificate Authority. One is integrated within an Active Directory (an enterprise root Certificate Authority), the other is a stand-alone CA. For each of those configurations, you can determine whether the CA is a root Certificate Authority (a CA that is not signed by another CA) or a subordinate CA that needs to obtain a certificate itself from another CA before it can start to issue any certificates.

We're going to talk about installing a root Certificate Authority—one that's not signed by another CA. On the Windows 2000 Server or Windows Server 2003 Control Panel, click on the Add/New Programs icon, select Add/Remove Windows Components, and choose to add Certificate Services. You'll see a wizard like the one shown in Figure B.4.

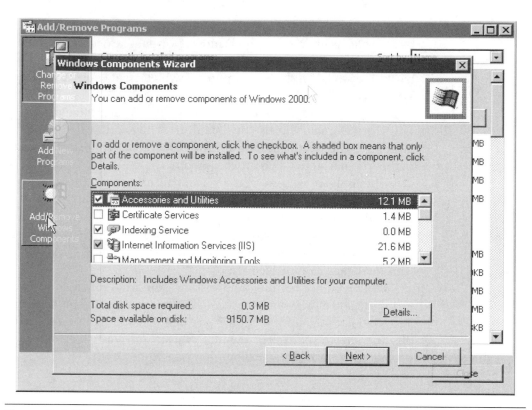

Figure B.4 The Windows Components Wizard

You'll be warned by the installation wizard that once you have installed Certificate Services you will be unable to rename the computer, or join or leave a domain. We suppose this means you won't be able to go home tonight....

The next step of the installation asks you to choose which type of CA you wish to install, as shown in Figure B.5. If you have an Active Directory Domain, you can select an enterprise Certificate Authority. If this is going to be the first CA in your domain, you'll want to choose the enterprise root CA. If you don't have an Active Directory Domain, you can choose to install a stand-alone CA, and if it's to be the first Certificate Authority you'd choose the stand-alone root CA. (Be advised if you install a stand-alone CA that by default no one at all—not even machines within the Active Directory

Domain—will trust any of its certificates, and you are going to have to take additional steps at each machine that expects to trust its certificates.) On Windows 2000 Servers, the main difference (as we'll see later) comes when asking the server for a certificate. Stand-alone Certificate Authorities on Windows 2000 Servers cannot be configured to automatically issue a certificate in response to a request. It requires the intervention of a Domain Administrator to explicitly issue certificates requested, but we'll see all that in just a minute.

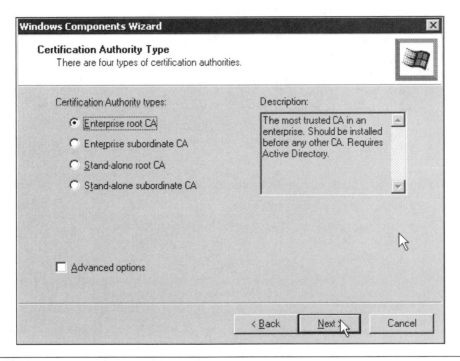

Figure B.5 Choosing a Certification Authority Type

The rest of the configuration options are similar. They simply prompt for information that identifies the Certificate Authority and the company that's creating it (see Figure B.6). Now is no time for levity, as this information will be presented to users when it comes time for them to trust certificates generated by the CA.

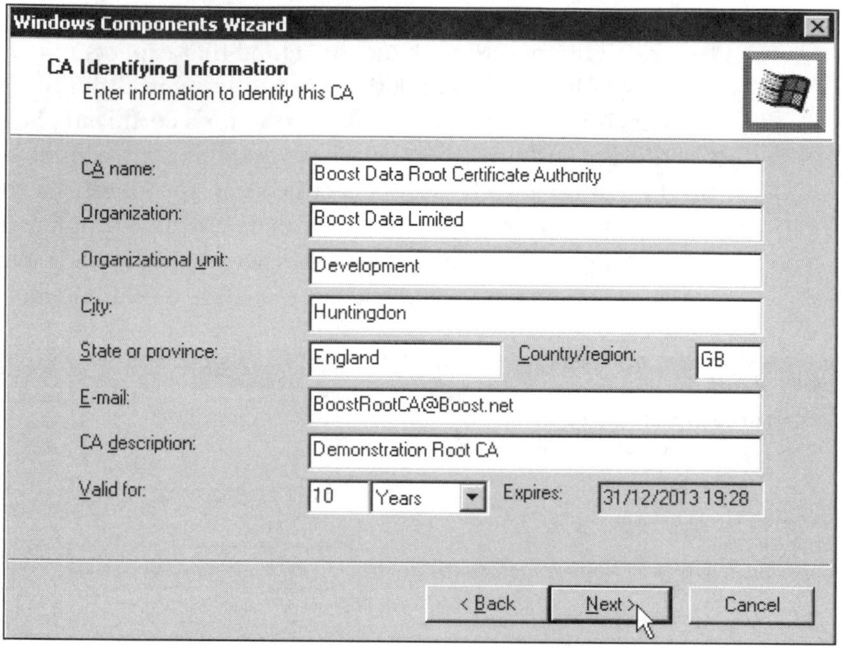

Figure B.6 Identifying the Name and Creator of This CA

And that is *it*. You can click through to the end of the wizard, which will stop IIS server and install a Certificate Services ISAPI to enable you to ask for certificates via a web interface. That interface will be on http://<server name>/certsrv.

By the way, make sure if you installed onto Windows 2000 Server that when you access the Certificate Services web interface you always use lowercase for "certsrv." There is a little quirk that causes it not to work if you don't. Thankfully, that quirk has been fixed in the Windows Server 2003 version.

Obtaining a Web Server SSL Certificate

Now that we have a Certificate Authority installed, let's get a certificate for our Default website that can then enable us to install Reporting Services with SSL checked. We practice safe computing in our enterprises, and we advocate to developers that they do the same. One of the things we ensure is that while our own personal accounts have Administrative rights over our own development domain workstations, our user accounts don't have Administrative rights per se on the domain. We mention this because when it comes to requesting a certificate from an enterprise Certificate Authority integrated with the Active Directory, the ordinary policy is only to accept requests and issue certificates for web server SSL certificates that have Domain Administrative privileges. This means you can either log in as a Domain Administrator, or you can use Run as… (as shown in Figures B.7 and B.8) and run the IIS MMC snap-in under the credentials of a Domain Administrator.

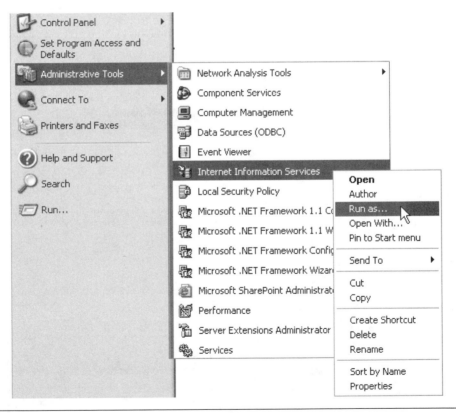

Figure B.7 Starting the IIS MMC Snap-In Using Run As…

Figure B.8 Providing Domain Administrator Credentials to Run As...

Once the IIS MMC snap-in is launched, navigate to the Default website and pull up its properties, as shown in Figure B.9.

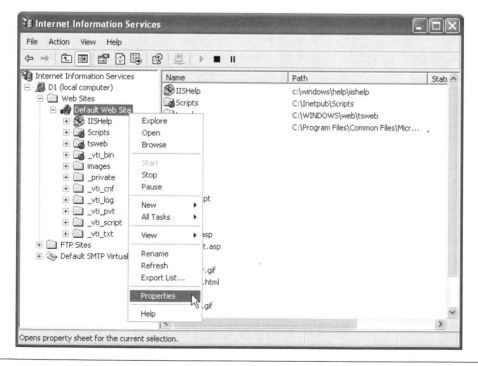

Figure B.9 Navigating to the Default Website Properties Dialog

Next, scuttle along to the Directory Security tab and select the Server Certificate button (as shown in Figure B.10).

Figure B.10 The Default Website Properties Page with the Directory Security Tab Selected

This launches the Web Server Certificate Wizard, as shown in Figure B.11.

We're creating a new certificate, so we'll select "Create a new certificate" as shown in Figure B.12.

Figure B.11 The Welcome Page of the Web Server Certificate Wizard

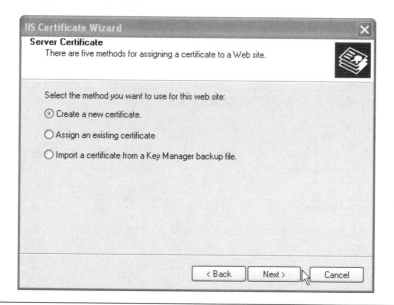

Figure B.12 IIS Certificate Wizard—Creating a New Certificate

At this point, we might have an opportunity to "Send the request immediately to an online certification authority" (as shown in Figure B.13). What this really means is that Active Directory has noticed that there is a Certificate Authority in the Active Directory Domain that can be a source for a new certificate. If you didn't install an enterprise Certificate Authority, this option will be grayed out. If you wish to request a certificate from a public Certificate Authority, you should select "Prepare the request now, but send later." This will prepare a request file for you. For our example, we're going to "Send the request immediately to an online certification authority," but keep reading because the next few steps are the same, regardless of which route you take.

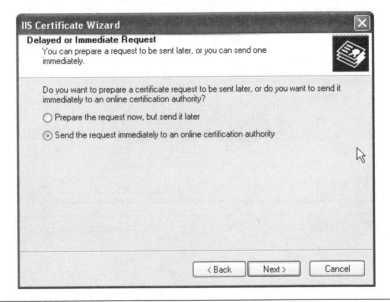

Figure B.13 IIS Certificate Wizard—Send the Request Immediately

At this point, you need to name the certificate (as shown in Figure B.14). This is not terribly important—it is only a memory aid to enable you to identify the certificate. What *is* important is the bit length. The longer the bit length the more difficult it is for malevolent people to decrypt any network traffic they might intercept—conversely, the longer the bit length the more load you put on the server encrypting and decrypting. It's a compromise.

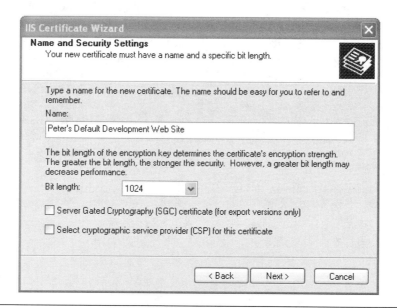

Figure B.14   IIS Certificate Wizard—Naming the Site and Setting the Encryption Bit Length

The next page of the wizard (as shown in Figure B.15) will ask for other identifying information of the organization and the organizational unit. Again, these are not terribly important to the functionality; they're just identifying information that will get embedded in the certificate.

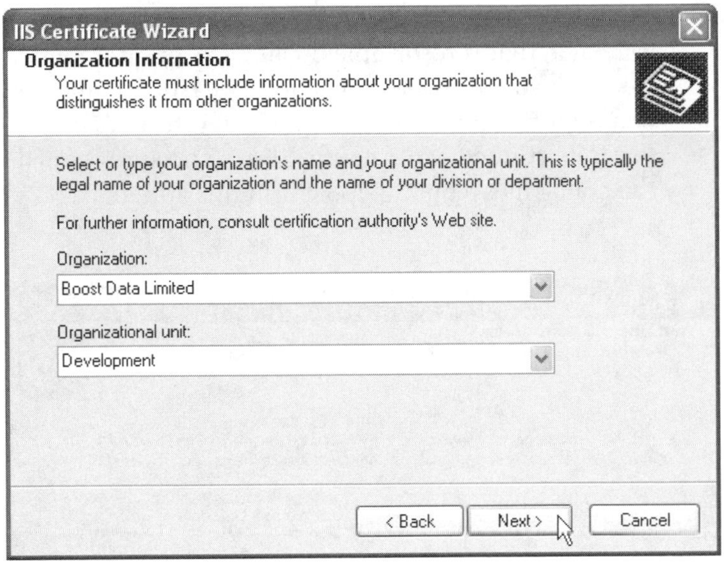

Figure B.15 IIS Certificate Wizard—Naming the Organization

This next part is probably the most important section of the certificate request to get right—naming the site. This name gets embedded in the certificate's *common name* property. By default, the wizard picks out the machine's NetBIOS name. This is all very well if the site is only going to be used with HTTPS on an internal network where NetBIOS names might be resolvable. Reporting Services version 1 was not really designed for Internet deployment scenarios, but even in intranet situations you may find that NetBIOS names are not always resolvable. In fact, if you've got the SSL checked during install, the NetBIOS name is embedded into the configuration files, irrespective of whatever you choose here.

If you decide to use a NetBIOS name as the common name (as shown in Figure B.16), we've found putting the name in lowercase leads to fewer problems. We chose to use a full DNS name, d1.internal.boost.net, which identifies a machine on our the internal intranet networks and means that when addressing that machine over HTTPS, we will need to do so in the form of `https://d1.internal.boost.net`. What we advise folks to use is a name that is resolvable on all parts of interconnected networks. Because we are requesting a non-NetBIOS name into the common name on the certificate, we are going to have to make changes to the Reporting Services config files, so be sure to read the section on the config files, coming up later in this appendix.

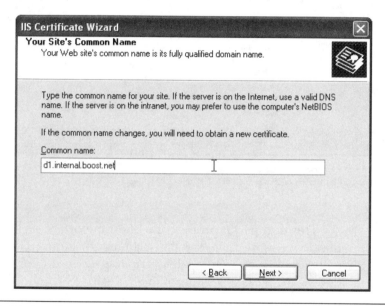

Figure B.16 IIS Certificate Wizard—Naming the Organization

Next, the wizard collects more identifying information (as shown in Figure B.17) that's not crucial but will get embedded into the certificate issued.

If we have an enterprise Certificate Authority in the Active Directory Domain, the wizard lets us choose which CA within the Active Directory Domain will source the certificate (as shown in Figure B.18).

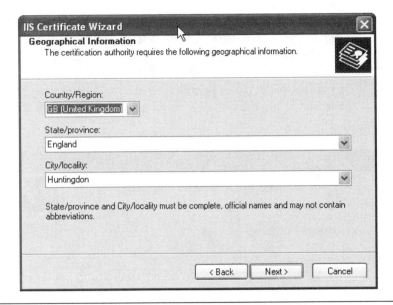

Figure B.17 IIS Certificate Wizard—Geographical Information

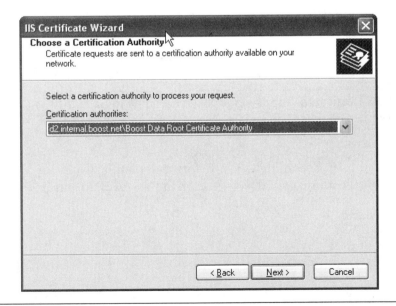

Figure B.18 IIS Certificate Wizard—Choosing a Certification Authority

Or, if we wish to request a certificate from a stand-alone certificate server or from a public root Certificate Authority, then at the dialog shown in Figure B.13 we'd have selected "Prepare the request now, but send it later." In that case, instead of getting a Certificate Authority to choose from we'd have the option to choose where to save the request file (as shown in Figure B.19).

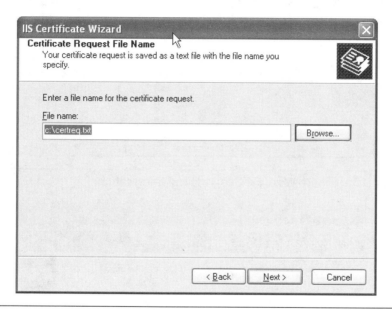

Figure B.19 IIS Certificate Wizard—Providing a Filename to Save the Certificate Request

Accordingly, just before completing you'll see either of these confirmation dialogs (shown in Figures B.20 and B.20A):

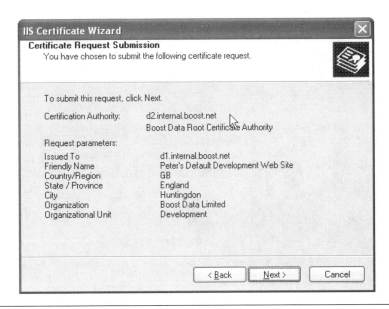

Figure B.20 IIS Certificate Wizard—Confirming the Online Enterprise Certificate Authority from Which to Request a Certificate

Or...

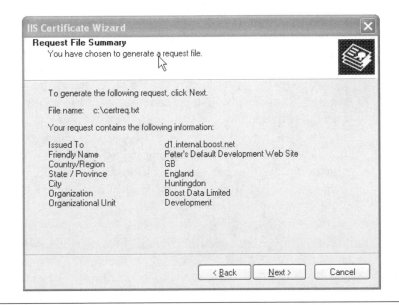

Figure B.20A IIS Certificate Wizard—Providing a Filename to Save the Certificate Request

And if you were requesting a certificate from an online Active Directory integrated certificate server, you'll hopefully get the confirmation screen shown in Figure B.21 and you're done. You have a certificate installed, so skip ahead to where we talk about testing it.

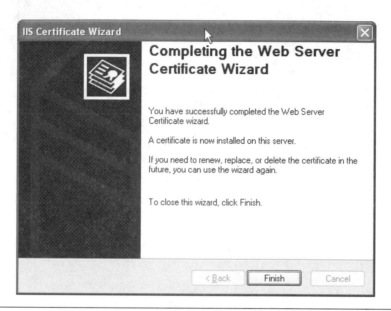

Figure B.21 IIS Certificate Wizard—Completion

If you were going down the request file route, you have a bit more work to do because you need to take the request file created and submit it manually to a certificate server (as shown in Figure B.22).

If you installed a stand-alone certificate server, you should be able to access that server's web interface via `http://<server>/certsrv`. Select "Request a certificate," as shown in Figure B.23.

Figure B.22 IIS Certificate Wizard—Passing the File to the CA

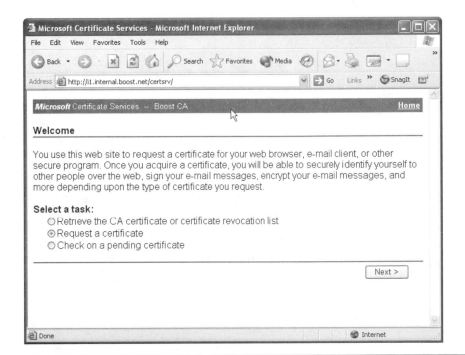

Figure B.23 Accessing the CA Certificate Services via HTTP

Next, choose "Advanced request" as shown in Figure B.24.

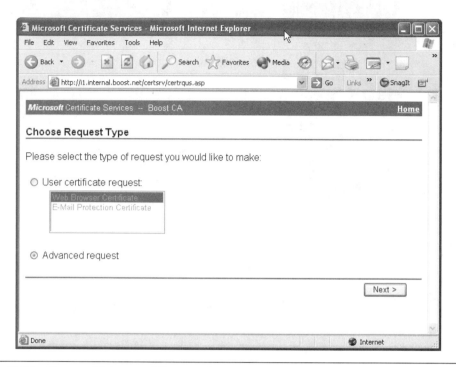

Figure B.24 Choose "Advanced Request"

Next, select that you want to submit a certificate request using a file, as shown in Figure B.25.

Use Notepad to open the request file that the wizard created earlier, certreq.txt, and copy the contents, including the lines "-----BEGIN NEW CERTIFICATE REQUEST-----" and "-----END NEW CERTIFICATE REQUEST-----" to the Clipboard to be ready to paste into the web form (as shown in Figure B.26), and then...

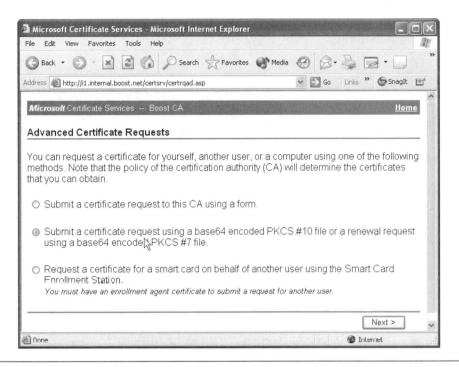

Figure B.25 Submit Certificate Request

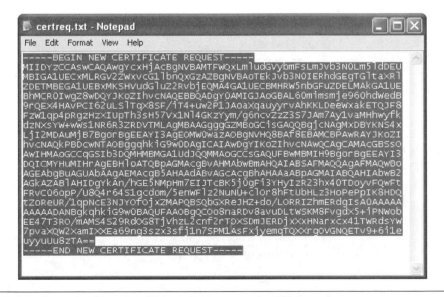

Figure B.26 Copy the New Certificate Request to the Clipboard

...paste it into the web form (as shown in Figure B.27), and click Submit.

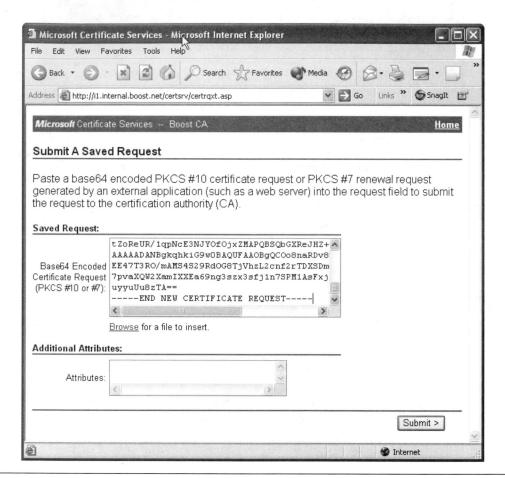

Figure B.27 Paste the New Certificate Request into the Base64 Encoded Request Dialog

At this point, you have submitted your request to the stand-alone Certificate Authority. You may have to wait for an administrator to approve the certificate request (as shown in Figure B.28).

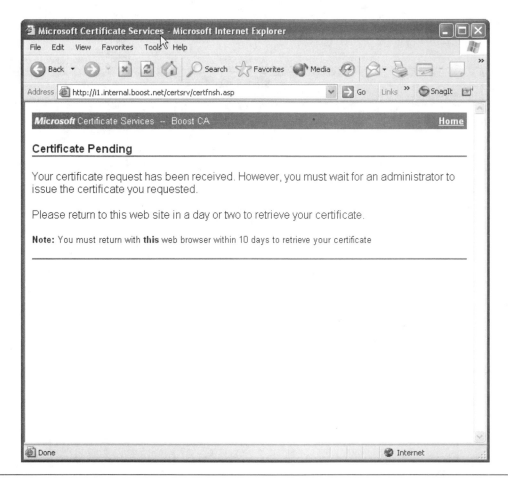

Figure B.28 Certificate Pending Approval

At this point, you need to get onto the server, launch the Certificate Authority MMC snap-in from the Administrative Tools menu (as shown in Figure B.29), and look up the pending requests. When you find the request for the web server certificate, select to "Issue" the certificate from the right mouse click context menu.

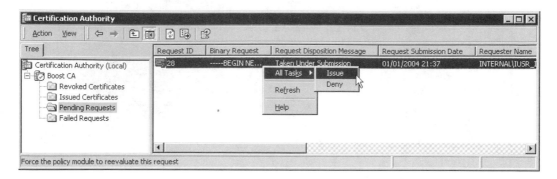

Figure B.29 Certificate Authority MMC Snap-In

You can then return to the browser and retrieve the certificate by checking on a pending request (as shown in Figure B.30):

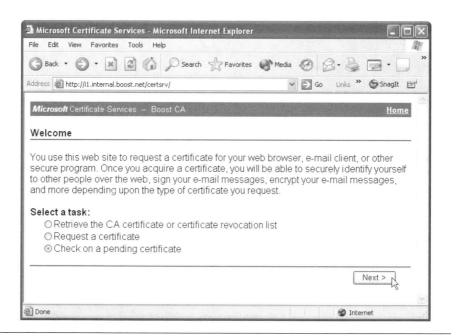

Figure B.30 Fetch the Status of the Pending Certificate

The Certificate Authority returns the saved certificate request (as shown in Figure B.31)...

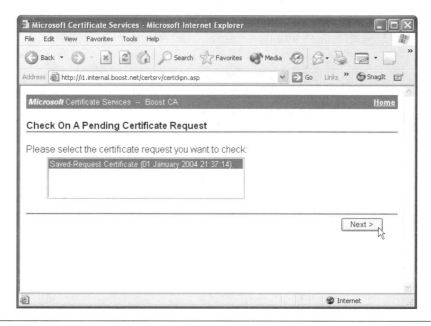

Figure B.31 Select the Certificate to Query

…which returns the status, as shown in Figure B.32.

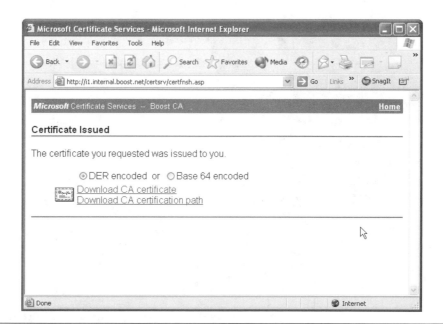

Figure B.32 Response from the CA

Clicking on "Download CA certificate" will download a certnew.cer file that contains the web server certificate you requested. It does not download the public certificate for the Certificate Authority that issued the certificate. This downloaded file will be "expected" by the IIS web certificate wizard, as we'll see in a moment. However, if the IIS machine doesn't already trust certificates from the certificate server, it is probably a good idea to download the CA certification path, which includes the SSL web certificate and the public certificate of the Certificate Authority in a certnew.p7b file.

If you're acquiring your SSL web server certificate from a public root Certificate Authority, follow the CA's specific instructions to send them the certificate request file, certreq.txt, and they'll provide you with your certificate in a file.

After making your choice and downloading the certificate file, you are ready to go back to the IIS MMC snap-in. Next, select the Default website's Properties dialog, navigate back to the Directory Security tab, and launch the Web Server Certificate Wizard again (as shown in Figure B.33). Notice that this time when you launch the Certificate Wizard it knows that it has an outstanding request.

Figure B.33 Relaunching the Certificate Wizard

Unless you want to delete the request, you should process it (as shown in Figure B.34).

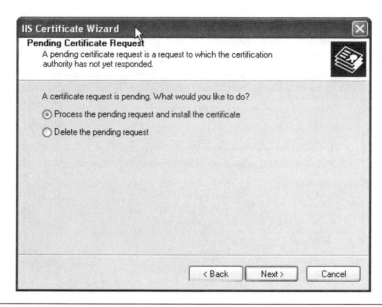

Figure B.34 Process the Pending Request

This gives you the opportunity to locate the downloaded certificate file—either the certnew.cer or the certnew.p7b file, as shown in Figure B.35.

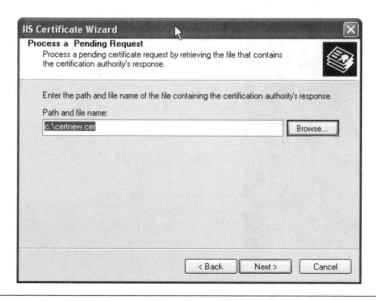

Figure B.35 Provide the Filename Containing the CA Response

This returns a confirmation dialog verifying that things are as you want them (as shown in Figure B.36).

Figure B.36 The Certificate Summary

At long last, you get the completion page (shown in Figure B.37).

Figure B.37 The Final Confirmation Page

Phew! Now you should have a certificate installed. It's a good idea to test that your certificate is installed by checking that you can access pages on the Default website over HTTPS using the NetBIOS name or the full DNS name you chose for the common name in the certificate.

Caveat About Stand-Alone Certificate Authority

If you installed a stand-alone Certificate Authority, no machine will by default trust certificates it issues. This means that you're going to have a huge deployment issue to address. You'll need to figure out how to enable each and every client machine to trust the certificates. Yes, there are mechanisms and contortions that you can go through. For example, you can navigate from each machine back to the `http://<server>/certsrv` interface and retrieve the CA certificate, as Figure B.38 shows.

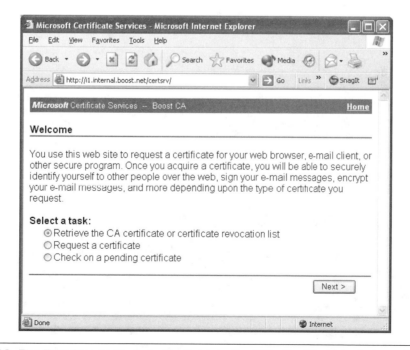

Figure B.38 The First Step in Choosing to Retrieve the CA's Certificate in Order to Trust It

Next select "Install this CA certification path," as shown in Figure B.39.

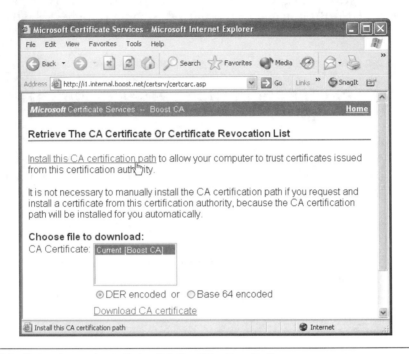

Figure B.39 Selecting to Install the CA Certification Path

And here we terrify users and take them into territory that their simple user accounts might not be permissioned to venture into, as shown in Figure B.40

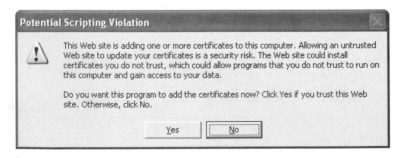

Figure B.40 Warning Dialog That Something's Going on with Your Certificates

If the install of the Certificate Authority's public certificate is successful, you'll get the confirmation page shown in Figure B.41.

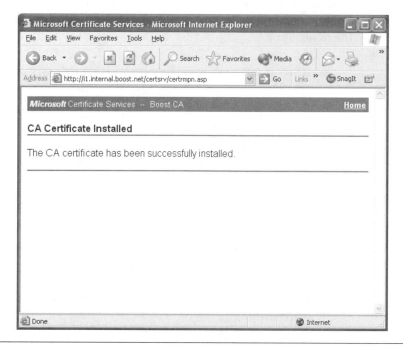

Figure B.41 All Done—the Certificate Authority Is Trusted by One Machine

Other mechanisms permit a stand-alone root Certification Authority to be trusted as well. However, it's all a *big* hassle, isn't it? It's so much easier to shell out $500 and get a certificate from a public root Certificate Authority—especially if you need to sign a website with a certificate that can be trusted outside an Active Directory Domain.

Install Reporting Services

At this point, you'll be able to complete the installation of Reporting Services and leave the SSL checkbox "on"—which is the reason for this article in the first place.

Reporting Services Configuration Files

If you used anything other than the NetBIOS name in the common name for the web server certificate, you'll need to make several changes to some configuration files. The following list details these changes.

- **RSReportServer.config:** In RSReportServer.config, which you will find in *Program Files\Microsoft SQL Server\ MSSQL\Reporting Services\ReportServer*, you'll need to locate the <URLRoot> element and update the NetBIOS name to the DNS name. Take care to use the same case for the letters as you used in the certificate. So in our example here we need to edit the <URLRoot> to be:
  <UrlRoot>http://d1.internal.boost.net/ReportServer </UrlRoot>.
- **RSWebApplication.config:** You'll find this config file in *C:\ProgramFiles\Microsoft SQL Server\MSSQL\Reporting Services\ReportManager*. The change needed here is to update <ReportServerUrl> to include the name used in the certificate:
  <ReportServerUrl>http://d1.internal.boost.net/ReportServer </ReportServerUrl>
- Finally, the master control over SSL is governed by the following line in the RSReportServer.config file: <Add Key= "SecureConnectionLevel" Value="2"/>.
  Acceptable values are:

  - 3 is the most secure—use SSL for absolutely everything.
  - 2 is secure—use SSL for rendering, but don't insist on it for all SOAP calls.
  - 1 is basic security—accept HTTP, but reject any calls that might be involved in the passing of credentials.
  - 0 is least secure—don't use SSL at all.

The value "2" is what the installation wizard will put in for you if you install and leave the Use SSL checkbox "on."

And now, drumroll, music, and drop the curtains.... That's all, folks. Oh, and don't forget if you are editing/deploying reports in Visual Studio .NET 2003, you need to put your https:// URL into the TargetServerURL once you have SSL installed, as shown in Figure B.42.

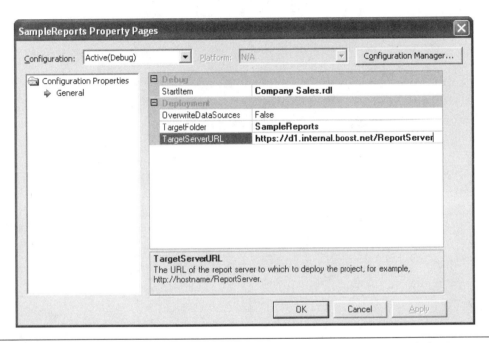

Figure B.42 Setting the TargetServerURL in the SampleReports Property Pages

Configuring SMTP

This appendix contains additional details about configuring SMTP. Generally, e-mail can be configured in two ways: first, in the default way, which the installation wizard sets up for you by programming the Report Server Windows service to squirt e-mail traffic to the e-mail SMTP server on Port 25. As an alternative, you can manually edit the elements under <RSEmailDPConfiguration> as follows:

- Set the <SMTPServerPort> element to program the SMTP service to use a non-default SMTP port.
- Set the <SMTPConnectionTimeout> element to increase (or decrease) the default connection timeout from 30 seconds.
- Change the <SMTPUseSSL> element to set SMTP service SSL authentication methods. You can specify that the connection to the mail server should use SSL—assuming that the mail server's SMTP demon has been signed. However, there is a big drawback to connecting using this default approach. What happens when the connection can't be made to the receiving SMTP server? For example, either it's not there, it's flooded with calls, or the server is busy rebooting. Well, in short, the mail fails and simply gets lost.

Configure E-Mail to Use the Pickup Folder

The default e-mail configuration can lead to e-mail getting lost in the ether. Once the <MaxRetries> has occurred, we recommend that you make the changes we describe here to use the pickup folder instead—this is much more robust, shouldn't lead to disappearing e-mail, and puts less pressure on the Report Server.

- Set the <SMTPServerPickupDirectory> element to address a pickup folder for your e-mail. To setup a far more robust mechanism to handle overflow e-mail, use the SMTP Service demon that comes with Windows 2000 and Windows Server 2003, or the demon used when you install Microsoft Exchange. In this case, you can configure Reporting Services to post overflow e-mail into the letterbox of its pickup folder. Typically, on a default install you'll find the pickup folder in *\Inetpub\ mailroot\Pickup*, but if you've installed Exchange Server, the pickup folder may be located somewhere like *\Program Files\ Exchsrvr\Mailroot\vsi 1\PickUp*.

In the RSReportServer.config file, you'll need to set this folder value in the <SMTPServerPickupDirectory> element, and set <SendUsing>1</SendUsing>. Once configured, the SMTP Service demon picks up overflow mail and moves it to its outgoing queue. With this approach, you can take advantage of the configuration options on the SMTP Service for things like a smarthost. This way delivery is first attempted directly, but if that fails the service can forward the mail to another SMTP server (in the hope that it is smarter).

Take Care Experimenting with SMTP Delivery!

The power that the Reporting Services tools provide is quite awesome. While experimenting in our labs, we setup a schedule to fire an e-mail notification every minute. Next, we setup a subscription to one of the sample reports using that schedule: the AdventureWorks catalog—yes, all 1 MB of an MHTML report! The Reporting Services engine posted the catalog in the inbox every minute. However, we forgot about it and left it running on a test server for several days. And it slipped our minds that the Report Server Windows service had been stopped, which explained why no reports were being e-mailed. But the SQL Server Agent Service was still running merrily away, adding an event to the Event table once a minute. When the server was restarted some days later, the Report Server Windows service started automatically, and unbeknownst to us, dutifully started processing those queued-up events—and relatively quickly too because we were adding more Report Servers to create a web farm. The popularized version of Murphy's colloquial law ("Anything that can go wrong will go wrong") comes to mind, but we think that Murphy was an optimist. The e-mail address was incorrectly entered (a simple typo), so the mail was being sent from a well-formed e-mail address within the domain but effectively from a nonexistent account, so the unmonitored administrator's inbox was being blasted with several thousand 1-MB nondelivery reports.

Okay, so now you've had a laugh at our expense. Hopefully, sharing our pain might help you to avoid repeating the same problem in your live production environment.

Configuring the SMTP Mail Pickup Folder

While it is probably best to use the SMTP Service's pickup folder on the same machine as the Report Server, it's possible to share the pickup folder on another machine and put the UNC pathname in the <SMTPServerPickupDirectory>. However, we don't recommend this approach. That's because you'll need to give special consideration to the share ACL and the user account under which the Reporting Services Windows service is running to ensure that there is access to the share, and at the same time remain concerned that this account could be misused.

If you have a look at the mail header of a report sent by Reporting Services, you'll see

```
X-Mailer: Microsoft CDO for Exchange 2000
```

embedded therein. And there lies a clue to what the Microsoft development team did; they used Collaboration Data Objects (CDO) to implement this feature. If you need more information on CDO, we suggest querying MSDN for CDO. If the default e-mail delivery provider doesn't cut the mustard for you, can encapsulate your own wrapper around CDO and create your own Delivery Provider extension.

Using the IIS Metabase Editor

Resolving 403.9 Errors on Windows XP

By default, the IIS server hosted on Windows XP is configured to a maximum of 10 concurrent connections. This limit can be debilitating when developing with Reporting Services on Windows XP because each web browser connection consumes more than one connection. Once you start to get 403.9 errors, it appears that even when IIS times out and closes those connections (as confirmed by the performance monitor), you can still get strange errors when opening a new connection. However, at this point, these errors are generated by Reporting Services rather than by IIS.

The solution for this problem is to increase the maximum number of connections to 40 by editing the IIS metabase. We used the IIS MetaEdit utility to make the change—this is one of those tools that like the registry editor comes with severe health warnings and disclaimers, such as "Beware a professional with a tool." To tune the IIS metabase on your development system, perform the following steps:

1. Find and download the IIS MetaEdit 2.2 utility. The Microsoft Knowledge Base Article Q232068, *"HOW TO: Download, Install, and Remove the IIS MetaEdit 2.2 Utility,"* should help you locate the tool. Install it and run it.
2. Next, locate LM | W3SVC in the Metabase Editor, as shown in Figure D.1, and double-click on the MaxConnections entry to launch a dialog, as shown in Figure D.2. Increase the MaxConnections (ID-1014) to a value no higher than 40. No, don't try to use a value higher than 40 because IIS will automatically revert the number to 10 if you do.

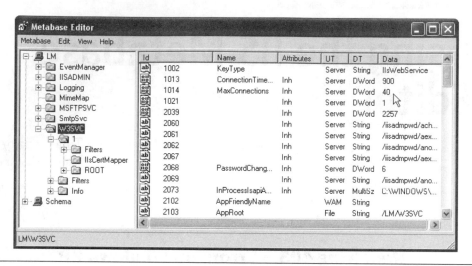

Figure D.1 The Metabase Editor and the MaxConnections (ID=1014) Value on the W3SVC (Web Server)

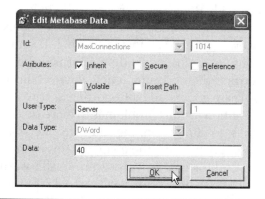

Figure D.2 Increasing the Value of the MaxConnections to 40

WARNING If you think you'll be smart and increase the MaxConnections to a value of above 40, you'll find that it will get the better of you. What happens is that a MaxConnections value entry is created directly in LM | W3SVC | 1 node, which is the "Default Web Site," and that value (which you'll find by its ID of 1014) will be set to 10. If this happens to you, you can safely delete the MaxConnections with an ID of 1014 in LM | W3SVC | 1, but only after you have set the MaxConnections value in LM | W3SVC to a number that is less than 40.

3. Finally, close the Metabase Edit tool and restart IIS.

Further Thoughts—IIS Timeouts

We've not had a problem with 403.9 errors once we increased the limit, but if you still are able to lock up the IIS in developer scenarios, you might investigate setting the Connection Timeout property to a lower value to decrease the time before IIS detects that a connection is idle and disconnects it, as shown in Figure D.3.

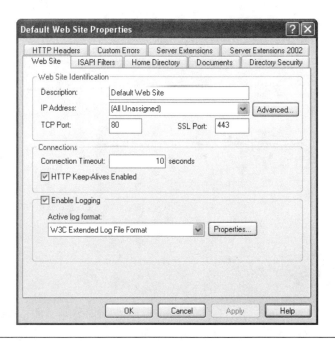

Figure D.3 Decreasing the Connection Timeout

Reporting Services Books Online

When you are developing reports in Visual Studio .NET, it is really useful to be able to search for help filtered to just those articles coming from the Reporting Services Books Online, rather than from the whole gamut of the online Knowledgebase. You probably don't want to be forced to wade through the hundreds of other interesting yet irrelevant articles that your search condition might match. Fortunately, within Visual Studio .NET you can generate a filter; we don't know why this wasn't part of the Reporting Services installation wizard—perhaps it's a globalization issue. Whatever the reason, you'll find the following can make your Reporting Services help more productive.

1. Open up Visual Studio .NET, and on the Help menu select Edit Filters.
2. Within the Form that loads into the client area, click the tab-like hyperlink labeled New.
3. Enter the following string into the Filter Definition area: `DocSet"="kbrepserv.`
4. Select the tab-like hyperlink labeled Save, and in the pop-up give the filter a sensible name such as "Reporting Services."

The resulting interface will enable you to search the Visual Studio .NET help, filtered to the just the Reporting Services Knowledgebase.

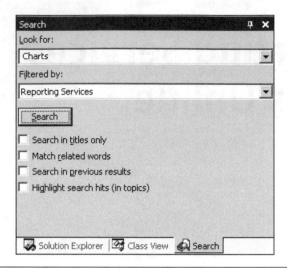

Figure E.1 Your New Reporting Services Knowledgebase Search Interface

Index

DVD-ROM Warranty

Addison-Wesley warrants the enclosed DVD-ROM to be free of defects in materials and faulty workmanship under normal use for a period of ninety days after purchase (when purchased new). If a defect is discovered in the DVD-ROM during this warranty period, a replacement DVD-ROM can be obtained at no charge by sending the defective DVD-ROM, postage prepaid, with proof of purchase to:

> Disc Exchange
> Addison-Wesley Professional
> Pearson Technology Group
> 75 Arlington Street, Suite 300
> Boston, MA 02116
> Email: AWPro@aw.com

Addison-Wesley makes no warranty or representation, either expressed or implied, with respect to this software, its quality, performance, merchantability, or fitness for a particular purpose. In no event will Addison-Wesley, its distributors, or dealers be liable for direct, indirect, special, incidental, or consequential damages arising out of the use or inability to use the software. The exclusion of implied warranties is not permitted in some states. Therefore, the above exclusion may not apply to you. This warranty provides you with specific legal rights. There may be other rights that you may have that vary from state to state. The contents of this DVD-ROM are intended for personal use only.

More information and updates are available at:

> http://www.awprofessional.com/
> http://www.sqlreportingservices.net/